NEWSWEEK CONDENSED BOOKS

JOANNA RICHARDSON

NANCY FRIDAY

RUTH KIRK

JAY ANSON

JOHN H. DAVIS

SARAH BERNHARDT AND HER WORLD

MY MOTHER/MY SELF
THE DAUGHTER'S SEARCH FOR IDENTITY

SNOW

THE AMITYVILLE HORROR

THE GUGGENHEIMS
AN AMERICAN EPIC

NEWSWEEK BOOKS, New York

NEWSWEEK CONDENSED BOOKS

Herbert Gilbert, Editor

Mary Ann Joulwan, Art Director

Elaine Andrews, Associate Editor

Alvin Garfin, Publisher

The original editions of the books in this volume are published and copyrighted as follows:

Sarah Bernhardt and Her World
Published by G.P. Putnam's Sons
Copyright © 1977 by Joanna Richardson

My Mother/My Self
Published by Delacorte Press
Copyright © 1977 by Nancy Friday

Snow
Published by William Morrow & Company, Inc.
Copyright © 1977 by Ruth Kirk

The Amityville Horror
Published by Prentice-Hall, Inc.
Copyright © 1977 by Jay Anson

The Guggenheims
Published by William Morrow and Company, Inc.
Copyright © 1978 by John H. Davis

CONTENTS

SARAH BERNHARDT

SARAH BERNHARDT AND HER WORLD

A condensation of the book by

Joanna Richardson

The "divine Sarah": one of the
best of the early photographs.

INTRODUCTION

"Madame Bernhardt has had an adventurous life, which is no business, and not much interest of ours." The comment was made by a woman writer in 1897. It was acid, prudish and envious. It was also unwise. For adventurous lives have perennial fascination. We enjoy their fairy-tale quality. We revel in the escape which they offer us from the everyday world. And, more important, we may learn from them. The lives of celebrated people give us an insight into human nature; they often show what may be achieved not merely by talent, or even genius, but by resolution. "You ask me my theory of life," said Sarah Bernhardt, once. "It is represented by the word *will*." In a life of nearly eighty years, a career of more than sixty, and in an age which hardly approved of the "liberation" of women, she showed, above all, what indomitable will could accomplish.

Sarah Bernhardt became an actress almost by accident; but she was a superb professional. She took infinite pains with every aspect of the dramatic art. She learned her technique not only from her teachers at the Conservatoire, but from her colleagues, from her own triumphs and mistakes, from her wide and vigilant observation of life. She could so identify herself with any part that her fury on stage struck terror into the most placid audience, and her pathos touched Queen Victoria. She could also be the most seductive among women. She conquered a world of admirers, and among them were the Prince of Wales (the future Edward VII) and Napoleon III. Victor Hugo knelt before her. Théophile Gautier sang her praises. Ellen Terry, Burne-Jones and Max Beerbohm, C. B. Cochran, Colette and Clémenceau: the list of Sarah's worshipers is glittering, and it is endless. She was not conventionally beautiful, but she remained all women in one. She kept this intense femininity to the end of her long life. She owed it not only to her physical appearance, to velvet and chinchilla, to the aura of perfume which hung about her. Nor did she owe it only to her powers as an actress. Her feminine magic was, above all, a quality of spirit.

She was, indeed, more than a woman: she was a symbol of womanhood, a symbol of beauty. And so she inspired not only the poets who wrote for her, but the artists who painted her. Sarah Bernhardt created a new beauty of her own; she set a style of beauty for *fin de siècle* France. And yet, of all her endowments, her voice was the most magical. "There is more than gold in it," wrote Lytton Strachey. "There is thunder and lightning, heaven and hell." As a girl, she could tame a hostile audience in a Paris theater by the enchantment of her voice. As an old woman, on a bleak November afternoon, in the undramatic setting of the Ritz Hotel in Paris, she could, without props or footlights, without resplendent robes or jewels, recite a poem by Victor Hugo and move a sober audience to tears. Sarah Bernhardt was a great actress, and, perhaps, an actress of genius. She had transcendent personal magic.

She led a flamboyant, eccentric, private life. Her delight in magnificent dress and outrageous conduct, her lovers, her quarrels, her latest escapade were the daily gossip of France. Her vitality was endless, her activities manifold: she was sculptor, critic, author, theater-manager. She made fortunes, lost them, and made more. She traveled tirelessly. There was, it seemed, no corner of the world so remote that Sarah Bernhardt had not acted there.

Sarah made her début at the Théâter-Français in 1862 at the height of the Second Empire. She gave her last performance in 1923, when she attempted to film *La Voyante* just before her death.

Rachel [the stage name of Elisabeth Félix, famed nineteenth-century actress acknowledged as the queen of tragic roles on the French stage] was the presiding genius in the life of Sarah Bernhardt; and there were similarities between those two Jewish actresses, fighting to achieve preeminence. They had both cast themselves, with fervor, into *Phèdre* and *Adrienne Lecouvreur.*. They had both astonished the world by the quality and distinction of their liaisons, by their emotional energy on and off the stage. They had both shown a Jewish devotion to their children and to their parasitic and unworthy families. They had both amazed the world by their triumphal tours abroad. They had both left a challenge and an aura in the theater.

Despite the number of parts Sarah played, despite the power and variety of her gifts, despite her all absorbing, progressive love of her art, Sarah's greatest achievement was her personal *mise-en-scène,* the part of Sarah Bernhardt. Her interests were vivid and many; her friendships and her passions were lasting and strong; but she always saw herself as the leading actress in the grandiose performance of life. She was as great an egoist as Napoleon. Like the Emperor, she proved enough to hold a world in fee, to inspire a cult and a legend. She affirmed her virtues, she did not seek to hide her weaknesses, she would tell enquiring journalists the wildest myths: not so much, one feels, to hide her real self from a prying world as to set the world talking, once again, of Sarah.

One cannot deny that she herself was the first high priestess of the Bernhardt legend. One cannot deny that her exhibitionism sometimes led her astray. Yet she lived so intensely, so constantly, in fact and in fiction, that she seemed to all men an epitome of all things.

That is why Sarah Bernhardt's life must be our concern. There remains a fraction of truth in Edmond de Goncourt's suggestion: "The life of Mme Sarah Bernhardt may prove the greatest marvel of the nineteenth century."

CHAPTER 1

FIRST PERFORMANCE

On October 23, 1844, at an undistinguished address in Paris, a girl of sixteen gave birth to a daughter. There was no rejoicing at the event. Indeed, there was probably regret, because the child was illegitimate and its existence might impede the mother's career. Judith Van Hard earned her living as a courtesan. Sarah-Marie-Henriette was her daughter by Édouard Bernhardt.

Judith Van Hard was Jewish, and she came from Haarlem in Holland. She was "ravishingly beautiful," Sarah wrote long afterwards, "like a Madonna, with her golden hair." As for Édouard Bernhardt, his daughter was to recall him (glorified, perhaps, by memory) as imposing and divinely handsome. He came of a good Roman Catholic family in Le Havre; he had abandoned his lawyer's career to travel about the world. But from time to time, like some homing bird, he would return to France to enchant her.

Judith Van Hard did not compensate Sarah for his absence. She soon deposited the unwanted baby with Édouard Bernhardt's old nurse, a buxom Breton who was married to a farmer near Quimperlé. Sarah long remembered the little white cottage with a low thatched roof on which wallflowers grew. She remained there for the early years of her life; and there, it seems, she developed her love for limitless landscapes.

Very suddenly the décor of Sarah's childhood changed. Judith Van Hard descended on the cottage and took her with the nurse and the nurse's ailing husband to Paris. She installed them in a little house in a garden full of dahlias, at Neuilly on the banks of the Seine. But, as Sarah was to write: "My mother adored traveling. She would flit from Spain to England, from London to Paris; from Paris to Berlin. From there she would go to Christiana [Oslo]; then come back and kiss me and set off again for Holland." Her constant travels were explained by her series of liaisons. Once she had left her daughter at Neuilly, she was off again. She acknowledged her maternity by random presents of money, by occasional parcels of sweets and toys. She did not trouble to leave an address. When the nurse's husband died, the nurse remarried and went to live with her new spouse, a Parisian concierge. She simply took the five-year-old child to her new home over the courtyard door of 65 rue de Provence. No doubt she did her best to look after Édouard Bernhardt's daughter; but she gave her a room without a window. Sarah was overcome by despair. She refused to eat, and she would have died had it not been for a chance event which might have come from a romantic novel. One day she was playing in the courtyard. She glanced up to see Tante Rosine, her mother's sister, who happened to be looking for an apartment.

> I uttered a cry of delight and of deliverance [remembered Sarah]. "Tante Rosine! Tante Rosine!" . . . I buried my face in her furs: I shuddered; I sobbed; I laughed; I tore her long lace sleeves. . . . Frivolous, and tender, and cajoling, and without love, she spoke sweet words to me; she stroked me with her gloved hands . . .

Then Sarah was led upstairs, in tears, to watch the carriage depart.

Perhaps she had already learned to mistrust the promises of adults. Perhaps she was simply desperate and wanted attention—or perhaps she really wanted to end her life. On a dramatic impulse she jumped out of the window. Her arm was fractured and her kneecap was broken.

She woke up in a large bed, in a room that was full of sunshine. Judith Van Hard was for once conscientious, and hastened to look after her; and Sarah found herself surrounded by solicitous aunts and cousins. It took her, so she said, two years to recover from her fall.

When Sarah was seven years old, and her mother was expecting another child, she was bundled off to a pension at Auteuil. She was not unhappy there: indeed she settled down cheerfully to her new and welcome independence. She grew accustomed to the routine. Suddenly, after two years, it was broken. On her father's orders, Tante Rosine arrived to take her away. Sarah fought for two hours to escape her. She fled to the garden and climbed the trees; she threw herself in the pond (it happened to be full of mud, not water). Exhausted, sobbing and frustrated, she was finally driven away to the rue de la Chaussée-d'Antin, and put to bed. She was in a fever for three days.

A few weeks later, accompanied by her parents and by a trunk of belongings all marked in scarlet cotton "SB," she was driven off to the convent of Grand-Champs at Versailles. Édouard Bernhardt promised her that four years hence he would come and fetch her, and take her away on his travels.

Yet another promise was to be broken. She did not see him again. Her mother vanished once more on her errant life, flitting from spa to spa, from boudoir to boudoir. It was Mère Sainte-Sophie, Mother Superior of Grand-Champs, who now guided Sarah's life.

Mère Sainte-Sophie was, naturally enough, the first person for whom the discarded, rootless child felt deep affection. Her kindness, courage and gaiety won Sarah's heart. It was Mère Sainte-Sophie who calmed her when she flew into rages; Mère Sainte-Sophie who roused the finer instincts that her father and mother had failed to encourage. Sarah only wanted some absorbing emotion. It was not surprising that she wanted to stay at the convent forever. Her mystic tendencies were confirmed by an epoch-making event. Monseigneur Sibour, Archbishop of Paris, arranged to visit Grand-Champs.

The news sent the convent into a turmoil. Mère Sainte-Thérèse wrote a short play in three tableaux for the occasion. Sarah, trembling with apprehension, waited to hear what part she had been assigned. She was given nothing. Outraged and furious, she created a part for herself: the shepherd's dog. But it was of no avail. She entered the competition to make the fish's costume; but, alas, her costume was not chosen.

And then, at the dress rehearsal, she was given her chance. The Archangel Raphael collapsed from stage-fright and declared that she could never say her part. And a triumphant understudy, who had carefully learned the words, scrambled on to the platform waving a willow branch in her hand, and continued: "Fear not, Tobias, I will be thy guide . . ."

Sarah Bernhardt was giving her first performance.

At last the day of the visit arrived. Monseigneur Sibour not only gave each child a holy medal, but promised to return in the spring for Sarah's baptism. From that day forward she became more studious, more serene. And then in January 1857, the horrified convent learned how, during a service at Saint-Étienne-du-Mont, a mad priest had murdered Monseigneur Sibour. The news was an acute shock to the sensitive child; her love of mysticism grew stronger than ever.

As the time of her baptism approached she would weep for no apparent reason, and she had irrational fears.

And then came Sarah's baptism and her first communion. She was pale and thin, wide-eyed, in perpetual ecstasy. It was only when her mother took her off to Cauterets in the Pyrénées that the excitement of travel and the change of countryside did their work. Her nervousness was overcome; so was her mysticism. For the first time she began to live.

She returned from Cauterets to Grand-Champs, where she stayed for another ten months. Then Judith Van Hard took her back to Paris; and the imposing Mlle de Brabender, who had once been governess to a Russian grand duchess, arrived each morning to supervise Sarah's lessons.

What was her future to be? One September morning in 1859, just before her fifteenth birthday, several guests assembled for *déjeuner:* Mlle de Brabender, M. Régis (Sarah's godfather), Tante Rosine and, finally an elegant, balding, dark-haired man with a moustache and an imperial, a worldly man in his forties, an imposing man who, within the last decade, had helped to lay the foundations of the Second Empire. He was the current lover of Judith Van Hard, the Emperor's half-brother, the Duc de Morny.

After *déjeuner,* one or two others joined the council to discuss Sarah's future. Sarah was still determined to take the veil. It was the Duc de Morny who ended the deliberation. Perhaps he made the suggestion from genuine percipience. Perhaps he saw it as a convenient way of ridding his mistress of an unwanted daughter. Perhaps he ventured a guess, at random, because he was growing bored. Whatever his motive, he decided Sarah Bernhardt's career. "You know what to do with the child?" he said. "Send her to the Conservatoire."

Sarah felt no longing to enter the theater. But the Duc de Morny had decided that Sarah was to take up a theatrical career, and on an evening in September 1859, with her mother, M. Régis and Mlle de Brabender, she went to see *Britannicus* at the Théâtre-Français. She had not been to the theater before, except to see the conjuror Robert-Houdin; and when the chandeliers grew dim, the curtain slowly rose, she thought she would faint with emotion. It was in fact the curtain of her life that was rising.

And soon the necessary volumes of Corneille and Racine arrived; and Daniel Auber, the composer, director of the Conservatoire, summoned her to see him. A month later came the entrance examination, and she found herself before an awe-inspiring board of examiners: Auber himself, Jean-Baptiste Provost, the tragedian, and a buxom, out-spoken woman in her thirties who studied Sarah mercilessly through her lorgnette: Augustine Brohan. Sitting with them was Joseph-Isidore Samson, a small, benevolent, white-haired man who had been the master of the great tragedienne Rachel.

She stood before them, strangely thin and frail, with an unruly aureole of fair hair, a slightly Jewish face dominated by compelling eyes. Sarah recited La Fontaine's fable *Les Deux Pigeons*, and her voice already astonished, already conquered. She was admitted to the Conservatoire. Beauvallet and Provost both asked to have her in their class, and Sarah was allowed to choose her master. She disliked Beauvallet's outspoken manner, and she chose Provost. "I have only one regret," said Auber. "It is that your lovely voice is not destined for music."

Sarah won the second prize for tragedy at her first examination. She took lessons in deportment. Every morning Judith Van Hard gave Sarah twenty sous for omnibus fares, and every morning Sarah saved the money so that she might return by cab on alternate days. Even now she enjoyed her exits and her entrances. Her favorite class was that of the gentle, courteous Régnier, who taught sincerity of diction. But she learned her grandiose gestures from Provost, her simplicity from Samson, whose favorite maxim was: "Gesture precedes and prepares for words." Sarah did not forget the lesson. "Never shock the spectator," she was to tell one of her pupils, May Agate, "by abruptness of speech or gesture. Register the thought before the action."

She entered for her second examination with the resolve that if she did not win the first prize for comedy she would renounce the theater and take the veil. Alas, she did not win the prize. It was a young actress, called Marie Lloyd, whom she saw acclaimed as Celimène. The lesson was to serve Sarah Bernhardt throughout her life. Marie Lloyd had won her prize as the incarnation of the coquette. She had realized Molière's ideal. "I have never forgotten the prize," Sarah wrote toward the end of her days. "And whenever I create a part, the character itself appears before me . . ." When Sarah at the height of her fame was playing Cleopatra, Mrs. Patrick Campbell asked why—since the audience would not see them—Sarah tinted the palms of her hand. "I shall see them," said Sarah. "I am doing it for myself. If I catch sight of my hand, it will be the hand of Cleopatra. That will help me."

She was helped, one must admit, in her early years by the distinguished men who frequented her mother's boudoir. After her second examination it was Camille Doucet, ministre des Beaux-Arts, and the Duc de Morny, who saw that she entered the Maison de Molière. She was received—and accepted—by M. Thierry, administrator-general of the Théâtre-Français.

Once Judith Van Hard had signed her daughter's contract with the Comédie-Française, Sarah threw herself into the theater with the ardor which she had once shown for religion. She determined that if she was to be an actress, she would be an actress of distinction; perhaps already, in her childish heart, she had decided to be the greatest of all actresses.

Unlike her predecessor, Rachel, she started with advantages. Her mother, it is true, lacked the warmth and affection of Rachel's mother, Mme Félix, and was always glad to dispose of her unwanted daughter. But Judith Van Hard was not a peddler's wife; she was the mistress of the Duc de Morny. Sarah's destiny had been decided by a duke, it was a duke who had quietly smoothed her way; and, a few days after she had entered the Comédie-Française, Tante Rosine gave a dinner-party that many débutantes would have envied. Morny was there, of course; and so was Comte Alexandre Walewski, the illegitimate son of Napoleon, from the Ministère des Beaux-Arts. So was Rossini. It was Gioacchino Rossini, the composer of *William Tell*, who invited Sarah to recite. It was for Rossini that she declaimed *L'Âme du Purgatoire* by Casimir Delavigne, and it was at Walewski's suggestion, with Rossini as accompanist, that she repeated the poem. The Comte de Kératry, an elegant young hussar, paid her many compliments and invited her to recite at his mother's. The girl who had left home embarrassed by her first evening dress went home again transformed. Some say that Kératry was the first of her lovers—and perhaps he was indeed the first in the long procession that was to pass through Sarah Bernhardt's life.

On September 1, 1862—more than sixty years before her last appearance—Sarah Bernhardt made her début as Iphigénie at the Théâtre-Français.

She took an infinite time to dress; and when the curtain rose she felt faint with apprehension. Provost, tall, grey-haired, paternal, was waiting in the wings to encourage her. It was he who heard Iphigénie's cue and pushed her on to the stage of the First Theater of France.

She flew to her father, Agamemnon, and clung to him; she hurled herself at her mother, Clytemnestra. She grabbed her part; and, when she came off stage, she fled to her room and feverishly began to undress. She had to be reminded that there were four acts still to come. Sarah conquered her nervousness and returned to the stage; but she was insignificant. "Mlle Bernhardt, who made her début yesterday in *Iphigénie,* is a tall, pretty young girl," wrote Francisque Sarcey in *L'Opinion Nationale.* "The upper part of her face is remarkably fine. She holds herself well and pronounces with perfect clarity. That is all one can say at the moment."

It is customary at the Théâtre-Français to make three debuts. Sarah made her second in *Valérie;* she made her third as Henriette in *Les Femmes savantes* and called forth another critical outburst from Sarcey. "This performance was very poor, and inspires some sad reflections. That Mlle Bernhardt should be inadequate does not matter, for she is beginning; but it is sad that the actors supporting her were not much better than she was. They had not many advantages over their young companion except a greater knowledge of the boards; they are today what Mlle Bernhardt will be in twenty years' time if she remains at the Comédie-Française."

Fate decreed that Sarah did not remain there. It was Molière's birthday and as usual the Comédie was to garland his bust on stage. It was the first time that Sarah had attended the ceremony, and her youngest sister, Régina, had begged to be taken.

The whole Comédie was assembled in the foyer; the call-boy announced that the ceremony was about to begin, and everyone crowded into the corridor where the busts of the great actors were displayed. In this confusion, Régina trod on Mme Nathalie's train.

Mme Nathalie, stout and pompous, pushed the child aside, and Régina fell and cut her face. Mlle Sarah Bernhardt boxed Mme Nathalie's ears.

The curtain rose that night twenty minutes late. Next morning Mlle Sarah Bernhardt received a summons from the administrator. She was asked to make a formal apology to the offended Mme Nathalie. She refused to do so, and resigned.

Sarah's violent break with the Comédie had its natural repercussions in her family life, and there were perpetual reproaches. But the family did not abandon its hopes for Sarah's future. Again the chain of wellwishers set to work; and in May 1863, she duly found herself in the offices of Montigny, director of the Théâtre du Gymnase. Montigny lectured her briefly on her flight from the Comédie and promised her many fine parts. Then he drew up her contract, and she signed it.

For the first few months he kept his word. And then, one day, he gave her the part of Princess Dunchinka, "a Russian princess, with nothing to do but eat and dance all the time," in a play by Raymond Deslandes, *Un Mari qui lance sa femme.* It was a disappointing part; but Sarah found it more than disappointing. Since she always went to extremes, she decided to give up the theater; and now that the thought of the convent had faded from her mind, she decided to go into business. A family friend advised her to take a confectioner's shop in the boulevard des Italiens. At the sight of it, Princess Dunchinka renounced the thought of commerce forever.

It must be admitted that there was a deeper reason for Sarah's vagaries than mere caprice or professional disappointment. Her mother was anxious to be free of an unwanted daughter. More than once she had suggested suitors for Sarah's hand; bourgeois aspirants, of course. Sarah had understandably turned them aside, and she had found herself a lover to fulfill her dreams of romance. By the early spring of 1864 she was the mistress of Henri, Prince de Ligne. He came from one of the oldest families in Belgium; he was young and indubitably handsome. There could be no question of marriage, but in March Sarah was pregnant.

Sarah Bernhardt was not even noticed in the first performance of *Un Mari qui lance sa femme,* except by her mother. "My poor child, you were ridiculous!" she said. "You were a great disappointment."

For all her mother's cutting indifference, Sarah was fond of her, and the comment hurt. No doubt she was also suffering from her pregnancy. The morning after her performance, she collected her savings and, snatching the crucifix from her bedroom wall, she was down the stairs and in a cab and on her way to Spain before her mother had drunk her morning coffee. When the news arrived at the Gymnase, Montigny simply said: "May the Devil take her!"

For a fortnight and more Sarah reveled in Spain. She might have settled there if she had not received a telegram from Mme Guérard, her friend and confidante in Paris, telling her that her mother was gravely ill. Sarah promptly took the train for Paris, where Judith Van Hard was recovering from pleurisy.

But the flight to Spain had taught Sarah the delights of independence; and now, as her child was about to be born, she learned that half the dowry bequeathed to her by her father would be given to her immediately. She moved to the rue Duphot with her sister Régina. A maid was installed, a cook was engaged, and Mme Guérard spent most of her days there. It was at the rue Duphot, on December 22, that Sarah found a new purpose in life, a new and permanent center for her affection. She gave birth to Maurice, her son by Henri, Prince de Ligne, and her only child.

CHAPTER 2

THE FLOWERING OF DREAMS

There were moments of triumph in Sarah's life. Yet, by the end of 1868, she found herself approaching twenty-five, and still (apart from her escapades) virtually unknown. She must have reflected bitterly on the destiny of Rachel, who, when barely twenty, had swept aside all prejudice and conquered the English public overnight.

One wonders how long Sarah might have waited for fame had it not been for a young clerk at the ministry of war by the name of François Coppée. That September he wrote a one-act poetic drama, *Le Passant*.

Silvia, the Venetian courtesan, is growing weary. She longs for young, pure love, and dreams beneath the stars one evening when the wind is warm. There comes a young boy playing a guitar and singing as he passes. Silvia feels her heart touched by new passion; then, seeing his innocence, she feels that she must save him from disillusion. She asks him to go and shows him his road. Zanetto takes his guitar and cloak and slowly goes into the distance, and the play evaporates rather than ends.

Mlle Agar, Coppée's mistress, heard the play with enthusiasm. She demanded the part of Silvia, and insisted on a young colleague at the Odéon as Zanetto. "Sarah Bernhardt is charming, and I think she was born for the part."

A few days after the first performance, the timid young clerk at the ministry of war, very ignorant of the ways of the world, was introduced by Théophile Gautier, at the request of Princess Mathilde, the high patroness of art, into the sumptuous salons of the rue de Courcelles. He was asked if *Le Passant* might be performed there in the presence of Napoleon III. On April 29 Princess Mathilde gave her annual reception for the Emperor's birthday. After this evening, Agar was received by the Emperor's command in the Comédie-Française. Sarah Bernhardt's sovereign future was assured.

Napoleon III was not to be Emperor much longer. On July 15, 1870, France embarked on the Franco-Prussian War. Sarah was shaken by the wild scenes she witnessed in Paris, the frenzied singing of *La Marseillaise,* the cries of *"A Berlin! A Berlin!"* The campaign soon proved to be disastrous; the Emperor surrendered to William I of Prussia at Sedan. On September 4 the Bonapartes were deposed. The Empress Eugénie fled to England. The Second Empire was over, and the Republic was proclaimed. But the catastrophic war continued. When the Siege of Paris began, Sarah sent Maurice and his nurse, her mother and her sisters to Le Havre, and she decided to organize a hospital. With the help of Félix Duquesnel, she installed one in the Odéon theater.

On December 27 the bombardment of Paris began. The hospital flag on the Odéon served as a target for the Prussian guns, and the patients had to be packed in the rat-infested cellars. They were only transferred when the cellars were flooded.

Clad in her pink bonnet and her little white apron, Sarah herself was now playing one of her finest parts. The war had taught her the smallness of individuals. It helped to tame her conceit, to teach her the importance of patriotism. "I am French," she was to say, "I am French by birth, at heart, in spirit, art and love." Her character became more subdued, her fits of temper more rare. She had long known her own importance, the importance of the theater; now she learned the pettiness of personal existence, even of personal triumph.

Sarah Bernhardt was awarded a gold medal for her work during the siege. And then the wretched peace was signed! "A terrible sadness took possession of everyone, even of the people who most ardently longed for peace. Every Parisian felt on his cheek the hand of the victor." Then came the Commune, and the hideous repression of the Commune. And then, at last, while Paris still breathed in the acrid smell of destruction, the theaters began to reopen. One morning Sarah received a rehearsal notice from the Odéon.

She was soon to have her initiation into the world of greatness. She was cast as the Queen of Spain in the revival of Victor Hugo's *Ruy Blas.* She made Hugo's acquaintance and was soon his devoted admirer. When he arrived for rehearsals it seemed as if the theater were illuminated.

Ruy Blas was revived on January 26, 1872. Francisque Sarcey, now theater critic for *Le Journal des Débats,* was in ecstasies; and Théodore de Banville, poet and critic, simply wrote: "Always, until the end of time, men will recall the image of Sarah Bernhardt when Ruy Blas says, 'She wore a little diadem of silver lace.'" Sarah remembered how, after the performance, the crowds of admirers suddenly made way, and Hugo himself came toward her. "Before I could say anything, he had knelt down, and, raising my hands to his lips, he murmured: 'Thank you, thank you.' He was so fine, that evening, with his noble forehead which caught the light, his stubble of silver hair like a crop cut in moonlight, his laughing, shining eyes . . ."

How far, one wonders, did enchantment lead them? Some say that Sarah was among his mistresses, but it is unlikely that there was a long liaison. Sarah herself, in later life, was to regret that she had not seen more of Victor Hugo. "I was stupid enough to prefer the company of a bunch of elegant fools to that of the superior men around me." So she lamented to the composer Reynaldo Hahn. "Just think of it! One day I left Victor Hugo in the middle of a conversation and went back to some men from the Jockey Club!" But Victor Hugo was not rejected for a few men-about-town. He had a much more dangerous rival. In 1872 Sarah was enamoured of Jean Mounet-Sully, a young actor who was made, it seems, to play romantic heroes, to be Hamlet or Orestes, "and to feel the moving plumes of Achilles shaking upon his brow." Mounet-Sully was thirty-one, dark, bearded, endowed with pensive eyes and the gift of speaking poetry as if poetry had been his native tongue. Victor Hugo was seventy, and he looked like an old carpenter. For all his gallantry, for all his towering celebrity, he could not match him.

A few days after Sarah's dazzling performance in *Ruy Blas,* there came a familiar envelope bearing the circular stamp of the Comédie-Française. The letter was from Émile Perrin, the administrator-general. He asked to see her.

Duquesnel urged Sarah to stay at the Odéon. He warned her that she still had a year of her contract to run, and he refused to increase her salary. Sarah ignored his warning, hurried to the Théâtre-Français, and entered Perrin's office with the words: "I have come to sign."

She returned to the stage of the Comédie-Française in November 1872. She took the title part in Dumas' *Mademoiselle de Belle-Isle.* War and civil war and her own peregrinations from theater to theater had made her almost a stranger in the rue de Richelieu. Théodore de Banville, watching her this November evening, introduced her to his readers as someone almost unknown, described her with a miniaturist's care:

> She has one of those delicate, expressive heads that the illuminators of the Middle Ages painted in the miniatures of their manuscripts. Deep, shining, liquid eyes, a straight, fine nose, red lips that open like a flower, revealing the sharp whiteness of the teeth, a long and flexible neck; and

all receive unheard-of brilliance from that rich, transparent coloring.
. . . To these strange charms, Mlle Sarah Bernhardt adds one that is
still more strange, for her brow is crowned with a heavy, enormous,
abundant head of hair, very likely the unruly tresses of goddesses, those
confusions of light and gold that the sculptors of the Renaissance accumulate on the brows of their Dianas. . . .

It was at about this time that Sarah began to rehearse the part of Berthe
de Savigny in Octave Feuillet's play *Le Sphinx*; and in Feuillet she found
yet another bewildered admirer. "A strange girl," he wrote home to his
wife. "It's the first time in my long career that I've met the real actress of
the novels, the courtesan-actress of the eighteenth century." When Mme
Feuillet attended the last rehearsals, she too was spellbound by Berthe de
Savigny. "Thin and diaphanous, she seemed to struggle to drag her im-
palpable body along. . . . She seemed at times like a wandering shadow. . . . This Sarah, of so fatal but so delicate a beauty, had extraordinary dramatic powers. She had unexpected feelings, too, and proved
most touching in the fourth act, as the sacrificed woman. This part of the
play was a real triumph for her at the first performance."

Sarah established herself at once in the rue de Richelieu and began to
dabble in power politics; indeed, there was constant conflict between the
new *pensionnaire* and the administrator-general of the Comédie-Française. Since Perrin did not give her enough work to satisfy her, she determined to become a sculptor. Wholehearted as ever, she rented a studio
near the place Clichy, where friends and lovers came to admire, take
counsel, and, at five o'clock, take tea.

One day[so Sarah remembered]Perrin came to see me in my sculptor's studio. He began by chatting about my busts, and said I should do a
medallion of him; and then, as if by chance, he asked if I knew the part
of Phèdre. Until then I had only played the part of Aricie, and the part of
Phèdre seemed formidable. None the less, I had studied it for pleasure.
"Yes, I know the part. But I think that if I had to perform it, I should die
of fright."
He laughed, his little nasal laugh, and said as he kissed my hand (for
he was very gallant): "Work on it, I think that you will play it."
And indeed, a week later, I was summoned to the director's office, and
Perrin told me that he was announcing *Phèdre* for December 21st, Ra-
cine's birthday, with Mlle Sarah Bernhardt in the title role.

Phèdre was the most demanding, most prestigious part in all French drama. Phèdre was the reef on which all but the greatest of actresses must founder; and though it was certain that Sarah would bring her poetic feeling, her magic diction, her sculptural, classic gestures to the part, it was felt that sometimes her physical strength might fail her.

This was indeed what happened; in the fourth act, in the terrible scene when Phèdre learns that Hippolyte loves Aricie, Sarah visibly weakened, her voice betrayed her, and she struggled to express the passions that she knew so well. The mantle of Phèdre was too heavy for her delicate frame. But in the scenes that exacted less evident strength, she was excellent, and some thought that the famous declaration had never been recited with more contained passion, with finer consciousness of the shades of meaning.

Sarah herself was convinced that Rachel's Phèdre was unique, could not have been surpassed; and this even though she had never seen Rachel on the stage. But if Rachel recalled the statues of ancient Greece, Sarah conjured before the eyes of the audience the living woman of antiquity, and she had no need to study her sobs. Her tears were always close to the surface, and they flowed easily, with heart-breaking realism. Sarah would always abandon herself to Phèdre as she abandoned herself to no other part. Perhaps her supreme achievement was her Phèdre. When she played the role she always needed to prepare herself with a long interval of quiet reflection. But, as Maurice Baring was to write, from the moment she staggered on to the stage, trembling under the load of her unconfessed passion, "the spectator witnessed the building up of a miraculous piece of architecture in time and space, and followed the progression, the rise, the crisis, and the tranquil close of a mysterious symphony."

It was in the New Year, 1875, soon after her first performance in *Phèdre,* that Sarah was made a *sociétaire* of the Comédie-Française. The honor did not wholly please her:

> From that moment[so she wrote]I felt as if I were in prison, as if I had agreed to stay at the Maison de Molière for many years. The thought of this made me unhappy. It was Perrin who had urged me to demand the societariat. And now I regretted it.
>
> For the rest of the year I performed only occasionally. I spent all my time supervising the construction of a pretty hotel which I was having built for myself. . . .
>
> My dream was to have a home that was really my own; and so I fulfilled it. M. Régnier's son-in-law, Félix Escalier, was a very fashionable architect, and he built me a delightful hotel.

> There was nothing I liked better than to go round the scaffolding with him in the mornings. . . . And then I used to climb up on the roof. I forgot my theatrical troubles in this new occupation. God knows, I even dreamed of turning architect. . . .

On February 14, 1876, Sarah appeared as Mistress Clarkson in *L'Étrangère*, the first acknowledged play by Dumas *fils* to be performed at the Théâtre-Français. "I confess," wrote Henry James, "that L'Étrangère strikes me as a rather desperate piece of floundering in the dramatic sea. . . . The *Foreigner* is played by that very interesting actress, Mme Sarah Bernhardt. . . . [But she] is like the heroine of an old-fashioned drama of the Boulevard du Crime who has strayed unwittingly into a literary work." Sarcey, like Henry James, considered the play an extraordinary medley. As for the famous speech in which Mrs. Clarkson told the story of her life, he considered it "a tissue of extravagances and useless vulgarities. If Mlle Sarah Bernhardt had not cast the fascinating poetry of her gesture and diction over such romantic idiocies, the public would have burst out laughing."

It was a measure of Sarah's powers that her next impressive part was a part she performed that autumn, the part of Posthumia in Alexandre Parodi's *Rome vaincue.* She had, in fact, refused the part of the vestal virgin and demanded that of the blind old woman of seventy.

Even Sarcey, who made and unmade the success of plays, wrote a panegyric about Sarah:

> She displayed qualities of energy and pathos that even her admirers did not suspect in her.
>
> She was wonderfully dressed and wonderfully made-up. A wasted, wrinkled face of extraordinary majesty: vague, dull eyes, a cloak which fell at her sides when she raised her arms and seemed like the vast wings of some gigantic, sinister bat. There could be nothing more terrible, more poetic. . . .
>
> It was no longer an actress; it was nature itself, served by a wonderful intelligence, a soul of fire, by the clearest, the most melodious voice that has ever enchanted human ears. This woman acts with her heart, with her whole being. She dares gestures that would in anyone else be ridiculous, and they sweep an audience off its feet. . . .

It was, however, Victor Hugo's *Hernani* which finally established Sarah with the public—the triumphant *Hernani* of November 21, 1877. Mounet-Sully, in all his beauty, all the splendor of his talent, played Hernani to Sarah's Doña Sol. And after the performance Hugo wrote to her: "Madame, you were great and charming; you moved me, the old warrior himself; and, at a certain moment, while a touched, enchanted public applauded you, I wept. The tear that you inspired is yours, and I lay it at your feet." With the letter came a gold bracelet with a diamond pendant. Sarah later lost the diamond at Alfred Sassoon's, but she would not let him replace it. No Sassoon could return her Victor Hugo's tear.

Sarah was not only now the darling of the public; she was the darling of the critics too. Her colleagues at the Comédie were, understandably, a little jealous, and Perrin—so she tells us—was constantly picking quarrels with her. It offended his sense of self-importance that she should not depend on him; and, as he always refused her requests, she now simply sent them over his head to M. le Ministre des Beaux-Arts, and they were promptly granted. During the Paris Exhibition of 1878 Perrin was given yet more cause for exasperation. In the *Doña Sol*, an orange balloon made specially for the occasion, she ascended from the exhibition site.

In a fantasy, published that year, *Dans les Nuages: Impressions d'une Chaise,* Sarah even described her flight as it might have appeared to the chair she used on her ascent. Rapidly they rose from the crowded exhibition, "and then nothing! Nothing! . . . The earth below, the sky above . . . I'm in the clouds, I've left Paris in the mist, I find a blue sky and a radiant sun. The little basket plunges into a milky vapor all warm with sunshine. Round us are opaque mountains with iridescent crests. . . . It's wonderful! Stupefying!" Over the Pont de la Concorde they drifted, over the Tuileries, where the crowd in the courtyard rushed towards the *quais* to follow the escapade. The balloon drifted on, over Père-Lachaise, and Sarah stripped the petals off her corsage and scattered them over the cemetery. At half past six she began to make foie-gras sandwiches; they uncorked a bottle of champagne and drank to the future of ballooning, to glory, to the arts, to what has been, is, and will be, and tossed the empty bottle into the Lac de Vincennes. After nightfall they landed at Verchère and returned to an apprehensive avenue de Villiers.

Perrin, that model of officialdom, fined Sarah 1000 francs for making a journey without leave. Sarah retorted that she would not pay, and that she would resign from the Comédie-Française. Once again M. le Ministre des Beaux-Arts intervened; he declared that Perrin had exceeded his rights, that the fine was canceled, and that Sarah should withdraw her resignation. Triumphantly she did so.

It was now, on April 2, 1879, at the apogee of her career, that Sarah first played opposite Mounet-Sully the part of the Queen in *Ruy Blas*.

She came on stage, as so often, stricken with fear, trembling so much that she could only indicate some of her gestures. But "Sarah Bernhardt, always so pretty, so elegant, so artistic, has never perhaps been so adorably dressed," wrote Arnold Mortier in *Les Soirées parisiennes*. "It was poetry in costume. Nor has a real queen ever been more queenly than this queen of the theatre in her magnificent dress in the second act: a white satin dress with silver embroideries, a train in figured silk; a little crown on top of her hair." And it was not only her appearance that enchanted the house. As she played that night opposite Mounet-Sully, she had, wrote Sarcey, "all the tender, languorous grace of the part. There are words that she said to perfection, with exquisite delicacy; others she hurled away with the impulse of a passion breaking its banks." Hugo's most lyrical passages seemed, as Sarah spoke them, like a long caress. "She only added the music of her voice to the music of the verse."

Flowers filled her dressing room, the corridor was heaped with roses, violets and lilac. And years later, inscribing a book to her, Victor Hugo could only inscribe it "to the Queen whose Ruy Blas I should have wished to be." Perrin, too, was glad that Sarah drew such multitudes to the theater; but he would have been even more pleased (so she considered) if the applause had been accorded to another. The more that Sarah triumphed, the more he understood his own ineffectiveness. Her independence drove him to silent fury.

It was evident that the tension could not last, that sooner rather than later there would be a dramatic change. It came with the arrival of William Jarrett.

> I heard the sound of argument in the next room [recalled Sarah]. I went out, palette in hand, determined to send the intruder away; but, just as I opened my studio door, a tall man came forward, so close to me that I had to step back; and he therefore came into my hall. He had bright, hard eyes, silver hair, a well-kept beard; he apologized, very correctly, for disturbing me, he admired my painting, my sculpture, my hall: so much so that I still didn't know his name.
>
> After ten minutes, I asked him to sit down and tell me the purpose of his visit. He began quietly, and with a marked accent. "I am Mr. Jarrett, impresario. Do you want to come to America?" "Never in my life!" I cried, fiercely. "Never! Never!" "All right. Never mind. Here is my address. Don't lose it."

As Jarrett left the room he mentioned that there would be a further fortune to earn if she gave private performances in London. Sarah had met her match, and signed the contract. Jarrett inspired her with confidence from the first; and that confidence, so she wrote some thirty years later, was never lost.

Perrin and the committee of the Comédie-Française had in fact arranged for a French season in London; they had signed a contract with John Hollingshead, manager of the Gaiety Theatre. No one had been consulted on the decision, and Sarah understandably disapproved of such high-handed behavior. Her tacit but very evident disapproval caused Perrin anxiety, and he asked her what she contemplated. Sarah demanded to be made an independent *sociétaire* for the length of the London season.

This agreeable status would allow her to give as many private performances as she wanted. But she made this demand of a Comédie already exasperated by her behavior; and the committee refused it. Sarah might not have crossed the Channel in this sultry, significant summer if John Hollingshead had not made his pronouncement. He simply said that if Sarah, Croizette, Coquelin or Mounet-Sully failed to appear in London, the contract would be annulled.

Sarah was for once alarmed at the damage she might cause the Comédie. She called on Perrin and declared she was ready to go to London on any terms. The committee promptly created both Sarah and Croizette independent *sociétaires* in perpetuity. Perrin and Sarah embraced each other, peace was once more restored and final preparations began.

CHAPTER 3

SARAH THE CONQUEROR

It was on a May morning in 1879, the day before the Whitsun holiday, that Sarah Bernhardt landed at Folkestone. "*Vive* Sarah Bernhardt!" cried a young man who looked like Hamlet and handed her a gardenia. It was Forbes Robertson. "They will soon be making you a carpet of flowers," said a jealous colleague. "Here it is!" cried another worshiper, casting an armful of lilies at her feet. This was Oscar Wilde; and he led the cheers as the Comédie-Française boarded the train for London.

From that moment, Sarah Bernhardt was the cynosure of every eye, and the favorite theme of every conversation. And at 77 Chester Square, where she was to live during her stay, the door stood open, the lights inside invited her to enter, and an enormous, radiant bouquet was waiting, with a card inscribed: "Welcome! Henry Irving."

Next day was devoted to receiving the press. Thirty-seven journalists came, and Jarrett spared her none of them. The thirty-seven journalists had hardly left Chester Square before a duchess arrived to pay a call. Sarah's social life had begun. And, from the first, Sarah delighted in it. She went to her first dinner party in London, at a peeress's house in Prince's Gate. "There were some twenty people there. . . . I had been told that the food was very bad in England; I found the dinner perfect. I had been told that the English were cold and formal; I found them charming, and full of humor. Everyone spoke French well. I was ashamed of my ignorance of English. . . . I came home very happy and very much an anglomaniac."

On June 2, 1879, at the Gaiety Theatre, the Comédie-Française were to open their London season with *Le Misanthrope,* the second act of *Phèdre,* and *Les Précieuses ridicules.* At a quarter past ten that night Sarah Bernhardt was due to give her first performance to an English audience. She brought her own enveloping aura of legends, passions and eccentricities, her own theatrical reputation. Far more dangerous, far more exacting, she also brought with her the aura and the legend of Rachel. It was twenty-four years since Rachel had last taken London by storm, and there must have been many in the audience who remembered her, many who instinctively compared. It was typical of Sarah that she began deliberately, defiantly, with the part that had been Rachel's most lasting triumph.

In her dressing room at the Gaiety, stagefright overcame her.

> Three times I put rouge on my cheeks and shadow on my eyes; three times I took it all off with a sponge. I thought I was ugly. I thought I was thinner. I thought I was shorter.
>
> I shut my eyes, to listen to my voice. . . . My voice was husky in the low notes, clouded in the soprano notes. I wept with rage.
>
> They came to say that the second act of *Phèdre* was about to begin. I was mad. I didn't have a veil. I didn't have my rings. My belt of cameos was not fastened. . . . I had stagefright. Not the kind that paralyzes, but the kind that sends you mad. It is quite enough, but it's better. You do too much, but at least you do something.
>
> The whole audience applauded for several seconds when I went on stage; and, as I bowed in acknowledgement, I said inside myself: "Yes, yes . . . you'll see . . . I'm going to give you my blood . . . my life . . . my soul . . ."

I suffered, I wept, I implored, I cried; and all of it was real; my suffering was horrible, the tears that flowed were burning and bitter. I implored Hippolyte for the love that was killing me, and the arms that I stretched out to Mounet-Sully were the arms of Phèdre, tense with the cruel longing to embrace. The god had come.

She had met London across the footlights—and she had roused it to fever pitch. Few audiences in her career were to be so impassioned. "We remember Rachel's sombre grandeur," said *The Times*, "the concentrated passion that seemed to be glowing at a red heat in the core of her heart. Her Phèdre might be more terrible and intense, but it was, perhaps, less womanlike, less sympathetic, than the Phèdre of Sarah Bernhardt." "When she advanced alone to the footlights," wrote another spectator, "in the speech in which she acknowledges and laments her unhappy love—there was deep silence. No one could clap; we could only pant and clench our hands. The slow, emphatic declamation, the small white muscular face, were too impressive—the tragedy was too awful a reality."

Sarah's determination to conquer London, the perpetual passion of her performance, had exhausted her. That night she was shaken by a fit of coughing. Dr. Parrot, who had long attended her, was summoned to London. He arrived next afternoon and forbade her to perform that evening. Parrot's orders decided her. She asked him to leave the room, dressed herself rapidly, and sped off in a hansom to the theater. Parrot went the way of all who failed to comply with Sarah's wishes. Half an hour later her maid brought a letter from him, full of affection and fury, reproaches and advice. He also enclosed a prescription in case of relapse. He was returning to Paris within the hour.

Parrot's reproaches were deserved. Three times Sarah fainted as she dressed for *L'Etrangère*. When at last she came on stage she was dulled with opium and she walked as if she were in a dream.

However strangely Sarah performed that night, the audience had no eyes for anyone else. Even Francisque Sarcey—who had bustled across the Channel—found that he was basking in her glory. "Nothing," he wrote back to Paris, "nothing can give an idea of the craze that Mlle Sarah Bernhardt is exciting. It's a mania."

Sarah's personal triumph in 1879 equaled that of Rachel in that London season of thirty-nine years before; but perhaps, this time, the triumph owed something to intense publicity. Sarah was not, like Rachel, exclusively given to her art; there was far more of the Barnum about her, and publicity methods had progressed in the last few decades.

Whatever the reasons for Sarah's triumph, every seat in the Gaiety was booked, now, for her Phèdre. The guinea stall on Sarah's nights was, we are told, "often sold by *abonnés* for five times the amount." Sarah was also enjoying a constant social triumph. She received hundreds of letters which she never answered. She accepted invitations and failed to appear, or disturbed all arrangements by preposterous unpunctuality. One of her first engagements, so we are told, was at the house of the octogenarian Lady Combermere. A roomful of guests, packed in several ranks of gold chairs, awaited her for an hour. At last there was the sound of an arrival. Sarah was slowly and nonchalantly mounting the staircase, when from the landing her manager "hurled an opprobrious epithet at her."

Sir Algernon Borthwick of *The Morning Post* (later Lord Glenesk) was more fortunate than Lady Combermere. He not only persuaded Sarah to give a private performance in Eaton Place, but even received a bronze inkstand modeled by herself and representing her head on the body of a sphinx. For years the "letters of friendship and gossip" were to speed to and fro between them.

While Sarah was appearing in *Andromaque,* she held an exhibition of her sculpture and painting in a gallery in Piccadilly. A hundred invitations had been sent out, and, much to her delight, twelve hundred guests arrived.

Sarah's immense popularity raised a storm of jealousy within the Comédie; and a swarm of malevolent rumors were soon buzzing in the press. It was said that for an admission fee of a shilling one could see Sarah Bernhardt in male dress; that she might be observed, free of charge, on her balcony, smoking giant cigars; that she dressed in pierrot's clothes, and took boxing lessons. An article by Albert Wolff in *Le Figaro* proved to be the finishing touch. On June 26 she answered: "My dear Monsieur Wolff, . . . if Paris is growing tired of the nonsense that is said about me, if they've decided to be frigid when I come home, I don't want to put them in a position where they have to do anything unworthy. I'm handing my resignation to the Comédie-Française."

There was consternation. Letters flew between London and Paris. And while the agitated correspondence continued, Mme Bernhardt herself, "the all too celebrated resigner," had second thoughts, postponed her resignation and gaily starred in a new and brilliant entertainment: the French Fête at the Royal Albert Hall. The Fête was arranged for July 7 and 8 in aid of the French Hospital in London. "Who knows," cried a journalist, "to what fabulous prices a rose will rise when coming from the hands of Mlle Sarah Bernhardt?" The Prince of Wales was expected on both days, the band of the Garde Républicaine, dispatched by the French government, was to be "conveyed without charge to London and back by the two Kentish railway companies." The Fête did not belie such enthusiasm. The Prince of Wales bought a portrait of Sarah, and the royal party lingered a long while at the stall where she "labored indefatigably all the afternoon, haranguing, writing, raising the price upon her admirers, till she had taken the largest earnings of any stall— £256. . . . The Prince of Wales threw down a handful of notes to settle his accounts as he left."

The Comédie gave its last performance on July 12. Sarah returned to Paris, and Perrin arrived at the avenue de Villiers in a paternal and conciliating mood. There was no question of her resignation. On August 2, the Comédie-Française paid its birthday tribute to Molière. Two by two, the actors came on stage, bearing palm or wreath to decorate the busts of the dramatist. Sarah chose to come on stage alone. She did not, like her colleagues, bow or curtsey. She advanced to the footlights, and gazed resolutely into the eyes of Paris. A tremor ran through the audience. Then, suddenly, there was a roar of acclamation.

Sarah was not to make many more entrances in the Comédie. On April 17, 1880, she played the part of Clorinde in *L'Aventurière*. She despised the part and the play, and she detested the author, Émile Augier. On the eve of the performance she asked Perrin to postpone it for a week. She had been ill and unable to study for three days. She had not even tried on her costumes. Perrin refused to postpone the performance. The result was disastrous. "You have only to see her eccentric costume," snapped *Le Journal des Débats*, "to see clearly that she had an imperfect understanding of her part. Her gestures and general appearance lacked nobility. . . . Let us be frank: in her outbursts in the third act, she was quite detestable." *Le Figaro* administered the unkindest cut of all and declared her vulgar.

This time the break with the Comédie was final. "It is my first failure with the Comédie-Française," Sarah wrote to Perrin. "It will be my last." "The Comédie-Française," wrote Banville, "does not know why Mlle Sarah Bernhardt has left it, and Mlle Sarah Bernhardt does not know why she has left the Comédie-Française." One of the reasons may have been the enmity of Augier; and no doubt Perrin, overwrought by her countless escapades, was glad when she departed.

The break was inevitable, but it was London that had taught Sarah Bernhardt her powers, given her her freedom. And she was too original, too tempestuous, too variable, too fired with a love of a measureless art, of universal travel and international glory, and (one must admit it) too much of an egoist to restrict herself to the rue de Richelieu. Thirty years later, in her memoirs, she herself confessed: "That first evening in London decided my future."

Did Sarah ever regret the Comédie-Française? Perhaps she did. Certainly Claretie tried to re-engage her. On May 16, 1892, she called on him to discuss her re-engagement, and he offered her what had been given to Coquelin, the best-paid *sociétaire*: 40,000 francs. Sarah was accustomed by then to her world-wide tours and fabulous receipts. She found the sum far too small. Besides, as she explained, she had her own company; she might be going to Scandinavia. She did not want to be tied to the Comédie for three years. She could only stay for a year. Perhaps in a year's time she would change her mind. Claretie listened sadly to Sarah's torrent of excuses; but he noted in his diary that when she left she had a melancholy air.

But in April 1880, when Sarah left the Comédie, she was far from melancholy. She called on Dumas *fils* and asked him for *La Dame aux camélias*. "The play is yours," he answered, without hesitation. "Do what you will with it."

It was at this opportune moment that Jarrett reappeared. Jarrett was formidable. Immune to Sarah's charm, ignoring her caprices, he was the only man who earned her trust and her unswerving respect. Now, again, he asked her to sign a contract for America; and this time he mentioned details: 5000 francs for each performance and half the receipts should the box office draw in a further 15,000. He offered her 1000 francs a week for hotels and a special Pullman for her railway journeys containing a bedroom with a fourposter bed, a salon complete with piano, four beds for her staff and two chefs. He himself would take ten percent of all she received.

She agreed to everything. Jarrett sent for Abbey, the American impresario; Abbey rushed from the New World to the Old. The contract was signed, and Sarah ordered twenty-five everyday dresses, six costumes for *Adrienne Lecouvreur*, four costumes for *Hernani* and one for *Phèdre* (this alone cost 4000 francs). And then, to fill in time, she signed a contract with Mayer and Hollingshead for an intermediate season in London.

On May 24, when Sarah began her second Gaiety season, she shone in a theatrical firmament which was resplendent with stars. At the Lyceum a few yards away, Henry Irving and Ellen Terry were playing in *The Mer-*

chant of Venice; at Covent Garden, Patti was singing in *Don Giovanni;* and at the Opéra Comique, every evening, the expectant crowd assembled to revel in "a new and original opera, by Messrs W. S. Gilbert and Arthur Sullivan, *The Pirates of Penzance.*"

It was, then, a critical audience that assembled that summer evening for Sarah Bernhardt, an audience accustomed to good theater. And many of them, again, recalled Rachel; for it was in *Adrienne Lecouvreur,* which Sarah would play for the first time that night, that Sarah's great predecessor had "for the first time crossed the well-marked line separating classic tragedy from modern drama. No doubt," considered the critic, "it is easy to conceive passion that should present more dignity and self-restraint, till it flashed out in some supreme revelation. This was possible and natural to Rachel, but it is not thus that Mlle Bernhardt renders the emotion of such a scene. In her case physical as well as emotional abandonment is the dominant note of love. But the audience yielded to its charm, and by the end of the act the actress had regained her empire of the public." She conquered them not only by charm, but by horrifying realism. The death of Adrienne Lecouvreur was considered one of Sarah's masterpieces. It was realistic to a degree which was rare even for her. It was a death by poison, and the effects of the poison could be seen. When, at last, she died, the audience burst into wild applause. Sarah did not achieve this triumph without suffering. Once, when she had prolonged her agony on stage, she almost collapsed in her dressing room and only revived with the aid of smelling-salts. "It's like that," muttered a colleague, "nearly every time she acts this blessed play."

On October 15, 1880, Sarah Bernhardt boarded the *Amérique* and set out, like Rachel before her, to conquer the New World. On October 27 the *Amérique* stopped in an icebound Hudson River. The icebreakers hewed a way for the ship to dock, and three small boats sailed out to greet Doña Sol. Then the crowd of admirers, sightseers and reporters burst on board. American publicity, and Sarah Bernhardt's American legend, had begun.

On November 8 she gave her first performance at Booth's Theater in *Adrienne Lecouvreur.* New York was conquered; and when she returned that night to her hotel she found a crowd assembled to serenade her. In *La Dame aux camélias* she was, they said, the greatest of Marguerites; and in *Phèdre,* when she was still and silent, there was the smell of sulphur in the air, proclaiming, that, though the crash had not come, it was coming—it was there.

33

Poster, above, by Alphonse Mucha, shows Sarah as Mélissinde in La Princesse lointaine. *Sarah, above, as Lady Macbeth, 1884. Below, cover designed by Willette for Marie Colombier's scurrilous book about Sarah, 1883.*

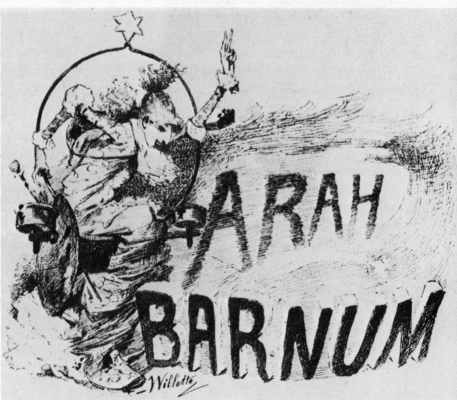

Above, Sarah Bernhardt in 1879, the year of her first of several appearances in London, from the portrait by Jules Bastien-Lepage. Sarah's first play in London, Phèdre, made her an immediate rage with both the critics and the public. Left, a photograph of Sarah by Nadar.

Opposite page, the divinity at home:
Sarah Bernhardt with a granddaughter
and a faithful friend. In 1889, Sarah
Bernhardt signed a twenty-five year
lease for the 1700-seat Théâtre des Nations, which she renamed the Théâtre
Sarah-Bernhardt. The English actress,
Lily Langtry, and Sarah, right, wearing a coat, in a photograph by Sarony.
The two great actresses were good
friends.

Sarah, age seventy-five, with her bust of the famous French playwright Edmond Rostand, from a photograph taken in her studio, 1919. Sarah Bernhardt's tomb, below, at Père-Lachaise, in Paris.

When she arrived at the theater for her last New York performance she found the street blocked by admirers. One woman took off an amethyst brooch and pinned it to Sarah's cloak; another enthusiast, trying to snip off a lock of her hair, only cut a feather off her Parisian hat.

After a triumphant appearance in Montreal, Sarah returned to America and the show went on. New Orleans, Mobile, Memphis, Louisville, Cincinnati, Columbus: through them all steamed the train, and Doña Sol on a rocking chair platform of her carriage saw the panorama of endless plains and forests ever changing. Dayton, Indianapolis, St. Joseph, Leavenworth, Quincy, Springfield. . . . The train puffed on its way. Chicago, Detroit, Cleveland, Pittsburgh, Bradford and Erie, over the frontier they went to perform in Toronto; back again they went to Buffalo, Rochester and Utica. Then off to Washington (where they had supper at the French Embassy), Baltimore and Philadelphia. Finally, and breathlessly, they returned to New York. Sarah bade farewell to America with *La Dame aux camélias*, and she took fourteen curtain calls. On May 4 she embarked in the *Amérique* for France.

Ambroise Aristide Damala was born on January 6, 1855. The Damalas were an aristocratic family from Syra, one of the islands of the Aegean. About 1860 they moved to Marseilles, where Ambroise Aristide was first educated; later he attended the Collège Royal de Louis-le-Grand in Paris. In 1869 M. Damala died, leaving some 300,000 francs to each child. Aristide became an adventurer. He was the handsomest subaltern in the Greek cavalry, and one of the bravest in the war of 1875–78. At one time he served with the Foreign Legion in the Sahara. He studied to be a diplomat, and finally came to Paris, where he spent the last thousand francs of his inheritance, and soon involved himself, it is said, in numerous intrigues. His Oriental parties, wrote Mme Berton, the actor's wife, at which the guests "divested themselves of their clothing and plunged naked into baths of champagne," were the talk of Paris. Perhaps Damala was already a victim of morphine; and perhaps it was in the world of drug addicts that he met Sarah's half-sister, Jeanne.

Was it Jeanne, or was it Delaunay, the actor, who introduced him to Sarah? We cannot tell. But Delaunay gave him drama lessons, and one September morning in 1881 Damala called at the avenue de Villiers. Sarah found herself in the presence of "a tall and handsome man with a pair of ferocious mustachios" and no acting experience. He boldly asked for a part, and she told him to learn Don Carlo's monologue in *Hernani* and to recite it to her three days hence. Three days later she engaged him, asked him to learn the rest of the part and to play it with her in Brussels. And so it was that Damala first appeared on stage in *Hernani,* in Belgium, in the Autumn of 1881. The tour continued in triumph through Vienna and St. Petersburg, Warsaw, Genoa, Basel and Lausanne, Lyons and Trieste. By the time they performed in Naples on March 31, 1882 Sarah was playing opposite her fiancé.

Probably Sarah was attracted by Damala's indifference. Sarah was always inspired by resistance, and he alone of all the men she had known had not been immediately conquered. "I made up my mind to marry him," she told a reporter years later; and, being Sarah, she had to be satisfied at once. Since French and Italian laws imposed delays on marriage, she and Damala had to be married in England; and since he was an orthodox Greek and she was a Catholic, and neither the Greek nor the Roman Church allowed marriage in mid-Lent, they had to be married in a Protestant church.

They paid a flying visit to London; and on April 4 the assistant curate at St. Andrew's, Wells Street, married a young man of twenty-seven "who resembled Mounet-Sully, but was better looking," and a woman of thirty-seven, very pale and fatigued with her journey.

It was, of course, a thronged theater that greeted her when, on May 25, after visits to Portugal, Spain, and Switzerland, she reappeared in Paris to perform in *La Dame aux camélias* opposite her husband. As often as Paris had seen her on the stage with her current lover, this evening presented her in a more dramatic light. Small wonder that this charity performance of Dumas' play proved to be "the greatest success that a Parisian manager could attempt." "I paid 25 louis for my box," said one satisfied spectator, "but I cried enough for 2000 francs."

It was on one of her frequent visits to London that the queen of the French theater was the guest of the reigning monarch of the English stage. Henry Irving, always conscious of his regal status, felt it incumbent upon him to extend an almost official welcome to distinguished foreign actors passing through London. After the last rehearsal of *Henry VIII* he gave a supper in honor of Sarah Bernhardt. During supper that night, Sarah leaned across the table to Ellen Terry and said: "My darling, there are two people who shall never be old—you and I."

Sarah was autocratic. She was insatiable. And she was infinitely alluring. No one disputed the crown with her. Her enemies and critics, like her myriad admirers, watched her with fascination.

Wider still, and wider, the bounds of legend were set. There were graphic accounts of the "nicely polished skeleton" admiring itself in the glass in her bedroom. There was certainly a skull inscribed by Victor Hugo. There were yet more tales of the coffin embellished with her initials and with her defiant motto *Quand même:* the coffin in which she was said to study her parts. It was rumored that Sarah was plotting to restore the Empire. It was said that she drank enormously, that she had ordered a coach in gold and ebony, that she was not a woman at all, but a boy masquerading in woman's clothes.

The year 1882 brought Sarah not only the new role of a wife, but that of a director of a theater. Some time ago she had agreed to open her new season at the Vaudeville in Sardou's *Fédora;* and now, despite her entreaties, Sardou refused to have Damala as Fédora's lover. It was a hard decision to break to a husband who was already envious and bitter: a man who was perhaps even now a confirmed morphine addict. Sarah solved the problem by commissioning *Les Mères ennemies* from Catulle Mendès. It was a play with a fine part for Damala. She appealed to her husband's pride and pointed out the advantage of taking an undisputed lead rather than an obvious second place. Then, in her anxiety to keep him, she leased the Théâtre de l'Ambigu regardless of the probable financial loss. In a further attempt to placate her son, who still firmly opposed the marriage, she leased the theater under the name of Maurice Bernhardt.

On November 17 *Les Mères ennemies* had its first successful performance. On December 11 the opening of *Fédora* at the Vaudeville marked the beginning of the collaboration between Sarah and that skillful, prolific dramatist, Victorien Sardou. Just as Bizet had composed *Carmen* to suit Galli-Marié, Sardou had written *Fédora* to suit Sarah. She found the part very hard; but that evening, in Paris, the god descended. Her feline charm, her violence, sent a shudder through the audience. In the fourth act, when Sardou had arranged for Fédora to die of poison, her pathos was superb.

Sarah saw herself triumph with mixed emotions. It was hard to know how her husband would receive this victory which eclipsed his own achievement at the Ambigu. She had not long to wait. On December 16, after a fierce quarrel, he accused her of trying to ruin his stage career and abruptly left the avenue de Villiers.

Then, in February 1883, he suddenly returned. His physical condition was now worsening; and one day in April, in sorrow and in fury, Sarah threw away all the morphine and syringes she could find. Damala left the house again, and she obtained a legal separation. She sought consolation, not for the first time, in the arms of a burly, bearded poet, the antithesis of Damala: Jean Richepin.

It was with Richepin that, in June, she returned to Copenhagen. The city was so festive in her honor that some inhabitants, unaware of what was happening, asked if the excitement meant a change of government. From Copenhagen they went to Stockholm, where King Oscar attended all her five performances of Richepin's *Nana Sahib* and awarded her a gold medal and a crown of brilliants. Yet it was perhaps in London that Sarah felt herself to be most surely the empress of the stage; and on July 9, at a Gaiety Theatre resplendent with the new electric light, she opened a one-week season in *Fédora.*

The failure of Richepin's *Nana Sahib* and of his crude prose version of *Macbeth* in May 1884 were to weaken his liaison with Sarah, and he went the way of all her lovers. On December 26, 1884, a year to the day after she had appeared with Richepin in *Nana Sahib,* she appeared with Philippe Garnier in *Théodora.*

Théodora was Victorien Sardou's greatest triumph with Sarah: indeed, it was one of the greatest triumphs in her career. It was the story of the ex-dancer taken to wife by the Emperor Justinian. Under the name of Théodora she remained a courtesan, only to learn one day that her current lover meant to assassinate the Emperor and Empress. Justinian discovered the plot and his wife's infidelity, and Théodora was put to death. "Heaven," wrote Jules Lemaître, "has endowed Mme Sarah Bernhardt with singular gifts. . . . And Mme Sarah Bernhardt marvelously exploits this air of a fairy-tale princess, of a chimerical and faraway creature. . . . In the first act, lying on her bed, the miter on her brow, a great lily in her hand, she looks like the fantastic queens of Gustave Moreau, those dream-figures by turn hieratic and serpentine, of a mystic and sensual attraction." *Théodora* was performed more than three hundred times, with a single break in the summer of 1885, when the Empress Sarah took the play to London.

In the autumn of 1887, after a thirteen-month tour of South America, Sarah appeared opposite Pierre Berton in a new play Sardou had written for her: *La Tosca.* The amount of electricity generated by one scene of this play would have been enough, so someone observed, to light the streets of London. Pierre Loüys, the future novelist and poet, was then a susceptible *collégien,* vainly seeking a goddess whom he might worship. Early in the new year he saw Sarah in *La Tosca,* and he was overwhelmed by his first passion. Two months later, still afire with adoration, he waited by Sarah's carriage to see her leave the Odéon where she had been rehearsing *L'Aveu.*

Sarah's first venture as a playwright, *L'Aveu,* was first performed on March 27, 1888. It is a short and cogent melodrama played round the bedside of a dying child. When the mother feels that the child is lost, she confesses to her husband that it is not his and that the real father is waiting in the next room for news. There is a violent quarrel between the two men, and then the baby dies and the quarrel ends.

For all Sarah's acting, *L'Aveu* was poorly received, and it was performed a mere dozen times that year. But it was not to be her only literary venture. She wrote a new and vastly successful version of *Adrienne Lecouvreur.* Her *Christmas Story* appeared in *The Silver Fairy Book* in 1895. She turned to the novel too; and in *Petite Idole,* that strange amalgam of fact and fiction, she was to project herself as Espérance Darbois, the child actress who died on stage at the Théâtre-Français.

At the end of March 1888, suddenly exhausted by the strain of endless tours, of perpetual playing, of personal unhappiness, Sarah was forced to interrupt performances of *La Tosca.* But she did not rest for long. After several weeks she had recovered enough to take the play on tour in the French provinces. In July she went to London, where she played *La Tosca* with such terrifying effect that men had to leave the theater in mid performance.

It was on her return that an event of profound domestic importance occurred: the marriage of Maurice. At the age of twenty-three he married a Polish princess, Terka Jablonovska, and left the avenue de Villiers. Maurice was the truly great love of Sarah's life, and he was her only lasting passion. To Maurice, a prince's son, who was as handsome as a prince, Sarah had given all the devotion that she had not been able to give to Damala and her lovers, all the affection that her family had not deserved. The shoes he had worn as a child had been with her on her prodigious tours of America; she wore his portrait and a lock of his hair in a gold locket at her neck. His frequent duels, his indolence, his complete dependence on her—all were forgiven him to the end of her life. Now for the first time he left her roof; and fond though Sarah was of Terka, warmly though she approved of the marriage, there remained a void in her existence.

There was some consolation. She spent August with Maurice and Terka at Belle-Île in Brittany. Then, refreshed by the country air, she set out on yet another European tour and went on to Egypt, Constantinople, and St. Petersburg. She returned home by way of Sweden and Norway. And back in Paris in March 1889 she received news of Damala. He begged her to come and see him.

She hastened to him, found him in a little *entresol* at the back of a courtyard in the rue d'Antin. The small, dark rooms were sparsely furnished, their only ornaments the sabre he had worn in *Les Mères ennemies,* a gold crown and a Greek flag. Damala was now taking cocaine as well as morphine; he stayed in bed most of the day, watching his mind grow increasingly unbalanced. Sarah was filled with maternal pity. She had him taken to hospital. On August 18, 1890, at the age of thirty-four, he died.

He was buried in Athens. But visitors to Sarah's *hôtel* always noticed in a place of honor a marble figure she had sculpted: "Damala lying on his back with his hands under his handsome head." She kept the greatest affection for his family and for his memory.

In January 1891 she embarked on the most prodigious tour of her career. In September 1893, after thirty-two months, she ended her odyssey at Lisbon with a profit of three and a half million francs.

It was at this moment of wealth that she became the manager of the Théâtre de la Renaissance, guiding it for five years, until 1898. During those years, among many revivals, she produced twelve new plays. Two of them, *Izeyl* by Eugène Morand and Armand Silvestre, and *Lorenzaccio* by Alfred de Musset, had little more than seventy performances. Only one, *Gismonda,* reached its hundredth performance. But if the Renaissance was not a happy school for dramatists, it was a brilliant nursery for actors. Sarah set three new actors at the head of her company. One of them, Abel Deval, was excellent; the others, Lucien Guitry and Édouard de Max, were outstanding. Lucien Guitry was thirty-three; but having spent nine years acting in St. Petersburg, he had not yet established himself in Paris. Under Sarah's management he rose to eminence. Édouard de Max was only twenty-four when she took the Renaissance; and it was Sarah herself who launched this admirable actor, her own ideal partner— indeed her best partner after Mounet-Sully. De Max was regally handsome, the incarnation of the prince of legend.

It seemed that Sarah, like Cleopatra, was not condemned by the years. And yet she was sometimes sad. Her perpetual activity, her manifold triumphs, her defiant motto *Quand même* were essential to her existence; but they grew increasingly difficult to maintain. And, so far as the press was concerned, the days of unqualified praise were already ending. "This

Sarah the Younger is a fascinating, seductive, supple and sinuous creature, with the smile of a Sphinx and the voice of a Siren," decided the critic William Archer, watching her in *Izeyl* at Daly's Theatre. "But ah! You should have seen her mother, twenty years ago! The daughter imitates her marvelously; but the copy is mechanical, and sometimes a little coarse."

A young poet, Edmond Rostand, now presented himself at 56 boulevard Péreire. He was to write some of Sarah's most conspicuous triumphs, and she was to give him his celebrity. On April 5, 1895, supported by Guitry and de Max, Sarah launched *La Princesse lointaine.* "It may not make a sou," she had said, "but I don't care. I think it is superb. No artist could fail to stage it."

La Princesse lointaine depended on Sarah's power of creating unearthly beauty, of realizing a dream. The first act described Mélissinde, Princess Far Away, a being of irresistible fascination and supernatural loveliness. In the second act she appeared, and fulfilled imagination. The verse was graceful though unremarkable; then, suddenly, there emerged a lyric which was strangely and hauntingly musical. Geoffrey Rudel, the troubadour prince, recited it in the first act; in the second act the Rhyme of Princess Far Away was spoken by Sarah Bernhardt herself. Everyone waited for that moment. At last the moment came.

The indifferent poetry of *La Princesse lointaine* turned, as Sarah spoke it, to gold; but her greatest triumph was a triumph of grace, and even Sarcey applauded the final vision of Mélissinde arriving, like Cleopatra in her barge, decked in her finest raiment and followed by a gorgeous retinue, to take the veil.

La Princesse lointaine was magnificently cast, spectacularly beautiful; but, as Sarah had feared, it was not popular. It had cost her more than 200,000 francs, and it ran for thirty-one performances. Despondently she revived *La Dame aux camélias.*

By 1895, Sarah was so tired of her theater that for a time she handed it over to Guitry. She had spent a fortune; she was constantly spending a fortune on her household with its numerous servants, its three or four carriages and six horses. Sarah was also spending a fortune on the ten to twenty guests who arrived for nearly every meal. It was time to make a fortune again. She prepared to return once more to America; this time she would go for ten months.

It was the queen of actresses who left Le Havre on January 3, 1896 for another tour of the United States. She made a royal progress through America. She received deputations from several cities where she could not play. In one they would have erected triumphal arches for her; in another they wanted to illuminate the town.

Late in July she returned to France; late in September she returned to the Théâtre de la Renaissance in *La Dame aux camélias,* a revival even more successful than usual, for, instead of playing it in modern dress, she staged it in the costume of its period. A week after her return, this triumph was briefly interrupted to let her appear at Versailles before the tsar; for Nicholas II, asked by the French ambassador what entertainment he chose for his official visit, had answered in two words: "Sarah Bernhardt."

In December she took the title role in the first performance of Musset's *Lorenzaccio,* and received a vigorous welcome from the critics. "She was," cried Catulle Mendès, "from beginning to end, and at every moment, incomparably sublime. And the fête that Paris is preparing for her will express all the gratitude of a century and of a nation." It was, in fact, a week after the opening of *Lorenzaccio* that the official glorification of Sarah took place in Paris. Henry Bauer, the journalist, organized *la Journée Sarah Bernhardt.*

Not since the various glorifications accorded to Victor Hugo had there been such a national event. On the morning of December 9, 1896, the elect assembled for a banquet in honor of Sarah Bernhardt. They were never to forget the emotion and applause as she made her entrance. Nobody ever moved better than Sarah. Jules Renard, the novelist, seeing her come down a spiral staircase, said that the staircase seemed to turn, and she to be motionless. Today she came down the stairs to the banqueting room, the huge Salle du Zodiaque, in the Grand Hotel, rue Scribe. They acclaimed her wildly.

After the compliments and embraces she took her place at the table of honor on the dais under a canopy of green velvet. Her delicate profile, the profile of a princess in legend, stood out against a tapestry which gracefully represented "Time in chains." On her right sat Victorien Sardou, on her left Henry Bauer. There were five hundred guests, all famous in science, politics and business, in literature and in the arts, in society and in the theater. There were three kinds of menu, each designed by a different artist. Among the dishes were *gâteaux Sarah* and *bombe Tosca.* After the banquet, Sardou proposed a toast to "the great and good Sarah." The Colonne choir (accompanied by the Colonne orchestra) sang a cantata composed to her greater glory. Then Sarah made her regal departure. "As she went slowly up the winding stairs, from time to time sending a smile or a wave of her hand to her admirers below, she seemed almost to be mounting in triumph towards the sky."

And then the assembly followed her to the Théâtre de la Renaissance, where Sarah performed the second act of *Phèdre* and the fourth act of *Rome vaincue*. Then the curtain rose to show her robed in white and gold and seated on a throne of flowers under a canopy of green palms, camellias and orchids. Women in peplums, crowned with roses, posed in adoring attitudes about her. Then a young student paid homage to the eternal youth of the artist. And then, in turn, poets read their sonnets in praise of Sarah Bernhardt. When the curtain fell on this apotheosis there were shouts, cheers, applause, stamping feet. Women tore flowers from their hair and from their corsages to throw them on the stage.

CHAPTER 4

A GREAT INSTITUTION

Half a century before, Rachel had magnificently played the part of Pauline, the Christian convert in *Polyeucte*. At Easter 1897, Sarah Bernhardt, who was also Jewish, again moved Paris by religious fervor in the first performance of *La Samaritaine* by Edmond Rostand. All the religious fervor which had possessed Sarah as a child seemed to come upon her now; and Rostand dedicated his play "to Madame Sarah Bernhardt who was a flame and a prayer."

Soon after *La Samaritaine*, it was announced that Eleonora Duse would perform in Paris that summer; indeed, her impresario was already negotiating with various theaters. Sarah promptly offered her the Renaissance free of charge, and a contract was signed for ten performances in June, to alternate with her own.

In May, when la Duse published the list of plays she would perform, there was stupefaction. Most astonishing, she had chosen to make her début in Sarah's theater in *La Dame aux camélias*. Sarah did not object to this provocative choice, but the press commented on it severely.

The early summer brought a battle that recalled the conflict of forty years ago between Rachel and la Ristori. Again an Italian actress came to Paris, again the audience was to watch a theatrical contest. Sarah was fifty-two, resplendent with her international triumphs; la Duse was thirty-eight, her reputation was not comparable, but she had the advantage of her years, the advantage of novelty and the greater advantage of pleasing Sarah's detractors. La Duse enjoyed a considerable success, largely due to curiosity, but the comparison she had sought was hardly made. There was no comparison to make.

It was said that the personality of Eleonora Duse sometimes impeded her portrayal, but that Sarah's always illuminated hers. La Duse so sublimated the part of Marguerite Gautier that she could play it with woollen spencers ill-concealed beneath her negligées. The approach was intellectual, and as far removed from reality as it could be. In the summer of 1894, in London, Sarah herself had seen la Duse as Marguerite Gautier. "Signora Duse's conception," she told a reporter, "strikes me as being absolutely original, and, if I may say so, particularly Italian, but I do not think we differ much as to essentials." In time she came to be less benevolent; and she published such a harsh judgment of la Duse that the Italian actress replied: "Tell Mme Bernhardt that I am not writing my memoirs, nor have I any intention of writing them; but she had better pray God I never change my mind."

October 1897 found Sarah performing in Belgium. She returned to France to produce a series of unfortunate plays. By the end of 1898, pursued by an inexorable series of failures, she was convinced that an evil spell had been cast on the Théâtre de la Renaissance. She put up her lease for sale and bade farewell with *La Dame aux camélias* in November and December. Then she signed a twenty-five-year lease, beginning on January 1, 1899, for the Théâtre des Nations near the banks of the Seine; a theater which, characteristically enough, she renamed the Théâtre Sarah-Bernhardt.

It was in this theater that on May 20, 1899, Sarah gave her first performance as Hamlet. Long before her appearance, rumor said, she had adapted herself to the part by wearing Hamlet's costume in the boulevard Péreire. Now, when she appeared on stage, she recalled to some the Hamlet of Delacroix. The translated *Hamlet* was—at least to Parisian ears—an immense success; and Maurice Baring declared that it was Sarah's performance which first gave the French public an exact idea of *Hamlet*. Her characterization was strikingly original, and roused such heated comments that Catulle Mendès fought a duel with an opposing critic, George Vanor, over the color of Hamlet's hair—or Sarah's hair, which was the same thing, that season. Then, in June, to allow the contractors to work on her theater, Sarah went to play *Hamlet* in London.

And so, on June 12, 1899, at the Adelphi Theatre, London witnessed one of the most remarkable performances in the annals of Shakespearean production. "You are so lucky in England," Sarah was to tell an English journalist. "You have Shakespeare. You can never quite forget him." She spoke, perhaps, more truly than she understood. It was an audacious venture to interpret the most controversial character in English drama during the reign of Henry Irving; and it was doubly audacious, for the young Prince of Denmark was not only to be played by a woman, and by a Frenchwoman at that, but by a woman fifty-four years of age.

> As a tour de force Mme Bernhardt's Hamlet was bound to be interesting [reported *The Times*]. As a success de curiosite it was bound to attract the town. But it is much more than this that Mme Sarah Bernhardt had to offer. Her Hamlet is a rendering worked out with a consistent grip upon the character as the actress conceives it. . . . No one who is an admirer of Mme Bernhardt's wonderful art and wonderful personality will come away disappointed.

There had been a time when Sarah enjoyed astonishing the world. She was not the only star to recognize the value of publicity; she had simply publicized herself better than most. She had created a legend for the public. Now, however, she had done with fostering absurdities. Yvonne Lanco, as a small child, used to see Sarah Bernhardt pass in her carriage. A black servant in scarlet livery sat beside the groom. But Sarah herself, always dressed in white, did not seem like Sarah Barnum. She seemed to the child a very great lady.

It was this very great lady who, in September 1899, returned to Paris to supervise the decoration of her theater. Parisian theaters had always been furnished in red. Sarah's auditorium was draped from ceiling to floor in buttercup yellow velvet framed in ivory white. In the public foyer, which looked out on to the place du Châtelet, ten murals represented Mme Bernhardt, life-size, as Lorenzaccio, Phèdre, Théodora, la Princesse lointaine, la Tosca and Gismonda. Mme Bernhardt's "dressing room" was not merely a dressing room, but an extensive apartment of five rooms on two floors. A double door and three steps led from the stage into an anteroom twenty-one feet long and twelve feet wide. Then came a large Empire drawing-room hung with yellow satin and furnished with Empire furniture. Finally came Sarah's dressing room with a tall dressing table, wardrobes enough to hold fifty costumes, a monumental washstand, a bathtub and a gigantic three-paneled mirror.

On December 16, 1899, Sarah reopened her theater. A brilliant audience, including President Loubet, admired some revolutions in theatrical design. Next day, on the stage of the Théâtre Sarah-Bernhardt, Edmond Rostand read *L'Aiglon* to her company.

Only a woman supremely sure of her public and her powers would have dared attempt what she attempted now. Thirty-one years before, Sarah Bernhardt had entered upon her glory as Zanetto. Now, at fifty-six, she would take the part of another boy: the son of Napoleon. The fact that Sarah was a woman, and a middle-aged woman, was forgotten once she had spoken. L'Aiglon stood before the audience. She carried off the lines with a pace and intensity which went through the theater like an electric shock. People were crying everywhere. When the final curtain fell, there was a rain of violets—the Bonaparte flowers—on the stage. Rostand and Sarah Bernhardt had touched the public heart: had stirred the public pride in Napoleon and his dynasty.

The triumph of *L'Aiglon* was to continue all through the summer; and Sarah, in her famous carriage with the chestnut horses, often went to visit the Rostands in the house they had taken near Montmorency. Sometimes, to the delight of Maurice Rostand, Edmond's son, she would bring her two little granddaughters, Simone and Lysiane; they both looked like Sarah at different periods in her life. Maurice Rostand was long to remember those magic days of childhood when Sarah tossed her chinchilla coat to her favorite greyhound, and proved that her tousled hair was naturally curly by pouring Heidsieck Monopole all over it.

With a break in August so that Sarah could rest, *L'Aiglon* ran for 237 performances. It might have continued until its five-hundredth performance had not Sarah undertaken a new six months' tour in the United States, from November 1900 to April 1901.

To the end of her long and arduous life, Sarah remained untiring. She would act till midnight, change when the curtain fell, and rehearse till five in the morning. Every morning, when she rose, she would throw off her nightclothes and exercise on a stationary bicycle in her bedroom (there was also a fixed "rowing boat" in the boulevard Péreire). She did many things, and indeed she learned many things—among them sculpture, painting and music—not so much for themselves as for their value to the theater. Sarah, as she said herself, was no musician; but music increased her sense of rhythm and gave her the control of breathing which was as necessary for elocution as it was for singing.

The theater was the sum and center of her interests. It was her true and perpetual home. Her life was spent upon the boards acting, and in rehearsing when she was not acting. That was all that counted. Day after day she would be in the theater before noon, and stay there for twelve or fourteen hours, using every moment to the full. She would eat her frugal *déjeuner* and dinner in her dressing room "with no relief of silence, and with little interruption of the flow of business." Sometimes in her work she was guided by impulse; but method was her mainstay, and concentration the key to it all.

The years 1902 and 1903 were not entirely successful for Sarah, and only in December 1903 did she achieve an uncontested success (her last with Sardou) in *La Sorcière*.

On April 8, 1905, she played Assuérus in a revival of *Esther*; and at the end of the month she left for London, where she played in Maurice Maeterlinck's *Pelléas et Mélisande* for the first time. Mrs. Patrick Campbell, who had already played Mélisande in English in England and the United States, now played it in French to Sarah's Pelléas. Alas, when they took the play on tour, a Dublin critic wrote succinctly: "Mrs. Campbell played Mélisande, Mme Bernhardt Pelléas. They are both old enough to know better."

CHAPTER 5

THE STRICKEN QUEEN

On June 5, 1905, Sarah embarked at Southampton for yet another American tour. On October 9, in Rio de Janeiro, she met with one of the great disasters of her life. She was playing in *La Tosca*. At the end of the last scene Floria committed suicide by leaping off the parapet of the Castel Sant' Angelo. Usually, of course, the stage behind the parapet was covered with mattresses; that night, for some unknown reason, the mattresses had been forgotten, and Sarah fell heavily on her right knee. She fainted with pain; her leg swelled violently, and she was carried to her hotel on a stretcher. Next day, when she embarked for New York, a doctor was called to her stateroom, but his hands were so dirty that she refused to let him touch her. In vain her friends protested, insisted that they would make him take a bath. Sarah would see no doctor until she reached New York three weeks later.

Her New York season had to be postponed for a fortnight. About mid-November, she was able to walk and to begin her tour in Chicago. But the three weeks' delay had proved disastrous; and, inexorably, her injury grew worse. By 1908 she could only walk with difficulty; by 1911 she could not walk unsupported; by 1913 the furniture had to be arranged on stage so that she never took more than two consecutive steps. In her dressing room she rubbed ether on her knee to deaden the pain; often she was given injections. And as she walked to her entrance she was helped by a handrail of rope round the back of the stage. When she made her exit she would fall exhausted into a chair and rest for several minutes before she was taken back to her dressing room.

Late in June 1906, Sarah Bernhardt returned to France and went to London for three weeks. Then, tired and ill, she spent a couple of months dictating her torrential, charming and frequently inaccurate *Mémoires*.

How astonishing, how admirable were these, her later years! The injured, defiant child of years ago, who had taken as her motto the challenge *Quand même*, had become the injured, aging but indomitable woman. And when, in May 1909, the actress Adeline Dudlay gave her farewell performance, Sarah made her only reappearance in the rue de Richelieu. She was sixty-four and she took the part of the young romantic poet in *La Nuit de mai* by Musset. That November, defiant as ever, she took the name part in *Le Procès de Jeanne d'Arc*. Twenty years earlier, in her forties, in a play by Jules Barbier, she had appeared as the Maid of Orleans. Now, at sixty-five, she played Joan of Arc again; and when, in the trial scene, she was asked her age, she turned slowly, very slowly, to face the audience. Gently but firmly she answered: "Nineteen." Every evening, at this point, she was given an ovation.

Fiercely, delightedly, Sarah moved with the times. She was, for instance, one of the few to recognize in the new-born cinema the embryo of the giant it would become. Such modernity was characteristic of Sarah. She did not disdain to appear, for the first time in her life, as a London music-hall attraction. In the summer of 1910 in London, at the Coliseum, a Turkey red carpet eighty feet long was laid from Sarah's dressing room to the stage, so that her feet should not touch the boards which, perhaps, performing elephants had just trodden.

On January 15, 1914, the President of the French Republic paid an official visit to the Théâtre Sarah-Bernhardt. He watched Sarah's performance in *Jeanne Doré*, and he invested her with the insignia awarded to every dutiful French functionary: the cross of Chevalier de la Légion-d'honneur. "Dear great friend," cabled Rostand, "I kiss you with all my heart"; and in a second telegram he added: "Every poet and artist has waited impatiently for the time when your huge mass of laurels should at last be found by this little bit of red ribbon." The minister of public instruction later recalled her qualifications for the honor. "Sarah Bernhardt served as a hospital nurse in the war of 1870, and she has made the French tongue known throughout the world."

Soon afterwards, Maurice Baring saw Sarah in *La Dame aux camélias*.

> She was suffering from her leg. . . . The Stage had to be marked out in chalk for her, showing the spots where she could stand up, for she was too unwell to stand up for more than certain given moments. I went to see her with a Russian actress who had seen her play in Russia and had not been able to endure her acting, thinking it affected and listless, and wondering what her reputation was founded on. We arrived late, after the second act, and I went behind the scenes and talked to Sarah, and told her of this Russian actress who was tone deaf to her art. Sarah played the last three acts with such agonizing poignancy and reserve that not only was my Russian friend in tears, but the actors on the stage cried so much that their tears discolored their faces and made runnels in their grease paint. I said I never would see her act again after that, and I did not.

There was little chance to see her perform. In May she began to tour France with *Jeanne Doré*, but her performances were interrupted at Lille, near the Belgian frontier, and on July 28 she returned to Paris. Within a week the First World War had begun.

Sarah spent August in Paris. She was suffering greatly from her knee and hardly left the boulevard Péreire. Late that month her family advised her to leave Paris, but she refused to listen to them. It took George Clémenceau himself to force her to the decision. Clémenceau (who, at the time, was out of politics) had been warned by the counterespionage authorities that Sarah was on the list of hostages who were to be deported if the Germans took the capital. At his urging Sarah set off in her car for the south on August 31.

She rented a villa at Andernos, about twenty-five miles from Bordeaux, and there she settled indefinitely; as the war news improved she would have liked to go back to Paris in October, but her knee had grown far worse and it was giving her acute pain. Her leg was put in plaster. After three months of immobility, it was found that the disease was no longer local but was actually threatening her life. Professor Pozzi came from Paris to consult with two local doctors; and after lengthy consultations they suggested amputation. "Since there is nothing else to be done," said Sarah, "why ask my opinion?"

She herself decided on the amputation.

At the age of seventy, with remarkable courage, she prepared herself for the operation. On the eve of the operation she sent a characteristic telegram to a friend in Paris. "To-morrow they are going to take off my leg. Think of me, and book me some lectures for April."

She was forced to spend about a fortnight in bed at Bordeaux before she went back to Andernos for her convalescence. She was already thinking of playing *La Princesse lointaine*. No woman, Sarah once said, need be as old as her years, but only so old as she thinks herself. "The same applies to death. I often think about death, but only to assure myself that I shall not die until I am ready."

She was never able to walk again after she lost her leg; she was never able even to stand on an artificial limb. Wherever she went she was carried in a folding chair; she traveled in a specially built car. She was so philosophical herself that she probably did not know how distressing it was for others to see her disabled.

She lost herself in work, and she appeared as a nurse in a topical film, *Mères françaises*. In the spring of 1916 she was carried round the front and performed for the Théâtre des Armées. On September 30 she embarked once again, this time with a very small company, for America. She took a new repertory to suit her condition, including the third act of *Le Procès de Jeanne d'Arc*, the fifth act of *La Dame aux camélias*, the sixth act of *L'Aiglon*. She was brave; but she returned to France weary and discouraged, knowing how disappointed the public must have been by her mediocre repertory, and saddened by the thought of the plays that were now forbidden her. One day in America she had met the magician, Harry Houdini. "Houdini, you do such wonderful things," she had said to him. "Could you bring back my leg for me?" And, seeing that he was startled, she added, "Yes, but you do the impossible. I never was more serious in my life."

CHAPTER 6

FINAL OFFERING

In 1920 Sarah gave a series of special performances of Racine's *Athalie*. She was carried on to the stage in a gold palaquin. Paul Géraldy, the poet and playwright, stood in the wings and saw her as she passed. She looked decrepit, a very old woman with chattering teeth and withered face. But no sooner had she said the opening lines than he felt the spell which she had cast over the whole theater. Her voice became the gate of a hundred sorrows, and her eyes had in them the retrospect and sadness of a resurrected spring. He and all the audience were ready to kneel at her feet and weep.

It was this year that May Agate saw Sarah in Paris. She was carried into the drawing room in the boulevard Péreire, and May Agate found her enormously changed. Her hair was now allowed to be its own natural white. She wore it loosely tied with a black bow. Her features had always been fine, but they were now more rugged than before; and, for the first time, she looked old.

On Saturday April 4, 1921, she arrived in London. On the way to Boulogne her car had broken down, and she had been forced to spend the night at Montreuil-sur-Mer and to leave there at five A.M. The crossing had been rough, and she reached the Savoy in a state of exhaustion.

Two hours later, she was rehearsing; for on Monday she was to perform at the Princes Theatre in *Daniel*.

That Monday, immediately before the second act, she was carried on to the stage; and there she remained until the final curtain; and *Daniel* "was wonderful, though more wonderful still was the intense emotion of the whole house while waiting for the curtain to go up." Children who heard little and could understand less were brought to the theater so that they might say one day that they had seen Sarah Bernhardt. For older generations, it was a strange evening of reminiscence "overlaying and almost obliterating experience." It was today that Sarah was promoted Officier de la Légion-d'honneur; and it was today that, led by Ellen Terry, the English acting profession gave her a golden book of signatures in homage and gratitude.

"You ask me my theory of life," said Sarah once. "It is represented by the word *will*. . . . Life is short, even for those who live a long time, and we must live for the few who know and appreciate us, who judge and absolve us, and for whom we have the same affection and indulgence. We ought to hate very rarely, as it is too fatiguing, remain indifferent a great deal, forgive often, and never forget."

On October 25, 1922, as she prepared in her dressing room for Maurice Rostand's *La Gloire*, she was overcome by the shuddering that announced an attack of uremia. The doctor forbade her to perform that evening; but "when the hour comes, she for whom the Swedes sowed the waves of the Baltic with roses, beneath whose feet the Peruvians spread their cloaks, must, like her comrades, obey the call of the prompter.

There lies her salvation." And there lay Sarah's duty. Devoted to Maurice Rostand, she continued like a soldier of the theater. And then the curtain fell between her and the world, enveloping her like a great purple shroud.

In December, rehearsing a play by Sacha Guitry, *Un Sujet de roman*, she collapsed. Her first words when she regained consciousness were: "When shall I appear again?" She did not succumb at once. A week later she attended the dress rehearsal of *Le Phénix* by Maurice Rostand, and all Paris filed through her dressing room in homage. But she had presumed too much on her strength; and from that moment she began to fail.

On March 15, 1923, Lysiane Bernhardt arrived at the boulevard Péreire to watch the filming of *La Voyante*. In the studio, facing networks of scaffolding, mercury lights and spotlights, was a decor of a fortune-teller's booth with a view of Montmartre from the window; and Sarah sat weary, expressionless, behind a table. Patiently she picked up her fortune-telling cards and went through her movements. Then she fell.

On March 20 the doctors declared that the poison had entered her system and that there was no hope. At first she was in despair. She had wanted to perform in Guitry's new play; she had wanted to finish her film. Then, gradually, she grew resigned, and resignation turned to torpor, and those around her knew that Sarah was going to die.

She knew it too. She knew that the journalists were waiting night and day on the bench in the boulevard Péreire facing her windows. It amused her to keep them waiting. On March 23 Mrs. Patrick Campbell came to dinner and found her wearing a long-sleeved dress of pink Venetian velvet sent by Sacha Guitry. Knowing that she had not long to live, Sarah sat there, white-faced, eating nothing and infinitely gracious. When dinner was over, she was carried upstairs on her chair; turning the bend of the staircase, she kissed one finger and held it out.

"How slow death is in coming," she said to Maurice on the morning of March 26; and again, "It is springtime, let me have a wealth of flowers." She had moments of serenity, moments of lucidity; moments, too, of delirium, when she recalled the great deaths she had played: the death of Marguerite Gautier, the death of l'Aiglon. And wildly, now, in identification, she recited the words.

At half past three that afternoon she received extreme unction; and at five past eight, in a deep coma, she died.

Sarah, who had received so many flowers in her life, was given them in death. Her pillow was covered with roses and white and purple lilac, her deathbed was surrounded by lilac and roses, forget-me-nots and Parma violets. The multitudes who came to see her walked through a house that seemed a very garden, into a room impassable for flowers.

Sarah was dressed, as l'Aiglon had been dressed, in white. She wore a white satin robe; on her breast was the insignia of the Légion-d'honneur, and round her neck was a gold locket on a black ribbon, holding a portrait of Maurice, a lock of his hair. In her hands was a crucifix of gold and ebony, and "her face, full of peace, was like carved ivory."

And then she was laid in the rosewood coffin, lined with old rose satin, that had waited so long.

Sarah Bernhardt was buried on Maundy Thursday, 1923, at Père Lachaise. She was buried with proper splendor, and a wealth of flowers.

Nancy Friday

MY MOTHER/MY SELF

THE DAUGHTER'S SEARCH FOR IDENTITY

A condensation of the book by

Nancy Friday

MOTHER LOVE

I have always lied to my mother. And she to me. Her denial of whatever she could not tell me, that her mother could not tell her, and about which society enjoined us both to keep silent, distorts our relationship still.

Sometimes I try to imagine a little scene that could have helped us both. In her kind, warm, shy, and self-deprecating way, mother calls me into the bedroom where she sleeps alone. She is no more than twenty-five. I am perhaps six. "Nancy, you know I'm not really good at this mothering business," she says. "You're a lovely child, the fault is not with you. But motherhood doesn't come easily to me. There are some things I know about. I'll teach them to you. The other stuff—sex and all that— well, I just can't discuss them with you because I'm not sure where they fit into my own life. We'll try to find other people who can talk to you and fill the gaps. You can't expect me to be all the mother you need. I feel closer to your age in some ways than I do my mother's. I don't feel that serene, divine, earth-mother certainty you're supposed to that she felt. I am unsure how to raise you. But you are intelligent and so am I. Your aunt loves you, your teachers already feel the need in you. With their help, with what I can give, we'll see that you get the whole mother package—all the love in the world. It's just that you can't expect to get it all from me."

A scene that could never have taken place.

For as long as I can remember, I did not want the kind of life my mother felt she could show me. Sometimes I think she did not want it either. The older I get, the further away she gets from my childhood, from her ironclad role as my mother—the more interesting a woman she becomes. Perhaps she should never have been a mother; certainly she was one too soon. I look at her today, and wish she had had a chance to live another life. But hers was not an age in which women felt they had a choice.

I have no idea when I began to perceive with the monstrous selfishness that dependency lends to a child's eyes that my mother was not perfect: I was not her whole life. Was it at the same age that I began to make the terrible judgment that she was not the woman I wanted to be? It seems I have always known both. It accounts for my guilt at leaving her, and my anger that she let me go. But I am sure that she has always known that my sister and I were not enough. We had not brought the certification of womanhood that *her* mother had promised. That, once in her life, sex and a man had been more important than motherhood.

A more dutiful daughter than I, my mother wanted to accept the view of reality my grandmother taught her. She subverted her genuine feelings, those burgeoning intimations of life's hope and adventure which she found in my father, and which induced her to elope with him against her family's wishes—all lost, in the name of being a good mother. Her mother's rules had the authority of the entire culture behind them. There was no such thing as a "bad mother"; there were only bad women. They were the explicitly sexual ones, who lived out the notion that what went on between themselves and their husbands had at least as much right to life as their children. They had little "maternal instinct."

We are raised to believe that mother love is different from other kinds of love. It is not open to error, doubt, or to the ambivalence of ordinary affections. This is an illusion.

Mothers may love their children, but they sometimes do not like them. The same woman who may be willing to put her body between her child and a runaway truck will often resent the day-by-day sacrifice the child unknowingly demands of her time, sexuality and self-development.

In our perception of our mother's unauthenticity—her own anxiety and lack of belief in over-idealized notions of womanhood/motherhood she is trying to teach us—anxieties about our own sexuality are born. There is the beginning of doubt that we will succeed as people with identities of our own, separate from her, established in ourselves as women before we are mothers. We try for autonomy, try for sexuality, but the unconscious, deepest feelings we have picked up from her will not rest. We will only feel at peace, sure of ourselves, when we have fulfilled the glorified "instinct" we have been trained to repeat: you are not a full woman until you are a mother.

It is too late to ask my mother to go back and examine evasions she made as silently as any mother and to which I agreed for so long—if only because she doesn't want to. I am the one who wants to change certain dead-end patterns in my life.

In my years of interviewing, how many women have repeatedly said to me, "No, I can't think of anything significant I've inherited from my mother. We're completely different women . . ." This is usually said with an air of triumph—as if the speaker is acknowledging the enormous pull to model herself on her mother, but believes she has resisted.

To be fair, if my interviewees and I talked long enough, they themselves began to see the similarities with their mothers' lives. First the superficial, outward differences had to be worked through. Mother lived in a house, the woman I was talking to lived in an apartment. Mother never worked a day in her life, the daughter held down a job. We cling to these "facts" as proof that we have created our own lives, different from hers. We overlook the more basic truth that we have taken on her anxieties, fears, angers; the way we weave the web of emotion between ourselves and others is patterned on what we had with her.

Whether we want our mother's life or not, we never escape the image of how she was. Nowhere is this more true than in our sexual lives. Without our own sexual identity, one we can put our full weight upon with as much certainty as once we enjoyed being "mother's girl," we are unsure. We have spurts of sexual confidence, activity, exploration, but at the first rejection, hint of loss, of sexual censure or humiliation, we fall back on the safe and familiar: sex is bad. It was always a problem between mother and ourselves. When men seem bright and alluring, we momentarily ally with them against mother's antisexual rules. But men cannot be trusted. We say the fault is our own: we go from mother to men, with no self in between. Marriage, instead of ending our childish alliance with her, ironically becomes the biggest reunion of our lives. Once we wanted to be "nice girls." Now we are "nice married ladies"—just like mother. Those quarrels with her over men are ended at last. The hardest thing to face in mother is her sexuality. She found it hardest to face in us.

Unless we separate mother's love from her fear of sex, we will always see love and sex as opposites. The dichotomy will be passed on to our daughters. "Mother *was* right," we say, and the fervor with which we deny our daughter access to her own body is fired with all the anger, confusion, and self-abnegation we have experienced in giving up on our own sexuality.

"If the mother has a genuine sexual relationship with her husband," says psychotherapist Leah Schaefer, "but pretends to her daughter that in some way all erotic life must be tied up with motherhood, the girl senses this. She gets the feeling she cannot trust her mother. In my psychoanalytic practice, *I have found again and again this is the basic lie.* Parents tell their kids, 'No, no, you mustn't'—but the little girl senses that the mother herself is doing the forbidden. It makes a certain aspect of the mother's life and personality a big secret to the girl—and yet the mother always wants to know everything about the daughter. She pries into the girl's psyche, she's always telling her daughter they are friends, they must tell each other everything—but once more the girl knows mother is keeping one big secret from her, one part of herself is out of bounds. It is a one-way relationship, supposedly based on trust, but which the girl experiences as manipulative. She resents it.

"What makes the situation more difficult for the girl is when the mother is not conscious of telling this lie. She rationalizes: 'How can you tell a child *that?*' You may choose to withhold certain information, but this is not the right to tell your daughter a lie. Some women work their own minds around to where they believe the only purpose of sex is motherhood. So they don't think they're lying at all. They think they are safeguarding the girl's 'morals.' What they're doing is setting up a lifelong distrust on the girl's part, and also a feeling of isolation, of helplessness. Sex is very confusing to the daughter, but if she gets the feeling that her mother is lying about it—whom can she ever trust? And trust of yourself and the other person is the basis of life, marriage, and sexual orgasm."

Mother's difficulty is not necessarily that she is a liar or hypocrite. She says one thing, does another, and yet communicates on a profound level that she really feels something totally different. Most of us have learned to live with this tripartite split in the people we know and take each other as a whole. As daughters, however, we are so focused on our mothers, that we take them literally and try to integrate all three warring aspects they present to us. Since this confusion permeates the mother-daughter relationship and will be seen again and again throughout this book, let me clearly separate the three ideas here:

1. *Attitude.* This is what we say, the outward impression we give people, and is the quickest aspect of ourselves to change. It is often a reflection of public opinion, books we've read, what our peers believe, etc. An example is the mother who decides that her daughter will not grow up in sexual ignorance, as she did; she buys the girl a copy of the latest book on sex education. How she acts when the girl puts the book's precepts into use is the difference between attitude and:

2. *Behavior.* Mother finds her daughter touching and exploring her vagina, just like the photographs in the book. She grimaces and pushes the girl's hand away.

Behavior has changed greatly in recent years, but it is a mistake to believe how we act always correlates with our up-to-the-minute attitudes. Dr. Wardell Pomeroy, Kinsey's foremost researcher, tells me that changes in behavior usually lag at least a generation behind changes in attitude. This conservatism is strongly influenced, if not determined, by our:

3. *Deepest (often unconscious) feelings.* These buried, basic forces or motivations are usually learned from our parents. They are the most rigid aspects of ourselves, carry-overs from the past which often nullify the other two. They may be denied or "forgotten" but will nevertheless often express themselves in irrational or distorted behavior. In a mother's behavior, she carefully does not "know" that the girl has gone off for the weekend with a man. But her deepest feelings are betrayed when the daughter comes home on Monday to find mother resentful, worried, and angry for no reason she can name out loud.

Saying one thing about sex and motherhood, feeling contrary emotions about both at the same time, mother presents an enigmatic picture to her daughter. The first lie—the denial that a woman's sexuality may be in conflict with her role as a mother—is so upsetting to traditional ideas of femininity that it cannot be talked about. The girl is left with perception of a gap between what mother says, what mother does . . . and what the girl detects mother feels beneath it all. Nothing mother really feels ever escapes us. Our problem is that because we try to live out all parts of the split message she sent us, our behavior and lives all too often represent a jangled compromise. We don't know what to do. We unbutton the top button on our dress and then button it back up again. That is a joke. But when we are in bed and feel the promise of orgasm, our unconscious and divided feelings assert their primacy, depriving us of satisfaction. That is no joke.

Our efforts to see mother clearly are frustrated by a kind of denial. It is one of our most primitive mechanisms of defense. Early on, children begin to avoid knowledge that mother is anything less than the "good mother" she pretends to be. Very often this is done by splitting the idea of mother into *good* and *bad.* The bad mother is the other one, not the real one. She is the one who is cruel, has headaches, does not like us. She is temporary. Only the good one is real. We will wait for her return for years, always convinced that the woman before us, who makes us feel guilty, inadequate, and angry, is *not* mother. How many of us who live away from home, periodically go back to mother, perhaps at Christmas or on a birthday, hoping that this time "Everything will be different"? Grown women ourselves, we are still looking for, still tied to the illusion of the all-loving, good mother.

Children think their parents are perfect, and if anything is wrong it's their fault. We have to think our parents are perfect because as children we are so totally dependent. We can't afford to hate mother, so what we do is turn our anger against ourselves. Instead of saying she is hateful, we say, "I am hateful." Mother *has* to be all wise and kind.

The truth is that while the child *wants* to believe her mother loves her unequivocally, she can live with disappointment at finding out it is not so. What is most necessary is that the child feel her mother is for real, *authentic*. It is better to learn as early as possible that while mother loves us, it is not to the exclusion of everything and everyone else. If the child is encouraged to enter into collusion with mother, to pretend that the maternal instinct conquers all, both will be stuck ever after with mechanisms of denial and defense which cut them off from the reality of their mutual feelings; gone is any hope of a true relationship between them. The daughter will repeat this relationship with men and other women.

Where does the child get this idea of perfect mother love? From what her mother says, if not from what mother does. Mother always presents herself as totally loving. Her verbal formulas tell the girl that there is no question of the ideal way she feels. The reason mother is so angry or upset or cold right now is that father has been awful, the groceries didn't arrive, there is little money in the house, or the girl herself has been bad. In the end, the child comes to understand that whatever it is, it is because *she* has been naughty. It is all her fault.

The hardest part of writing this book will be giving up the illusion that if I myself had just said or done the right magical thing, the illusion of perfect love between my mother and me would have been made real.

There *is* real love between most mothers and daughters. There is real love between my mother and me. But it is not that kind of love she always led me to believe she felt, which society told me she felt, and about which I have always been angry and guilty. Angry because I never really felt it, guilty because I thought the fault lay in me. If I were a better daughter I would be able to take in this nourishing love she had always told me was there. I have recently found I could get angry with my mother and that it would not destroy her or me. The anger that separated me from her also put me in touch with the real love I have for her.

I have heard daughters say that they do not love their mothers. I have *never* heard a mother say she does not love her daughter. She can be honest about anything else, but the myth that mothers always love their children is so controlling that even the daughter who can admit disliking her mother, when her own time comes, will deny all but positive emotions toward her children.

"I love you, it's for your own good," mother says when she forbids us to play with a friend. "If I didn't love you so much, I wouldn't fuss so about you wearing galoshes." "Of course I love you, but that's why I want you to go to camp. I want you with me always, but it's better for you to enjoy a summer of fresh air." All these explanations seem reasonable on the surface. We want to believe that love is the motivation for everything mother does. Often it is not love, but, respectively, possessiveness, anxiety, and outright rejection that is being expressed in sentences like these. We cannot afford to believe this on a cognitive level. Way down deep we feel it.

To take mother's words about love at face value is to distort the rest of our lives in an effort to find again this ideal relationship. We learn our deepest ways of intimacy with mother; automatically we repeat the pattern with everyone else with whom we become close. Either we play out the role of the child we were with mother, and make the other person into the mother figure, or we reverse: playing mother to the other person's "child." "All too often," says Leah Schaefer, "what we play out with this other person has little to do with them or who we are today." This is why arguments or frictions between some people can never be resolved: they are not reacting to what is going on between them, but to old, unhealed hurts and rejections suffered in the past.

Intimacy is just an old record we replay. "First," says psychoanalyst Richard Robertiello, "we *introject*—take into ourselves—mother's tangled-up notion of what love is. Then we *project* it upon our lovers, husbands, and our own daughter."

Perhaps mother was very possessive and tried to live through us, but at the same time did give us a lot of cuddling, satisfying physical contact and affection. It is all too easy for us forever afterward to buy the whole package—clutching dependency and physical warmth are both tied into an inextricable knot and labeled *love*. Our husband may be physically affectionate; unless he is possessive too, we decide he doesn't "really" love us, something is missing from the perfect love he is supposed to feel for us.

Another example is the mother who tells her daughter she loves her, but is always sending her away to stay with grandmother, leaving her in the care of nurses, or packing her off to boarding school. Is it surprising that a girl like this will often grow up convinced that the only people who love her are the ones who don't want her around? Rejection and affection have become inextricably mixed.

Sometimes we are so hurt by mother's ambivalences that we reject the entire package—throwing out the good, positive aspects mother presented to us, along with the painful ones.

Says Dr. Robertiello: "What we must do is break down the specific components of mother's love—analyze exactly the ways she did not love us, but also the ways in which she did. Did mother give you a kind of basic security—a structure of stability, shelter, nurturing? Did she give you admiration—a genuine feeling that you were worth plenty in your own right? Did she give you warmth and physical affection, cuddle, hold and kiss you? Did she really care what happened to you and accept you—my daughter right or wrong? These are some of the components of real love."

Spontaneous, real and honest love admits errors, hesitations, and human failings; it can be tested and repaired. Idealized love ties us because we intuit that it is unreal and are afraid to face this truth.

"I only tell my mother what she wants to hear," women say. The inference is that the lie is an outgrowth of love; the daughter is merely translating into action her desire to protect her mother. The fact is we become our mother's protectors not because we are such good daughters but to protect ourselves. In some part of our psyche we are still children who are afraid to risk losing mother's unbroken love even for the short space in time of an argument. Telling the truth is a test; it lays bare what in fact goes on between two people.

Our mutual refusal to show our true selves, good and bad, to each other does not allow either woman to explore her separate life, her own identity. The unspoken fear is that if one partner leaves, if either questions the perfection of mother-daughter love by being "different," we are both destroyed. How many grown women dread the idea of living alone, being alone? There is only one thing in this world that approaches the pain of letting go of our mothers, more wrenching than giving up the illusion that she loves us unambivalently. It is separating from—letting go of—our daughters.

"I needed and loved my mother so intensely at times," says a young mother of a five-year-old daughter, "that I remember saying to her when I was eight, 'I will never love my child as much as you love me.' Now I know that I meant *smother*, not love. My mother seemed so selfless, so giving. But I didn't want her to live for me. It piled too much guilt on me. And yet, I didn't dare ask for any space. It would have made me guilty.

When I was seventeen I couldn't wait to get away from home. When I married and had a daughter of my own, I became just as possessive of her as my mother was of me. I was a working mother, and thought that meant I was giving my daughter the space I never had. But I used to telephone home all the time from work, and when I got home, guiltily made up for being away by smothering her. Just like my mother, I called every possessive, overprotective thing I did 'love.'"

The maternal instinct says we are all born mothers, that once we are mothers we will automatically and naturally love our children and always do what is best for them. If you believe in the maternal instinct and fail at mother love, you fail as a woman. It is a controlling idea that holds us in an iron grip.

I propose to use "maternal instinct" as it is emotionally experienced by most women. Whether you call it "instinct" or not, most women enjoy having children, want to, and do. For this majority, the trouble begins not with being mothers, but with the emotional propositions contained in the notion of maternal instinct—that being a good mother is as natural and undifferentiated to humans as it is to a she-wolf with her cubs.

"I tell mothers on the first day," says pediatrician Dr. Sidney Q. Cohlan, "it's not having the baby that makes the relationship, it's the day by day living and caring for the infant that makes the relationship. You can't love your baby twenty-four hours a day, seven days a week. Taking care of a baby in the first few months can be hard work and at times a monumental bore. The rewards begin to come after the mother and infant have lived through a period of adjustment and responsiveness to each other's needs. But she has read all the poetry in the magazines and expects 'instant motherhood,' and thinks there is something wrong with her if she doesn't respond at first sight to her new baby in picture-book fashion."

The split between what mother says, the way she behaves with her baby—*and what she unconsciously feels on the deepest level*—leaves her unsure of herself. Says Dr. Robertiello: "Women walk around feeling they have something to hide, that they are secretly 'unnatural' or 'bad mothers.' The act of giving birth does not set up an ability in you to be a mother, you will not necessarily feel this marvelous 'maternal instinct' welling up in you, telling you what to do with your baby at every moment. Women must have this myth taken off their backs. It puts them at the mercy of a male chauvinistic society. Men are 'sure' that women are meant to be mothers. But each woman, when she has a baby, is not so 'sure.' She looks to other people to tell her what to do. Male supremacy uses the myth of the maternal instinct to reinforce its power position."

71

The first thing it can be said a mother honestly feels in relation to her child is a kind of self-love. The child is essentially a narcissistic extension of herself. The child used to be a part of her, inside her. It is now external but is still closely connected with her own body. Whatever investment she has in her body is continued in the child. If the infant is all she hoped it would be, she may more easily live up to society's injunction that she love the child more than herself. But if there is something about the baby—if it's a boy instead of a girl, too fat, too thin, too lethargic—that makes her feel less than the exaltation she has been led to expect, she must deny it. Any wound to her narcissism—that tidal basin out of which all maternal emotions flow—must go unacknowledged.

The glorification of motherhood demands that when her child is born, autonomy over her own emotions must end. She must ignore her own subjectivity, her real pleasure in physical beauty if her child is not pretty, her boredom with stupidity if the child is slow. Above all, she must not let the sex of her child make any difference to her. She must shut her eyes to the very first item of information we take in about any new person we meet, and which colors every transaction we have with them thereafter.

And yet the truth is that when one woman gives birth to another, they are linked together for life in a very special way. When a daughter is born, fears a woman thought she had conquered long ago are re-aroused. Now there is another person, not simply dependent on her, but *like* her, and therefore subject to all the dangers she has fought all her life.

The mother's progress into a larger sexuality is halted. She retreats and entrenches herself in the cramped female stance of security and defense. The position is fondly hailed as mother-protector. It is the position of fear. She may be only half alive but she is safe, and so is her daughter. She now defines herself not as a woman but primarily as a mother. Sex is left out, hidden from the girl who must never think of her mother in danger: in sex. It is only with the greatest effort that the girl will be able to think of herself that way.

"I think what frightens me most is my daughter's vulnerability," says a mother of a six-year-old. "It's my own fear that I would be exploited sexually. I know I overprotect her. But I'm so afraid she'll be hurt, taken advantage of. She's so naturally unguarded." How is she going to protect this pitifully vulnerable female infant until she reaches the safe haven of marriage? The mother just doesn't know. What she does know is that for a little girl—as opposed to a little boy—sex is a danger. It must be denied, suppressed. Her daughter will not be raised a sexy hussy, but "a lady." No erotic stimuli must intrude into the little girl's consciousness, no dirty jokes, no daring clothes, no indication that the mother's own body responds sexually. If mother doesn't mention it or think about it or respond to anything herself, it will go away. In order to keep the child's attention from turning to the anxious-making topic of sex, the mother goes the final step and desexualizes herself.

From the girl's earliest years, her emergent sexuality will be a cause of anxiety, seeming to make her not more like her mother, but unlike her. If mother denies her own sexuality, and reacts to mine with such shame or fright, how big an asset is it? How difficult it is to be a woman! Better to remain a child, a good little girl. Thus the lifelong puzzle between mother and daughter has begun.

When women's lives were more predictable, when we had no alternative but to repeat our mother's life, our mistakes and disappointments were pretty much confined to her margin of error and unhappiness. I do believe our grandmothers, even our mothers, were happier; not knowing as much as we do and not having our options, there was less to be unhappy about. A woman might give up her sexuality, hate being a housewife, not like children, but if every other woman was doing it, how could she articulate her frustration? She could feel it certainly, but you can't want what you don't know about. Television, for instance, gave them no sense of thwarted expectations. Today women's lives are changing at a rate and by a necessity we couldn't control if we wanted to; we need all the energy that suppression consumes. If we are going to fill more than women's traditional role, we can't afford the exhaustion that goes with constant emotional denial. There are pressures on women other than the "maternal instinct." They are the new economic and social demands.

If women are going to be lawyers as well as mothers, they must differentiate between the two, and then differentiate once again about their sexuality. That is the third—and *not* mutually exclusive—option. As the world changes, and women's place in it, mothers must consciously present this choice to their daughters. A woman may incorporate all three choices within herself—and even more—but at any given moment she must be able to say to herself and her daughter, "I chose to have you because I wanted to be a mother. I chose to work—to have a career, to be in politics, to play the piano—because that gives me a different feeling of value about myself, a value that is not greater nor lesser than motherhood, only different. Whether you choose to work or not, to be a mother or not, it will have nothing to do with your sexuality. Sexuality is the third option—as meaningful as either of the other two."

Actually, the woman and the mother are often at war with one another—in the same body. Dr. Helene Deutsch, in *The Psychology of Women*, takes the classical Freudian view on the "passivity" of women, one in which many analysts today do not join (nor do I myself), but I think she gives us an important clue here: "The origin of this longing in primitive, unsublimated instinctual drives," she says, "manifests itself in various ways. Ardent wishes to be desired, strong aspirations to exclusive egoistic possession, a normally completely passive attitude with regard to the first attack . . . are characteristic attributes of feminine sexuality. They are so fundamentally different from the emotional manifestations of motherhood that we are compelled to accept the opposition of sexuality and eroticism on one hand and reproduction instinct and motherhood on the other."

Like so many women since the world began, my mother could not believe in this opposition of the two desires. Tradition, society, her parents, religion itself told her that there was no conflict; that motherhood was the logical and natural end product of sex. She took as her act of faith the proposition that if she were a real woman, she would not be a good mother and I would grow up the same. If I repeated her path and pattern of motherhood, it would show I did not blame her for her choice. It would justify and place the final stamp of value on what she had done.

Some women do make this choice gladly. They may be the majority, but my mother was not one of them. As I am not—her daughter in this too. Even in a good marriage, many women resent the matronly, nonsexual role their children force them to play. My mother didn't even have a good marriage; she was a young widow.

Frightened as she was, as much in need of my father as my sister and I were of her, mother had no choice but to pretend that my sister and I were the most important part of her life; that neither fear, youth and inexperience, loss, loneliness or her own needs could shake the unqualified and invincible love she felt for us. My mother had no body of woman-to-woman honesty and shared experience to use in her fight against the folk wisdom that said just being a woman carried all the inherent wisdom needed to be a mother—that it was either "natural" to her, or she was a failure as a woman.

In all the years we lived together, it is a shame we never talked honestly about our feelings. What neither of us knew then was that I could have stood honesty, no matter how frightening. Her angers, disillusionments, fears of failure, rage—emotions I seldom saw—I could have come to terms with them if she had been able to speak to me. I would have grown

74

used to the idea that while mother loves me, at times other emotions impaired that love. I would have developed trust that in time her love for me would always return. Instead, I was left trying to believe in some perfect love she said she had for me, but in which I could not believe. I did not understand why I couldn't feel it no matter what her words said. I grew to believe that love itself, from her or anybody else, was a will-o'-the-wisp, coming or going for reasons I could not control. Never knowing when or why I was loved, I grew afraid to depend on it.

The older I get, the more of my mother I see in myself. The more opposite my life and my thinking grow from hers, the more of her I hear in my voice, see in my facial expression, feel in the emotional reactions I have come to recognize as my own. To say her image is not still a touchstone in my life—and mine in hers—would be another lie. They have stood in the way of my understanding myself all my life. I have always known that what my husband loves most in me is that I have my own life. My work, my marriage, and my new relationships with other women are beginning to make his assumptions about me true—that I am an independent, separate individual. They have allowed me to respect myself, and admire my own sex. What still stands between me and the person I would like to be is this illusion of perfect love between my mother and me. It is a lie I can no longer afford.

CHAPTER 2

A TIME TO BE CLOSE

I grew up in a house of women. It's a different way to begin life, but I didn't allow myself to feel the loss of the father everyone else had. I would later theorize that perhaps my kind of childhood had its advantages: not having seen a man diminished by women's impossible demands on him, I grew up believing all things were possible between a man and a woman. Of course I missed him.

In our house there were always four women: my mother, my older sister Susie, and myself; at first, the other woman was my nurse Anna. I loved Anna so much I let her slip out of my life as painlessly as my father. The day she left I told myself I felt nothing. I had learned everything about love and separation in the first years of my life.

Anna was fearless, and she loved me in a way I can still feel. She was as tough and dependable as my mother was timid and out of her depth. "My poor mother"; why do I think of her that way even today, with my stepfather and a world of friends around her? I suppose in the same way that she still sees me as a child, I still see her at twenty, a widow with two baby girls. But what did I feel then? With the terrible injustice of children who know that to be fair can cost them their lives, I always wanted her complete and unswerving love and attention; all she had to offer was her vulnerability and sadness.

In the space between what I demanded and she could give, I lived. From there it was not a far step to decide that my demands made her unhappy, that in some way I was the cause of her unhappiness. It's why I hated her to braid my hair: I could hear her sighing behind me. Her sadness was my guilt. Whenever she talks about her own mother, whom I never knew, that look comes over her face. It's worse when she talks about my father. She only does when I ask, and I was twenty-two before I dared. We believe that if we had been better children, or even right now could do or say the right thing, we could make it go away. I cannot bear to be in the same room when my mother's face changes from the look I love to that maddening unhappiness. My intellect tells me the guilt I feel whenever I say good-bye to her has nothing to do with what I did or didn't do. My mother is a reasonably happy woman, other people would say. I've been a reasonably good daughter, my mother would say. But until I understand my guilt, I will not be free of her.

"Oh, Nancy," she'll begin, "I wish you had known Mama. She was such a wonderful woman . . ." and her voice will drift away to some distant image which she sees beyond me, and we'll talk about something else. I'd like to see that image, to share anything that may tell me more about my grandmother—and so about my mother, and so about me. But the stories my mother tells about her mother, lovely as they are, much as I like to hear them again and again, are as diffused with sentiment as the faded, misty Bachrach photos in the leather volumes at my grandfather's house that I have pored over every summer of my life, looking . . . for what? My mother is the oldest child, but in all the photos, even the sister eleven years younger looks more self-assured than she. How dizzying it must have been to be picked at seventeen by my handsome father, she the thorn among the roses in her father's stern eyes. She eloped with him against that father's wishes, though I wonder if even her elopment didn't express her silent dutifulness as a daughter: if she did not find favor in her father's eyes, she was prepared to leave. How unprepared she must have been for motherhood a year later, and two years after that for my father's death. So much loss for a person who never had a sense of self.

As we both grow older I see how suited she was to be a wife, how grace-fully she moves now that she has a second chance and my sister and I are grown, leaving her role as our mother almost negligible beside her life as a woman. I am sure much of her talent as a wife comes from her mother, as does mine; again and again she tells me what a strong influence her moth-er was on all her children—this woman who has taken on almost mythic magnitude in my imagination. But in fact my grandmother died suddenly and mysteriously of an incurable disease called sleeping sickness when my mother was sixteen.

As much as I want my mother to go beyond the pretty pictures of her mother ("so beautiful, so kind"), and of my father ("so handsome, so charming"), I have come to realize she needs her own protection against loss and pain. She will see in those early years only what she can afford to live with.

My grandmother left my grandfather and went to Florida with the youngest of their five children. It was a stunning thing to do in that era. I've often stared at her self-portrait that now hangs in my living room and wondered, angry as she was with my grandfather, how she could have left her children—none of whom to this day can speak of her without a kind of adoration and longing. But then, given my grandfather, I would prob-ably have married and left him too. In the portraits of him which she painted, he looks like the young F. Scott Fitzgerald. He was easily twice as difficult. They met at an amateur theatrical, and though I'm told he never loved any woman as he loved her, they never stopped arguing.

My grandfather made his fortune in steel alloys in Pittsburgh, lost it in the Depression and made it all back again. He loved power, horses, tro-phies, and beautiful women. He never forgave my mother for not being one. She grew into beauty too late. As a little girl I would stand in the room with the silver cups, the red and blue ribbons, the stuffed swordfish, the photos of yachts and fox hunts, and I would imagine myself beautiful and winning them all for him. On those evenings when my grandfather dined out with the Mellons and the Carnegies, I'm told my grandmother cooked spaghetti for her arty friends in her studio at the top of the house.

My mother, her three sisters, and brother loved and feared my grandfa-ther until his death a few years ago. Their feelings about their mother are totally unambivalent. From their stories I have a picture of a woman who was every child's dream, a beauty with large eyes and dark hair who wrote plays for her children, who dressed up with them and was as capable of entering their world as she was of taking care of them. She was as roman-tic and sensitive to life as my grandfather was ambitious and incapable of demonstrating the love he felt for his children. Still, she would not go through all her short life celebrating only self-abnegation and the maternal emotions. She loved other ideas and people besides her children. She was their mother, but would not be their martyr—which is one reason they loved her so. I have never heard one word from my mother, aunts or uncle of any guilt she ever made them feel.

We are the loving sex; people count on us for comfort, nurturing warmth. We hold the world together with the constant availability of our love when men would tear it apart with their needs for power. We feel incomplete alone, inadequate without a man, devalued outside marriage, defensive without children. We are raised for love, but when love comes to us, somehow it is not as ultimately satisfying as we dreamed. We are being loved for being a part of a relationship, for our function—not for ourselves.

He asks us out for dinner, and even as we hang up the phone, hot with pleasure, we wonder who else he asked before us. As he holds us in his arms, we are already half afraid he will forget us tomorrow. On the day he marries us, we ask him yet another time: "Do you really love me?"

The seed of our disbelief goes back to our first love, a time we can't remember. The lessons learned from mother in the way she loves us and the way she loved herself stay with us for life.

All my life I've resented the tyranny of infancy, the notion that my adult behavior was determined by a stage of life that I couldn't remember, that was past, and therefore beyond change, regret, or control. I believed in learning from experience, that we could make ourselves up out of whatever material had been handed us; that we could change our lives if we were strong enough.

Strong—the very word has always been glamorous but mystifying to me. If I am "strong," why is there so much anxiety in my life? Why am I so haunted by fear that my work isn't good enough? Above all, why can't I enjoy what my husband and friends tell me—that they love me? Ever since I can remember, I have been, outwardly at least, a winner—good in school, good at sports, people liked me, I did accomplished work. Why then do I still feel insecure? We get our courage, our sense of self, the ability to believe we have value even when alone, to do our work, to love others and to feel ourselves lovable from the "strength" of mother's love for us when we were infants.

If as a tiny child we didn't get the kind of satisfying closeness and love that gives an infant the strength to grow on, we do not evolve emotionally. We become older but a part of us remains an infant, looking for this nurturing closeness, never believing that we have it, or that if we do, soon it will be taken away.

Freud, Horney, Bowlby, Erikson, Sullivan, Winnicott, Mahler—the great interpreters of human behavior—may disagree profoundly in some ways but are as one about beginnings: you cannot leave home, cannot grow up whole, separate and self-reliant, unless someone loved you enough to give you a self first, and then let you go. It begins with our mother's touch, smile and eye: there is someone there whom she likes to touch, there is someone there she likes to see. That's me. And I'm OK!

It used to be thought that if you loved a child too much, you would spoil her. We know now you cannot be loved too much—not in the first years of life. In the depths of that first closeness to our mothers is built the bedrock of self-esteem on which we will erect our good feelings about ourselves for the rest of our lives. An infant needs an almost suffocating kind of closeness to the body whose womb it so recently and reluctantly left. The technical word for this closeness is *symbiosis*.

It is especially important for women to understand the meaning of this word because for so many of us it becomes our lifelong way of relating. Very early on, the young boy is trained to be independent. As young girls, we are trained to see our value in the partnerships we form. To symbiose.

At the beginning of life, symbiosis is of prime, positive importance to both sexes. It begins as a growth process, freeing the infant of the fear of being vulnerable and alone, giving her the courage to develop. If we get enough symbiosis in the beginning, we will later remember its pleasures and be able to look for it in others; to accept and immerse ourselves in it when we find it, and *move out of it again* when we are sated, knowing that we will always be able to re-establish it. We will trust and enjoy love, take it as part of life's feast—not feel we must devour every crumb because it may never come again. If we do not experience this first symbiosis, we look for it the rest of our lives, but even if we do find it, we will not trust it—hanging on so desperately that we will suffocate the other person, boring him to death with our cries of, "You don't love me!" until, in fact, we have made it come true.

The first meaning of symbiosis is found in botany, where it means two organisms who cannot live without each other. In the animal world, it often means a slightly different relationship, one of mutual help; the bird that wins its food by obligingly picking the hippopotamus's teeth clean is a partner in symbiosis. In human terms, the meaning shifts a little once again. The most classical symbiosis is the fetus in the womb. Here we have an illustration of two different kinds of symbiosis.

The fetus is in *physical* symbiosis with the mother; literally, it cannot live without her. The mother (most of the time) is in *psychological* symbiosis with the unborn baby. She can live without it, but pregnancy gives her the feeling of more abundant life. In this way, the fetus nourishes her. In our earliest symbiosis with mother, both partners win.

At birth we don't know there is anything outside of ourselves. Our unfocused eyes cannot differentiate shapes, we don't know where mother ends and we begin. When we reach out our hand, she is there to touch. When we cry, we are fed or picked up. We rule the world! No wonder we are so reluctant to give up mother; she sustains this wonderful feeling of total power, "infantile omnipotence." In a sense we continue to be physically connected to her, just as mother psychologically still experiences us as almost a part of her body, her own narcissistic extension. The symbiosis is mutual, complete, and satisfying.

Gradually, our eyes begin to be able to focus. Things, people, are near or far. We become aware that another person is there—mother—but she is so close that we still see her as merged with us, not separate.

In this early stage of symbiosis, the good mother sees her needs as entirely secondary to her infant's. This is to mutual advantage: the infant is enabled with gradual comfort to get used to the idea of powerlessness; nor is it presented as very terrible anyway: mother is always near to fix things. For the mother, knowing what the child wants gives her an almost mystic sense of union and being needed. It is an experience of transcendence.

In the next stage, we may begin to distinguish our body from mother's, but can't separate our thoughts from hers. When we are wet, she changes us. Hungry? She knows it almost as quickly as we do, and food arrives. But now anxiety begins to enter. When mother is not around, the blanket isn't pulled up, the breast or bottle isn't offered. Our power has begun to erode. Anxiously we keep watch for her. If she's around, everything is OK. If she's not, we can die. When mother's love is steady and uninterrupted, we gradually come to be able to do without having her around for longer and longer periods of time. Trust is being born.

Instead of clutching at mother in fear that she will leave, the infant lets her go, secure in the knowledge that she always comes back when needed; meanwhile, there are those colored toys to play with. But if the fear should ever strike that mother may not come back, that she may be inattentive to our needs, growth stops. Interest in bright lights or playing with crib toys disappears. The self has been swallowed by fear. The baby can think of nothing else in the world but that mother must never go away again. We must not be left alone. The foundations of a lifetime of uncertainty have been laid.

The word for the next stage of development is *separation*. The child, more or less secure in the symbiotic love of her mother, wants to venture out into a larger world. As important as it was for the mother to symbiose with her infant when that was all baby could understand, it is equally important now for her to begin to let her child go, to let the daughter proceed into her own life according to her inner, psychic timetable. The long march toward individuality and self-reliance has begun.

In the normal course of events, a sense of self begins to emerge at about three months. The child shows she is reacting to specific events or faces: she smiles. Around eight months, the child can tell the difference between mother and a stranger. At the age of one and a half (give or take), the growth process away from mother picks up momentum. We start to separate from her more and more. It's a beautiful, exciting world, and there are so many things other than mother to bite, touch, taste, see. The self is becoming more and more conscious. By age three or three and a half, if we are lucky and mother has been loving, we emerge with a sense of ourselves as separate people—still loved by mother, but with a life of our own that is not hers.

"The first demonstration of social trust in the baby," says Erik Erikson in *Childhood and Society*, "is the ease of his feeling, the depth of his sleep, the relaxation of his bowels." The child has begun to trust his mother, to relax; he doesn't have to keep awake or sleep with one ear open for fear she will go away. "The infant's first social achievement, then," Dr. Erikson goes on, "is his willingness to let the mother out of sight without undue anxiety or rage, because she has become an inner certainty. . . ."

This need to feel a basic trust of life is essential for both males and females. But because of the inevitable modeling relationship between mother and daughter, we are not just stuck for life with the sense of basic trust she did or didn't give us. We are also stuck with the image of her as a woman, *her* sense of basic trust that *her* mother gave her. A boy will grow up, and following his father's lead, leave home, support himself, start a family. He may or may not be successful. Much of his success will depend upon the basic sense of trust his mother gave him; but he will not identify with his mother. He will not base all his relationships on what he had with her (unless he is a certain kind of homosexual).

But a girl who did not get this sense of basic trust, though she may leave her mother's house, get a job, marry and have children, will never really feel comfortable on her own, in control of her own life. Part of her is still anxiously tied to her mother. She doesn't trust herself and others. She cannot believe there is another way to be because this is how her mother was. It is also how most other women are. If our mothers are not separate people themselves, we cannot help but take in their anxiety and fear, their need to be symbiosed with someone. If we do not see them involved in their own work, or enjoying something just for themselves, we too do not believe in accomplishment or pleasure outside of a partnership. We denigrate anything that we alone experience; we say, "It's more fun when there's someone else along."

Emotionally unseparated from mother, just as afraid as she was, we repeat the process with our own daughter. An unfortunate history, a way of growing up female that our society has amazingly left unchallenged. Being cute and helpless, clinging, clutching, holding on for dear life, becomes our method for survival—and ultimate defeat.

It is important to understand it is not the mere number of hours that mother spends that assures the child of those early, satisfying, symbiotic feelings of warmth and life assurance she needs. "It is better," says Dr. Robertiello, "that the child doesn't get her mother's full attention than a charade of a mother who would rather be at her office or out having lunch with her friends. Inauthentic behavior, especially when it comes disguised as love, creates the worst problems."

It is the *quality* of attention we get from mother that counts. Incomplete, unsatisfying, or interrupted symbiosis stamps a woman for life. We missed something from our mothers; despaired; grew guarded—and learned early a cramped line of defense: not to expect too much from the world. Even as our lovers hold us we cannot believe they will not leave. Our husband complains that we are suffocating him: "What more do you want of me?" he cries. We cannot give it a name but we feel a distance is there.

Society plays us a dirty trick by calling us the loving sex. The flattery is meant to make us proud of our weakness, our inability to be independent, our imperative need to belong to someone. We are limited to need and nurture, leaving erotic love to men. A "lovesick" man makes people uncomfortable because the condition weakens him, jeopardizes his manhood, cuts down his productivity. But a woman who can't think clearly, who dreams over her law books, loses weight and walks into brick walls arouses warm feelings in everybody. Men and women both know how good it feels to be knocked out by love, but someone has to mind the store. Since women haven't got anywhere to go anyway, and a needy woman makes a man work harder in order to provide for two, romance itself becomes fuel for the economic mill.

A good mother finds it very hard to let her baby fall on its face the first time it takes a few steps, but she knows that it is the way you learn. A little boy will crawl away, try to maneuver the stairs, even push his mama away when she interferes because the impulse to grow is so strong. She is afraid for him but knows she must train him in courage. Mom has already begun to teach him not to cling to her, much as they both may still want it. "Don't baby him," her husband says. The boy is emerging from symbiosis into the pleasures of separation. Through experience, practice, and repetition the boy learns that accidents happen but are not fatal, rejections are lived through, the self goes on.

Little girls, on the other hand, get the opposite training. When a little girl ventures into the backyard and hurts herself, mother doesn't encourage her daughter to try again, as she would her son. She holds the girl tighter, fearing for them both because she's been there; she has been hurt, anxious, and afraid much of her life.

Other elements of the mother-daughter relationship inhibit the little girl's sense of adventure: she seeks kisses but expects rejection. In mother's earliest and usually unconscious efforts to handle feelings of competition with her daughter, she teaches the little girl not to expect too much physical attention from daddy. "Come away. Daddy has important papers to go over." Mother is teaching us that men don't have "our" need for love. Brothers, sisters, friends—they are all unreliable. Only mother will be ever constant.

"You can see why a little girl may cling to her mother through fear of the threatening outside world," says Dr. Robertiello, "but what must be realized is that mother isn't an ogre, keeping the girl locked up for spite. Mother has real fears and needs too, which seem to be met by symbiosis with her daughter. Too often, the mother never separated from *her* mother, and as the grandmother gets older and mama begins to feel the loss of that secure tie, she substitutes a bond to her daughter. She fears more than anything she may end up alone, with no one to tell her what to do.

"Because of this primary, unconscious tie to her own mother, the wife/ mother was never free to give her first loyalty to anyone new, including her husband. Oh, she may have had a sudden spurt of separation on getting married, a fine new flush of sexuality for a while. But all too often, when her daughter was born, she settled back into that less exciting, but known-and-safe feeling she had with her mother . . . only doing it this time with her daughter. She cuts off her independence, diminishes her sexuality, her intellect; she is no longer a young woman but a 'matron' instead; a mother. Now she's safe forever. She's got a guarantee against ever being alone again for the rest of her life because her daughter is going to outlive her."

To explain separation, how we build an identity, we must go back once more to symbiosis, just as the tiny child who is learning to be on her own keeps going back to mother. The urge that brings baby, in panic at being alone, suddenly crawling back, to see that mother is "there," that "everything is all right," is inevitable.

Technically, this is called "the rapprochement stage," but I prefer a more familiar term child psychologists use: "refueling." Having touched base with mommy, thus refueled, the child is confident and ready to venture out again. The good mother understands the frightened return, but does not use it as a warning not to leave again; in fact, once she sees the child is refueled, she encourages it to go off again. The clinging mother magnifies the child's fears: "Ah, poor baby. It's so scary out there. Don't ever go out again unless I come with you."

A mother like this is so unseparated from her daughter that she cannot figure out if the anxiety is her own or her child's. In the end, it doesn't matter: the girl will pick up the mother's fear and make it her own. The outside world comes to seem threatening, forbidding. When she grows up and is away from home, she worries that the gas was left on, that somebody is sick or dying. Above all, she does not like to do anything alone. She wants to feel *connected* at all times, at any cost.

However, every action has an equal and opposite reaction. Beginning around fourteen to eighteen months and continuing to about the third year, the child begins to experiment with resistance to mother's demands on her. This try at self-assertion is marked by the almost constant use of the word *NO*.

This is a very important experience for the child, separating out what she wants to do—even if it is not to make up her mind yet—and what mother wants her to do. "*We* want to go to the park, don't *we?*" says mother, using the symbiotic pronoun. "No," says the little boy, asserting an early step toward individuality and separation. "*I* don't want it." Everyone who hears him applauds—even mother. Girls get the opposite treatment.

Says child psychiatrist Sirgay Sanger: "Boys have an easier time in this period because mother thinks, 'Well, I don't know enough about boys. I'd better leave him alone.' There is also a cultural bias against mothers who keep their sons tied to them. But if her child is a girl? Well, she knows all about girls. So she rides like a steam roller over her girl's individuality. 'Come on,' mother will say to the little girl. 'You always like to go shopping with me, so we're going to do that now.' Right away the little girl becomes less assertive. She loses a lot of her gumption. This starts as early as the time between the first and second year."

Separation, outgrowing the need for degrees of symbiosis inappropriate to the present stage of development, is not a case of black or white. Theoretically, separation from mother should be completed by age three or three and a half, "but I think it goes on as long as we live," says Dr. Robertiello. "I've never met anyone yet for whom it has ended, man or woman. We are all very much connected to our mothers or some substitute. I think it's especially acute with women because the girl has that constant image of her mother from which she never escapes." Vital as it is in our first years of life, the only way to describe symbiosis between mother and daughter after age three is unhealthy. It is a sticky issue because our culture confuses symbiosis and love; *but when we are grown, symbiosis and real love are mutually exclusive.* Love implies a separation. "I love you" can only have meaning if there is an "I" to love "you."

In a symbiotic relationship, there is no real concern for the other person. There is just a need, a craving to be connected, no matter how destructive. Marriage is often seen as releasing the daughter from her symbiotic tie to her mother. In fact, it may be merely a switch to her husband. Now he must support her, supply her with life, make her feel good about herself. Unless we have separated from mother long before marriage, it is almost impossible to set up a healthy relationship with a man.

The best definition of love I know is psychoanalyst Harry Stack Sullivan's: love means you care almost as much about the other person's safety, security, and satisfaction as you do about your own. I feel this is a realistic definition; you *can't* love somebody else more than yourself. The truly loving mother is one whose interest and happiness is in seeing her daughter as a person, not just a possession. It is a process of being so generous and loving that she will forgo some of her own pleasure and security to add to her daughter's development. If she does this in a genuine way, the mother will have someone who cares about her forever—not a guilty, resentful love, but a daughter who gives her love freely.

Most of the time it is too difficult to examine what we really have with mother because there is not enough distance between us. Are those telephone calls to mother done out of real love or a need to maintain symbiosis? If we call her happily, voluntarily, because we get a lift out of talking to her—that is love. If we move to the phone—though it be daily—with a heavy feeling of constraint and duty, with an anxious need that these calls never seem to fill, if they leave us in tears, angry, defensive, or guilty, then, though the culture may call ours a loving mother-daughter relationship if only for the sheer size of our telephone bill, I would not.

I have known women whose mothers loved them for themselves and then let them go. They have a certainty about themselves.

On the other hand, uncertain people often make their fears come true. A woman friend with a beautiful figure constantly complains about her "huge" hips. She tells me how lucky I am not to have to worry about such things. She is my height. Finally I ask what her hips measure. I tell her mine are two inches bigger. "But they can't be!" she cries. We refuse the facts today because the image was set at a time we can no longer remember by someone who knew everything. We do not spend all those hours in front of the mirror because of anxiety. Something is wrong with our basic narcissism.

Until recently, narcissism was thought to be a dirty word. Today, we make a sharp distinction between this faulty sense of self, which is called "secondary narcissism," and healthy, primary narcissism.

Secondary narcissism is pathological because it attempts to fill the void in the healthy self-image with an intense preoccupation with the self. This can be expressed through an excessive focus on appearance, or physical and emotional symptoms (hypochondria). A person like this is trying to make up for a lack of attention in childhood—most especially in the first year of life—by paying the same kind of exaggerated attention to herself that she needed from her mother but did not get at that stage of development.

Healthy, primary narcissism is rooted in infancy. Mother is the first "objective" voice we hear; her face is our first mirror. When we are born, she cannot hear enough wonderful things being said about us. She absorbs the praise of friends and relatives as they coo and gurgle about our beauty, size, and amazing agility. At this stage she is rightly so tied to us that she doesn't know where praise for us leaves off and admiration for her giving birth to such a miraculous baby begins. We feed her narcissism and she feeds ours. It is the height of symbiosis at its best, primary narcissism functioning as it should. Our ego is being born.

Out of this experience will come a person who is going to have a good image of herself. Someone who will be able to walk into rooms without undue shyness, believe that other people like her, accept praise for her work as her due, and smile at the nice reflection of herself in other people's eyes just as she smiles back at what she sees in the mirror. When a man says, "I love you," she is pleased, not gripped by disbelief and fear.

Does this describe you, or women you know? What happened? What becomes twisted, even when life begins with strong primary narcissistic gratification? Why do we either not continue to seek it in later life, or, if we do, cannot enjoy it—take no nourishment from it to feed our self-esteem?

Take this as a familiar enough occurrence: a mother who could not hear enough praise for her infant suddenly begins to say to admiring friends when the girl is three or four, "Now, that's enough. We don't want a conceited little girl on our hands." Primary narcissistic gratification stops.

What has happened to turn mother off praise and begin to make the little girl self-conscious about getting it—and unable to take it in when she does—is that the mother has begun to project upon the child her own fear of seeming irrationally conceited. Now that we are no longer infants but have become active people instead, mother identifies with us. She knows how she would feel if she were getting this extravagant praise. *She projects herself into our minds because she is not separate*—and brings with her *her* own damaged narcissism, *her* inability to believe compliments, *her* fear that if she let herself think they might be true for one moment, *she* would get a swelled head. This is the way in which *her* mother began to undermine and make her feel embarrassed about her own healthy narcissism. Now she is doing it to us.

How many mothers have you heard say to their daughters (of any age), "You look absolutely wonderful!"—without any however, buts, or qualifiers like,"—but must you wear so much eye shadow?" When did your mother last say to you, "You did that perfectly, darling!" with the absolute certainty of one individual admiring another?

Says Dr. Sanger: "Almost from birth, we see mothers conveying to their daughters that they aren't good enough as is. Mom doesn't fuss much with her son, but she is constantly adjusting, fixing, trying to perfect this little female picture of herself in the same way she fiddles with her own never-perfect appearance."

In the name of fairness, and reality too, let me add an important postscript which is true not only for this chapter but of this whole book: looking over our shoulder at what mother may or may not have done so many years ago locks us into the past. "She did it. There is nothing I can do about it." *Blaming mother keeps us passive, tied to her.* It helps us avoid taking responsibility for ourselves.

"One of the major resistances in analytic work," says child psychiatrist Aaron Esman, "is the notion, 'It was my mother's fault.' Patients don't want to see their own responsibility, so they blame mother. Parent-baiting, mother-baiting uses up energy that might better go into examining the wrong choices one has made oneself." Brooding over past injustices, we have little emotion left over to create a better future.

Those of us who had rejecting mothers are often drawn to men with the same cold temperaments. We try to manipulate warmth from them. This is merely to repeat the past. We would be better off giving up the sour comfort of recriminations and finding someone who doesn't have to be cajoled but gives warmth easily and gladly. Our job as adults is to understand the past, learn its lessons, and then let it go. Blaming mother is just a negative way of clinging to her still.

CHAPTER 3

A TIME TO LET GO

In an interview with a young mother in Detroit which lasts five hours, she smiles and talks easily about how she is raising her daughter to be "an individual person." "You don't think then that mothers have problems separating from their daughters?" I ask as we are parting. She laughs nervously: "When you first said that word, I felt goose flesh up and down my arms." Separation—the word sounds so final, fraught with loss, abandonment, and guilt that mothers don't want to talk about it.

"Letting go" is perhaps a friendlier way to put it. It implies generosity, a talent a good mother needs in abundance. Separation is not cutting yourself off from someone you love. It is giving freedom to the other person to be herself before she becomes resentful, stunted, and suffocated by being tied too close. Separation is not the end of love. It creates love.

It is hard for women to let go. We are born collectors. We live in the treasured bits and pieces of past life. Mothers collect the memorabilia of their children's past, shoes from the time they possessed baby most totally. Grown women collect match covers and menus from nights when a man held us close, when we felt most possessed, and we count the hours dead until he calls and brings us back to life. A woman and a man exchange Valentine cards; he opens his, smiles, kisses her and then throws the card away. "You're not going to keep it?" she cries. She's saved every card since she was fifteen. But men don't need our collections; their future may be uncertain, but they feel they have a hand in its creation. They are not dependent on the past. When we cut our hair, mother cries, "You've changed!" It is not a compliment to growth but a fear of disloyalty and separation: "You're leaving me!"

Motherhood is also a good excuse for giving up sex. Mother has "more important" things to worry about than the ambivalent emotion which has tempted but troubled her all her life long; she stops thinking of herself as a sexual woman. "This is usually unconscious," says educator Jessie Potter, married thirty-four years and mother of two daughters. "She may in fact have been an interesting sexual partner until her child was born, but now she is too tired, too busy, she says the children take up too much of her attention. It's all culturally induced, but the result is that she goes underground sexually until the kids are grown. As for the daughter, she grows up seeing a mother who has no sexual life at all."

Little wonder that physical love comes to seem frightening to young girls. "If mother has given up on a sexual life," says Dr. Mio Fredland, "she will send the little girl bad vibrations. When the daughter asks questions, as four-and-five-year-olds do, the mother will denigrate the subject or communicate her embarrassment. The daughter soon comes to think her own sexual feelings and fantasies are bad."

Nobody knows a mother like her daughter. Mother says sex is beautiful. When her words go in one direction, but the music is going in another, the daughter listens to the music. "It is extremely important," says Wardell Pomeroy, "that the five-year-old girl be enabled to recognize that mother has something very warm and special with daddy. Studies show that teen-agers overwhelmingly complain, not that their parents did not give them the technical facts but that they never presented their children with an image of physical affection between mother and father." The girl develops an image of sex, not as something to grow up to and hope for but as something to fear.

The emergence of our sexuality arouses in mother all the pride she ever felt about her body and her sex . . . but all the shame, fear, guilt, disgust, dirtiness, and rejection too. Grown women, we ask ourselves why instead of our putting his hand on our vagina or guiding his mouth there, we feel an almost instantaneous reflex of rigidity when he touches us. We want to enjoy sex; our mind tells us we are free to. We examine and re-examine our anxieties, wondering if the inhibition is in us, in him—is the fault in our social system that sets the sexes at war with each other? The truth is you cannot be sexual with another person until you accept yourself. Another person doesn't make you sexual. Often with the best intentions in the world—to protect us—mother denies our sexuality, loading sex with a fear that makes us want to cling to her all the more. Only in partnerships, in mergers, in marriages like hers—runs the silent message—can we be safe.

Sexuality is one of the first forces to forge our identity. "A kind of inborn timetable," says Dr. Aaron Esman, "brings children to a sexual polarization around five or six. Little boys talk about wanting to marry mother. Little girls can become extremely feminine and seductive with their fathers." But while mother may fondly recognize and even enjoy her son's "romance" with her, she will deny the little girl's open flirtation with her father. The denial may take the form of, "Stop bothering your daddy!" Other mothers practice avoidance, ignoring what the little girl is doing even as she parades naked in front of daddy, dances for him, or falls into the flirtatious poses she's picked up from watching TV or mommy herself.

This early interest in daddy is a childish but meaningful rehearsal; it is practice opposite the one man who loves us enough to applaud what we are becoming. That's all we want at this stage; we may come on as if to steal him away from mommy, but we'll happily settle for his smile, his fond kiss, his lighthearted acknowledgment that we're just about the prettiest little girl he's ever seen. But if he ignores our gleeful dance or worse yet, dismisses us with embarrassment, a fearful, frigid personality is being born. "This kind of woman often marries early," says Dr. Sanger. "Having been oedipally rejected by her father, she is afraid to take risks. She marries the first man who asks."

It is important that the daughter feel there is room for privacy from her mother by the time the oedipal stage is reached. But while she wants to feel she can shut the door on mother, she also has the seemingly contradictory wish that from the other side of that closed door mother approves.

The girl wants to feel that mother acknowledges and approves whatever signs of sexuality she may show. If she can react to her experience, life, and body without guilt, she can learn to enjoy and be proud of her sexual self. But the symbiotically tied girl picks up on her mother's fear or dislike of sex. She is afraid to enjoy these new feelings; they would mark her as *different* from mother, separating her from the only source of love she had been taught she can depend on.

Ever since we were four months old we knew there was a wonderful sensation if we rubbed ourselves between the legs. When mother changes her baby's diaper and inadvertently touches its genitals, the infant feels pleasure. The tiny hand naturally goes to the source of that pleasure; mother automatically pushes the hand away. She does this whether the baby is male or female, but the way she does it—her deepest, perhaps unconscious feelings behind the gesture—will already be different depending on the sex of the child.

Four years later her boy's sexual awareness may worry or frighten her, but what does she know about male sexuality? She is reluctant to meddle in male business, maybe to set up inhibitions in him as a grown man. In her hesitation, she gives him space.

She feels no such hesitation conveying her feelings to her daughter. Without mother having said a word, by the time we are four we know that touching ourselves makes her angry. "Women say to me, 'But I never masturbated,' " says Dr. Mio Fredland. "We know from clinical experience that a child's natural impulse *is* to masturbate. 'Can you remember why you didn't?' I ask. 'Were you told not to or were you punished for it?' The standard response is, 'Oh, nothing was ever said to me.'

"Of course it *was*," says Dr. Fredland, "but it has been repressed. Maybe something as mild as, 'Ladies don't do that,' which is quite enough, if they're afraid of losing their mother's love—enough for them to feel humiliated, frightened."

Had we learned the ABC's of masturbation before boys entered our lives, we might have explored our sexuality and our fantasies. We might have learned there are different things you can have with men, some of them sexual, some of them romantic, some warm and friendly, etc. We might have learned to trust and follow our feelings so that we knew when it was sex we wanted, when it was romance and loving comfort. There is a difference between love and sex; it is nice when they are combined, but they needn't be. You can have and enjoy one without the other.

CHAPTER 4

BODY IMAGE AND MENSTRUATION

The day I began to menstruate it was raining. A paralyzing Saturday, smothered in heat and the indecision of whether the rain would cancel my riding lesson. Another niggling worry was the discomfort in my lower stomach. Once before I'd talked my mother out of the need to have my appendix removed; it would have meant missing basketball season. Now the entire summer was threatened. When I saw the little brown spots on my pants, I breathed a sigh of relief. So that's all it was. The rain stopped. I could go riding. The summer was mine.

There was no one but mother to instruct me how to put on a Kotex. My sister was away at boarding school. If my horse had not been waiting, I might have lain in bed and bled to death rather than go to her for such intimate help; I still remember the unmentionable discomfort between us of that moment.

She got me a pink elastic belt and showed me how to hook the ends through the metal hooks. I sucked in my stomach away from her fingers and rushed her through her patient explanation. "All right, all right, I understand, I can do it." I couldn't wait to get out of the house. Beginning menstruation meant two things to me: relief that it wasn't appendicitis, and deep embarrassment at having to go through the initiation rites with my mother. I didn't tell her about my stomach ache, and she didn't cancel my riding lesson. I was used to telling my mother as little as possible and getting my way. Years later I was to accuse her of indifference. Mothers cannot win.

Driving me to a friend's house the next day, she caught me off guard with a new voice: "Well, how does it feel to be a woman?" I hated the friendliness those strained words offered. I leaned far out of the car window, my pigtails flying behind. My answer was appropriately lost in the wind. They were the last words my mother was to utter on the subject.

I am still working on her question how it feels to be a woman. But I never have understood secrecy about menstruation.

Our attitude toward menstruation is a vivid example of the power of emotion over intellect. My mother wanted to give me the information she had. I needed that information. I am certain she tried, but our crossed emotions got in the way. As I think back to that crucial moment in our lives, I feel we were enacting a universal mother-daughter drama. She could not give me the facts in a way I could hear; because listening was hard for me, she became even more inhibited. For most of us the results are the same. Grown women of twenty-five or forty-five, we are not easy about a function which more than any other sums up what we've subliminally been taught to feel about that part of our bodies: it is not nice.

In my entire research on the mother-daughter relationship, I have found no aspect more ruled by contradiction, loss of memory, confusion, and denial than menstruation. There is no behavior about which we express such cool certainty, but over which we have less control.

Long before we are eleven or twelve we have been aware that mother bleeds once a month—something that is difficult not to learn in any household. (If by some extraordinary arrangement, mother has kept us from knowing it, that speaks perhaps loudest of all.) By the time we reach puberty, we already know how mother feels about *anything* connected with sex. If she likes her own body, takes care of it, is proud of it, we too may feel pride in becoming a woman. If she enjoys men, if she doesn't become someone we don't recognize when she's around them—then, when she takes us to lunch and tells us that we are beginning "the most beautiful part of a woman's life," we may believe her.

But psychiatrist Dr. Lilly Engler says: "Many mothers don't want to face their daughter's menstruation because it means the girl is now sexual. If there's another woman in the house, it makes her the 'older' woman. I've known mothers who really want to prepare a daughter and even think they *have* done it . . . but have not. We don't like to admit this, but it often has to do with jealousy."

On the other side of the oedipal door, "menstruation reminds a young girl that her mother is sexual in a way she cannot deny," days Dr. Schaefer. "A girl of fourteen came to see me. She could not understand her own reluctance to discuss menstruation with her mother. She said she 'hated' it, that suddenly her mother was 'connected with the whole business.' She was worried, guilty that she no longer felt as close to her mother."

Until we begin to menstruate, we have some distance from mother. We identify with her, but we are not like her. The gulf allows us to ignore the facts of her life we don't yet want to face. But once we begin to menstruate, we can't look away. Her life is ours. Having to understand what the periodic cycle means to mother makes us unable to avoid any longer recognizing that mom is not merely the kindly, "pure," and totally unsexual being we had always assumed, but is as irrationally taken by the same erotic desires as we. She feels our emotions and knows the same excitement as we do within our own bodies. It is disturbing. Obscure oedipal conflicts are stirred up. She is not only our mother, she is a woman too. And a rival.

The excitement of becoming "one of the girls" quickly disappears. Suddenly we are back in touch with emotions we haven't felt in years, the primitive shame that went with wetting our bed, bad odors, soiling our clothes. The humiliation of involuntary or untimely excretion has been so pounded into us by years of zealous toilet training that to avoid it we have learned absolute control, control so rigid that neither our bladder nor sphincter dare to let go even while we are asleep. Abruptly, we are back in the middle of all that.

Menstruation is the elimination of a waste product. All women go through it. Why then should it not be something we share, a common experience that ties women together? "If men menstruated, they would probably find a way to brag about it," writes a male reviewer of a recent book on menstruation. "Most likely they [men] would regard it as spontaneous ejaculation, an excess of vital spirits. Their cup runneth over, their sexuality supererogates. They would see themselves as 'spending' blood in a plenitude of conspicuous waste. Blood, after all, is generally considered a good. 'Blood sports' used to be the true test of manhood and at the successful conclusion of a boy's first hunt, he used to be 'blooded.' It is turned around when it is the woman who bleeds. Bleeding is seen as a sign of infirmity, inferiority, uncleanliness, and irrationality."

We pretend disinterest in a function that begins on an hour and day of its own choosing, that may make us irritable, that can cause pain, public embarrassment, that makes us reject our men sexually or feel rejected by them. Again and again I warn my husband about my evil temper prior to my period; again and again I am aware of how true it is—after the fact, after my period has begun, after the quarrel.

Medical research shows that the brain affects our menstrual cycle; it may even control it. We also know that what goes on hormonally at the time of menstruation feeds back into the brain. But no doctor can tell you exactly how or why. The amount of control menstruation has over our lives is indeed so profound emotionally and physically that we can only deal with it in silence and denial. "A whole book about menstruation?" women said to Paula Weideger when she began her research for *Menstruation and Menopause*. "How do you find enough to say about that?"

Dismissed: a function that has been the subject of myth, speculation, mystery, and taboo since the world began, a function that is unique in every woman's life and that ends one day just as it began: unannounced. We prefer superstition to knowledge.

"Not many people thought menstruation worth a course on its own," says Paula Weideger about her experience teaching women's health. "The attitude was you just give women the nuts and bolts stuff about the egg and the uterus and that's it." Her book, published in 1976, was the *first* on menstruation ever brought out by a major publishing house with intent to reach a large popular audience. Nevertheless, when she began to publicize her book, TV talk shows invariably focused the discussion less on menstruation than on menopause. They said it was because their audiences were "health oriented." What does that say? That they found menstruation unhealthy?

We are so embarrassed about menstruation that we cannot abide to hear it spoken about even if in a complimentary manner. We believe the words must be merely flattery, and only fools are taken in by flattery.

Men have always been willing to play the clown. A little boy will fart in class. It is thought to be embarrassing perhaps, but essentially funny. It is no laughing matter when a little girl farts. It is dreadful.

When men go through a humiliating experience, they may get mad, curse, or fight. Then they have a drink, make a joke about the whole thing, and laugh it off. "You know those terrible roast programs they have on TV, where all the men make fun of the star?" a woman says to me. "Well, last week they had a woman as guest of honor. When they began knocking her for being ugly, about her shape and her funny hair, I got terribly uncomfortable." When a woman is insulted, made fun of, if she gets drunk or stains her clothes, we look away. It is so painful, it hurts. Low self-esteem, rooted in notions that there is something wrong with our body, makes us more the prey to feelings of humiliation than men. There is no space for light-hearted kidding.

The strongest feelings of humiliation, according to all the psychotherapists I have consulted, are those associated with soiling ourselves in public, with loss of body control. In the end this is perhaps the most difficult barrier to accepting menstruation: we have no control over this new body function. What is worse, nobody has warned us about this aspect of it.

Perhaps, too overcome by the excitement of the awaited event, we don't feel shame the first day we bleed. Eventually it surfaces. In all the talk about beauty and being a woman, why has nobody warned us, for instance, about the smell? And if nobody has mentioned it, it must be the most terrible smell of all. The surprise of it, the silence in which we experience it, our isolation in feeling we alone are fouling the air of everyone near us—all double the shame.

Men offer one of our great opportunities to dissolve the maternal inheritance of negative feelings about our body. How they feel about menstruation is therefore significant. "Men get their attitudes about menstruation from women," says Dr. Robertiello when I ask his opinion on this subject. "That it is something secret, not to be discussed, to be avoided as much as possible. Women can be insane about not wanting men to know they are menstruating. The analytic explanation is that they make the man into the parent who is going to judge them as being 'dirty children.' Even without menstruation women see the man's organ as being cleaner than their own. For instance, a menstruating woman may try to conceal the evidence of her 'waste.' She will wrap her sanitary napkin in layers of paper, and carry it outside to his garbage can rather than leave it in his nice clean wastebasket. It is also why most women don't want to have sex with men at this time. In a woman's eyes, since he doesn't share this dirtiness with her, he will look down upon her with tremendous contempt. The woman projects onto a man this demandingly 'clean' parent, unconsciously left over from the toilet-training period, who is going to see her as dirty, disgusting, not acceptable.

"What creates men's anxiety is not only that it is a mystery connected with female anatomy. It is also a reminder of another feminine mystery— allied, but not the same. It is the power to reproduce. Men don't have this power, so it makes them edgy. And finally, women's mysterious powers rearouse another unconscious anxiety in men: at one time, a woman was all-powerful in every man's life . . . when he was a baby. Her sex once gave her power over him, and now that he's grown up, do you think those humiliations are all forgotten? Not in the unconscious, they're not. Also, if her sex gave her power over him then, might it not happen again? Men's safest bet was never to give women a chance to have power again. And they went right to the heart of any person's strongest feelings of identity —the power of total sexual acceptance and freedom."

Our feelings about menstruation are the image of what it is to be a woman in this culture. While menstruation and the fear of revealing evidence of loss of body control bear possibilities of humiliation for women of which men are not aware, it is humiliating too to be that sex whose voice and presence carry less significance. It is humiliating to speak the same words as a man and have his heard, and not yours. It is humiliating to feel invisible when God gave you a body as solid as his. It is humiliating that women are accorded little dignity unless they are married. We twist these humiliations around, of course, and say it is glorious to have a man fight our battles for us, put us on a pedestal, take care of us. It is, if you enjoy being dependent on someone else.

There are other emotions as secretive as the shame that surrounds menstruation. They are the feelings that remind us of life, that we can give life, and that we are still alive, young—sexually capable of reproducing ourselves. It is difficult to tell an eleven-year-old daughter about these inchoate and complex stirrings of sexuality, life, and death which are hers to live with. How do you describe the awe that has always surrounded reproduction, the mystery and emotion that such a gift (the power to reproduce) and such a curse (to bleed once a month) must arouse in those who do not share them?

How do you not?

CHAPTER 5

COMPETITION

In the stereotyping of the sexes, men are granted all the competitive drives, women none. The idea of competitive women evokes disturbing images—the darker, dykey side of femininity, or cartoons of "ladies" in high heels, flailing at each other ineffectively with their handbags. An important step has been left out of our socialization: mother raises us to win people's love. She gives us no training in the emotions of rivalry that would lose it for us. With no practical experience in the rules that make competition safe, we fear its ferocity. Never having been taught to win, we do not know how to lose. Women are not raised to compete like gentlemen.

The young girl does not begin by thinking of it as competition at all. The adolescent merely wants what mother has. Well, then, why doesn't she just step aside and give us daddy, and let us succeed her as the woman of the house? It has nothing to do with wanting to hurt her. Our biology is our logic. Competition only enters when mother resists.

Freud defined the Oedipus complex as the sexual feelings of the four-, five-, or six-year-old child, directed toward the parent of the opposite sex, accompanied by competitive urges against the parent of the same sex. But contemporary psychoanalytic theory believes the contest between mother and daughter isn't only for daddy. It is the girl's struggle for recognition, for the limelight, for her place in the world, with or without daddy's presence.

Alas, the entire literature and folklore of the oedipal conflict is written from the child's point of view. Nobody tells mother what she should feel. All she knows is she is supposed to have only nice, story-book, motherly emotions. There is no place here for jealousy of a young girl, anger that the person who always obeyed you, *and whom you love*, now demands to do things her way, and makes you feel old.

Mother recognizes these feelings with anger and shame: they are a rearousal of her old, buried, oedipal competitive wishes against her own mother. She is not evil; how can she admit to feeling these evil things?

97

We go through life denying we are competitive, while feeling other women's gains somehow bar us from life's feast. "Competitive? *Me*? I'm not competitive!" we hotly deny as if we've been accused of murder—even as we blindly race against the only people who count: other women. The exercise is to win the prize, but perhaps more urgently, to test once again the limits of the contradictory reality which hems us in: can you beat out the other woman and still have her love?

Mother denies any rivalry on her side, and acts instead on the emotions that surround and protect her from competition. It is irritation, motherly concern, and exasperation she feels at our adolescent behavior. We are her "little girl," not her rival. When we grow up and another woman gets a dazzling new job, we aren't as comfortable around her. We say she "irritates" us. She is our best friend; we didn't want the job anyway. What is irritating is that her promotion threatens to make us conscious of our competition with her.

In a similar manner, to avoid acknowledgment of competition, we declare it no contest and put ourselves down before anyone else can pass judgment. When our husband talks too long to another woman, we say, "I know I'm not as interesting as she . . ." Feelings of inferiority are a classic defense. We feel diminished by her, frightened, we could kill her. Or him. But we do not feel competitive. Do you understand? *We are not competitive!*

There is much a father has to offer a daughter at adolescence. But what a tightrope he must walk! He must give attention to the needs of both wife and daughter, while being careful not to set one jealously against the other. "My husband is crazy about our daughter," says psychologist Liz Hauser, "but initially he didn't realize what he was setting up. For instance, if she and I were having a quarrel, he would come in and give her a little sign: don't worry about what mommy is saying, I'll fix it up. That wasn't good, he realized. The child doesn't know where her loyalties should be." It arouses mother's jealousy, but may also instill in the child the doomed desire to win out over her mother permanently.

Many mothers try to keep their daughter and husband apart by denigrating the father. Says Dr. Robertiello, "It's their way of competing with the girl while keeping both the daughter and father for themselves. Divide and conquer." "You know your father can never handle that kind of problem," says mother. "Why didn't you come to me in the first place?" Mother remains the friend of both sides, always firmly in the middle.

It is a destructive situation, leaving room for all sorts of oedipal fantasies to enter. If mother doesn't want him, if she doesn't understand him, maybe the girl can win him after all. But even if mother is a bitch, the girl can't afford to lose her primary alliance. Father may be the spice of life, but mother is the bread and butter. The relationship to mother was formed earlier, and runs deeper, than anything the girl has with father.

Many women can only fall in love with married men. They say they want the man to leave his wife—just as they wanted father to leave mother for them. But when the man is ready to divorce his wife, the woman loses interest. She didn't really want her father to leave her mother, it was just a wish. If mother and father should get divorced, and the daughter goes to live with daddy, she is guilty. She didn't want the wish to come true. "*Some oedipal wishes are very ardent but are not meant to be fulfilled,*" says Dr. Deutsch.

Father has his own oedipal feelings to contend with. When we were five, he may or may not have felt nervous about our sexual overtures. "Little girls can be terribly seductive," says Dr. Esman. "At least, fathers can experience it as such." But when we are thirteen, there is no way he can dismiss our advances as the games of a little girl. Nor do we want him to. We press up against him as daddy, the one person who loves us so well we can try behavior with him we wouldn't dare with boys our age. We expect him to run the show, to be able to know the difference between actions that say, "Treat me as a woman," and our continuing need to be loved as a daughter. We expect the world of him since he's daddy. Therefore, we are terribly hurt if he is threatened, if he precipitously withdraws and says, "Get off my lap, you're a big girl now." We are thrown back onto mother. The healthy sexual thrust of adolescence toward men has been dammed up or even reversed; the major movement of our lives remains focused on women.

Father is not the only man who arouses oedipal competitions. "There was a man, my father's best friend," says a woman of thirty-five. "We called him Uncle Steve. Years later I was to find out that my mother was very attracted to him. But to her dying day my mother patted herself on the back for never having had the slightest affair with this man. I was fourteen when this incident happened. We were out on the terrace. I was lying alongside Uncle Steve on a redwood chaise. He was a very affectionate man. The whole family was there . . . my brother, father, my sister and mother. Out of a clear sky my mother said, 'Helen, you're a bit too old for that now.' I remember going scarlet. I instinctively knew there was something between my mother and him. She was jealous. I was utterly embarrassed, but nothing further was said."

Later in our interview, this woman tells me that when she and her husband were living together before they were married, she always dreaded that her mother would telephone while he was there. "I was afraid she would know he was in my apartment, in my bed. I just didn't want her to." How could her mother know? Because her mother lived on in her head. Love for the man she was to marry was pushed aside by fear of her competitive, No-saying mother.

The hard but necessary lesson to the loser in the oedipal competition is that she just can't continue to hang out around her rival's house forever. She has to grow up and get out if she is ever to find her own man. But mother dismisses our efforts at sexuality as silly, brushes off our independence as foolhardy, and denies our growing ability to want and feel what she does. She says it is for our own good, but we are not so sure.

The family that was once felt to be lovingly close, now seems claustrophobic and boring. We want to get out, to get away. We are often drawn to people and activities mother doesn't like. With her grudging permission, or behind her back, we do them anyway. *An identity is being formed*—but we feel it is in the teeth of her opposition. Guilt piles upon anger, we twist and double back on her. How can you hate your own mother?

It is a dilemma; we are between worlds. We have not yet arrived at the safe harbor of discovering we can love men, and that they will love us back—and that in this new, exciting (but still frightening) kind of sexual love, we will find feelings of warmth, intensity, arousal, and power that in their different way are as rewarding as what we had with mother. We look to boys for the confirmation of the burgeoning sexuality mother doesn't like, and the reinforcement which daddy would not give us. But the acceptance we get from boys never holds the deep reassurance we had with mother. Often, we ask too much; they resent our demands or feel insufficient to meet them. They hurt us and depart. Unlike the promise mother makes, their love is conditional. They have been raised to see us as appendages, symbols of their success, sex objects. They want us for something we don't wholly believe in.

We went looking for love, but somehow sex came with the package. The whole business becomes tinged with anxiety. Wouldn't it be wiser to retreat? If we go back, become "good" again, mother's girl, mother would stop being angry. These endless arguments about whether she doesn't like this boy or that would end. We would have her love forever. There would be no competition.

Instead of asserting our individuality, our needs and desires, we become more like mother; join in her protest that sex isn't important to us after all. Pretty soon, the sexual drive is tamed, symbiosis wins. We grow up, we marry and have children, but never really left home.

On a realistic level, mother is not afraid we are going to steal daddy away from her. But there is a difference between a six-year-old who can fit into a man's lap, and a thirteen-year-old who fits perfectly into your clothes, who vies for the only man in the house and elicits from male visitors the kind of smiles you haven't seen in years—all the while, making plans of her own for a future you will never see again. Perhaps mother has come to terms with her fantasies of motherhood—but nobody ever mentioned treating her daughter as another woman. Certainly her own mother never treated her as one. Another wife, another mother, yes. But another *woman?* Never.

Some women have always felt overwhelmed by their more glamorous friends, that other women were more sexual. Now their daughter too is more beautiful, and younger. They withdraw from the competition by letting themselves go, becoming even more of a mom. Other mothers become so sexual that the daughter doesn't dare compete.

Says psychoanalyst Betty Thompson: "People tend to keep on being whoever they are. Becoming a mother doesn't change that. So a woman who is more concerned with her own feelings than anyone else's can be unreasonably competitive with her daughter. I've known mothers who forget they are twenty years older than the girl the minute their daughter starts bringing boys home. They compete as if the man were their own age. It's habit. Any time a man comes in the room, they have to feel attractive."

"I've been wondering if I should get Penny a bra," a mother who is thirty-four says to me. Her daughter is thirteen. "No, she hasn't asked for one, but I've noticed that people are beginning to look." What kind of people—men, women? What kind of look? I don't ask. But what is this pretty young mother feeling? Fran is a good mother who sees her work as caring for children and husband. Feelings of envy, competition, would be out of the question. At the dinner table that night, the daughter scolds the father: "Daddy, do you know how many calories there are in that dessert?" It is her mother's voice. She starts to take the dessert away from him, playing the stern mother (wife), but her father draws the line. "Sit down, Penny," he says. He is smiling. Fran watches from across the table. It is difficult to read the expression on her face. Where does she fit into this? The challenge comes on all levels, from the girl she loves, but also from everyone and everything that would take the girl or her husband away from her. Psychiatrists say we should air these feelings, maybe joke about them. But Fran's mother didn't joke with her about feelings of jealousy, competition. So Fran too is silent. The husband says privately to me, "My wife and daughter argue about everything and anything. I don't think they even know what it's about. I find it kind of amusing because I know it's about me. It's nice to have two women fighting over you, though they'd deny it to the death." Meanwhile, Fran sighs and confides to me, "I must find some exercises for Penny, she's getting round-shouldered."

I remember being round-shouldered, not because I needed a bra, but because I didn't. I hated the nasty pink one my mother finally bought me after kindly pointing out that I didn't need one. Seeing my humiliation, she'd tried to cover it up by telling me how lucky I was: I wouldn't have strap marks on my shoulders when I was her age. *I wanted strap marks!* The battle of the bra is an adolescent classic.

Mother knows what breasts mean in our culture. If she likes hers, if she allows us the peculiarly female rite of passage of the first bra when we want it, and not when she does, we too grow to like our breasts. If not, our round shoulders try to hide the inadmissable truth: at one time in our lives, our breasts were the focal point of anxiety about the new sexuality we wanted to be proud of, but which mother feared and shamed us into hiding. "The classic mistake mothers make with adolescent girls," says Dr. Fredland, "is that they won't let them become women."

Skills and abilities that once gave us recognition and self-esteem now also betray us. "Up to the age of puberty," says Jessie Bernard, "the young girl does all right, but now she traditionally begins to fall behind in school." We used to raise our hand enthusiastically for teacher's attention, to speak out loudly and clearly when we knew the answer. Now we hide our intelligence and bite our tongue. We want to attract boys, we want to be "feminine," and the way you do this is the same way mother taught us to keep her love: submission and passivity.

Adolescence is a tempestuous time, filled with rivalries, crushes, rages, disappointments, and unreal, giddy exultations of new relationships. We slam doors, stay out late, go out and get pregnant, or rush into early marriage—but it is stasis. We have done nothing for ourselves, only something in reaction to mother. Rebellion implies a break.

In adolescence we want rules, if only to assert ourselves by breaking them. The girl who complains about her mother's strictness is disturbed by her friend whose mother doesn't lay down any rules at all.

"I hated only having the backs of cars, dark hallways," one mother says. To give her daughter the privacy she missed, this mother goes out when her girl has a date. "I don't want her to think I'm playing the heavy chaperone, spying on her." Privately, the girl tells me that when she has a date, she always spends the night at a girl friend's house. "They are a big family, there's always someone at home." The daughter wants her mother around in case she needs the control, in case she wants to tell the guy, "We can't do that, my mother's home." The irony is that the mother never asked if the girl wanted her there. She didn't consider that her daughter's needs might be different from hers. *She made the assumption that the daughter wanted what she wanted.*

"There is a cliché which I tell mothers of girls of this age," says Dr. Esman. "You have to resign yourself to the fact that between the time your daughter is twelve and fifteen, whatever you do will be wrong. It is my effort to give them a sense of humor about the situation to help them— the mothers—survive." A mother who finds she must play the square for her daughter's own good, even while her daughter protests, needs a certain appreciation of irony.

We may bitch at mother's rules but we will accept them if something at the back of our mind tells us they are sensible, consistent, and in accord with reality. But if we perceive her decisions as arbitrary and/or phony, we will resent her and them. We fight to win ground for ourselves but she shifts the argument from the content of our request to the tone of our voice: we are rude and unladylike. We want to be popular and have our own friends, separate from her; she says certain girls aren't good enough and are just taking advantage of us. She feels left out of our decisions, rejected, and becomes punitive about the high cost of the telephone calls we make. We want a string bikini, but the argument becomes one about the clutter in our room. Years later when we fly home to visit, her first words at the airport are, "Oh, darling, what a short skirt!"

What is confusing is that part of mother does worry about our well-being. Half of us knows that is so. When this is genuinely the case, the criticism is not so unceasing; sometimes there is none at all, just pleasure in seeing us again. But if time after time, the first words we are met with make us feel like naughty little girls, the pattern is clear: more than our welfare or beauty, mother wants to put us in our place.

In adolescence the sexual drive is an explosion of energy that tries to break through, once and for all, the sticky, little-girl ties that bind us to mother. Sex is an expression of our own individual needs and desires. "I am a woman who likes this, does that, and goes for the other kind of man." It says who you are—and takes no account of mother at all.

If mother's fear of sexual self-assertion has made us reluctant to assert our own, our growth will stop. To deny that we are in sexual competition with her, we will say we are not sexual at all. The processes of separation and individuation slow or cease; we merge with mother instead and become what Mio Fredland calls one of the "latency girls."

These are the women whose lives express a certain safe, nonsexual quality. It is as if they are living still in that period—between eight and ten—that is characterized by palships with other girls and not too great interest in boys. "There are millions of women," says Dr. Fredland, "who are very successful at jobs and careers, even as wives and others, but who never really got into adolescence. They are well organized, get along fine with other women, not too competitive on a 'female' level. Psychosexually they are still back in their latency years. They have a different 'feel,' a kind of Girl Scout quality."

Many mothers do not see this kind of behavior as arrested development but as a process that has produced exactly the kind of daughter they want. A "nice girl," pal to girls and boys alike, who will dutifully get good grades at school and never be seen by mother as any kind of sexual competitor. She won't be heavily involved with men until it is time to marry, and then she will choose an equally "nice" boy who himself will carry none of the anxiety provoking overtones that mother distrusts.

Unless we learn the rewards of being our own women now, we will ever need to merge with a man as we did with mother, rather than expand his life and our own by joining in a union of two separate individuals. It may look like sex, but it will be symbiosis. Never mind that it is taking place with a man; it is modeled on what we had with mother during latency.

True sex can exist only between two separate people, each aware of herself/himself as individual entities and therefore of the alien magnetism of the other. There is no passion in symbiosis.

CHAPTER 6

THE OTHER GIRLS

After mother and before we are ready for men, there are the other girls. At five and six, they appeared in our lives like life rafts, bright welcoming alliances to carry us away into a new identity. We could never have left mother on our own. Father had failed us. Little boys weren't interested in our overtures—but little girls! They are our great chance to separate. They have all the safety and familiarity of home: they are female and needy, just like us. All of us are eager to find something more than mother, to embrace life, but the prospect is frightening. We rush into one another's arms the first day at school. Those arms close round us as tightly as the pair we just left at home. We don't struggle. We went looking for freedom, but found something too good to resist: tightness and closeness. We think we've left home. We have only changed partners. Symbiosis with a new face.

What human relationship contains as much ambiguity and ambivalence as women with women? We have so much to offer one another, but our history is one of mutual inhibition. The bond that ties us to other women parallels what we had with mother. She too began in our life as a loving friend. She became a no-sayer and a rival. Her very success in helping us grow through the difficult early stages of development brought us to the threshold of sex. Dad was the first man we saw. Mother was in the way. All her goodness and patience did not help. Within the family, there is only one prize. She had him. We wanted him. In one way, our desire was as natural as a river finding the shortest way to the sea; in another, guilt was the inevitable result. The irony is, the better mother she was, the greater guilt. It is one of the inexorable, situational tragedies of human nature.

The fear of competing against mother and the guilt at wanting to beat her out anyway spreads to the entire female sex. We like the little boy who sits next to us in class and want to win him away from Sally. But to go after him might incur Sally's anger, so we defend against wanting him at all. Instead of being jealous of Sally, we telephone her to come spend the night.

Clinically, this is called reaction formation. It is a way of denying an unconscious impulse; the act comes masked as its opposite. Instead of expressing our anger and competition toward women, we join with them and express love.

"Girls can be merciless," says Dr. Sanger, "organizing vendettas against other girls, suddenly turning on each other. A girl needs all the help her family can give her. The tears I have lived through with my own daughters and the young girls who come to see me . . . what they go through is terrible. Boys do it, but it doesn't have that personal, poignant cruelty. Boys have defeats to deal with too, but they don't have this sense of violation, betrayal: "This morning, I thought she was my friend, and this afternoon I found out what she was doing to me."

With no outlets for feelings of envy, competition, or jealousy, our emotions become compressed, escaping like steam through cracks in our nice-girl veneer. Before we know it, we have dealt the stab in the back, said the unkind word. We don't want to be bitches. Where did we learn it? Even as she separated us from our own body mother smiled and said she loved us. Blending love and anger, smiles and deceit, she taught us that our only rejoinder was to love her back no matter what she denied us— daddy, independence, sexuality—or we could suffer even worse loss.

Within our friendships with women, a larger and freer framework than the stultifying one at home, we might explore ourselves with people who are subject to our own anxieties, curiosity, and joys. We want confirmation that it is all right to go, to separate, to seek our identity on our own and with men. We ask one another for encouragement, for community and a boost up out of childhood. We want the other girls to tell us that it's OK, that they too feel what we feel. What we get instead are The Rules.

The Rules institutionalize the anger in our reaction formation. I've never met a woman of any age who could tell me when they were drawn up. No woman I interview can list them, but The Rules run our lives at thirty-five as they did at fifteen. They make us push men away, edit our opinions, dress like everyone else. More than anything, The Rules make us choose: which do we want—sexuality or the love of other women?

The group's job is to find outlets for those pressures society does not yet want to see in us. Slumber parties, romantic gossip, covert and overt sexual relationships with other girls substitute for sex with boys. *The group must keep the woman a girl for a few more years.*

Like some ten commandments of the flesh, The Rules are a list of Thou Shalt Nots: no kissing, no touching, no sexual expression, except to the degree the group allows. "The rules are made so none of the girls can outdistance any of the others sexually," says Dr. Schaefer. Those who break The Rules, walk around like pariahs—living examples of the punishment for making us jealous, bringing our competitiveness to consciousness. Exclusion is the sentence girls mete out to rule breakers now.

When the mysterious tides turn in the group and one girl is suddenly left out, she cannot retaliate: the girl who is out at the moment must wait, bottle up her anger and pain. Once more, we are acting out a parallel to the lesson mother began to teach us almost from the day we were born: nice little girls don't get angry.

How mother reacts to our new alliances determines not just the wholeheartedness with which we form them but what we come to expect from these new friendships. If mother is afraid for us, controlling, prying, telling us who we can or cannot see, we will try to control our friend, unable to expect more from her than we get at home. If mother is jealous, we will be jealous too—fearful of other people taking our friend away.

If mother said, "I love you but I want you to love other people too, to have relationships with them as rich as you can make them, and to try other lives than the way I live," our discovery of life's variety would not seem a betrayal of her.

Mother is inhibition; things and people she doesn't like have come to represent life and excitement. In fact, much of what we do with other girls is thrilling only because we know mother would disapprove. In time, when we break the group's rules, the exploit will be all the more thrilling for being forbidden. When we are grown, how often the best sex will be that which mother and other women wouldn't approve. Stolen sex with the wrong kind of man, in the wrong kind of place, all the more electric because he's married or we're flying home tomorrow. What kind of grown-up sexual people are we when our greatest moments are in ratio to their disobedience to The Rules? The bottom line is that when we marry, when we have the kind of sex mother would approve, sex goes stale. Our true excitement was not purely erotic. Underneath was the greater adolescent kick of rebelling against mom and other women too.

If it were really sex we wanted, if it were our strongest drive, we would break the adolescent rules and join with men in a sexuality that reinforced us. If it was a realistic fear of sex and its consequences (such as pregnancy) that held us back, we would be more intelligent about the use of contraceptives. But it is not sex we want most, nor sex we fear. It is the loss of our place in the society of women.

Sociologists speak of a cult of domesticity that once existed, a special "woman's sphere." "It was a secure place," says Jessie Bernard, "in which women had warm ties with one another. It was a woman's world, and they loved it."

Perhaps the woman's sphere of our grandmother's day belongs to a time we will see no more. That does not mean a community of women cannot be formed today which would be relevant to contemporary life. "Men always have had their old-boys' network," a woman tells me, "which gives each man within it a feeling of place and identity. In this way, they don't have to see someone younger as a terrifying rival, but as someone it is a pleasure to help out. Since I've become successful in my work, I've gone out of my way to help younger women. It's a great satisfaction. It makes me feel close to women, close to life, part of something larger than my own narrow ambitions."

I do not think that the passing of the old "woman's sphere" alone explains why we are such emotionally hungry people. Our problems of emotional deprivation go back too early in both our collective history as women, and in our individual biographies as daughters.

The woman's sphere was secure precisely because it was so small. Today a woman's world is as large as she can make it—but that means she has larger yardsticks by which to measure herself. It is from this sense of competition and potential loss that our anachronistic, adolescent fears come back to haunt us.

How grand is our success when we know other women would love us more if we were less—less beautiful, sexual, successful? We give up our will and initiative. We say to the man, Here I am, defenseless, vulnerable, take care of me. More than sex, we have always wanted symbiosis. We think men will reward and love us forever for giving ourselves over to them. Instead, when we get pregnant, they leave us. If we marry, they get bored with our suffocating clinging and look for more adventurous partners. Hurt, we regress to the only real protection we could ever trust: other women.

CHAPTER 7

SURROGATES AND MODELS

On a day that began like any other, my dentist removed my braces. Losing those wires marked my entry into puberty more significantly than menstruation. What had my vagina ever done for me? We were not even on touching terms. It was my mouth that carried the full potential for excitement: I had recently discovered kissing when my friend Daisy's older brother—who had nothing better to do that evening—put his tongue in my mouth.

Grinning and astonished, I moved my lips over my naked teeth and ran all the way to the Memminger Auditorium, where we were rehearsing *The Wizard of Oz*. My Aunt Kate was the Cowardly Lion and I was the Tin Woodsman. She took one look and wrapped her arms around me.

Aunt Kate was the only woman, after my nurse Anna, whose embraces I welcomed. I knew her perfume and the smell of her skin and when the world threatened to be too much in those years, her voice, her presence, the mere idea of her was something to hold on to. "You're just going through adolescence," she once said, and because she had a name for it, I believed it would end. She was the way I wanted to be when I grew up.

Kate was my mother's youngest sister. She had come to visit us after graduating from Cornell and had stayed on to live in our house. She saved my life. If that sounds overly dramatic, understand that it wasn't just the pain of adolescence that she got me through. She also gave me my present life. She got me ready for my husband and my work. The idea of her life, the picture of her, how she was physically and mentally, were my motivation and goal for years when I wanted everything and didn't know what it was I wanted. Long after adolescence, things she had told me, ideas she believed in, ways I observed her to be, were my guideposts. We are very different women today, but I am her child. My whole family knew that, including my mother.

Aunt Kate was different from anyone I had ever known or seen. All my girlhood years I had wanted nothing more than to blend, to melt into "the group" and be like everyone else. She had a style, a self-assurance, a truly original spirit that made being "different" a glorious prize. She didn't try to control me, but her opinions and knowledge were incorporated into the self I was forming. Even as I stuffed falsies into my bra and made myself shorter by dancing with my knees bent under the conveniently long skirts of the New Look, I was beginning to take pride in being smart, to question whether there might be more to life than chasing boys. I wanted boys too, desperately; I wanted to be popular and to kiss in parked cars until the music station went off the air and my white panties with the lace trim were soaked through. But I wanted more than the standard conclusion of this southern dream—to wear graduation-and wedding-white on the same day. I wanted to act, to write, to travel, to be Kate.

She was my height and had my mother's beautiful auburn red hair. There was nothing in grown women's usual clothes that I coveted; they were a boring sea of shirtwaist dresses and spectator pumps. Kate wore ballet slippers. Her dirndl skirts were cinched at the waist with wide belts, and a gold Egyptian coin dangled from her wrist. During the day she wrote copy at the radio station and in the evenings she went to the Dock Street Theatre. She didn't just act in plays, she wrote them as well. And she painted. "Painter or not," my mother said with caution, "no one in Charleston has a loft, Kate." A grand piano, easels, old velvet couches and candles filled the loft Kate rented on the waterfront. I would go there alone and sit for hours, inhaling the turpentine like a promise.

It was the summer after Kate had come to live with us that I dropped out. I stayed home, refused to see my friends, followed Kate around like a shadow. My sister was away at boarding school that year; a time that was to be a grievous experience for her too. I felt abandoned, but more to the point, I felt I was going crazy. I shrank from my mother, rejecting her touch, answering in monosyllables. Reading was the only way of marking time until Kate came home for two o'clock dinner.

Kate didn't just tolerate me, she included me. I followed her everywhere, to her studio, to the theater, out to dinner. Kate drew up book lists for me. She bought me water colors, and on weekends we would sit in St. Phillips graveyard with our sketchbooks on our knees. While she typed her first play on the card table in her bedroom, I wrote my first story about a girl and a horse. She did not mind my interruptions when I asked how to spell a word—interruptions I can see now must have been maddening. When she read my story, she suggested I put in a description of the girl. I did and she said it was good. When her own play was finished, I was given a small part.

That time in my life when I stayed home to read to avoid my "thoughts" and clung to Kate as to life itself ended as quickly as it began. Summer was over, school began, and once again I only came home to eat and sleep. As I was on my way out the door one day to meet a friend, Kate called after me, "Hey, how about a chocolate sundae?" I was late, but I must have heard something in her voice that reminded me of myself: she missed me. We walked to Byer's Drug Store like we used to when I couldn't live without her. During the next years I would run into her on my way out to chase boys, to meet boys, to talk to boys, and I would avoid her eyes. I didn't need her anymore. She never said a critical word.

How simple it was when we were three, or even nine and ten. Whatever else we wanted, we wanted "to grow up like my mother and have children." Says Jessie Bernard: "Our society makes a much greater effort to masculinize boys than to feminize girls. It is not necessary for girls. The model each girl lives with is female." But adolescence and the advent of sexuality change our ideas. Even if we want to be mothers, we don't want to get there mother's way. In our eyes, mother is not sexual.

For the girl who genuinely wants to re-create her mother's life, the repetition comes with a sense of peace and fulfillment. Her path goes straight through girlhood, early marriage, pregnancy, with mother's smile and society's approval every step of the way. The daughter who wants something different has a harder time; the idea goes against her mother's model.

Either way, most of us repeat our mother's emotional life. When we are young and energy flows in the veins like wine, we have no intention of giving up vitality, humor, adventurousness. It is unthinkable that we will ever be as anxious and conservative as mother. Then one day we hear ourselves telling our husband not to drive so fast, nagging our children to clean up their room, and know we've heard that voice before. The degree to which we can forge our own emotional selves depends greatly on the help we get from other people who love us, people whose lives offer a pattern we can follow.

When we meet an old friend of mother's, who recounts how daring and exciting mother was before she married, it is as riveting as a fairy tale. It has the power of truth in a framework of the mythic. We both want to believe and don't.

During family reunions when I was growing up, I loved my aunts to tell stories about my mother as a young woman. My mother—with different men, making conquests! I still pore over old photos of her jumping horses in dangerous steeplechases. It is thrilling to think of her taking chances. By the time I came along, she had changed.

If she could have offered herself to me as a model of daring, independence, and sexuality, would it have availed? I've known so many admirable women whose daughters reject their lives. Other women's daughters may emulate them, but the girl under their own roof will look elsewhere, *outside* the immediate family, for someone who stands for a different, roomier world, simply because mother is not in it. What I did learn from my mother was her other side: overcaution, anxiety, fear. I have tried to hide these traits behind the more daring qualities I learned from others. I know the world sees me as independent. I know myself as my mother's daughter. Mother is love and life itself, and we want to hold on to that, but a model for sexuality and independence is a bridge toward separation. Mother cannot be that for us.

"Getting unstuck from even a 'good enough' mother," says Dr. Robertiello, "is best accomplished if you can form an alliance with someone else, someone close, like your grandmother or father. To separate, you have to ally yourself with a person you feel knows the way, who is stronger, wiser or more independent than you." These people give us a source of power and strength outside of mother. They need not physically take care of us, but in a sense psychologically stand *in loco parentis*. They have many names in the technical vocabularies, least awkward among which are identification figures or role models.

"I can't think of any woman I admire, that I want to be like," says a fourteen-year-old whose mother is one of the most admirable women I know. "Except this older friend of mine. She's seventeen. She's very creative. I think she's wonderful. She's got her own opinions, which doesn't mean she doesn't hear other people out. But she doesn't let them make her go against herself." A couple of days after our interview, this girl telephones me long distance to tell me she has remembered another woman who is "sort of a heroine of mine." It is Katharine Hepburn.

Katharine Hepburn. She was one of my models too. Unmarried, childless, flat-chested—she is the antithesis of what mother and society want for us. And yet my mother adores her, and men too seem to sense something heroic in her. She transcends looks, style, or whatever particular circumstances the scriptwriter places her in; through force of character, by making it on her own, by never giving up and keeping her integrity intact, she wins us all. She is an image of the separate person.

Until recently, the women to whom young girls turned for role models during adolescence were almost stock figures. There were so few areas in which women were, by the nature of their work, assertive and self-affirming, that school teachers and camp counselors appear with regularity. Today, my woman editor, my woman literary agent, or any of the dozens of admirable women you and I know if only on television are available models.

As yet, the women with whom an adolescent is most likely to come into contact, to get a real feel of, remain the tried and true favorites. A gym teacher embodies the idea of aggression in the best sense, of being very connected with selfhood: if you play tennis with style and can throw a basketball well, that is a self-affirming kind of activity. Drama teachers are attractive because they direct people; in fact, anyone "in charge" is helpful, people who put things together and furnish direction but leave room for you to bring your own talents to the role. They allow autonomy to grow because they do not do the whole job for us. It is wonderful when your heroine returns your affection and respect, but you don't want her living through you the way mother did. Ideally, she is there when you need her, but she doesn't cry Betrayal when you walk away. She has her own life, and allows you to have yours.

If we cannot find models who will safely help us separate and become our own women, we may just give up and retreat back to where we started. A return to mother at this stage of development is a significant defeat, sapping our self-confidence and undermining our will to try again.

I am not saying that women would be better off not to marry, nor that it is a defeat to become like your mother. What matters is whether your life is your choice. If you have won independence first, so the decision to follow your mother's life comes of your own volition, and not out of a sense of passive inevitability, duty, or fear, that is a victory. It is a self-affirmative life, as valid as anyone else's.

In all fairness, it must be said that our view of mother makes it almost impossible for her life to aid our separation. An independent woman is one who has a totally different relationship to life, to men, to work, and to herself than we were ever willing to perceive in mother. If she has an existence independent from us, we dislike it, discredit it. *She is our mother!* She should be *there,* attached, waiting for us when we got home from school or from a fight with our friends. It is our privilege to leave her, not hers to leave us. The lament is almost universal among the daughters of successful women I've interviewed. I am guilty myself: I've said that I used to be thrilled by photos taken before I was born of my mother as an intrepid horsewoman; but I also remember—with greater emotional intensity—my silent recriminations that she was often out for the evening, was younger than the mothers of my friends, that she didn't wear an apron and have gray hair.

We insist that mother be homey, unglamorous, "Like everybody else's mother." Then with the unfairness of children, once we have safely imprisoned her in the stereotype, we reject her as lacking excitement and jaunt off looking for someone else—someone who will be different, who will give us an idea on how to leave home, an arm to lean on while we try on our shaky new identities.

What makes the mother-daughter relationship so poignant is its bewildering reciprocity. "Even with all my professional training," says Dr. Leah Schaefer, "I can't help getting these feelings of rejection and abandonment about my adolescent daughter. Katie had always loved going everywhere with Thomas and me, to the theater, to friends' houses. She was wonderful company and we loved to include her. Suddenly, she didn't want to go anywhere with us. The phone rang endlessly for her, and she only had time for her friends. A friend would come to visit, they'd immediately go up to Katie's room, the door would close, and that would be that. Of course I was happy for her to be growing up, but it took terrific objectivity on my part plus Thomas's repeated assurance that she was just going through a phase, and that she hadn't rejected me. I just could feel the surge of retaliation in me, the desire to be punitive about the telephone or to set strict hours in which she could see her friends. If you have been close with your daughter, it is very, very hard when she turns to other people for what she almost exclusively used to find in you."

An important ethical point arises. If it is mother's duty to let us go, the responsibility for our going rests with us. I agree with Mio Fredland that "a mother should be a good loving consultant," but among the first signs of maturity is to know the difference between what your mother should be told about your experiments in new life-styles, and what should be kept to yourself. If we tell her everything, more than she's asked to know, it is a sure sign we are not serious about our efforts to be independent. Too often the complaint, "I wish I could talk to my mother," really means, "Why can't I tell her I'm smoking dope or drinking in bars and get her approval for it?"

The wonder is not that so many of us fail, but that so many succeed—that we aren't all walk-around, wind-up children, sexual pygmies for life. When you think about it, how do we get through all that denial? The areas of conflict with mother that we've learned to avoid—our bodies, anger, masturbation, aggression, sexuality, competition—read like a program for retardation. And yet there we are: me writing this book, you raising your children, working—most women on the whole making a pretty satisfactory job of their lives.

Among my own friends, the most interesting people had difficult parents and stormy adolescences. Basic temperament and other mysteries of the personality cannot be dismissed in trying to explain that so many of us *do* move against all the odds to find a larger world. And while I believe that role models make up a great part of the answer, it is fascinating to wonder why we choose some people to serve as this bridge toward growth and ignore others—who, to the outside eye, would seem to be very glamorous indeed. In my research, for instance, I have found that people like Gloria Steinem and Jane Fonda don't "take" the imagination of most women. We may admire them, but I've never heard a woman say she wanted to be like them. They are the revolutionaries; we are still our mother's daughters.

Our model of self-individuation is not always our sexual model. In a society that denigrates explicit female sexuality, we will be lucky to find any sexually defined woman at all. Little wonder that the people we look to for sexual models are often the "bad" girls our own age. Their spirit is just too much to resist. By being "bad" they are demonstrating what we long to achieve: separation. Even if we ourselves are not yet ready to "go all the way," we want to know there are people who do. They are our future.

Adolescent boys have an easier time finding sexual models than we do. They may not think of their fathers as Don Juans, but at least they see them responding to women, turning to look at a pretty girl in the street, talking about sex. We may not like this, it may be done in bad taste, but it gives the boy a sense that it is OK to be sexual. But when did you last hear a mother remark to her daughter about the sexual appeal of a good-looking man? Oh, we talk about his hands, his eyes, the cut of his suit, but what about the seductive line of his hip or shoulder? How does mother react to an off-color joke? No wonder women have no background, no models, for response to blue movies. We have no sexual camaraderie.

Women may not yet be aroused by the nude male centerfolds in magazines. Psychologists report we are not as sexually stimulated visually as men. The implication is that this is biological, that we are born non-voyeurs. My own feeling is that it is learned behavior. Once women are given an unprejudiced start as sexual people, we will know at last if the eye alone can turn women on. We will also know *what* turns us on, and instead of men's ideas of what women want, we will produce our own erotic imagery. Meanwhile, young girls today still turn reverentially West, to Hollywood, for an image of sexuality.

At least, films fill the aching void. At worst, they give us an idea of woman and sex so overly romanticized that when it does come at last, we wonder why it doesn't feel the way it did when Robert Redford held Ann-Margret in his arms.

Between mother's great No to sex and the false sexuality we see in the commercial world we live in, little wonder that one of the biggest jobs we have in adolescence is to establish that core of self which psychiatrists call "gender identity."

Gender identity can be defined as the way we see ourselves as either male or female—subjectively, not anatomically. And one of the measures of our lives is the degree of certainty we feel in this identity. Until recently, how a woman felt about her femaleness didn't matter. If her anatomical identity said she was female, there was a rigid set of personality and character traits she was expected to have, and they corresponded exactly with how others reacted to her. Today we are beginning to see that by strictly defining emotional or behavorial patterns as *masculine* or *feminine,* we put straitjackets on both sexes.

"Everyone has the potential to have the qualities we think of as masculine or feminine," says Jessie Bernard. "I would like to see both sexes have them—sons who are gentle and tender, daughters who can be strong and assertive. Perhaps with men becoming involved with the raising of children today we will see this happen." The contemporary idea of gender definition is more complex and richer for women than it has ever been. Given a modicum of ease about her gender identity, a young girl in the process of formation will try to strengthen those feelings about herself she likes best, borrowing character traits from the most admirable female and male figures around her. She may choose to be a girl-girl, as pop lyrics put it, an old-fashioned, clinging creature; or she may take on the characteristics of a woman so contemporary she has not yet been given a pop-tune name—someone sexually giving, who possesses what used to be called masculine assertiveness. Or any mixture of the two.

But let me add an important caveat here. While I do believe notions of gender identity are changing to allow all of us to take in more of life's complexity, that change has not yet become a universal gut feeling. We live an almost schizoid sense of values. Right along with our assent to the latest manifesto on sexual freedom, says Dr. Robertiello, "we find that a woman's idea of her gender identity, her subjective feeling about herself as a woman, is much more connected with her concept of herself as a mother than it is with her concept of herself as a sexual person.

"For instance, say a woman is divorced and has a number of lovers. She still isn't to be able to think of herself as an adequate woman if she isn't fulfilling her mothering functions with her child. Can you have good sex if you think of yourself as a bad woman? You might have a good time in bed, but you would put a pejorative connotation on it. Instead of saying, 'Aren't I an exciting, sexual woman?' you would say, 'I'm a bad person. I should be home taking care of my daughter.'"

I would go even further than Dr. Robertiello. We do not even have to be mothers to see our gender identity more connected with motherhood than sexuality. So long as we have not repeated the model of our mother's life, most of us will live with a suspicion of failure, of being incomplete.

For instance, I would have told you that I was totally committed to my decision not to have children; and yet when I was writing the first chapter in this book, my argument against the maternal instinct was so strong and out of proportion that I was almost unable to get past it. I could not give it logical emphasis because I was defending myself. All the intellectualizing in the world hasn't yet convinced me that in going against my training I have not abandoned my true gender identity, true femininity.

While role models and identification figures help us separate from mother, surrogates play a different role in our lives. They were the nurses, housekeepers, grandmothers and older sisters who gave us warmth and intimacy when mother was physically or psychologically not available to us for any of a variety of reasons. In that dependent time of life, before we were ready to separate, surrogates taught us many of the emotional and personality traits we carry through life.

There is a big difference between the surrogates of childhood and those we find during adolescence. It is choice—ours. Our nurses and older sisters who comforted and held us when we were babies did so by their choice. The surrogates of adolescence, the people whose bodies, approval, touch, and esteem become so vital to our continued growth, are chosen by us. We are old enough by now to have some notions of what we want. Our needs are more psychological than to be fed, held, and bathed. And yet both early and later surrogates often share a similar fate in the end: oblivion. We tend to forget them, to play down their importance.

A woman I interview speaks of the influence of a teacher in her life, but says she felt compelled to hide it. "My English teacher when I was fourteen changed my life," she says. "She taught me to read and to value being intelligent. She was not pretty, which was what all the girls in my crowd prized. I am ashamed to say that I never told anybody how much I admired her. I just took what I wanted and ran. I never thanked her, never, and I've always been sorry about that."

This is just one example. Again and again in researching this chapter, I come upon evidence of this denial. Even when directly asked if there isn't someone who mothered them, or with whom they identified while growing up, most people will pause, shrug and say no, there was nobody.

"It is often the case," says Dr. Helene Deutsch, "that if a woman cannot remember how important a nurse or housekeeper was to her emotional development as a child, it was because of guilt toward the mother, that she allowed herself to have these feelings of love toward another woman."

It is a guilt born of symbiosis. To people who are attached, admitting there is someone else opens them to fear of the symbiotic partner's anger, retribution, and possible abandonment. We can no longer afford to live in this squeeze. Today, when mothers are involved in more than one job, children need more than one mother.

But mother first must give up her illusory gains from symbiosis carried on too long. Perhaps the easiest person to whom she can cede at least part of mothering is her husband. Says Mio Fredland: "It really doesn't matter what the gender of the mothering person is." Some men are maternal. Some women are not. To the child, it does not matter where the warmth comes from. "Motherhood is too important to leave to women," says Jessie Bernard. "It's got to be shared."

There is no doubt however that most fathers have not yet learned to accept responsibility for children to the same degree as women. "When I'm at work, I can't help worrying about whether he's given Susie her lunch," one woman tells me. "I know that when we're both at home and the baby cries, he sleeps on. It's me who hears it. How can I rely on him?" How can she not? The fault is not entirely with men. Never given full responsibility, father soon takes less than his half.

While many women today have to take on all the risks, fatigues, and drudgery of what used to be the male workaday world, they cannot give up any of the risks, fatigues, and drudgery of being a mother too. Some women can combine full-time careers with being full-time mothers, but they are the superhumans among us, and you cannot base a rational society on all women being super people. Other young women recognize they can combine marriage and a career, but decide they can't be mothers too.

How destructive that anger at mother should take up so much of our adult lives. We may say, "I'm not angry at my mother!"—but why do we go into such a rage when our daughter doesn't clean up her room, or our husband is late? The fury is not appropriate. It has been displaced from mother onto someone "safer." This is unfair and bewildering, leading to arguments that cannot be resolved because the real target for our furies is never named or even made conscious; to examine our unresolved angers even now would mean to reawaken those infantile emotions of loss and retribution we never outgrew.

The truth is that once faced, we could live with that anger today. Unfaced, it contaminates any real love we may have for our mother. As the models and images of independence and life we once found so attractive slip through our fingers, we find ourselves becoming more like the anxious, critical, sexually frightened woman we never intended to be. Anger at the person who inhibited our trust in any model but herself works on us in the disguise of passivity, conservatism, and resignation.

Says Dr. Betty Thompson: "Passivity in women can be humiliation, fear, lack of ego strength, terror that you're going to be found wanting. All too often it is anger." Unlike men, who get points for being tough and hot-headed, women have their anger termed unladylike. We start to get angry, but feel guilty about it, and tamp it down. The passive-aggressive personality is the result: someone who expresses her anger in a seemingly civilized disguise. "Where do you want to go tonight, honey?" the husband says, not so much wanting to get the name of a restaurant from his wife, but wanting to hear in her emotional tone that she is pleased to be going out with him. "Anyplace you want," his wife says, depriving him of the real answer he hoped for but disguising her desire to frustrate and annoy him by seeming to comply with the overt question put to her.

Anger is negative, but still it is a tie. It retards separation because as long as we are angry at mother, she is uppermost in our thoughts, and we are still her daughter.

One day when I was talking to Robertiello, he said as an afterthought, "Why can't you accept the fact that your mother doesn't love you?"

For a moment, I thought I was going to hit him. Instead, I went through one of those instantaneous, self-protective reflexes, and changed the subject. But his sentence thundered around in my head.

For weeks I would think about it, wince, retreat, and then return to it again. How could he have said such a thing? It became a familiar pain, until one day, like a weight lifted, I felt relief. Of course she didn't love me! Not in the perfect, idealized way I'd wanted all my life.

I couldn't wait to tell Dr. Robertiello of the feeling of freedom that had come out of this understanding of his disturbing statement. "But, Nancy," he said, "you've twisted my words. I didn't say your mother didn't love you 'perfectly.' From all you've told me about your relationship, I said she didn't love you, period."

Perhaps the reason I have always felt free to acknowledge the importance in my life of my nurse and my aunt was that my mother so easily accepted them. She has never hesitated to give them credit for what they gave me, never made any reluctant show of her gratitude to them. How many times have I heard her tell other people how much she owes them, how glad she is for me that I found them. Isn't this love?

The lunatic other side of the coin is that I am angry at her for not giving me herself what I found in them. It is the case of the woman with the too-liberal lover. She is grateful that he takes her back after he learns of the other man, but why didn't he throw her out? Did he value her so little?

I have never wanted to confront my mother with my anger. It would be to little avail. She wouldn't understand, and if she did, what could she do now? It is too late for nursery angers, but I will be left with them for all my life if I do not accept that they are there, and why. Otherwise I will be in the position of those people who, as Dr. Sanger puts it, "endlessly try to shake love out of their mothers by the lapel."

The possibility that mothers may come not to resent but to welcome the necessity for role models and surrogates in their daughters' lives is a thrilling idea for the future. Equally remedial in raising the mother-daughter relationship to an adult level is to see our own lives become a model for mother.

The reversal of roles in which the child teaches the parent seems to release both women from the fixed demands of anger and symbiosis. Even
if we have outgrown her, we can forge a new and loving tie by becoming
her role model. "My mother worked from the time I was fourteen," says a
twenty-nine-year-old woman. "Whatever my mother achieved was subor-
dinated to make my father happy and seem successful. I married when I
was a sophomore in college. I wanted a family, I expected to be a traditional wife, like my mother. The stereotype didn't work out that way. The
man I married never found a career—he was just like my father. I followed my mother's model and did everything so this man could be successful. I got a part-time job, I went to graduate school, I wanted to be as
strong as my mother. Eventually I couldn't take it. I left him.

"I was glad to be out of a bad marriage. I found a good job, everything
should have been rosy, but I felt this terrible anger in me. I thought it was
at him. I soon realized how much of it was at my mother. I had been a
good daughter, I had done everything she had trained me to do, and it
hadn't worked. She had lied to me about what life was all about.

"I'll tell you something that has helped relieve the anger. I have recently come to see how much my life has influenced my mother. She makes
choices now she never could have before, without me. Like saying to my
father, after thirty-three years of marriage, 'You can do as you like, but
I'm not going to turn down promotions because you'd feel like a failure.
I'm going to go as far as I can in this career.' She couldn't have said that
without having watched what I've been through. I am proud of my mother when I see her growing and doing things she should have done years
ago. It gives all those years she spent raising me significance and meaning. I am prouder of this than anything, that my life has given mother a
second chance."

If mother believes in our new identity enough to trust her weight on it,
we can believe in it too. We have not lost her. The debt is paid.

CHAPTER 8

MEN THE MYSTERY

I can't help wondering how relevant to my mother's decision to remar-
ry was the emergence of all the women in our house into a time of
sexuality. It would have been an unconscious pressure, of course, but
timing is so much. There we were, four women: my mother, Aunt Kate,

my sister, and I, each needing her own man, her own identity. My aunt married within a year of my mother. My reaction to the news of my mother's remarriage was childish but much less important than my own need to solve the mystery of men.

Sexuality is the great field of battle between biology and society, and mother is the first regiment pressed into battle.

When mother takes our hand away from between our legs, when, as we grow older, she lets us know by look, tone of voice, attitude and gesture, that it isn't nice, she is being what society considers a good mother. *The effect is to cut us off from our own bodies.* "In our culture," says Dr. Robertiello, "women are trained to expect that in some magical way, men will make them sexual people. They can't do it to themselves." Little wonder then that men seem mysterious to us. Who can understand creatures so powerful that they can command sexuality itself? "Invariably," says Dr. Schaefer, "the way women put it is, 'He gave me an orgasm.' I tell them, 'Someone doesn't give you an orgasm. You give yourself an orgasm." Usually, words like these are treated as if they were merely semantic tricks, not to be taken seriously. A woman thinks she needs a man to bring her to life. Passivity is indoctrinated and reinforced.

"When a mother hinders or arrests a daughter's sexual activity, she is fulfilling a normal function whose lines are laid down by events in [her own] childhood, which has powerful, unconscious motives, and has received the sanction of society," wrote Freud in 1915. "It is the daughter's business to emancipate herself from this influence and to decide for herself on broad and rational grounds what her share of enjoyment or denial of sexual pleasure will be."

Freud's dictum seems to be fair enough. It lays the responsibility for our sexuality where it belongs—with us. But he is talking about the years when we are old enough to decide "on broad and rational grounds" how much sexuality we should allow ourselves.

For most of us in our teens, that time is not yet. Mother's inhibition of our sexuality re-creates in each of us the myth of Sleeping Beauty, and a complementary myth becomes our future: some day my prince will come, the knight in shining armor who will awaken my dormant sexuality. Our parents smile at our teenage acned Lancelots, but in our eyes, they arrive trailing clouds of glory. We become pinned to them, braceleted, chained and enslaved to how we feel when they hold us in their arms. They release us for a time from prison, from waiting, sleep, and passivity. When not in their arms, we live on fantasies, until they hold and release us once more. I am not talking of the release of orgasm, but of the release from tension—the fear that no man will want us as much as we need him. Of course this tension is sexualized, is itself part of the rhythmic build to orgasm, but we learn to satisfy it without the forbidden climax. We come to find more release in the certainty that he will never leave us than in having him inside us. *That certainty becomes more important than orgasm ever can be.*

The real thing, the penis inside, for many women never does live up to that early substitute: security. And tight security—control—is the antithesis of orgasm—letting go. After hours of fondling and kissing, young girls go to their rooms with their pretty panties soaked through, but do not lie awake in sexual frustration. We sleep sound in our virginal beds because we have lain in his arms long enough to believe again, at least for tonight, that "everything will be all right, I'll never leave you, I'll love you forever." Who he is, what he wants—*sex itself*—is never so important as the fantasy of permanent security he gives us. Is it any wonder that after a year or two of marriage, so many women wake up with a stranger? "Why did I ever marry him?"

"I was an only child growing up in a house full of women," says actress Elizabeth Ashley, "so men were always mysterious to me. My mother had been damaged, but, like so many women of her generation, she felt impelled to hide her scars. To show pain would have been a fall from dignity. She was really an early and very private feminist, strong, idealistic and brave. Her mission was to raise me to be independent. And she succeeded in that, but those mysterious men still had this huge power.

"In a way, men to us were like drugs are to this generation. The kids are told, 'If you take them, you'll be addicted forever.' Men were our 'reefer madness.' They became imbued with this mystical, dangerous, irresistible romance. And romance is, of course, the cornerstone of any addiction."

Young women today tend to have friendships with men where ten or twenty years ago there could only have been romantic love. It is a significant change. However, when sex does enter, the pregnancy and abortion rates among teen-agers are frightening. Young girls still expect something wonderful, magical, mystical, and dreamy from their sexual partners.

"Our lives as women," says Dr. Schaefer, "are filled with fantasies. You have the fantasy of what you think your father is, and the fantasy of what your mother says he is. You have the fantasy of the kind of man you think you should marry and the fantasy of the kind of man you actually do marry. You have a fantasy of what life is going to be like. A lot of us end up not being able to cope with the reality we live because we always have that fantasy in our mind of what it should have been."

"How will I know if it's really love?" a girl asks her mother. "You'll know when it comes along," mother says. And then one day, astoundingly, it turns out to be true. Being held in our lover's arms creates a feeling of warmth, love, and happiness we have never felt before—or have we? We are pervaded by an eerie sense of having been here before. We have always known this feeling existed, and have merely been waiting for it to come along again. *It feels right.*

"The reason the feeling of love at these moments is so satisfying," says Dr. Robertiello, "is that in a perfectly acceptable, heterosexual situation, the woman has re-created the intensity of satisfaction she once felt at being held like this. It was when she was a baby in her mother's arms." Since this thought is vaguely unpleasant, somewhat threatening to our gender identity as women, it is repressed. For all their masculinity, men can give us moments in which they remind us so much of the love we once had with mother that we are afraid to recognize it. We cloud the feeling in mystery.

But they give us sex too! When both elements are present—the nurturing plus the explicitly sexual—the marriage or affair is said to be serious, and continues for some time. If the unconscious nurturing we learned to expect from mother is missing from a relationship, we say it is "merely sexual," and it soon ends. The ultimate richness of life depends, in my experience, more often on satisfying our unconscious needs than meeting the demands of the physical.

Whether we like it or not, in the vast majority of American families the major figure for the child—male or female—is the mother. Our entire pattern of relating to others is set up first with her. Women who perceive that their mothers didn't like men in general or their father in particular suffer a devastating effect. "If the girl does like her father," says Dr. Schaefer, "mother's negativism sets up conflict in her. She doesn't feel free to like him if mother doesn't, if mother is always finding fault, nagging him. She may ally with her father, but it will be a guilty alliance. Her relationships with men often repeat the way her mother was with her father: nagging. Father didn't make enough money, he wasn't as smart as other people—that is how the daughter remembers family life."

Just who daddy is, is never quite so clear as what he does for mother . . . and by extension, for us. He is this mysterious outside force, he "brings home the bacon," showers the family like Santa Claus with the goodies of life—the house, the car, the washing machine, summer vacations, money for that special pretty dress for a dreamed of occasion. Even in those families where mother also works, she usually contributes less than he to the income. It is a feeling that she reinforces for her own reasons: most women need to feel that their husbands are the major providers, and this is the feeling they pass on to their daughters.

Little wonder then that long before the question has arisen as to how or whether mother should prepare us for the sexual experience of men, she has given us a picture of life in which they are indispensable. Like those photos in fashion magazines where the men are either out of focus, characterless, or homosexuals, *who* they are is never so important as what they give the women in the picture: stronger definition. The dress costs $200, but without a man, whole gaggles of men lolling at her feet or helping her out of the car, the image of the woman in that dress would be far less significant *to other women.*

The thrust of our development today is away from this; and yet the notion that men are absolutely vital to any value we may have is so woven into feminine reality that most women think to reject it would be like trying to reject the law of gravity. When I say women still need men "to take care of us," the idea sounds dated and old-fashioned. It is too easy to dismiss if taken only at its superficial meaning. Women do not need men to pay our bills or repel marauders. We need men to take care of us because we don't believe we are visible, that we exist, without one . . . much as we felt lost, abandoned, near death as infants if mother did not appear when we became frightened at being alone.

By turning men into Father Christmas, mother deals an enormous blow to the problem of competition between us. Daddy isn't this sexual person, this attractive man we both want. He's really a nice, big, warm provider, as comfortable and nonerotic as a hot-water heater. What could be sexual about a person who works his way to an early heart attack, who comes home so tired and grumpy he barely has the strength to peck a kiss on Mommy's cheek? Mother further cements the alliance between us: Daddy is not the competitive prize we both want but a fuddy-duddy opponent whom we league together to fool: "We'll tell him the dress only cost twenty-five dollars, not forty-five."

There is an enigma in this nice, safe, domestic picture she is presenting. Here she is, telling us what a nice man daddy is, how hard he works for us, how much he loves her, what an ideal marriage they have. But why is she always up to these sly little manipulative tricks that make him look like an oaf? Doesn't she remember they just had that frightening quarrel last week? Doesn't father usually seem bored with her, spending more time than she likes away at the office or bowling with his friends?

When she talks of the rewards of marriage (as opposed to the dangers of sex), we feel a loss of reality. Part of us does want to get married, but her own marriage turns us off. Something is missing. Sex is problematic, she's always telling us; brutish boys are only out for one thing. We may be young but we already know that life is not worth living without the excitement boys give us. How can we buy mother's promises? She presents boys in such a dangerously attractive light that sex becomes the one thing we are always thinking about too.

Mother did not deliberately lie. She wishes us to repeat her life because thus she is validated herself. She keeps life a mystery because if we knew the little she knew, we might not repeat the cycle.

Says Dr. Schaefer: "The only way for a mother to prepare her daughter for the reality of living with a man is by being honest about her life with her husband. If you try to tell your daughter one thing, but you are living something else, the split creates the biggest hardship."

Our difficulty begins with mother's ambivalence. If it is hard for her to say, it is impossible for us to listen. "Nobody tells you about the feelings you will have when you get close to someone," says Dr. Schaefer. "In fairness to mother, how can anybody prepare you for the enormity of orgasm? Many women are so unprepared they don't want it. They resist it. It is not that they can't reach orgasm, they can't handle all the feelings."

Dr. Schaefer continues: "Take the problem facing a mother if she tries to get specific with her daughter. Just because the older woman can accept certain sexual ideas—even welcome them—doesn't mean they don't frighten the hell out of her when she thinks of them in connection with her daughter. Now the boy friend has come around to pick up the daughter in a car. The mother knows that they'll park sooner or later tonight. She knows her daughter's fantasies are about the good feelings she gets from kissing. But she also knows that the boy's fantasies are about the girl touching his cock. How does she explain that to her girl if she is still guilty about sex herself?"

"A lot of women are objective about a man until they go to bed with him," says Sonya Friedman. "Then they literally get all screwed up. They become inappropriately bonded to him. He assumes an emotional importance out of all proportion. Here is this woman, so calm and rational yesterday, agreeing with the man that it is just a little flirtation, a roll in the hay, a limited affair . . . and today she's crying, 'I want him, I want him, I'll die without him!' I hope this kind of thinking is dying out.

"One of the things that happens as you mature," continues Dr. Friedman, "is that you gain the ego strength to remain intact. You can enjoy someone physically and emotionally without becoming bonded to him, sitting beside the telephone waiting for it to ring. This is what I hope my daughter is learning, that if she has some significant skills, a good opinion of herself as someone all by herself, she won't have to trade that off for a relationship dominated by the notion that she can't live without him.

We expect marriage to liberate us from this sexual guilt. The contradiction is that while the wife wants the man to be strongly erotic and magically male, to awaken us sexually, we want him to do this within the emotional framework of warmth, nurturing, cuddling, affection. "No, don't touch me there!" we exclaim when something he does threatens to take all tenderness out of the erotic. The man is bewildered: if she doesn't think that's sexy, what the hell does she want? We have kept our hands off our body for the past twenty years. How can we tell him what we want, when we have never been allowed to explore the idea ourselves?

What is puzzling and frightening is when mother says in one breath that men are bad, they aren't trustworthy, they're children who will selfishly let you down—and then in the next breath tells us of the marvelous future we will have married to one of them! In our culture, a good mother never, never admits to her daughter that she may not marry, or that it may not be the best idea in the world. The fear and distrust of men that some mothers lay on their daughters is later projected on each man in the girl's life as he comes along.

When the romance and fantasy fade, when we see men defrocked and their great mystery turns out to be that they are merely human like us, we grow angry. When we were fifteen, mother seemed archaic; we were sexual heroines, breaking ground that would have terrified her had she known. What happened? Suddenly, the glow has left our lives and we realize we have gone no further than she did. *We are just like her!*

CHAPTER 9

THE LOSS OF VIRGINITY

From the primitive to the most sophisticated cultures, the unconscious wisdom of the race has seen the need for young men to be confirmed in the assumption of manhood through puberty rites, Bar Mitzvahs, hunting ordeals, etc. Today you are a man. In complex civilizations, sex may still be delayed a few years. Nevertheless the youngster has been signaled: it is time for you to put away childish ways and begin to separate from your family. He has looked forward to this ceremony of separation for so long that when it comes he has no doubt of its value. His mother weeps for joy, his father is proud, he himself knows he has reached life's next lofty step. When sex comes, it is the inevitable outgrowth of the rest.

There is almost nothing comparable for girls. There is no ritual, no step-by-step training for womanhood. No celebration of our sexuality. Our one symbolic act is loss of virginity, which is done in secret and without applause. Should we wait until we are married, the act of sex like marriage itself is meant to accomplish what should take years of process and preparation. What should be an act of separation becomes but another form of symbiosis: now that he's "taken" our virginity, will he love us forever, call us tomorrow, leave us for another woman? Instead of making us free, curious, experimental about the future, sex fills us with regressive postcoital anxiety. "Hold me, love only me as I will love only you, forever. Promise."

Everyone remembers the first time. What we were wearing, the lighting fixture in the ceiling, the feel of the car upholstery. It is set apart in an airtight compartment of memory. The initiation rite has been experienced. One act that says we are children no more, and have pushed aside mother's rules. We are adult, grownup, sexual—synonyms for separate. Except we are not.

More than in any other area of our lives we expect sex to grow us up. Much as mother may not have wanted us to leave home or take a career, she forbade nothing so much as she did sex. We are right to think of it as a step away from her, but it cannot do the job alone. "Because women have no other formal preparation for sexuality," says Dr. Robertiello, "the act of losing your virginity comes to bear an impossible load. It just cannot accomplish what people think it will. Separation is not a physical act, like breaking the hymen. It is an emotional one. It must begin during the first years of life and be progressively strengthened all during development. It's no wonder so many women grow disappointed and lose interest in sex. They have feared it so long and then expected it to do so much in one fell swoop. Nothing makes you independent all at once." Separation is not something that "happens" to you one night in the back seat of a car or is given to you by a husband in a honeymoon suite.

What a blessing if women could be relieved of their virginity at birth. One simple act to get rid of a label which more than anything else confounds our thinking about sexuality; the marketplace for virgin brides wiped out once and for all, mothers relieved of an anxiety that has nothing to do with their daughters' essential heart, soul and character. Instead of cops, they could function more easily as loving nurturers. Instead of thinking that in one night we "lose" some mysterious treasure between our legs, we might come to understand that our sexuality lies between our ears and is won by us alone.

Every free act, every victory over fear and inhibition, leaves an increment of courage, making it easier to try again the next time. Therefore, let's imagine an area of development in which a young person *could* practice her sexuality and learn to feel separate from her mother. Ideally, it should be safe, cheap, quiet, private and hurt nobody's feelings. It should be self-motivated and self-performed—a self-satisfying pleasure with no possible consequences to anyone but yourself: masturbation. Nature is cunning.

And yet, Kinsey reported in the early '50s that "No other type of sexual activity has worried so many women as masturbation." In 1964 Dr. Schaefer found every woman in her study on female sexuality—which included some who were professionally trained psychotherapists—felt anxiety about masturbation. Nor did the sexual revolution of the last decade profoundly change our ideas. According to Robert Sorenson's 1974 research, women today may masturbate more, but still describe what they feel as "defensiveness and discomfort."

The topic itself continues to be anxiety-laden, whether women do or do not masturbate. Why? Says Dr. Schaefer: "The anxiety is connected to an unwillingness to be responsible for one's own pleasure—one's own fantasies—even to be responsible for one's own orgasms."

If we do not understand why we do not masturbate, we cannot understand why we do not ask for what we want in bed. If we do not feel free to touch ourselves, how can we open ourselves to pleasure with another?

"When I was six," says an eighteen-year-old college sophomore, "I never connected masturbation or childhood sex games with intercourse. I remember lying on my stomach, spreading my legs and wiggling until what I called 'the good feelings' came. I felt no guilt about it and even tried to turn my friends onto it. The guilt only started when my mother caught me and I was scolded. I didn't connect the pleasure I gave myself with sex. I thought sex was a very fast maneuver when you wanted a child. I'm still too tense to use Tampax. Last year I fell in love with a smooth talker who finally talked me into going to bed with him. My God, but it hurt! The only thing I enjoyed was being close to him. He left and I never heard from him again. I haven't let myself get close to anyone since."

This young woman enjoyed masturbation until her mother connected it with sex and told her it was bad. She continued to masturbate but she feels so uneasy about that part of her body that she can't even use tampons. If she doesn't like to touch herself, how can she believe anyone enjoys it? What chance did she have of actively choosing a partner for sex? He chose her, he smooth-talked her into it, he hurt her, he deserted her. A "good girl" to the end, she sounds as if she were hardly there at all. "The only thing I enjoyed was being close to him." Symbiosis.

Little wonder then that most women do not think of entering into sexuality as a break with the symbiotic patterns of childhood; it becomes instead a search for that old togetherness, even if in a new, sexual mode. "I'm glad I saved myself for Steven," a young woman says. "My first time was wonderful. It made me feel part of him." These are beautiful sentiments, sincerely felt. But there is a confusion of two important ideas here. Closeness and sex are not synonymous. As long as we mesh one with the other, we jeopardize our chance of having the best of either.

I believe that sex is an absolute, an end in itself. If "making love" does that for you, it is a bonus, not the *raison d'être* of sex. Sex with love is marvelous, but sex can be exciting without love or closeness. If we enter into it only to heighten the symbiotic union, we soon find we have been using sex for a function it cannot perform well. Sex gets its energy from connecting two people; the spark needs a gap to jump. If it is used to hold together two people already meshed like a layer cake, you may stay together, but the sex is smothered in sweetness.

In spite of our training, many of us do feel at least a momentary thrill of separation. "I had a great feeling of power after that first night," one woman says. "I felt exhilarated, relieved of a burden," says another. "It was wonderful!" says a third. "I'd arrived; I was a woman at last!" Despite the commonplace phrases, these words have terrific emotion; they give us the sense of people living in their authentic selves if only for the moment, doing what they wanted, walking into the den of fear they had been warned against and finding it instead a fountain of pleasure. They were living in their own experience, not mother's.

But this sudden confirmation of self is unsettling. The experience of reveling in this body, this skin, these breasts, my vagina is joyous but scary too. Nothing says you can make it on your own more clearly than a shot of sexuality. Good as it feels, we retreat instinctively. It is too foreign to the only identity we have been taught is acceptable for women: I am a nice girl, not really sexual at all.

"After I lost my virginity, I felt free," says a twenty-eight-year-old woman. "I felt more attractive, but it didn't change my sexual pattern. I went out with the next man for nine months before I went to bed with him. I still didn't think sex was nice. In my head, I was still a virgin. I'd had sex with one man but that didn't mean you shouldn't wait until you were married."

If you've smiled with recognition at what this woman says, you will understand the rest. Part of her had agreed to go to bed with a man, but a more important part had not. She still wanted to be nice, to obey mother's rules, to be loved for not entering sexuality. We want to be women. We want to remain daughters too. In this split we live. Sex has failed to do its magic thing.

The world sees us as women; we have the sexual experience of the female race. Why don't we feel it? Why aren't we the sexually mature people we dreamed of becoming when we were still virgins, saving ourselves for this glorious event? We hasten to confirm the legitimacy of our title of woman. Props are hauled in, a stage production is being born. Who are you? Are you that little girl you fear you still are? No, I am the woman everyone envies for having that wonderful man, this fantastic house, those tickets-around-the-world, six lovers, sixteen Halston gowns, a Christmas card family. Some of us use men and sex like props too, piling up numbers to bolster our subjective fears that we are a sham. Is there anything missing from your sex life? No, I am the woman who had four orgasms last night and seventeen different men in the past month. And yet late at night—even though we lie beside a beloved man and count our blessings and tell ourselves we have everything a woman could ask for—the doubts go on. Is this all? We decide that sex is overrated. We do not realize that by trying to make it function as a form of symbiosis we never gave sex a chance.

The beginning of menstruation and the loss of virginity are doors into the adult world. "Menstruation," says Dr. Schaefer, "is stepping into it biologically, while loss of virginity should be the emotional step into adulthood." Menstruation is something over which we have no control. Sex, when it happens, where, with whom and whether we take responsibility—these are things we can choose to control. Most of us do not.

I am not saying that outwardly we do not say yes, nor that the man rapes us. On an overt level, we do consent, but a distinction must be made between consent that is the signal of active choice, and consent that is hesitant, passive or no choice at all. To the camera eye, the woman chooses the man, decides to uncross her legs. Subjectively, from the inside, we don't look at it that way: we want to feel carried away. Do we want him to touch our breasts? Not a word is breathed. Do we wish he would move more rapidly or slowly? More silence. We communicate with our lover by hope and by prayer. Would we like him to kiss us between the legs? The thought is so unsettling we aren't sure we do want it. Better to let the moment take us where it will, let him push our body here, put our legs there. He did it, not me.

"If women could subjectively say, 'I choose to do it, and this is what I want'—and mean it—they would make a developmental jump," says Dr. Robertiello. "But this would increase their separation, and that is frightening." When we were mother's little girl and living under her roof, it was appropriate to be aware of her strictures. How appropriate is it for a woman old enough to be in bed with a man still to be bound by rules to the point where she hesitates to do and ask for what she wants?

The next morning we question the mirror: Am I now a woman? We go over that first time like an unsolved mystery: what was missing? It was our sense of choice. We did not choose to enter sex. The experience was not *ours*. We just let it happen.

"What a letdown after all those years of waiting," a woman recalls. "I'd been expecting an earthquake. I didn't even get a tremor." After years of saying No we decide to go! In one jump we go—but stop too. It's like being shot from a cannon and falling down a foot or two from the cannon's mouth. A big decision to go nowhere.

Who are the men we choose for this momentous occasion? We choose a nice boy. A boy who has a familiar feel; who is, in fact, like us, not too experienced. Should we by some chance choose a sexy devil, you can be sure that either he or we are just passing through town: he won't be around tomorrow to remind us of our secret indiscretion, to suggest to our friends, or mother, that we are anything less than good girls.

We decide to let a man touch our breasts. For years we have felt ashamed of our bodies. We have been taught to cover them up. Our breasts aren't right, too big, too small. We expect that his hand will now give us a magically different feeling about them than we ever had. Stupidity. A man enters our vagina, the battleground of our emotional lives; we expect what we feel to have nothing to do with toilet training, masturbation, menstruation. Arrogance. Seductive as is its promise of pleasure, our vagina has also been the source of our greatest humiliations and anxiety. It is over this very part of our body that we almost lost mother. We try to compromise: we will let him touch our vagina, but we won't enjoy it.

We will go to bed with him, but won't come.

A moment's introspection tells us that his reality has begun to blur. We are turning him into a shadowy figure, a projection. He is more "mother" than lover. We are afraid that if we showed him we had those "dirty" sexual appetites and desires mother disliked, he would reject us. Mother did—until we hid them from her.

We explain all this to ourselves as "guilt"—that catchall word that merely gives a negative name to what we feel but explains nothing. "What is important," says Dr. Robertiello, "is the feeling behind the 'guilt.' The real anxiety is the woman's fear that the sexual act has made her separate, on her own, cut off from her upbringing and so having to take responsibility for the course of her life. To do the traditional thing is always easiest. To strike out on a new road, to try to be independent, is difficult. To most people, facing the fact that they are still tied to their baby needs is the most shameful thing in the world. So the word 'guilt' is brought in. It gives a serious, grown-up sound to the childish anxiety."

It is not guilt we feel, but fear—fear of having made the break from the girl that mother wanted us to be. Fear that if she finds out, she will angrily widen the break, and we will not be able to go back. Fear of separation.

For instance, when you secretly had sex or went too far and felt "guilty," didn't you feel better when you got home and found mother washing the dishes as if nothing had happened? The turmoil was due to your unseparated self being *sure* mother would know. How could she? When you were a baby, she knew when you were hungry, when you were wet—she was so tuned in to you that she could "read" your mind. The unseparated self fears she still can.

To continue: when you had sex a second and third time didn't the "guilt" diminish? The first time, sex gave us a feeling of separation from mother. We lived through it. We got used to it. It wasn't so bad. In fact, the pleasures of sex were so nice that it was worth it. When we have sex a second and third time it doesn't increase our degree of separation. We are simply repeating at the same level, and so we don't feel so guilty.

But let's say we introduce a new element, and conduct two affairs at the same time. Once again we feel that old stab of "guilt." Once again we are relieved when we get home and find that our lover/husband is sitting there reading the paper as if nothing has happened. Our degree of separation has been stepped up by having sex of a more "forbidden" nature than before; once again we are reassured when we find the world has not come to an end. It is not postcoital guilt from which we suffer, but postcoital anxiety. Sex has cut us off from being the nice girl mother once loved. Because the fear is free-floating, we may not associate it with the loss of the early, all-approving mother. In fact we will most likely connect it with fear of loss of the man, loss of self-respect, loss of our women friends or roommate (should we have been too sexually explicit) . . . but it's loss, loss, loss.

What is being discussed here is not the morality of sex or even the wisdom of conducting two affairs at the same time. That is private business. What is common to most of us is fear of loss of the beloved because of the notion that in some uncanny way what we are up to is no secret. True guilt resides in the conscience, and you feel it whether or not anyone else knows what you've done. Nonseparated anxiety means you are afraid your partner *knows*. You are afraid you'll lose him.

Even now, in the final quarter of the twentieth century, the act of intercourse remains a very powerful symbol. It puts you in a new category. It implies a break, loss, separation. That is its thrill and its fear.

When we were learning to walk, mother helped us practice, and her confidence in our success encouraged us to keep trying. When it came to sex, her emotions became communicated to us too; this time what we learned from her was anxiety and failure. Our practice in masturbating, sexual fantasy, pleasure in our body became secret, repressed. Since mother had always denied there could be competition between us, we have not learned through experience that we can win ground that she did not want to yield to us, and that the battle will not destroy her or us.

A nineteen-year-old is talking about her mother. They are very close, but like most of us she cannot put her finger on what is wrong between them. "When I was eleven," she says, "I wanted a bra. All my friends had one, but mother wouldn't let me. One night we were having dinner with friends and she started saying in front of all those people how ridiculous it was that someone my age should want a bra. I was so ashamed." Later in the same interview, she says, "My mother is the kind of person who talks a great deal. In a group, she is always the center of attention. When I bring a guy home who is older than me, for instance, she'll just take over. I can't get a word in. It really disturbs me."

If you told this mother she was acting competitively with her daughter, she would deny it. Her major criticism of her daughter's behavior is, "She is not responsible enough."

How could she be? Every time the young woman has tried to be separate, to be sexual, her mother has interfered—all the while denying interference. With no practice in seeing herself as a woman, in finding she can be sexual and still keep her mother's love, the girl avoids competition by being irresponsible. She tells me that when she lost her virginity, she did not use any contraceptive. "See, mother," this kind of act says, "I don't understand about all that. I may be entering sex, but only timidly. I don't

133

have your expertise. Don't be mad at me. I'm still a little girl."

The authentic self is not born. It is won. Regression into fear ever beckons. If you let some childhood limit keep you from doing something you know is your right, you are diminished; you have to fight to keep clear what you won last week, last month, last year. Sex does not make a woman of you. It is your reward for having made a woman of yourself first.

And yet, some people who do not have sex are marked by that very fact as autonomous. "If a girl feels she is still too young to handle sex," says Dr. Robertiello, "and says no—that is very self-confirming. She is more separated than her friends who get into sex because everyone else is." If we choose to remain a virgin until marriage, not because mother or society wouldn't approve but because chastity until marriage is one of the principles of our inner value system, that is an act of independence—much more so than with girls who leap into bed for fear of losing the man.

Autonomy enables a girl to say *No* as meaningfully as *Yes*. "Very often," says Gladys McKenney, "the girls who don't have sex in high school are the ones who have well thought-out goals, like going to college. They're not ready for sex yet, and they resist all peer pressures to get into it because everyone else is doing it. They will look at the other girls and maybe they wonder what these girls are doing, but they don't condemn it. You don't get the feeling they are holding back from sex because they are frightened of it. They just don't want it for themselves yet."

To ask, "What will he think of me tomorrow?" is to put the power into someone else's hands. The right question is, What will I think of myself tomorrow? Autonomy is making up our mind, not accepting the values or timetables of other people.

Most sociologists I interview agree that young men today are more amenable than their fathers to women being independent and assertive—traits once deemed for men only. But it does not follow that these same young men are prepared to grant equality in sexual experience to their women. In her recent study of college men, *Dilemmas of Masculinity*, Professor Mirra Komarovsky found most men still felt more comfortable when they were the more experienced partner.

The media message goes out to women: "It's a great, big, free, sexual world out there!" The real one is: "But you better not believe it."

Is it any wonder that even when we "choose" to have sex our lifelong internalized *No* is still with us? We can make our bodies do this or that, but our minds and emotional consent lag behind. And so there is this absolutely uncanny, almost suicidally foolish manner in which women enter sex. What it says is that the solution to our problem is not to have to face it at all. It is the great Swept Away phenomenon.

"You don't want to be ready for it," says an eighteen-year-old. "You just want it to take over and happen, especially the first time. You want it to be spontaneous. You want to get carried away. There's a free clinic in town, where you can get advice and your first contraceptive free, but if you plan—that takes all the romance out of it."

Swept Away: it is not merely a phenomenon of the very young. Women of all ages give it as rationalization. The underlying message is always the same: I don't usually do that kind of thing. I'm not that kind of girl. I had no choice. I was just carried away.

Even our daydreams—the safest possible playground to toy with new ideas—are written along symbiotic lines. In over seven years of research on women's sexual fantasies, the more prevalent themes I found were rape, domination, and force. Good girls to the end, we make the other person *do it* to us.

I want to say this emphatically: not a single woman I ever talked to said she did want to be raped in actuality. What is wanted is something only in the imagination, release from the responsibility of sex. Only the terrible force of the brute can free us from the fear of wanting the sexuality he represents. "Women are almost as strong as men," says Dr. Sonya Friedman, "or at least, they could be. But they like to make the disparity seem enormous. Their feeling of almost total helplessness is used to keep themselves children, not responsible, needing to be taken care of." It wasn't our fault. If we hadn't drunk so much, if things hadn't gotten out of hand, if the moonlight hadn't been so bright. . . . *He made me do it!*

How many women lose their virginity or have their most abandoned moments with a stranger, the steward on the cruise ship, the handsome translator in Rome? "These women are compartmentalized," says Dr. Schaefer. "They go to Europe and have all sorts of adventures, and then they come back home and are back to being good little girls. They may not have sex again for months. They've said, Europe is not reality, it's fairyland, it doesn't count. What counts is when I'm home in my mother's domain, and here I am a 'nice girl.' Yes, they've done better than the ones who never have sex, but they've only allowed it because it was in a place that let them keep the all-important tie to mother."

Young women today are more likely to have their first sex with someone they are emotionally involved with. Vera Plaskon works with teenagers in the Family Planning and Gynecological Clinic at Roosevelt Hospital. She is twenty-nine but remembers only too well how girls lost their virginity when she was growing up. It was usually "on vacation," she says, "with some stranger, rather than with the boy back home. Today, kids have sex within the important relationship. There is more caring with sex. That doesn't mean however that they are more responsible. It's so rare that I will get a young woman who will say to me, 'I'm planning to have sex, tell me what to use.' They prefer to let it come without thinking about it in advance, to be swept off their feet."

Even the scientific organization SIECUS (Sex Information and Education Council of the U.S.) cites the Swept Away phenomenon as a seemingly valid reason so many reject using a diaphragm or the pill. " . . . they cannot conceive of themselves as being prepared for coitus all the time. They must be emotionally carried away for coitus to occur."

Incredible! Never before in the history of the world has so much contraceptive information been available to young women. And yet the rate of premarital pregnancies is higher today than twenty-five years ago. In the '50s, Kinsey found that 20 percent of the women who had sex before marriage became pregnant. In more recent studies a full generation later, Zelnik and Kantner found 30 percent of such women got pregnant. That is a full 50 percent increase in rate of unwanted pregnancies!

"Every woman knows about contraception, or could if she wanted to," says anthropologist Lionel Tiger. "In our book *The Imperial Animal,* Robin Fox and I compared the drugstore cosmetic counter with the contraceptive counter. Young women seem perfectly capable of understanding the 25,000 different items on the cosmetic counter, which can be used in millions of permutations and combinations on many different parts of their bodies. But they very often appear not to know how to—or be willing to—manage the contraceptive counter, though it involves a quite simple business. When one looks at this behavior, one must say there is something strong driving these people to do what is often far removed from their rational plans."

There are many explanations, of course. Each one a logical, seemingly sufficient reason for a young woman's lack of decision or skill in using contraception. "If you are raised to be a passive partner," says educator Jessie Potter, "you do not get fitted for a diaphragm. If you raise girls not to touch themselves, they make rotten contraceptors. If you teach them to think sex is beautiful only when the right man comes along and does it to you, then you are raising them to wait, to avoid taking responsibility for themselves." Other explanations for not using contraception include rebellion, religion, getting pregnant in order to get the man to marry you, or to prove to yourself that you are capable of getting pregnant. Boys promise girls that they can control it, withdraw in time. Many women have a phobic avoidance of contraceptives. Dr. Helen Kaplan, a psychiatrist at the Payne Whitney Clinic, says women have a deep, unconscious wish to be impregnated by a man they care about. The list grows with every authority I interview. The fact is that all these explanations fit right into, and work along with, the need to be Swept Away—a need every professional worker in sexuality mentioned in addition to any other specific reason he/she gave.

From the day we are born there is a bit of what society calls *male* in all of us. It is our lust. Mother did her best to keep it in check. As we grew older she passed the job on to us. To be sexual was to be "out of control," like an animal, like a man. Badgered to be "feminine," we grew up afraid of our lust. We learned control instead, iron control—of ourselves, of him, of the situation.

It is hard for men to understand women's problems with control. A young boy is baffled by a girl's fear of being touched, her reluctance to touch him back. "Girls in the sixth grade are horrified that a boy wants to finger-fuck," says Jessie Potter. "I try to explain to the boy, 'Look, she hasn't even allowed *herself* to put her finger there.' He can't understand that because he's touched his penis every time he pees and a lot of other times besides. Boys masturbate in front of each other, but there is no 'show-and-tell' for girls. He expects her to be as eager to touch him as he is to touch her. I say to her that she must understand that his desires don't say anything judgmental about her or him, he is not 'gross' to have these wishes. Because he wants to do it to her, she isn't any less the nice girl she wants to be. They meet like two strange people from different planets. When he wants to touch her breasts, he has no way of understanding her feeling about this encroachment on the body she has been taught to keep so private. So he perceives himself as being rejected and unlovable. In self-defense, to gain back some of his lost ego, he decides she must be frigid. She, not understanding how she was taught to withhold, frequently sees herself as unloving."

Many young women have a tremendous fear that if we allow ourselves to become sexual, we will become promiscuous, whores. Why else would society/mother put on these ten-ton chains if sex weren't so titanically strong and dangerous? If we once let the barrier down, we will become sex addicts. "We have a whole cultural fix," says Dr. Robertiello, "about how sexuality is such a powerful urge that it overcomes all other forces. Men aren't afraid of this sexual force or of loss of control; they get points for being sexual. Women do not."

A controlling relationship is what we know best. We may say we want the man to be stronger, brighter, taller, and that we want to be dominated in bed. That doesn't mean we don't want to control him. What we know about intimacy, how to gain and keep it, is how mother was with father—and with us. Mother's control proved she cared. Some men don't mind our moving in with ideas of eternal togetherness, others jump like rabbits. To be fair to both sexes, many women aren't aware of the manipulation involved in control. It comes disguised as love. "If you really cared for me," we say . . . Guiltily, he does what we ask.

"I was afraid of having sex," says a college senior. "Afraid that once I went all the way, that I would have no more leverage with him. If I couldn't hold out on him any more, I'd have no more control. Once you have sex, you never know if it's you or the conquest that was important; when you're growing up, ninety percent of the time it's the conquest."

Increased experience does not lessen our fear of the overwhelming power of sex. "Oh, no, the adolescent rules didn't affect my later sexual life," says a woman of twenty-eight. "When I started I really started. But I've always been monogamous. It is a kind of self-protection. The only way you can protect yourself is to mind your behavior . . . . or it just slips away."

As we move out of mother's area of control, and the man is gradually allowed to enter our vagina in the one-step-at-a-time ritual loss of virginity, we make a trade. We construct with him the kind of bargain we had with her: if I allow you to touch me there, promise you will never leave me. If I reject mother's laws for your sake, and give up my once-in-a-lifetime power as a virgin, promise nothing bad will happen and that you will take care of me as she did.

The man is being made to assume the protective stance of the absent mother. Symbiosis is continued. Forbidden sex, the source of anger for as long as we can remember, need not destroy us after all! We thought men were so powerful, so self-sufficient, but we can use sex to control them. "Withholding sex," says Sonya Friedman, "is women's greatest source of power."

The price to the woman is high. To preserve our bargaining position, we must control our own desire first, hoarding lust like a miser, never spending it on pleasure. "When I'm with a guy for the weekend," says a twenty-seven-year-old woman, "it's heaven while I'm there, while we're in bed. But Monday morning when I go to work, the good feeling fades and I get this funny idea I've lost something. I'm in a weaker position with him, and I can't help myself . . . I begin these maneuvers about when am I going to see him again. I hate myself for it, but I have to do it." The bitter irony is that having got rid of mother's control, we are unhappy without it. We long to set it up with the man. Under these circumstances, we are not taking on a lover. We just switch mothers.

My own sexual ideas are different from what they were ten or fifteen years ago, and so I expected to find dramatic changes in behavior and attitudes toward virginity in young women today. Even my mother's attitude—unswerving for all of my life—has been affected by what she has seen and read, and perhaps most of all, by her neighbors' attitudes—those whose children have come of sexual age in the sixties. "When your child runs away to San Francisco," says Dr. Sidney Q. Cohlan, "or becomes pregnant, or marries a hippy or goes on drugs, you must accept some of the changes in the life-style of her generation if you want to keep a relationship with her. You may not like these changes, but it is easier for you to accept them nowadays because you find your neighbors are accepting them too."

Surely if I lost my virginity today, instead of in the sex-taboo fifties, I'd do it differently. "In 1963, only twenty percent of adults said it was OK to have intercourse in some circumstances before marriage," Dr. Ira Reiss tells me. "That was a national sample. By 1970, it had jumped to fifty percent. If we took a new national sample today, I'm sure we'd get more than half the parents saying it was OK under some circumstances."

Therefore I am not surprised when gynecologist Sherwin A. Kaufman tells me that the mothers who consult him today are not so concerned with their daughter's loss of virginity as they are afraid of her becoming pregnant. "They have come to accept that a girl who goes off to college," he says, "may not graduate without sexual experience. It's an idea they didn't want to think about ten years ago." And though Dr. Kaufman is quick to add that the New York women who consult him are a special subculture, I wonder if these liberal mothers aren't in tune with what college girls in their teens and early twenties are feeling all across America. They are a special subculture too.

"What *has* changed are attitudes," says Wardell Pomeroy. "The real change is more in approach than practice. A lot of people talk a bigger game than they play. From this big change in attitude will come later changes in behavior, in what people do (and not what they say they do). But it really hasn't shown up yet with statistical significance. People develop certain norms and ideas, but it takes more than a film or book to change their behavior. It is a gradual process. Change usually comes between generations, not within one."

Statistics must be read in context. There are over 200 million people in the U.S. today, double the number fifty years ago. When twice as many people do something, we are prone to believe "everybody" is doing it, that something new is going on. It is merely more visible. We are changing, but not all that rapidly. There is more talk and general acceptance of sex today. Nonvirgins used to keep it a secret. Today, they go on TV talk shows. "Everything is different nowadays," we tell each other.

We want so badly to be easier about sex. As mothers, we don't want our children to grow up with our sexual inhibitions. We change *our* attitudes and think that will change *their* lives. We look at them behaving far more guiltlessly than we'd have dreamed ten years ago, and identify more with their generation than the one we grew up in. We talk of multiorgasms and bisexuality and glibly think something as primary and emotive as loss of virginity is old-fashioned, tame stuff. But for all our new attitudes, the liberated poses we strike, our children don't believe us. They are still uncomfortable when we bring up sex. We are hurt. Haven't we made enormous efforts to understand their world?

A parent who asks such a question is being as sincere as she knows, but once again is confusing the difference between attitude and gut feeling. Children may listen to mother's words; what they really take in is how mother feels on the deepest level. Our ideas about our bodies, our eroticism, our sexual limits, are so much a basic part of us that we may not be aware how they determine the things we *say* to our daughters. We got them from our mother; she got them from hers. When we talk to our daughters about sex, or when we have sex—what we feel is a mixture of the old and new, of what our mothers felt about it, and what we would like to feel.

Two girls both know about the pill. One takes it methodically, in advance of sex. When, sooner or later, she enters the bedroom, it will be with the fear of pregnancy (at least) diminished. The other girl doesn't take it, or does so sporadically. Statistics say neither is a virgin, and that both are members of the liberated seventies. But the quality of their sexual experience is totally different. Why? Because the first girl's attitude toward sex, her behavior and gut feelings, acted together. Faced with no conflicting double message, she felt free to choose the pill. All too often girls in therapeutic counseling sessions for unwed mothers know about the pill but do not use it or use it incorrectly. They have one attitude in their head about sex. In their gut, they are entirely different, much more judgmental.

"In their hearts, the parents of girls who come to the Family Planning

Clinic," says Vera Plaskon, "are against early sexual activity. At the same time, they are middle class, they want to be IN. So these mothers rerun their own fantasies of what they would have liked to have done—or what they would do if they were their daughters today. They push these fantasies onto their kids before they are ready. 'Just let me know when you want the pill,' they tell their thirteen-year-old. They don't stop to think maybe the girl is not ready to hear this. It can be a lot more subtle. The mother may be fully unaware that by buying her daughter the latest seductive clothes and make-up, she is pushing her into what *she* would have liked to have done when she was young, before the sexual revolution. Once she has the girl living out her fantasy, there is also the mother's competition with the girl, *plus* her own guilt at what she has done. It may be unconscious, but it is very confusing to the daughter. Recently I was talking to a girl who is very sophisticated for her fifteen years. She laughingly said her mother always told her that if and when she needed birth control, to come to her. 'But you should have seen her face when I actually did!' she said. Most girls are not so sophisticated, and they don't laugh about it. They don't know what to do. And finally, there are many girls who really wish their mothers would say, No, *and mean it*. They can't handle all this freedom at fifteen or seventeen—their own growing up, and often their mother's as well. The girl doesn't know what the mother wants from her. The mother doesn't know herself. So she sends out the contradictory message to her daughter: 'This is the modern age, do what you like!' But when the girl comes home at three in the morning, the mother screams at her that she is acting like a whore."

A double message undermines our reasoning powers and gives us no clear-cut line of separation. In our middle, not knowing which way to go, we surrender our will. Either we allow ourself to be swept away by the man, or we turn back to mother. Neither is an autonomous choice. It is just a need to depend on someone. We listen to mother's contradictory commands, and in true symbiotic fashion, act out both halves of mother's conflict. One day we are "good," and say No to the boy. The next day we are "bad" and become pregnant. What more could mother want?

I ask Dr. Robertiello how a mother could possibly be sending out a message for her daughter to get pregnant. "Pregnancy and intercourse," he said, "are often confused and tied together in people's minds. Getting pregnant is proof of getting laid. If you are thirty-five and married and six months pregnant, that is not a sexual idea. But if a girl has a friend, let's say, who gets pregnant at fifteen, she can read the light in her mother's eyes: Boy, that is a sexy, bad girl."

If mother tells us that she is not certain that 2 and 2 are 4, we smile and say we have no doubts ourselves. In the area of arithmetic, at least, we are separate from her. If her words about our pregnant fifteen-year-old friend are negative, but we see that excited light in her eyes, we respond to her excitement. Despite all our own real fears and attitudes about getting pregnant, down deep we don't think it is so bad at all. We have taken in mother's unconscious wishes and act on them as if they are our own.

In a survey of girls who went to a campus contraceptive clinic versus those who did not, Ira Reiss found the clinic girls believed they were attractive to men twice as frequently as nonclinic girls. The clinic girls also more frequently felt they had as much right as men to initiate sex. "What the pill does," says Dr. Reiss, "is put choice in the hands of the female. It tells her, 'Look, if you don't want to have intercourse, that's your right, but you have to have a different reason to say No than fear of pregnancy. That can be taken care of. You are going to have to make up your mind without pretenses.' "

Choosing to use the pill is evidence of a good deal of integration. The clinic girls are saying by their behavior that they are entitled to sex. By acting on what they say, and going to the clinic to be prepared for the consequences of their actions, they show their behavior, attitude and gut reactions are in line.

To my mind, their autonomy is illustrated in another area in which most women usually betray great insecurity: *they did not wait for a man to tell them they were sexually attractive.* Their actions tell me that they made their own evaluation of their looks and bodies, and, having decided they were attractive, decided to reap the reward for it by getting into sex.

I would emphasize however that it was not going to the clinic that made them more autonomous than the girls who did not. That is reverse reasoning, confusing cause with effect. They were more separate *before* they went. That is *why* they went. The pill did not make them autonomous. Their autonomy enabled them to decide to use the pill.

Psychoanalytic theory used to say that if a girl entered into premarital sex, especially if it were an unhappy experience or ended with pregnancy, it was an expression of rebellion. Sex was seen by the girl as a way of getting back at the restrictor, doing exactly the opposite of what mother wanted. That is still often the case, but nowadays psychiatrists have come to see that rebellion is one of the symptoms, not the complete statement of the overall problem—which is lack of separation. Rebellion becomes separation when the goal is self-fulfillment, not mere frustration of something the parent wants us to do.

The difficulty in understanding rebellion begins with the romantic glow that folklore has given the world. To researchers in human development, it has a very specific, time-related meaning. When we are two, rebellion is appropriate. This is the No-saying stage children go through. Another rebellious period comes in adolescence, but by this time, just saying No is not enough. Certain moves toward autonomy have to accompany the sixteen-year-old's rebelliousness or it is inauthentic, a sign of attachment. We may have more sex than we really want, a drink too much, but at the same time, if we are meeting our academic requirements, handling money responsibly, it can be said that the rebellious elements are in the service of separation.

But at twenty-five, thirty-five, the time for rebellion should have been long over. If we are not taking care of ourself, not paying our bills, turning up late for work, having a lot of sex without really enjoying it, then rebellion is immaturity.

We look at the very young today and envy them their sexual ease and apparent lack of guilt. Despite all that has been written, said, experienced, and thought in the past decade, most of us have not reached the kind of free-flowing sexuality young people seem to have been born with. They seem to be so accepting of their sexuality; the word used for them is "liberated"—which is another way of saying they are separated.

It is the old philosophical problem of appearance and reality. To the outside eye, they may indeed seem free. They appear to have won the rebellion against those antisexual rules which cost us so much. In our fight for autonomy, sexuality was the one battlefield above all others. To have won any degree of freedom there, was more difficult than anywhere else.

For those of us raised before the sixties, the rules were hard and fast—especially about sex. Mother made no bones about wanting to repress and inhibit our sexuality—or our retaliatory anger. She gave us firm ground on which to plant our defiant feet. In the anger and quarreling, separation between mother and ourselves gains definition; we may not have attained autonomy, but at least we knew where she stood.

It we've been raised in too permissive a manner, separation can become difficult. The rules are vague and elastic. Rarely is the permissively raised child out-and-out forbidden to do this or that. We were merely presented with more attractive alternatives. In this way our own desires were manipulated and used against us. We weren't told not to play with that nasty little boy next door. Whenever he appeared on the horizon, mother took us to the drugstore for an ice cream instead. If we got kicked out of college, that was unfortunate, but a new school was found which was more tolerant of our special temperament. If we broke the parental rule about sex (if there was one), it was not the end of the world. Even if we insisted on a fight, wanting to clarify the difference (separation) between us, mom once again quickly shifted ground, to join us. "Oh, I'm so glad you feel free to express anger at me! What a healthy thing to do!" How do you separate from somebody so glued to you with admiration? Anger is not allowed to do one of its principal jobs: separate me from you. You never get a clear-cut No; no firm ground is offered from which to push yourself off.

It is difficult. We love mother, but there she is, *surrounding* us. We want to separate from her (even if we don't use the word) but we can't get a fix on the problem. If we want to run away to India, she'll pay for the ticket and remind us to phone collect when we want to come home. Never having been let go of, we can't let go ourselves. Permissively reared people have had no experience of separate relationships, and so never look for them. We gravitate to what we know.

On the surface, relationships like this seem freer, easier than those between sharply defined people. If one partner wants to go to a movie and the other wants to go to a ball game, neither insists on dominance; it needs hardly any discussion to decide to compromise and go ice skating. This is not the first choice of either, but the relationship has not been roiled, even for a moment. Everything is soft, blurred, hazy, friendly. Even sex becomes non-differentiated. (It is no coincidence that the permissive era is the Unisex era.) Young people do not regard each other today across the differences of sex as if the other were from Mars. They have been raised to relate to other people without fuss, without fighting, *without separation.*

People who come out of a background of being coddled, who are not allowed to develop separately, indeed often do have sex—but it doesn't mean they are autonomous. It can mean the opposite: that they are using sex—which is one of nature's methods of helping us grow up—to remain childish instead, to create a nice, warm relationship with this other person which is similar to that one they once had with mother, which they never had to outgrow, and which is all they know. Proof of this is that such "sexual" relationships between young people often cease to be sexual at all; they soon become fond and fondling palships. Is being "free" of sex such an unqualified good?

Some sociologists have gone so far as to suggest the days of the double standard may be coming to an end. That too is a gain, but if monogomy is settled on without choice, where is freedom? "It used to be that only girls were like this," says Betty Thompson, "but today we see boys acting the same way, refusing even to look at another girl." On the surface it may look like love and fidelity. In a few years, we may see it differently. That is when symbiosis has so killed off whatever degree of sexuality there was between them that they flood the divorce courts. Freedom to have sex together has been bought at the price of never giving each other air to breathe.

If people raised in nonpermissive times envy the freedom from sexual guilt of young people today, Spock-reared people seem to have lost their elders' ability to work toward well-defined goals and aims in life.

Says Betty Thompson: "When you are indulged, when everything is done for you, you do not grow up with a recognition of the realities of life. You break your bicycle, and mother says, 'Don't worry, we'll buy you a new one.' If mother and father saw to it that you got everything you wanted, there just hasn't been any practice in being responsible for yourself. What is not available is a recognition that everything in the world cannot be bought. When a girl says, 'I don't want to carry a diaphragm when I go on dates,' it is an evasion of responsibility, it is regressive in the sense of character development. It is not romantic, it is not being separate and adult. It is babyishness." Carelessness, lack of forethought and disorder may masquerade as freedom to the outside eye. But they tie us with chains of consequence.

At seventeen our problems with autonomy arise from one direction; at thirty-seven they come at us from another. Lack of separation is where both lines meet. Autonomy is the declaration and affirmation of the self; sex is one of its expressions. "I am a woman and this is my body and my life. I will do what I want with both because that is what I want, not because I want to get back at you."

It took me twenty-one years to give up my virginity. In some similar manner I am unable to let go of this chapter. Unanswered questions run endlessly through my head like ticker tape: how does the daughter's loss of virginity affect her relationship to her mother? Shouldn't she wait until she has left home to lose her virginity so that her mother won't be involved? Doesn't the fact that a girl hasn't yet left home mean she is not yet ready to have sex?

It is August. Everyone is at the beach but me and, luckily, Richard Robertiello. Once more I trudge past the baseball players in Central Park to see him. Dr. Robertiello hears me out. "Nancy," he says, "you are asking the wrong questions. They show you are still trying to protect some false structure. You are trying to place the issue of a woman's sexuality within the framework of her relationship to her mother. Sex, more than anything else, should have nothing to do with mother. Why should losing her virginity have anything to do with what goes on between her and her mother? You talk as if the mother *knows* the girl is having sex, that she is inside the girl's head, the way she was when the girl was a baby and thought mother could read her mind. *That is symbiotic thinking.* So what if someone has sex while she is still living at home? Privacy and secrecy do in fact aid in separation. Your questions, the inability to finish this chapter, are all about how to continue the tie to mother while being a sexual person. No wonder you can't answer them. There are no answers—you can't be sexual and symbiotic with mother at the same time."

This chapter has revealed a split in me. Intellectually, I think of myself as a sexual person. Subjectively, I don't want to face what I have written: that the declaration of full sexual independence is the declaration of separation from my mother.

The shame of still needing, still wanting to be tied to mama even after we're grown, is universal. "I feel it myself," Dr. Robertiello once told me. "I'm always pointing to my sexuality as proof of my autonomy." Separation is a process nobody completely attains. We can only keep trying.

CHAPTER 10

THE SINGLE YEARS

Our single years! The first time on our own, our second chance to form ourselves. This is our chance to outgrow mother's training in passivity, her fear that without someone to lean on, we are nothing.

"I think it's important for a woman to have time on her own after high school or college, and before she marries," says an eighteen-year-old. "You can find out that you can support yourself. That you don't have to have a man to survive. So many girls get married right away. It's frightening never to find out you are able to take care of yourself. You think you must always depend on somebody else."

Here's the other end of the spectrum:

"I love my marriage," says a thirty-two-year-old woman, "and yet it has made me more frightened than when I was single. Without my husband and children, who am I?" Neither her husband's arms around her nor her child's head on her shoulder can ease the anxiety: what would she do when/if they leave her? She has attained the goal her training promised would end all insecurity, but it hasn't. When this woman's daughter grows up, how can she be expected to encourage the girl to leave?

In poignant form, these two women recapitulate different stages of our early drama of separation from mother. At first we are hungry for a life of our own, for freedom, no strings, to go our own way. Behind our youthful vigor and eagerness to explore, a lifelong anxiety waits for us. Children and a husband are a fulfillment, but they are also hostages to fortune. We regress; we grow as dependent on them as once we were on mother. Pop radio is filled with songs about girls aching with loneliness, but statistics show that never-married young women with college educations, earning decent salaries, are the least depressed segment of population. On the other hand, TV commercials show us smiling young mothers, supposedly secure in their marriage, home and family—but the same statistics say that married women with small children in the household are among the most depressed people of all.

The eighteen-year-old rushes into life. Who is to say she will not end up with the thirty-two-year-old's hopelessness?

The fear of freedom—which we dress up and call the need for security—is rooted in the unresolved half of us which is still a child, still looking for a man to replace the mother we never successfully left. So long as we have our need for symbiosis, we will not believe we can make it on our own. The child thinks that if she becomes too "strong," too independent, mother will decide she can make it on her own and neglect her. We keep ourselves little. It means we must continue to live as a child: powerless.

Love puts the child in us back to sleep. When we doubt love, lose love, or become inappropriately afraid that in a world of 4 billion people we will never find love again—we must learn to look back to that little girl. The fear is hers—which is why it baffles us so. Rather than railing at fate or the perfidy of men—which is easy but not the real issue—it would be better to reexamine the relationship of that child to her mother of long ago.

"The pervasive problem for many women," says sociologist Cynthia Fuchs Epstein, "is their basic low opinion of themselves." If so many of us are dependent, helpless, anxious creatures, how can we believe that men may love us? Of course they will wise up and get out sooner or later. The work of our single years is to turn this opinion around.

The first job is to prove to ourselves that we are agents in our own lives, not passive patients forever operated on by other people. Marriage may be beautiful, but all too often it is a call back into symbiosis: the desire to lose our identities in someone "stronger," more valuable than ourselves.

Says Dr. Schaefer: "Women's desire to subordinate themselves to the man is the pattern of dependency learned from mother. To escape the feeling that she may be ornamental but nevertheless fundamentally valueless, she becomes the 'woman who is behind the successful man.' She will not try on her own. But even as she succeeds, even as she makes the man more successful, more valuable, her own feelings of self-worth diminish. The bigger he gets, the more frightened she becomes that he will leave her, a nobody."

In our single years we have our first chance to act so that the existential evidence of our lives tells us that we are new—helpless children no more. If we can successfully make the break away from home and discover we can live without the immediate emotional backup of mother and family; if we choose friends who reinforce our individuality rather than because they are "nice" or live nearby; if we meet men with whom we can explore pleasures mother never allowed; let the experiences of life happen and find in even the painful ones that there is an excitement in knowing an existence larger than we dreamed possible; and get a job which not only delivers the thrill of economic self-sufficiency but builds up our self-esteem because we do it well—we have set up a bank account in our own name on which to draw for the rest of our lives. *I enjoyed living by myself once. If I have to, I can do it again. My world does not stop if other people leave. Their going will sadden me. It will not finish me.*

In our single years, we have a powerful ally in the fight to separate and grow up. It is our sexuality. It makes us take chances, pulls us here and there, brings us into a world larger than the family, fills our life with excitement, dangers, pleasures, and disappointments that make us grow even as we learn to handle them. That is why mother's house now seems too small for the two of us. So long as we live with her, we must do so by her rules. It is almost impossible for her to give us more space within the same rooms, under the same roof, where she protected and ordered us about for eighteen or twenty years.

The moment it was born in us, mother singled out sex as her enemy; she knew it would separate us from her. She could not even call it by its right name. Instead she would say, "You're so irresponsible," "Don't talk back to me," "Why must you close your bedroom door, wear those tight sweaters, those high heels," etc. Now when we want to leave, to have a place of our own, we too cannot say it has anything to do with sex. We are her daughter and lust is not ladylike.

"My mother couldn't come out and say it, but I knew when I left home she was thinking, 'You want to move out so you can sleep around!' What she said was, 'Why do you want to move out? You have a nice home here.'" The speaker is a twenty-six-year-old woman who is writing her master's thesis on the difficulties women find in leaving home.

When her daughter leaves, mother is often caught between what she knows and what she feels. The graduate student continues: "Of the forty women I interviewed for my thesis, every one had trouble leaving unless it was to get married. The women's movement hasn't really reached all that many people, even in a supposedly liberal place like New York. The great majority of mothers who responded to my questionnaire equated the daughter's moving out with rejection. A typical mother said, 'I can understand a person needing to live alone.' *A person*. Not her daughter. These mothers don't want to act this way but they are driven to it."

According to the U.S. Census Bureau, 40 percent of women aged twenty to twenty-four were single in 1975, almost double the number for 1960. These figures seem to suggest a revolution. In terms of real estate, they may be: an apartment of our own gives the illusion of separation. Emotionally, how independent are we? We may feel a kind of emotional blackmail from mother when we leave home, or she may help us furnish the new one-room apartment and wave bon voyage as we pull away to a new life. Either way, we pack her anxiety along with our suitcases.

With mother's fears roiling uneasily beneath our surface, it is not surprising that the revolution so far is mostly skin deep. Once she's left home, the daughter is delighted to have a job and money of her own, but when she's offered a promotion, she hesitates. She doesn't want to become so career-minded men will feel they have little to offer her. She experiments with sex, but still wants to be swept away: she is contraceptively unprepared almost a third of the time. When she is with her friends, she is the brave new person she always wanted to be. When she goes home, she reverts to the dutiful daughter she wanted to leave behind. (She even speaks differently.) When she meets new people, she tells them what she thinks they want to hear, not what she feels. At a party, she does not think, Who is there here who interests me? Instead, she wonders, What do these people think of me? The morning after a satisfying date or a good sexual experience, the pleasures of the night before have turned to anxiety: will he call again?

We talk a brave game of independence and make a point of lighting our own cigarettes. Underneath, we still doubt the authenticity of what we project. Mother may have talked a good time too. Underneath she is afraid her daughter cannot make it on her own. (She never was good at it herself, when she was single.) We live not with mother's official declarations of confidence but with her inarticulated fears.

"More girls may be living on their own today," says Sonya Friedman, "but the umbilical cord is still there. It is the telephone." To relieve our "guilt" we phone mother. The cure is never complete because what we feel is not guilt. After all, we have not committed some dread crime. What the symbiotically tied daughter calls *guilt* is really *fear*—fear that with every step toward independence, every step away from mother, we have lost her.

"What arouses the most guilt in you?" I ask a woman.

"My mother."

"What is the worst thing you can imagine?"

"A phone call in the night telling me she died."

I had a chance to interview this young woman's mother. From *her* side, the story runs this way: "I know my daughter feels guilty about not coming home for Christmas. I felt the same when I was her age. So this year, I went and spent Christmas with her. I love to see her, but I felt underfoot at her place. I'd really rather stay home with my friends. I love my daughter and I'd have felt guilty if I left early, so I stayed till the end of the holidays." So much *guilt,* so much *love.* The semantic confusion is only surpassed by the emotional confusion in which mother and daughter place one another.

Before we marry, for the first time in our lives a bond is being formed which can be more powerful than the one we had with mother. It is the bond with men. "It used to be a bit of folk wisdom," says Dr. Robertiello, "that men should try out all sorts of sexual experiences before they married. The same now applies to women. Sexual experience doesn't have to be unbridled. If you are Catholic or Southern Baptist, for instance, you will have stricter limits than others. If you don't let yourself do anything else, then at least go to church where you can sit opposite or near a man. Women should try to give themselves experience *vis-à-vis* a number of men so that the male sex becomes less frightening and remote—so that the woman can learn she is able to attract and interest a man. For some people this might mean holding hands . . . for others, a series of orgies. The single years are the time to be as experimental as possible."

The single years are the time to enlarge and reinforce whatever degree of separation has been so far achieved. Otherwise, we will make our new ties with men into a form of regressive symbiosis, and sexual excitement will give way to safety. What we have with him will no longer be electric and powerful, but at best warm and friendly; at worst, merely a bargain in mutual control and dependence.

Experimenting with a number of men, different relationships, helps put the finger on what is "always" going wrong. Men hurt us. Men leave us. At least half the fault must be ours: *we chose them.* "Even if you have a psychological compulsion to make it only with bad guys who do you in," says Dr. Robertiello, "it is better to go through it ten times than not to get involved with men at all for fear of being hurt. That way, you will at least get a feeling of the location of your problem, and look around for ways to solve it." In the privacy of our single years we have time and opportunity to begin the work.

Privacy aids separation. For the first time in our lives, nobody knows what we are doing. Unless we tell them. "My husband and I always told our daughter Katie that some things are private," says Leah Schaefer. "Not hidden or denied, but private. Now she understands when we close our door. Sometimes she locks her own door and says, 'I want privacy.'"

Without practice in privacy when we are very young, we are ever after uncomfortable with it. If our closed bedroom door was meaningless, if mother was always "straightening" our bureau drawers, asking questions about our friends and telephone calls, we grow up with the uneasy feeling that privacy is a guilty idea. We suspect no secret of ours is safe, that someone always knows what we are thinking. As if in reaction, some women rush to tell their mothers everything. We may say that sharing our lives with mother, keeping closely in touch with her, is gratitude, paying her back for all she did when we were little. And yet, under the guise of being dutiful and loving, aren't we asking her to be a collaborator and condoner of our sexuality?

"Has my mother asked if I'm still a virgin?" says a twenty-two-year-old. "I told her I was, but I lied. I'm not. When she asked if I would tell her when I did have sex, I said No, it was my own business." This young woman only lives a few blocks away from her mother; she is shy, self-effacing and has not been much involved with men. But her degree of separation, her efforts to establish it, are superior to another woman who travels constantly around the world and has sex frequently with many different men: "My mother and I are really great friends, though we're very different women. We talk constantly on the phone. I even called her from France the first time I had sex. Recently, I had bad luck and got pregnant. I called her and said I had to have an abortion. She was sweet about it, but she didn't give me the feeling of support I really wanted. I wanted her to call me three times a day, or even get on a plane and come take care of me."

This woman wants it both ways, to tell her mother about her sex life, to be a buddy, and to have her mother take care of her too—as her mother did when she was a child. "Sex should be something you do on your own," says Dr. Schaefer, "and for which you take responsibility. Telling your mother about your sexual life respects neither her privacy nor your own. It opens you up to her influence, one way or the other. You are giving her too much power to comment, to give or withhold approval, in an area in which she doesn't belong."

It is a difficult issue for both parents and children. Says Dr. Robertiello: "I'm not against my daughter having sex. That is her separate decision to make. But if she brings the boy home to spend the night with her, that's different. She's invading *my* privacy, bringing me into a situation I don't want to be part of. Liberal parents who don't like kids to bring their lovers home are often called hypocrites. I don't believe they are. If it bothers parents, they have the right to say, 'Don't do it in front of me. It's not my business.' Children have a right to their sexuality, but parents have a right not to be made party to it."

Some mothers want their daughters' sexual lives to be private, because it gives them a freedom too. "Sometimes my daughter tells me more than I want to hear," says the mother of a twenty-four-year-old. "All the excruciating details of her romances. When she was nineteen, she asked me to go with her to get a diaphragm. I said no. It seemed *too* intimate. She knew I didn't disapprove, but I thought some of her life as a woman has to be her life. If you aren't prepared to go without your mommy to get a diaphragm, then you're too young to be getting one."

A twenty-five-year-old woman tells me that she doesn't mind her boyfriend sleeping over at her apartment, but she is nervous if her mother calls while he is there. "I have this uncanny feeling she can see over the telephone, and knows he is naked in my bed while I'm talking to her. I don't want her to know. I guess I have a real double standard." This young woman has turned a healthy situation around and criticized herself for keeping her sexual life private from her mother. She should keep it private. And yet, if she is still so symbiotically tied that, like a child, she feels her mother can read her mind over the telephone, is it not surprising that the experience is filled with anxiety. Dr. Schaefer's comment is that she is doing the right thing. "In time, simple repetition of the experience will rid her of this anxiety."

Meeting and knowing a variety of men in our single years can help us see our capacity for life was greater than we ever dared think. One man, grabbed on to too soon, can ground us in the way we've always been. The symbiotic dependency of most marriages does not allow women to grow.

The divorcée or widow is alone again in the world at age thirty or fifty, dealing with men as if she were a teen-ager. "If he leaves me, I'll die!"

Most of us will marry. No one can promise it will last. Our love may be in other people. Our security is in ourselves. If we goof our way through our single years, not paying our bills, losing our keys, writing home for the rent money, our days filled with little more than waiting for Mr. Right, basing our value not on achievement but on the men who didn't work out—we will have established an ominous memory of ourselves. Mother was right: we are too frail to survive on our own.

Things seem to be changing. The single woman looks down at us from every billboard—the symbol of our time. Reach out, and success, love, independence and freedom too—they can all be yours.

And yet there is a built-in lie to the single girl as heroine. It is the hidden agenda—habits of dependence we have been trained to think of as our central feminine core. It is based on our first role model and is backed up by the entire culture. It says the single woman is "unfinished."

I interview a 33-year-old woman: "My mother was pleased at my success in my job, she'd wanted me to go to college. But among her friends, she is the only mother whose daughter hasn't married. Finally when I got promoted and a story about me appeared in the hometown paper, she had something to show them. I was pleased that she was proud of me, but it hurt a little too that her neighbors' opinions are so important. I know the best thing I can ever give my mother will be my marriage . . . if I ever do."

Many men today have begun to say they believe women have a destiny outside the nursery and kitchen. But sociologist Mirra Komarovsky points out in her book *Dilemmas of Masculinity* that the same liberal male who says he believes in the women's movement often wants to marry a woman who will stay home and keep house for him.

And yet I would like to add a word here in men's defense. One of the great cries of our time is that women are held back because "men won't let us." Sometimes this is true. Very often it is neither men nor society which holds us back. We do it ourselves. If the goal for women is self-reliance, we must understand why we succeed or fail in terms of ourselves—without the convenient, catchall excuse of male malevolence.

Says Smith College economics professor Jeanne McFarland: "We send young women ambivalent signals. We give them this terrific education so they can compete. On the other hand, we say—what you really need is to find a husband. So go slow on competition. Men don't like women who compete. Men like their women on the pedestal—goddesses of nurturing and socialization and all the other 'good' things men don't have time to be. It's a mixed signal: compete, but don't do it too well." Can we be surprised if despite all the current talk about women making it, down deep we are afraid? We have more to lose than to gain from autonomy.

For most of us, the end of the single years comes none too soon. Even if we had a broken or unhappy home, we still have at least the fantasy of family life. We have an unforgettable model of how to be a wife, patterned not just on how mother was with father but, more significantly, on how we were with her. We are the couple—mother and me—that we will try to reestablish with others. The more we needed her, the more she rewarded us. When we are grown, dependency is still the norm ever held before us. "What happens," says Dr. Robertiello, "is that the cultural idea of women's dependency reinforces the women's own childhood training. This is the single greatest trap held out to women. It might be called *the* feminine option."

Like many traps, it is baited with honey.

This option says that any time a woman wants, she can give up on herself and find a man to take care of her—so why struggle to establish herself in the first place? This supposed privilege is so deeply planted in our psyche that we are often not aware that we use it as our ace in the hole. "Men are so competitive. I don't see the point in working so hard." Of course society applauds the woman who feels this way, who just marks time until she takes the option. She is one less competitor to worry about, someone who will take on all the unpaid work of housekeeping, etc., that men don't like to do. Dropping out on ourselves, giving responsibility for our life to a man, is not the mark of a woman but of a child.

Says sociologist Cynthia Fuchs Epstein: "Most women don't think they have any alternative to being a wife and mother. They just don't think success is possible for them. It's not in their spectrum of expectations. Not until they get into the marketplace and get decent jobs do they see there is some possibility for success."

Often, it takes the experience of a failed marriage for a woman to realize that the supposed lifelong security of having a husband can be a painful myth. "Women like these," continues Dr. Epstein, "often become very career-oriented. They don't necessarily stop seeing men, but their anger at a shattered illusion has opened their eyes. They learn they can't look to men to be their sole gratification."

Work-oriented women, however, face problems that men do not. Says Dr. Epstein: "There are few supports for women to say to a man, 'I can't see you tonight, I have to work late.' . . . Women are very torn in work situations. They have to make a whole set of decisions based on different priority systems—including love, friendship, marriage and children—not all of which co-ordinate." If a woman becomes involved with her career, she's afraid love will suffer. If she gives too much time to her love life, she is afraid it will be at the expense of her career.

I feel these pressures myself: walking past a mirror today, I saw my mother. On my face was the expression of hers I like least: anxiety. The harder I work, the less womanly I feel.

I plan a dinner party so that I may at least hear some praise for my feminine accomplishment at cooking, but I am working so hard at writing that I cancel it—feeling more depressed, less womanly than ever. My husband and I have a terrible row and I bury myself in the papers on my desk, depriving myself of his company. Why? The repression lifts for a moment: I am leaving him before he leaves me—a game I first played with mother when I was six.

Psychoanalysts have long become accustomed to the necessity of *working through* these bits of insight, making patients aware of the repressed connections again and again before they are truly grasped—the liberating, emotional truth integrated for good. We women resist knowledge of ourselves and our mothers. We prefer our fantasy relationship and so we cannot put to work what we know about the two of us.

The fear of losing mother doesn't even require having had an emotionally nourishing relationship with her in the first place. Sometimes, in fact, the hardest mother-daughter relationship to face is the one that is only a wish-fulfillment fantasy.

For women like this, the culturally idealized mother-daughter relationship is more important than reality. As children we miss the symbiosis we didn't have so acutely that we are perhaps even more desperate for it than women who were less deprived. It is too painful, too humiliating to admit.

"My parents are very uptight about sex," says a twenty-nine-year-old single woman. "I don't want sex always to have to be part of some big, emotional intimacy, some ongoing relationship. I like to be able to have sex without strings. Recently I met a guy I liked a lot and went to bed with him the first night. It bothered me that he didn't call again. When I did get a note from him he didn't even refer to that night." When I suggested that it had been a humiliating experience, she protested adamantly. "No, no, it wasn't humiliation. It's just that I haven't wanted to see other guys since." As I am leaving, she stops me: "Goddamnit, I did feel humiliated." The curtain of repression had lifted for a minute. Will she ever be able to integrate her attitude—wanting sex with no strings—with her gut reaction of despair when a man takes her up on it?

"When a woman goes to bed with a man and he doesn't call," says Dr. Robertiello, "she feels humiliated. It's like being used, duped, conned. It goes back to that early feeling of betrayal and loss of that first person who led you to believe that if you 'gave' to her, she would always be there for you." In her conscious mind, this woman has made a personal, rational decision about men. On the unconscious level she is still reacting to them as if they were her mother.

Men don't share our conflict. The more successful he is, the more a man feels he can get the best women, sex, and love. Where the sexes differ is that *we get involved with men symbiotically*—displacing our need for mother onto our husband or lover. No wonder we have more difficulties apportioning our time—so much for love, so much for work—than men do. In symbiotic love, the need is so great it swallows all time and nothing is left over for anything else.

"I always believed I could have love and work," says Dr. Schaefer, "and therefore I did have them. I was brought up with this belief because both of my parents loved to work. It just seemed natural to love *and* to work. Their training makes women think they must exclude men from their lives to have interesting work. What we believe is what we make happen."

In terms of work that builds independence, there is no reason to think of jobs merely in snobbish or elitist terms. The woman who can run a switchboard gets a feeling of mastery and competence. If we can do small repair jobs around the apartment—unplug a drain or fix a blown fuse—it is one more area in which we have learned to dominate the nitty-gritty details of life, without depending on a man. The woman who is proud of her position as an irreplaceable secretary gets as much feeling of value from her job as does the woman vice-president. The world may put different monetary or status value on what they do, but as far as helping to confirm feelings of autonomy, both are equally desirable.

While the value of earning a paycheck that supports you cannot be overestimated, some women find that their most emotionally nourishing work lies outside an office. They may paint or write on weekends, go into politics or put in time with the Red Cross. But the activity must be important enough to be worth the sacrifice of extra time, labor, and social activities. Otherwise, it isn't emotionally valuable enough for us to gain feelings of autonomy. Without real commitment, it is only a game. If it doesn't matter if you lose, you gain little if you win.

Today's cry is freedom; none cries it more loudly than the single woman who demands it even while she is out finding someone to surrender it to. "Why can't I find a man to take care of me?" is a common complaint, even among Leah Schaefer's women patients who have jobs or careers. "I tell them," Dr. Schaefer says, "that the world is filled with men who feel more manly by taking care of women. But there is a payment you must make; you can't expect a man to take care of you, and also tell him what to do. The way you pay for being taken care of when you are little is to be the kind of person mother wants you to be. The same price must be paid to a man. Many women want it both ways. There is nothing wrong with wanting to be taken care of, I tell them, just as long as you know the price of what you are getting."

Matina Horner wrote her doctoral thesis on women's "motivation to avoid success" in 1968. "Of course!" we exclaimed, "that explains my anxiety, my failures, my ambivalence about work. I am a woman just like any other. I have the feminine fear of success!" Our fears were not biological but socially conditioned. What was learned could be unlearned. Besides, it was all the fault of the paternalistic society anyway.

I sometimes wonder if Dr. Horner's conclusions haven't done women more harm than good. Having the zippy phrase—fear of success—in advance of trying, it becomes a self-fulfilling prophecy. We recognize failure as an old friend, the very mark of our womanliness. We make the same mistake in reading certain feminist fiction. Eager for identification with other women, we recognize ourselves in the heroines—beaten down, harassed, often humorous even if self-deprecatingly so. It is nice to know we aren't the only ones who feel uncontrollable rage when our husband comes home late, loss of identity if he doesn't come home at all. It doesn't follow, however, that identification with someone else's failures makes us better equipped to overcome our own.

Nevertheless, I feel Dr. Horner was right. We do fear success; but the phrase is useless unless we see it in context. Fear of success used to be explained with emphasis on oedipal retribution: if you beat mommy out for daddy, she will seek her revenge. I think this is true of both sexes, but women do not fear mother's rivalry and anger as much as her loss. There is a shading of emphasis here that runs along sexual lines. Our problems of separation are not parallel to men's. A man doesn't have to leave another man to gain his independency. A boy can be a rival to his father and/or use him as a model—but in either case, continue to get love and support from mother. A daughter, however, often feels she must choose a field distant from mother's in order to reinforce separation. For many women, competition with men is much easier to face than competition with another woman.

"In developing strategies for winning, women have much quicker understanding than men," says George Peabody, who is a doctor of Applied Behavioral Science. He invented The Powerplay Game, by which corporations try to teach employees on the way up methods for success in business. "But again and again, we find women hesitate—to the point of stupidity—to put what they know into play. They aren't stupid, so you have to ask why. They think their superior strategic and political planning is somehow cheating. When they enter the office, they park this kind of skill at the door. In Powerplay, they tend to want to give back all their winnings when the game is over. Many are afraid to beat out the other girls. They don't want to destroy relationships."

I know a travel agency staffed by women that has "eliminated" competition by doing away with titles. "When a senior position is open," one of the partners says proudly, "we don't make a big deal of it. Competitive feelings don't get stirred up. Someone gets the position and that's that." The story makes my heart sink.

Who is fooling whom? When there is no open power relationship, it does not mean there is no power relationship at all. Everybody knows who decides that the office will open a branch in Florida, who decides Mary Anne will get that lush assignment to Paris while Sally will type up the reports. Some people want to run organizations, some do not. Unless the rules of competition are spelled out, nobody is comfortable. The dominant personalities rule the roost by their own rules, and usually for their own comfort, while paternalistically (!) telling the subordinates they are one big happy family with the good of all as the common goal. Nor do the people at the top win totally: because their place in the hierarchy is unacknowledged and thus nonlegitimate, they suffer from anxiety too.

To deny women their right to feel competitive reinforces old stereotypes of passivity. Power is being exercised, but everyone pretends it is not. Only we are nasty enough, competitive enough to feel angry. Better shut up, pretend not to be competitive at all. To do anything else is to risk being labeled unwomanly. We think we will be rewarded for being good girls, for not making waves. The other guy gets the promotion.

"Why has there never been a woman who has been the bridge or chess champion of the world?" asks Dr. Robertiello. "The way this question is usually put by male chauvinists is, 'Why haven't there been more great women artists, scientists,' etc.? The answer is a function of the culture in which women are brought up. After all, in comparative IQs, women come out brighter than men."

Working for yourself, getting ahead, usually means beating out another person, *breaking a bond.* Says Dr. Peabody: "Women have been trained to be somebody's 'other,' not to have an independent sense of identity. When you get to be Number One, you can't be somebody's other. If your lifelong habit is to think of your identity only in terms of being somebody's wife, somebody's secretary or assistant, it is scary not to be in that position. It means you have no identity. But as soon as you can tell women that it's not cheating, not naughty, to go after what they want, that they can do it and still be feminine—that assertiveness does not mean putting other people down—then women can give themselves permission to use their great skills and they move marvelously. It is almost a shock to them to find people don't fall apart when they say No."

We have been trained not to initiate, but to respond—not to choose but to be chosen. "My job," Dr. Peabody continues, "is to help women over the fear of clear self-definition and self-responsibility; it's the only way to move into top management. Sometimes it takes six to eight months to get even the best women through that knothole. But they can learn!"

"You're terrific!" says the boss. "What a job you did!"

We blush. He really didn't mean it. It was a fluke; we'll never be able to pull it off again.

This is the split in which we live. We may hear praise when it is given. We just can't believe it. We see recognition of our accomplishments as a kind of flattery, mistaken or insincere. But if you cannot take in praise and recognition during the uphill battle to get a hold on who you are, how long are you going to stick with it? We have been trained to gain confidence not through efforts for ourselves but through meeting the needs of others. "Women," says Jessie Bernard, "are the ones who keep families together. All the studies show that women are the mediators in kinship relations." We are good at compromise. Men take the extreme positions that, right or wrong, define identity. They let people know "where they stand."

Says psychoanalyst and sex therapist Helen Kaplan: "We are in a transitional period. We want to be successful on our own, but we still look for superdaddy, who will be more successful still. In terms of numbers, there are more men available to the career-oriented woman. She is more likely to be sexually active than the home-oriented person. But the great number of work-oriented women are thrown by the notion that most men they meet are less successful than they are. For women like these, a man who is less powerful than they may not be attractive."

Women marry up, men marry down. Says sociologist Cynthia Fuchs Epstein: "For all the talk about the women's revolution, there are no figures to indicate this is changing." And yet if women could get over our learned need to attach ourselves to someone more powerful than we—and accept the more democratic notion of a relationship between peers—new numbers of men would become available to us. "I won't even go out to dinner with a man who makes less money than I do," says a divorced woman who is an advertising copy chief. She eats dinner, night after night, alone.

Symbolically, nothing says you are big and strong as forcibly as money. The last thing I want to do here is set up money as the kind of value for which men have thought it worth killing themselves—but it is vital that women understand their choices regarding money, how often unconscious separation anxieties get played out in our attitude toward the dreamy stuff.

From the time we are children, we begin to learn not how to earn money but how to manipulate for it. Half the fights between mother and father are about money. We sense her feeling that if he loved her more, there would be more money available for him to give her. Money is proof he wants to take care of her. If mother had to earn money for herself, that would mean she was not so dependent on daddy, not nearly so loved by him. What we must do is turn the whole game around. Instead of making money ourselves, which means we are separate, unloved and independent, we want to have our husband put us on an allowance, as mother did. This uses money not to threaten the symbiotic connection but to establish it more firmly.

The man thinks setting up a reward system of giving the woman something extra to buy a new dress is his idea; the woman is at least complicit in this maneuver from the start. When we are grown and have a "big daddy" of our own, we still like to get that nice little extra something for being "a good girl." In this way, money becomes involved with closeness, rather than separation. "Nevertheless," says Professor Jeanne McFarland, "while the wife is proud of how she can cajole money out of [the husband] she knows the real money power is with him. When the man threatens to leave her, instead of quickly thinking of ways to support herself, she feels the old paralysis. By the time you're a wife, you don't really have economic options because you've bought the model that says you're dependent."

One way to solve our childish need to have a man more powerful than we is to "choose" to make less money ourselves. Very rarely have I heard a woman say she wanted to make a million. I can't count the number who've told me, "I want to marry a millionaire." By deliberately deciding to leave the issue of making money to someone else, by marrying *up* so we feel we have someone powerful to lean on, we have not strengthened the grown woman within, but reinforced the baby.

A paycheck is proof we can make it on our own. Once we have succeeded in a job, once we have the feel of money, it loses much of its awe. We know how much it costs to earn; how to spend it, save it, what it can do for us. It no longer is some mystery that only men can understand. Money in your pocket gives you firm ground on which to stand. Until we have an economic alternative to marriage, we have no alternative at all.

CHAPTER 11

MARRIAGE: THE RETURN TO SYMBIOSIS

So sweet is the first feel of marriage that we give up everything. We abandon our names, say good-bye to old lovers and friends, and close our savings and checking accounts, putting everything in our (his) name. We are losing our credit rating for life—should this man ever die or leave us—but we don't want to hear this. We have come full cycle. We are home. Nothing has ever felt so right as putting ourselves in his hands.

Our marriage puts mother's heart at rest too. It is proof that she has been a good mother. Accomplishments prior to marriage may have made her proud, but they also put distance between us. Marriage builds a bridge back. She helps us decorate the house, sends us *The Joy of Cooking*, lends us money. *She is available.* We think the change is in her. It is we who have changed, taking a step back in time to meet her again.

Very often the new mother-daughter friendship comes at the expense of what should be our prime union—with our husband. We do not mean to ally with her, but whose standards are we living up to when we give up our identity? Did he ask it of us? When a husband is unfaithful but the wife does not take the same freedom for herself, to whom is she remaining true? If sex once divided mother and daughter, The Rules in marriage make us friends again. Monogamy is the vow made for our husband but even more to placate the introjected mother within.

"After we'd been married six months," a thirty-year-old woman recalls, "my husband said he didn't want me to talk to my mother on the phone so much. 'I don't want you to see her,' he said, 'until you understand a new habit you've gotten into. If I want to put a chair here, a table there, the two of you get together and decide they would look better in a third place.

She's done it for years to your father. I won't have you lining up against me with your mother. You and I will decide and then we'll tell her how we want things done, if we tell her at all.' He was right. I wasn't even aware of slipping into this thing with mother—which, in a way, was against him."

For some people, the blissful "in love" stage of the honeymoon may go on for years. We idealize the other person—and through him, ourselves. The unspoken self-flattery here is that we must be pretty special too, to have been chosen by this incredible being. For others, reality presents its harsh face when the two weeks in Bermuda end and he calmly goes back to his job or golf foursomes. He walks out the door alone, and doesn't think of it as betrayal at all. When he leaves home for work in the morning, his feeling of doing the right thing is unmistakable. Much as we love our new house, our new name, they have not brought us what we expected of marriage. The rational self knows the mortgage must be paid, but somewhere within we feel his 9 to 5 life—*anything separate from us*—is a rival. We want love, more love, love without end. Doesn't he want it too?

We are told we are womanly to need love so badly but the issue is not love. It is the longing to be merged. If we take a job for a salary our new family needs just as much as it does his, why don't we feel as wholeheartedly right about working as he does? "Everything is OK," he says reassuringly. We don't believe him. The independence of a job, life in the office with other people, do not seem to complement what we have at home, but carry jeopardy. New friends and adventures when we were little, sex itself, were all the more exciting because they were *away* from mother, but that was why they were tinged with anxiety too. We didn't tell her about these experiences because we believed they would frighten her; the truth is we were frightened that if she knew, she would get angry. Our tie to her would be weakened. This way of thinking was confirmed when we found out later that more men, more success and accomplishment often lost us the love of other girls. They experienced our gains as somehow leaving less of the pie for them. How can our husband be any different? How can he not fear the added life we get from work as a betrayal too? Won't he love us less, even leave us?

A successful career woman tells me she feels no conflict at all between marriage and career. "It was my husband who encouraged me to continue my job," she tells me proudly. But when we part, she calls back: "I've been thinking," she says. "Sometimes I do feel guilty that I'm not there with a hot meal when Jim comes home from work. It's irrational, but there it is. There's this niggling fear that maybe I'm disenfranchising myself from my femininity. He's never said anything, but I feel it."

The anxiety here is not between husband and wife but within the woman herself. On TV, she sees commercials of families moving together in tight, compact groups. She has her own history of closeness within her childhood family. She and her husband may have worked out more economic divisions of time; she may be getting rewards more real and appropriate from her marriage—but it is not what she was raised to look for. The majority of American divorces—higher than ever last year—come in the second year of marriage. The third year is almost as bad. More women than ever are working outside the home, but our culture has taught us so successfully that a woman's place is tied to a man as securely as once we were tied to mother that we are guilty about our efforts to be free. Men too have been raised to think of women in this way. Though they may give our work separate from them verbal encouragement, the other half of the unspoken double message is often there too: why aren't you the way my mother was with my father?

It is important to emphasize that wanting to be taken care of is not always negative. Men and women are drawn together because we all need a close, intimate relationship. In a good one we can satisfy each other's needs with pleasure, or at least at low psychic cost. To be held in someone's arms, to be able to say, "I'm scared, lonely, tell me everything will be all right. Comfort me and I'll do the same for you when you feel this way"—that is not asking to be guaranteed against all the vicissitudes of life. The woman who says this to a man is merely asking for a resting place, a fueling station in which to gather her strength to go on again. It is not quitting adulthood, nor is it submitting to a superior-inferior relationship.

When "take care of me" means asking someone to permanently interpose himself between us and reality, the wish is destructive to the self, and therefore to the marriage. This behavior is often found in women whose total orientation toward life is a kind of reliving out of the dissatisfactions they experienced from a cold, nongiving mother. Even in sex, such a woman expects to be passively gratified at all times, with little concern for the man's needs or satisfactions. If her primary aim is to be nurtured, to be petted, soothed, *suckled* (in any of its unconscious disguises including the sexual), it is not orgasmic satisfaction she is looking for. I've heard men say sex with women like these makes them feel, not refreshed, renewed and satisfied, but exhausted.

A psychiatrist describes a sexual problem she often sees in women: "She won't do anything during sex because that means giving. All she wants is to receive. She speaks of sex as 'letting him make love to me.' The idea that she might make love to him is inconceivable. She just wants to lie there. The typical mother of a woman like this simply hadn't been there, emotionally or physically, when the woman was little. Therefore, the daughter's orientation toward life was that she had to be constantly reassured, told how good she was, to be nurtured and done for. She can't give, partly because she was afraid she would be smacked down if she did, but mostly because she has very little to give." You can't learn to give without having been initially given to.

No wonder so many couples who have lived together worry that marriage may ruin what they have. "We're as much as married now," one of them may say, "what would be different if we went through a legal ceremony?" But marriage does change us; it brings a formal element into our lives, the rigidity of the model of our parents.

Women have an important confusion about being taken care of emotionally, and being taken care of financially. It compounds the problem of symbiosis, and so will be discussed here at some length. The difficulty begins with the fact that men and women see money's role in their lives in different ways. This causes almost hopeless frictions compounded by the fact that all of us have been trained to think there is something intrinsically not nice in talking about money at all.

By the time a man is old enough to think of marriage, he is usually on his way to having solved the material side of living. Socialized masculinity tells him that as long as he is a good provider, women will tend to his emotions for him. "Take care of me," he says when he comes home from the office. He means he is exhausted by the battles of the day, and wants his wife to help him feel better. He is asking for emotional support.

The wife too is exhausted by battling it out with the carpool, the repairman, the PTA, and her loneliness. "Take care of me," she says. Her emotional request is as legitimate as his, but she wants more from him. You might say there is a hidden clause in her request. In defense of women, it must be added that this usually operates outside our conscious knowledge: mixed in with any request to be emotionally taken care of is the expectation that this includes being taken care of financially as well—an assumption men do not fully understand. From here, it is easy to fuse and confuse emotional and material needs: we expect that meeting one need implies the man is ready, willing, and able to meet the other too. That is what love "means." If he buys us expensive gifts, a house on the lake, or takes us for a trip to Paris, the economic half of the gift becomes suffused with a romantic, emotional glow: he has "proved" he loves us.

"I will marry for love," a woman says, but the unspoken half of her definition is that love will make her feel free of material anxieties. It is only after marriage that many women become aware that what they love is not just the man but the material security he is supposed to bring. Married couples fight over money more than any other single cause.

On the other hand, a marriage in which all bills are paid promptly is not necessarily a happy one. It is only a negative event, an anxiety subtracted. The cliché is old and tired, but that is because it is so often true: a man often works so hard and long to make the money for the marriage that he has little time or energy left for emotions.

Money is the rub, and when marriage fails, often enough it is money which women use to "get back at him." How much of the unrealistic amounts asked for in divorce settlements are meant for support, how much for revenge? When they were in love, she told him money didn't matter, love was all. Now that the unrealistic promise of symbiotic love has failed, money matters very much. But, says lawyer Emily Jane Goodman: "When I tell women that if they do not own and control their own money, they do not control their lives, I always meet resistance. 'Oh, no,' they say. 'I'm the one who keeps the checkbook, pays the telephone bills on time, we have a joint account,' etc. They never want to face that when he stops putting money into the joint account, everything stops."

A common defense wives adopt against economic powerlessness is to live by a kind of unspoken formula. "Your money is our money, but my money is mine." Feeling sneaky and sly, she squirrels away part of the housekeeping money in a cookie jar or secret account. She has some unconscious feeling that money—keeping money, hiding money, *her* money—is not nice. Saddest of all, the amount being withheld is not going to give her autonomy anyway.

My own feeling is that far from behaving childishly, women who defend the unspoken formula "Yours is ours and mine is mine" may be showing a certain amount of common sense. Says psychologist Sonya Friedman: "I don't think it's unrealistic for a woman with no income to put money away as a margin of safety. In marriage counseling, I often see men who are getting ready to leave their wives. He sells the home, then puts her in a new $80,000 house with a $70,000 mortgage and departs, keeping most of the cash realized on the sale of the old house. A woman must ask herself, 'Am I being financially wise to depend on him totally?'"

Millions of women do contribute to the family income. More than 30 million women work outside the home today—over one-third the labor force. A recent University of Michigan survey shows that a third of working women are the sole wage earners of the family. Some women have been raised by their mothers to think of themselves as providers and take pride in it. Other women find feelings of deeply satisfied symbiosis with the husband and children when they hand over their paycheck for the good of the family. "It is when the money in the family rises above the baseline of survival," says Dr. Friedman, "that the trouble starts. It's up to him, the wife thinks, always to provide the economic baseline on which they live. If she earns anything, it is on top. He is not supposed to count on it. She thinks she is entitled to do whatever she wants with her money." She has been raised to think she needn't earn any money at all, so if she does, it is extra, hers alone. And if a money need should arise that she considers to lie within his province of day-to-day family expenses—like a repair bill for the car—and he asks her to help pay for it, she may stubbornly resist.

She usually gives in to him on everything else. Why does she balk here?

Ever since we can remember, mother has held out marriage as the grand payoff for all our sacrifices and restraints. It is put as a kind of reality principle: deferring satisfaction today will lead to a greater reward tomorrow. If we curb our temper, deny ourselves sex, give up assertiveness—all will bring a better man, a safer marriage, one in which it is the man's job to support us. For the wife to contribute money to her own support is to break the symbiotic illusion that the husband will always take care of her.

Money is power, the woman without money is a victim. Most wives realize this means they are living on the edge of a financial precipice. It is difficult to tell a husband: "I'm not getting enough emotion from you." It sounds neurotic and childish. It is easier to say, "Why don't you ask for a raise? Why can't we take a trip to South America? The people next door have a new car. Can't we?" Asking for pleasures that money can buy when what we really feel is emotionally poor makes money arguments family-killers. Trapped in role-playing postures, talking about one thing when they mean another, and unable to understand the difference between emotional and material "taking care of," both husband and wife are doomed to endless Rashomon arguments. Each is defending unnamed positions the other doesn't suspect.

A woman may resist the new tide of feminism and reject all its tenets, but she cannot forget she has alternatives her mother did not. Grandmother may have gotten enough narcissistic gratification through identification with her husband, his achievements and her status as his wife. Today, television makes it impossible not to know many women out there are getting a lot more out of life. This is not to say being a housewife and mother is not enough for millions of women. It obviously is. But if you are the sort of person who wants more than being *Mrs.* Harry Brown, living through him may not be enough. He is not taking in enough air, life, success and/or achievement for two.

"But the insufficiency," says Dr. Schaefer, "is not seen by the woman as her problem. She thinks it is his. She may feel like a nobody, but the way she puts it is: 'Oh, I'm very happy, but I wish George were better organized so he could get a better job.' Her implication is, If I were George, I could do it better."

Dr. Schaefer continues: "A woman like this is afraid to take the risks her husband does. She would like a more interesting, stimulating life, but she sees it as something only he can get for her. It never occurs to her the problem is hers. She is so meshed, so dependent on him, she can't see where he begins and she leaves off. She fears that separating out a problem as her own will divide them—that it will force her to act on her own. 'Why not get a job?' I suggest to a woman like this. 'You're terrific with clothes, you could sell dresses in a boutique.' But she is terrified. 'Oh, no, I could never fill out one of those sales slips!' she says. She clings to him and complains instead."

To people like this, the contemporary message that women have a responsibility for their own gratification in life seems like so much theoretical hooey. A woman who is as talented as her husband will put him through school because she has been trained to feel the life she will get from his success far surpasses what she could get on her own.

In those marriages where roles are shared—where women help carry the financial load and men help in the housework and raising the children, studies show, says sociologist Jessie Bernard, "that women end up working at least 25 percent more than the men."

There has been a recent backlash among certain male writers who warn that unless women return to traditional roles and get out of the male marketplace, a whole new generation of frustrated and angry males will be unleashed upon the world.

I would like to talk about the rage of women.

We bear a burden of anger all our lives. Just like men, some of us are more angry than others. Although some authorities would like to convince us that men's greater potential for anger is sex-linked (hormones, testosterones, etc.), I remain unconvinced. The difference between the angers of the sexes is that women's are the more repressed.

If I choose to discuss anger within the context of marriage, it is not because I believe there are no happy marriages. I know many. And yet any institution sold to women as a reward for lifelong inhibition must cause anger and disappointment. "The more I talk to a woman," says Sonya Friedman, "the more anger I uncover. All the depression, the going to sleep early, not having energy, the fact that it's three in the afternoon and she is still sitting around in her housecoat—all these are various forms of anger. 'I'm bored,' she says, 'I went through all this schooling, I used to have dreams but now I know they aren't going to be met. I'm even afraid to go back to school, to get out there and compete.' Most of the anger has to do with the ways she was raised. Marriage, she was told, would be the answer to all problems. The typical American housewife has no identity apart from her husband, so can't let the anger out. Her only way to deal with it is to turn it upon herself. That is why so many women are depressed."

Speech is the least harmful outlet for anger. The easiest way to dissipate it or to change the environment in a beneficial way is with words. But one of the first things girls are deprived of is the direct translation of thought into speech. While we are little, the clever, articulate child is mother's darling. It is the commonplace experience of pediatricians that little girls learn to speak earlier and more fluently than boys. As we become young women, this changes. The subtle training in silence begins.

We learn that spontaneity in speech can lose you people. We learn to edit our thoughts, to reduce strong emotions to bland euphemisms. "When I go places with my husband," says a thirty-year-old woman, "I'd like to participate more in the discussions. But by the time I've formed a sentence in my head, the talk has already gone on to a new subject."

We are not practiced in spontaneity. What fluency in speech this woman picked up in college has been lost in the ten years she has spent at home raising children. She does not regret the choice of motherhood; she just can't understand her uneasiness about joining in dinner-party conversation. "Many men aren't necessarily bright, but that doesn't stop them from going nonstop. Why can't I let myself get in a word?"

Like any other facility, the conduit between brain and tongue requires use if it is not to go rusty. Without practice, the prospect of humiliation, fear of saying the wrong thing and finding ourselves stranded midsentence, keeps us silent.

We also have the social disadvantage of a woman's voice. I've often sat in my own living room and heard my opinion ignored as if I were invisible; the same idea spoken five minutes later in a sonorous male voice is applauded. These experiences do not equip us to handle differences of opinion about a movie or even teasing about a tennis game. How can they equip us for the sudden and violent emotions of anger?

How many women have you ever heard express hostility intelligently? Our voices become charged, not with anger's force and determination, but with an anxious quality that makes listeners turn away. They are afraid we will lose control; they are "bored" by our overemotional delivery. "That's how women are. They can't argue logically." What drives us to fury is not the illogic of our argument, but inexperience in speaking aggressively. We ourselves fear hysteria. I have watched socially organized groups of intelligent women disintegrate into anxious little knots of dismay when faced with someone's inability to speak her anger at another woman who is present. It is easier to show anger to a man: it was a woman who taught us to suppress our rage. Tears and weeping are the only sound of anger we are allowed.

Because society would rather we always wore a pretty face, women have been trained to cut off anger. "Help me," we cry, running to psychiatrists, surgeons, doctors, priests, or even back to mother. We say we are "nervous" and take tranquilizers, aspirin, gin and courses in Total Womanhood. We say we are "happy" but find ourselves unaccountably suffering from headaches, ulcers, or chronic fatigue. We say we are bored and gamble, take lovers or spend too much money in the department store. We say we are not in the mood and deny our husband sex. We say we are menopausal and live in states of chronic physical and/or mental anguish for a decade. There is a respectable body of medical opinion which believes that our buried, long-smoldering anger can even lead to the silent explosion of the body against itself: cancer. Our anger against the false idealization of marriage is so unacceptable that we have turned it against ourselves in the profoundest sense of the word.

Says Dr. Schaefer: "I see so many women whose lives are dominated by the idea, 'He won't let me.' The whole women's movement is based on personal responsibility, but many people think as soon as they've liberated themselves, all the goodies will drop in their lap. They think: Now that I've dumped the old man who was holding me back, now the boss will give me, the world is going to give me, the sisterhood is going to give me. Because women were never raised to be autonomous, they don't understand the personal responsibility needed to make the liberation slogans mean something."

The bottled-up fury resulting from overidealizing marriage as the solution to all our problems makes for a kind of agoraphobia. "You might even call it 'housewife phobia,'" says Sonya Friedman. "It is not uncommon, and describes the great number of women who don't like, or are afraid, to leave the house alone. It has to do with the fear that once she gets out there in the wide-open spaces, she'll get this irresistible urge to run away."

A private detective who works for a large agency in New York gives me a description of the average runaway housewife. It reads like someone in a TV soap opera: she got married at nineteen, had children shortly thereafter, and has had little or no work experience. She's thirty-four when she differs from her more conventional sisters and disappears to find a new life.

In a symbiotic marriage, you feel protected, close—in fact, so close that no separation can be tolerated. Any emphasis put on individual choice, any anger expressed, is betrayal. Men have long run away from it. Women are beginning to.

Our culture rewards women for swallowing their anger and/or directing it away from its source. The compulsive housekeeper, the lioness of the Anti-Porn Society, the nonstop charity-worker, the overprotective and critical mother who does it all for someone else's good—who can fault these people out loud? We don't know where they get their energy, we don't know that they get out of it. We may avoid them and their company; but we can't call them bad women/wives/mothers.

Very often, these women are obsessive/compulsive—suffering from forms of behavior that seem to have nothing to do with anger. Unlike depressed people who turn their anger within, against themselves, the obsessive/compulsive express theirs outwardly—but in such an indirect way they never need face their furies at all.

While usually discussed together, compulsions and obsessions differ slightly. Compulsions are repeated acts of behavior, like contantly emptying ashtrays while the smoker is using them, or fluffing up the sofa pillows the minute somebody gets up. If you've ever been around compulsive people and seen how they fray the nerves of anyone they come into contact with, you will recognize that a great deal of hostility is being loosed nonspecifically into the environment. On the other hand, obsessions are not actions, but thoughts. Obsessional people have their minds constantly flooded with repetitive ideas—like the woman who is ever worried that something terrible has happened to the children, that her husband will leave. Once again, anger has taken on a disguise, a constant conjuring-up of pain, loss and death. Nobody has happy obsessive thoughts. Both obsessions and compulsions are repetitive because underground anger must be defended against, over and over.

Says Sonya Friedman: "Women have problems with anger because they don't have a sense of security within. Women go from being an extension of their families to being an extension of their husbands. Most marry before they complete growing. The man usually has more power, so whatever sense of identity she has can easily be snuffed out. Men don't *do* this *to* women, they do it *with* women's compliance. Women have been so conditioned for marriage that they buy the contract, the trade-off of autonomy for dependence. Later they cry: 'What can I do to save my marriage?' You have to tell these women there are no ready-made answers. Maybe in time they get in touch with their anger, but that means going back to the beginning to when they first learned the double-edged reward they got from mother was paid for by playing down their self-confidence and independence."

We have trouble understanding that we can be angry and forgiving at the same time. The two are not mutually exclusive. We think if we hate someone we hate them all the way through. This is to misunderstand the split between the conscious and the unconscious, between the adult self and the child.

Besides headaches, depression, ulcers and other illnesses, repressed anger can also take the form of sexual masochism. As an example, take the mother who says to her child: "You've been naughty. Wait till your father gets home." Says a young mother: "In our house, discipline was always handled by my father. I'd be sent to my room to wait until he got home, and I'd sit there quivering. I was terrified of my father, and I would say that my fear of rejection from men stems from him. But even more than I feared him, I needed my mother's approval. It seemed she was the only bulwark I had against him. She dominated the household, including him. And so having established him as the fake authority figure, the bad guy, she would then use him. We would conspire together. If I were going out she'd say, 'Be in by twelve, but if you're really having a good time, call me and I'll tell him it's not as late as he thinks.'"

In time, this woman came to regard her mother as a victim of this terrifying male creature who had to be cajoled, lied to, and above all, controlled—or his savage temper would be loosed. She goes on:

"It was only when I got far enough away from home in distance and time that I began to see what a raw deal my father had. I used to think he was such an ogre, but my mother *ran him*. There is a parallel in my own marriage, in that I accepted the face-value aspect of my parents' marriage. When my husband would storm and rage at me—for ten years he told me I was frigid, castrating and sexually nothing at all!—I accepted it. That's how men were supposed to be—perpetually storming and angry. I never could get mad back at him because my mother had shown me that a *real woman* handles a man with the soft answer and the cunning trick. If I stormed back at him, it would be acting like a man!"

When mother sets up the father as the daughter's disciplinarian, the unspoken message is: "I'm mad at you, but I'm not going to express it because women don't. The bad guys, the sadists of the world, are men. That's what daddy is—he's going to hurt you." Later, when the daughter is married, she does what she has been taught is woman's role: she looks to the man to put her down, to hurt her psychologically or even physically. She may hate it, but it's what she's been taught to expect.

On the other hand, if our needs are to be as symbiotic and unseparate from our husband as possible, we will not do anything that might arouse his anger. Instead of using him to express our anger, we turn it inward. We feel we are failures, become insomniacs, compulsive housekeepers, victims of obsessive ideas of aging, death. One very frequent face this inner fear and anger wears is that of the controlling woman. The nagging, critical, hen-pecking little woman.

Says Dr. Friedman: "We think the controlling wife is so sure of herself. The opposite is true. Very often there is such a terror of *being* controlled or abandoned that she assumes control."

In human relations, fear is almost always counterproductive. The more a wife fears the husband will leave her, the more she nags, the more she will try to run him like a child. He gets fed up with all the tears, the going through his pockets for evidence, the anxiety. He goes.

As the girl watches her mother play martyr rather than express her anger directly, she learns techniques of masochistic manipulation.

"Oh, that's all right," mother tells father, "don't worry about me if you have to work tonight. I'll just have dinner alone." This kind of nonexpressive, nonassertive behavior once again tells the girl she must bow to men's evil ways. The message is: "Any resentment or anger that women might show is nothing compared to men with their tempers, ruthless business ethics, their delight in wars and the mayhem of Sunday pro-football games." Techniques of passive-aggression are being taught—a method of letting the man know you are angry at him, all the while denying you are, giving him no handhold with which to grasp the problem. Passive-aggressive actions may be very subtle, not conscious or even verbal: withholding an appropriate response, for example. A classic case is the man who becomes aware that he has said or done "something." "What's wrong?" he says to his wife, who has gone dead and silent on him. "Oh, nothing," she replies. She says it without feeling although everything about her—her face, body, her attitude and posture—is screaming that everything is wrong.

These methods of avoiding expression of anger create an alliance between the women in the family; often it is a method of avoiding sexual competition. Setting daddy up as the bogey man warns the daughter off from wanting to be close to such a stormy, hurtful creature. Only mother is unfailingly kind and nice. It is a way for mother to win the almost universal competition between the parents as to whom the child loves most.

After marriage, in any quarrel, the man is set up as the agressor, we are the victim. We knew it would come to this. Men only bring pain. Men can't love. Men don't understand. A basic insecurity is being expressed: it all depends on this other person. His anger, loss, disappearance, or death wipe us out. We would be unnatural if we did not at times resent needing someone so much. But our very dependency forces us to smother any hostility. If the marriage breaks up, we have more to lose than he. Says Dr. Sonya Friedman: "Mothers tell their daughters, 'It's up to you to make the marriage work. It takes 80 percent from you, only 20 percent from him.'"

Except for sex. That is the man's job, 100 percent. If this is so, how is the wife to cope when sex doesn't run smooth? "Sam couldn't keep his hands off me before we were married," a young wife sadly says. "Now he couldn't be less interested." The only advice she gets from popular wisdom is to experiment on the safe margins: try a new perfume, go off for "a second honeymoon" to Hawaii. Says Dr. Schaefer: "The wife is not conditioned to realize that she's just as responsible for their sexuality as he is. She can't imagine initiating sex in totally different ways, to vary the usual active/passive roles." "You're cold and frigid!" cries the man, his anger at peak because he knows he is at least half at fault. But he is the sexual expert. If he labels us a sexual dud, we believe him. It is *all* our fault.

It is only in some buried, central core of being that we know better. It is here where the residual anger lives.

There is little we can do about it. The power relation has been set since adolescence: we are the malleable clay, he is the master sculpture. Do with me as you will. The tyranny of the orgasm begins: true sex, real sex, orgasmically fulfilled sex with your husband will make a different woman of you, a real woman, a prettier woman, one more relaxed, more energetic, happy to be alive. In our secular society, a kind of sexual mysticism is one of our last faiths, and the "right" orgasm comes to be its tangible sign.

It is a medical fact that many women report having wonderful feelings about sex without orgasm, just as it is true that many women have orgasms without sexual pleasure, or happiness. "A very dependent and neurotic woman can be very orgasmic," says Dr. Robertiello. "In my clinical experience I have found women in the back wards of psychiatric hospitals who are multiorgasmic. There are other women who are well-functioning, who enjoy sex, but who have never had an orgasm in their lives. When we say there is a diminution of sexuality with the loss of the self in symbiosis, we must not confuse sex with orgasm. We don't know what makes some people have orgasms and others not. There are no exact correlations between sexual pleasure and orgasm."

"The reason a woman chooses sex to demonstrate her rage," says Sonya Friedman, "is that it is the only weapon she has. On the surface her tendency is to accept the blame, but underneath, because she can't be assertive in any other way, she withholds sex."

A significant number of women do not hold out on their husbands totally but use sex as a form of barter—candy for getting something she wants from him, when she feels guilty or afraid he might leave her. The penalty of turning sex into a commodity in this manner is that it—and she—are reduced to a cheap bribe, and the man who takes that foolish bribe is a chump. Respect is gone from the marriage. So is romance and genuine excitement.

Withholding sex is not always a coldly conscious maneuver. The wife may get sudden headaches; she is tired, fatigued, she says the children may hear them, etc. It doesn't matter that by denying the man she is denying herself. She is gaining something preferable to sex in her state of dependency: the poisoned joy of control.

Says Dr. Friedman: "When a woman turns her anger upon herself and becomes nonsexual or nonorgasmic, she is doing several things. On an unconscious level, she refuses to give him the deepest part of herself, perhaps the only area in which she feels full control. Many women simply don't want to share sex with the man they are married to. I see a lot of women who are selectively orgasmic—just as some men are selectively impotent. It has nothing to do with technique. She is angry, bitter. She doesn't want to give this pleasure to him, to let him see her abandon herself. She doesn't want to enhance his pleasure. If a woman goes into marriage thinking he must take care of her, including making her sexual, orgasmic and fulfilled, she's too frightened to tell him what she wants."

It is a common enough idea that orgasm correlates very strongly with the trust a woman feels for her sexual partner. "If you are angry, wary or suspicious," says Dr. Engler, "then you feel you must control yourself. You have to control him too. If you are constantly trying to control, you can't let go and be spontaneous in sex or anything else."

CHAPTER 12

A MOTHER DIES. A DAUGHTER IS BORN. THE CYCLE REPEATS

During our honeymoon in Rome I began to menstruate two weeks early. It had never happened before. I took it as a sign: the mystery of marriage was full upon me. Ten months later, I had a pregnancy scare.

The words are apt because I was as terrified as a sixteen-year-old. Marriage had once loomed like The End of adventure. Now pregnancy threatened like the finish of life itself.

I went to a young American doctor on one of those pretty, shady streets just off the Via Veneto, who confounded me still more with his disdain for a married woman who did not want to be a mother. Afterward I met Bill at the Café de Paris. I was shaking. What was so terrible? Why were we acting like two conspirators hiding from the consequences of a dubious act? We thought it had to do with not being able to afford a family yet. We wanted more time for ourselves. Or so we said. The idea that we simply did not want to be parents was something neither could voice.

I don't think I was really married until two or three years after we'd gone through the ceremony. "Playing at marriage" was how I'd describe that first year in our pretty apartment in Rome. Play-acting in a foreign country. How can the mere signing of a document change a life? Young girls imagine being married so long; when reality comes, it seems a dream. It took me time to become a wife, to give up my fantasies of what marriage would be. I did not love Bill that first year or two, not as I would grow to. I was right to be worried that day. Children, Bill and I had decided, would come later. We were both still absorbed in our marriage. Bill was beginning a new career, as a writer. We were young. We never doubted that one day we would be parents.

Four years ago I went off the pill. We were living in England and a close friend was having a baby. My London doctor kept pointing at the clock and making doomsday noises: I was not getting younger. What is frightening is that I don't remember Bill and me sitting down to have a discussion about parenthood. We seemed to have come to this crossroad of our lives by an almost negative route: since we had always assumed one day we would have children, when the time struck me as right—a friend of my own age having her first baby—he just went along with it.

"We drifted into that decision-without-making-a-decision," Bill recently said. "Neither one of us was expressing his own wishes. We had not gone along with conventional ideas about jobs, career, money, where and how to live, or what we wanted out of marriage. But this one was too big, too deeply implanted in us. In our own defense, we have to remember this was before the whole nonparenthood movement came to consciousness. Still, backing into that decision to have a child meant we'd lost confidence in ourselves. We were surrendering to unconscious assumptions about what the world seemed to be asking of us. Never to have a child was too large a decision to question by our own values. As for me, I was undercut in my reluctance by feeling I must be strange, inhuman, not to want to be a father. Alienation from my true feelings made me indecisive and passive. I didn't feel I had the right to make you live by my strangeness."

The whole exercise wasn't an idea I entered into passionately either, merely one I assented to, and with less weighing of the pro and con than the decision to move to another country. I set about getting pregnant.

I was passionate about one aspect of motherhood: it must be a boy. The idea of a little Bill with dark hair and big brown eyes was a wonderful fantasy. Growing up without a father, I told myself that I'd had enough of living with women. Nothing but a boy would do, I said to Bill, as we were driving to Mexico on a shaky assignment that might enable us to live there a year. Infrequent as our talks were about children, joke as I might about my insistence on a boy, I was deadly serious about not wanting a daughter. Something in me knew I would never, for instance, let her take journeys like this into the unknown. I would be a mother more afraid for her daughter than for herself.

Two months after I went off the pill I was back on it. Once again it was not really a conscious decision about motherhood. Work demanded we return to New York; starting a family was being postponed as haphazardly as it had been entertained. A year later I switched from the pill to a diaphragm, and about two years ago Bill and I decided not to have children. No, to put it correctly, the decision went like this: One day he said, "Isn't it a good thing that we didn't have children?"

When I was interviewing Helene Deutsch for this book, she spoke of the maternal instinct. "Are you telling me, Dr. Deutsch," I asked with some incredulity, "that one day I'm going to wish I'd been a mother?" "Yes," she said without hesitation, "You will always regret never having had a child." Even now words like this fill me with anxiety. I will always have a fantasy of a son. Because I have decided not to have a child doesn't mean I never dream of what might have been.

Let's begin with a story of classical mother-daughter role-modeling:

Peggy is cooking her first big meal for her parents since her marriage—a glorious Virginia ham. Standing up to carve, her new husband asks Peggy why she sliced off three or four inches from the shank end before baking. Peggy looks surprised. "Mother always does it that way."

Everyone at the table looks at Peggy's mother. "That's how my mother did it too," she says, a bit puzzled. "Doesn't everyone?"

Peggy phones her grandmother the next day, and asks why has the shank end always been cut off before baking. "I've always done it that way," grandmother says, "because that is how my mother did it."

It happens that four generations of women are still alive in this family. A call is put in to great-grandmother, and the mystery is solved. Once when her daughter—Peggy's grandmother—was a little girl and learning to cook, they were baking a large ham. The family roasting pan was small, and so the shank end had been cut off to make it fit.

Four generations of women, each one ignoring present reality, each one conforming, unquestioningly, to a circumstance that was no longer relevant; each one certain in her mind "that's how you do it" because she had seen her mother do it that way. An amusing story, an illustration of how we incorporate those parts of mother we choose to imitate—like her skill in cooking—but right along with them we also take in less rational and unexamined aspects all unaware.

It is here that one of the great feminine mysteries begins. Everyone else can see we've taken in many of mother's most negative character traits; we cannot. We deny it, treat the imputation as an accusation, get angry. And yet one day we realize that we are acting to our daughter exactly in the same repressive way mother once acted on us. How did it happen? We swore we would show our child only the wonderful warmth and love we got from mother. As for the rest—mother's nagging, anxiety, sexual timidity and general lack of adventurousness—why, we would just leave them out. And yet, generation after generation of daughters become women still carrying the inheritance of mother's sad luggage, passing it on to daughters of their own.

Why do daughters repeat in their lives many aspects of mother, including those they hated? Says Dr. Robertiello: "Two mechanisms are at work. *Role-modeling* is largely conscious, and has a lot to do with those parts of the 'good' mother we liked. For this reason, it is usually the work of a moment's introspection to see that mother's ease with strangers, and our skill at entertaining, are connected. At some point, role-modeling shades into *introjection*. This process is harder to understand because it is mostly unconscious, and is marked by a lot of repressed anger directed against the 'bad' mother. We take in her negative aspects in order not to see them in her. If they are in us, we don't have to hate her—and run the risk of her retaliatory anger. We are the bad ones. The evil, split half of mother has been introjected."

An example might be when mother refuses to let us go to the movies with friends. We hate her, splitting her off from the good mother who bought us a pretty dress yesterday. However, should one of our friends say, "That's mean, your mother is too strict," we rush to mom's defense. We don't like to hear our parents, especially mother, criticized by others. It externalizes the bad mother, threatening release of our pent-up rage, which would destroy the relationship. It is easier, safer to feel we are bad, not she.

This process is unthinking, unconscious and inevitable. The child cannot take the fearful loneliness that hating mother brings. Introjection is an almost mindless union in the depths of being, a merger at the level of the baby who could not bear—and indeed could not survive—being separated from mother.

In ideal developmental circumstances, by the end of the first year the child will have fused the image of the good and bad mother into one person—she will have come to the realistic conclusion that mother is a mixture of both. This is a highly sophisticated idea, a judgment of such difficult and mature perception that even adults have difficulty with it. We get stuck with a kind of dichotomous view of the people with whom we are intimately involved, repeating with them the split we never resolved with mother. If we get mad at our husband, he becomes the biggest bastard in the world, and our entire marriage to date has been a mistake; the next day, when he brings us flowers, we realize that he's really the sweetest guy of all time. It is a child's way of seeing the world—the way we liked to see movies when we were little. The white hats were all good. The black hats were all bad. Any effort on the screenwriter's part to show us that there were shades of gray in the good guys, some redeeming features in the bad, ended by confusing us. It is only when we are able to achieve a higher level of psychic integration that we can accept others as a mix of good and bad and not swing to extremes when they disappoint or hurt us.

As we grow up, we both know and don't know there are parts of mother we dislike. We can afford to see them because separation anxiety is not too great: we are both living under the same roof. We may hate or rage at mother, but there she is, waiting. An hour later, a kiss and a few tears, and symbiosis is back, strong as ever. Even if we are not affectionate, she is physically near, available.

As we get older and the tie to mother is weakened by physical or psychological separation, introjection gathers momentum. When we move into an apartment of our own, when we find a job, take a lover, get married and have a child of our own—in all these important rites of passage away from her, as we take one step forward, we take another one back, and find ourselves doing things her way. *Becoming like her overcomes our separation anxieties.*

It is a kind of symbolic rapprochement. Just as the infant who crawls away from mama into the next room gets frightened and rushes back for confirmation that she is still there, so, emotionally, as we edge away from mother in our adult lives, do we incorporate parts of her. Having her with us—*in* us—makes the journey less fearsome.

The process of introjection continues even if we never see mother any more, even if she is dead or living in Paris. It is not the present mother who is being introjected, but that bad one of long ago, whom we could not afford to "know" was making us so unhappy we hated her. When we have an outburst of fury at someone, how often is it because what that person is doing makes us aware of something we dislike in ourselves?

When we were little and saw mama running her house, we admired how firm she was with the repairman who did a bad job, the department store that sent the wrong bill. She spoke her mind, got the job done. We're as good at these things as she. But we also remember her panic when father was driving and took a wrong turn, how angry she got over spilled milk, her fear of noises in the house when alone. Above all, we have introjected her anxiety about sex.

Marriage is our chance at last to become as sexually daring as we would like. Instead, we are preoccupied with furniture, neatness, entertaining. The clothes we wore when we were single had plunging necklines. Now we run to suburban styles that don't raise an eyebrow. The reason sex was easier when we were single was that we had never seen mother unmarried and without a child. This was a role we could create on our own. She was far away—emotionally, at least—and we felt the zip of at least temporary separation. Marriage reunites us with her. To openly declare our sexuality now would make us too different from the picture of how she was as a wife. We would have to face our anger at last at that frustrating mother who hated the sexual pleasure we wanted from the time we were infants, who made us renounce it to keep her love.

When we become mothers ourselves, introjection speeds up even more. When we hold our little girl in our arms, we are reminded of mother, feel at one with her, as never before. Since sex was always a powerful force toward individuation, it is hardly surprising that sex is one of the first things to go.

To please mother, we gave up the right to our bodies and erotic gratification when we were little. Now when baby touches her genitals, we don't just frown. As mother did to us, we take her hand away. We become child-centered caretakers, madonnas, "not always thinking about sex." Mother used to be the enemy of sex. We are tired of the war. For our daughter's sake, and our own, we join her. Continuity is preserved.

Most women I interview are aware they became less sexual after motherhood, but cannot say why. They were too tired, they had to listen for the baby's cries, etc. Good reasons, but not convincing. If you want something badly enough, you establish priorities so you get it. Child psychologist Helen Prentiss looks at the issue subjectively and objectively:

"Before my daughter was born, I had been very proud of my sexual union with my husband. More than anything, I felt this distinguished me from the kind of woman my mother was. But when I became pregnant, I began to lose this contact with him, with the feeling I'd always had opposite him. I knew Jack loved my body, but that was my old slim body. How could he be turned on by this fat lady? He would put his arms around me, start kissing me, but I would make excuses. It felt wrong, sex, and me almost a mother. I was into this whole other picture of myself—one of those warm clean, dedicated mothers you see in women's magazines. Those pretty women don't have sex! They're good mothers, and I was going to be one too.

"My own mother being around a great deal speeded this idea. She was always dropping by with clothes for the baby, helping me fix the nursery. It was very reassuring to have her around because I was a little scared.

"As she and I became closer, my physical thing with Jack diminished. It was as though I couldn't have both—my closeness with her and with Jack. Sex became something silly or frivolous, perhaps a bit shameful, that you did before you became a mother. Now that I was pregnant, well, this was serious business, and those long hours in bed, those nights and mornings

Jack and I used to spend exploring one another, they seemed like selfish devilishness, kid stuff. Unwittingly and without any hesitation in the world, I gave up one of the most important things in my life and with my husband—our sexual tie.

"It was as though I'd been programmed from birth like some female Manchurian Candidate. I just allied with my mother in this feminine mystery she and I shared, and Jack was left out—some Dagwood Bumstead who perhaps had been necessary to get the whole thing started, but now it was time for him to get out and let us women handle the realities of life. It was almost as though what I was setting up with my mother was against him!"

Dr. Prentiss went on to say that while she knew—theoretically, intellectually, from everything she had read and lectured on herself—that it is necessary for a mother to be as symbiotic as possible with her baby during the first months of life, this union should not be allowed to interfere with what goes on between husband and wife. "There's a six-week prohibition against sex after the baby is born. Well, in my case six grew into ten, and what with me listening for the baby every time Jack touched me and feeling like this Super Mother, I would say, *Jack, please!* in this tone of indignation, as though he'd touched the Holy Grail.

"In my mind, I knew that without a connection to your adult identity, you stay symbiotically tied to your baby long beyond the period when you should let your child start to separate. Sex is the call of the adult world, reminding you of who you are. Reminding you that you may be a mother, but you are a woman too, a wife. But deeply as this knowledge was planted in me, something deeper, more unconscious, was working on me to get out in the world, to leave home and become my own person. I loved my mom but I wanted a bigger life, and when I met Jack, sex with him became the final definition that divided me, in my mind's eye, from the picture of my mom. I was a different kind of woman, or so I thought. Holding this baby in my arms changed all that. It never occurred to me that Jack might like to be included in taking care of Sally during those first months. And since I seemed to have no confidence in him, he lost whatever confidence he might have had in himself. He stopped volunteering. So there I was—a case out of one of my own textbooks. Symbiotically tied to my baby, reunited with my mother, and excluding my husband from 'our' (me, my baby and my mother's) life!

"I got an enormous amount of emotion from this thing with my baby. And my libido, if you want to use those kinds of terms, was very much directed toward the baby. My body was still not the beautiful body it used to be, my narcissistic view of myself was diminished. I just didn't feel like a sexual woman. I can see now that all my old notions—all my mother's old notions—had come back: that sex was dirty, or selfish. *It was unmotherly.*

"If you don't think about sex during those first months when you are so meshed with your baby, you wake up six years later not a woman, but a mom. Being sexual and being a person with a strong sense of who she is are ideas that are very tied together. Women cannot focus on this enough. It is hard enough to be sexual people before we become mothers. The outside world may see us as sexual women, but inside we are not at home with that idea ourselves. It's so easy—and dangerous—to lapse back into being a 'nice lady,' a mother. Giving yourself to union with your child at the beginning of your baby's life is healthy and necessary. After that, it is resignation from the problems, joys, and pleasures of an adult life of your own."

Resignation or not, it is what most women do. "Not in front of the children," sounds like a musical-comedy joke, but it is a fact of marital life. We gladly make the sacrifice because it is "for our child's good." The idea is debatable. Frustration and anger lie just behind the curtain we have pulled down between ourselves and our sexuality.

If we have to sacrifice so much for her good, well—she'd better be damned good. We are determined not to be as inhibiting as our own mother, but much stricter codes of conduct are enforced on our daughter than our son. After the latest outburst at the girl, we sit down and get hold of ourselves. Never again! How frightening it used to be when we were little to have mother furious. And so we start out once more with the best intentions: to be calm, cool, kind, to let her do things her way. But even as we act out this part, an inner anger comes up to sabotage all good intentions. It is not possible to be this "perfect" mother without comparing the ideal way we are trying to act, with the restrictive way mother used to be. To see this comparison too clearly would be to become furious at the old "bad" mother hidden in the unconscious. This rage would separate us from her. That is intolerable. The anger gets diverted, back onto ourselves, onto our husband, the unfairness of the world in general. Part of it inevitably spills out onto the daughter.

One part of our anger becomes subverted, and is experienced as a kind of forgiveness. "When women have children of their own," says Dr. Mio Fredland, "they begin to feel much more empathetic with their mothers. They make up old quarrels. They realize what their mother's life was like. They forgive whatever obscure angers have plagued them in the past, and they become loving and close. Especially if they have a daughter."

"A major reason," says Dr. Sirgay Sanger, "why women's anger at the mother often diminishes when they have a child is that the good mother image can now be acted out in real life. The negative, internalized image can be repressed, and there is the existence now of a new capacity—to love the new baby with a pure, unfettered giving of one's self. This is the mother one wished to have and to be. There often exists a euphoria after birth that women radiate. It casts a glow of warmth over her family, her husband and friends. It is also biologically necessary for the early growth and development of the infant. The desire—'I want to be the good mother to my infant'—explains why some women who never asserted themselves before can say no now in the name of that infant. The wish for a perfect mother has been transformed into becoming that perfection."

To nobody's surprise, the new mother finds the need for her own mother increasing. By this I don't mean the need for physical help and practical advice so much as the longing for an emotional reconciliation, a bonding with her. Now, more than any other time in our lives, when we hold our helpless baby in our arms, we cannot afford the old angers at mother. Ironically, mom herself is mellowing, becoming more like the mother we always hoped she would be. But not to us—to our little girl.

Before motherhood, we tried to find with men and other women what we missed with mother. Our husband may have failed us in that search for a perfect, blissful union. (How could he not?) Becoming a mother ends the search. We will never be alone again.

"As a new mother," says psychologist Liz Hauser, "part of what you're looking for in this heavenly blurring of dependency and closeness between you and your child is the desire to be taken care of yourself. If you didn't get enough mothering when you were a baby, this is your chance to do the mothering. It is as if you can make up to the baby for what you didn't get yourself. So in your befuddled, symbiotic way, you get the feeling of tight attachment and unending love. *But you are not the one being taken care of.* The child is getting it all. There is an immense satisfaction in being a mother but not the kind of satisfaction you wanted. You are not the child in this relationship. You are the mother. This is the problem of symbiosis: undefined boundaries. You don't know where you leave off and the child begins. Eventually you become angry because your child is not satisfying your needs. . . .

"This is why women should be aware of separation before they decide to become mothers. They should run checks on themselves after the baby is born. For instance, when you get terribly angry at a child that's been crying and won't stop, ask yourself if the intensity of your anger at that moment isn't derived from your own frustrations that the baby is making you miserable when you want *her* to make *you* happy. All those feelings of closeness and security and mother love you've been dreaming about—where's your payoff?"

Motherhood furnishes great feelings of worth and value, function and pleasure. But a question some women are beginning to ask is, Is there something else I would rather do with my life that would be more satisfying still? In a recent public-opinion poll, three out of four people—men and women alike—thought it OK for women not to have children. My own feeling is that this reflects our changing attitudes—most necessarily our deepest feelings: *it's OK for other people, not me.* But if most women don't think of marriage without children as a permissible option, can it be said that they *chose* to be mothers?

Having a child is still so expected of us, so programmed into our development, that we drift into what is perhaps the most important act of our lives. Our reasons for becoming mothers—difficult as they may be to get at—are the first clue as to whether we will maintain our own identity, and let our child grow into a person—individual and separate from us.

The manner in which a woman relates to her child is one of the marks of her development—or arrested development. If she related symbiotically to her mother, and does the same with her husband, it cannot be said she has grown. Only the cast of characters has changed. In time, the wife may become a bit more independent of her husband, but when their daughter is born, the symbiotic switch is made to the girl.

Cutting the symbiotic tie between mother and daughter can be best begun through an effort of absolute honesty, introspection, and memory. We have to see who mother was, and who we are. What was mother really like when we were little? Was she withholding, not quite attentive enough? Or did she overprotect, intrude, and make us fearful of life without her? Have we been able to face both the good mother and the bad, to know what we love and what we hate, and begun to fuse them all at last without sentimental gloss?

If the reason for having a child is to give yourself an identity, to replay childhood over again the way it should have been, to preserve the marriage, to have someone to live through, or a half dozen other crippling reasons, separation will be very difficult. The daughter cannot be let go because *she is doing something for you.* If she leaves and becomes her own person, you lose your identity, function, the chance to live life all over again.

Making a conscious decision about motherhood is one of the most liberating things that can be done both for ourselves and the unconceived child. Even if we want to become a mother for unrealistic reasons, *just knowing it,* says we are more separate than someone who doesn't make a decision at all, who passively slides from growing up into getting married and then automatically has a child. That kind of sequential thinking—or nonthinking—says we have no real feeling of self. The woman who says, "I want a child because I want to hang on to my husband," has been proved again and again to be acting for wrong and self-defeating reasons, but even she is ahead of the wife who gives birth because that's what you do if you're a woman. Right or wrong, the first woman has decided, she has been active, and taken the responsibility for becoming pregnant.

Deciding that we want a child, knowing why, helps us escape the feeling "they" made us do it. If motherhood is disappointing, if the work of having a baby is more than we reckoned, remembering it was our own idea helps put a damper on making the child feel responsible for being alive.

If the inexorable pattern of repetition between mother and daughter is to be changed, all the denied aspects of our mothers and ourselves must be faced. We have the right to acknowledge at last the fury felt when we were five and she neglected us. But she has the right, now that we are twenty-five, to be allowed to be less than perfect. Seeing mother plain, a mixture of good and bad, is in itself an enormous step toward separation. It helps us from cutting ourselves off from her so totally that we throw away all our good inheritance from her, as well as the parts we don't like.

There are two times in women's lives when the unconscious drive to become the mother we dislike speeds up. The first is when we become mothers ourselves. The second is when our mother dies.

Even beyond the grave, mother continues to be split. The person who died was good. The bad person lives on in us, vile daughters who did not appreciate mother enough while she was still alive.

"My mother died six years ago," says Leah Schaefer, "and I'd had problems of separation from her all my life. I think I took my biggest step toward autonomy when my daughter Katie was born. In my years of psychoanalytic study and practice, I'd come to an intellectual grasp on the symbiotic problem between my mother and me, but I'd never been able to resolve it. When Katie was born, I was forty-two. Only then was I ready to take this giant step in separation from my mother. If I say I did it for the sake of my daughter, I know it was I who benefited from it most. I had always thought it was my mother who insisted on keeping this symbiotic hold on me. Typical wishful thinking, the sheerest projection. I learned I was the major contributor to keeping alive this suffocating attachment between my mother and me.

"All my life I had never denied my mother anything. If I wanted to do something she might not like, I did it secretly. I always believed something terrible would happen if she knew of this other me, my secret self. She would die or reject me if I defeated or denied her. When Katie was born, she wanted to come live with us. I realized that if she did, it would be the end of me. If I gave in to her, as I always had in the past, she would just take over my life and my child. I understood the symbiosis between my mother and me, I could handle that. But now I was a mother and I wanted to raise my daughter to be the individual I was still trying to become. Telling my mother No, that she could not move in with us, was one of the major turning points in my life—a lifelong dependency on her broken.

"It didn't kill her, she didn't reject me. In fact, it was the best thing I ever did for both of us. We think we cannot be straight with our mothers, that they can't take the honesty of who we really are. But it is we who are afraid that if we stand up to them, they will abandon us.

"It was a terrible confrontation when I told my mother No. We both cried. I felt miserable, as though I'd put a knife in her heart. Then several days later, she announced she was returning to California. 'I think married people need to live alone,' she said to me, as though she had come to this decision herself. She was perfectly content with the explanation. She was basically a very independent person, but she had this terrific tie to me, her only daughter. When we said good-bye she was as light-hearted as I'd ever seen her. I felt miserable. You know what my biggest emotion was after she'd left? One word kept running through my mind: *rooked!*

"All my life had been one big compromise because I'd believed that if I ever denied my mother anything, it would mean a withdrawal of her love. I'd had my secret life where I did those things she wouldn't approve of anyway, but it had been paid for by all this guilt. The revelation that I could be myself in front of my mother, tell her No, and that she didn't die and I didn't die, that nothing terrible happened—was incredible. I was married and the mother of a daughter of my own, but emotionally I was still acting like a child who had to have her mother's approval. It was the purest symbiosis. All those years I spent being less of the person I wanted to be because I also felt I had to be her kind of person. Now, here she was tolerating my separation from her very happily."

Dr. Schaefer continues:

"The break with my mother that began when my daughter was born allowed me to begin to see in myself, before she died, the good things I had inherited from her. My mother's dedication to her work made her effective and admirable. I had hated it as a kid because it left me out. Now that I had gained some distance from her, I could see this wasn't 'compulsive' but rather, it was professionalism. Without this dedication to my work, I would not have been able to support myself, to make her last days in the hospital easier, or to pay her financial bills. Unless I had separated from my mother, I would never have allowed myself to see the value of how I am like her in the best ways."

The idea of *melancholia*—in connection with the death of someone toward whom we have ambivalent feelings of love and hate—was developed by Freud and one of his disciples, Dr. Karl Abraham. It is very different from genuine mourning.

In the melancholic, grief is not whole-hearted because the ambivalent rage at the bad mother of infancy has not been resolved. Sorrow cannot be fully expressed and so gotten out. Old feelings of infantile omnipotence come to plague the daughter: her unconscious conscience accuses her of murder.

It is too terrible an idea. We must deny our hatred for the bad mother more strongly than ever. This repression seems to solve the problem. We begin to walk like mother, talk like her; *we become her.* We take in all those parts that once we hated. In this way, we can answer the self-accusation that we are glad she is dead: we are keeping her alive!

By turning our aggression inward, hating those aspects of her we have introjected, we do not have to see it is really directed at her. We hate ourselves instead. The result is a sadness and self-hate that goes on and on, feelings of futility and bewilderment, flashes of seemingly pointless rage amid a general air of depression. Melancholia.

The usual way to avoid the fear of seeing there are parts of mother we hate is to sentimentalize her. Literature tells us very little about what really goes on between children and their mothers. The saccharine sweetness of Mother's Day poetry protests too much.

Most of us need to get over the fear that separation is going to kill mother. Part of this fear of hurting her is puffing up our own importance. Another part is wishful thinking, maintaining the symbiosis. Both may be summed up by the thought, "She cannot live without me." Another part is, "My anger is so terrible, that if I show it to her, it'll kill her."

The Greeks had a word for all this: *hubris.* It meant a kind of overween-ing self-importance, pride, and arrogance. It always led to destruction. Now that we are grown, to decide that mother must be protected as if she were the child—isn't that hubris too?

Guilt is the name we give anxiety at the fear of losing symbiosis with mother. Guilt is what we feel when we leave her ourselves. All our lives, whenever we say good-bye, there is this feeling we have not been able to give her something she wanted. What does she want from us that we can't provide? Next time we meet, we promise ourselves, we will try harder, we will be "a good daughter," we will give her this magic something that will make her happy. But the next time we fail again, and after she dies we know we have failed forever.

I heard ideas like these from women, and in a recent talk with Dr. Ro-bertiello mentioned how often I'd felt them myself. We'd been talking about introjection, and about his father's death; it had occurred while I was writing this chapter. I went on to say that I hoped what I'd learned from my research would "help me avoid all that old sadness and guilt the next time I go home and it comes time to say good-bye." Richard shook his head in mock despair: "Ah, Nancy," he said. "You still haven't inter-grated what you know intellectually with what you feel down deep. It is not guilt you feel, that you cannot make your mother happy. You feel *anxious* that you do not say the right thing, open the magic door, through which all the love you once wanted from her would come flooding through. You still cannot let go of your infantile need of that magic mother of long ago. Your mother is still vigorous and alive, but if you don't come to understand what you are doing, you will continue to blame yourself after she dies. The forsaken feeling will not be that you didn't make her happy, but that you did not do or say the magic thing that would force her—in the sense of infantile omnipotence—to love you as you have waited for all your life.

How many times have I said in this book that my mother and I are to-tally different women? Oh, I acknowledged certain minor virtues I got from her—housekeeping, an easy hostess, etc. But compared to those qualities of hers I have always disliked but taken over anyway—her anxie-ty and the fear which lies beneath my surface independence—how paltry appeared my "good" inheritance. I have always thought I had to leave home to reinforce the qualities in myself I wanted because I felt by nature my mother is a very timid person.

For every step I have taken away from her—my sexuality, my work, the whole dramatic design of my life which overshadows her conservative one—I have been aware of her tugging at my heels, pulling me back. Maybe I "made myself up," but there is not a daring thing I have ever done that has not been accompanied by anxiety. At the beginning of this chapter I had said that one of my strongest reasons for not becoming a mother was I did not want to turn into the kind of nervous, frightened mother she had been to me. Alone, I can control the helpless mother who lives inside me. A mother myself, I would become just like her.

Helpless? Why do I automatically associate that word with her? A woman who raised two daughters on her own, who ran her house smoothly, paid her bills on time, and never set a table or planned a trip where anything was left out? Is she indeed so timid and afraid, so unlike me—the adventurous daughter? To turn that around: am I so unlike her?

It has taken me the entire writing of this book to acknowledge in my heart that the qualities I am proudest of in myself I learned from her. It is unbelievable to me now to think I did not know them last week. "Why, you look just like your mother!" a woman said to me recently. I thought she meant I was wearing my mother's tight, anxious look. But she was thinking of something else. "The last time I saw her," this woman went on, "your mother bid a grand slam. It was four o'clock in the morning, and she made it!"

Stories of my mother's courage have always excited me. The photos of her I love so much hang over my desk—jumping a horse over a high brick wall, wearing a daring two-piece bathing suit twenty-five years ago when she was my age. Why have I refused to credit her for the abilities and emotions I have tried to incorporate in myself?

At one time I would have told you that more than anything else, my sexuality differentiated me from my mother. But she likes men tremendously, and they her. When we are together, I am usually the one who calls the evening to an end; she'd prefer to dance all night. More important, why have I always discounted that when my mother was seventeen she ran away with the handsomest man in Pittsburgh, and married against her father's wishes? I used to make her elopement sound like some out-of-character phenomenon, as if the idea had been totally my father's and she had only passively gone along. The fact is, my "asexual" and "timid" mother was into sex *four years younger than I, who didn't give up her virginity until twenty-one!*

In my absolutism about having made myself up out of no cloth taken from her, I have disinherited myself from my grandmother too. Didn't she leave her dominating husband and their oldest children when she could no longer stand the tyranny—and that in the 1920s, long before liberation, long before the time when a decision like this could be thought anything but mad and irredeemably unfeminine?

There is a strong current in the women in my family that I am bound and determined not to recognize. I come from three generations of sexual, adventurous, self-sufficient women. Is this not more exciting, more profound, than the shallow notion of making myself up? Aren't these the qualities I want most to reinforce in myself? In the service of maintaining a childish tie to a mother who never existed, I have turned my back on the best of my inheritance.

I am suddenly afraid that the mother I have depicted throughout this book is false.

Does this mean that everything I have written so far is false?

"No!" says Dr. Robertiello. "Like everyone else you keep changing your idea of your mother. One day she's good, kind, and loving. The next day, she's frightened, timid, and asexual. One day all you can see is your anger. Right now you want to go into a period of seeing her as all good. Either way, it means you are still avoiding the job of seeing her realistically. You are determined to invest your mother with magic importance—to see her, not as a human being, but in some childlike, monolithic, total way. *That is the way the baby sees her mother.* You are still lost in that first attachment to her, as you were when she was the Giantess of the Nursery."

Seeing mother divested of the symbiotic glamour she once held for us means she becomes another person, someone else, outside of us. Which means we have separated at last. As long as we remained symbiotically linked, there was always hope that it was not too late to get from her the perfect love we always wanted. Now we are grown, and know we never will. We must give up the fantasy and look elsewhere. The idea is sobering. It is maturing too. Most important of all, it is the truth.

I can see now that while I liked my sexuality and wanted to give my mother no credit for it at all, that part of me rested on an uneasy base: if my mother, my image of femininity, was "asexual," then my own sexuality must be "masculine." I was proud of it, but didn't trust it. In this way, until we learn to fuse our mother into one person, we will be at war with ourselves. The cries and slogans of liberation from outside can serve at best to cheer us on. There is no changed history for women until each faces her own.

I said in the first chapter of this book that I'd often wished my mother had had my life. Hubris again, snidely competitive, and damned imperti-

A condensation of the book by

Ruth Kirk

CHAPTER 1

THE ROLE OF SNOW

Try to describe snow, and immediately there arises a question of context. Shall it be the snow that falls as a veil and gently closes a household in upon itself, or the snow that streaks slantwise past the window and blows along the ground, blurring the surface and obscuring even the most familiar landmarks? The snow that to hydrologists is the near-perfect water storage system, or the sort that gives small boys ammunition for snowball fights? The snow used by Eskimos as a building material, or that which becomes the headache of highway maintenance men?

Patterns of snowfall can't always be depended upon. On the night of December 30, 1976, Seattle skiers met to burn skis and chant a supplication for snow; yet that entire winter so little fell on nearby slopes that by the end of January a Puget Sound yacht outlet was advertising: "Skiers, surrender. There's no snow. Your skis accepted as trade on a sailboat." Meanwhile, kitty–cornered across the country, the *Miami News* issued a souvenir edition with a headline three inches high proclaiming snow.

Northward, snow halted winter traffic. The city of Buffalo welcomed a twenty-man "Snow Liberation Crew" from New York City's Sanitation Department, flown in with snowblowers and a scoop loader aboard a U.S. Air Force C-5A transport. Drifts twenty feet deep buried cars and, even where the snow was less deep, nothing moved. Businesses of all kinds slowed, then stopped, prostitution included. "We work only in cars," one hooker complained, "and all the streets are blocked." Thus erratically did North America's winter of 1976–77 enter the record books. Eastern hookers and western skiers were stymied equally by the vagaries of snow, whether an excess of it or a lack.

195

Snow can be valued highly. During the Tokugawa era of Japan, which corresponds to the European medieval period, the powerful daimyo Akimoto regularly curried favor with the shogun by sending snow from Mount Fuji to the court at Edo (the old name for Tokyo). Each summer his horses and porters started from the high slopes heavily laden, and each summer they arrived at the end of the eighty-mile journey with little more than snowballs left. Nonetheless, there was enough to ice drinks and to shape into snow cones over which syrups could be poured, welcome delicacies on hot lowland days and a distinctive touch for the ruling court of the day. In a far more prosaic way, Japanese farmers even now value snow as a way to "read" how far along the season is. Those living in the mountainous region of central Honshu, northwest of Tokyo, set out their rice seedlings when melting snow on the flank of a certain peak takes on the shape of a man holding a hoe. In the Innster district of the European Alps farmers similarly watch for a snow pattern called the White Scythe to appear on the slopes above their fields in late June. Then they mow their hay. In Great Britian archaeologists have identified sites worthy of excavation by photographing from the air right after a light fall of fresh snow has accentuated irregularities of the earth's surface.

Military men have a long history of using snow to their advantage, or of having battles inadvertently affected by its presence. Snow in the mountain passes stopped Alexander from continuing east into India in 330 B.C., and a century later, Hannibal with his elephants incurred losses in the Alps because of the "white enemy." In the thirteenth century, snow blocked the Moors from Spain in their effort to enter France. In the fifteenth century, troops crossing St. Gotthard Pass to aid the Duke of Uri were "wretchedly devoured by an avalanche," and four hundred years later Napoleon crossing the passes en route to the Battle of Marengo instructed his advance guard not to "cry or call out for fear of causing a fall of avalanches." During World War I, Austrian and Italian forces purposely released avalanches in the southern Tyrol, once killing thousands of enemy soldiers in a single day.

Among World War II situations involving snow perhaps the greatest long-range effect came from the Finns' near–defeat of the Russians in the three-month "winter war" of 1939–40. Observing it, the Nazis realized that although Russia ultimately forced its will onto Finland, the war nonetheless very nearly had been a case of David downing Goliath. From this they assumed the Russians to be weak, a grave miscalculation. On the contrary, the bitter Finnish experience taught the Kremlin that coping with snow must be fitted into army training and tactics, and by the time Hitler invaded the Russian homeland in 1943, Stalin's troops were as prepared as the Finns themselves had been earlier.

Across Siberia, Alaska, arctic Canada, and Scandinavia, people living close to the land invariably regard snow as an ally. A few years ago my husband and I flew into Kotzebue, on the Alaskan coast, in late April and found Eskimos sad because there soon could be no more visiting of family and friends across the water. The snow was getting soft. Visiting would have to wait three months, until the ice went out in July, and travel by boat became feasible, whereas through the long winter they had zipped over the snow at will by dog team and snowmobile.

In the past, northern people knew all the varying attributes of snow and employed them. For example, pieces of snow are helpful when you're thirsty, not for eating, but to use as blotters to soak up water from spots that can't be reached directly with lips or a dipper. A good place to look for such water is close against rocks that jut up from a frozen pond; such rocks absorb heat from the sun and melt the ice in immediate touch with them. Or, if you fall through ice into a lake or river, or the ocean, snow can draw the water out of your clothing before it wets through to your skin. All you need do is roll in a snowbank immediately. Cold dry snow will freeze the liquid water onto its crystals and solve your problem.

Snow is remarkably varied. For example, consider hue. There is the glistening white of wet spring snow and the dull powdery white of new-fallen dry snow, the glitter of sequin crystals following a bitterly cold night, and the forlorn grime of snow soiled by city dirt and country dust. Snow can be gray and invisible against the horizon on an overcast day, or it may turn violet-blue as the rays of incoming light are filtered out except for the blue end of the spectrum. Frank Debenham, a geologist in the Antarctic with the explorer Robert Scott, once told of showing the expedition ornithologist, Bill Wilson, a polar landscape he had painted in tones of dull white. Wilson, himself an accomplished artist, asked, "Is that what you really saw —white snow? It's very rare, you know." Thereupon Debenham stepped outside and realized that it was not an all-pervading whiteness that dominated his senses. Instead the snow was shadowed and textured, reflecting tints of the sky.

Usually the exact hue of snow is a matter of lighting. But it can be built in. Pink snow regularly patches the alpine country of western North America from California's Sierra Nevada to Alaska's Brooks Range, and it is scattered throughout the world's high elevations and high latitudes. In this case the color comes from the chilly counterparts of hotspring algae, well known for their brightening of steaming pools at Yellowstone and

Mount Lassen. Algae are among the planet's most adaptable life–forms, surviving from nearly boiling to well below freezing. Of species living their whole cycles in snowbanks, the most abundant forms tint the snow from faintly rosy to decidedly watermelon-red, depending on concentration. At times such snow even takes on the aroma of watermelon (although not the taste). Other forms of algae turn snow yellow or green, and at least in Europe one type turns snow blue.

More than one hundred species of algae have been identified in snow and mapped geographically. Investigators now find a whole ecological chain of minute life-forms in snow, dependent ultimately on algae as the bottom of the food pyramid. For instance, the snow worms that Robert Service immortalized are real. Living at Mount Rainier, Washington, where my husband served as park ranger, we occasionally observed the conversion of colleagues from skeptics in this matter into believers. In one case a ranger who was stationed close to the six-thousand-foot level of the mountain, where snow usually lasts into August, customarily chilled drinks by reaching out the window for handfuls of snow. He did this with a ritualistic flair intended to impress guests with the romance of ranger life. Then came an evening of sad truth when worms were found in the bottoms of the glasses!

Worms, as algae, are common in snow and ice, several species of them strictly limited to such a habitat. All belong to the one genus *Mesenchytraeus*, a distant relative of earthworms. Sometimes these worms congregate by the thousands, writhing at the surface of a snowbank like so many fine, inch-long bits of thread. Black is the most common color, although some are brown. The pigment evidently lets the worms melt their way up and down through the snow by absorbing heat from the sun. Algae supply food through the hot months and when cold comes the worms vanish, as well as the algae. Probably they, too, go beneath the snow, although nobody knows postively. Springtails, or "snow fleas," are another form of small animal life that thrives in snowfields. There also are minuscule rotifers and protozoans, a decomposer chain of bacteria and fungi that breaks down the organic debris of all the life-forms, and a predator chain including spiders that feed on the snow fauna and birds that feed on the spiders. Sterility, often associated with snow, really isn't one of its inherent characteristics.

Neither is the common assumption that snowflakes never duplicate one another necessarily true. No dictum of nature keeps all snowflakes from being identical, however renowned their variety; and, since no physical force imposes differences between them, mathematical odds probably favor duplication. Such twins haven't been reported, but the sheer number of flakes that fall and their fleeting existence as separate crystals augur against enough observation to say for sure one way or the other.

It takes more than one million crystals to blanket a two-square-foot area with snow ten inches deep. Multiply this by the nearly one quarter of the world's land surface that is whitened each winter and by a total annual snowfall that in places amounts to two hundred feet or more, and the possibility of duplication—if not the certainty of it—becomes impossible to deny. Having thus computed volume, next add to it the number of snowflakes that reach the earth yearly and also of those that turn into rain on the way down; then multiply this by the eons snow has fallen, and the odds favoring duplication rise still more. Yet the wonder of snowflakes' formation and pattern remains undiminished whether or not a crystal caught this year on a gloved finger may possibly have had an identical counterpart that millennia ago became part of the Greenland ice cap.

If not infinite, the variety of snow crystals is nonetheless great—and correctly speaking, snow crystals should be distinguished from snow-flakes. A flake is an assemblage of individual crystals, both whole and broken, joined together in falling. Such flakes may be as much as an inch, or even two or three inches, in diameter. They form only at relatively mild temperatures. The polar regions, for instance, never receive snowflakes but only separate crystals, usually so fine and simple as to be virtual snow dust.

In 1951 the International Commission on Snow and Ice proposed a classification scheme recognizing seven basic forms of falling snow crystals plus ice pellets, hail, and graupel (crystals heavily coated with rime). These seven are star, plate, needle, column, column with a cap at each end, spatial dendrite, and irregular. Partly to sort out the "irregulars," C. Magano and C. U. Lee a few years later classified 101 types of snow crystals, making fine distinctions such as hollow bullet, solid bullet, column with dendrites, cup, pyramid, hexagonal plate, stellar crystal with plates at ends, and so on. Of these the stellar crystals are the ones most commonly known. They are assumed the most typical and are the form behind the "no two alike" belief. Beyond question such stars, often perfect and intricately patterned, rate as the most beautiful of all. But they also are not the most common. Irregular, unsymmetrical crystals and aggregates formed into flakes are far more typical.

Wilson A. Bentley, an American farmer-photographer, a century ago gave the public its first magnified look at the exquisite intricacy of individual snow stars. For forty years he photographed, producing over six thousand photomicrographs, one-third of which were published in 1931 in a book called *Snow Crystals*. Bentley selected his subjects largely on an esthetic basis and even retouched some negatives to enhance the crystals' beauty. His results, thus, are more selective and idealized than truly representative of snow as it falls. What form a crystal will take depends largely on temperature and the availability of water vapor. Bentley knew this and commented that the crystals he concentrated upon fell only under certain conditions. But the beauty of his images overshadowed the truth of his words so far as the public was concerned, and, seeing representations mostly of flawless stars, popular belief mistakenly began to consider them the most frequent type.

From early times men have pondered the singular nature of snow. Among early Chinese scholars the six-sided nature of snow crystals was attributed to water, and both snow and water were given an association with number six. In Germany the seventeenth-century astronomer Johannes Kepler published a small pamphlet speculating at length on the "six corneredness" of snow, but without realizing its true crystalline nature. About the same time the French mathematician and philosopher René Descartes, who was living in Holland at the time, published the first scientifically accurate drawings of flakes and commented on various shapes in addition to six-sided, single-plane crystals.

It is known that six sides are basically inherent in the atomic structure of snow crystals, although some are three–sided or five–sided. Form and growth rate are the product of environmental conditions. At a given saturation of air and with a certain type of nuclei present, hexagonal plates form at temperatures from freezing to 27° F.; needles at 27 to 23°: hollow prismatic columns at 28 to 18°; hexagonal plates again, but of a different type, at 18 to 10°; fernlike stars at 10 to 3°; plates at 3 to -13°; and hollow prismatic columns at -13 to -58° F. At least snow-crystal growth works this way in a laboratory cold chamber. Simply lowering or raising a hair within the chamber to move from one temperature zone to another will change the form of a crystal growing on it.

Artificial production of snow in cold chambers has greatly eased study because working only with natural snow often is troublesome. Snow generally is studied at the earth's surface, yet it forms high in the atmosphere and changes constantly while falling and after alighting. What happens as snow forms in the clouds probably never can be as fully understood as what happens in a cold chamber, but since the same kinds of crystals are produced under both circumstances certain statements can be made confidently.

Snow is unique as a chemical compound capable of a great variety of crystal habits. Its basic structure consists of molecules with one oxygen atom at the corner of two hydrogen atoms held by electric charges at 120-degree angles from the oxygen atom. A single snow crystal may have 100 million such molecules, each with this 120–degree arrangement. To start growing, a crystal needs a nucleus with a suitable molecular structure. This may be dust from a farmer's field or a volcanic eruption, exhaust gas from city traffic, salt spray from the ocean, a tiny splinter of ice broken from a falling snow crystal, or even a micro-organism. Given some such suitable nuclei, crystals will develop, providing droplets are present within a cloud of the right temperature or that there is an excess of water vapor present. If these conditions are met, droplets will sublimate onto the nuclei, in the process setting up minuscule currents that catch additional vapor molecules which also whirl onto the surface of the crystal and become part of it. Depending on temperature at the time of nucleation, growth may be dendritic, platelike, or columnar; and whatever form a crystal takes at first its final growth will be determined by temperature, humidity, and barometric pressure, all of which vary with altitude.

In general, large intricate crystals form at relatively warm cloud temperatures when ample moisture is present, and small elementary crystals form at low temperatures when the air holds less moisture. If a falling crystal drops into air warmer than itself, sublimation quickens. Rays shoot out until the crystal warms to the temperature of the new air layer. Then, differences lessened, a new growth pattern starts. Since crystals fall with their broad surfaces roughly horizontal and they usually rotate, their edges are in contact with the most water vapor, and growth takes place primarily there. If a crystal, or a flake, passes through a layer of supercooled droplets while falling, it will be coated with rime. Droplets remain liquid at below freezing temperatures only so long as they stay suspended; they freeze the instant they touch anything solid, including falling snow. If enough droplets coat a crystal it becomes graupel, a tiny soft lump so heavily rimed that the underlying crystal form can't be seen.

Snow changes as it forms and falls, and it continues to change after landing. On the ground snow passes through stages of metamorphism that lead ultimately to glacial ice if conditions are right, but the process may—and probably will—be interrupted at any stage. The fluffy blanket of new snow that falls without wind and softens the winter earth is an unstable emulsion of air and flakes. It is a froth. The larger the flakes, the looser they lie and the more quickly they change. The more intricately branched they are, the larger their surface in proportion to volume, which in itself carries a tendency for the redistribution of mass and energy. A rounding of form results, lessening the ratio between surface and mass. Apparently this occurs primarily as molecules sublimate away from the points of stars, where vapor pressure is greatest, and are redeposited into the notches between rays. The hollows of a crystal thus fill in at the expense of points and edges. Intricate pattern and surface detail are lost, and small round grains eventually result. Each may retain the mass of the earlier crystal, but the form is changed forever. Or, in a similar way, small crystals may lose their molecules to large ones; fine projections have higher pressures than large ones, and so small crystals with the sharpest angles lose molecules to adjoining large crystals with blunter angles. In this way snow settles and becomes denser. At this stage it is called "old snow," a term that applies to the stage of crystal growth rather than to the passing of time.

If metamorphism continues, *firn* develops from old snow. This is a further compaction and hardening, with bonds from grain to grain tighter and mechanical strength and density increased, but with spaces still remaining between the grains. If the process continues still farther, firn becomes glacial ice. Individual grains touch, and air is present only as bubbles within the crystals, not in spaces between them. At this stage what once was snow takes on a vitreous character.

Snow layers close to the ground usually are warmer than upper layers because of heat given off by the earth. The effect of this is that vapor moves within snow from lower and warmer layers to upper and colder layers, and new crystals form. Their shapes may be hollow cups, prisms, scrolls, columns, or hexagons, depending on conditions of growth. Near the bottom of a snowpack, depth hoar may form, a layer so porous as to amount to little more than a latticework of ice walls and space. Depth hoar can't bear much of a load without collapsing and may be highly susceptible to shearing. It is the bane of cross-country skiers, since its hidden layers continually give way; but for the same reason it is the blessing of animals such as northern lynx which easily break into it and feed on voles they hear scampering about at the ground surface.

Of external forces affecting snow, none outranks wind. It may pack falling flakes into a firm crystalline blanket rather than a soft airy one, or it may drift already fallen snow into gentle ripples or sharply pinnacled *sastrugi*. It may build cornices that curl over mountain ridges, or etch graceful saucers around tree trunks and boulders and chalet corners as eddies first spiral particles upward, then bring them back into the main wind stream. Wind mechanically rounds snow crystals by shattering delicate rays and spikes, simplifying their outline and fitting them together more tightly. It also steps up the rate of sublimation, eating away molecules along the points and margins of crystals by evaporation. Wind brings atmospheric vapor to condense onto snow and freeze, thereby enlarging grains and bonding them. It sorts grains by size and deposits them into layers that vary with density, permeability, and thermal character.

Layering persists throughout the life of a snowpack and even after its transformation into glacial ice. Cores taken at Byrd Station from as deep as four hundred feet within antarctic ice show distinct layers representing centuries. On the Blue Glacier of Mount Olympus, Washington, I remember one night descending a seventy-foot vertical shaft dug through five years' worth of snow layers which, toward the bottom of the shaft, had been compressed into ice. The shaft was large enough for one person at a time to be winched up or down in an oversize canvas bucket while a fluorescent tube was raised or lowered in a second, smaller shaft separated by eight or ten inches from the main shaft. The tube's glow backlit the ice and disclosed the layering in a manner all the more dramatic because of the night's inherent blackness and one's own awareness of descending through the snowstorms of the past as well as through the inner structure of a glacier.

Living at Mount Rainier showed us how much snow varies according to exact conditions. Through the winter, wet snow piled like pillows onto every horizontal surface, from the crossbars and seats of our sons' swings to the rough ridges of tree bark. On cold days it squeaked underfoot as individual crystals rubbed against each other and broke, and on days close to freezing, or above it, silently compressed beneath boot soles and skis. When summer came, climbing the mountain was simplified by crusted snow that would bear our weight, or made harder by crust so icy that the points of crampons and ice axes wouldn't bite in or so soft that if broke beneath each step. Even worse was no crust, when we sank ankle-deep in slush or found our crampons balling up with snow stuck to their spikes. Adhering snow then must be repeatedly knocked off by hitting the side of your foot with your ice ax every other step or so. When one is weary, this added effort can seem too much, and I remember on my first Rainier summit climb that I fell again and again on the descent as my crampons balled up.

From a scientific standpoint a litany of terms describes the differences and changes within snow: allotriomorphic-granular, hypediomorphic-granular; paratectonic perecrystallization, regelation, congelation, infiltration, densification. The words precisely describe the variations and continuing stages of state within snow, only slightly suspected by most of us who stand at the top of a ski lift or shovel a walkway clear after a blizzard. Certain properties of snow, ill defined within our minds though they may be, nonetheless, evoke characteristic human responses. The urge to slide, for instance, seems nearly universal, whether on skis or sleds or with the simple wooden clogs traditionally soled with metal for the delight of children in nothern Japan or the "sliding shoes" that coastal Eskimo parents made for their children (ovals of skin worn under the boots and held with straps).

The ready compressibility and cohesiveness of snow also elicit a predictable response: snowballs. Even those who never before have seen snow may become instant boys. Three African dignitaries once came to Mount Rainier following a summer international conference, their faces elaborately tattooed, their teeth filed and set with diamonds, their robes richly brocaded, their bearing totally regal. Yet the moment they saw snow the air filled with snowballs. Gold slippers wet and robes of state flapping, the battle was on. So irresistible is this urge that Eskimo children in a village along Alaska's Kobuk River whom I asked about their feelings toward snow invariably answered in terms of play. They mentioned sliding, snow fights, snowmen, tunneling in snow, making snow dolls, mounding snow into targets to shoot arrows into, and drawing in the snow with sticks.

Perhaps not surprisingly, animals as well as humans seem to delight in snow. Hiking in the Olympic Mountains one July, I watched a black bear slide down a snowpatch on its belly, them lumber back up and repeat the pleasure. In similar fashion polar bear sows stand to catch their cubs at the bottom of a snow slide and wait indulgently while the young run up to slide again. Otters are renowned for their snow slides, and evidently snowshoe hares also play in snow. When the whitened world gleams in the moonlight they sometimes gather in considerable numbers to bound and leap in a pixilated dance that is apt to end abruptly as the silhouette of an owl glides silently overhead.

All who have experienced snow more than once or twice know that some kinds will do for snowballs—or any other specific purpose—whereas others won't. Snow isn't simply snow; it is different kinds of snow. English expresses this poorly. A language developed in a moderate climate, it lacks the subtleties needed to speak adequately of snow. Northern peoples, however, have the words for fluent, concise description. For instance, an English speaker might talk about "a place that has been cleared of snow by the wind," but a Soviet tribal hunter of the Altai or Transbaikal could use the single precise word *vyduv*. English speaks of "an accumulation of snow blown into a depression and likely to remain there well into the summer," whereas *zaboy* says the same thing. Furthermore, these single snow words are more than labels; they carry amplifying connotations. A vyduv is where reindeer graze in winter; a zaboy is where they lie in summer to escape from flies.

Probably the greatest linguistic finesse of all belongs to the Eskimos whose lives are so filled with snow that they phrase the question "How old are you?" by asking "How many snows-there-is-none have you seen?" Their language—so similar around the entire arctic basin that a seal hunter from Greenland can understand one from Alaska—distinguishes two dozen or more kinds of snow. There is new-fallen, soft snow; fluffy deep snow that fell without wind; wind-packed snow firm enough to walk on; wet snow belonging to springtime; the walk-anywhere crust of an early morning that comes after a cold night; and the same crust after it has thawed to corn snow but is still fine for traveling; dry sugary snow; snow for igloos; long tapered drifts in the lee of objects; rounded smooth drifts; snow lying on the slope of a hill; local ground drift; extensive ground drift—and more, more, more.

Ironically, snow brings warmth of a sort, for the earth's white "blanket" is literally that, a blanket. It holds in the warmth of the earth and wards off the frost of winter air. This affects the wild plants of the tundra and taiga and alpine meadows, and it presents an immeasurable boon to nothern farmers. Where snow is lacking across the prairies and steppes, soil regularly freezes to a depth of several inches. One Russian comparative study showed that with a six-inch blanket of snow, frost penetrated less than an inch into the soil, whereas adjoining snow-free fields were frozen for more than a foot. Futhermore, snow not only insulates against low minimum temperatures but also against fluctuations. A bare soil surface may be heated by direct sunshine, then cooled in seconds as clouds pass overhead, and its temperatures often surge drastically from day to night. Snow moderates these swings and that can be a crucial advantage, depending on plants' hardiness, for winterkill and stunted growth can occur without actual freezing.

Surprisingly, snow also benefits plants directly by supplying them with fertilizer. One investigator places the value of this to prairie farmers at around twenty dollars an acre in nitrates spread on the fields by an average winter's snow. French peasants have a proverb to the effect that a proper February snowfall is worth a pile of manure. Sulphate, calcium, and potassium, as well as nitrates, are delivered to the earth by snow (and rain). These ions—and others in lesser amounts—come from ocean air masses, dust from the earth, atmospheric gases, and industrial pollution.

Not all growth fostered by snow is a blessing to farmers, however. Snow mold is a curse throughout the cereal belt of the world. If snow falls early, especially on unfrozen soil, certain fungi may become active enough to menace young plants. Even if the plants are only moderately affected, they may lose so much nitrogen from blighted leaves that they respond slowly to spring warmth, which ultimately increases problems of weed control and delays harvesting. Snow favors the growth of fungi by holding soil surface temperature close to freezing and maintaining a high humidity. Ample oxygen is present even when snow lies deep, and since fungal growth thrives on dim light anyway the near-darkness doesn't matter. A foot and a half of snow has been found to reduce light by 99.5 percent, which is ideal for snow mold. Green plants can't photosynthesize under such conditions, however, and the longer they go without manufacturing food the more their leaf proteins break down, weakening them and making them susceptible to disease.

Hastening snowmelt by spreading whitened fields with fine peat, wood ashes, lamp black, powdered graphite, or coal dust mixed with talc is one way to reduce the danger of snow mold. But to be effective, whatever material is used should be insoluble in water and coarse enough to stay on the snow surface and ride it down as melt takes place. If it dissolves or sinks into the snow and disappears, it is useless. Dusting from planes makes this method of speeding up snowmelt feasible, but the process is a gamble at best. New snow may bury a freshly blackened surface, or a warm spell may melt a shallow snow cover and render the dusting just that much money wasted. Furthermore, any speeding of melt to control fungus must be balanced against its effect on soil moisture, for snow acts as a natural reservoir. In fact, pamphlets for farmers on how to accumulate snow on their acreages far outnumber those for melting it ahead of schedule.

Drift fences and barriers of vegetation with strong, flexible, close-set stalks can control where snowdrifts form and how deep they get. Without such management, snow may blow and be lost, carrying away a major source of water. Even low stubble catches about four times as much snow as fields left fallow.

Snow can be manipulated. Where it is to fall and when it should melt can be decided by man to a considerable degree. To some extent even glaciers—the fossil snow of past millennia—can be pressed into our service. The potential of this control is enormous. Three quarters of the earth's fresh water is stored in glaciers, the equivalent of about seventy-five years' worth of snow and rain for the whole globe at current rates. By far the greatest glaciers are located in the polar and subpolar regions—remote, yet perhaps not beyond reach of technological man if agriculture or industry becomes thirsty enough. At present southern California researchers, financed by the National Science Foundation, have proposed towing icebergs north from Antarctica to meet water needs in the Los Angeles basin, and the Saudi Arabian government has asked French engineers to work out the feasibility of towing antarctic bergs through the Indian Ocean and the Red Sea to the port of Jidda.

Antarctic bergs are fairly smooth and manageable in shape, and as big as 150 miles across and 1,000 feet thick, an incredible volume even allowing for melt on the long trip north. (And melt would be minimized by covering the ice with plastic quilts almost two feet thick, calculated to hold the loss to no more than 10 percent of a berg's volume). Tugboats of the type used to haul oil-drilling platforms would tow the icebergs, probably making only about one knot an hour. This would mean an eight- or ten-month trip from McMurdo Sound to Los Angeles, about six months to Jidda. On arrival close to port, the bergs could be tethered and quarried by a scoop. It would feed great chunks onto a conveyor belt for delivery into a submerged pipe connected to the shore. Stockpiled in cold storage on land, the ice then could be melted as needed. Its water would be the purest available to any major city, and the cost for Los Angeles should be about one-third of what the city now pays for water brought by aqueduct from nothern California. For the Saudis the cost would be far less than that of desalinization.

In a long-range sense ancient snow, compressed into glacial ice, constitutes the major potential water source for a world faced with a probable doubling of population within the next two generations and a need of water for everything from drinking and bathing to growing corn (ten thousand gallons per bushel) and producing steel (sixty-five thousand gallons per ton). On a current basis, without stepping up ice melt, our yearly blanket of fresh snow constitutes a sort of placental support for humanity linked by aqueducts and irrigation ditches and transmission wires from the mountains to cities and fields. The wheat that grows in eastern Washington and the electricity used by Puget Sound communities depend on snowfields in Canada, which give birth to the mighty Columbia River. The lettuce from southern California and the cotton from adjoining Sonora, Mexico, and even the bright lights of Hollywood, are the products of snow that falls in the Rocky Mountains and flows through the desert as the muddy water of the Colorado River.

Until recent years nobody dreamed of harnessing glacier water, but the concept of surveying winter snowfields for their probable moisture yield originated decades ago. Oddly, one man's personal exuberance for the winter mountains got events underway—and he wasn't an engineer cannily assessing possibilities but a professor of Greek and Latin: Dr. James Church of the University of Nevada.

Mount Rose, a few miles south of the university campus in Reno, drew Dr. Church like a magnet. In 1895 he and a friend celebrated New Year's Eve by climbing the 10,800-foot peak equipped with "nothing but rubbers and one pair of webs [snowshoes] for the two of us." Mountaineers today might well call such an ill-prepared ascent irresponsible, but at the time no communications or rescue networks existed to concern themselves with other people's routes and itineraries. At Christmas six years later Church and his wife spent a week in a cabin at the 9,000-foot level of the mountain, each evening setting a dead pine afire to let friends below in Reno know that all was well. In 1906 a winter climb of Mount Whitney in California drew him. Whitney, at 14,495 feet, is the highest peak in the United States outside Alaska.

Personal enjoyment—adventure—prompted these treks into the snowy heights, but after Church returned from Whitney he talked with power company officials in Reno about putting his obsession to work. They wanted information on the upper reaches of the watershed; he offered to climb Mount Rose each month and take temperature readings. He had no particular instruction in such undertaking, only some experience in climbing through snow and a boundless enthusiasm. The power company thought the proposal worth a try, and Church arranged for horses to haul a small instrument shelter over the snow to the summit of Mount Rose. He and a colleague then commenced bi-weekly ascents, leaving sleeping bags hanging from the limb of a giant pine at nine thousand feet, so that they could sleep there one night, then climb on to read the instruments the next morning.

The scientific community and the press followed the readings from the mountaintop with interest, for at the time few specifics of high-elevation conditions were known. From that point of origin, the methods developed by Dr. Church became the standard not only for the western United States but for the continent and abroad in nations such as Norway, Sweden, Switzerland, India, Chile, and Argentina. His Mount Rose Sampler, as first designed, consisted of steel tubing in lengths of up to ten feet. These could be screwed together to reach through a snowbank and extract a sample of snow from its entire depth, clear to the ground. Through the years various aspects have been modified. Aluminum tubing, fitted with steel cutting teeth, now reduces the weight by about half, and tube lengths are reduced to thirty inches for ease in handling. Fiberglass and plastic lining minimize sticking and simplify getting samples from deep, dense snow. Oversnow vehicles have been added to skis and snowshoes as a means of running snow courses, and telemetry, helicopters, and satellite photography now increase still more the reliability and sensitivity of snow readings.

Surveys have become a matter of men closeted in warm offices surrounded by electronic scales and calculators that are recording the conditions of distant, cold slopes. One system relies on a series of stakes set out in snow courses for which long-range data already are known. These are photographed from the air to provide readings of snow depth for comparison against the overall mean. Another system involves metal pillows that register the weight of snow falling onto them. A third relies on gamma emissions from lead-shielded packets of cobalt–60 set at ground level before the first snowstorm of the winter. A counter suspended above each packet measures the rays emitted by the cobalt and beamed straight upward, and, because water impedes their transmission, the resulting electronic pulses can be correlated to the moisture content of the snow.

Satellites orbiting the earth now map snow cover and, although depth and moisture content can't yet be detected by this means, what they tell about the extent of snow has proven extremely accurate both in mountainous terrain and across flat land. This is true despite the interference with some readings from clouds and thick canopies of coniferous forest. Radar can be used to estimate the water equivalency of snow while it is falling and to map the thickness of glacial ice. Seismic waves also measure glaciers from their surface to bedrock, and ice buried beneath the rock and gravel of a moraine can be detected by how it radiates infrared energy from deep within the earth.

Myriad complications interfere with all of this modern wizardry but, even so, its cumulative accuracy is relied upon for an ever-escalating range of applications and, rather than tasting triumph in their ability to read the hitherto undecipherable, today's forcasters more nearly feel concern over the possible consequences of misinterpretations. Should ski resorts prepare for a severe avalanche season? The answer lies in assessing the amount of snowpack and its nature. Will there be water enough for farmers, or should they reduce their planting? What of floods? And what of the prospects for hydroelectric power generation? How about increased roof load on buildings throughout the snow belt? Is there a threat of serious pollution if spring melt lags behind normal and fails to dilute adequately the effluent carried by rivers? Such pollution has occurred. The social and economic impacts of snow surveys are crucial for the technological world.

Increasingly also, men today are served by information from the snows of the past. Lying layer on layer within glacial ice, they can be "read" for a surprisingly large amount of baseline data with which to compare our present conditions with those that have gone before. Volcanic eruptions through the centuries have left signatures in the form of ash fallen onto what at the time were the surfaces of the snow. Ice cores taken from Antarctica revealed two thousand such ash deposits during the last seventy-five thousand years. Radioactive snow gives incontrovertible proof of nuclear explosions in the atmosphere. Extraterrestrial fallout also shows up in glaciers—part of the more than nine million metric tons of micrometeorites that shower the earth each year at present rates. Most of these tiny fragments are hopelessly difficult to differentiate from the earthly dust they fall onto, but not so with the fragments that land on snowfields. They show plainly, and continue to do so as layers of fresh snow and of additional micrometeorite showers build on top of them.

A possibly alarming increase in the lead content of the environment has been noticed by ecological sleuths analyzing the icefields of Greenland. It correlates with human contamination of our planetary nest. A fivefold increase in lead shows up for snow layers dated from 800 B.C. to A.D. 1750, and another fourfold increase is recorded from 1750 to 1940. The percentage rise since 1940 is even sharper. The figures reflect man's activity beginning with the Industrial Revolution, particularly widespread coal burning and metal smelting, and also a wholesale use of leaded gasoline in automobiles since World War II (most of it attributable to the United States alone). Analysis of snow layers within antarctic ice presents a different picture. Even recent lead levels there so far are scarcely above those of ancient ice, and the difference from one hemisphere to the other seems to be the concentration of industrial activity in the north.

A large portion of the earth falls within the realm of snow. If the cold regions are defined as where the coldest month averages freezing or below, then about half of the land in the nothern hemisphere is included. For the United States, the line angles down the Cascade Range of Washington and Oregon and continues slightly west of the California–Nevada border, then about at Reno starts wavering across the continent between the thirty-fifth and fortieth parallels. The spectacular red sandstone country of northern Arizona and New Mexico is included. The Texas panhandle and Arkansas are barely inside the line, which then continues eastward across southern Kansas, the middle of Missouri, southern Illinois, Indiana, and Ohio. From there it follows below the Pennsylvania border and goes out to sea beyond New Jersey, New York, and Connecticut. New England is within the cold region, both coastal and inland.

In Europe the line strikes southward along the fjord coast of Norway, runs along the German and French border, follows the Alps practically to Monaco and eastward across the top of Italy, then swings down through Yugoslavia, across Bulgaria to the Black Sea, on across Iran, north India, Tibet, and into China just north of Shanghai. Japan lies largely outside the line, except for the nothernmost island of Hokkaido plus Honshu from Sendai, north. From the Asian coast the line crosses the Pacific to the Aleutians and starts south along the Alaskan panhandle and the British Columbia coast. Plotted along a zero-degree Fahrenheit line, instead of a freezing line, this nothern cold region leaves out all of the United States except for a narrow arc of North Dakota and Minnesota. Europe is entirely out, and the line enters Siberia from the Arctic Ocean following the Ural Mountains, at sixty degrees north longitude. This puts the whole of Siberia inside the line (except for the Kamchatka Peninsula), and Mongolia and Manchuria also are included.

Almost equally vast regions are delineated by plotting the realm of permafrost, permanently frozen ground which causes soil to swell and settle, and buildings to cant off plumb and highways to buckle. Permafrost reaches as deep as one thousand feet into the earth in places, and where it does facilities as basic as water supply become major problems. A deep well may be mechanically unsound, and a shallow one will freeze up. Pipelines cannot be exposed to freezing, and they also must not be allowed to transfer heat into the ground and disturb its thermal regime. The upper ground, which may freeze and thaw each year, will change from rock-hard in winter to oozing mud in spring, and during fall freeze-up stresses as great as fourteen tons per square inch can be expected.

Still another way to define the cold regions of the earth is by snow. It blankets half the land surface of our planet at least temporarily and 10 percent of the ocean surface. About forty-eight million square miles of the earth's surface lie under a constant blanket of white; about six million square miles ice-covered, the rest snow-covered, sometimes deeply so.

Within the United States the record for deep snow belongs to Paradise, situated on a mile-high shoulder of Mount Rainier, where the winter of 1970-71 brought 1,027 inches of snow. Even in nonrecord years winter entry into the patrol cabins throughout the high country of the park is by digging down to a second-story window. The next heaviest snowfalls recorded in the United States have been at Thompson Pass, Alaska, with 974 inches for the 1952-53 season, and near Lake Tahoe in Tamarack, California, with 884 inches in 1906-07. In the single month of January 1911, Tamarack registered 390 inches of new snow. In a single storm, from February 13 to 19, 1959, the Mount Shasta Ski Bowl in nothern California was covered with a 189-inch snowfall, and in one 24-hour period, during April 1921, Silver Lake, Colorado, received a 76-inch blanket.

Such record amounts, however, have relevance only for our time. In broad perspective they are as fleeting as the snowdrifts themselves, for climate doesn't hold steady, and the land that lies white and cold today may well have grown tropical plants in the past and will do so again. Major snow celebrations as diverse as Alaska's 1,150-mile Iditarod sleddog race from Anchorage to Nome, and Japan's festival of snow sculpture held in Sapporo each winter, belong strictly to the present, from a climate standpoint as well as culturally. So do everyday events, from prairie farmers tying a rope between house and barn to prevent getting lost during blizzards to snow-country mothers the world around endlessly dressing their tots for snow play, then a few minutes later undressing them. For Buffalo hookers and Seattle skiers—and Bronx Zoo reindeer—the pattern of expected snowfall is based on a period of time so brief as to be indistinguishable within the full flow of earth history. And it is this broad scale that determines present-day climate.

It is one we have only begun to grasp.

CHAPTER 2

THE CLIMATE PENDULUM

Freak storms from time to time dump snow onto dismayed Floridians and whiten the lowland deserts of Arizona and California. A February 1887 snowfall is on record as having blanketed San Francisco with four or five inches, resulting in arrests for snowball attacks on cable cars.

Such storms may be one-time occurrences, or they may portend change. Many signs and many years of data have to be combined before a trend can be read accurately. Recently, climate has shown signs both of warming and of cooling. Farmers in southern Ontario a few years ago began to experiment with cotton, Icelanders to plant oats, and New England lumbermen to lose their stands of white birch. Why? Because of worldwide warming—which apparently now may be ending, for other signs point to the onset of cooling. British farmers have seen their growing season decline by about two weeks since 1950, with a resultant serious loss in grain production.

Perhaps the best place on earth to grasp firsthand the alternate gripping and releasing of the land by cold is at Glacier Bay, Alaska, not far from Juneau. There the white sterility of active ice is edged by the raw brown mineral debris of land newly free from glaciers and in process of green reconquest by plants. Sixteen glaciers thrust as walls of ice into the water of today's fjords, splitting off great slabs that ride as icebergs until they melt.

The birds feed close to the calving glaciers, fluttering to the water to dine on crustacea that get churned to the surface by the belly flopping of the freshly calved icebergs, and by the torrential flow of meltwater. The mineral nutrients of the water are increased where glaciers reach to the sea, disgorging the rock flour they have scoured from the land and the organic debris accumulated within the ice because of the life-forms living in it and the material blown or washed onto it. Thus enriched to a veritable broth, the water supports abundant small life-forms which, in turn, sustain larger forms, even to whales. Harbor seals frequent the ice-choked upper reaches of the inlets, hauling out on pan ice to give birth to their pups in early summer, and to sun and nap. Tlingit Indians took seals within Glacier Bay in ancestral times before advancing ice forced them to move to new land. With the ice again now pulled back, men from Hoonah Village returned to hunt, their new, efficient weapons gravely threatening the seals until recently when a protective agreement was signed.

Ice is withdrawing from parts of Glacier Bay at a rate believed faster than anywhere else in the world. It pulls back as much as a quarter mile per year, releasing land to lie as a primal moonscape of bare silt and gravel and rock. Captain George Vancouver explored this part of the coast in 1794, but he could sail only ten miles into Glacier Bay. Ice four thousand feet thick choked the rest, walling it so spectacularly that Vancouver referred in his log to "solid mountains of ice rising perpendicularly from the water's edge." In the time that has passed since then—a period that is no time at all geologically—the ice has withdrawn from forty to seventy miles up the bay and, overall, continues to retreat each year.

Born of yesterday's snows and nourished by those of today, several glaciers that feed into Glacier Bay now measure a mile wide at tidewater. Their cliff faces rise one hundred to two hundred feet above the surface, and an equal or greater extent rests unseen beneath the water. In summer the main current of the large ice tongues moves forward as much as ten feet a day, while for the glaciers as a whole, movement holds to somewhere around one-third that amount. Yearly discharge is from five million to nine million cubic feet of ice from a single tidewater glacier, a stupendous amount in itself, let alone multiplied by the full complement of such ice in Glacier Bay and elsewhere on the Alaskan coast.

The sight and sound of the icebergs' birth rate is one of the world's great nature experiences. Twice my husband and I have surrendered to the allure and stayed for a few days at Reid Inlet in upper Glacier Bay. One of these times we slept aboard a small cruiser anchored close to the beach. Bergs repeatedly hit us, a thundering crash separated from the eardrum by no more than the quarter-inch fiber glass of the hull. Had ice ridden into the anchor line we might have been in trouble. But none did. Instead the icy world seemed pervaded by peace.

On our second trip we watched the calving of icebergs off the Margerie Glacier, several inlets distant from Reid. A mounting series of thundering and cracking noises would herald blocks breaking loose and, since we were in a boat a mile off the ice front, the sounds reached us a while after the action was over. Falling ice would shoot up plumes of water as it slid into the bay; then we would hear the cannon report that actually had accompanied its first break from the active front. By the time the shock wave generated by its fall had begun to subside and the sea was starting to quiet, we would hear the deep boom of the ice hitting the water.

Nowhere is the raw power of snow-turned-to-ice more apparent than at Glacier Bay—power and also the seesawing of consequences as climatic pulsations extend the reach of the ice, then withdraw it. Clusters of silvered stumps stand upright on a few beaches and erode from loose slopes. They are western hemlock trees that were overwhelmed by gravel deposits and suffocated from two thousand to seven thousand years ago, as shown by radiocarbon analysis of the wood. Glaciers were locking up a great deal of water at that time, so the ocean stood lower in relation to the land than it does today. Where there now are beaches, the trees then were growing on upland benches. The fact that they are hemlock stumps suggests a long period of forest conditions. Hemlock is not a tree to pioneer raw land.

Seemingly, gravel washed from an advancing glacier and smothered the trees during a local "little ice age," or maybe they drowned as the enormous weight of expanding glaciers depressed the land below sea level. Either way, the roots of many presently are washed by each day's tides, clear indication that they couldn't have grown recently. Such a habitat would be impossible for living trees. But at the time these hemlocks sprouted and grew, salt water stood twenty feet lower than now. When the land was lowered, the ocean encroached. Now the beaches again are rising. The general melting back of the ice is causing a rebound of an inch and a half per year at Bartlet Cove in Glacier Bay, a remarkably rapid rate of change.

This line between livability and unlivability is a fine one, and it is ruled by a very few degrees of temperature difference. In Glacier Bay the wavering of the line is easy to see; the glaciers come and go rapidly. But on a global basis and a great time scale, the evidence can be difficult to read.

Perhaps the first understanding came from the Swiss. Peasants noticed glaciers carrying boulders and concluded that large stones in their fields also might once have ridden the conveyor belt of ice. Similarly they noticed scratched and polished rock and smoothed knobs emerging from the edge of current ice, and they reasoned that these same characteristics elsewhere must be associated with glaciers of the past. By the nineteenth century, scientists led by Louis Agassiz felt sure that ice on an enormous scale previously must have blanketed much of the land. They recognized its signs on the plains of North Germany, dotted with erratic boulders from Scandinavia, and in America where rocks from Canada rested in United States wheat fields.

As the twentieth century opened, investigators realized that the presence of the great ice sheets had not been a single occurrence: on the contrary, they more than once had come and gone, the cold interspersed with periods of warmth. Reindeer antlers were recovered along the Mediterranean, and woolly mammoth and arctic fox fossils came from central Europe. All gave some indication of past cold. Conversely, the remains of macaques and hippopotamuses also were found there, positive witness to previous semitropical conditions. Only sweeping changes in past climate could account for such divergent animal species within the same general region, and identification of pollen recovered from successive strata bore this out. It revealed plant species known only in cold climates interlayered with those strictly from warm climates.

Actually, ice ages are rare; our human time span simply happens to fall within one. It may be nearing its close, or it may be on the verge of resurgence. Either way, the most recent ice age, the Pleistocene, began one million to two million years ago and was preceded by other ice ages. These are known to have recurred ten million, twenty–five million, three hundred million, and six hundred million years ago, and there probably were other ice ages, as well, not yet well documented. Yet, regardless of these repeated ice ages, temperate conditions have prevailed throughout most of the earth's five-billion-year history.

Various theories seek to explain why snowfall periodically increases enough to sheathe so much of the globe in ice. One possibility is associated with the recently accepted geologic concepts of drifting continents and the accompanying shifts of the polar regions. The differing distributions of land these explanations postulate would affect climate drastically, and indisputable evidence now establishes that the pattern of continents and oceans familiar on today's maps had not held constant. On the contrary, until mid-Mesozoic time about 180 million years ago, North America, Greenland, and Eurasia were joined as a single landmass; and South America, Africa, India, Australia, and Antarctica formed a second supercontinent.

The name Gondwanaland has been given to an ancestral southern supercontinent; Laurasia, to a northern supercontinent. Under today's circumstances it is the northern latitudes that have the most land and the most ice (except of course for Antarctica). We don't associate much ice with Australia, Africa, India, or South America. Except in their mountain ranges, these lands have no glaciers—yet they show evidence of former heavy glaciation. Gondwanaland was mantled by such thick ice that present-day south and central Africa may have been more frequently glacier-covered in the past than any other part of the world. Antarctica and Greenland are still so blanketed by ice that geologists have little chance to see the rocks and study the distant past.

During Gondwanaland's ice ages, tropical swamplands dominated northern-hemisphere Laurasia, giving rise to the great coal forests of the Carboniferous period in late Paleozoic time. The North Pole lay somewhere in what now is the northwest Pacific Ocean. How long the two supercontinents prevailed is not known, but it is apparent that something less than two hundred million years ago their plates began to separate. At the same time the earth's surface seems to have cooled. Ice started to accumulate at both poles, which by then were in their present locations. When the poles are in mid-ocean or are surrounded by low, flat land, the entire world's climate stays fairly moderate, including the poles themselves. This had been the case earlier, when the antarctic-African amphibians and reptiles were alive, and when early horses were browsing the vegetation of today's Arctic and falling prey to saber-toothed cats.

Then the pendulum swung, and sweeping changes gradually took over. The flatness of the land was followed by the birth of mountains, and the overall average elevation of the continents more than doubled from about one thousand feet to twenty-six hundred feet. This contributed to cooling, which slowly intensified over a period of tens of millions of years. By five or six million years B.P. ("before present," the term used for geologic time instead of B.C. or A.D.), the world had begun to slip toward another ice age. Around one million years ago it definitely crossed the threshold, and glaciers began another inexorable advance, this time chiefly in the northern hemisphere, the erstwhile Laurasian lands.

Some critical new factor must have been added to bring about the advance of the ice, but what? The rising of the mountains alone seems an insufficient cause. One possibility is that the cold was ushered in by a change in the energy output of the sun, perhaps associated with the sunspot cycle. During about 90 percent of the past half billion years worldwide temperature has averaged 72°F. but it presently is 58°, and at least four times since the onset of the Pleistocene age it has fallen to 45° or less. The magnitude of such oscillations could come from a mere 8 or 9 percent change in the output of the solar furnace, and this might possibly be the outcome of either an expansion or contraction within the sun's core, which would affect the nuclear burning of its hydrogen. According to this concept, it would take only a 13 percent drop in the sun's heat to encase the earth in ice a mile thick, assuming enough water evaporated from the ocean to fall as snow; or a 30 percent rise in the sun's heat to destroy life on earth.

But perhaps the pendulum of world climate hasn't swung in response to changes in solar energy output. Perhaps it has been to differences in the amount of that energy reaching us. Water vapor hanging above the earth could reflect back as much as 90 percent of the sun's radiation, insulating and chilling the entire planet. Concentrated clouds of dust also might block the sun's rays or might provide nuclei around which vapor could condense, setting off increased rainstorms and blizzards. Volcanic eruptions seem to contribute to such dust veils.

Recent support for belief in a tie between such dust veils and lowered temperature has come from deep sea-bottom cores, which indicate markedly increased volcanism during the last two million years, a period characterized by successive ice ages. On the other hand, despite this correlation, a major problem is that possible causes can't be distinguished from effects with any real certainty. Volcanism may lead to global chilling, or it may be the other way around. Climate fluctuations could contribute to volcanic eruptions by indirectly causing stresses as the ocean basins are alternately unloaded and reloaded, with water first withheld by glacier ice, then returned to the ocean because of melting. A possible response to this could take the form of explosive eruptions.

Or, regardless of the interrelationship between volcanic dust and climate, it may be that a dust zone farther above the earth than is likely from volcanic eruptions sets off global chilling. Satellite investigation now shows such zones, probably caused by meteors. Nearly one million tons of fine meteoritic debris falls to earth scarcely heeded each day, and an equal or greater amount may hang far above our planet, augmented by dust raised as large meteors collide with the moon. If the concentration of this screen were sufficient it might reduce incoming heat enough to chill the earth.

Still another explanation for periodic world temperature changes may be the variations inherent within our orbit. Three distinct cycles affect earth's exposure to the sun's rays. The first of these operates over a period of about 93,000 years, the second on a 21,000-year basis, and the third on a 41,000-year basis. The longest and shortest of these cycles occur because of the elliptical rather than circular nature of our orbit. If we truly circled the sun, winter and summer would be equal in length; but the actual path of the earth is elliptical with an eccentricity that varies over a 93,000-year cycle between zero and 4.3 percent. This changes the angle of segments of the earth's surface in relation to the sun. While the orbit is elliptic, as at present, we come closer to the sun each time around than is true during a circular orbit. Furthermore, at present our northern hemisphere reaches closet to the sun in January, but in 10,500 years this timing progresses again into July. This matter of varying distance from the sun constitutes the shortest cycle.

The third cycle stems from our orbiting the sun not only erratically and at a changing distance, but also with a varying angle of tilt. Sometimes the earth's spin axis is more nearly perpendicular to the direction of the sun than at other times, and the farther off perpendicular this tilt gets the greater the seasonal differences on earth. The closer to perpendicular, the less the differences. This shift swings back and forth over a forty-thousand-year period and combines with the two other cycles to affect distribution of the sun's energy and initiate and rescind the earth's accumulation of snow.

The superimposed fluctuations couldn't have produced an ice age in the temperate world of the late Mesozoic or early Tertiary, but they may have finished ushering in the cold after mountain building and overall elevation of the continents, together with a related general cooling, already begun in late Tertiary. A circular orbit exposes the earth to less total solar radiation each year than an elliptical orbit does, and a low degree of tilt, with minimal seasonal differences, lets snow accumulate because summers aren't warm enough to melt winters' deposits. Icefields form, and once they are present they act as heat sinks, absorbing a great portion of the calories reaching our planet from the sun. Furthermore, ice and snow bring an additional chilling by bouncing back from 60 to 98 percent of the sun's incoming rays. Vegetated land, by way of comparison, reflects only about 20 percent of incoming radiation, depending on the angle of slope, type of plants, and so on. The reflectance figure for calm water is from 5 to 10 percent.

Multiply this effect of snow and ice by the area of the earth whitened, and the magnitude of the mirroring becomes apparent. Today far less of the earth is mantled than was true at times of maximum glacial advance; yet the total area is immense, and it reflects enough incoming warmth to be a major force powering the world's climate machine. In 1968 satellite surveillance showed more than 7 percent of the planet covered with snow and ice in August; in late December the figure rose to 15 percent. Over the next three years northern-hemisphere photographs showed a decided increase, and by the winters of 1972–73 and 1973–74 this had risen to 11 or 12 percent over what the first satellite maps had shown. The increase brought the total snow-and-ice-covered surface of the northern hemisphere to twenty-three million square miles. Furthermore, this cover had started to build nearly a month earlier in the fall and was lasting a month later into spring. So much additional bouncing away of incoming radiation potentially could bring on a rapid chilling. Will it? Nobody can say. The oscillations now have been identified but discovery alone says little about how they fit into the patterns of climate. By themselves the fluctuations of a few years mean nothing within the scheme of geologic time, and indeed overall snow cover began to diminish again in 1974–75.

For snowfall to be heavy, open water must be located where prevailing winds can pick up moisture that eventually is precipitated. A theory developed by American geologists Maurice Ewing and W.L. Donn contends that Pleistocene glaciations correlate with times that warm water is flowing from the Atlantic basin into the Arctic. This warmth prevents an ice lid from covering the Arctic Ocean and, without a lid, the water evaporates. Snowfall increases. When it becomes sufficient, continental ice sheets form. They withhold water from the ocean. This lowers sea level and in time causes the flow of Atlantic water to be cut off by a submarine ridge lying between Iceland and the Faroe Islands. Without the warm water, the Arctic Ocean freezes over. Evaporation slows, which lessens snowfall, which diminishes the ice. The glaciers begin to melt. The sea rises. The warm flow resumes. And the cycle starts anew.

No matter what the reasons behind the onset of Pleistocene glaciation may have been, the nature of the ice advance itself is known fairly well. Worldwide warmth had lasted for two hundred million years, but it ended. Winter began to linger longer each year; rains changed to snow. The white blanket from one year remained to be covered the next. Ice on the high ground of Eurasia, Greenland, Iceland, and North America inched down mountain valleys, propelled by the enormous and increasing pressure of its own weight. Ice also spread in all directions from accumulation centers on plateaus and plains. When these ice caps started to wane about fourteen thousand years ago, they were covering nearly one-third of the earth's land surface. Europe lay frozen in a glacial grip from Scandinavia across the Baltic Sea into Germany, Czechoslovakia, and Poland. To the west the British Isles were covered by ice, and to the east ice reached as far as the Kola Peninsula and blanketed additional portions of the Siberian, Kamchatkan, and Asian plateaus. Offshore even the high peaks of Taiwan and Hawaii lay beneath ice.

In North America a continental glacier as much as ten thousand feet thick stretched from Alaska south to the state of Washington; another spread from Hudson Bay to Kansas and Iowa and down the east coast to New York. Boulders carried by that ice lie today in Central Park. Six million square miles were glaciated by the two North American ice caps, the Cordilleran of the west and the Laurentide of the east.

For the southern hemisphere fewer details are known, although it is clear that the last ice advance sheathed parts of Africa, New Zealand, Tasmania, the Patagonian plains, and the peaks of the Andes with glaciers. Pollen evidence is beginning to permit the tracing of climate shifts, in the southern hemisphere as well as in the northern, and carbon-14 dating is providing a skeletal time clock in radiocarbon years before the present. From this evidence it appears that the two hemispheres may have experienced slightly reversed phases of glaciation, with events in the north setting the tempo. When ice advanced there it retreated in the south, and vice versa.

Despite this phase difference, however, most geologists consider the recent glaciations of the two hemispheres as roughly contemporaneous. They point to evidence of an equal degree of glaciation in Greenland and Antarctica, and to comparable present-day recessions of ice in both the northern and the southern hemispheres. Furthermore, the rebound of land slowly freed from the weight of so much past ice shows significant similarity from one hemisphere to the other.

As might be expected, each successive glaciation largely obliterates evidence of its predecessor—and within the Pleistocene ice age alone there have been at least five major advances interspersed by warm periods. Yet even with most of the land now lying open to the sun and revegetated, the signatures of the ice endure. In the United States these vary from the magnificent sculpture of Yosemite Valley and the sharp horn peaks of the Teton Range to scratch marks and polish left on bedrock outcrops along the New England coast. Glaciers caused the formation of Niagara Falls, shaped Cape Cod and Bunker Hill, and deposited the mineral debris that plains farmers cultivate for wheat. By melting, ice left the pothole lakes of the prairies. Half the duck population of North America now frequents them, migrating in response to inner urgings that may themselves derive from the time of the glaciers. The lengthening reach of ice drove birds before its harsh sterility, according to this reasoning. Then, as the glaciers retreated, the flocks returned to their ancestral latitudes. The pattern became established and now repeats itself on a seasonal basis.

Nearly five million square miles of North America were glaciated during the last ice age; so were more than two million square miles of Eurasia. In Antarctica, South America, Africa, India, and Australia perhaps another five million square miles lay beneath ice. Most of the vast weight of these glaciers now has been lifted, and the earth's crust is rising at a rate perceivable within a single human lifetime.

Changes of sea level in relation to the land are reported from all over the world. They are not localized occurrences but global. Their mechanisms are complex and only partly understood, although it seems likely that the level of the water is a direct response to the transfer of volume and weight from ocean to land and back to ocean again as water is held by ice, then released. The most recent worldwide glacial maximum accounts for a theoretical ocean-level drop of about 360 feet. By 6,000 years ago melting had brought the level up to essentially what it is today. Then 3,000 years ago a climate warmer than today's raised the ocean nearly seven feet above what it now is, and sea ice in the Arctic may have melted each summer. If all the ice presently remaining in the world should melt, a rise of 150 to 200 feet above the current ocean level could be expected. This would be offset partly, however, by the isostatic rebound of the land freed from the ice's weight.

A variety of additional factors also may contribute to the repeated submergence and reemergence of land. Sediment deposited from the continents onto the ocean floor displaces water and raises sea level, although nobody knows for sure the magnitude of this in the past. Estimates are that if present–day land were torn away and carried into the ocean, water level would rise a possible eight hundred feet, but so far as is known nothing even approaching such a wholesale deposition ever has occurred. Besides, sediment loads on the sea floor also trigger crustal displacements along fault zones, complicating the task of tracing their specific effects. Also, cooling or heating of the entire ocean must affect water level, although a full ten degrees either way are calculated to bring about only a seven– or eight–foot rise or fall.

The fairly newly discovered bombardment of our planet by protons from the sun may furnish raw material for new water, which at least theoretically could raise the level of the ocean. The effects of this aren't really known—some scientists aren't even sure the phenomenon exists—but it may be that the incoming protons, which are hydrogen nuclei, combine with oxygen in the outer atmosphere to form water which precipitates to earth. This would increase the global supply of water, previously believed an unchangeable and eternally cycling amount. What the potential increase from this source may be isn't yet speculated upon.

Contractions of the earth are another possible cause of raised sea level, because of reduction in the size of the ocean basins. Conversely, a general expansion would stretch the basins and lower the water level, and the spreading of ocean-floor plates now is known to occur. This apparently isn't affecting the size of the world, however, because as new magma is added to the ocean plates, continental plates undergo compression and mountain building, and they also have their edges driven back down into the mantle.

Of the various explanations for major ocean-level shifts, the tying up of water in glacial ice remains the most plausible, and it alone is enough to account for radical coastline changes known to have taken place. For instance, the Bering Strait, even now only about fifty miles across, once was a sagebrush-covered steppe. The sea bottom beneath today's northern Bering Sea and almost all of the Chukchi Sea is one of the flattest, smoothest expanses known anywhere. Known as Beringia, this drowned plain is about nine hundred miles wide from north to south, which is considerably greater than the width of Alaska along the Canada border.

Evidently Beringia has alternately stood above the ocean and been flooded. Once it belonged to Laurasia, and turtles and alligators lolled at ease in its marshy lakes and lemurs clambered through its forests. The flora and fauna of today's eastern Eurasia and North America were then essentially one, as was true for the fauna of Antarctica and Africa. Subsequently Laurasia broke apart on a line about along the present-day Lena

River, then rejoined. Since then Beringia has at times been awash and at times above the water. By the onset of the most recent glacial advance its land repeatedly had emerged and been inundated and was about to make still another appearance. This most recent ice advance, known as the Wisconsin in America and the Würm in Europe, began somewhere around 100,000 to 80,000 B.P. It reached a maximum about 40,000 B.P. and by 14,000 years ago started to wane.

Sometime during this period, while glaciers were holding water in their icy fastness and Beringia was above water, man arrived in America. He hunted his way across from Asia seeking woolly mammoths, giant bison, elk, moose, caribou, and other animals which were grazing and browsing the broad steppe that joined what now are two separate continents. Just when the first Americans arrived, exactly where they came from, what they were like at the time, and how they populated the New World are questions only beginning to be understood. Little more than hints of man during these millennia are ever likely to be glimpsed, for the early arrivals must have been few and must have lived in scattered family groups.

Nonetheless, camps and hunting sites belonging to these ancient new-comers have been found in every nation of the New World. Fragments of human skulls more than ten thousand years old have come from Marmes Rock Shelter in southeastern Washington, the oldest actual New World human remains discovered so far in a context that can be positively dated not only by radiocarbon but also geologically and by cultural, faunal, and floral association. Artifacts, animal kill-sites, and fire hearths of equal and greater age have been found at various locations scattered all the way to the tip of South America, with hunting camps in the highlands of Peru dated at nearly 22,000 B.P. and cultural deposits in caves along the Strait of Magellan at about 8,000 B.P. North American dates, as determined by radiocarbon means and geologic context, are as old as 40,000 B.P., and ar-chaeologists believe there must be still older sites they haven't found yet.

Lowered ocean level eased man's arrival in America, and today's level determines the location of port cities such as New York, London, and To-kyo. Yet if the glaciers now present were to melt, water would rise three hundred feet, and unless the land also rose, barnacles would grow on the Empire State Building and sea anemones would wave from Buckingham Palace and the Ginza. Practically every culture has a myth chronicling a flood of such magnitude. New evidence linked to glaciation even lends possible credence to the story of Atlantis in the Mediterranean region.

Our globe still wears an ample glacier mantle. Whether it now is grow-ing and will lower the ocean level, or is shrinking and will substantially raise the ocean, isn't really known. Greenland alone is weighted by ice two miles thick, its bedrock depressed like a saucer. Only the highest peaks are exposed. Snowfall there yields a yearly equivalent of 107 cubic miles of water, and even more melts than falls. Antarctic ice exceeds Greenland's volume by about seven times, a total calculated as seven million cubic miles. This mentally staggering quantity seems to be neither increasing nor decreasing greatly, although the statement is based on too little evidence to be more than tentative. Assuming the figures to be reasonable, the combined antarctic and Greenland ice represents 99 percent of present-day glacial ice which, in turn, amounts to no more than one-third the volume of ice at the height of the most recent ice age. No other solid component of the earth's surface is as widely distributed as ice. Glaciers cover more than 10 percent of the land surface: a little over six million square miles, which is about the same as the amount of land that is farmed, or of the tropical rain forest belt. Sea ice is distributed over more than twice the area of terrestrial ice, and if icebergs broken from glaciers are added to this figure the total for floating ice becomes more than twenty-eight million square miles—23 percent of the ocean's surface and 14 percent of the entire globe's surface.

Is the ice now dwindling? Or is it building?

"Maybe so," answers both questions. Studies are too recently begun and lines of evidence too conflicting for anybody to feel confident one way or the other. The broad outlines of what we know suggest that the earth is vastly cooler now than when it first formed and, from the standpoint of life, that its temperature has been oscillating between moderately warm and intensely cold for the last one or two million years. We may be finishing one of the moderately warm periods now. Indications of this have been the recent thickening of some mountain glaciers, first noticed on the Coleman Glacier of Mount Baker, Washington, in 1948 and on Mount Rainier's Nisqually Glacier in 1951. Prior to that, world climate had seemed for fifty years or so to have been about as it was during the time of the great Viking expeditions: warmer than average.

The most recent—now possibly ending—period of warmth and the earlier warmth that favored the Norse were separated by hundreds of years of biting cold. Napoleon's problems in Russia were compounded by the bitter cold of winters during that period. A third of a century before his time, the British forces occupying New York City also had cursed the problems of winter. The American revolutionaries were worse off, hunkered around their campfires at Morristown, New Jersey.

During those times all that anybody could do was to get on with the tasks at hand despite the cold, or give them up because of it. Climate, which is long-range weather, swung on a pendulum beyond man's reach. Soon this may not be true. We may be able to alter the weather, and quite possibly the climate. Some of this is intentional. Experimental cloud seeding was begun in 1946 by Vincent Schaefer, now head of the Atmospheric Science Research Center at New York State University, and Irving Langmuir, a Nobel laureate. Their work established that substances such as silver iodide can be dispersed into the atmosphere to act as nuclei for ice crystals which ultimately grow into snowflakes or raindrops. These introduced substances may even function more effectively than naturally occurring nuclei, which often are sparse.

Examples of man's intentional efforts to increase precipitation are legion. Even more numerous, and potentially more far reaching, are his unintentional effects. Add lead particles to the atmosphere, as our automobile exhausts and industrial chimneys do by the ton, and ice–crystal formation is stimulated just as effectively as by the dispersal of silver iodide particles. Add too much lead, and clouds may even be prevented from releasing snow and rain. The ice crystals form but stay too small to gather vapor droplets, grow, and fall to earth. They don't collide with one another, collecting and merging into a size that can overcome gravity. Laboratory tests from around the world repeatedly have produced such overseeding, although precisely what is happening currently on a global scale isn't known. One likelihood is increased cloudiness and suppressed precipitation as ice particles too tiny to fall ride the winds above the earth. Or, if they meet an infusion of warm moist air, the effect may be devastating blizzards and rainstorms. Artificial cirrus cover similar to that produced by automobiles and industrial pollution also results from lingering—and increasing—jet airplane contrails. Their vapor lasts in the upper atmosphere an estimated eighteen months.

The consequences of what we are doing aren't known well but the statistics of the actions themselves are beginning to come in. Human-caused pollutants presently constitute a frightening 326 million tons of particulate matter spewed into the atmosphere each year. Dust rising from earth accounts for another 100 million to 300 million tons per year. This comes from the mechanical tilling of ever more acreage as demanded by increasing human population, plus recent wholesale drought conditions and the man-induced advance of deserts. Smoke from agricultural and slash burning adds a further 45 million to 65 million tons of matter. What are the implications? One may be to screen us from the warmth of the sun's rays. If the natural swing toward a colder climate, which many experts believe they detect, is actually the case this human–caused atmospheric veil may hasten and intensify the recurrence of an ice age.

On the other hand, global chilling may be offset by other factors. Gases from our aerosol spray cans may diminish the protective ozone layer high in the stratosphere and condemn us to too much ultraviolet radiation. Billions of pounds of aerosols per year have gone into the air from America alone as householders have sought odor-free bodies, clean ovens, and shiny paint jobs on cars. The real result of all the spraying may be a slow incineration of earth, or at the least an alarming increase in skin cancer.

An effect that can be stated definitely is a marked warming above cities. Stone and concrete and asphalt store up more heat than vegetation does. As a result urban temperatures range as much as four degrees Fahrenheit higher than those surrounding rural areas in summer and two degrees higher in winter. Plumes of hot air reach for half a mile above some cities. A survey in the United States shows an increased rainfall of from 9 to 27 percent in nine cities, seemingly as a result of such heat islands. This is because the heated air rising from cities reaches altitudes high enough to condense its moisture. Rain now seems to be more likely than snow over cities because of this new, artificial warmth. Conversely—and typical of interlocking and contradicting bits of evidence—the recent five-year drought in the northeastern United States also is attributed to urban heat barriers. Rain clouds that otherwise would have drenched the region were forced to flow around the sprawling megalopolis.

Another factor possibly acting to warm the world is the renowned greenhouse effect produced by a floating blanket of carbon dioxide. Our air now holds 10 percent more carbon dioxide than a century ago, most of it added since World War II because of accelerated fossil fuel consumption. This source currently feeds twelve billion tons of carbon dioxide into the atmosphere every year, which may keep heat from continuing to escape normally from the earth. Incoming shortwave solar radiation passes easily through the natural atmospheric veil and can keep on doing so even with the increased carbon dioxide concentration; this is similar to the way heat comes through the glass of a greenhouse or the windshield of a car. The earth sends the heat energy that it doesn't absorb back out as long-wave infrared radiation, and normally this is lost to the atmosphere. Some observers believe that a change now is underway. Infrared waves are absorbed by carbon dioxide, not transmitted. Consequently excess carbon dioxide may hold heat against the earth rather than let it escape, just as glass holds heat within a greenhouse. Some feel that they see the beginnings of this now.

If true, many Cassandras of climate predict that the heat will melt the world's ice. But whether they are right, or their counterparts who argue for an imminent return of the glaciers, isn't ours to know—at least yet. Whichever way it goes, the fragile balances of the high latitudes will show the first drastic effects. The vigils kept in the white nether reaches of the earth by today's scientists beyond question carry great import.

CHAPTER 3

TO THE POLES

The great snow realms of the Arctic and Antarctic have drawn men to them ever since early whispers of their existence began to reach temperature-zone adventurers and scholars. Traveling across the frozen wastes held horrors beyond ordinary imagining until recent decades, yet men went and persevered.

Few men from those heroic days of polar exploration remain to talk with today, to ask what it was like and what drew them to the snowy nether reaches of the world. But one lived quietly on Salt Spring Island in British Columbia until his death in 1975: Sir Charles Wright. Through introduction by a mutual friend I sat by his hearth one drizzly day that turned out to be only a few months before his death. He had been a Canadian scholarship student studying physics at Cambridge when he heard Captain Robert Scott lecture on his first antarctic expedition, 1902 to 1903. The second expedition was then forming; Wright decided to apply for it and was accepted as one of ten men comprising the scientific staff.

Nobody yet had reached the South Pole, and hope ran high that this expedition would be the first to get there. Reaching the Pole ranked as Scott's primary goal, but, for him, scientific observation and the collection of specimens came second only because of the limited time and energy available, not because of less interest. Meteorologists, physiographers, geologists, a biologist, an oceanographer, an ornithologist, even a helminthologist (an expert on one type of worm) belonged to the scientific staff. Wright was a physicist who became a glaciologist, one of the world's first, for study of the physics of ice had barely begun in the European Alps at the time, and little was known of the nature of polar ice caps. Sir Charles had no special training in the field; virtually none was to be had. But he was a scholar, and observation and study soon made him knowledgeable.

In Antarctica each day's travel demanded enormous stamina. How much so varied according to peculiarities of the snow surface. Where wind had done no packing and polishing, individual grains of snow tended to be coarse and had about the effect of sand so far as the sleds were concerned. In a similar way, if temperatures were too low for the friction of the runners to melt the points of the crystals and smooth the way, progress came only as grains moved against one another, creating a dreadful drag rather than permitting a glide. At other temperatures, warm enough to melt the snow, water would freeze onto the runners in hard lumps that interfered terribly with travel. Upending the sled and knocking them off was the only way to get rid of them; that meant stopping, then starting up again with desperate, energy-sapping jerks to break the sled loose and get it sliding. Most of the time Scott's party hauled the sleds themselves, hitched to them by canvas bands worn across the abdomen. They pulled in pairs, the weight of their loads as much as 250 pounds per man.

From Scott's base camp at Hut Point, the Pole lay nearly nine hundred miles away. Sixteen men, including Sir Charles, set out for it with ten ponies, twenty-three dogs, and thirteen sleds. The plan called for establishing food caches on the outward journey so that the men could supply themselves on their return journey. All would travel to within striking distance of the Pole; then a small team to be picked by Scott would press on while the others turned back. The ponies were expected to give out, whereupon they would be sacrificed to feed the dogs, each providing food for an additional four days. When the dog food thus augmented ran short, both dog teams would turn back with four men. The other twelve would continue, man-hauling the sleds loaded with food, oil for the primus stove, tents, and spare sled runners.

New Year's Day, 1912, found the party of twelve 180 miles from the Pole, and Scott that day decided on four men to join him in the final push. On January 4 the support party traveled a few miles with the polar team; then, all seeming in order, they turned back. "A last handshake and good-bye, I think we all felt it very much," Apsley Cherry-Garrard wrote. "They wished us a speedy return and safe, and then they moved off. We gave them three cheers, and watched them for a while until we began to feel the cold. Then we turned and started for home. We soon lost sight of each other."

As it turned out the loss was forever, the good-bye final. Scott's diary, found with his body, told of the journey. On January 16, twelve days after the others had turned back, the five men of the polar party found ski and dogsled tracks and with sinking hearts estimated them to be about three weeks old. They knew that Roald Amundsen also was pushing toward the Pole. The tracks had to be his, and they meant the race already was lost. "The Norwegians have forestalled us and are the first at the Pole," Scott wrote. "It is a terrible disappointment and I am very sorry for my companions. Many thoughts come and much discussion we have had. Tomorrow we must march on to the Pole and then hasten home with all the speed we can compass. All the daydreams must go; it will be a wearisome return. . . . Great God! this is an awful place."

The five men had been underway for two and one-half months at the time Scott wrote. Barely more than two months later all lay dead, three of them only eleven short miles from a cache with ample food and oil to have sustained them. Edgar Evans fell into coma and died in mid-February, following a fall. Titus Oates perished a month later. His feet were hopelessly frostbitten,and he asked to be left rather than imperil the others. They refused. So Oates stepped out of the tent saying, "Well, I'm just going outside and I may be some time," and he hobbled off into the blizzard. His body never was found. Searchers led by Sir Charles found the bodies of Scott and the two others inside their tent, the records of their observations kept to one week before they made that last camp and found themselves pinned down by blizzards and creeping weakness. With the men were a last few personal letters, several rolls of film, and thirty-five pounds of geologic specimens including fossil impressions of plants found in a coal seam. There also was a note for King Haakon from Amundsen, which had been left at the Pole with the expectation that Scott would carry its message to the world should the victorious Norwegians themselves perish on the return trip.

At the Pole Scott had written: "He [Amundsen] has beaten us. . . . We have done what we came for all the same and as our programme was laid out." So they had. They had completed two major geologic expeditions aside from the work accomplished on this last tragic journey, and there had been a winter ornithological expedition with temperatures as low as −70° F. even at high noon.

Scott and his men had accomplished their "programme." But Amundsen had beaten them to the Pole. He started from a base sixty miles closer to the goal than Scott had chosen. Also, Amundsen's men had been skiers from childhood and they started their last push for the Pole in top condition, rather than already half-exhausted from man-hauling sleds. They rode their dogsleds for the first one hundred miles of their journey and for the next three hundred were towed on skis behind them. They weren't strangers to snow. They knew how to make it count as ally, not enemy. And they happened to pick a much better route for weather than Scott's which lay over the Beardmore Glacier, the world's largest glacier and now recognized as squarely in a blizzard zone.

On the outward journey from England, Scott had received a telegram forewarning him of the competition to come. It read: "Am going south. Amundsen." Initially Amundsen had been outfitting for a northern expedition across the Arctic Ocean in the Norwegian explorer Fridtjof Nansen's old ship *Fram*. Before he could set sail, however, reports told of both Frederick Cook and Robert Peary having reached the North Pole and with that news, interest in Amundsen's planned northern exploration dwindled. So did financial backing for it. Consequently he announced that rather than continue with the Arctic Ocean plan he would round Cape Horn and sail up the coast of the Americas to Bering Strait; but instead from Maderia he cabled Scott that the two of them were in a race for the South Pole.

Actually the "race" for knowledge of the snowy extremities of earth had begun two thousand years before the time of Scott and Amundsen. It focused first on the Arctic. A Greek navigator named Pytheas in the year 325 B.C. reached as far north as Iceland and then sailed still farther until blocked by ice. Irishmen, Scotsmen, and Shetland Islanders may have preceded Pytheas in the north, traveling in simple but sea–worthy vessels of hide stretched over a wooden frame. Certainly after Pytheas' time Irish and Norse monks seeking escape into a life of isolated contemplation settled in the Orkney, Shetland, and Faroe islands; and some, following the route of migrating geese, eventually landed in Iceland. Sagas dated about A.D. 870 tell of their colonies and of a new wave of northern settlement by the Vikings. These newcomers had the stage of polar exploration to themselves for five centuries.

By the 1400s educated men were accepting the Greeks' knowledge of the earth as a sphere, and the concept of circumnavigation was on its way. Land prevented eastward voyages to Cathay, so ships' captains decided to try westward routes. When Columbus made a landfall in Cuba he thought he had arrived in Japan, and he even sent emissaries with a gift for the emperor and a letter of greeting from their Royal Highnesses Isabella and Ferdinand. Five years later John Cabot, a Genoese from Bristol, also sailed westward to reach the East. He arrived in Newfoundland and Labrador, realized that their coasts couldn't possibly be outriders of Cathay, and acknowledged that a previously unknown continent must lie between Europe and the spices and silks of the Orient. The route westward was blocked by land, he reported, as was the route eastward.

Perhaps the way lay to the north. By the sixteenth century successive arctic expeditions left from England to find out. The only real question lay in whether the Orient might best be found via a northwest passage or one to the northeast. The northeast route held favor. A widely accepted, although fallacious, map showed it as best; furthermore, the waters were familiar to British seamen at least as far as North Cape, about five degrees beyond the Arctic Circle, and they knew that Russian fishermen regularly sailed eastward to the River Ob and possibly beyond. Also they believed that *"Civill* people" lived along the coast, and this gave hope for brisk trade opportunities en route to Cathay, however distant it might prove to be. In comparison, the northwest route seemed unpromising. Cabot's experience was discouraging and, although Jacques Cartier returned from Canada and discovery of the St. Lawrence in 1536, his report was not published for nearly thirty years.

Whichever route was tried, the sixteenth-century voyagers outfitted with utmost care. The expedition of Sir Hugh Willoughby in 1553 furnishes an example. Lead sheathed the bottoms of the vessels to repel the voracious attack of worms believed one of the main hazards of the torrid waters off Cathay—this for what in reality proved the misty ice-choked domain of polar bears.

In 1554, a year after they had sailed, the bodies of Willoughby and those of all the officers and men of his command ship were found near Murmansk on the Kola Peninsula, barely beyond the Finnish border. The "torrid seas" had given Willoughby a frigid reception. Blown off course, he had made landfall as best he could in a raging blizzard and resigned himself to wintering over. Death came, probably from scurvy. The route Willoughby had hoped to establish actually remained unnavigated in its entirety for nearly a century after his attempt. In 1648, during a rare ice-free summer, the Russian Cossack Semen Dezhnev seemingly reached the Bering Strait via the north Siberian coast. Some authorities question the authenticity of the evidence, however, and the final claim for the Northeast Passage may belong to the late nineteenth century when Nils A. E. Nordenskjöld sailed from Kolyna to Okhotsk in 1878-79.

After Willoughby's tragic failure, the northwest route began growing in favor. Martin Frobisher was one of the first to make the search. He went seeking new geographic knowledge, yet also thirsting in the old way for trade, which remained an incentive for financial backing. On August 19, 1576, two months after leaving England, this expedition reached the southeastern shore of Baffin Island and made contact with Eskimos. By trickery Frobisher brought one aboard ship and took him back to England partly as proof of arrival in exotic northern lands. Thus did Londoners first meet the people of the snows whom they believed to live along the route to Cathay. Within days the Eskimo died of a cold, but Frobisher insisted that his presence gave evidence that the new land his expedition had reached must be the entry of the long-sought Northwest Passage.

The following year Frobisher commanded a second voyage north, this time returning with his holds filled with two hundred tons of supposed gold ore. Success led to a third expedition of fifteen ships which sailed from England on May 31, 1578, but this time the promise proved illusory. Two months later, off Baffin Island, "there fell so much snow with such bitter air that we could scarce see one another for the same, nor open our eyes to handle our ropes and sails." The storm was a harbinger of disaster, for when Frobisher arrived home again his only welcome was word that the prized ore from his previous voyage was worthless iron pyrite. The news meant that Frobisher's present cargo of thirteen hundred tons of ore also was worthless, a shattering substitute for the glory he had expected and a bitter end for his voyages.

Public fascination with the north continued strong, however, despite Frobisher's folly in mining there. William Barents, a Dutchman, led three successive arctic voyages commencing in 1594, and his experiences were reported in England "as so strange and wonderful that the like hath never been heard of before." In a sense Barents' expeditions marked the transition from one era of polar exploration to the next. The map still was mostly blank for the high latitudes of both north and south, but knowledge at last was beginning to replace fantasy. Europeans had contacted the Eskimos, had wintered in the north, and knew enough about it to realize that as a route to the riches of the East it was neither short nor easy.

Through the seventeenth century and into the eighteenth, knowledge continued to grow. A breakthrough in understanding magnetism enormously boosted the effectiveness of exploration techniques, and ways of preventing and treating scurvy at last were discovered. England, France, Holland, and Russia each hoped to outdo the other in trade and in glory, and to that end mounted expeditions. One of the most significant was that of Vitus Bering, a Dane belonging to the Imperial Russian Navy, who journeyed by horse-drawn sledge from St. Petersburg to Okhotsk on the Siberian Pacific and from there coasted the Kamchatka and Anadyr peninsulas in 1729. This led ultimately to establishment of the Russian-American Company, which began operation on the American side of the Pacific by the end of the century.

In England, the British Admiralty of the early nineteenth century was looking for new missions and found one in northern exploration. One of the important ventures of the time was Edward Parry's. He departed from the Thames on May 11, 1819, heading for Kamchatka via the northwest but destined instead to hear the crack of his ship's timbers as winter ice held him fast off the east coast of Canada with "not an object to be seen on which the eye could rest with pleasure." In 1821, Parry headed northwest on a second voyage, and in 1824 on a third. He added overland exploration to coastal charting, specially equipping his ships' boats with iron runners and carrying lightweight sledges and provisions for two and one-half months of oversnow travel. Snowblindness forced the party to move only at night, and pack ice kept drifting away with them at a rate faster than the progress they could make northward. Yet by July 26, 1827, Parry reached to within 435 miles of the Pole, a northern record that stood for fifty years.

More new equipment and methods were tested—worthwhile ones and foolish ones, half workable ones and half impossible ones. The Arctic became a successful testing ground for the new screw propeller, a great step forward in marine design although not an immediate triumph. Sir John Franklin's expedition, an ironically important one, helped to pioneer use of the propeller. His ships were even equipped with the added refinement of being able to raise their propellers to protect them from the ice. Converted railroad engines provided power, leading to a comment from one of Franklin's men that "Our engine. . . has a funnel the same size and height as it had on the railroad and makes the same dreadful puffings and screamings, and will astonish the Esquimaux not a little." In late spring 1845, the expedition cleared the shores of Britain and by the end of June crossed the Arctic Circle off Greenland's west coast, intending to pass into Bering Strait by autumn. Franklin, his men, and the public expected a great deal of new knowledge to be gained. But it was destined to happen only indirectly as would-be rescuers searched vainly for survivors. In July the captain of a whaling ship that was moored to an iceberg spoke with the men of the Franklin expedition, then watched the two vessels, *Erebus* and *Terror*, steam off. No one outside the Arctic ever saw them again. The entire expedition—134 men—vanished and little trace ever was found despite more than two decades of looking.

In all about forty searches were made. Each party charted and mapped the maze of arctic islands and waterways as they went and in this way contributed to basic understanding of the Arctic.

Emphasis now shifted to the race for the Pole, as such. The search for Franklin led to recognition that the Northwest Passage was an impractical link between Europe and Asia. The geographic pole, however, that elusive northern point—at which all lines of longitude converge and the only direction is south—remained enticing and unknown, although the techniques of arctic exploration were showing steady improvement. Charles Hall, an eccentric Bostonian who sought futilely for evidence of Franklin during the 1860s, had called attention for the first time to the advantages of dressing, eating, and traveling the Eskimo way. Rather than impose oneself on the snow and ice, Hall pointed out, wisdom lay in adapting to the realities of the Arctic and seeking to fit in harmoniously. Trying to bludgeon the North into submission by sheer determination and technology was foolish. Fridtjof Nansen with three other Norwegians and two Lapps furthered these recommedations by getting Eskimo help in designing equipment, then testing it in 1882 by skiing across the Greenland ice sheet, a four-hundred-mile trip that included climbing nine-thousand-foot mountain passes.

Late in the century attempts on the Pole were made under the flags of England, America, Australia, and Norway. Many said such a prize scarcely could be worth the cost of reaching it, but no long-held goal is that simply—or rationally—dismissed. The expeditions continued. As the nineteeth century closed, the American explorer Robert E. Peary determined to stand at the Pole itself, and on a third try he succeeded. In July 1908, he steamed out of the New York harbor and ultimately shoved off across the ice on a course set west of north to compensate for drift. On April 2, 1909, he commenced the last stage of his journey. Accompanying him were Matthew Henson, a black, and four Eskimos. The party raced the full moon and the tides, which threatened to open impossible leads in the ice—and they won. "The Pole at last," Peary wrote in his diary on April 6. "My dream and goal for twenty years."

On April 7 Peary and his men started back from the Pole, and soon he cabled his triumph to the world. "This work is finished, the cap and climax of nearly four hundred years of effort, loss of life, and expenditure of fortunes by the civilized nations of the world. I am content." His contentment was short-lived, however. On arriving home he immediately found himself embroiled in a controversy of such magnitude that to this day it is not resolved fully. Dr. Frederick Cook, a polar pioneer who had been with Peary in Greenland in 1898-1902, claimed to have reached the North Pole the year before, on April 21, 1908. By the time Peary returned, feeling exultant, he found Cook's report published with the title "My Attainment of the Pole." Congress investigated. So did a special committee of the National Geographic Society. Peary emerged the victor, but the edge was forever gone from the final glory that so long had lured men north. "Polar exploration is at once the cleanest and most isolated way of having a bad time which has been devised," a colleague of Peary's wrote. Few who had experienced it would disagree.

In the North, however, the search for the Pole at least had been backed by a long acquaintance between man and Arctic. For no matter how elusive the Pole itself, or how slow Europeans and Americans had been in adapting themselves to its white wilderness, man has lived in the Arctic for at least thirty thousand or forty thousand years and possibly for untold millennia more. In the Antarctic, no such familiarity exists. Instead man and land only recently have met. Amundsen's and Scott's achievements came as the swift climax of only a few centuries of speculation concerning the South Pole rather than after millennia. The aborigines closest to Antarctica lived at Tierra del Fuego, the large island off the tip of South America named for the fires of the Indians, but so far as is known these people never ventured to the continent south of them. The only legend of such a voyage comes from a very different quarter. Polynesians tell of a warrior who sailed so far that he entered a dismal realm of fog and boundless ice. On his return to the sunny palm islands of home he recommended against anyone's traveling so far again.

Until the eighteenth century, geographers had little knowledge of the far south latitudes, although they believed that a huge continent spread across "the bottom of the world." They expected it to be fertile rather than desolately white. Great navigators from Columbus' time on added fragments of understanding, but it wasn't until 1768 when the great British mariner James Cook strode onto the stage of history that scattered bits of observation at last could be fitted together. Cook had immense drive and ability, and at the time he began his explorations he was in his late thirties and therefore with enough years of life remaining to settle major questions of world geography. On his first voyage, 1768–71, he navigated from Cape Horn to Tahiti, circled New Zealand, coasted Australia to the east, and returned to England by way of New Guinea. He reported that no continent lay in the region of the fortieth parallel and that if such a discovery ever were to be made the search would certainly have to be made farther south. The public, however, paid little attention to these words, preferring instead to believe that Cook had found the fabled land of the south and that it was inhabited by people "hospitable, ingenious, and civill." The government actually was questioned concerning its involvement with colonies in America when so clearly a more spacious and richly endowed land lay to the south. In time, Cook's full account and true viewpoint gained general acceptance, but by then he was off on his second voyage.

On January 17, 1773, his two little vessels crossed the Antarctic Circle, the first known with certainty to have done so. Turned back by pack ice on January 26, he wrote that while perhaps it was possible to get farther south, the effort seemed rash. "It was, indeed, my opinion, as well as the opinion of most on board, that this ice extended quite to the Pole. . . . And yet I think there must be some [land] to the south beyond this ice; but if there is it can afford no better retreat for birds, or any other animals, than the ice itself, with which it must be wholly covered."

In spite of Cook's observations most men refused to replace their long-held vision of a green southern continent with the actuality of white desolation. In part this was because Cook had mentioned seals and whales in abundance, a clear invitation to wealth as commercial seafarers saw it. Furthermore, so men reasoned, where there was ocean life there must also be gentle lands fit for human settlement. British, French, Russian, and American governments and private companies responded to what they saw as new opportunity and, although no rush to southern waters immediately ensued, discoveries by navy men, whalers, sealers, and would-be colonizers extended an understanding of extreme southern geography.

William Smith, an Englishman, sighted the antarctic mainland on February 4, 1820, and claimed it for Britain, naming it Graham Land. That same year an American sealer, Nathaniel Palmer, also sighted the same shore with the result that American maps referred to the Palmer Peninsula rather than to Graham Land. By chance, Russian claims also date from 1820—and in fact can be said to predate those of England or the United States by a few days. Baron Fabian Bellingshausen, German-born but sailing for the czar, came within sight of Graham Land/Palmer Peninsula a little before the English and American sightings, but he arrived during a snowstorm and couldn't see through the bleak whiteness to recognize his position.

An expedition commanded by the Scotsman James Clark Ross saw and named Mount Erebus and Mount Terror, volcanoes that astonished them in the seemingly endless snow and ice. Erebus, 12,400 feet, was in eruption, "a most grand spectacle." The party also found Ross Island, which they called High Island, and the Ross Ice Shelf, which they called Victoria Barrier, adding the comment that a man "might with equal chance of success try to sail through the Cliffs of Dover as to penetrate such a mass."

In a sense Ross closed the era of major antarctic exploration by sea and raised the curtain on the land exploration that would culminate with Scott and Amundsen and lead to our own day of sophisticated research. In another sense Ross's reports added specific impetus to the probes already begun by seal and whale hunters. He commented on the abundance of life encountered in antarctic waters and thereby quickened the thirst for riches to be made from sealskin and whalebone and from rendering the oil of the animals' carcasses. With the opening of major whaling and sealing came the beginning of detailed geographic knowledge as replacement for the speculation of previous centuries. The white realm of the south, as that of the north, was becoming known. By 1912 both poles had been won; man had reached the ends of the earth at last.

CHAPTER 4

ARCTIC AND ANTARCTIC

The two poles differ greatly. The ancients who thought of the Far North as the land of Arktos, the Great Bear (Big Dipper) were right to name its counterpart the Antarctic, for in many ways the southern polar region opposes the Arctic. It is an ice-covered continent set in a partly frozen ocean, whereas the Arctic is an ocean choked with drifting ice, dotted with islands, and nearly ringed by continents. The North Pole must be located by instruments because its character changes from day to day as the pack ice clashes and grinds in its slow clockwise drift. Because of water's moderating effect the mean annual temperature at the Pole is a mere −9° F., and the winter mean for the Arctic as a whole varies from −20° to −40° depending on elevation and latitude. Conditions are such that a wide range of life can thrive, including large land mammals.

Not so the Antarctic where the annual mean temperature of the Pole is −58° F., and in the entire region the biggest land animal is a wingless fly less than a quarter-inch long. Antarctica is a continent capped by so much glacial ice that the sheer weight in places is pushing bedrock to sea level and below. Nowhere else on earth is there so much ice. It overrides the land as an incredible blanket up to three miles thick. Only the greatest peaks rise free. The elevation of the continent as a whole averages about six thousand feet, which is higher than any other continent, and peaks soar to nineteen thousand feet.

This height of the Antarctic almost is matched in magnitude by the depression of the arctic basin, which averages 4,200 feet and has a maximum depth of 17,500 feet. This is much more than men at first supposed. Late in the nineteenth century Nansen sailed north to test ideas of arctic drift by letting his sturdy little vessel *Fram* freeze into the pack ice and be carried with it by the slow circling of the current. At the time nobody knew most of the Arctic first-hand, and geographers disagreed as to its character. With *Fram*, Nansen firmly established the wholly oceanous nature of the highest north latitudes, which were expected but not proven, and also their great depths, which weren't anticipated.

The tragic voyage of the *Jeannette* a few years before Nansen sailed had established the clockwise drift of the ice. Lieutenant George Washington De Long of the United States Navy left San Francisco on July 8, 1879, and by September 6 his vessel was frozen helplessly in the ice. For twenty months it drifted with the pack; then the ice opened, only to close back and crush the already battered ship. De Long and most of his men perished, but not even death stopped the accomplishment of their expedition. Three years after the disaster, wreckage unmistakably from *Jeannette* was found on an ice floe off the southwest coast of Greenland, the opposite side of the polar basin from where ice had smashed the ship. Discovery of the wreckage, along with the fact that driftwood believed to have come from Siberia also had been found in Greenland, made it clear that a great current rotated around the polar sea.

Nansen knew of this and decided to test the drift empirically and directly, hoping it would take him to the Pole itself. That didn't happen, but his technique of making observations while drifting was to become standard. In 1918 the American anthropologist Vilhjalmur Stefansson manned the first scientific station to be established on an ice floe, drifting with it for eight months to record data on the pack and the tides. Today such iceland stations are regularly maintained by both the United States and the Soviet Union, and have been for forty years.

The 1920s and 1930s brought real understanding of the nature of both polar regions as men increasingly penetrated them. As early as 1926 Amundsen flew over the North Pole in a dirigible, thus becoming the first man ever to attain both poles. Two years after that flight Sir Hubert Wilkins made the first airplane crossing of the Arctic Ocean. In Antarctica similar advances were made. Admiral Richard E. Byrd flew his Ford trimotor monoplane from Little America to the Pole and back in one day—sixteen hundred miles—in 1929.

Yet even with the overall character of the white nether–reaches of earth now known, certain basic statements remain complex. For instance, the size of the polar regions can be given generally as about five and one-half million square miles for the Arctic Ocean, closely matching the slightly more than five-million-square-mile expanse of the antarctic continent. But try to define the boundaries of the two and a problem arises. The Arctic Circle at 66°33' north latitude is of course the exact counterpart of the Antarctic Circle at 66°33' south latitude, but these imaginary lines really aren't satisfactory delimitations. Each girdles the earth at the position of the midnight sun, marking the latitude where for one twenty-four-hour day each winter the sun never comes above the horizon and, conversely, where it never sets for one day each summer. This means that the Arctic and Antarctic circles are relevant to astronomical events but say nothing about the topography of the earth or the nature of its habitats.

Climate considerations are more valid. The widely recognized Koppen system of climate defines Arctic and Antarctic as regions where the warmest month averages below 50° F., and the coldest month never rises above freezing. From a biological standpoint this line, in the Arctic, corresponds fairly closely with the northern limit of trees—although defining a tree isn't easy at that latitude. A genus that clearly produces trees elsewhere may in the Arctic amount to nothing but brush or even less. Certain willows stand no more than an inch high when fully mature. The Antarctic has no trees by any definition. Lichens and mosses are its major vegetation, and they are sparse.

Another approach to defining the polar regions is to use the limit of floating ice as the beginning of the Arctic or Antarctic. The concept is reasonably appropriate in the polar south but not in the north since it leaves out parts of the Greenland coast and the Barents Sea along with all of interior Siberia, Alaska, northern Canada, and Greenland—yet the coldest temperatures within the Arctic are recorded not at the North Pole but in the highlands of eastern Siberia where the winter minimum has sunk as low as −93° F. In the Antarctic ice does form a distinct boundary. By itself, the pack amounts to a virtual physical barrier, and in addition its outer edge coincides with the point at which warm salty water flowing down from the north merges with cold Antarctic water, chilled and freshened by ice melt. Where the two meet, a great upwelling takes place as the cold water sinks and the warm water rises to replace it. This stirs nitrates and phosphates to the surface, enriching the nutrient broth of the water for the few species of plankton adapted to the dominating cold. Unadapted species from the north die, their crucial temperature and salinity requirements no longer met. The presence of the plankton, whether living or dead, makes the convergence zone a rich feeding ground for birds, fish, seals, and whales as well as for deep–water sponges, mollusks, and other filter feeders nourished by the organic rain from above. So dintinct are the effects of the waters' meeting that a mariner usually knows without looking at his chart that he has arrived at about 50° south latitude in the Atlantic or Indian Ocean, and between 55° and 62° in the Pacific. A gray bank of fog will lie ahead, and crossing into it voyagers soon find the fog turning to mist and the mist to snow. Such wet weather is all but perpetual as vapor held by warm moist air increasingly surrenders to the bitterly cold southern air.

In both polar regions sea ice forms when surface water temperatures drop to about 28° F. Snow weights the thin new ice and causes it to sag, which sends water flooding over it. This quickly freezes, thickening the ice. In the north, pack ice amounts to a shifting, grinding lid that covers the ocean several feet thick from fall into spring. In the Antarctic, pack ice is very different. There the winter pack rims the continent for nearly five hundred miles and is a combination of sea ice plus immense icebergs calved from glaciers. The summer pack retreats to a comparatively narrow band except for semipermanent ice in much of the Ross and Weddell seas and off the Pacific side of Lesser Antarctica.

In addition to the pack, the Antarctic has two other types of ice—and a total ice volume that exceeds the Arctic's by about eight times. Aside from pack ice there also are shelf ice and glaciers. The shelf ice forms as layers of snow blow from the land onto the frozen sea and compress. This ice stays attached to the land because it is continually replenished from that direction. The best known example is the gigantic Ross Ice Shelf which covers inner McMurdo Sound, an area the size of France. This ice stretches nearly 400 miles across the sound, and at its outer edge is 350 miles from the innermost shore. Its glistening cliffs tower 200 feet above the water and reach four times that far beneath the surface. In places glaciers augment shelf ice. They stretch across the land and into the water like gigantic frozen tongues floating at their lower ends. Antarctic glaciers as a whole account for the greatest part of the ice that whitens the entire south polar region.

High in elevation and far removed from a moderating effect of the ocean, the continent experiences temperatures as low as −127° F., the coldest known anywhere in the world. This reading was taken in 1960 at Vostok, a Soviet research station situated on the ice cap eleven thousand feet above sea level. A standing rule there is that men should be outdoors for only fifteen minutes at a time when the temperature falls to −112° F.;

when it drops to −121° F. or lower, the time is cut to ten minutes. The buddy system of course prevails, as it does at all antarctic stations: no man ventures forth alone. When going out, multiple layers of clothing, including furs, are standard attire, and in addition men carry battery heaters to warm hands, feet, and chests. They also wear face masks which are fitted with hoses to allow breathing warm air from inside clothing. Thus equipped, they carry out their observations.

Actually, despite harsh conditions, Antarctica in many ways serves as a more convenient high-latitude observatory than the Arctic Ocean is ever likely to be. Although the southern ice cap remains wholly inhospitable, it at least offers a solid base for permanent stations, and its most remote reaches are easier to get to than corresponding points in the Far North. This had made the Antarctic the primary location for study of many characteristics common to both polar regions. In 1961 nineteen nations signed a treaty of cooperative international scientific study in the Antarctic with all individual political, economic, and military gain forever forsworn.

Both polar regions are dominated by ice and snow and cold—yet both are deserts. Precipitation is scant. Less falls in the Arctic and Antarctic than in Arizona's Sonoran Desert; the yearly polar average resembles that for parts of California's Mojave Desert. This seeming incongruity has a simple explanation: the moisture capacity of air increases with warmth and, at the poles, there is very little warmth. Air at −40° F. holds one-tenth what it can at 50° above zero, and this alone augurs against much polar precipitation. It means that the Arctic and Antarctic are snowy not because of what falls each winter but because of what has fallen already and not melted. In the central Arctic and on the Greenland ice cap yearly precipitation totals less than five inches. Over the whole of the antarctic continent the amount is five or six inches of water equivalent (from a snowfall of about sixteen inches).

This lack of available moisture greatly restricts life. The few truly polar land mammals that exist, such as polar bears and arctic foxes, belong exclusively to the north. They guard against the cold with thick fur and various adaptations in behavior. They get moisture from their food, much of which comes directly from the sea. Antarctica has no terrestrial animal life except for invertebrates such as the fly, plus springtails, mites, and similar simple life-forms. The seals and penguins of the Antarctic really belong to the water. Plant life also is scarce and stunted. Only three species of flowering plants live in all the vastness of the continent, compared with nearly one thousand for the Arctic. There are two kinds of wire grass and an herb related to carnations. More common are algae, lichens, and mosses which crust rocks and tuft sterile ground. Their nutrients come from saltwater spray and from the dropping of birds that feed in the sea but come ashore to nest. In almost all of Antarctica the only source of moisture for plants is melting snow, and the incessant, utterly dry winds rapidly evaporate what little of this there is. Light summer snowfalls melt at about the thirty-five-hundred-foot level and leave a fleeting legacy of moisture that becomes clearly marked by a line of crustaceous lichens. The drainage patterns of longer-lasting snowbanks are faintly outlined by rosettes of green algae. A few mosses have managed to spread around the coastal rim of the continent, where moisture is relatively abundant, and liverworts also are present on the Antarctic Peninsula, which is character-ized by summer mildness and frequent drizzle.

Among the best growth situations are minute spaces between rocks and the ice or snow that abuts them. Such niches provide both warmth and moisture. Three hours of summer sunshine can raise the air temperature within them from zero into the low eighties F. and melt enough snow to create fragile zones of moisture. Additional windblown snow sifting in contributes still more life-giving liquid. Springtails and mites, the most abundant and widespread of antarctic land fauna, also utilize the minus-cule warmth of rocks. They gather beneath them and under clumps of moss and lichens, alternating between activity and dormancy, and know-ing no fixed cycle of seasonal growth or breeding periods but only the fickle coming and going of the warmth.

Around the rim of the continent but not in the interior, meltwater pools harbor populations of microscopic rotifers, diatoms, and water bears, which are primitive relatives of scorpions, spiders, mites, and ticks. On the Antarctic Peninsula tiny crustaceans called fairy shrimp are pres-ent, as well, and brackish ponds there are the breeding grounds of the wingless flies.

Antarctic soil is scarce and poor. Much of what there is holds no organ-ic carbon except near penguin rookeries where guano provides enrich-ment, or where decomposition from patches of lichen or moss has left a bit of humus. Bacteria are present within the soil, however, including two strains capable of fixing nitrogen from the air. Some bacteria probably are transported on dust that blows to Antarctica from other continents, but they are present in sufficient numbers to indicate a true population that belongs specifically there. Even permanently frozen sediments fourteen hundred feet below the surface have been found to hold bacteria, the old-est known anywhere. Their depth within the earth indicates at least ten thousand years of existence and possibly as much as one million years. Remarkably, when brought to a laboratory and placed in a nutrient solution some have become active.

The largest stretches of ice-free soil on the continent are in the dry valleys near McMurdo Sound. These valleys lie in the lee of a mountain range, evidently carved by glaciers, although the ice is long gone. Jumbles of boulders alternate with sand and square miles of polygons that resemble the well-known patterned ground of the Arctic (and are caused by the same freeze-thaw action of waterlogged silt and gravel). A few streams flow through the dry valleys, and there are lakes, many of them ringed by successive shoreline terraces left as water levels have changed. Each lake has its own unique character. One is covered by ice ten feet thick; yet, for reasons unknown, the bottom stays about 80° F. Volcanic heat once was believed to be the cause, but underlying strata have proven cold. Another lake doesn't freeze despite low winter temperatures. It is too salty.

Most surprising, the remains of seals have been found in some of the valleys. Men on Scott's first expedition came across two such Weddell seals more than fifty miles inland and at an elevation of five thousand feet. The second Scott expedition found thirteen mummified seals on the Ferrar Glacier and its moraines, together with the fleshless bones from so many others as to suggest their presence over a long period. More recently, American researchers found ninety crab-eater seal mummies in Taylor Dry Valley. These are especially mystifying. Weddell seals occasionally are seen as far as thirty-five miles from the coast, usually aged bulls that seemingly go inland to escape sea leopards and killer whales. But crab-eaters are practically unknown away from the shore except for this discovery. All the mumified seals are believed to have traveled inland centuries ago when ice floored the valleys. Radiocarbon dating shows them to be as much as twenty-five hundred years old, although the dates are somewhat suspect because upwelling of ancient carbon could have entered the food chain of the ocean and made its way into the seals' tissues. Probably it never can be known just when or why the seals made the journeys, but their mummies and bones in the silent, cold, dry valleys emphasize the essential sterility of the continent. Found inland they seem drastically out of place. In Antarctica only the ocean can support vertebrate life, not the land.

Among the aquatic life-forms of the Antarctic are penguins, birds peculiar to the southern polar realm which come ashore only to nest. Forty-three bird species are known south of the Antarctic Convergence, seven of them penguins. The others include twenty-four species of petrel, five species of gulls, skuas, and terns, two cormorants, two ducks, two wading birds, and one songbird, a pipit. These are all water birds and all but the last five are seabirds.

The Antarctic Ocean exceeds the yield from the world's most fertile agricultural land in carbohydrates, fats, and proteins. Its food production is quadruple that of any of the world's other oceans, so rich that men are considering turning from the hunting of whales, now overkilled, to harvesting the chief food that has sustained them. This is krill, small crustaceans that feed on diatoms. About two inches long, these clawless "lobsters" reach a density as high as one for each cubic inch of water. Fecundity of this magnitude readily supports the shadowy forms of fishes and mammals swimming and feeding within the water and of birds by the hundreds of thousands wheeling and calling above the waves, then plunging within to feed. But the teeming life belongs only to the antarctic summer, to the period of sunlight when the microscopic plants of the phytoplankton can photosynthesize and thereby form the key link in the food chain. When the sun disappears below the horizon most of the conspicuous life-forms of the Antarctic also vanish. The minute sink into dormancy, and most of the large forms migrate. A very few tough it out.

Even those species that forsake the antarctic winter find the southern continent far from temperate. The mildness of its summer season is unendurably harsh by most standards. For example, silver-gray petrels nesting on exposed rock faces often work with their beaks for hours to clear snow from the crevices where they have laid their eggs and, when blizzards delay the return of adults feeding at sea, hatchlings starve or freeze to death. Elephant seals breeding among the grass tussocks of South Georgia Island, which lies north of the true Antarctic, also are plagued. The warmth of their bodies sometimes melts holes in the snow crusting between tussocks, and pups drop for several feet to lie helplessly trapped and beyond any chance of suckling. Such is the legacy of the mild season. In winter the elephant seals and the petrels are gone.

Weddell seals, on the other hand, stay. They maintain breathing holes through the ice with their teeth, although not by biting. The seals open their jaws and use their teeth like ice picks, driving with their shoulders and swinging their heads to chisel holes open. In winter when the thickness of the ice reaches ten feet and more, they use the same method to haul out. They can't shoot up in their holes high enough to get their flippers over the edge when the ice is that thick, so they rasp an inclined trough with their teeth and work their way up. Once on top they dry off by rolling in the snow. Otherwise they soon would be sheathed in ice. For the most part Weddell seals meet the antarctic winter by avoiding its fury on land. They stay under the ice, or among the hummocks and caverns of its pressure ridges. In this way they escape the wind and the temperature fluctuations of the terrestrial world.

This isn't true of emperor penguins. For them winter is nesting time—the coldest, darkest, stormiest part of the year. Their chicks need months to fledge fully, and if they hatched in summer their plumage still would not be complete when autumn cold set in. They might die. But by hatching in winter they have the benefit of parental brooding through the ferociously hostile period of the year. By the time they have grown too big to fit under a parent's body the warm season has come, and they can be left safely while the adults forage for food. Zoologists believe that penguins, which are flightless, evolved from more conventional birds perhaps as long as one hundred million years ago when Antarctica was part of Gondwanaland. The outlines of their behavior were sketched in during that gentler time, and as living conditions worsened penguins adapted to meet them. Now they are locked into established patterns. Any variance means death, given the harsh conditions of the present Antarctic. For penguins the cold and the blasting of the accompanying wind and drifting snow are routine. They endure such conditions for weeks at a time and do it without shelter and without food.

The emperor penguins, largest of all penguin species, stand more than three feet tall and weigh up to eighty or ninety pounds. They feed mostly on fish and squid, diving as deep as 885 feet, which is more than double the deepest dive recorded for a scuba-equipped human. Furthermore, they can stay under water for eighteen minutes at a time.

To breed, these birds leave the ocean and march to their established rookery sites on the ice close to land. They arrive in late autumn, always returning to the same place. As many as one hundred thousand may congregate, their weight amounting to thousands of tons. Since the ice isn't stable this late in the year, chunks sometimes break under the weight of the birds and carry great numbers of them to sea. If it merely sags instead of breaking the penguins shift location a bit to save themselves from being flooded by seawater. Selecting a suitable situation on the ice is crucial. The rookery needs to be where the bond between new sea ice and land will be secure, so that winter storms won't set the colony adrift. At the same time it should be where leads will open in the summer. And it can't be too desperately far from open water through the winter or the adult birds can't make the incredibly long feeding journeys that are needed while brooding their young. Even at best, the extent of the ice increases through the winter, and these treks commonly become fifty to one hundred miles long. They can't be longer than that or the parents haven't time to walk to the ocean, feed, and return before their young starve.

Courtship begins soon after the penguins arrive at the selected nesting site, and sometime during May or early June, which is the onset of the southern winter, the females each lay a single egg. By this time the journey to the rookery, mating, and laying already have kept the birds two months without food, and they have lost a quarter of their body weight. The females feel an urge to feed, and they need the males to take over nesting responsibilities. To achieve this each female begins to parade with her egg on her feet, snugly held against her warm belly. The male notices and follows. The female then gives a wag of her head, spreads her feet apart, and melodramatically rolls the egg onto the ice. Seeing it, the male uses his bill to hoist it onto his feet against his brood patch. He vocalizes a bit, tries to follow the female as she walks through the rookery, gives up, and settles down to incubate the egg. The female heads for the sea, walking and tobogganing on her belly.

For the male a nine-week vigil begins, perhaps the greatest regularly occurring survival feat in all of nature. Egg temperature must be kept at about 85° F. regardless of the buffeting experienced by the parent bird. To make this possible the lower abdomen of the male has a special flap of skin richly supplied with blood vessels, which covers the egg and holds it fairly firmly in place. He can shuffle about and even toboggan without losing the egg or crushing it, but he can do nothing to escape the tempestuous weather. He can protect his developing embryo but not himself. The only defense for the males is to huddle close together and, peaceable birds, they endure this massing. It gives a rookery the look of an endless series of backs hunched as a living shield over the precious eggs. When penguins on the outer ring get too cold they shoulder into the huddle, and others take their turn at bearing the full impact of the weather.

A layer of blubber initially an inch and a half thick provides built-in nourishment for the male penguin during his ordeal, and he eats snow for water. His feathers insulate so effectively that if the temperature chances to warm anywhere close to freezing, he starts to suffer heat stress. He then fluffs his curious stiff feathers to release the dead air next to his skin and let body heat escape. Each feather is curved at the tip to almost interlock with an adjoining feather, and each has a tuft of down at the base. As many as seventy to the square inch, the feathers ordinarily overlap like tiles on a roof and ward off cold by holding life's warmth within.

In July, the time of the worst blizzards, chicks begin to hatch. Male birds by then have lost nearly half of their weight but haven't yet completed their duty. They must continue brooding until the females return with full gullets to feed the hatchlings and take over warming them. In an emergency the males can secrete a whitish mucus for the young which is rather like pigeon milk, but having to produce it drastically diminishes their own reserves. Usually, the timing is such that the female returns soon after a pair's lone egg hatches, and the male's milk isn't needed. She brings about seven pounds of fish and krill, which is enough for the chick while the male at last ends his fast and leaves her with the brooding. He starts for the ocean to feed with two strikes already against him: He has starved himself for four months and, while this is happening, the ice has widened. His return to the sea is a longer journey than his trek inland from it. Yet despite the seeming odds, the system works. The male succeeds in reaching the water, feeding, and returning to the rookery.

Chicks weigh less than one pound when they hatch but by the time they fledge at the end of summer they have gained thirty–five or forty pounds. Through all these weeks their parents take turns caring for them, and here again the advantage of winter breeding is apparent. As increasing summer warmth lessens the distance to open water, the parents can accomplish their fetching and carrying with greater and greater ease, even though eight or ten pounds of food are needed for a meal by the time the young reach adolescence. The adults are faithful parents. Every mature emperor penguin seems to covet a chick, so much so that a high mortality results from overattention. A chick that strays from its parents' feet may be trampled as six or seven adults that have lost their own chicks bear down upon it. Some chicks get directly loved to death; others crawl under a chunk of ice to escape and end up freezing to death. Even dead chicks are given care. Adults carry them around until their down wears thin. The same impulse during incubation prompts any adult that has lost or broken its egg to snatch a neighbor's egg if it can find one unguarded. That failing, it may work a chunk of ice onto its feet and brood it until it melts. No more than one chick from every ten to twelve eggs laid survives to venture to the sea, but an emperor penguin that lives this long is likely to survive another thirty to thirty-five years.

Man, a newcomer in the Antarctic, is an enemy of the penguin. His helicopters and snowmobiles scare penguins from their nests, leaving eggs and young vulnerable not only to cold but also to opportunistic skuas, which move in quickly. His buildings create lees where such large snowdrifts accumulate that no amount of rearranging stones can ward off ruinous flooding of nests. More directly, men kill penguins to feed their dogs. In early whaling days, thousands of the birds' fat bodies were burned as fuel while rendering oil from blubber. Some breeding colonies seem not to have recovered yet from these depredations, and there is concern that man's predation may overwhelm penguins and eliminate them as a life-form.

In the Arctic penguins quite cetainly would be too vulnerable, not just to man but to polar bears and arctic foxes. Eight species of birds stay in the high north latitudes year round, but all are capable of flight and thereby relatively safe from land carnivores. Penguins, on the other hand, would be defenseless. In the Antarctic they are virtually the only form of vertebrate life ashore for any length of time. The numbers and variety of arctic land vertebrates of course fall far short of those belonging to temperate latitudes; there is little jostling for space, and ecological webs tend to be relatively simple. Nonetheless, arctic life is abundant compared to that in the sterile Antarctic. Lemmings and voles by the million and separate caribou herds numbering in the hundreds of thousands thrive. So do musk ox, bears, wolves, wolverines, and foxes. Each summer the low-elevation, ice-free, ocean-moderated lands so resemble temperate regions that geese and ducks flock there from far away to nest. They have no particular adaptation beyond this ability to travel distances, and they need none. The Arctic is Eden, in season.

Through the endless days of summer, birds and mammals search for food practically nonstop, many of them needing only two or three hours of sleep out of each twenty-four. All need to store part of summer's abundance either in food caches beneath the snow or as layers of fat on their own bodies. To do this arctic species forgo choosiness. Snowy owls, which hunt live rodents during times of plenty, settle for carrion if need be. Purple sandpipers at times give up the search for larvae and eat plants. Arctic foxes, normally sustained by rodents and birds, may instead feed on mollusks. Reindeer nibble seaweed if deprived of lichens and may even devour lemmings. If polar bears can't find seals they turn to fish, birds' eggs, starfish, dead whales washed ashore, grass, or sedge.

The greater the latitude within the Arctic, the fewer the species equipped to cope with winter. Most northerly of those that can are polar bears and arctic foxes. The bears, as the penguins of the Antarctic, are conspicuous on the ice, yet actually depend on the ocean for sustenance. The foxes, in their northernmost range, depend on the bears and hence are also beholden to the ocean. The character of water doesn't fluctuate as that of air does. Its moisture is constant, its temperature relatively so, and no wind blows within its deeps. Diving in it penguins and polar bears lose the insulation of their feathers and fur as pressure drives out entrapped air. Yet water penetrating practically to the skin poses no problem that a layer of fat and metabolic heat can't answer. On the ice surface and exposed to the air, however, plumage and pelage are indispensable as shields against the cold. The body temperatures of polar mammals and birds stay about the same as those of mammals and birds elsewhere. Feathers and fur and fat hold in warmth with remarkable effectiveness.

Polar bears range as far as 80° north latitude, never far from drift ice and in fact preferring the region of the greatest ice movement. They seldom wander more than a mile inland, and they avoid sheltered inlets where the ice is relatively stationary. Huge animals up to ten feet long and seven hundred to one thousand pounds in weight, polar bears nonetheless are extremely agile. They lope along at twenty to twenty-five miles an hour, easily leap ice ridges five to six feet high, and jump from lookout posts as much as twelve feet high. Even on polished ice they move confidently, gaining traction from close-set stiff hairs on the soles of their feet. In soft snow their ten-to twelve-inch paws act as snowshoes and, when the surface won't support their weight, their long and powerful legs still let them travel through snow better than any other arctic animal. On thin ice they spread their legs until their bellies drag and in this position slither along for considerable distances. As swimmers they are nearly as successful as seals. They can travel four or five miles an hour and stay under for two minutes, eyes open, ears and nostrils closed. Their paws provide paddles, and if they choose they can swim porpoise-style, leaping ten to twelve feet out of the water at a time. Their leg bones are filled with buoyant oil rather than marrow; their skin is spongy and oily; their fur is oily enough to be waterproof for short periods at negligible depths.

Neither hearing nor eyesight is highly developed in polar bears. It is smell that the bears most rely on, for most of their kills are seals taken at breathing holes. Snowed over, the holes are not apparent to the eye, but bears (and dogs) can detect them by smell. A hunting bear abruptly changes direction to angle off directly to a hole as soon as the odor of seal is detected. Polar bears remain motionless by a hole as long as three days and nights if need be. Before settling down to wait, however, a bear scoops out the seal's breathing hole enough to reach in easily with its paw. Then it refills the crater so the approaching seal will see nothing amiss. Next the bear lies down with its nose buried in the snow, seemingly to diffuse its breath so that the seal will have no warning of a predator's presence, or perhaps to hide the black dot of the nose which flaws otherwise perfect camouflage. Seals stay below water only seven or eight min-

utes at a time, or up to twenty minutes in an emergency, but they each
have nearly a dozen holes so no particular one is sure to be visited very
often. When a seal does come to a hole it lets out air in a bubbly gasp—
and the waiting polar bear pounces with claws and teeth and pulls the
prey onto the ice.

Sometimes two bears hunt together, one waiting by a breathing hole
while the other stops up all the others nearby, thus raising the odds of a
seal's returning to the hole where the first bear waits. Or both bears may
walk almost carelessly to a selected hole; then one leaves, letting any lurking seal think danger has passed. Another technique is to lure a seal to a
hole by scratching and patting at the snow in imitation of seals lying out
on a summer ice floe.

Seals occasionally are captured out of water. In fact, polar bears stalk
with impressive stealth and effectiveness. In winter their clean white
coats blend well with fresh snow, and in summer their soiled yellowish
coats match the hue of old ice. Creeping catlike, a bear lowers onto its
belly, pulling along with its forelegs and letting its hind legs drag. Or it
may push with its hind legs, holding its forelegs tucked under its chest like
sled runners. Sometimes a bear even pushes a chunk of ice ahead with its
nose as a screen. By these means it glides to within twelve or fifteen feet of
its prey, then lunges. Or, while still some distance away, the bear may
choose to slip into the water by backing to the edge of an ice floe, putting
in one hind leg, then the other, holding onto the ice with its forepaws all
the while. Once in the water it submerges all but its snout and swims
practically without a ripple until close to its quarry. Then it dives and
shoots up out of the water, or even through thin ice, and lands on the seal
and crushes its skull with a single well-aimed stroke.

Polar bears don't really hibernate. The female lives on fat reserves for
four or five months and swallows mouthfuls of snow for water. She wakes
to give birth to her young—usually to a single cub but occasionally to
twins—which weigh only one or two pounds each, and to suckle. She also
rouses if an avalanche damages her sleeping chamber or, when denned
on the pack ice, she wakes if a berg starts to tip and threatens disaster.

Adult male bears, barren females, and yearlings may or may not den
for the winter. If they do, it seldom is for long unless the temperature
drops exceptionally low, or seals are particularly difficult to hunt. During
blizzards all bears seek shelter. Once in a while they even enter Eskimo
igloos. More commonly if there is no shelter, they pivot round and round
in the snow to gouge out a hollow large enough to curl into, and then
they sleep.

Polar bears once were believed to drift haplessly with the ice, rotating clockwise with the current. This now is known to be untrue. Males and females find one another at traditional breeding grounds on a regualr seasonal basis, and dens are used almost every year. The geographical rhythms of their lives thus are not at the mercy of drift ice, but bears nonetheless may float great distances with the pack. They have been found on floes two hundred to three hundred miles from the nearest land, and a polar bear tagged in Svalbard a few years ago turned up a year and a half later in southern Greenland, a distance of two thousand miles. Some bears pass through the Bering Strait on the ice and drift down the Alaskan coast to Nome.

How many polar bears remain in the Arctic currently isn't known accurately. Estimates are around ten thousand to twelve thousand, and their number no longer is dwindling thanks to the treaty that resulted from the polar bear conference held in Oslo in 1973. In it Canada, Denmark, Norway, Russia, and the United States agreed to prohibit the killing or capturing of polar bears over what amounts to about 95 percent of their range. The use of aircraft and ships is specifically banned in hunting bears; snowmobiles are allowed only in Canada and there only when used by natives engaged in subsistence hunting. No hunter in any category may travel more than one day onto the ice of the Arctic Ocean to hunt.

Arctic foxes, the only other animal to feed as far north as polar bears, have escaped profound threat to continued survival. Their range extends to every tundra coast and island of the Arctic, and in winter they commonly travel the sea ice with bears. Inhabiting such a variety of ecological niches gives them an advantage as a species, yet their fur is the thickest in proportion to size of any mammal in the Arctic and is prized accordingly. Eskimos in Canada alone presently market from ten thousand to eighty thousand pelts per year, each valued at around thirty dollars. For trappers the arctic fox is akin to a cash crop, and money is the new Eskimo open-sesame for everything from snowmobiles and rifles to boxes of cake mix and packets of steel needles.

Arctic foxes have an additional advantage in being adaptable in their food habits. When food is in short supply, coastal arctic foxes follow polar bears on their seal hunts, and inland foxes follow wolves which, in turn, follow musk ox and caribou.

The relation of arctic foxes with polar bears is one-sided. The foxes benefit from it; the bears are unaffected one way or another. A fox will follow polar bear tracks, then curl into the snow and sleep until a seal has been caught. Often a raven perches nearby, also waiting. When the bear makes its kill, it usually skins the seal by biting around snout and flippers and jerking off the hide to expose the rich blubber. This the bear feasts upon, then it ambles off, leaving the seal carcass to be scavenged by the waiting fox and the raven.

Feeding thus without spending much energy in hunting is an essential part of survival for arctic foxes. Their incredibly rich fur is another part. Long outer hairs lie as a shield over woolly inner hairs, seemingly held in position by opposite electrical charges between the two layers. Legs, neck, and tail are short, which minimizes circulatory heat demands. Ears and nose are small and furry. The combination lets foxes survive even in the high Arctic without shelter and without raising body temperature higher than that of foxes anywhere else, about 100° F. If it weren't for this remarkable fur and compact body shape, an unsheltered arctic fox would have to generate about ten times the body heat of a desert counterpart. As it is, even when the air drops more than 150° F. below body temperature, these northern foxes are comfortable. In comparison, an unclothed man starts to shiver and thereby increases metabolic heat production when the air temperature falls about thirty–five degrees below his body–core temperature.

Of all the species living in the Arctic and the Antarctic, man is the most vulnerable. He stands tall and receives the full buffeting of the wind. His body has no natural insulation or water repellency. He can't cosset himself from the bite of the winter air by dropping into torpor or diving into the constancy and relative warmth of the ocean. Clothing and shelter are essential for survival. Yet, though he lacks innate adaptation to the polar realms, man can dictate their ecological future.

CHAPTER 5

SHELTER AND CLOTHING

The white expanses of the polar realms remain today, the blizzards howl, and the cycle of light and dark continues through the months first one way, then the other. The land hasn't changed, but man's position within it has. None of the polar pioneers would stand incredulous before the changes, of course. They were too much men of vision to permit such disbelief, and they worked too hard to improve the ways of coping with what is perhaps the most forbidding environment on earth. Yet how could they dream of trees grown on the arctic coast purposely to lift morale, or of men running naked in Antarctica to break the monotony as an expression of the blithe "streaking" fad that flared into fashion in the early 1970s. At the American polar research station the exclusively "200 Club" limited its membership to those men who sat for fifteen or twenty minutes in a sauna, then donned only boots and dashed 150 feet to the exact spot of the Pole for a photograph. Requirements stipulated that the temperature difference between the steam bath and the outside air must be at least 200 degrees.

The home base for this particular elite club was the New Pole Station, completed in 1974 at a cost of six million dollars. Four metal tunnel-ways like gigantic corrugated sewer pipes 44 feet high and 180 feet long house a generating plant, a depot with 150,000 gallons of fuel stored for winter use, a maintenance shop, and a biomedical research laboratory. A separate geodesic dome 164 feet wide and 50 feet high shelters three additional prefabricated buildings from such climatic realities as temperatures potentially lower than -100° F. and snow loads of 120 pounds per square foot of roof surface. Included in these buildings are living quarters, scientific work space, a library, a communications center, and a post office. This new marvel of a station, one quarter mile from the Pole, replaces the nearby Old Pole Station which now lies covered with forty feet of snow. The old buildings date from 1957 and were intended for three years' service, yet actually continued in use until 1975.

Much the same thirst for knowledge that activated the early explorers prompted establishment of this new base and the others in Antarctica. Scientists from a dozen nations and scores of academic disciplines today work together toward a common goal of understanding. In the North the situation differs somewhat. On the arctic slope of Alaska and Canada's Northwest Territories, hunger for oil and gas gives the thrust for current development, and instead of governments and scientific institutions financing the undertakings, costs are borne by the oil companies. Aspects of the old Klondike gold rush are reborn and updated. How all the bonanza of black gold and gas will get to market remains another matter, as does what it may do to the environment en route.

In the arctic hinterland of North America and the Soviet Union, in Greenland and Iceland and in Antarctica, attention focuses on snow and ice not as a construction problem but as a building material. Probably the origin of building with snow lies somewhere back in the white dawn of arctic prehistory, and peoples living at high elevations elsewhere also may well have built with snow. It is Eskimo snow technology that is best known and seems to be man's most highly developed.

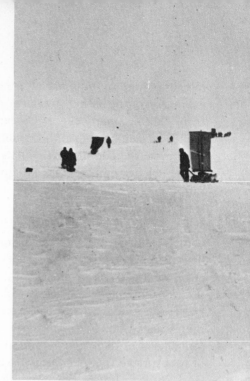

Snowmobiles greatly ease a variety of tasks such as checking traplines and logging for firewood. Below, a Lapp brings his reindeer to hitch to a sleigh. Use of deer as draft and saddle animals is widespread across Eurasia, though few are fully domesticated. Human urine is used as bait for catching wild reindeer.

Careful mushers tie booties onto their sled dogs' feet when traveling across icy snow. Otherwise the animals' paws get torn. Sail-powered sleds cross frozen Crater Lake en route to Dawson, Alaska. With a snowmobile, below, a man can travel a hundred miles, make his game kill and return home in the same day.

Top, seal mother and pup, Glacier Bay, Alaska. Yellowstone elk, left, helpless in the deep snow of Hayden Valley, winter of 1894. Elk are chioneuphores. In normal snow depths the elk's long legs give it a chance to outrun predators and to reach the twigs they favor for browse. Their long legs act as stilts holding the body above the snow surface.

Mew gull perched on iceberg, Glacier Bay, Alaska. Buffalo swing their heads from side to side to brush aside snow and reach down to winter grazing. If snow isn't crusted, they can bulldoze through drifts three to four feet deep, belly submerged, swinging their great shaggy heads from side to side to plow a trench into the snow. Bottom, monkey sitting on snowball it has rolled.

ABOVE AND BELOW: RUTH AND LOUIS KIRK

G. GRAY EATON

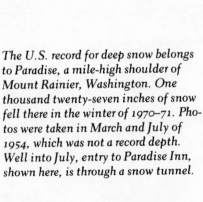

The U.S. record for deep snow belongs to Paradise, a mile-high shoulder of Mount Rainier, Washington. One thousand twenty-seven inches of snow fell there in the winter of 1970–71. Photos were taken in March and July of 1954, which was not a record depth. Well into July, entry to Paradise Inn, shown here, is through a snow tunnel.

Roald Amundsen, Norwegian explorer, headed the expedition that was first to reach the South Pole, below, December 16, 1911. Amundsen beat the British explorer, Royal Navy Commander Robert Scott, to the South Pole by a month and two days. Of Scott's party of five who reached the pole, all died on the return journey, three of them only eleven miles from enough food and oil to have sustained them. Opposite, the U.S.S. Bear on arrival at Bay of Whales, Antarctica.

Like a great forking superhighway, the Yetna Glacier, one of the ice rivers coming off Mount McKinley, Alaska, the highest summit in North America.

Snow houses never were universal among Eskimos. They provided the standard winter dwellings along the central arctic coast of Canada and in parts of Labrador where families wintered on the sea ice to hunt seals. Greenland and northern Alaskan people built them when traveling or hunting. The word *igloo* actually means any kind of house, not just one built of snow, and most Eskimos lived in sod houses built with driftwood or whalebone frames and set halfway into the earth, for warmth. In his book *Hunters of the Great North,* Stefansson tells of his introduction to "the real Eskimo snowhouse," although he previously had camped in a shelter of snow blocks set as vertical walls and roofed with skins. The first step was finding the right snow. As night approached Stefansson's Eskimo companion, Ovayuak, and his wife began checking drifts until they found a promising one. Their footprints gave the first sign that the snow was suitable: too hard, and fur mukluks leave no mark; too soft, and they sink in so that the outline of the whole foot shows; just right, and the imprint is barely plain enough that a man's trail can be followed. Ideally a drift should be around four feet deep and uniform. To check, Ovayuak probed with a rod (traditionally of caribou antler), driving it with a steady motion. If it alternated between slipping in easily and being a bit hard to push, the snow would not do; it was too stratified and blocks cut from it would break into layers. But if the probe slid in evenly, the business of cutting blocks began.

For this task Ovayuak used a special snow knife with a caribou–antler blade about fifteen inches long. He cut vertically, producing blocks twenty-five inches long by fourteen inches wide, and any blocks that came out thicker than others were trimmed until all were about four or five inches through.

The trick in building an igloo is to produce a spiral and to undercut the inner edge of the blocks so that each one tilts slightly inward when set into position. Ovayuak had the first course of blocks to form a ring ten feet across, and then he tapered the upper edges of three of the blocks into a sharp diagonal. This was to force the second tier to begin rising at an angle, setting a spiral for the entire house. Each successive round was tilted inward slightly more than the preceding one, a key factor in producing a smooth dome as the roof blocks were placed. Ovayuak worked from the inside. His wife busily cut new blocks, and Stefansson handed them in, first over the rising walls and, when that became awkward, by passing them through a hole cut at ground level. Five tiers totaling forty or fifty blocks were needed to complete the house. The final closing of the roof is "easier than anything," Stefansson wrote. "When you get near the roof the circle you are working on is less than half the diameter of the original ground circle. The blocks, therefore, meet at a much sharper angle and you can lean them more squarely so they support each other better." The last block is fitted into a hole trimmed to give a perfect match. The builder "takes up a particular snow block, trims it so it is a little thinner than average, puts it on end and lifts it vertically through the hole, so that if you are outside you can see his two arms sticking up through, holding the block. He now allows the block to take a horizontal position in his hands and lowers it gently down upon the opening so as to cover it like a lid."

With this, the basic house is done except for gently rubbing soft snow into the chinks and shoveling additional snow over the outside to bank three feet deep around the base, thinning to eight or ten inches by the third tier of blocks. The roof is left with only the thickness of the original blocks. The entry is fashioned both from the inside and the outside. As the final block was fitted into the roof, Ovayuak was completely shut inside, for he had filled the hole through which Stefansson earlier had passed blocks. Consequently, "with a shovel his wife now dug a trench about three feet wide [tunneling] under the wall of the house to meet a hole that Ovayuak was digging down through the floor." The trench later was roofed to provide a typical combined porch, entryway, and storage anteroom. Ideally this entry tunnel should include a right–angle turn, to deflect wind. Better yet, it may be T–shaped to provide for closing either doorway, or neither, as the wind changes.

Furnishing a snow house calls only for platforms, also built of snow. A large one, taking up two–thirds of the floor space provides a bed and working and lounging area. A smaller, adjoining platform serves as kitchen table. To build these, rows of blocks are first set on edge to make the fronts of the platforms, and then loose snow and fragments of blocks left from the house construction are filled in behind. This material is packed down hard and smoothed and, if available, wood or bone may be added as an edging to prevent wear from climbing and sitting. A double layer of caribou furs is laid onto the sleeping platform as a lining, the first one placed hairside down, the second hairside up; sometimes an insulating layer of caribou ribs or waterproof kayak covers goes underneath. Blankets or more furs are laid on top as bedding. Other linings are rarely used by the Eskimos, except for the Baffin Island and Igloolik (central Canada) groups who hang skins from the inside of the walls. Reducing the temperature differential between men and icy walls this way theoretically reduces the heat loss radiated from the occupants' bodies. Such liners also lessen glazing, an advantage since glazing decreases the insulation of snow walls. It also strengthens walls, however, and makes them more windproof. Dripping is not a major problem even without wall liners. Water tends to run down the curve of the dome, providing it free of irregularities, and snow at the base of the walls, which is too low and cold to glaze, blots it up.

A window of freshwater ice about three inches thick used to be set into the wall near the cooking area, sometimes in conjunction with a snow block mounted on the outer wall as a reflector. Freshwater ice is clearer than sea ice and consequently was so much preferred that Eskimos often carried a panel of it from an inland caribou camp to the coast where fresh water, frozen or liquid, is not easy to come by. If heat from cooking grew excessive, the ice window could be curtained temporarily with a skin to prevent its melting.

Occasionally a cluster of snow houses would be built with a common entry to simplify visiting back and forth and sharing routine indoor chores without going outside. Similarly, construction of communal dance halls consisted of roofing over four circled igloos and then knocking out the inner walls. Sometimes single igloos were built thirty feet in diameter and ten or eleven feet high in the center. Because of their dome shape such houses, large or small, have great inherent strength. When first built, the walls are fragile and even chinking with loose snow is done gently lest blocks be broken. But once the snow has age–hardened the dome shape is capable of holding up despite great weight and pressure. Polar bears weighing half a ton have been known to climb onto snow igloos as vantage points in a flat land.

For the men of early polar expeditions living in huts and tents, ventilation posed a serious problem, and sometimes it does so today when tents get so ice-coated that their fabric loses its porous nature. On the other hand, in a snow house no one need worry. With a hole in the roof and the entryway left open fresh air circulates constantly. In fact a standing man may experience all of the world's climates simultaneously: his feet will be in a polar zone, his middle torso temperate, and his shoulders and head tropical. Eskimo children up to five or six years old customarily went naked, and adults often wore only knee-length breeches. "A hot house is good for you," Eskimo people used to maintain. "You can go outside and cool off." Sweating was no bother in the old days. When wood was at hand, men shaved blocks of white spruce into quantities of long, excelsiorlike curls that were piled into corners and used to wipe the sweat from faces and bodies. When white men's towels became available they replaced the shavings—and grew increasingly soiled with no way of washing them, whereas the shavings were used a clean handful at a time, and afterward discarded.

A single blubber lamp traditionally furnished heat for the snow houses. It consisted of a piece of soapstone about a foot across carved as a shallow bowl among the western Eskimos and as a rimmed, flat crescent to the east. Oil filled the depression, and a slightly raised platform held a wick of dry powdered moss, wood sawdust, or fine scrapings of walrus ivory. Seal blubber most commonly furnished fuel, although walrus, beluga whale, and narwhal blubber were preferred in some districts, shark liver oil in others, and haddock oil in an emergency. Inland people got along with caribou or musk-ox tallow, poor substitutes for the rich oil of marine mammals both in quality and quantity. A seal weighing two hundred pounds may yield half its weight in blubber, a luxurious ratio of fuel to food. Except in starvation times, coast Eskimos had light and heat freely available. For cooking, a soapstone kettle hung suspended above the lamp, near the blubber. Above it was an open latticework of sinew held by a wooden or bone frame something like the web of a crude bearpaw snowshoe. Here the woman of the house dried clothing, virtually a life-and-death responsibility since wet mittens or parkas could bring frostbite and perhaps ultimate freezing for a hunter or anyone else, whose work kept him outside.

The traditional dwellings of the North were extensions of the land itself, whether built of snow or of earth, wood, whalebone, or skin. Not so today. The conditions of the arctic environment still rule but even native peoples no longer adapt to them as in the old days. For Eskimos this has been acutely true. Overall they have lost heir own way, yet until recently have lacked the affluence needed for the new, outsiders' way. Their own houses, built small, low, and thick-walled stayed warm, yet not stuffy. Then white men arrived and introduced architecture intended for temperate latitudes. The new style meant flimsy walls too vertical and high to bank with sod or snow as insulation even if custom favored such practice. Convection currents in the old houses brought in air through the open doorway without chilling the whole interior, because the entry always was sunk below floor level, and the cold, heavy air tended to hang there. The new houses, however, lose heat by conduction through their thin walls, and occupants must squander fuel trying to stay warm.

When did man first encounter snow? No sure answer exists, but it may have been as long ago as two or three million years while he was barely beyond the cradle as a species. The place would have been somewhere within the shadow of icy Mount Kenya, Mount Kilimanjaro, or the Ruqenzori Range. Certainly by half a million years ago man had adjusted to the frigid realities of life at the edge of the glaciers that then were sheathing the ice-age Eurasian continent.

Physiologically his survival in a realm of perpetual snow and ice seems unlikely: thin skin, little protective blubber, no fur, spindly limbs. Unclothed and unsheltered he shivers miserably at around freezing, a poor performance compared, for instance, to an arctic fox that can doze snugly in extreme cold, or to a polar bear that simply lets its metabolism drop for the winter and enters the peace of hibernation.

Man can make few adjustments to cold within his body, although Eskimos differ somewhat in this from unacclimatized Caucasians or blacks. Eskimos' hands stay warmer. More than half again as much blood flows to the fingers, which keeps them dextrous even while in slushy snow or water. Tests show that human fingers chilled to a skin temperature of 68° F. are only one-sixth as senstitive as at normal temperatures. This makes the hands next to useless and easily could cost a man his life in the Arctic, but the Eskimos' circulation avoids the problem. Also, Eskimos maintain higher body-core temperatures than Caucasians do during exposure to severe cold, and they recover from the chilling quickly, whereas Caucasians' temperatures not only fall lower at the outset but continue to drop for a while after the exposure to cold is over. Slightly more adipose tissue among Eskimos may help. Probably more significantly, their basal metabolism stays above that of temperate-zone people.

At the opposite end of the globe from the Eskimos, Alacaluf Indians of Tierra del Fuego also demonstrate a high metabolic rate. Walking barefoot in snow was common among the people of Tierra del Fuego and also is reported for Aleuts and Bering-Strait Eskimos. Seemingly, in the Arctic, the practice was to save wear on boots, for coarse or wet snow is hard on footgear, and replacement took hours of work. The Alacalufs and Yahgans had no footgear, although particularly for the Yahgans, who lived in the southernmost part of the archipelago, snow fell frequently even in summer. Nonetheless, these people's only real concession was to tie on shin guards of stiff guanaco hide when walking through crusted snow. Their feet they left bare, and they wore no clothing beyond a breechcloth or apron augmented by a scrap of sea-otter or fox skin no bigger than a handkerchief. This small garment was tied around the torso with a cord and shifted from front to back and side to side as token protection against wind and driving snow or rain.

Such instances notwithstanding, man's life in cold regions depends largely on contriving ways to spare himself its effects. Physiologically he is doomed. Behaviorally he manages. How comfortable he is, and how favorable his survival odds become, depend in large measure on his success in selecting the right clothing and caring for it properly, as well as in providing himself with shelter. In the North reindeer skin was more commonly used to make clothing than any other. (Reindeer in the Old World and caribou in the New World are the same animal called by different names.) Among Eskimos sealskin also was of great importance, and various Siberian people preferred dog skin. Fox, hare, and eider-duck skins went into clothing, but not for everyday wear; they are too delicate. Polar-bear skin was too heavy for general wear, although hunters stood on pieces of it as they waited in the snow for seals to return to their breathing holes. Musk-ox fur is too shaggy to keep clean.

In areas where sealskin was important for clothing, the animals' intestinal membranes also were used to make waterproof parkas and pants, forerunners of today's rubberized and plasticized outer wear. In other areas the skin of whales' tongues, or the outer membrane of the liver, was favored for this use; so were the bladders of halibut and the intestines of sea lion, bear, and caribou. Fish skin provided still another waterproof material and reports of Siberian journeys in the eighteenth-century mention clothing of pike and turbot skins among the Ostyak people, suggesting that these were their only garments part of the year. So common were fish skin garments that for the Arctic as a whole they ranked second after those of reindeer/caribou hide in importance. They were worn more widely than were garments of sealskin or dog skin.

For boots the skin of reindeer legs was best, and the tough hide of bearded seal was especially prized for soles because of durability. In some areas sealskin was used for uppers as well as soles. It made boots more watertight than was true for those of reindeer hide, even allowing for removal of most of the seal oil in tanning. This waterproof quality offered great value during times of wet snow, such as in fall before the arctic world froze hard and in spring during the thaw. Sealskin boots are said to be as watertight as modern rubber boots.

Continual care of native garments accounted as much for their effectiveness as did the design and materials themselves. Clothing simply was not allowed to get damp or ripped. Baffin Islanders had a saying that a woman with children knew no moment's freedom, so busy was she drying and repairing her family's clothing and sleeping robes. Rips and beginning weak places were corrected immediately, and every flake of snow or trace of rime was shaken or beaten out before parkas and pants were put on in the morning, or robes snuggled into for sleep. A special flattened stick was kept handy by the door expressly for the purpose.

Avoidance of sweating was important, too, and the cut of clothing helped in this regard. A layer of dead air was held between clothing and the wearer's skin and, warmed by the body, it stayed in place. Furthermore, cold outside air couldn't come in so long as a parka was worn closed at the waist (or hips) and throat. If ventilation was wanted, the bottom edge or neck, or both, could be opened to provide a regulated flow of air. This would cool the body and evaporate sweat, extremely important not only for comfort but also to keep the clothing from getting damp. Without pulling his second parka on or off, an Eskimo hunter could be warm enough to ride in a sled, or cool enough to cut blocks for a snow house or to paddle a kayak against the current without sweating.

Clothing serves three purposes in the white world of the polar and subpolar regions and the high mountains: it insulates the body, keeps it dry, and protects it from wind. The whole idea is to hold in body heat and, whether with an Eskimo's caribou parka or a mountaineer's down jacket, this is accomplished by compartmentalizing air into small, separate units within the fur, fiber, or fabric of each garment and between layers of clothing. Getting wet from the melting of snow or from sweat can be disastrous in part because the moisture fills the dead–air spaces and destroys the insulation. Wind spells trouble because to be effective dead air must stay "dead"—stationary.

The principle involved in dressing for snow and cold is the same whether for an Everest climber caught by nightfall, or avalanche, or for an Eskimo hunter waiting by a seal's breathing hole or a city dweller who has forsaken his apartment in favor of a weekend on the ski hill: provide insulation and control moisture.

CHAPTER 6

BLIZZARDS AND AVALANCHES

Records of snow disaster date well back into history. Hannibal crossing the Alps with his elephants in 218 B.C still comes readily to mind because of the avalanches he experienced. The crossing took place "at the setting of the Pleiades," probably late October. His entourage included at the outset thirty-eight thousand men, eight thousand horses, and thirty-seven elephants, but before the crossing was completed nearly half of the men, a quarter of the horses, and "several" elephants had fallen victim to mountain snows. For two days Hannibal's expedition camped at the top of the pass; then they started on. A blanket of fresh snow covered the crusted snow of an earlier storm—notorious avalanche conditions— and, as the descent began the animals' feet perforated the upper fluffy snow. That layer gave away and men, horses, and elephants plunged helplessly downslope. The tragedy has become one of the world's classics.

The human refusal to surrender to reality runs a stubborn thread throughout the literature of snow, for most persons caught in the white disaster of blizzards, or avalanches somehow deliberately court their fates. The turn-of-the-century Klondike stampeders furnish an example. As someone has written, God must have chuckled when he created gold: Nothing, not even women or drink, turns men into greater fools. Certainly in thirsting for wealth most of those involved in the gold rush of 1897-98 disregarded topography, climate, and their own human frailty.

Announcement of the newly discovered riches of the Klondike prompted a rash of advice on how to get there, and chartered boats began unloading would-be miners at a variety of unpromising access points. Best known is the route over Chilkoot Pass which led thirty-two miles from the coast at Dyea, near the top of the Alaskan panhandle, to Lindeman at the headwaters of the Yukon River. Seventy feet of snow fell at the pass during the first winter of the stampede; one single night brought an awesome six-foot snowfall. Tents collapsed beneath its weight, smothering occupants and burying caches of goods stacked layer on layer and futilely marked with poles by men relaying loads up the long slope to the pass.

Two of the routes alternate to the Chilkoot led over glaciers: the Valdez and the Malaspina. Twice the number of men who braved Chilkoot Pass that first winter after the strike set out over the Valdez Glacier, even though as an approach it led across a giant tongue of crevassed ice that stretched for twenty miles from Prince William Sound lowlands to a forty-eight-hundred-foot mountain crest, then down for nine miles to a series of streams and lakes that fed ultimately into the Copper River. The river, in turn, could be followed to the gold fields. Best estimates place success via the Valdez Glacier at about one half of 1 percent of those who tried it.

Fortunately, not as many Klondikers attempted the Malaspina Glacier as the Valdez. At fifteen hundred square miles it is the largest piedmont glacier on the continent and an incredibly rough route. Nonetheless, perhaps one hundred men landed at the Malaspina in the spring of 1898, forty-two of them destined to die there and others to be crippled for life. One party of eighteen recruits who had answered a *New York Herald* advertisement spent three months crawling over the ice in company with the man who had placed the ad. They slept in the lee of their equipment because nights were too windy for tents, and all were so weary they didn't speak for days at a stretch. "It was like traveling with deaf-mutes," noted the leader, Arthur Arnold Dietz. One sled, loaded with the party's most valuable possessions, disappeared into a crevasse along with four dogs and Dietz's brother-in-law, who was driving. A second sled and dog team fell behind in a blizzard, then vanished after the driver had gone insane from snowblindness and frustration. With the provisions of these two sleds gone, dried beans remained the only food, and a third man soon died of malnutrition accompanied by agonizing indigestion. Ice cut the feet of all, yet all not only continued but even dragged a quarter-ton motor up the glacier only to abandon it on the other side when winter's darkness and snow settled in. Crazy with boredom of a bivouac, four men struck out for Dawson and were lost. The other twelve huddled into a log shanty and spent the brief, gloomy subarctic days and the long nights cutting wood and stoking the fire. When spring came they started back over the mountains, hoping for escape.

An avalanche took three, scurvy a fourth and fifth. This left seven who somehow made their way back to the beach, where men from the revenue cutter *Wolcott* found them. By then three of the seven lay dead in their blankets and of the four who lived, two had totally lost their eyesight from snowblindness and the other two could barely see. All were dazed and uncomprehending. Despite this, a *Seattle Times* report of the rescue mentioned the men's "success," for somehow they had managed to acquire and keep a little gold dust.

To South American gauchos the word for blizzard is *el tormento*, expressive of the winter anguish experienced around the world each year. Suffering can be dreadful during violent snowstorms, yet Stefansson, writing in *My Life with the Eskimo*, says that a blizzard need not be dangerous even for one stranded out in it. The main thing is not to fight the storm foolishly; if visibility is nil, wait for a bit of clearing. He gives four rules to follow during the wait: Keep still, moving only enough to stay warm. Take care not to overexert and sweat, which dampens clothing. Contrive a shelter of some sort, preferably of snow, if the temperature drops to −10° F. or lower. Sleep as much as possible. This last counters all usual advice, but Stefansson insists it is the Eskimo way.

Blizzards can blot out even the closest and most familiar of landmarks, and snow may fall so thick it is hard even to breathe without sucking in its flakes. If the temperature is low under these conditions the snow usually is fine and dry and sifts into any least opening. With a wet blizzard the problem usually is sticking rather than drifting. Crushing snow loads build onto roofs and "shoveling" means using a saw to cut it into icy blocks that can be toppled from the eaves.

Perhaps ranchers have the hardest time of all with blizzards, for they must try to care for livestock as well as for themselves. Stefansson, born on a Dakota farm in 1879, at about age eighteen started a ranch with three other boys. Their first Thanksgiving a storm from Canada turned the world to swirling white. Somehow the boys had not strung a rope from house to barn, as was the custom, but Stefansson decided to brave the blizzard and care for the animals anyway. He thought he could use the wind direction as compass and, since the barn was a long one standing broadside to the house, he was confident he could find it. He did but then couldn't find the door. It was on the lee side of the building, and a drift there hid all traces. Shoveling would be pointless; snow would drift back as fast as any amount of digging could clear it. Besides, the shovel was buried. Stefansson thought of breaking through the roof but realized he still couldn't carry hay to the animals. The haystack was totally inaccessible. Chastened, he reversed course and arrived safely back at the house.

Years later, writing about the Arctic, Stefansson referred to this event which he had given little thought at the time. "I now consider it one of the most foolhardy enterprises of a career that has been in considerable part devoted to similar things," he wrote. Defying the blizzard and going to the barn wasn't what Stefansson had come to see as foolhardy; it was his unknowledgeable handling of the effort.

Wild animals have certain safeguards for the snow they are sure to encounter. Polar bears' eyes, for instance, are equipped with a nictitating membrane that passes sideways across the eyeball and clears slush, which blinds prairie cattle and arctic sled dogs. At the onset of winter, sables outside Moscow grow forty-four fine underhairs for each longer bristle hair, twice the number of underhairs they have in summer and marvelous protection against cold and wind-driven snow. Arctic foxes turn white in winter, as camouflage, and the soles of their feet become furry, which helps keep the paws warm and acts as built-in "snowshoes."

Against one aspect of winter, however, there is little protection for animals that chance to be exposed. This is the white fury of an avalanche. Popular belief holds that mountain-dwelling animals instinctively save themselves from avalanches. This isn't true. They often recognize the deep roar of onrushing snow for what it is, but they can't always save themselves. Some mammalogists believe that avalanches take a greater toll of these animals than any other one cause of death.

Avalanches affect wide areas during winters of heavy snow and in such years mountain-animal deaths increase. In the Alps chamois graze where avalanches recently have run, exposing dry vegetation, and while feeding they get hit by new avalanches. As many as thirty carcasses have been found in the snow of a single slide.

The Alps, five hundred miles long by one hundred wide, have for centuries been the world's most inhabited mountains and they also have the longest written record of mountain conditions. In his *Geography* the Greek-raised Strabo, writing a century and a half after Hannibal's battle with mountain snow, speaks of danger in the Alps "which comes to all, including the beasts of burden, who travel the passes on foot." He concludes that "these places are beyond remedy, so are the layers of ice that slide down from above—enormous layers capable of intercepting a whole caravan and of thrusting them altogether in the chasms that yawn below." Regardless, travelers continued to cross the Alps.

By the middle ages many of them were on pilgrimages to Rome. In December 1128 the abbot Rudolf from Saint-Trond, which is near Liege, led such a band over Saint Gotthard Pass. "As though fixed in the jaws of death we remained in peril by night and by day," he wrote. Avalanches had them terrified to proceed and equally terrified to lingering. Guides in the little village where they had stopped refused to risk going on, then finally were bribed into it. Wrapping felt cloths over their faces and pulling on heavy jackets, mittens, and spiked boots, they set out against their own judgment to scout the route while the abbot led a mass for their safety. Soon, Rudolf's history continues, "a most sorrowful lament sounded through the village, for, as the guides were advancing out of the village in one another's steps, an enormous mass of snow like a mountain slipped from the rocks and carried them away. . . ."

Such events must have been commonplace and well known. Yet both travel over the passes of the Alps, and settlement in the high valleys, showed no letup. Men are said to have muffled the bells hung around their mules' necks to silence the clanging lest noise set off an avalanche, and village children learned not to shout or slam doors on days when the snow hung precariously to the slopes. In Bavaria villagers each spring painted the sign of the cross onto eggs and devoutly buried them at the foot of known avalanche paths, praying divine protection; and a 1652 court of law officially pronounced witches as the cause of avalanches and set death as the punishment.

Human action often actually did contribute to avalanching. Villagers in need of lumber and firewood cut forests on slopes conveniently at hand and thereby created avalanche infernos where the hazard would otherwise have been moderate. Families then grazed cattle or sheep on the cutover slopes which stopped all possible forest regeneration and destroyed bushy growth that might have helped to anchor winter's buildup. Disaster commonly resulted.

Today in parts of the Alps man's effect is even more critical. Where ski resorts have taken over farm villages, livestock no longer is led to pasture on the high slopes, and the removal has influenced avalanche conditions in two ways. Paths formerly cut into the earth by the animals' hooves gently terraced the slopes every foot or two, and this was corrugation enough to help hold the snow. Also stock ate the grass to stubble, which left a serrated mat to bond well with snow. But in recent years grass has been growing tall in summer, drying in autumn, then bending to the ground beneath the weight of winter's first snow. This produces a slippery surface that contributes to avalanching. To prevent this some resorts and many peasant villages strictly enforce the mowing of autumn grass regardless of grazing. Forest practices also are closely and specifically linked with avalanche prevention programs, since snow is much less likely to break loose on a forested slope than on a bare one, and trees lessen the force of any slides that do slam down into them.

The siting of villages in the Alps long has avoided known avalanche paths, and as added precaution all residents join in maintaining barriers built on the most troublesome slopes. These are a series of platforms angled out from mountainsides where there are no trees. Formerly the barriers were built with stones brought down by previous avalanches or from wood, but now they usually are of aluminum which is lightweight, sturdy, and weatherproof.

Such work is done cooperatively; village life—in fact survival itself—has little place for individualism. Communal action dominates, several aspects of it quite directly linked to avalanche danger. Men get together to stamp paths into snow threatening village cows, then move them to safer elevations. Land ownership is so fragmented that a typical holding seldom totals more than ten acres which may be divided into fifty separate, widely scattered parcels. In case of avalanches this has advantages. A farmer might find one or two of his plots covered by snow or rocks and rendered worthless until he can clear them. But he never will be cut off from his farm altogether. Several plots are sure to remain unharmed, and he can work at a steady pace through the whole growing season.

Snow can flow almost as a liquid, or stretch elastically, or compress—all without losing its structure as a solid. It can cling particle to particle, layer to layer, and snowbank to ground surface; it also can abruptly lose all semblance of such cohesion. As much as one million cubic yards of snow have been known to give way and thunder downslope at a time. This amount would fill the beds of 10,000 ten-yard dump trucks, so many that if they were lined up bumper to bumper they would reach for about 200 miles. Such a slide may be triggered by nothing more than a falling stone, the hopping of a rabbit, thunder, the sonic boom of a jet airplane, or a man slicing across a slope on skis. Results sometimes are instantaneous, other times delayed. Several skiers may safely cross a poised slope before the cumulative effect of their passing sets off the snow and catches the last members of the party.

The middle elevations of the mountains tend to be the hardest hit. Comparatively little snow falls at lower elevations, and also those slopes usually are forested and for that reason alone somewhat protected from avalanching. Higher evelations tend to be barren and faceted with crags and steep faces that unload themselves before snow builds deep enough for major avalanching. Also, in these highest reaches, winds blow so ferociously that they sweep snow away rather than pack it into great slabs and cornices. Consequently the middle elevations with thirty- to forty-degree slopes generally produce the most avalanches. Convex slopes are the most deadly of all; snow on their steep lower portions tends to pull at the rest of the cover and set up enormous tensile stress. Steepness isn't requisite to sliding. If enough meltwater or rain lubricates individual grains, wet snow may avalanche no matter how gentle the gradient. A mere six or seven degrees can be enough. Or, sometimes instead of lubricating individual grains, the water seeps between layers and causes them to slip. On a moderate slope avalanche danger is likely to be great whenever the liquid content of the snow reaches 10 percent or more. If a handful of snow packs easily in the hand and feels slippery, it probably had reached this point.

No one can guarantee whether or not avalanching will occur simply by adding this condition and that. Nonetheless certain rules of thumb are now well established, and the magic and divine supplications of previous days have given way to knowledge. One might think, for instance, that a well-cohered snow layer poses minimum risk of avalanches: it is holding together and should be secure. Actually, the opposite tends to be the case. Great slabs of snow lying like immense tiles on a roof can rocket downslope en masse in response to the least disturbance. Such conditions present the greatest danger. Loose snow, whether wet or dry, tends to stabilize itself by sliding before enormous pressures accumulate; but where slabs of compact snow are involved, avalanching comes as the final collapse of what may be an enormous mass. Sometimes with a sound no greater than a click, sometimes with a thunderous crack heard for miles, such snow breaks loose.

Slab avalanches of this sort often start out huge. A whole slope starts into motion virtually at once, leaving a low vertical face to mark its line of fracture. Each storm will have built its own distinctive snow layer with a crystalline structure and water content all its own. Each surface will have been tailored by weather conditions before fresh snow falls and builds an overlying layer. Sometimes a slick rind of ice from a rainstorm is sandwiched between an old layer and a new one, or the sugar-crystals of depth hoar act as ball bearings and ease the breaking away of a slab whose time has come. A layer may be ten inches thick, or ten feet; it doesn't matter. If it is cohesive it will slide as a unit. Loose-snow avalanches, on the other hand, occur when cohesion within the snow is slight. Individual grains start to slip at a point near the surface and, once moving, these grains sweep others along with them.

Wet snow or dry powdery snow can be involved in either type of avalanche. Wet-snow avalanches take place most often in spring, frequently starting near a sun-warmed cliff. Moving snow may ball up and produce boulder-sized lumps that keep rolling and sliding until they grow as big as houses. Rocks and soil and trees first get shoved ahead of such a hurtling snow mass, then engulfed in its plunge. Avalanches gather, swallow, and transport everything in their path—yet their speed seldom exceeds ten or fifteen miles per hour. Once halted, they turn to instant "concrete," often tens of feet deep. In the Alps there is record of snow from a wet avalanche so thick it took fourteen months to melt.

Dry snow avalanches behave differently. They travel faster: Almost three hundred miles an hour has been clocked on a forty-degree slope in the Swiss Alps. Speeds are so great that dry snow becomes airborne as it avalanches. Slabs usually start to disintegrate along the leading edge as soon as their speed reaches several feet per second. After that, fragments of what had started as a single slab begin to tumble and may whirl into the air. Progressing downslope these powdery clouds disturb the air in front of them, and this whirls more loose snow into frenetic suspension. Trees and buildings may be blasted by this wind and toppled before the snow hits them. There are cases of damage occurring after an avalanche has stopped; the dreadful wind alone packs all the devastating potential needed. Death has struck men untouched by the racing snow; yet, when autopsied, their lungs show lesions of the sort produced by explosions.

Best advice if swept into the seething morass of an avalanche is to "swim" with it, not against it, and to move toward the surface and the sides where velocity is least. Try to keep the head uphill and the mouth closed and either by standing upright or lying face down when the sliding stops. Both positions help avoid swallowing snow, which is dangerous because it may put water in the lungs and bring death by drowning. Hands held boxer-fashion in front of the face give a chance for having breathing space. Struggling is folly. It's too likely to cause sucking in snow and choking. Don't waste energy shouting unless voices can be heard close by, and even then don't shout if buried. Curiously enough, sound carries downward in snow quite readily, but not upward.

Survival odds vary. Perhaps the all-time record for mass burial by avalanche belongs to villagers from Blons, near Arlberg Pass in Austria. Precautions had been taken. The ravages of snow were all to familiar. Each winter the village councilmen ordered removal of the crucifix that stood close to a certain ravine, lest it be damaged; and while crossing the bridge over that ravine villagers automatically walked in single file and quit talking whenever the snow seemed threatening. By spacing out they knew fewer would be taken should an avalanche roar down upon them. By not talking they knew it at least would not be their voices that set off the slope. Nonetheless on January 11, 1954, avalanches such as Blons never before had known broke loose, the first at 9:36 in the morning and a second at 7:00 in the evening. By the time the devastation was totaled, twenty-nine homes out of the ninety in the village were listed as demolished. Of 376 residents, 111 were caught. Of the people who had been buried, thirty-three extricated themselves, thirty-one were dug out alive by rescuers, and forty-seven were found dead. Eight of those found alive later died, and two persons never were found. The dividing line between a fair chance of rescue alive and very little chance is about one hour; very few victims survive under snow for more than three hours. A rule of thumb is that survival odds are halved by the passing of each thirty minutes.

The first rule for anyone present when an avalanche roars downslope and swallows other members of a party is to mark where victims last were seen. Branches from a tree will do, or a ski pole—anything! But do the marking immediately, before shock compounds mental confusion and falling snow changes contours and disguises small landmarks. Next, quickly search below the point of disappearance for any sign of a buried person such as a protruding ski, or an arm, or some avalanche cord (which is bright colored nylon cordage worn trailing from the waist). Finally, send someone for help while the rest of the party continues to search. When found, an avalanche victim probably will be in shock, suffering from the effects of cold, and suffocating. There may well also be head, neck, back and/or internal injuries. Initial treatment should include opening the mouth, clearing it of snow, and employing mouth-to-mouth resuscitation if indicated.

Rescue systems are so well coordinated in resort areas nowadays. Led to the scene by a witness to the avalanche, they work fast. Their search involves moving in a line across the avalanched snow, each man scuffing the surface and scanning for clues. That failing, still in a line, the team uses rods to probe coarsely along the fall line below the victim's last-seen position and also at the tip of the slide, in its eddies, along its sides, around any obstructions such as trees or boulders, and wherever abrupt changes in the slope may have altered the flow mechanics of the snow. The intent is to locate the victims quickly, checking the snow depths where the chances of survival are best. If possible more than one coarse-probe line may be in operation at the same time, or a single line may repeat its quick check an added time or two before going to the next stage of fine probing.

The fine probing is almost sure to locate the victim, but it is slow, and the chances of finding a body instead of a survivor are great. For the fine probe, men stand practically shoulder to shoulder with their feet about twenty inches apart. They gently thrust in their rods in unison, first by the right toe, then in the center between the feet, finally by the left toe. Everybody takes a short step ahead, and the process repeats. This methodically grids a slope every ten or twelve square inches. The rods are sections of steel or aluminum tubing ten to fifteen feet long and half an inch in diameter. They can be carried in short sections and fitted together at the site. Anyone who feels something within the snow leaves his probe in place, and the team leader, more experienced, makes additional tests. If shoveling is called for, care is taken to stop about a foot short of the detected object and change to digging with the hands. Harsh probing and frenzied use of shovels only add to the misfortune of victims. Success requires a sense of touch to feel the difference between rocks, frozen ground, wood, and human bodies. It takes an hour for twenty men to make a fine search of five hundred square meters of snow, probing to a depth of six feet. By using a coarser grid pattern, a greater area can be covered faster and victims' chances of survival shoot up. Unfortunately so do their chances of being overlooked.

Dogs can effectively speed the search, especially those trained to sniff a human odor carried through snow. Saint Bernards were the forerunner of today's avalanche dogs, equipped for the task by size and strength rather than by any particular training. Furthermore, legend aside, they didn't carry flasks of brandy strapped to their necks. As a breed the Saint Bernards seem descended from Tibetan mastiffs brought to Greece in the fourth century B.C. and then on into western Europe by the Romans. Their fame—and name—comes from their association with monks at the Saint Bernard hospice atop Saint Gotthard Pass.

Monks brought dogs to the hospice as defense against highwaymen. A few seem also to have been fitted with packs to carry milk from cowshed to kitchen, and it quickly became common practice for monks to take along dogs when they patrolled the pass for wayfarers. The dogs gave companionship, had a valuable sense of direction, and could easily plow through deep snow. They also could scent a man buried beneath snow. In this way dogs and monks became the world's first mountain rescue teams, extending help to all comers whether rich or poor, traveling alone or in groups. At Saint Gotthard and at other passes where the Augustinians also had monasteries, monks would go each winter morning to meet travelers approaching the passes from either direction. The constitution of the Saint Bernard hospice, dated 1436, directs this to be done from mid-November until the end of May "as the monks always have done," indication that the practice already was long established at the time the constitution was written.

CHAPTER 7

THE WINTER BATTLE

The whole audacious idea of overcoming winter snow was new as the twentieth century opened. Until then men had accepted submission to nature as their lot. Nor was this necessarily negative. Snow, far from an impediment, was utilized. Winter's blanket eased the problems of getting around. Webbed snowshoes in America and wooden skis across Eurasia made winter by far the easiest time of the year for travel. Snow smoothed terrain and opened limitless routes apart from established trails and waterways. Furthermore, it rendered the tracks of game animals visible even to inexperienced eyes and silhouetted the beasts themselves for marksmen of whatever skill. As modern living patterns replaced indigenous patterns, men still saw snow as a transportation ally not an enemy.

Villagers of the European Alps kept travel routes open by hitching six or so horses—or in some areas cattle—to an empty sledge. A heavy chain dragged from the back to cut the path through new-fallen snow, and additional horses followed behind with empty sledges to firm the course. Men on foot added finishing touches with shovels. All day might go into opening five or six miles of road. Such winter travel as there was depended on runners, not wheels, and men groomed snow to ease their glide rather than pushing it aside or hauling it off.

In Canada and in the northern United States road departments developed rollers to pack snow in place and provide smooth roadways. Shoveling or plowing snow off the road left a trench that was likely to blow shut or at least close in so narrow that teams scarcely could pass. Rollers worked much better. They provided a wide road easy and cheap to maintain partly because instead of being sunken it stood high and exposed, and fresh snow tended to blow off. Also packing the snow throughout the winter extended the sleigh season into spring, thereby shortening the weeks of sloppy travel through mud. In some cases winter crews used plank drags to supplement rollers, but overall the rollers did the job. They were enormous. Most were of wood, three to six feet in diameter and twice that long. They weighed two tons or more.

The coming of World War I brought the need for War Department trucks to keep rolling regardless of winter, and to accommodate them horsedrawn blades and motor plows began to gain favor over the rollers. Snow needed to be cleared, not compacted, and municipal street departments, as well as their rural counterparts, switched from packing and smoothing to shoveling and plowing.

Ice causes the worst removal headaches. Even where snowfall is heavy and troublesome the cost of getting rid of it runs a tenth or less the cost of removing ice. Unless the temperature hovers near freezing, ice can't be handled mechanically: the bottom half inch will be bonded so tightly to the pavement that scraping it damages the road surface.

Ice presents such problems that highway and street departments struggle to eliminate snow before it compacts or melts and refreezes. Salt once appeared a cure-all but alarming side effects give reason for considerable disrepute. Snow control in the United States alone consumes one-sixth of the world's total supply of salt. This represents ten million tons applied annually to sidewalks, streets, highways, and byways. The use averages from 400 to 1,200 pounds of salt per mile, per application. Cumulatively in a winter many roads receive more than 20 tons per lane mile.

This reliance began after World War II with acceptance of a bare–pavement policy. Previously, traction on snowy surfaces simply had been enhanced by spreading abrasives such as sand and cinder, but salt seemed to promise a better way. In the first years its use totaled about half a million tons for the whole nation—enough to demonstrate effectiveness and spark such acclaim that the volume applied has doubled every five or six years since. Road salting now amounts to a 150-million-dollar business, with Pennsylvania, Ohio, New York, Michigan, and Minnesota leading the way. Salt speeds the melting of snow and ice, weakens the bond to pavement, and by lowering the freezing point minimizes the formation of new ice. It turns two or three inches of snow, or an ice crust, into heavy slush that passing traffic splashes off onto the sides of the road. Cheapest and most widely used is rock salt, sodium chloride. Calcium chloride is the next most commonly used. Its costs is triple or quadruple that of sodium chloride, but it has considerable advantage because it works faster and stays effective at lower temperatures.

Damage to road surfaces became noticeable as soon as heavy salting began. Concrete needs multiple coats of boiled linseed oil and petroleum mineral spirit or kerosene to protect it from salt. Asphalt seems less affected, although baring pavement instead of leaving it insulated by snow increases damages from frost heaving. Corrosion of automobiles and trucks owing to salt costs an average of sixty dollars per vehicle per year in snowbelt states. Along roadsides excess salt damages plants as drastically as if drought had struck them. Wholesale scorching, stunting, and defoliating are part of the cost of present–day snow-free pavement—a high price in dollars as well as in amenity loss and nuisance.

Animal and human life suffers too. Deer drawn to roads to lick salt have been struck by cars. Dog owners protest damage to pets' feet. Widespread contamination of municipal wells has become commonplace and a few communities have been forced to close water supplies that had served for generations. Some of the trouble comes from snow scraped off streets and roads and dumped into rivers, lakes, and ponds; some is from seepage through the soil.

What are the alternatives to salt? Burlington, Massachusetts, recently returned to plowing and sanding, and reports an immediate 22 percent lowering in the cost of snow removal. The figure can't mean much until it represents more years, but it may be a harbinger. Oregon never switched from abrasives to a primary reliance on salt. Their system is to mix just enough salt into sand or cinders to ease loading and handling and to speed their imbedding into highway ice.

In regions where drift causes the greatest problems, road maintenance headaches can be minimized by building snow fences, baffles, and walls. How much snow the wind can carry depends on the cube of its velocity and any lull may cause it to drop its load. Thus, if the position of obstacles is deliberately manipulated, the formation of drifts can be controlled.

Heat is used to melt snow from critical short sections of pavement such as toll plazas and bridge ramps, but it is too expensive to warrant general use. Heat sources vary from overhead infrared lamps to electrically charged wire mesh imbedded in the pavement. The Road Research Laboratory in England is experimenting with graphite and other electrically conductive substances mixed into asphalt to permit heating entire road surfaces. At Klamath Falls, Oregon, the heat for keeping streets clear is geothermal. Water is piped into a hot zone within the earth, and steam is piped back up and into a grid beneath the streets. Mountain villages in Japan also use geothermal heat to control snow, but they spray the hot water directly onto the streets, flushing away the resulting melt in open ditches. A Russian system taps into the steam heating of buildings, using a hose to connect a street-level network of perforated pipes to rooftop steam vents.

Researchers throughout the world's snow belt are trying to develop additional approaches to the winter battle. Whatever the odds, man seems intent on continuing to roll. The days of surrendering to snow are past.

CHAPTER 8

SNOW AND LIFE

Snow has to be shoveled. It makes driving dangerous. Avalanches bring sudden death. Blizzards kill cattle. Say the word *snow* and modern man reacts negatively. But the tie between snow and life is ancient and not wholly malevolent.

Most insects time their cycles to be in dormant, pupal phases while snow mantles the land and food is unavailable, yet ladybugs by the millions have been found hibernating beneath snow. Birds generally migrate, but some species are superbly adapted to life in a cold and snowy world. Ptarmigan change their plumage to camouflage white and grow special feathery tufts on their feet as snowshoes. For insulation from the cold, they dive within snow's protective blanket. Grouse similarly snuggle beneath snow, growing special spurs to help them dig their way in.

Humans—even those who live in cities and those who escape to Caribbean islands in winter—depend on snow. It grows crops to feed the cities and turns the turbines of industry, which provide the dividends that permit the escapes. Clouds are seeded to increase winter snow accumulation, and regions argue over who rightfully "owns" the clouds and has the right to seed them and so increase their mountain snowpack at the expense of others elsewhere. Even forests are being tailored to manage the snowfields beneath the trees for their water content.

Trees markedly affect the buildup of snow. So, too, the buildup affects the trees and other forms of life. Let a spruce in the northern taiga tip slightly off vertical, and it will catch more snow than those still standing upright. Eventually the load breaks the tree or causes it to fall, leaving an opening within the forest. Other trees ringing the opening then grow most luxuriantly on their sides facing the extra light. In time the weight of snow caught on their branches overweights and breaks them, and the opening grows. Shade and the rain of dry needles from the branches are gone, which soon affects the plant community. Mosses die out and willow, alder, aspen, and birch take over. In time, snow bends these new branches and brings their tips within reach of snowshoe hares and ptarmigan. The surface of the glade becomes hummocky with caves formed beneath snow-weighted branches, and there small creatures take refuge. Nitrogen from their fecal pellets enriches the soil, and eventually spruce seedlings gain a new start. The succession of plants has come full circle.

Human understanding of the fine tuning of such relationships between snow and life has only barely begun. The elk of Yellowstone National Park, Wyoming, furnish an example. Massive winter die-offs during severely snowy years are normal for herd animals, but not even biologists have known or accepted this until recent decades. Judging from fossils, elk, also called wapiti, have been roaming the mile-high Yellowstone country for at least twenty-five thousand years. They are a North American species that migrated over the Bering land bridge during the last ice age. In time they ranged the continent from coast to coast and from the far north of Canada practically to Mexico. By early in this century they had decreased so that only about seventy thousand were left, perhaps half of them in the Yellowstone region. Establishment of the national park in 1872—the world's first such preserve—gave the elk sanctuary at what probably was a crucial time in their survival as a species. Man's knowledge of how to help them was faulty, however. The urge—and need—to protect domestic livestock extended to management of the wild elk herds. In those early years all predators from wolves and coyotes to cougars and

grizzlies were categorically branded as "bad," and systematically poisoned, trapped, and shot. As a result elk herds within the park increased.
So did winter die-offs.

The only correction seemed to be for firing lines of hunters to form
along the north boundary of the park each fall and shoot elk migrating
out of the snowed-in high country toward their traditional wintering
grounds at lower elevations around Gardiner. Park managers and the
public believed the die-offs came because the elk herd was too large.
More accurately the problem lay in men having usurped land the animals
needed for winter survival and having killed the predators that in nature's
scheme help to check burgeoning overpopulation. In fact, the "problem"
wasn't a problem except in men's understandable reaction to the die-offs
as cruel and wasteful of life. Actually they were normal. Die-offs forceful-
ly assure herd turnover, hard on some individual animals but an advantage to the herd in the long run.

Today's elk management in Yellowstone has become a planned non-
management. Herd size now is maintained as it was through the long millennia before men tried to alter the system. Predators have been allowed
to return to the park, and winter die-offs are accepted as a natural result
of heavy snow. During the winter of 1969—70, when snow came late and
lasted long, one of the park's elk herds lost perhaps a quarter of its number. As for the dead, their flesh gives life to the community as a whole.
Creatures from bears, wolves, coyotes, foxes, shrews, and mice to ravens,
jays, magpies, and chickadees depend on such deaths for their own lives.

A Russian ecologist has classified mammals as chionophobes, chiono-
philes, or chioneuphores, using the Greek word for snow *chion*. The
-phobes are those unable to adjust to snow: most cats, for instance, and
opossums. The -philes are those few with specific adaptations to snow
such as caribou and snowshoe hares. The -phores are those that can survive in snow but lack delicately tuned adjustments of either physiology or
behavior.

Elk and moose are chioneuphores. Their long legs help them move
about in snow. They also give them a chance to outrun predators and to
reach the twigs they favor for browse, which probably means that the
length didn't develop specifically in response to snow. Nonetheless long
legs act as stilts holding the possessor's body above the snow surface, and
moose are probably the next best snow travelers after caribou. Under
some conditions they too do everything possible to avoid the "wrong"
kind of snow. When it is deep they may stubbornly follow a packed sled

trail, even refusing to give way to an oncoming dog team, which guarantees pandemonium. Around two and a half to three feet seems to be the maximum snow depth moose will tolerate. If there is more than that their bellies drag. To avoid deep snow many moose make seasonal shifts in altitude or latitude. For instance, an altitude drop of 4,000 feet may require a British Columbia moose to travel 30 to 40 miles. To gain the same effect by shifting to a more southerly latitude it would have to travel for 350 miles.

Another means of avoiding excessive snow depth is to "yard up." Moose need an enormous quantity of food to survive; they have to get through the winter with nothing more than frozen willow tips, just like ptarmigan. Picking a place with ample forage and staying there helps. Otherwise the energy cost of fighting "wrong" snow may be greater than the gain of whatever food is found. Trampling packs the snow of the yard. An ideal location is a grove of willow or aspen sheltered from midday sun so that the snow surface won't melt in the morning and refreeze into a hard crust by afternoon. Eight or ten moose typically yard together in such a spot, staying within a fifteen- to twenty–five–acre area. Snow falling from the tree branches overhead contributes erratic compaction to the white blanket on the ground, and new snow sifting from the clouds bends branch tips into convenient reach for nibbling. Or, that failing, moose will rear up and pull down what they need with their forelegs. How well the animals fare depends on how much forage is available there.

In winters of deep and frequent snowfall moose may yard in spruce and fir thickets rather than in stands of birch, aspen, or willow which provide more nutritious browse. Or, they may migrate through coniferous forest in preference to broadleaf forest. This is placing a greater survival importance on minimum snow than on optimum forage.

Another means of getting around in snow—other than with the help of built-in stilts or snowshoes—is the battering ram approach. This is the method used by bison. Their legs aren't long; their hooves are small and sharp. But their strength is prodigious. If snow isn't crusted, bison can bulldoze through drifts three or four feet deep. You see them plodding with belly submerged, swinging their great shaggy heads from side to side to plow a trench into the snow. Cows and young string out behind the most massive bulls of the herd, following closely in their footsteps. This is an advantage that herd animals have over solitary animals such as moose. Within a herd the lead position can be rotated as the exertion of breaking trail takes its toll, so no individual has an undue burden, and all benefit. Herd members follow one another so exactly that it can be difficult to tell whether a lone animal or a considerable number have passed.

In Yellowstone bison and other animals have an additional—unusual—means of coping with snow. Some of them spend the winter in hot–spring basins where geothermally heated earth minimizes snow. Such opportunity, of course, is rare, and it is more common for many species to avoid snow by seeking exposed ridges that are swept free by wind. Mountain sheep, mountain goats, mountain antelope, chamois, and turs are well equipped with strong legs and hooves that give them unexcelled footing on steep slopes, or on loose surfaces such as rock scree and snow. They are inept in deep or crusted snow but are eminently well adapted to staying mobile and adequately fed among the high cliffs. There is no competition there from other grazers and browsers.

Musk oxen also depend on vegetation blown free of snow, so much so that they will crop an exposed slope until little food is left rather than feed in lush vegetation only a few yards away but lightly covered with snow. If proper grazing isn't to be found, or the energy needed to find it would exceed that likely to be gained from it, musk oxen have no real problem. They live off fat reserves built by around-the-clock feeding during the fleeting weeks of summer largesse.

Winter snow poses a problem, however. If a raging storm swirls around them and builds deep drifts of snow all musk oxen can do is to form a defensive knot with the young at its center where the warmth of the herd will provide maximum protection. If necessary they stand for days waiting out the storm without even lying down.

Musk oxen are the only land mammal that can bear the full blast of a far-north storm by doing nothing beyond standing and waiting for it to end. Other northern mammals, such as sled dogs, arctic foxes, and polar bears at least curl into the snow for protection if no better shelter is possible. But musk oxen survive with no shelter or fodder. Their wondrously warm coats are the key. An underlayer of fine wool covers their backs and hangs practically to the ground. It is thick and felted and serves as an airtight fringed rug of the best quality. Over this soft layer is a dark brown fleece of long guard hairs, slender at the roots and swelling toward their tips. They lie as as a close-fitted armor at the surface, holding air along their shafts and also protecting that within the underfur.

Beyond question man is the animal with the greatest impact on other life-forms in the North, but next in importance is the wolf. Snow gives both certain advantages. A wolf's track load is only a little over half that of a caribou and one-fifth that of a moose. Wolves hunt when snow crust supports their weight but not their prey's. If such crusts are too few during a winter wolves may starve. In fluffy snow, wolves also have something of an advantage over their prey because escaping animals must break trail for themselves, yet they leave a packed track behind them for their pursuers.

Men have feared, hated, and persecuted wolves only in recent centuries. Indian and Eskimo peoples don't feel this way, although they have lived with wolves long and closely. It is man as herdsman, not as trapper or hunter, who detests them. In nature, wolves don't decimate the wild herds they depend upon. Observe a hunt, and you see a pack give chase for perhaps an hour; then if there are no stragglers they turn to other pursuits. If necessary they can go for days without feeding. When they do make a kill nothing is wasted; wolves even lick blood from the snow while they circle a wounded animal. Parts of a carcass they don't immediately consume often are covered with snow to be fed upon later. Sometimes they make these caches under their beds, so as to conceal them from ravens, crows, jays, mice, weasels, martens, fishers, wolverines, and foxes, scavengers that raid wolf kills whenever they can.

Once wolves roamed all of the northern hemisphere except for the densest rain forests and driest deserts. Today their numbers and range are mere fractions of what they were. Wolves are practically eliminated from the United States, except for Alaska, and there and in Canada their fate alternates between policies of protection and of bounty-subsidized extermination.

Lemmings follow a built-in cycle which, about every four years, prompts what ends as a kamikaze stampede. Such migrations seem to occur only in Eurasia, not in North America, and they are not deliberate suicide marches to the sea. Rather they are great nervous millings about. If the most natural route of travel funnels seaward, the lemming hordes flow that way and, ultimately, with no more land ahead of them they continue into the water and swim as long as they can, then die. Many small herbivores with short life-spans experience comparable population excesses alternated with mass die-offs.

If food is abudant, reproduction takes place at an extraordinary rate; if not, it doesn't. A lemming litter born under the snow in March can produce its own progeny before the spring is out. But if the snow cover is thin while winter's cold still prevails, female ovulation will cease, and there will be no births. If snow lasts late and spring vegetation is meager, reproduction also will decline. There may already be a surplus population, however, product of a previous fecund year; and, if so, the famous migration to oblivion may start even before food has given out. Lemmings basically are not sociable, and when crowding brings them together the resulting stress sets up a hormone imbalance that causes some to move out. Jammed together by vagaries of topography they run with insane feistiness, chattering their teeth, snapping at one another, and panicking at any unexpected situation.

Similar in habit and sharing the same range are voles, slightly smaller than lemmings. Neither lemmings nor voles hibernate or have sufficient reserves of fat to survive winter without its blanket of snow. Even beneath it they must scuttle about continually to feed on whatever roots and stems and carrion they can find. This seldom is any problem. Most tundra plants carry growth buds through winter just above the ground surface, safe from freezing because of snow's insulation but readily available to lemmings and voles. Also, because these plants must sprout, grow, and reproduce with great haste as soon as summer begins, they maintain a dense mass of roots and rhizomes rich with stored carbohydrates.

The animals' need to feed actively beneath snow's protection works out well, as is true of all of nature's systems. Specially adapted to the task of finding winter food, the claws of lemmings and northern voles elongate and divide into prongs as autumn days shorten and turn cold, thus providing built-in snow shovels.

Foxes hunt also by zigzagging over the snow surface listening for faint squeals and scratchings, which they can hear through ten or twelve inches of snow. When a signal is picked up, the fox leaps high into the air to land stiff-legged with nose and forepaws held together. The sudden pressure breaks the snow crust, and the fox's jaws instantly close on its prey. Deep or compact snow thwarts such hunting.

Weasels and their European counterpart, stoats, hunt much the same prey that foxes do, but they go about it differently. They are small and supple enough to follow lemmings and voles into their burrows. They essentially swim through snow to initiate their chases, diving in and staying submerged until they succeed. None of the fox's energy expenditure of listening and pouncing, failing, and listening and pouncing again is required of the weasel family. They are at ease in the subnivean realm of their prey.

Lynx are another predator of the snow, the only American cat well adapted to the white world of winter. They are small cats despite the apparent larger size their fluffy coats give them. Broad and densely furred paws combine with fairly long legs to help lynx get around well in snow. Snowshoe hares are their main fare. They hunt by alternately leaping, then freezing in their tracks and crouching stationary and silent. Their sudden motion startles hares into bolting for safety, and their equally sudden disappearing act as they freeze the motion lures hares into hopping closer to investigate. It is, of course, their last hop. For lynx the ruse is necessary. They flounder if they try active pursuit of hares, but their bound-and-stop techniques work well.

Wolverines often victimize lynx. When snow is deep they trail them, then steal kills. Lynx are afraid of wolverines and retreat as soon as they see one. Wolverines also raid carcasses cached by wolves. In fact trappers often make their sets by such caches—and occasionally succeed in taking a wolverine. Man, in his long relation with snow and the life on it and in it, traditionally has understood the links between one species and another, and one snow condition and another. He himself has belonged to the web, and today's pioneering studies of snow ecology are only explaining what trappers and hunters have sensed empirically: that snow for many species is the key element in survival.

CHAPTER 9

SLED DOGS AND REINDEER

Fly into any Eskimo village in winter, and you are likely to find human villagers congregated in the warmth of church or school or home, or running errands on their snowmobiles or by taxi if there are roads. The village dogs, however, will be out in the snow, chained just out of reach of one another. If they are to be run, or if someone's passing excites them, they will be leaping and howling, their din filling the air with wild crescendos. If the day is cold, or at night, or if snow is falling or blowing, they will be lying curled with their tails wrapped around legs and noses. In this compact position dogs reduce body surface and lose less heat; also, their thickly furred tails protect their lightly furred lower legs and feet. No matter how cold or stormy they can survive outside without shelter.

Under similar circumstances wolves and polar bears and arctic foxes tunnel into snow banks. Dogs usually can't dig in. Their chains, only six to eight feet long, hold them short-tethered to stakes and their own constant presence packs the snow around the stakes to ice. Digging is impossible, and it's not needed. When storms come, dogs simply let themselves get buried by snow, thereby effortlessly achieving the insulation that other animals gain by tunneling. Even with snow lying directly against them, their fur doesn't get wet. It holds in body heat so remarkably that not enough escapes to melt the snow. This is essential, for wet fur is a poor insulator, and if it were to get wet, then freeze, it would encase the dogs in ice. But this doesn't happen. Instead the dead-air spaces of the fluffy snow are added to those of the fluffy fur, wind is excluded, and the dogs' warmth is enhanced.

Even without the advantage of snow, northern dogs can withstand intense cold. They don't need even a wall of snow to break the wind, nor do they need to be moved to the lee of their owner's house during a blizzard. On the trail they sometimes must endure wind-chill temperatures of −100° to −125° F., yet keep pulling.

Using dogs for haulage seems confined to the northern hemisphere, and especially to the arctic and subarctic regions, although Europeans until fairly recently hitched dogs to wheeled gigs and delivery vans, and Indian peoples of the North American plains used dog travois, which are long poles worn with a harness and dragged. Sledding, and the deep dependence of man on dogs, however, belongs exclusively to the Far North and to breeds within the spitz family, mostly malemutes, huskies, and samoyeds.

Sleds pulled by dogs varied depending on type of use and available building materials. Wood is scarce in most of the northern Arctic and Eskimos often substituted bone, whale baleen, or even frozen hides for it. One of their simplest methods was to soak a skin in water, fold it hairside out, press it flat, and let it freeze. Bearded-seal, polar-bear, musk oxen, beaver, and caribou skins were all fashioned into sleds, which with luck could serve for a winter or even two if kept dry when not in use. Caribou antler or small pieces of wood or whalebone, or even chunks of hard-frozen meat, were lashed onto the folded and frozen hides as crosspieces.

When possible, sled builders used wood. To get it many Eskimos in the central Arctic traveled great distances inland to forest lands. Others relied on driftwood brought to their barren shores from rivers draining faraway interior lands. Wooden sleds were of two main types: flat-bottomed toboggans and sleds with runners. The toboggans worked best in soft snow that runners would sink into, but on packed snow or ice only a small running surface was needed, and runners were best. This meant that people who lived in forested regions, where snow stays fluffy, used toboggans. Those who lived on the windswept tundra, where snow generally is crusted, used sleds with runners.

Regardless of type, aboriginal hunters pulled their own sleds and when moving camp had their womenfolk help pull them. Dogs, which were small compared to modern spitz, helped in hunting and maybe also acted as pack animals; quite clearly, they were eaten. But they weren't hitched as draft animals until late prehistoric time and weren't commonly used that way until the fur-trade era. Its culminating demand for pelts led to traplines as much as six hundred miles long, and men no longer could pull their own sleds. They needed too many supplies, and their traps produced too many furs to haul without help. Furthermore, using dogs to pull the sleds meant more speed, which meant more pelts and therefore more money. The money, in turn, meant more food for more dogs.

In spite of great environmental differences between regions, sleds of from eleven to fourteen feet generally were—and still are—favored throughout the north. Shorter sleds pound too much on rough snow. Longer ones are hard to turn in soft snow and unmanageable. Width typically is a foot and a half to two feet, about equal to the width of trail a man on snowshoes can pack most efficiently. The bed of most sleds rests six to ten inches above the runners, high enough to clear the surface of the snow and low enough to hold down the center of gravity. Upright stanchions line the sides of the bed, and a railing tops them. It projects beyond the rear of the sled to form handles for the driver to hold onto. Between stanchions a crisscrossing of rawhide or a lattice-work of short sticks keeps the load from falling out.

Construction can't be rigid. Sleds continually flex as they glide over irregularities, and their pieces must be lashed together rather than rigidly joined. This lets the sled "give" with the snow surface. A rigid sled would pound to pieces quickly. Runners are two or three inches wide curving up to the level of the bed, or higher, in front and extending out straight at the back to give the driver a place to stand.

Sapwood from a newly cut tree was (and is) best for runners, just as for toboggans. Steel runners work well at relatively mild temperatures, and some modern racing sleds even have a Teflon coating added to the steel. But when the winter temperature begins to hover below zero, most mushers replace steel running surfaces with hardwood, or switch to a sled with the appropriate surface already in place.

A sled with wood runners that has been gliding smoothly across inland snow will stop abruptly when brought onto sea ice. This is because the overlying snow soaks up brine and, consequently Eskimos who take their sleds onto the sea ice shoe their runners with strips of whalebone, which is unaffected by brine. The practice is both ancient and still in use today. This matter of precise snow conditions largely determines the ease—and even the feasibility—of sledding. Ideal temperatures are just warm enough for the pressure of the sled to melt the uppermost snow surface and provide a film of water for the runners to move on.

Wind and temperature both affect snow. Eskimos put off travel for a few days after a deep snowfall, waiting for wind to rework the surface into a crust and to drift loose snow over the rough places and smooth them. Such blessings can turn into liabilities, however. Often a breakable crust forms, or sastrugi turn tundra snow into a hopeless sea of sharp pinnacles.

Even when traveling on land under favorable conditions there can be moments when progress seems akin to making way through loose drifts of icing sugar. Dogs flounder in soft snow, and a driver often has to go ahead on snowshoes to prepare a trail. He may even have to go over it again and again before it can hold dogs and sled. Freshly made tracks are soft, but by the following day the snow will have recrystallized and the trail become firm. To take advantage of this, drivers often snowshoe a trail a day ahead of time. Even if it gets drifted over and doesn't show well, the dogs' paw can find it. So can human feet. You feel the firmness. But step off, and in you go.

To keep dogs pulling, a driver continually claps his hands and whistles, clucks and chirrups to them. He keeps them aware of progress by his voice, and holds their interest in order to buoy their morale. Beyond question a dog team runs with high spirit. Our driver on a dog-sled trip in Alaska claimed that the hardest commands to teach are "Stop" and "Stay stopped." In the excitement of running, dogs reinforce each other's behavior and prompt still more running. Overcoming this is hard. One is likely to keep on going or to start up again after a short pause, and they all take off again. Unless dogs are tired, they want to run.

On warm days some mushers stop and let their teams eat snow to replenish body moisture. The dogs pant furiously during these rests, as they also do while running. This is their normal way of cooling off, although they also lose excess body heat from the thinly furred skin of the groin and "underarms." To keep their dogs' paws from getting cut on the sharp edges of snow crystals, women in some parts of the Arctic make little shoes of sealskin or reindeer hide for the dogs, cutting a hole for the nails of the two front toes to stick out through. Careful drivers watch the snow and put these booties on as soon as it becomes abrasive. Others wait until they notice bloody footprints. Traveling through a wet blizzard it sometimes is necessary to stop and brush snow from the dogs' eyes.

Even when all is going well the chances are it won't last long. There may be no snow falling to blind the dogs, or rough snow to cut their feet, or crusted snow to break beneath their weight, but almost surely, sooner or later, two dogs will start to fight, or the whole team will chase off after caribou or a moose. If not this, the snow may well need to be packed ahead by snowshoeing, or the sled will burrow its nose into a snowdrift and have to be jerked free. Once everything is ready to go again, the runners may stick and need vigorous rocking and lifting to overcome their bond with the snow and get the sled back in motion. Not even passengers simply tuck into the folds of caribou robes and ride for hour after hour. Nothing muscle-powered can be that simple. Besides, days cold enough for good sledding are too cold to sit for long. Dogs can haul sizable loads in reasonable time, however, with distances, speeds, and weights varying a great deal. Probably a load of around seventy–five to one hundred pounds per dog is representative and, given that weight and pulling under reasonably favorable snow conditions, a nine-dog team can travel thirty to forty miles a day for weeks at a time.

The process of getting a nine-dog team unchained from the stakes and hitched to a sled takes a person working alone from fifteen minutes to half an hour if all goes well. On return from a trip the process has to be reversed, and the dogs fed. One of the main advantages of snowmobiles over dogs is eliminating this time spent hitching and unhitching. With a snowmobile the only preliminary to getting underway—usually—is to pull the starter cord. On return all that is needed is to stop and climb off.

Another reason many arctic people have switched to snowmobiles is that pouring gas into a machine is easier than getting food for a dog team, then storing, preparing, and dispensing it. A sled dog weighs about fifty pounds and needs half as much protein per day as a man does. Multiply this by keeping five to ten dogs, and it is obvious that as much work goes into fishing and hunting for a dog team as a family. Two or three tons of flesh may be needed each year.

Most of all, ease of travel and speed have led arctic peoples to abandon dogs for snowmobiles. A man on a snowmobile can go two or three times as far in the same number of hours as he formerly could by dog team. He also can pull a longer, heavier sled and do so under a greater range of snow conditions. He seldom even has to snowshoe ahead to pack a trail; all he need do is uncouple the sled and roar out on his machine, then come back after a double pass over the trail and hitch on the sled.

The machines haven't totally simplified life, however. They break down and wear out, often on the trail. Dogs took time to get underway, but always started. Also, if one dog gave out, the others still pulled. But let even a small part of a snowmobile break, and the whole machine may be useless.

Frostbite injury is far more common among snowmobilers than dog mushers because the machines' speed creates a chilling wind that drivers steadily face into, whereas handling dogs means getting on and off the sled, riding awhile and running awhile. Even fingers move constantly while sledding but not when gripped around snowmobile handlebars. The noise of snowmobiles is another disadvantage, so significant that hearing loss has become common in the Arctic. The concentrated weight of snowmobiles also is a problem. They break through weak ice and immediately sink, whereas dogs generally avoid such places instinctively, and they keep pulling if caught. Nonetheless, snowmobiles' advantages so markedly outweight drawbacks that acceptance has burgeoned throughout the north.

The practice of reindeer herding stretches from Lapland in northern Scandinavia, across all of Eurasia to the Chukchi Peninsula and Sakhalin Island, but seems never to have crossed to America (until the none-too-successful introduction among Alaskan Eskimos in the 1890s). Seemingly this is man's most recent domestication, occurring around two thousand years ago.

How did it start? Some say domesticating reindeer was an outgrowth of keeping cattle and horses in the Lake Baikal area, as tribes simply added deer to their other herds. Others say the beginning probably was on the headwaters of the Amur River. Tungus there would have observed domesticated camels and yaks, as well as cattle and horses, and when they subsequently pushed northward to the Yenisei region they may have taken along cattle and horses and substituted reindeer for camels and yaks, which couldn't adapt to the new environment. Or it may be that tending deer grew out of hunting them. Certainly an element of wildness remains in the tamest reindeer, and much of man's relation to them is more like hunting than usual herding.

Probably man's first advantage in gaining mastery over deer was to use those he tamed as decoys. At the outset, the main value of spending time in taming deer was to insure success in hunting wild deer. Once that relationship had begun, other aspects of herding were borrowed from cattle and horse cultures. Reindeer used as saddle animals and for packing seem to have derived mostly from Mongolian and Turk horsemen, although Lapps may have acquired saddles from Scandinavians.

Pulling sleds with reindeer probably was adapted from dog-sledding. Reindeer harnesses show no similarity to those used with horses or oxen but are like Siberian dog harnesses. Deer have advantages over dogs in greater strength and also in their self-sufficient manner of feeding.

Reindeer herding remains the economic key in much of Eurasia. Reindeer and their herders across a northern swath of Scandinavia constitute Lapland; it has no other territory, no political entity. Lapland is a tradition more than a land: By consent, those of its people who wish to do so still follow their herds from the Norwegian coast and islands, where the deer summer, to the woods of Sweden and Finland, where they winter.

In Alaska reindeer herding never really has caught on. Most Eskimos continue to prefer wild caribou to tame reindeer, a tie to hunting that still contributes to their livelihood and recently has received legal recognition for both Eskimos and Indians in Canada and Alaska as part of native-claims settlements.

Hunting methods vary throughout the Arctic but always have centered on the animals' migration. Stone cairns set in a row fifty yards apart for five or six miles formerly would lead to a lake where women and children waited along the shore and men on the water in kayaks. When the caribou approached drifting along the line of cairns, the women and children howled like wolves, or leaped from hiding, to stampede them into the water or onto thin lake ice. There the men speared them. Or, instead of leading to a lake, some fences funneled into a rocky defile or a river crossing where hunters waited. In forested country, poles set upright served instead of piled stones. Deadfalls also were used widely, usually with drift fences leading to them. Eskimos built pits entirely of snow. They mounded it up with an easy incline for walking to the top of the mound, and an abrupt drop into a pit that was concealed with snow and moss. Often they set knives upright into the snow at the bottom.

In Alaska, snowmobiles have prompted at least behavioral change, whether or not genetic. Just the sound of a motor sets caribou fleeing and, in the few years since snowmobiles' arrival, they already have learned that the machines can't follow up a steep slope, into a rocky place, or across snow-free ground. Only those that grasp this truth survive. Herd animals can learn from experience in a way that solitary animals such as moose or bear cannot. For these creatures the first chance to learn what happens when a snowmobile gets close may well be the last chance. But with caribou some survive even a considerable slaughter, and a leader that has learned from the experience will be followed as later snowmobiles approach. Caribou now even can discriminate between the mail plane's engine and a snowmobile's. They become alert when the plane passes over, but if the whine of snowmobiles comes into range, they are off.

The efficiency of the snowmobile, and earlier the rifle, has brought waste. With a convenient and assured power to kill, hunters have over-killed and seemingly mostly from this one cause caribou herds have de-clined. Canadian barren-ground caribou once numbered two or three million but by 1955 biologists counted only 278,900. Today the count is back up to half a million. In Alaska the arctic herd, which stayed at about 250,000 caribou, has dropped to only about 60,000. For the barren-ground herd the rifle is largely to blame; for the arctic herd, the snowmo-bile. Other factors may be involved, as well. Perhaps man's battle against wolves contributed to an unnatural excess of caribou, which now has trig-gered a built-in population adjustment. Maybe the die-off is in part owing to some little–recognized natural cycle. Hopefully, restricted hunting will let the caribou rebuild whatever the reason for their decline. The tradi-tional arctic triumvirate of men, dogs and deer never again will be as it was; times have changed. But, if all goes well, it will endure and even prosper along new lines not yet known.

CHAPTER 10

SKIING

Not only in the Far North but throughout the snow belt of North America and Europe, the two-cycle whine of the snowmobile be-came the sound of winter through the 1960s—a sound in the late 1970s or the 1980s perhaps destined to be at least partially silenced by the energy crisis. Where man once depended on sledding, snowshoeing, or skiing, his technology now provides effortless zipping about by machine. No training is needed to operate a snowmobile, no particular coordination or license, not even a road. Just go.

Northerners have come to rely on the machines for winter transporta-tion, law enforcement officers and wildlife wardens make their rounds by snowmobile, and children are "bussed" to school by them. Millions of dollars go into snowmobiling as recreation. Alaskans even air-freight their machines to enter the 160-mile race from Nome to Teller and back. Con-testants in it have careened across the land as fast as 90 miles an hour de-spite temperatures of -45° F., thus creating their own awesome wind-chill factor. The effects of literally millions of snowmobiles unleashed upon the winter world are legion—and notorious. Wildlife suffers from distur-bance and from mechanical alteration of snow cover, as well as from increased vulnerability to hunting. Plants get broken by passing machines, crushed by their weight overhead, and damaged by cold, since compacted snow offers little insulation. Snowmobiles break through the ice of frozen lakes and rivers, bringing death. They are costly and noisy, wholeheartedly disliked and equally wholeheartedly welcome. For many who live where winter is long and snowy the machines have brought welcome revolution; for others they have brought an unconscionable desecration of winter purity. For better and for worse snowmobiles have done to today's snow country what tin lizzie automobiles of yesterday—also for better and for worse—did to greener lands and in milder climates. The human impulse is to go and to do, and snowmobiles make it easier in winter.

Yet the machines aren't the first device to facilitate travel over snow. Man has had proper equipment for millennia and with it long ago divorced himself from dependence on the sea for travel and for food even in the snowbound north. Wearing snowshoes or skis he learned to walk along river valleys and across bogs when winter brought its yearly gifts of cold and snow. Frozen rivers then become highways to travel with equal ease in either direction, and the bottomless ooze of boggy ground no longer acts as an obstacle. Even forest travel is simplified once brush disappears beneath the snow. The long story of transportation has no more important chapter than that concerning the invention of snowshoes and skis. They underlie northern culture with one major exception: most Eskimo peoples stayed along the wind–blown arctic coast where snow is crusted and firm, and their hunting was for seals and walruses. They traveled across the sea ice, not the land, and didn't need elaborate gear for their feet. Some groups had crude snowshoes but on the whole Eskimos had no such basic reliance. Most other northern peoples did.

Curiously, southern hemisphere peoples had no snowshoes or skis. The Ona Indians of Tierra del Fuego sometimes tied small bundles of bushy twigs to their moccasins when walking in fluffy, new-fallen snow and their name for this translates as "shoe snow." Their whole approach to the problem was crude and temporary. Andean mountain people similarly developed no notable snow technology. That distinction belongs to the northern hemisphere, where it is fundamental from Japan across Asia and Europe to America. In general wood-plank footgear, or skis, belong most fully to Eurasia and webbed footgear, or snowshoes, to North America. Probably the earliest use of each was in central Asia, although evidence is skimpy. Wood and fiber webbing seldom last long and even archaeological traces can be expected only from dry caves or continually wet mud where chance preservation is possible. Regardless of origin, however, the practice of enlarging the feet to ease travel over snow is a natural concept for inventive peoples and individuals, and the fact that a few snow-country groups lack this technology is perhaps more remarkable than that most have it.

Snowshoes probably came first. In simplest form they are easier than skis to make and to use, whether no more than a tree bough added to the feet or a crude frame with some sort of crisscrossing. Snowshoes were used by early farmers in Sweden and Norway and pastoralists in northern Spain. They are known in ancient Tibet, on the Amur River, and among the Ainu of Sakhalin and Hokkaido. In America they range from the Atlantic to west of the Rockies, and from Arctic to desert. Frames were of everything from willows to spruce to whalebone. Shapes were rounded or oval or hour-glass, with a blunt toe and pointed heel, or pointed at both ends. Some European styles even are ladder-shaped—two straight boards connected with crossbars and left open at toe and heel, a stiff and clumsy contrivance but better suited to snow than the mere booted human foot. Webbing also has varied widely. Best is babiche, but sinew or even fish skin will do. Ainus and Mackenzie delta Eskimos simply used six crossboards and practically no webbing, and Mesa Verde Pueblo Indians sandwiched yucca leaves and roots between crude twig frameworks.

The oldest known wooden skis belong to late Neolithic times, four thousand to five thousand years ago. They are two types, arctic and southern. In the earliest southern styles, thongs pass through holes in ridges along the sides of the footrest. Tied to the foot, these thongs hold the ski on. This design was poor, however, because even in moderate use the side ridges broke easily. To correct this, men soon started thickening the footrest and passing the thongs through it horizontally, then bringing them up around the foot. Skis of this type have been found in bogs from the Ural Mountains to Norway.

Arctic skis had no raised footrest. They were held to the feet by thongs strung vertically through the skis themselves, and sometimes the bottoms of the skis were grooved between the holes to accommodate the thongs, so that they wouldn't interfere with sliding and would wear well. The oldest known skis of this type come from Sweden and have been dated at 2000 B.C., and, since time would be needed for such refinements to develop, these particular skis must have had forerunners unknown today. The Holmenkollen Museum on the outskirts of Oslo displays several ancient skis discovered in Scandinavian bogs, six of them older than one thousand years. In style and proportion they look about like the wooden downhill skis of the 1950s.

The earliest written record of skiing is a petroglyph chipped into the rock near Rodoy on the west coast of Norway. It shows a man skiing, his feet shod with long boards upturned at the toes. The silhouette is unmistakable and could as well belong to a modern skier as an ancient one. The skis are perhaps a little long even for cross–country skis today and the toes more sweeping, but not much. Skiing is one of mankind's oldest modes of transportation, and basically it has changed little. With the early skis at Holmenkollen are ten ski quotations from the years A.D. 920 to 1120. Even older written mentions are known in the seventh–century annals of China's T'ang dynasty. These speak of fishing and hunting peoples who wore "wooden horses" on their feet and used "props" under their arms. Thus wondrously equipped the people "went forward at least one hundred paces with every stride."

As is true of snowshoes, the styles of skis varied from place to place according to differences in snow and in human need. The widest and shortest were developed by the Siberian Evenki people who live in a forested zone of notoriously fluffy snow. The Holmenkollen collection has a pair of these only four and one-half feet long by ten inches wide with the toes only slightly bent up. Among the Nivkh people at the mouth of the Amur River and on Sakhalin Island the mark of a good hunter was to foretell accurately which type of skis to use according to season and weather. Fairly long, plain board skis were fine for winter trips to cut wood, for fishing through the ice, or for visits to villages not too far distant. They worked well in deep snow or on spring crust. But for hunting, where speed and silence were important, skis lined on the bottom with fur worked much better. Men attached strips of hide layer on layer along the whole length of the ski using fish glue, and sometimes they added whalebone edging. Skin of moose, deer, and seal worked best, each for a specific use in certain type of snow. Linings of moosehide slid poorly on winter snow but were fine in the warm fall or spring weather, and were particularly valued for sliding on the granular snow of spring without making noise. Deerhide slid smoothly on ice or snow in cold weather; skis lined with sealskin were equally usable but wore out sooner. A man needed to have a pair of each kind to live successfully.

In North America skis remained crude compared to those of Eurasia or to the continent's own highly developed snowshoes. The concept was distributed fairly widely in aboriginal times but never refined. Modern skiing came to North America as a European import little more than a century ago. The first colonists came mostly from England and France and Germany where skiing was little known, but when Scandinavians began arriving in America they brought their winter "long shoes" with them.

Today winter and skiing go together so naturally that even those who know the sport only through television have difficulty realizing how novel it was to most people just recently. Best estimates are that even by the mid-1940s there were only about two hundred thousand skiers in the United States. The figure now is ten million, and rising.

Scattered beginnings must have introduced modern skiing to the Americas but records are scarce. In the 1850s California experienced a ski craze—and it wasn't the legendary Norseman known as Snowshoe Thompson who first started it, as commonly is believed. Thompson made his first trip skiing mail from Placerville, California, to Carson City, Nevada, in January of 1836, a ninety-mile four-day feat with a heavy rucksack of letters and packages on his back. But six years before that skiing had begun in the Sierra gold fields at Rabbit Creek, a boomtown now known as LaPorte. The first skis, fashioned of barrel staves, evidently were the idea of Scandinavian sailors who had jumped ship in San Francisco and joined the stampede to the mines. Soon everybody had a pair, with the initial design quickly improved upon. "Long snow shoes" were standard winter equipment throughout the district from infancy into dotage.

Perhaps as early as 1853, and certainly by 1857, LaPorte was hosting downhill ski races. Each town in the mining district had its own club, and there never was a problem in attracting contestants to line up for prize money collected mostly from local saloons. Skiers stood at the top of a slope, someone hit a circular saw with a hammer, and at that signal a flagman dropped a red kerchief to signal timekeepers at the finish line to start stopwatches. When racing hit its peak in the late 1860s and into the mid-1870s, contestants used skis ten to fourteen feet long, about four and one-half inches wide, an inch and a half thick under the foot, three-quarters inch at the back, and one-quarter inch at the front. With these strapped to their feet they responded to the gong by shoving with their poles and striding to get up speed. They bent to a squatting position to cut wind resistance, held their poles parallel to the snow, and schussed. If both the snow and the choice of "dope" applied to ski bottoms were right the men shot downslope at speeds reported as eighty or ninety miles an hour, a speed that sounds high now may be accurate considering the nature of the race courses.

East of the Rockies skiers seem to have taken to New England slopes for sport by 1880, and a ski club was organized in Minnesota a few years later. By the 1900s organized sport skiing began to build popularity in America. A National Ski Tournament was held at Ishpeming, Michigan, in 1905, replete with a Suicide Hill jump 393 feet high. By the late 1920s clubs in New York City and Boston had persuaded the New York, New Haven, and Hartford Railroad to run special night ski trains to New England slopes, and a ski school, the first in America, had opened at Franconia, New Hampshire. In 1932 ski jumping and cross-country competition figured in the winter Olympic Games held at Lake Placid with Franklin Delano Roosevelt present for the opening ceremonies.

The Games added greatly to public interest in skiing, partly because in attendance there was Lowell Thomas, the renowned broadcaster. At Lake Placid he met Erling Strom, a young Norwegian who had come to the United States from a position in the King's Guard, which had included teaching skiing to the royal family. Thomas signed on for lessons with him, and became addicted to the sport. Under contract to make nightly news broadcasts from New York City, he began taking his wife, a secretary, a radio engineer, and a telegraph operator from ski slope to ski slope, broadcasting from whatever make–do studio he could contrive and paying the wire charges to New York himself.

Lowell Thomas skied his way from the Canadian Laurentians to the California Sierra winter after winter, his reports bringing a bonanza of publicity to ski resorts, most of which were just getting underway in the 1930s. For example, the Union Pacific Railroad Company had scouted Mount Rainier, Mount Hood, Yosemite, Reno, Jackson Hole, and supposed meccas in Colorado and Utah, then decided on Ketchum, Idaho, as location for a ski development. They christened an outlying stretch of countryside Sun Valley and hit on a new way to move skiers from valley floor to the tops of slopes: a chair lift. Rope tows recently had been pioneered at Woodstock, Vermont, and the only other lifts in use were gondolas suspended from moving cables. There was nothing between the two extremes. An engineer with the railway, who previously had worked in the tropics loading bananas, got the idea of adapting the type of endless cables he used there into a ski lift. All that was needed was to replace the banana hooks with hanging chairs. Sun Valley opened in 1936, its chair lift the first in the United States.

The adventurous, somewhat hazardous character of downhill skiing has been notorious from the outset. The names of ski runs tell the story: Suicide Six, Nose Dive, Devil's Hangover, Devil's Dip. One of the major forces for safety in the midst of such derring–do, where wearing a leg cast is akin to a badge of honor, is the National Ski Patrol Service. It was born largely of one man's injury and another man's death. Minot Dole, one of the true fathers of modern North American skiing, fell while skiing in the rain at Stowe, Vermont, in 1936. His ankle was badly broken, and he had to lie in the snow for hours while one friend tried futilely to keep him warm and two others went for help. A few weeks later, while Dole still was hobbling around on crutches, one of the friends who had helped rescue him was killed in an interclub ski meet. Grieved and shocked, Dole and others in his ski club decided to study the causes of accidents, then find a way to lessen them.

Out of this grew the present-day National Ski Patrol. An attempt at such a system had been made before, but it operated ineffectively. Dole determined to have a model system of safety and rescue ready by the time of the 1938 downhill and slalom ski races to be held at Stowe. Competitors and spectators were coming from all over America and Europe, and he planned to impress them and set a precedent for future races. Instead of patrolmen simply "being around" and helping if they saw an accident, the new organization put separate teams in charge of definite sections of trail and equipped each with its own toboggan, splints, bandages, blankets, and vaccum bottles of hot coffee. The result is the highly respected volunteer Ski Patrol, which assures reasonable safety and rescue for all.

Minot Dole also was responsible for launching a second organization singularly important in the annals of American skiing. This is the U.S. Army's 10th Mountain Division. In a way it stemmed from the Ski Patrol. In 1939 patrolmen were enjoying beer after races at Manchester, Vermont, and their talk turned to the Finnish ski soldiers who that winter were dismaying the Russian invaders of the Karelian Isthmus. What if foreign troops were to attack the east coast of the United States? Shouldn't there be American ski troops trained for such eventuality? The National Ski Association offered the idea to the War Department, which answered politely with "thanks for your suggestion" and did nothing.

Dole wasn't to be put off by this brushoff, however. He knew his idea was good, but it took two sets of contacts through former Yale classmates before he managed to reach General George Marshall and successfully present his proposal. Military thinking at the time held that if Germany were to attack the United States, the most likely route would be down the St. Lawrence River and into the Champlain Valley, as the British had done in 1779. If such an attack were to be stopped, the Adirondack, Green, and White mountains would become the line of defense, and in winter that meant ski troops. Skiers native to New York, Vermont, and New Hampshire who knew the overall terrain and the back roads could be organized into patrols and used as scouts and guides.

By April 1941 the Winter Warfare Board approved specifics for ski-troop equipment. The following winter the United States declared war, and ski training started at a special camp set up for the purpose in Colorado: Camp Hale. The rest is history. Men there skied hard and trained hard, and when the volunteer 10th Mountain Division was sent to Italy they fought hard. Three months of combat brought four thousand casualties among seven thousand men. Press coverage of the valiant troops for the first time drew the entire nation's attention to skis.

After the war the exuberance of 10th Mountain Division men together with their heroes' stature added impetus to the growth of skiing, which had reached its time for mass popularity. Some of the men returned to lives as ski instructors, others as five-days-a-week working men and two-days-a-week skiers, or ski bums. All acted as catalysts.

New Orleans and Dallas have ski clubs, if no snow slopes. Even Hawaii rides the ski bandwagon. On the Big Island the white slopes of Mauna Kea float above the green of palms and the blue of the ocean, and enthusiasts forswear wet suits in favor of ski parkas. Jeeps climb to the 13,784-foot summit with skiers, then grind back down to bring them up again after their downhill runs. The snow often lasts into July.

The world's longest groomed slopes are at Savognin in the Swiss Alps, where even a mini run is more than a mile long, and anybody who can stave exhaustion can get in fifty miles of lift-served downhill skiing in a day. Iran has some of the newest major resorts. Or, if the Caspian region holds no allure, skiers now can try the Caucasus. Russian's Citizen Exchange Corps arranges ski trips to Chegut, largest winter resort in Russia, with six chair lifts, runs featuring vertical drops of 3,400 and 4,300 feet, and a lodge at 13,500 feet on Mount Elbrus, Europe's highest peak, elevation 18,481 feet. If all of this isn't enough, skiers can shuttle back and forth between nothern and southern hemispheres; July in the Rockies corresponds to January in the Andes, in Australia, or on Mount Kilimanjaro and professional skiers and Olympic aspirants regularly head south when the ski slopes of North America, Europe, and Japan melt.

Equipment has become as elaborate as has getting to the slopes. Read an advertisement for "high performance ski-wear," and you know that the baggy pants of the 1950s and the stretch pants of the 1960s have no place in the 1970s or 1980s. Today's fashion calls for "Racy, high-waisted suspendered pants with stretch inserts to give ski-flex." Also fashionable are "Feather Weather parkas of down. The color: pale Olympink for her, darker burgundy Skianti for him."

Leather boots are scarcely even a memory. Plastic boots have replaced them on the slopes, with attention on flow padding. This is a layer of silicon with particles, such as cork, floating in suspension. Heat and pressure from the foot cause the silicon to flow and presumably to accommodate to the individual foot. Skis themselves also have changed. Their evolution has been from wood to metal to fiber glass to laminations of all three. Metal gives strength for quick, high-powered turns. Fiber glass cuts down on vibrations and clatter and damps excess springiness. Both are lighter than wood, but wood still is used for skis in combination with the newer materials.

Even ski slopes are now the product of technology. Wholly artificial slopes offer year-round skiing. Los Angeles has seven-acre Ski Villa with plastic snow made of interlocking tiles, each six inches square and shaggy with bristles that provide a surface skiers say is smoother than actual snow. Not even real snow is free of the artificial touch. For example in Michigan, which draws about 10 percent of all U.S. skiers, most winter resorts add artificial snow to whatever the clouds deliver naturally. Special machines spew a fine spray of water that freezes into an acceptable facsimile of snow. For many resorts the machines are the only assurance of snow as early as Thanksgiving and as late as Easter, and that long season is needed for profit.

Race speeds now have reached 100 miles an hour and over. In 1970 Yuichiro Miura with $3 million of backing and a retinue of thirty–one comrades and eight hundred porters skied for 6,600 feet and tumbled for 1,320 feet down the South Col of Mount Everest, beginning less than 2,000 feet below the 27,890-foot summit. He wore a parachute, in fact two of them. The first chute, a small one, popped open when Miura was traveling at 111.8 miles an hour, six seconds after starting. This chute triggered a much larger drag chute which offered his only hope of controlling speed and ultimately stopping. A crosswind spilled the air from it, however, and its effect became that of a whiplashing kite string instead of a brake. Then the wind stopped, and Miura managed to dig in a heel and arrest his fall. He had skied Everest for 98 seconds and skidded, fallen, for another 142 seconds. Eight cameramen recorded the event on 350,000 feet of film, photographing the eighteen-day trek to reach Miura's chosen ski course as well as his climaxing moments.

One early spring not long ago I decided to join the last Snow Survival course of the season to be given at Yosemite. By afternoon nine of us had skied a few miles beyond Badger Pass and begun to dig our caves for the night. At one point I remember thinking I'd probably always stick with a tent, given a choice. Snow caves aren't difficult to dig but they are slow.

They are worth the bother in an emergency or for prolonged camping in one place, but too time-demanding for one-night camps. You think this mostly at first, struggling to dig without enough space for working. A snow cave starts with sinking a well into the snow, then tunneling horizontally to hollow a sleeping niche with a smoothly domed ceiling, to prevent dripping. A shelf notched into the cave wall a foot or two above the floor protects you from the downward drainage of cold air and assures a comfortable night, given a warm-enough sleeping bag that has been successfully kept dry and is well insulated underneath. Novices sometimes forget the insulation, but it is necessary to prevent losing your body heat to the snow. A pack or a movable snow block set in the doorway will stop wind, and you must slope the entry away from the cave, not down into it. This is to let cold air spill out rather than in. Add a vent hole through the roof and you are done, although it's wise to keep a ski pole stuck through this hole for jiggling at night to break through any new-fallen snow.

This first cave of mine took four hours of work. Experience can cut that time in half—and, oddly, one snow cave leads to another. They are habit forming. You leave the warmth of campfire and companionship and crunch through the snow to where you remember your hole awaits. The pines and incense cedars stand as giant black plumes against white slopes and starry sky. You wriggle into your nest, taking all gear with you except skis which are standing upright in the snow, too tall to be covered by any new-fallen nighttime blanket. Then you slip into your sleeping bag fluffed out on the bench. A single candle gives ample light if you care to read. The porous nature of the snow and your vent assure fresh air. You sleep sealed off from outside sounds and cold.

I remember lying there that first night thinking of ptarmigan also sleeping within the snow, and of ages-old Eskimo snow igloos lived in for months at a time and enlivened with the births of babies and the drumbeats of dances. Thoughts came to mind of Sir Charles Wright navigating with Scott across the antarctic barrens by feeling the sastrugi with his feet and using only one eye at a time, keeping the other shut and in reserve in case of injury. I thought of dogsled races in Alaska today, and of North Dakota blizzards, and of skiing to remote patrol cabins at Mount Rainier to cut snow from the roofs; also about proliferating snowmobiles and ski developments that impact village traffic and require elaborate sewage drain fields and disposal plants. Snow now fosters complicated human actions and aspirations. Snow also still cradles simple responses and serene awareness of winter's purity.

Sleep within a Yosemite snow cave, and you find peace.

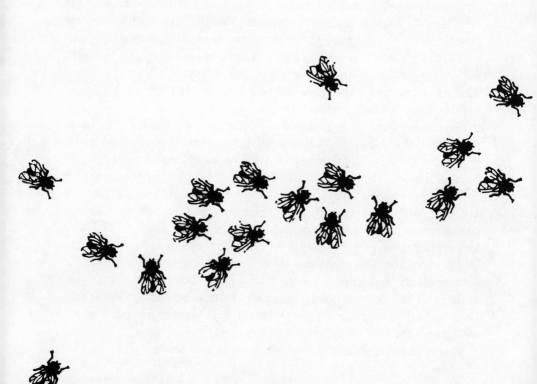

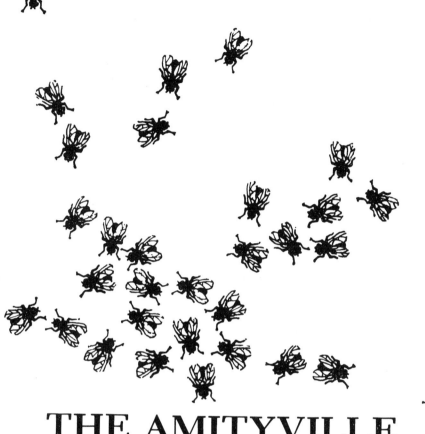

THE AMITYVILLE HORROR

A condensation of the book by

Jay Anson

1
December 18, 1975

George and Kathy Lutz moved into 112 Ocean Avenue on December 18. Twenty-eight days later, they fled in terror.

George Lee Lutz, twenty-eight, of Deer Park, Long Island, had a pretty good idea of land and home values. Himself the owner of a land surveying company, William H. Parry, Inc., he proudly let everyone know that the business was a third-generation operation: his grandfather's, his father's, and now his.

Between July and November, he and his wife, Kathleen, thirty, had looked at over fifty homes on the Island's South Shore before deciding to investigate Amityville. None in the thirty- to fifty-thousand-dollar range had yet met their requirements—that the house must be on the water and that it must be one to which they could move George's business.

In the course of their search, George called the Conklin Realty Office in Massapequa Park and spoke to broker Edith Evans. She said that she had a new house she wanted to show them and that she could take them through the place between three and three-thirty. George made the appointment and the broker—an attractive, warm woman—took them there at three in the afternoon.

She was very pleasant and patient with the young couple. "I'm not sure if this is what you're looking for," she told George and Kathy, "but I wanted to show you how the 'other half' of Amityville lives."

The house at 112 Ocean Avenue is a big, rambling, three-story affair, with dark shingles and white trim. The lot on which it stands is 50 by 237, the 50 feet facing the front, so that as you look at the house from across the street, the entrance door is down the right side. With the property comes 30 feet of wooden bulkhead that stands against the Amityville River.

On a lamppost at the end of the paved driveway is a small sign bearing the name given the house by a previous owner. It reads "High Hopes."

An enclosed porch with wet bar looks out at a preferred, older residential community of other big homes. Evergreens grow around the narrow grounds, partly blocking off the neighbors on either side, but their drawn shades can be seen easily enough. When he looked around, George thought that was peculiar. He noticed the neighbors' shades were all drawn on the sides that faced his house but not in front or in the direction of the houses on the other side.

The house had been on the market for almost a year. It was not in the paper but was fully described in Edith Evans' agency listing:

> *Exclusive Amityville Area*-6 bedroom Dutch Colonial, spacious living room, formal dining room, enclosed porch, 3½ baths, finished basement, 2-car garage, heated swimming pool, and large boathouse. Asking $80,000.

Eighty thousand dollars! For a house described like that, it would have to be falling apart, or the typist could have left out a "1" before the "8." One might think the agent would want to show a suspect bargain after dark and from the outside only, but she was glad to show them inside. The Lutzes' examination was swift but thorough. Not only did it meet with their exact requirements, but contrary to their anticipations, the house and other buildings were in fine condition.

Without hesitation, the broker then told the couple it was the DeFeo house. Everyone in the country, it seems, knew about that tragedy: the twenty-three-year-old Ronald DeFeo killing his father, mother, two brothers, and two sisters in their sleep on the night of November 13, 1974.

Newspaper and television accounts had told of the police discovering the six bodies, all shot by a high-powered rifle. All—as the Lutzes learned months later—were lying in the same position: on their stomachs with their heads resting on their arms. Confronted with this massacre, Ronald had finally confessed: "It just started; it went so fast, I just couldn't stop."

During his trial, his court-appointed attorney, William Weber, pleaded for Ronald's insanity. "For months before the incident," the young man testified, "I heard voices. Whenever I looked around, there was no one there, so it must have been God talking to me." Ronald DeFeo was convicted of murder and sentenced to six consecutive life terms.

"I wonder if I should have told you which house this was *before* or *after* you saw it," the broker mused. "I'd like to know for future reference with clients looking for a house in the ninety-thousand-dollar range."

Clearly, she didn't feel the Lutzes would be interested in such an affluent property. But Kathy took one final look about the house, smiled happily, and said, "It's the best we've seen. It's got everything we ever wanted." Obviously she had never hoped to live in such a fine house. But George vowed to himself that if there was a way, this was the place he wanted his wife to have. The tragic history of 112 Ocean Avenue didn't matter to George, Kathy, or their three children. This was still the home they had always wanted.

During the remainder of November and the early weeks of December, the Lutzes spent their evenings laying out plans for minor modifications to be made in the new house. George's surveying experience enabled him to rough out suitable layouts for the changes.

He and Kathy decided one of the bedrooms on the third floor would be for their two boys, Christopher, aged seven, and Daniel, nine. The other upstairs bedroom they gave to the children as a playroom. Melissa, "Missy," the five-year-old girl, would sleep on the second floor, across the hall from the master bedroom. There would also be a sewing room and a big dressing room for George and Kathy on the same floor. Chris, Danny, and Missy were well pleased with their room assignments.

Downstairs, on the main floor, the Lutzes had a slight problem. They didn't own any dining room furniture. They finally decided that before the closing, George would tell the broker they'd like to purchase the dining room set left in storage by the DeFeos, along with a girl's bedroom set for Missy, a TV chair, and Ronald DeFeo's bedroom furniture. These things and other furnishings left in the house, like the DeFeos' bed, were not included in the purchase price. George paid out an additional $400 for these items. He also got for free seven air-conditioners, two washers, two dryers, a new refrigerator, and a freezer.

There was a lot to be accomplished before moving day. In addition to the physical move of all their belongings, there were complicated legal questions, relative to the transfer of the title, that required sifting and sorting out. The title to the house and property was recorded in the names of Ronald DeFeo's parents. It seemed Ronald, as the sole survivor, was entitled to inherit his parents' estate, regardless of the fact that he had been convicted of murdering them. None of the assets in the estate could be disposed of before being legally settled in Probate Court. It was a difficult maze that the executors had to travel, and more time was still needed to provide the proper legal administration of any transactions related to the house or property.

The Lutzes were advised that provisions could be devised to protect the legal interests of all concerned if the sale of the house was consummated; but to arrive at the proper procedure to accomplish this could take weeks or longer. Eventually it was resolved that for the closing, $40,000 was to be put in escrow for the mortgage until a legal deed could be completed and executed.

The closing date was set for the morning George and Kathy planned to move from Deer Park. They had arranged to close on the sale of their old house the day before. Confident that everything could be worked out, and probably influenced by their anxiety to get settled in their new home, they decided to try and get everything done on the same day.

Packing was to be mainly Kathy's job. To keep the children out of her hair and away from George, she assigned them minor projects. They would gather their own toys and arrange their clothing for packing. When the chores were completed, they were to start cleaning their rooms to make their old house presentable for the scrutiny of new owners.

George planned to close his office in Syosset and move it into the new house to save on the rent money. He had included this item in his original estimate of how he and Kathy could afford an $80,000 house. Now he figured that the basement, a well-finished layout, might be the best place. Moving his equipment and furnishings would be time consuming enough, and if the basement was to be the location of the new office, some carpentry would be needed.

The 45 by 22-foot boathouse, out behind the house and garage, was not there just to be ostentatious and as an unused decoration for the Lutzes. George owned a 25-foot cabin cruiser and a 15-foot speedboat. The facilities at his new house would save him a lot of the money he normally had been paying to a marina. The task of getting his vessels to Amityville with a trailer became an obsession with him, despite the priorities that he and Kathy were constantly discovering.

There was work to be done at 112 Ocean Avenue, both inside and outside. Although he wasn't sure where the time was going to come from, George planned to attend to some landscaping and the garden, and put in some bulbs, and after that, spread some lime on the lawn.

Handy with his tools and equipment, George made good progress on many interior projects. Now and then, pressed for time, he got his hopeful projects confused with his musts. He soon dropped everything to clean the chimney, then the fireplace. After all, Christmas was coming.

It was quite cold on the actual moving day. The family had packed the night before and slept on the floor. George was up early and singlehandedly piled the first full load into the biggest U-Haul trailer he could rent, finishing in barely enough time to clean up and get to the closing.

At the legal ritual, the attorneys used up more than their usually allotted heretos, whereases, and parties of, and dealt each other long sheets of typewritten paper. The Lutzes' lawyer explained that because of the impediments on the house, they did not have a clear title to the property, though they'd have the best that could be fashioned for their mortgage. But remarkably, the closing was all over a few minutes past noon.

At one o'clock, George rolled into the driveway of 112 Ocean Avenue, the trailer crowded with their belongings and the DeFeos' refrigerator, washer, dryer, and freezer that had been in storage. Kathy followed with the children in the family van with their motorcycle in the back. Five of George's friends, young men in their twenties and husky enough to help move bulky items, were waiting. Furniture, boxes, crates, barrels, bags, toys, bikes, motorcycles, and clothing were taken from the truck onto the patio at the rear of the house and into the garage.

Then George walked to the front door, fumbling in his pockets as he went, searching for the key. Irritated, he returned to the truck and thoroughly searched it before admitting to his assistants that he didn't have it. The broker was the only one with the key, and she had taken it with her as she left the closing. George called her, and she went back to her office to fetch it.

When the side door was finally open, the three children leaped from the van, made straight for their respective toys, and began a parade of unprofessional movers in and out of the house. Kathy designated the destination of each parcel.

It took time to maneuver furniture up the fairly narrow stairwell leading to the second and third floors. And by the time Father Mancuso arrived to bless the house, it was well after one-thirty P.M.

2
December 18

It was past one-thirty when Father Mancuso arrived. The Lutzes' driveway was so cluttered that he had to park his old blue Vega on the street. It was an enormous house, he noted. Good for Kathy and the children that her husband had been able to provide such a fine home!

When the priest finished his ritual blessing, the Lutzes thanked him for his kindness and asked him to stay for supper, such as it would be that first night. He politely refused, explaining that he planned to have dinner with his mother at her home in Queens. She would be waiting for him; it was getting late, and he still had a bit of a drive. Once in his car, Father Mancuso rolled down his window. Repeated thanks and well-wishes were exchanged, but as he spoke to the couple, his expression turned serious. "By the way, George. I had lunch with some friends over in Lindenhurst before coming here. They told me that this was the DeFeo home. Did you know that?"

"Oh, sure. I think that's why it's such a bargain. It was on the market for a long time. But that doesn't bother us at all. It's got the best of everything."

"Wasn't that a tragedy, Father?" said Kathy. "That poor family. Imagine, all six murdered in their sleep."

The priest nodded. Then with repeated goodbyes from the three children, the family watched as he drove off to Queens.

It was nearly four by the time George had completed the first unloading at 112 Ocean Avenue. He drove the U-Haul back to Deer Park and into his old driveway. As he opened the door to his garage, Harry, his dog, leaped out and would have made a getaway if he hadn't been snared by his lead. The fast and sturdy half-malamute, half-Labrador retriever had been left behind to guard the rest of the family's belongings.

When they reached Amityville, George took Harry to the dog compound next to the garage and chained him with a 20-foot steel lead. Now that it was after six, George was almost exhausted and decided to leave the rest of his possessions in the truck, even though it was costing him fifty dollars a day to rent the vehicle. He worked inside, placing most of the living room furniture in its approximate position.

Coming to almost the very end of his strength, George decided to complete the day's labor with something more pleasurable for himself. He'd rig his stereo up with the hi-fi equipment that the DeFeos had built into the living room. Then he and Kathy would have music to add to the joy of their first night in their new home.

By eleven o'clock that night, the Lutzes were ready to settle down for their first night in their new home. It had gotten colder outside, down to almost 6 degrees above zero. George burned some now-empty cardboard cartons in the fireplace, making a merry blaze. It was the eighteenth of December, 1975, the first of their twenty-eight days.

3
December 19 to 21

George sat up in bed, wide awake. He had heard a knock on his front door.

He looked around in the darkness. For a moment, he didn't know where he was, but then it came to him. He was in the master bedroom of his new home. Kathy was there, beside him, hunched down under the warm covers.

The knock came again. "Jesus, who's that?" he muttered.

George reached for his wristwatch on the night table. It was 3:15 in the morning! Again a loud rapping. Only this time, it didn't sound as if it was coming from downstairs, more from somewhere off to his left.

George got out of bed, padded across the cold, uncarpeted floor of the hallway and into the sewing room that faced the Amityville River in the back. He looked out the window into the darkness. He heard another knock. George strained his eyes to see. "Where the hell's Harry?"

From somwhere over his head came a sharp crack. Instinctively he ducked, then looked up at the ceiling. He heard a low squeak. The boys, Danny and Chris, were on the floor above him. One of them must have pushed a toy off his bed in his sleep.

Barefoot and wearing only his pajama pants, George was shivering now. He looked back out the window. There! Something *was* moving, down by the boathouse. He quickly lifted the window, and then the freezing air hit him full blast. "Hey! Who's out there?" Then Harry barked and moved. George, his eyes adjusting to the darkness, saw the dog spring to his feet. The shadow was close to Harry.

"Harry! Go get him!" Another rap sounded from the direction of the boathouse, and Harry spun around at the noise. He began running back and forth in his compound, barking furiously now, the lead holding him back.

George slammed the window shut and ran back to the bedroom. Kathy had awoken. "What's the matter?" She turned on the lamp on her night table as George fumbled into his pants. "George?" Kathy saw his bearded face look up.

"It's all right, honey. I just want to take a look around out back. Harry's on to something near the boathouse. Probably a cat. I'd better quiet him down before he wakes the whole neighborhood." He slid into his loafers and was heading for his old navy blue Marine parka lying on a chair. "I'll be right up. Go back to sleep."

Kathy turned off the light. "Okay. Put your jacket on." The next morning, she wouldn't remember having awakened at all.

When George came out the kitchen door, Harry was still barking at the moving shadow. There was a length of two-by-four lumber lying against the swimming pool fence. George grabbed it and ran toward the boathouse. Then he saw the shadow move. His grip tightened on the heavy stick. Another loud rap.

"Damn!" George saw it was the door to the boathouse, open and swinging in the wind. "I thought I'd locked that before!"

Harry barked again.

"Oh, shut up, Harry! Knock it off!"

A half hour later, George was back in bed, still wide awake. As an ex-Marine, not too many years out of the service, he was fairly accustomed to emergency wake-up calls. It was taking him time to turn off his inner alarm system.

Kathy shifted in her sleep, so that her arm fell across George's neck. Her face burrowed deep into his chest. He sniffed her hair. She certainly smelled clean, he thought; he liked that. And she kept her children the same way, spotless. *Her* kids? George's now. Whatever the trouble, she and the children were worth it.

George looked up at the ceiling. Danny was a good boy, into everything. He could handle almost anything you gave him to do. They were getting closer, now. Danny was now beginning to call his stepfather "Dad"; no more "George." In a way he was glad he never got to meet Kathy's ex-husband; this way he felt Danny was all his. Kathy said that Chris looked just like his father, had the same ways about him, the same dark, curly hair and eyes. George would reprimand the boy for something, and Chris' face would fall and he'd look up at him with those soulful eyes. The kid sure knew how to use them.

He liked the way both boys looked after little Missy. She was a little terror, but smart for a five-year-old. He'd never had any trouble with her from the first day he met Kathy. She was Daddy's girl, all right. Listens to Kathy and me. In fact, they all do. They're three nice kids I've got.

It was after six before George finally fell into a deep sleep. Kathy woke up a few minutes later.

She looked around this strange room, trying to put her thoughts together. She was in the bedroom of her beautiful new home. Her husband was next to her and her three children were in their own bedrooms. Wasn't that marvelous! God had been good to them.

Kathy tried to slip easily from under George's arm. The poor man worked so hard yesterday, she thought, and today he's got more ahead of him. Let him sleep. She couldn't; she had too much to do in the kitchen and she had better get started before the kids got up.

Downstairs, she looked around at her new kitchen. It was still dark outside. She turned on the light. Boxes of her dishes, glasses, and pots were piled up all over the floor and sink. Chairs were still sitting on top of the dinette table. But, she smiled to herself, the kitchen was going to be a happy room for her family. It might be just the place for her Transcendental Meditation, which George had been practicing for two years; Kathy, one. He had been into TM ever since the breakup of his first marriage, when he had been attending sessions of group therapy; out of that grew his interest in meditation. He had introduced Kathy to the subject, but now, with all the work of moving in, he had completely ignored his established pattern of going off by himself into a room and meditating for a few minutes each day.

Kathy washed out her electric percolator, filled it, plugged it in, and lit her first cigarette of the day. Drinking coffee, Kathy sat at the table with a pad and pencil, making notes for herself on the jobs to be done around the house. Today was the nineteenth, a Friday. The kids would not go to their new school until after the Christmas holidays. Christmas! There was so much still to do. . . .

Kathy sensed someone was staring at her. Startled, she looked up and over her shoulder. Her little daughter was standing in the doorway. "Missy! You scared me half to death. What's the matter? What are you doing up so early?"

The little girl's eyes were half-closed. Her blonde hair hung across her face. She looked around, as if not understanding where she was. "I wanna go home, Mama."

"You *are* home, Missy. This is our new home. C'mere."

Missy shambled over to Kathy and climbed up on her mother's lap. The two ladies of the house sat there in their pleasant kitchen, Kathy rocking her daughter back to sleep.

George came down after nine. By that time, the boys had already finished their breakfast and were outside, playing with Harry, investigating everything. Missy was asleep again in her room.

Kathy looked at her husband, whose big frame filled the doorway. She saw he hadn't shaved below his jawbone and that his dark blonde hair and beard were still uncombed. That meant he hadn't showered. "What's the matter? Aren't you going to work?"

George sat down wearily at the table. "Nope. I still have to unload the truck and get it back out to Deer Park. We blew an extra fifty bucks by keeping it overnight." He looked around, yawning, and shivered. "It's cold in here. Don't you have the heat on?"

The boys ran past the kitchen door, yelling at Harry. George looked up. "What's the matter with those two? Can't you keep them quiet?"

She turned from the sink. "Well, don't bark at me! *You're* their father, you know! You do it!"

George slapped his open palm down on the table. The sharp sound made Kathy jump. "Right!" he shouted.

George opened the kitchen door and leaned out. Danny, Chris, and Harry, whooping it up, ran by again. "Okay! The three of you! Knock it off!" Without waiting for their reaction, he slammed the door and stormed out of the kitchen.

Kathy was speechless. This was the first time he had really lost his temper with the children. And for so little! He hadn't been in a bad mood the day before.

George unloaded the U-Haul by himself, then drove it back to Deer Park, with his motorcycle in the rear so that he could get back to Amityville. He never did shave or shower and did nothing the rest of the day but gripe about the lack of heat in the house and the noise the children were making in their playroom up on the third floor.

He had been a bear all day, and by eleven o'clock that night, when it was time to go to bed, Kathy was ready to crown him. She was exhausted from putting things away and trying to keep the kids away from George. She'd start cleaning the bathrooms in the morning, she figured, but that was it for tonight. *She* was going to bed.

George stayed down in the living room, feeding log after log into the roaring fireplace. Even though the thermostat read 75 degrees, he couldn't seem to get warm. He must have checked the oil burner in the basement a dozen times during the day and evening.

At twelve, George finally dragged himself up to the bedroom and fell asleep immediately. At 3:15 in the morning, he was wide awake again, sitting up in bed.

There was something on his mind. The boathouse. Did he lock the door? He couldn't remember. He had to go out and check. It was closed and locked up.

Over the next two days, the Lutz family began to go through a collective personality change. As George said, "It was not a big thing, just little bits and pieces, here and there." He didn't shave or shower, something he did religiously. Normally George devoted as much time to his business as he could; two years before, he had had a second office in Shirley to handle contractors farther out on the South Shore. But now he simply called Syosset and gave gruff orders to his men, demanding they finish some surveying jobs over the weekend because he needed the money. As for arranging to move his office to his new basement set-up, he never gave it another thought.

Instead, George constantly complained that the house was like a refrigerator and he had to warm it up. Stuffing more and more logs in the fireplace occupied almost his every moment, except for the times he would go out to the boathouse, stare into space, then go back to the house. Even now, he can't say what he was looking for when he went there; he just knew that somehow he was drawn to the place.

It was practically a compulsion. The third night in the house, he again awoke at 3:15 A.M., worried about what might be going on out there.

The children bothered him too. Ever since the move, they seemed to have become brats, misbehaved monsters who wouldn't listen, unruly children who must be severely punished.

When it came to the children, Kathy fell into the same mood. She was tense from her strained relationship with George and from the efforts of trying to put her house in shape before Christmas. On their fourth night in the house, she exploded, and together with her husband, beat Danny, Chris, and Missy with a strap and a large, heavy wooden spoon.

The children had accidentally cracked a pane of glass in the playroom's half-moon window.

4

December 22

Early Monday morning, it was bitter cold in Amityville. The town is right on the Atlantic side of Long Island, and the sea wind blew in like a nor'easter. The thermometer hovered at 8 degrees and media weathermen were forecasting a white Christmas.

Inside 112 Ocean Avenue, Danny, Chris, and Missy Lutz were up in the playroom, slightly subdued from the whipping the night before. George had still not gone to his office and was sitting in the living room, adding more logs to a blazing fire. Kathy was writing at her dinette table in the kitchen nook.

As she worked over a list of things to buy for Christmas, her concentration wandered. She was upset about having hit the children, particularly about the way George and she had gone about it. There were many gifts the Lutz family still hadn't bought, and Kathy knew she had to go out and get them, but since they had moved in, she never had any desire to leave the house. She had just written down her Aunt Theresa's name when Kathy froze, pencil in midair.

Something had come up from behind and embraced her. Then it took her hand and gave it a pat. The touch was reassuring, and had an inner strength to it. Kathy was startled, but not frightened; it was like the touch of a mother giving comfort to her daughter. Kathy had the impression of a woman's soft hand resting on her own!

"Mommy! Come up here, quick!" It was Chris, calling from the third floor hallway.

Kathy looked up. The spell was broken, the touch was gone. She ran up the stairs to her children. They were in their bathroom, looking into the toilet. Kathy saw that the inside of the bowl was absolutely black, as though someone had painted it from the bottom to the edge just below the rim. She pushed the handle, flushing clear water against the sides. The black remained.

Kathy grabbed the toilet paper and tried vainly to rub off the discoloration. "I don't believe it! I just scrubbed this yesterday with Clorox!" She turned accusingly to the children. "Did you throw any paint in here?"

"Oh, no Mama!" all three chorused.

Kathy was fit to be tied; the incident in the breakfast nook was forgotten. She looked into the sink and bathtub, but they were still gleaming from her scouring. She turned on the faucets. Nothing but clear running water. Once more, she flushed the toilet, not really expecting the horrible black color to disappear.

She bent down and looked around the base to see if anything was leaking through to the inside of the bowl. Finally she turned to Danny. "Get the Clorox from my bathroom. It's in the closet under the sink."

Missy started to go. "Missy! You stay here! Let Danny get it." The boy left the bathroom. "And bring the scrub brush, too!" Kathy called after him.

Chris searched his mother's face, his eyes watering. "I didn't do it. Please don't hit me again."

Kathy looked at him, thinking of the terrible night before. "No, baby, it wasn't your fault. Something's happened to the water, I think. Maybe some oil backed up the line. Didn't you notice it before!"

"I had to go. I saw it first!" crowed Missy.

"Uh-huh. Well, let's see what the Clorox does before I call your father and he. . . ."

"Mama! Mama!" The cry came from down the hall.

Kathy leaned out the bathroom doorway. "What is it, Danny? I said it's under the sink!"

"No, Mama! I found it! But the black's in your toilet, too! And it stinks in here!"

Kathy's bathroom door was at the far end of her bedroom. Danny was standing outside the bedroom, holding his nose, when Kathy and the other two children came running down.

As soon as Kathy stepped into the bedroom, the odor hit her—a sweetish perfume smell. She stopped, sniffed, and frowned. "What the hell is *that?* That isn't my cologne."

But when she entered her bathroom, she was struck by a completely different odor, an overpowering stench. Kathy gagged and started to cough, but before she ran, caught a glimpse of her toilet bowl. It was totally black inside!

The children scrambled out of her way as she headed down the stairs. "George!"

"What do you want? I'm busy!"

Kathy burst into the living room and ran over to where George was crouched by the fireplace. "You'd better come and look! There's something in our bathroom that smells like a dead rat! And the toilet's all black!" She grabbed his hand and tugged him out of the room.

The other bathroom toilet bowl on the second floor was also black inside, as George discovered, but it had no smell. He sniffed the perfume in their room. "What the hell's that?"

He began to open the windows on the second floor. "First, let's get this smell out of here!" He lifted the windows in their bedroom and ran across the hall to the other bedrooms. Then he heard Kathy's voice.

"George! Look at this!"

The fourth bedroom on the second floor—now Kathy's sewing room— has two windows. One, which looks out at the boathouse and the Amityville River, was the window George had opened that first night when he had awakened at 3:15. The other faces the neighboring house to the right of 112 Ocean Avenue. On this window, clinging to the inside of the panes, were literally hundreds of buzzing flies!

"Jesus, will you look at that! House flies, *now?*"

"Maybe they're attracted by the smell?" Kathy volunteered.

"Yeah, but not at this time of year. Flies don't live that long, and not in this weather. And why are they only on this window?" George looked around the room, trying to see where the insects had come from. There was a closet in one corner. He opened the door and peered in, looking for cracks; for anything that would make sense.

"If this closet wall was up against the bathroom, they might have lived in the warmth. But this wall's against the outside." George put his hand against the plaster. "It's cold in here. I don't see any way they could have survived."

After shooing his family out into the hall, George shut the door to the sewing room. He opened the other window overlooking the boathouse, then took some newspapers and chased out as many flies as he could. He killed those that remained, then he closed the window. By then, it was freezing on the second floor, but at least the sweet perfume odor was gone. The bathroom stench had also diminished.

This didn't help George in his efforts to warm his house. Though no one else was complaining, he checked the oil heating system in the basement. It was working fine. By four o'clock in the afternoon, the thermostat just off the living room read 80 degrees, but George couldn't feel the heat.

Kathy had scrubbed the toilet bowls again with Clorox, Fantastik and Lysol. The cleansers helped somewhat, but a good deal of the black remained, stained deep into the porcelain. Worst of all was the toilet in the second bathroom next to the sewing room.

The outdoor temperature had risen to 20 degrees, and the children were out of the house, playing with Harry. Kathy warned them to keep away from the boathouse and the bulkhead area, telling them that it was too dangerous for them to play there without someone around to watch them.

George had brought in some more logs from the cord stacked in the garage and was sitting in the kitchen with Kathy. They began to argue violently about who should go out to buy the Christmas gifts. "Why can't you at least pick up the perfume for your mother?" asked George.

"I've got to get this place in order," Kathy erupted. "I don't see you doing anything but harping!"

After a few minutes, however, the squabble petered out, and that night when they went to bed, George made his usual check of all doors and windows, latching and locking, inside and out. So, when he woke once more at 3:15 in the morning and gave in to the urge to look downstairs, he was stunned to find the two hundred and fifty pound wooden front door wrenched wide open, hanging from one hinge!

5
December 23

Kathy awoke to the noise of George wrestling with the wrecked front door. When she felt the chill in the house, she threw on a robe and ran downstairs to see her husband trying to force the heavy wooden slab back into its frame.

"What happened?"

"I don't *know*," George answered, finally forcing the door closed. "This thing was wide open, hanging on one hinge. Here, look at this!" He pointed to the brass lock-plate. The doorknob was twisted completely off-center. The metal facing was bent back as though someone had tried to pry it open with a tool, but from the *inside!* "Someone was trying to get *out* of the house, not in!"

"I don't understand what's going on around here," George muttered, more to himself than Kathy. "I know I locked this before I went upstairs. To open the door from in here, all you had to do was turn the lock."

"Is it the same way outside?" Kathy asked.

"No. There's nothing wrong with the knob or the outside plate. Somebody'd need an awful lot of strength to pull away a door this heavy and tear it off one of the hinges. . . ."

"Maybe it was the wind, George," Kathy offered hopefully. "It seems to get pretty strong out there, you know."

"There's no wind in *here*, much less a tornado. Somebody or something had to do this!"

The Lutzes looked at each other. Kathy was the first to react. "The kids!" She turned and ran up the stairs to the second floor and into Missy's bedroom.

A small light in the shape of Yogi Bear was plugged into the wall near the bottom of the little girl's bed. In its feeble glow, Kathy glimpsed the form of Missy lying on her stomach. "Missy?" Kathy whispered, leaning over the bed. Missy whimpered, then turned over onto her back.

Kathy let out a sigh of relief and tucked the covers up under her daughter's chin. The cold air that had come in while the front door was open had made even this room very chilly. She kissed Missy on the forehead and silently slipped out of the room, heading for the third floor.

Danny and Chris were sleeping soundly. Both were on their stomachs. "Later, when I thought about it," Kathy says, "that was the first time I could ever remember the children sleeping in that position—particularly all three on their stomachs at the same time. I even remember I was almost going to say something to George, that it was kind of strange."

In the morning, the cold spell that gripped Amityville was still unbroken. It was cloudy, and the radio kept promising snow for Christmas. In the hallway of the Lutz home, the thermostat still read a steady 80 degrees, but George was back in the living room, stoking the fire to a roaring blaze. He told Kathy he just couldn't shake the chill from his bones, and he didn't understand why she and the children didn't feel that way too.

The job of replacing the doorknob and lock assembly on the front door was too complex for even a handy individual like George. The local locksmith arrived about twelve, as he'd promised. He made a long, slow survey of the damage inside the house and then gave George a peculiar look but offered no explanation as to how something like this could have possibly happened.

He finished the job quickly and quietly. Upon leaving, his one comment was that the DeFeos had called him a couple of years before: "They were having trouble with the lock on the boathouse door." He had been called to change the lock assembly because once the door was closed from the inside, it would somehow jam, and whoever was in the boathouse couldn't get out.

George wanted to say more about the boathouse, but when Kathy looked at him, he held back. They didn't want the news spreading around Amityville that again there was something funny going on at 112 Ocean Avenue.

By two in the afternoon, the weather had begun to warm. A slight drizzle was enough to keep the children in the house. George still hadn't gone to work and was in constant transit between the living room and the basement, adding logs and checking on the oil burner. Danny and Chris were up in their third floor playroom, noisily banging their toys around. Kathy was back at her cleaning chores, putting shelf paper in the closets. She had worked her way almost to her own bedroom on the second floor when she looked in Missy's room. The little girl was sitting in her diminutive rocking chair, humming to herself as she stared out the window that looked toward the boathouse.

Kathy was about to speak to her daughter when the phone rang. She picked up the extension in her own bedroom. It was her mother, saying that she would be over the next day—Christmas Eve—and that Kathy's brother Jimmy would bring them a Christmas tree as a housewarming gift.

Kathy said how relieved she was that at least the tree would be taken care of, since she and George had been unable to rouse themselves to do any shopping at all. Then, out of the corner of her eye, Kathy saw Missy leave her room and enter the sewing room. Kathy was only half listening to what her mother was saying; what could Missy possibly want in there, where all the flies had been the day before? She could hear her five-year-old daughter humming, moving about some still-unopened cardboard boxes.

Kathy was about to cut her mother short when she saw Missy come back out of the sewing room. When the child stepped into the hallway and returned to her own bedroom, she stopped her humming. Puzzled by her daughter's behavior, Kathy wound up her conversation with her mother, again thanking her for the tree. She hung up, walked silently toward Missy's room, and stood in the doorway.

Missy was back in her rocking chair, staring out the same window and humming again, a tune that didn't sound quite familiar. Kathy was about to speak when Missy stopped humming, and without turning her head, said, "Mama? Do angels talk?"

Kathy stared at her daughter. The little girl had known she was there! But before Kathy could step into the room, she was startled by a loud crash from overhead. The boys were upstairs! Fearful, she raced up the steps to the playroom. Danny and Chris were rolling on the floor, locked in each other's arms, punching and kicking at each other.

"What's going on here?" Kathy screamed. "Danny! Chris! You stop this right now, you hear!" She tried to pull them apart, but each was still trying to get at the other, their eyes blazing with hate. Chris was crying in his anger. It was the first time, *ever*, that the two brothers had gotten into a fight.

She slapped each boy in the face—hard—and demanded to know what had started this nonsense. "Danny started it," Chris sniffed.

"Liar! Chris, *you* started it," Danny scowled.

"Started *what*? What are you fighting about?" Kathy demanded, her voice rising. There was no answer from either boy. Both suddenly withdrew from their mother. Whatever had happened, Kathy sensed it was their affair not hers.

Then her patience snapped. "What is going on around here? First it's Missy with her angels, and now you two idiots trying to kill each other! Well, I've had it! We'll just see what your father has to say about all this. You're both going to get it later, but right now I don't want to hear another peep out of either of you! You hear me? Not another sound!"

Shaking, Kathy returned downstairs to her shelving. *Cool down*, she told herself. As she passed Missy's room again, the little girl was humming the same strange tune. Kathy wanted to go in, but then she thought better of it and continued on into her own bedroom. She'd talk to George later when she had a chance to be calmer about the whole affair.

Kathy picked up a roll of shelf paper and opened the door to the walk-in closet. Immediately a sour smell struck her nostrils. "Oh, God! What's that?" She pulled the light chain hanging from the closet ceiling and looked around the small room. It was empty except for one thing. On the very first day the Lutzes moved in, she had hung a crucifix on the inner wall facing the closet door, just as she had done when they lived in Deer Park. A friend had originally given her the crucifix as a wedding present. Made of silver, it was a beautiful piece about twelve inches long and had been blessed a long time before.

As Kathy looked at it now, her eyes widened in horror. She began to gag at the sour smell, but couldn't retreat from the sight of the crucifix—now hanging upside down!

6

December 24

Every once in a while, Kathy Lutz felt the need for some time to be by herself, and the spare bedroom was to be her own personal room. She had also considered the room, along with the kitchen, for her meditation. That third bedroom on the second floor would also serve as a dressing room and storage place for her and George's growing wardrobes.

Among the cartons in the sewing room were boxes of Christmas ornaments that she had accumulated over the years. It was time to unwrap the balls and lights, get them ready to put on the tree her mother and brother had promised to bring over that evening.

After lunch, Kathy asked Danny and Chris to bring the cartons down to the living room. George was more interested in his fireplace logs and only halfheartedly worked on the Christmas lights, testing the many colored bulbs and disentangling their wires. For the next few hours, Kathy and the children were busy unwrapping tissue paper that enclosed the delicate, bright-colored balls; the little wooden and glass angels, Santas, skaters, ballerinas, reindeer, and snowmen that Kathy had added to each year as the children grew up.

Each child had its own favorite ornaments and tenderly placed them on towels Kathy had spread on the floor. Some dated back to Danny's first

Christmas. But today, the children were admiring an ornament that George had brought to his new family. It was an heirloom, a unique galaxy of crescents and stars wrought in sterling silver and encased in 24-karat gold. Crafted in Germany more than a century before, it had been given to George by his grandmother, who in turn had received it from her grandmother.

In the living room, Kathy began wrapping the few Christmas gifts she had accumulated before moving to Amityville. She had gone to sales at Sears and to the Green Acres Shopping Center in Valley Stream, picking up bargains in clothing for her children and other items for George and her family. Sadly, Kathy noted that the pile of boxes was rather small and silently berated herself for not leaving the house to go out shopping. There were few toys for Danny, Chris, and Missy, but it was too late to do anything about it.

She had sent the children up to the playroom so she could work alone. She thought about Missy. She had not answered her daughter's question about talking angels—Kathy had put it off by telling Missy she'd ask Daddy about it. But it never came up when she and George went to bed. Why would Missy come up with such an idea? Did it have anything to do with the child's peculiar behavior yesterday in her bedroom? And what was she looking for in the sewing room?

Kathy's concentration was broken when the front doorbell rang. She looked around, startled. "It must be my mother! George, they're here already and I haven't even started supper!" She hurried toward the kitchen. "You get the door!"

Kathy's brother, Jimmy Conners, was a big, strapping youth who genuinely liked George. That evening, his face exuded a special warmth and charm. He was to be married on the day after Christmas and had asked George to be his best man. But when mother and son entered the house, Jimmy lugging a sizable Scotch pine, both their faces changed at the sight of George, who hadn't shaved or showered for almost a week. Kathy's mother, Joan, was alarmed. "Where are Kathy and the kids?" she asked George.

"She's making supper, and they're up in the playroom. Why?"

"I just had the feeling something was wrong."

This was the first time his in-laws had visited the house, so George had to show his mother-in-law where the kitchen was located. Then he and Jimmy hefted the tree into the living room. "Boy! That's some fire you've got going there!"

George explained that he just couldn't warm up; hadn't been able to since the day they moved in, and that he had already burned ten logs that day. "Yeah," Jimmy agreed. "It does seem kind of chilly around here. Maybe there's something wrong with your burner or thermostat?"

"No," answered George. "The oil burner's working fine and the thermostat's up to 80 degrees. Come on down to the basement and I'll show you."

The Christmas tree was up at the Lutzes' home. Danny, Chris, and Missy were helping their Uncle Jimmy trim it, each urging him to hang his *own* ornaments first. George had returned to his own private world by the fireplace. Kathy and her mother were in the kitchen. This was her "happy" room, the one place in the new house where she felt secure.

She complained to her mother that George had changed since they moved in. "Ma, he won't take a shower, he won't shave. He doesn't even leave the house to go to the office. All he does is sit by that damned fireplace and complain about the cold. And another thing—every night he keeps going out to check that boathouse."

"What's he looking for?" Mrs. Conners asked.

"Who knows? All he keeps saying is he's got to look around out there—and check on the boat."

"That doesn't sound like George. Have you asked him if there's anything the matter?"

"Oh, sure!" Kathy threw up her hands. "And all he does is throw more wood on the fire! In one week, we've gone through almost a whole cord of wood."

Kathy's mother shivered and pulled her sweater tighter around her body. "Well, you know, it *is* kind of chilly in the house. I've felt it ever since I came in."

Jimmy, standing on a chair in the living room, was about to fix George's ornament to the top of the tree. He too shivered. "Hey, George, you got a door open someplace? I keep getting a draft on the back of my neck."

George looked up. "No, I don't think so. I locked up everything before." He felt a sudden urge to check the second floor sewing room. "I'll be right back."

Kathy and Mrs. Conners passed him as they came in from the kitchen. He didn't say a word to either woman, just ran up the stairs. "What's with him?" Mrs. Conners asked.

Kathy just shrugged. "See what I mean?" She began to arrange the Christmas gifts under the tree. When Danny, Chris, and Missy counted the meager number of prettily wrapped packages on the floor, there was a chorus of disappointed voices behind her.

"What are you crying about?" George was back, standing in the doorway. "Knock it off! You kids are too spoiled anyway!"

Kathy was about to snap back at him for yelling at the children in front of her mother and brother when she saw the look on his face.

"Did you open the window in the sewing room, Kathy?"

"Me? I haven't been up there all day."

George turned to the children near the tree. "Have any of you kids been in that room since you brought down the Christmas boxes?" All three shook their heads. George hadn't moved from his position in the doorway. His eyes returned to Kathy.

"George, what is it?"

"A window is open. And the flies are back."

Crack! Everyone in the room jumped at the loud sound that came from somewhere outside. Again came a sharp knock, and outside, Harry barked. "The boathouse door! It's open again!" George turned to Jimmy. "Don't leave them alone! I'll be right back!" He grabbed his parka from the hall closet and headed for the kitchen door. Kathy began to cry.

"Kathy, what's going on?" Mrs. Conners said, her voice rising.

"Oh, Mama! I don't know!"

7
December 25

For the seventh night in a row, George awoke at exactly 3:15. He sat up in bed. Once again, the urge to check out the boathouse came over him, and George quietly slipped from the room.

He was almost upon Harry in his compound when the dog awoke, springing to his feet. "Shhh, Harry. It's all right. Take it easy, boy."

The dog settled back on his haunches and watched George test the boathouse door. It was closed and locked. Once more he reached down and reassured Harry. "It's all right, boy. Go back to sleep." George turned and started back toward the house.

George circled around the swimming pool fence. The orb of the full moon was like a huge flashlight, lighting his way. He looked up at the house and stopped short. His heart leaped. From Missy's second floor bedroom window, George could see the little girl staring at him, her eyes following his movements. "Oh, God!" he whispered aloud. Directly behind his daughter, frighteningly visible to George, was the face of a pig! He was sure he could see little red eyes glaring at him!

"Missy!" he yelled. The sound of his own voice broke the grip of terror on his heart and body. George ran for the house. He bounded up the stairs to Missy's bedroom and turned on the light.

She was in bed, lying on her stomach. He went to her and bent over. "Missy?" There was no answer. She was fast asleep.

There was a creak behind him. He turned. Beside the window that looked out at the boathouse, Missy's little chair was slowly rocking back and forth!

Six hours later, at 9:30 in the morning, George and Kathy sat in the kitchen, drinking coffee, confused and upset with the events that were taking place in their new home. They had gone over some of the incidents each had witnessed and now were trying to put together what was real and what they might have imagined. It was too much for them.

It was December 25, 1975, Christmas Day all over America. The promised white Christmas hadn't materialized as yet for Amityville, but it was cold enough to snow at any moment. Inside, the children were in the living room, playing with what few new toys George and Kathy had managed to accumulate before moving in eight days earlier.

George figured out that in the first week he had burned over 100 gallons of oil and an entire cord of logs. Someone would have to go and buy more wood and a few groceries such as milk and bread, and it was Kathy who volunteered.

Sometime later George heard Kathy return from her shopping. He could tell she was backing the van in because of the grinding sound the snow tires made in the driveway. For some strange reason, the noise bothered him and he became annoyed with his wife.

He went out to meet her, took two logs from the van, put them into the fireplace, and then sat down in the living room, refusing to unload any more. Kathy fumed; George's attitude and appearance were getting on her nerves. Somehow she could sense they were heading for a big fight, but she held her tongue for the moment. She took the bags of groceries from the van and left the remaining logs stacked inside. If George felt cold enough, Kathy knew, he'd get them himself.

She and George had cautioned Danny, Chris, and Missy to stay out of the sewing room on the second floor, without giving them any reason. That made the children even more curious about what might lie hidden behind the now closed door.

"It could be more Christmas presents," Chris suggested.

Danny agreed, but Missy said, "I know why we have to keep out. Jodie's in there."

"Jodie? Who's Jodie?" asked Danny.

"He's my friend. He's a pig."

"Oh, you're such a baby, Missy. You're always making up dumb things," sneered Chris.

At six o'clock that evening, Kathy was preparing supper for her family when she heard the sounds of something tiny and delicate striking against the glass of her kitchen window. It was dark outside, but she could see it was snowing. White flakes were tumbling down through the reflection of the kitchen light, and Kathy stared at them as the rising wind whipped the snow against the pane. "Snow at last," she said.

Christmas and snow: it brought a reassuring sense of familiarity to the troubled woman. She recalled her own childhood days. There always seemed to be snow at Christmas time when she was young. Kathy kept looking at the little snowflakes. Outside, the multicolored lights from neighborhood Christmas trees gleamed through the night. Behind her, the radio was playing Christmas carols. She became peaceful in her happy kitchen nook.

After supper, George and Kathy sat silently in the living room. The Christmas tree was all lit up and George's tree-topping ornament made a beautiful addition to the decorations. Reluctantly he had gone out to the van and brought in more of the wood. There were now six logs in front of the blazing fireplace, just enough to last through the night at the rate George was shoveling them in.

Kathy worked on some of the children's clothes—patching the boys' trousers that were forever wearing through the knees, letting down a few of Missy's denim pants. The little girl was growing taller, and already the hems were above the tops of her shoes.

At nine o'clock, Kathy went up to the third floor playroom to get Missy ready for bed. She heard her daughter's voice coming from her bedroom. Missy was talking out loud, obviously speaking to someone else in the room. At first Kathy thought it was one of the boys, but then she heard Missy say: "Isn't the snow beautiful, Jodie?" When Kathy entered, her daughter was sitting in her little rocker by the window, staring at the falling snow outside. Kathy looked around the bedroom. There was no one there.

"Who're you talking to, Missy? An angel?"

Missy looked around at her mother. Then her eyes went back to a corner of the room. "No, Mama, just Jodie."

Kathy turned her head to follow Missy's glance. There was nothing there but some of Missy's toys on the floor. "*Jodie?* Is that one of your new dolls?"

"No. Jodie's a pig. He's my friend. Nobody can see him but me."

Kathy knew that Missy, like other children of her age, often created people and animals to talk to, so she assumed it was the child's imagination at work again. George had not yet told her of the incident in Missy's room the night before.

There was another surprise waiting for Kathy when she got to the top floor a few minutes later. Danny and Chris were already in their own bedroom, changing into their pajamas. Usually both boys fought to stay up past ten. This night, at nine-thirty, they were getting ready without being told. Kathy wondered why.

"What's the matter with you two? How come you're not arguing about going to sleep?"

Her sons shrugged, continuing to undress. "It's warmer in here, Mama," Danny said. "We don't want to play in there anymore."

When Kathy checked *in there,* she was struck by the freezing chill in the playroom. No windows were open, yet the room was ice cold. It certainly wasn't uncomfortable in Danny and Chris's bedroom, nor in the hallway. She felt the radiator. It was hot!

Kathy told George about the cold in the upstairs playroom. Too comfortable by the fireplace to want to move, he said he'd check it out in the morning. At midnight, Kathy and George finally went to bed.

8

December 26

George Lutz vividly remembers the day after Christmas because that was the date set for Jimmy's wedding. It was also the beginning of a severe case of diarrhea he developed after checking out the boathouse. The pain was intense at first, almost as if a knife had pierced his stomach. George became frightened when he felt nausea rising in his throat. As soon as he reentered the house, he made a dash for the bathroom on the first floor.

It was daylight outside when he settled back into bed. The abdominal cramps were intense, but finally he fell asleep out of sheer exhaustion.

Kathy awoke a few moments later and immediately roused him to remind him of the wedding affair that evening. There would be a lot of arrangements to be handled before her brother came to pick them up. She would be busy with her clothes and hair. George groaned in his half-sleep.

Before going down to prepare breakfast for herself and the children, Kathy went up to the third floor to check the playroom. It was still cold inside when she opened the door, but not as icy as the day before. George might not like to move from his fire, but he would just have to in order to check the radiator. It was working all right, but there was no heat in the room. Certainly the children couldn't stay in there any length of time, and Kathy wanted them out of the way until it was time for them to dress for the wedding. She looked out of the window and saw the ground covered with slush from the melted snow. That settled it. The three would remain indoors today. She decided they would have to play in their own bedrooms.

After they were fed, Missy obediently started up to her own bedroom. Kathy warned her that she was not to go into the sewing room; that she was not even to open the door. "That's okay, Mama. Jodie wants to play in my room today."

"That's my good girl," Kathy smiled. "You go and play with your friend."

The boys wanted to play outside, arguing that this was *their* Christmas vacation from school. It was the way they persisted and answered her back that angered Kathy. Danny and Chris had never questioned her requests before this, and she was becoming more aware that her two sons had also changed since they had been in the new house.

But Kathy was not yet aware of her own personality changes, her impatience and crankiness.

"That's enough out of both of you!" she yelled at her sons. "I see you're asking for another beating! Now shut your mouths and get up to your room like I said, and stay there until I call you! You hear me?

Sullenly, Danny and Chris mounted the stairs to the third floor, passing George on his way down. He didn't acknowledge them. They didn't say good morning to him.

In the dinette, George took one sip of coffee, clutched his stomach, and headed back upstairs to his bathroom. "Don't forget you've got to shave and shower today!" Kathy yelled after him. Considering George's speed in running up the stairs she wasn't sure he had heard her.

Kathy returned to her breakfast nook. She had been making up a shopping list, checking items in the refrigerator and cabinets that had to be replaced. Food was again running low, and she knew she just had to get herself up and out of the house. She couldn't depend on George to do it. The big freezer in the basement, one of the free items they had received from the DeFeo estate, was clean and could be filled with meats and frozen foods. Her cleaning materials were almost exhausted, since she had been scrubbing the toilet bowls day after day. Most of the blackness was gone by now.

Kathy planned to go to an Amityville supermarket the next morning, Saturday. She wrote "orange juice" on her pad. Suddenly she became aware of a presence in the kitchen. In Kathy's current state of mind over the eroding situation of her family, the memory of the first touch on her hand flooded back, and she froze. Slowly, Kathy looked over her shoulder.

She could see the kitchen was empty—but at the same time, she sensed that the presence was closer, almost directly behind her chair! Her nostrils caught a sweetish scent of perfume, and she recognized it as the odor that had permeated her bedroom four days before.

Startled, Kathy could actually feel a body pressing against hers, clasping its arms around her waist. The pressure was light, however, and Kathy realized that as before, it was a woman's touch—almost reassuring. The unseen presence didn't give her a sense of danger—not at first.

Then the sweet smell became heavier. It seemed to swirl in the air, making Kathy dizzy. She started to gag, then tried to pull away from a grip that tightened as she struggled. Kathy thought she heard a whisper, and she recalls something deep within her warning her not to listen.

"No!" she shouted. "Leave me alone!" She struck out at the empty air. The embrace tightened, hesitated. Kathy felt a hand on her shoulder, making the same motions of motherly reassurance she had felt the first time in her kitchen.

Then it was gone! All that remained was the odor of the cheap perfume.

Kathy slumped back into her chair and closed her eyes. She began to cry. A hand touched her shoulder. Kathy jumped. "Oh God, no! Not again!" she opened her eyes.

Missy was standing there, calmly patting her on the arm. "Don't cry, Mama." Then Missy turned her head to look back at the kitchen doorway.

Kathy looked too. But there was nothing there.

"Jodie says you shouldn't cry," Missy said. "He says everything will be all right soon."

By eleven A.M., George Lutz had no thoughts for Kathy or his brother-in-law's wedding. He had just made his tenth trip to the bathroom, his diarrhea unrelieved.

Jimmy's wedding and reception, an expensively catered affair for fifty couples, was to be held at the Astoria Manor in Queens. George would have a lot to do at the hall, but right now he couldn't have cared less.

He dragged himself back down the stairs to his chair by the fireplace. Kathy came into the living room to tell him his office in Syosset had telephoned. The men wanted to know when George planned on coming in to work. There were a number of surveying jobs that needed his supervision, and more and more of the building contractors were beginning to complain.

Kathy also wanted to tell him about the second eerie incident in the kitchen, but George waved her off. She knew it would be pointless to try and reach him. Then, from upstairs, she heard the noise of Danny and Chris fighting in their bedroom again, both boys screaming at each other.

She was about to shout up the staircase at them when George bolted past her, mounting the steps two at a time.

Kathy couldn't bring herself to go after her husband. She stood by the bottom of the stairs and listened to George's shouts. In a few minutes there was silence. Then the door to Danny and Chris's bedroom slammed and she heard George's footsteps coming back down. He stopped when he saw Kathy waiting. They looked at each other, but neither spoke. George turned and went back up to the second floor, slamming the door to his and Kathy's bedroom.

George came down a half-hour later. For the first time in nine days, he had shaved and showered. Dressed in clean clothes, he walked into the kitchen where Kathy was sitting with Missy. The little girl was eating lunch. "You get her and the boys ready by five," he said. Then George turned and walked out.

At five-thirty, Jimmy came to pick up his sister and his best man, and the children. They were due at the Astoria Manor by seven. From Amityville to Queens, the Sunrise Highway was the fastest way, and the trip to Astoria normally took an hour at most. The roads were reported to be icy from the recent light snow, however, and it was a Friday night. Traffic would be heavy and slow. Jimmy had played it safe by arriving early at the Lutzes'.

The young bridegroom looked resplendent in his military uniform, his bright face was shining with happiness. His sister kissed him excitedly and invited him into the kitchen to wait and to chat with her while George finished dressing.

Jimmy took off his raincoat and then, from his coat pocket, proudly pulled out an envelope packed with fifteen hundred dollars in cash. He had paid out most of the money at the Manor some months before; this was the balance due. He said he had just withdrawn the money from his savings account and it just about wiped him out. Jimmy put the money back into the envelope and returned it to his raincoat pocket, leaving the coat on the kitchen chair beside him.

George came down, neatly clad in a tuxedo. His face was pale from the diarrhea, but he was freshly combed, his dark blonde beard framing his handsome face. The two men went into the living room. George had let the last of his fire burn itself out, and now he poked around the ashes looking for any leftover embers to tamp out.

The children were dressed and ready. Kathy went upstairs to get her coat. When she came down, Jimmy disappeared into the kitchen to get his raincoat. He returned a moment later, hoisting it over his shoulders. "Ready?" George asked.

"Ready as I'll ever be," Jimmy answered, automatically patting his side pocket to check on the envelope of money. His expression froze. He shoved his hand into the pocket, it came out empty! Jimmy searched the other pocket. Again, nothing. He tore off the raincoat, shaking it, then turned out every pocket in his uniform. The money was gone!

Jimmy ran back into the kitchen, Kathy and George following. The three looked all over the room, then began an inch by inch search of the foyer and living room. It was impossible, but Jimmy's fifteen hundred had completely disappeared!

Jimmy became frantic. "George, what am I going to do?"

His brother-in-law put his arm around the distraught Jimmy's shoulder. "Take it easy. The money must be around here somewhere." George moved Jimmy to the door. "Come on, we're running late now. I'll look again when I come back. It's here, don't worry."

Everything welled up within Kathy and she began to cry. As George looked at his wife, the lethargy that had gripped him over the past week fell away. He realized how hard he had been on Kathy; for the first time he wasn't thinking only of himself. Then, in spite of the calamity that had just befallen Jimmy, regardless of the weakness he still felt in his loins from the diarrhea, George wanted to make love to Kathy. He hadn't touched her since they had moved into 112 Ocean Avenue. "Come on, honey. Let's go." He gave his wife a pat on her behind. "I'll take care of everything."

9
December 27

The Lutzes returned home from the wedding at three A.M. It had been a very long night. It began with the mysterious disappearance of Jimmy's fifteen hundred dollars, and several other incidents during the evening hadn't added any particular joy to George's appreciation of the event.

Before the wedding ceremony, George, the other ushers, and the bridegroom had taken Communion in a little church near the Manor. During the ritual, George became violently nauseated. When Father Santini, the pastor of Our Lady of Martyrs Roman Catholic Church, gave George the chalice of wine to drink, George started to sway dizzily. Jimmy reached out a hand to his brother-in-law, but George brushed it off and dashed toward the men's room at the rear of the church.

After he had thrown up and returned to the hotel, George told Kathy he had actually become queasy the moment he had entered Our Lady of Martyrs.

The reception ran fairly smoothly. There was plenty of the food, drinking, and dancing usually associated with an Irish wedding, and everyone seemed to be having a good time. George had to go to the bathroom only once, when he thought his diarrhea might be returning, but generally he wasn't too uncomfortable. Kathy's brother and his new bride, Carey, were leaving for their honeymoon in Bermuda directly from the Manor and would take a cab to LaGuardia Airport. George would be driving Kathy and the children back to Amityville in Jimmy's car, so he didn't drink too much.

Then came the unpleasant moment of settling up with the hall's catering manager. Jimmy, his new father-in-law, and George told the man of the unexpected loss of all the cash, but promised they would pay him his money out of their wedding gifts. Unfortunately, when the traditional "Congratulations are in order" was spoken, most of the envelopes left on the table in front of the bride and groom contained personal checks. The actual cash amounted to a little more than five hundred dollars.

The manager was upset, but after a few minutes of haggling, agreed to accept two checks from George for five hundred dollars each—one from his personal account, the other drawn on his company's account.

George knew he didn't have the five hundred in his personal checking account, but since the next two days were Saturday and Sunday, he would have time to cover the draft on Monday.

Jimmy's father-in-law quickly conferred with his relatives and scraped up enough cash for his new son-in-law to pay for the honeymoon. Luckily, the plane tickets were already paid for. The wedding party broke up around two, and the Lutzes headed back to 112 Ocean Avenue.

Kathy went up to bed immediately while George checked on the boathouse and the dog's compound. Harry was still asleep, stirring only slightly when George called his name. When he bent to pat the dog, George wondered if Harry was drugged, but then dismissed the thought. No, he was probably just sick. Must have eaten something he found in the yard. George straightened up. He'd have to take Harry to the vet.

The boathouse door was secure, so George returned to the house, locking the front door. As he went to the kitchen, he glanced down at the floor, hoping to spot the missing envelope of money. No luck.

The kitchen door and windows on the first floor were all locked. George climbed the stairs to his bedroom, thinking about his wife and their warm, soft bed. Passing the sewing room, he noticed the door was slightly ajar. He thought of the children. One of them must have opened it before they left the house. He'd ask them the next morning, when they woke up.

In the morning, Kathy took the van to go shopping in Amityville while George drove the children, and Harry, in Jimmy's car to pick up the mail at his office in Syosset. He told his employees he would be in on Monday for sure.

They came home to find Kathy putting groceries into the kitchen refrigerator. She had also brought back a load for the basement freezer. Kathy bemoaned the fact that prices were higher in Amityville stores. "I thought they would be," George shrugged. "Amityville is more affluent than Deer Park."

By then it was after one o'clock. Though Kathy wanted to make lunch, she still had to transport the additional frozen foods and meat into her freezer in the basement. George volunteered to put together sandwiches for himself and the children. A short time later, Danny and Chris came in with another young boy. "This is Bobby, Mama," Chris said. "We just met him. He lives up the street."

"Hello, Bobby," Kathy smiled. The little dark-haired boy looked about Danny's age. Hesitantly, Bobby stuck out his right hand. Kathy shook it and introduced George. "This is Mr. Lutz."

George grinned at the boy, shaking his small hand. "Why don't you three all go upstairs and play?"

Bobby paused, his eyes darting about the foyer. "No. That's all right," he said. "I'd rather play down here."

"Here?" asked Kathy. "In the foyer?"

"Yes, m'am."

Kathy looked at George. Her eyes carried the unspoken question: what's wrong with this house that makes everybody so uncomfortable?

For the next half-hour, the three boys played on the foyer floor, with Danny's and Chris's new Christmas toys. Bobby never took off his winter jacket. Kathy went back to the basement to finish making the closet into a pantry, and George returned to the living room fireplace. Then Bobby stood up and told Danny and Chris that he wanted to go home. That was the first and last time that the boy from up the street ever set foot in 112 Ocean Avenue.

The basement of the Lutzes' house was 43 by 28 feet. When George first looked it over, he came down the stairs and saw off to his right batten doors that led to the oil burner, hot water heater, and the freezer, washers, and dryers left from the DeFeo estate.

To his left, through another set of doors, was a playroom, 11 by 28 feet, beautifully finished in walnut paneling, with recessed fluorescent lights in a dropped ceiling. Directly in front of him was the area he planned to use as his office.

A small closet opened into the space beneath the stairs, and between the staircase and the right-hand wall, plywood panels formed an additional closet, extending out about seven feet, with shelving that ran from the ceiling to the floor. This walk-in area, George thought, made good use of what would otherwise be wasted space, and its proximity to the kitchen stairs made it a most convenient pantry.

Kathy was working in these closets. When she stacked some large, heavy canned goods against the closet wall, one of the shelves creaked. One side of the plywood paneling on the rear wall seemed to give a little. She moved the cans aside and pushed against the panel. It moved farther away from the shelving.

The closet was lit by a single bulb, hanging from the ceiling. The bulb's reflection shone through a small slit opening just enough to give Kathy the impression that there was an empty space behind the closet, under the tallest section of the stairs. She went out to the basement and called to George to come down.

He looked at the opening and pushed against the paneling. The wall continued to give a little more. "There isn't supposed to be anything back there," he said to Kathy.

George removed the four wooden shelves, then shoved hard against the plywood. It swung all the way open. It was a secret door!

The room was small, about four by five feet. Kathy gasped. From ceiling to floor, it was painted solid red. "What *is* it, George?"

"I don't know," he answered, feeling the three solid concrete block walls. "It seems to be an extra room, maybe a bomb shelter. Everyone was building them back in the late fifties, but it sure doesn't show up in the house plans the broker gave us."

"Do you think the DeFeos built it?" Kathy asked, holding nervously onto George's arm.

"I don't know that either. I guess so," he said, steering Kathy out of the secret room. "I wonder what it was used for." He pulled the panel closed.

"Do you think there are any more rooms like that behind the closets?" Kathy asked.

"I don't know, Kathy," George answered. "I'll have to check out each wall."

"Did you notice the funny smell in there?"

"Yeah, I smelled it," George said. "That's how blood smells."

She took a deep breath. "George, I'm worried about this house. A lot's happening that I don't understand." George saw Kathy put her fingers in her mouth, a sign she was scared. Little Missy always did the same thing when she was frightened. George patted his wife on the head.

"Don't worry, baby. I'll find out what the hell that room is all about. But we *can* use it as an extra pantry!" He turned out the light in the closet, shutting out the sight of the rear wall-panel but not obscuring the fleeting vision of a face he glimpsed against the plywood. In a few days, George would realize it was the bearded visage of Ronnie DeFeo!

10
December 28

Kathy was waiting for George to come home. She sat in the living room by the Christmas tree, not wanting to be in the kitchen nook by herself for fear of meeting up with that invisible something that reeked of perfume. The children were up in the boys' bedroom, watching television. They had been quiet most of the afternoon, absorbed in an old movie. By the delighted laughter that drifted down to her, Kathy was sure it was Abbott and Costello.

Now she was trying to concentrate on where Jimmy's money could be. Again Kathy and George had gone over every square inch of the kitchen, foyer, living and dining rooms, and closets looking for the envelope. It *couldn't* have just vanished into thin air! No one would have possibly been in the house to take it. Where the devil could it have gone?

Kathy thought about the presence in the kitchen and shuddered. She forced her mind to think of other rooms in the house. The sewing room? The red room in the basement? She began to get out of her chair, then stopped. Kathy was afraid to go down there alone now. Anyway, she thought, sitting back down, she and George hadn't seen anything but the red paint when they were in there.

She looked at her watch. It was almost four o'clock. Where was George? He had been gone over an hour. Then, out of the corner of her right eye, she saw movement.

One of Kathy's first Christmas gifts to George had been a huge, four-foot ceramic lion, crouched, ready to leap upon an unseen victim, and painted in realistic colors. George thought it a pretty piece and had moved it to the living room, where it now sat on a large table beside his chair near the fireplace.

When Kathy turned and looked fully at the sculpture, she was sure she had seen it move a few inches closer toward her!

When George finally returned he told his wife that he had taken a very long walk around the town and was convinced the street they lived on in Amityville was the nicest. Kathy thought George looked better for having gotten out of the house and she felt foolish about wanting to mention the lion. Then Geroge shivered a little. "Don't you think it's getting chilly in here again, Kathy?" He left the kitchen for the living room. "I'd better put some more wood into the fireplace," he said.

Kathy watched her husband shamble out of the kitchen. She began to get that depressed feeling again. Then she heard a loud crash from the living room. It was George!

"Who the hell left this lion on the floor? It almost killed me!"

11
December 29 to 30

The next morning, Monday, George's ankle was stiff. He had taken a nasty tumble over the ceramic lion and had fallen heavily against some of the logs by the fireplace. He also had a cut over his right eye, but it hadn't bled much after Kathy put a Band-Aid on it. What disturbed

Kathy was the clear imprint of teethmarks on his ankle!

George limped out to his 1974 Ford van and had trouble turning over the cold motor. With temperatures in the low twenties, George knew he could anticipate ignition problems. But finally he got the van going and headed across the Island toward Syosset. His first order of business was to cover the check he had written to the Astoria Manor. That meant drawings funds from his company's account.

Halfway to Syosset, on the Sunrise Highway, George felt a bump in the back of the van. He pulled over and inspected the rear end. One of the shock absorbers had come loose and fallen off. George was puzzled. This was a mishap that might occur after the shocks were old and worn, if then, but the Ford had gone only 26,000 miles. He drove on again, intending to replace the part once he returned to Amityville.

In Syosset, George found a caller waiting for him. The man introduced himself as an inspector from the Internal Revenue Service and explained he was there to examine the company's books and past tax returns. George called his accountant. The IRS agent spoke with him and made an appointment to return on January 7.

After the agent left, George got on with his priorities: withdrawing five hundred dollars from the company account and depositing it in his personal checking account; going over the plans that had been completed for several land surveys; deciding how to handle the few assignments that had come into the office since he had been away; and then doing some research into the DeFeo family and the background of 112 Ocean Avenue.

When the men on his staff asked why he'd been out so long, George told them only that he had been sick. He knew that was untrue, but what other explanation would make any sense? By one o'clock, George had completed his duties in Syosset. He planned to make one more stop before heading back to Amityville.

Long Island's largest daily newspaper is *Newsday*. George reasoned that *Newsday*'s Garden City office would be the most logical starting point to learn some facts about the DeFeo family.

He was referred to the microfilm department, where a clerk checked the cross-index files for the dates of the DeFeo murders and Ronnie's trial. George only vaguely recalled the details of the way the son had slaughtered the whole family, but he did remember that the trial had been held in Riverhead, Long Island, sometime in the fall of 1975.

George put the microfilm of the newspaper into the reader and ran it down until he came to November 14, 1974. One of the first items he noticed was a photograph taken of Ronnie DeFeo at the time of his arrest, the morning after the discovery of his family's bodies. The bearded twenty-four-year-old face staring at him from the picture could have been his own! He was about to read on when it hit George that *this* was the face he had seen fleetingly on the closet wall in his basement!

The first articles told how Ronnie had run into a bar near his home, calling for help, saying that someone had killed his parents, brothers, and sisters. With two friends, Ronald DeFeo returned to his house where they found Ronald Sr., 43; Louise, 42; Allison, 13; Dawn, 18; Mark, 11; and John, 9. All were in their beds, all were shot in the back.

The story continued that at the time of DeFeo's arrest the following morning, Amityville police said that the motives for the murders were a $200,000 life insurance policy and a strongbox filled with cash hidden in the parents' bedroom closet.

The last item explained that when the prosecution was ready, the trial would be held in the state supreme court at Riverhead.

George inserted another microfilm reel, this one containing the day-by-day record of the seven-week trial held from September through November. The record included charges of police brutality in forcing a confession from Ronnie DeFeo and went on to attorney William Weber's parading psychiatrists to the stand to substantiate his plea of Ronnie's insanity. However, the jury found the youth sane and guilty of murder. Imposing a sentence of six consecutive life terms, Judge Thomas Salk called the killings the "most heinous and abhorrent crimes."

George left the *Newsday* offices thinking of the coroner's report that pinpointed the time of the DeFeos' deaths at about 3:15 in the morning. That was the exact moment George had been waking since they'd been in the house! He would have to tell Kathy.

George also wondered if the DeFeos had used the red room in the basement as a secret hideaway for their money. As he drove back to Amityville, George was so absorbed in thought that he never noticed or heard his left tire wobbling.

As he stopped for a red light on Route 110, another car pulled alongside. The driver leaned over and opened his window on the right side. He tooted his horn to catch George's attention, then yelled that George's wheel was coming off!

George got out and examined the wheel. All the bolts were loose. George could feel them turn easily in his fingers. With his windows closed, he had dimly heard the racket, but being wrapped up in his thoughts, he just never considered it was coming from his car.

What the devil was going on? First the shock absorber had fallen off, now this. Was someone fooling around with the van? He or Kathy could be killed if the wheel came off while driving at any speed.

George became even angrier and more frustrated when he looked for the jack handle in the rear of the van. It was gone! He'd have to tighten the bolts by hand until he could get to a service station. By then it would be too late to do any further checking on the background of 112 Ocean Avenue.

The next day, the Amityville Historical Society had some interesting information for George, particularly about the very location of his house. It seems the Shinnecock Indians had used land on the Amityville River as an enclosure for the sick, mad, and dying. These unfortunates were penned up until they died of exposure. However, the record noted that the Shinnecocks did not use this tract as a consecrated burial mound because they believed it to be infested with demons.

For how many uncounted centuries the Shinnecocks carried on in this manner, no one really knows; but in the late 1600s, white settlers eased the first native Americans out of the area, sending them farther out on Long Island.

One of the more notorious settlers who came to the newly named Amityville in those days was a John Catchum or Ketcham who had been forced out of Salem, Massachusetts, for practicing withcraft. John set up residence within 500 feet of where George now lived, continuing his alleged devil worship. The account also claimed he was buried somewhere on the northeast corner of the property.

From the Real Estate Tax Assessment Office in town, George learned that the house at 112 Ocean Avenue was built in 1928 by a Mr. Monaghan. It had passed through several families until 1965, when the DeFeos purchased it from the Rileys. But in spite of all he had read in the past two days, George was no closer to a solution of what the mysterious red room was used for or who built it. There was no record of any improvements being made to the house that resembled the addition of a basement room.

It was the night before New Year's Eve. The Lutzes went to bed early. George had checked the sewing room for Kathy, as he had done the night before, after returning from *Newsday*. Both evenings the windows had been shut and locked.

Earlier they had discussed what George had discovered about the history of their property and house. "George," Kathy asked nervously, "do you think it's haunted?"

"No way," he replied. "I don't believe in ghosts. Besides, everything that's happened around here must have a logical and scientific explanation to it."

"I'm not so sure. What about the lion?"

"What about it?" he asked.

Kathy looked around the kitchen where they were sitting. "Well, what about what I felt those two times? I told you I *know* somebody touched me, George."

George stood up, stretching. "Oh, come on, honey, I think it's just your imagination." He reached for her hand. "I've had that happen to me too, when I was sure my father had put his hand on my shoulder in the office." He pulled Kathy out of her chair. "I was positive he was standing right beside me. It happens to a lot of people, but it's, it's—I think they call it clairvoyance, or something like that."

The couple had their arms around each other's waists as George turned out the light in the kitchen. They passed the living room on the way to the stairs. Kathy stopped. She could see the crouching lion in the darkness of the room.

"George. I think we should continue with our meditation. Let's do it tomorrow, okay?"

"You think that way we can find a logical explanation for all that's happened?" he asked, drawing her upstairs.

12

December 31

The year 1976 was just around the corner. The last day of the old year dawned on a heavy snowfall, and to many people it was the signal that a fresh, clean start would usher in the new.

In the Lutz household there was a completely different mood. George hadn't slept well, even though he had been active enough for the past two days, inside and outside the house. He awoke during the night, looked at his watch, and was surprised to find it was 2:30 A.M., not 3:15, as he anticipated.

George awoke again at 4:30 A.M., saw it was beginning to snow, and tried to fall back to sleep under the warm covers. But, tossing and turning, he couldn't find a comfortable position. In her sleep, Kathy was bothered by his restlessness and rolled over against George so that he was pushed to the edge of the bed. Wide awake, he kept having visions of discovering secret caches of money around the house and using them to solve all his financial problems.

George was beginning to choke with the pressures of mounting bills; for the house he had just taken on, and for the office, where he would shortly have a very serious payroll deficit. All the cash he and Kathy had saved had gone toward the expense of the closing, an old fuel bill, and paying off the boats and motorcycles. And now the latest blow—the investigation of his books and tax returns by the IRS. Small wonder that George dreamed of a simple magical solution to the bind he was in.

He wished he could find Jimmy's money. The fifteen hundred would be a lifesaver. George stared at the falling snow. He had read in the newspaper account that DeFeo had been extremely well off, with a big bank account and a good position with his wife's father in a car dealership.

George had examined the bedroom closet and discovered DeFeo's secret hiding place under the door jamb. The police had found it first at the time of Ronnie's arrest and now it was empty. He kept wondering where else the DeFeos could have stashed away some of their cash.

The boathouse! George sat up in bed. Maybe there was a meaning behind his being drawn there every night. Was some—some *thing* dragging him there? Was the dead man somehow urging him to look in there for his fortune? George was desparate, he knew, even to contemplate such a screwy idea. But why else *would* he be driven to go to the boathouse, night after night?

At six-thirty, George finally gave up and got out of bed. He knew he would never fall asleep again that morning, so he quietly slipped from the room, went down to the kitchen, and made some coffee.

It was still dark outside at that hour, but he could see the snow was beginning to pile up near the kitchen door. He saw a light on the ground floor of his neighbor's house. Maybe the owner also had money problems and couldn't sleep, he thought.

George knew he wouldn't go to the office that day. It was New Year's Eve and everybody would be leaving early anyway. He drank his coffee and planned to search the boathouse and basement for some clues. Then George began to feel a chill in the house.

The thermostat automatically dropped the temperature between midnight and six in the morning. But now it was almost seven and the head didn't seem to be on. George went into the living room and put some kindling and paper into the fireplace. He noticed that the brick wall was black from all the soot accumulated from his almost constant fires.

A little after eight, Kathy came down with Missy and made her daughter breakfast, but she couldn't eat anything herself. She had coffee and a cigarette. George didn't want any food and took only another cup of coffee. He had to get it from the kitchen himself because Kathy didn't want to come into the living room. She told George she had a bad headache. Kathy was frightened of the ceramic lion and planned to get rid of it before the day was out. But it was true that she did have a sick headache.

By nine o'clock, George had built the living-room fire to a roaring blaze. At ten o'clock, the snow was still falling. Kathy called out to George from the kitchen that a local radio station had predicted the Amityville River would be completely frozen by nightfall.

Reluctantly, George got up from his chair by the fireplace and dressed, put on his boots, and went out to the boathouse. He hadn't had the money to take the cabin cruiser out of the water for the winter. If the river froze, ice would eventually crush the boat, but he had prepared for just this kind of emergency.

George's mother had given him her paint compressor, and he had drilled holes in its plastic hose. Now he sank the hose in the water beside the boat and turned on the compressor. It acted as a bubbler system that would keep the water inside the boathouse from freezing.

Later that afternoon Danny and Chris threatened to run away from home. The first time had been when they lived in George's house in Deer Park. He had restricted them to their room for a week because they were lying to him and Kathy about small things. They had revolted against his authority; both boys refused to obey his orders, threatening to run away if he also forced them to give up television. At that point, George called their bluff, telling Danny and Chris that they could get out if they didn't like the way he ran things at home.

The two youngsters had taken him at his word. They packed all their belongings—toys, clothes, records, and magazines—into bed rolls and dragged the bundles out the front door. When they were about half-way down the street, desperately trying to move the heavy load, a neighbor spotted them and talked them both into going back. For a while, they stopped their childish fibbing, but now had come a new eruption.

Hearing them fighting, Kathy had gone up to their room and found the two boys on one of the beds. Chris was straddling Danny's chest, ready to clobber him. On the other bed sat Missy, a broad grin on her little face. She was clapping her hands with excitement.

Kathy pulled her sons apart. "What do you think you're doing?" she screamed. "What's the matter with you two? Are you going crazy?"

Missy chimed in, "Danny didn't want to clean up the room like you told him to."

Kathy looked sternly at the boy. "And why not, young man? Do you see what this room looks like?"

The room *was* a mess. Toys were scattered all over the floor, intermingled with discarded clothes. The tubes of an oil paint set had been left uncapped, the pigments oozing onto the furniture and rug. Some of their new Christmas toys had already been broken and were discarded in corners of the bedroom. Kathy shook her head. "I don't know what I'm going to do with you. We bought this beautiful house so you'd have your own playroom, and look at what you've done!"

Danny tore himself loose from his mother's grip. "You don't want us to stay in that dumb old playroom!"

"Yeah!" Chris chimed in. "We don't like it around here. There's nobody to play with!"

Kathy and the boys bickered back and forth for another five minutes until Danny threw down the gauntlet and challenged his mother with the threat of running away. Kathy, in turn, suggested corporal punishment for their behavior. "And you know who dishes it out around here!"

By dinner time, the Lutz family had settled down. The boys had cooled off, though Kathy could still feel the undercurrent of tension at the table. George had told Kathy he preferred staying home this New Year's Eve rather than facing drunks on the road home from her mother's house. They had made no plans to be with friends, and it was too cold to go out to a movie.

After they had eaten, Kathy convinced George to move the ceramic lion back up to the sewing room. Again there were some flies clinging to the window pane facing the Amityville River. George angrily swatted them to death before slamming the door shut.

By ten o'clock, Missy had fallen asleep on the living-room floor. She had exacted a promise from Kathy to awaken her at midnight, in time to blow her party horn. Danny and Chris were still up, playing near the Christmas tree and watching television. George was attending to his fire. Kathy sat across from him trying to lose her depression by looking at an old movie with the boys.

On television, Guy Lombardo saluted the New Year from the Waldorf-Astoria Hotel. The Lutzes watched the ball fall from the Allied Chemical

Building in Times Square but did not share the countdown with announcer Ben Grauer while he tolled off the last ten seconds of 1975.

Danny and Chris had gone up to their room about a half-hour earlier, and Kathy had put Missy into her bed and then come back downstairs to her chair across from George.

It was now exactly one minute after twelve. She stared into the fireplace, hypnotized by the dancing flames. Something was materializing in those flames—a white outline against the blackened bricks—becoming clearer, more distinct.

Kathy tried to open her mouth to say something to her husband. She couldn't. She couldn't even tear her eyes away from the demon with horns and a white peaked hood on its head. It was getting larger, looming toward her. She saw that half of its face was blown away, as if hit with a shotgun blast at close range. Kathy screamed.

George looked up. "What's the matter?" he said.

All Kathy could do was to point into the fireplace. George followed her gaze and he saw it too—a white figure that had burned itself into the soot against the rear bricks of the fireplace.

13
January 1, 1976

George and Kathy finally went to bed at one in the morning. They had been sleeping for what later seemed to them no more than five minutes when they were awakened by a howling wind roaring through their bedroom.

The blankets on the bed had been virtually torn from their bodies, leaving George and Kathy shivering. All the windows in the room were wide open, and the bedroom door, caught by the drafts, was swinging back and forth.

George leaped from the bed and ran to close the windows. Kathy gathered the blankets off the floor and threw them back onto the bed. Both were breathless from their sudden awakening, and even though the door to their room had slammed shut, they could still hear the wind blowing in the second floor hallway.

George wrenched open the door and was hit by another cold blast. Flipping on the light switch in the hall, he was startled to see the doors to the sewing room and dressing room wide open, the gale rushing freely through the open windows. Only the door to Missy's bedroom remained shut.

He ran into the dressing room first, fighting against the gale that hit him, and managed to force the windows down. Then he went to the sewing room and, with the cold now bringing tears to his eyes, closed one window. But George could not budge the open window that faced the Amityville River. He banged furiously on its frame with his fists. Finally it gave and slid to a close.

He stood there, trying to catch his breath, shaking. The wind was no longer blowing through the house, but he could hear it gusting violently outside. The chill remained. He took one more look around the room before he remembered Kathy. "Honey? You all right?"

When Kathy followed her husband out into the hallway, she too had seen the open doors and that Missy's door remained shut. Her heart thumping, Kathy had run to her daughter's room and burst through the doorway. She turned on the light.

The room was warm, almost hot. The windows were shut and locked, and the little girl was fast asleep in her bed.

There was something moving in the room. Then she saw it was Missy's chair beside the window, slowly rocking back and forth. Then she heard George's voice. "Honey? You all right?"

George came into the bedroom. The heat struck him; it was like stepping in front of a fire. George took it all in at once—the little girl safely asleep, his wife standing at the side of Missy's bed, the incredulous look of fright on Kathy's face, and the small chair teetering back and forth.

He took one step toward the rocking chair and it immediately ceased its movements. George stopped in his tracks, stood absolutely still, and motioned to Kathy. "Take her downstairs! Hurry!"

Kathy didn't question George. She lifted Missy off the bed, blankets and all, and hurried from the room. George came out behind them and slammed the door, not even bothering to turn off the light.

Kathy went carefully down the steps toward the first floor. It was ice cold in the hallway. George ran up the staircase to the top floor where Danny and Chris were sleeping.

When he came back down from the third floor a few minutes later, he saw Kathy sitting in the dark living room. She held Missy in her arms.

Kathy turned from the fireplace to look up at George questioningly. "They're all right," he nodded. "They're both sleeping. It's cold up there, but they're okay." Kathy let out her breath. He saw its vapor hang in the cold air.

George hurriedly started a fire. His fingers were numb and he suddenly realized that he was barefoot and hadn't thrown anything on over his pajamas. George finally got a small blaze going with newspaper, then fanned the flame with his hand until some of the old kindling caught fire.

Crouched in front of the fireplace, he could hear the winds howling outside. Then he turned and looked at Kathy over his shoulder. "What time is it?"

That was the only thing he could think of to say, George Lutz recalls. He remembers the look on Kathy's face when he asked the question. She stared at him for a moment, then replied, "I think it's about. . . ." But before Kathy could finish, she burst into tears, her whole body shaking uncontrollably. She rocked Missy back and forth in her arms, sobbing. "Oh, George, I'm frightened to death!"

George stood up and walked over to his wife and daughter. He crouched down in front of the chair and put his arms around both. "Don't cry, honey," he whispered, "I'm here. Nobody's going to hurt you or the baby."

The three remained in that position for some time. Slowly the fire burned brighter and the room began to warm up. It seemed to George that the winds were diminishing outside. Then he heard the oil burner click on in the basement and he knew it was exactly six o'clock in the morning on New Year's Day.

By nine A.M., the temperature in 112 Ocean Avenue had risen to the thermostat-controlled 75 degrees. The icy chill in the house had dissipated. George had made an inspection tour of each window, from the first floor to the third. There was no visible evidence that anyone had tampered with the locks on the windows of the second floor, and George remained completely baffled as to how such a bizarre event could have taken place.

Looking back at the episode, he claims that at that time, he and Kathy couldn't think of any reason for the windows behaving the way they did except for a freak of nature—that the hurricane-strength winds had somehow forced the windows up. But he can't answer why it happened only to the second-floor windows and not to any others in the house.

Suddenly George felt an urge to go to his office. It was a holiday, no one would be in, but he felt compelled to check on his company's operations.

By noontime George was in Syosset, working with his adding machine. He had discovered that the money coming in didn't balance with what was going out. The accounts-payable column was becoming too one-sided lately, and he knew he would have to cut back on his personnel.

George hated the idea of depriving men of their livelihood, particularly when he knew they'd have a hard time finding other jobs in the suffering construction industry. But it had to be done, and he wondered where to begin. George didn't dwell too long on the subject, however, because he had other pressing problems. Before banking week was up the next day—Friday—he would again have to transfer funds from one company account to another to cover checks issued to suppliers.

Deeply involved in these manipulations, George didn't notice the passing time. For the first moments since December 18, George Lutz was not thinking about himself or 112 Ocean Avenue.

The morning snowfall had made traveling on the roads hazardous. As the day wore on, it got colder, and cars began to get caught in drifts and skid on icy spots all over Long Island. But the snow had stopped falling while George was driving back to Amityville from his office, and he made it home all right.

The driveway of 112 Ocean Avenue was heavy with fresh snow. George saw he would have to clear a path to the garage before moving the van into the driveway. I'll do it tomorrow, he thought, and left the vehicle parked on the street, which had been recently plowed.

He noted that Danny and Chris had been playing in the snow. Their sleds were parked up against the steps leading to the kitchen door. As he stepped inside, he saw that they had left a trail of melting snowy footprints through the kitchen and up the staircase. Kathy must be upstairs, he thought. If she'd seen the slush they'd tracked into her clean house, there would have been hell to pay.

George found his wife in their bedroom, lying on the bed, reading to Missy from one of the little girl's new Christmas story books. Missy was gleefully clapping her hands. "Hi gang!" he said.

His wife and daughter looked up. "Daddy!" they chorused together, leaping off the bed and encircling George with delight.

For the first time in what seemed ages to Kathy, the Lutz family had a happy supper together. Unknown to her, Danny and Chris, forewarned by George, had sneaked back down to the kitchen and wiped away all traces of their snowy entry. They sat at the table, their faces still ruddy from hours spent romping in the cold air, and wolfed down the hamburgers and french fries their mother had prepared especially for them.

Missy kept the family in smiles with her aimless chatter and the way she kept sneaking fries off the boys' plates when they weren't looking. When caught, Missy would turn her face toward her accuser and flash a mouthful of teeth, minus one, to disarm him.

Kathy felt more secure with George home. Her fears had momentarily calmed and she gave no further thought to the latest whiff of perfume earlier that afternoon. Maybe I'm getting paranoid about the whole thing, she thought to herself. She looked about the table. The warm atmosphere certainly didn't portend a visit from any more ghosts.

As for George, he had let his depressing business operations retreat to the furthest recesses of his mind. It was as though he had entered a little cocoon at 112 Ocean Avenue. This was the way he wanted life to be all the time in his new house. Whatever the world outside had to offer, the Lutzes would tough it out together from their home. He and Kathy shared a steak. Then, lighting a cigarette, George wandered off to the living room with the boys.

George had brought Harry into the house to feed him and then let him remain to rough it up with the two boys in front of the fireplace. The Lutzes had eaten early, and so it was only a little after eight when Danny and Chris began to nod.

While the boys marched upstairs to bed, followed by Missy and Kathy, George took Harry out to the doghouse. Wading through the snow that had piled up between the kitchen door and the compound, he tied Harry to the strong lead line. Harry crawled into his doghouse, turned around several times until he found his right spot, and then settled down with a little sigh. While George stood there, the dog's eyes closed and he fell asleep.

"That does it," said George. "I'm taking you to the vet on Saturday."

After putting Missy to sleep, Kathy returned to the living room. George made his usual tour of the house, now double-checking every window and door. He had already inspected the garage and the boathouse doors when he took Harry outside.

"Let's see what happens tonight," he told Kathy when he came back down. "It's not blowing at all out there."

By 10 P.M., George and Kathy were feeling drowsy. His blazing fire was running out, but the heat was affecting their eyes. She waited until George had poked out the last embers and had poured water over some still-smoldering pieces of wood. Then Kathy turned off the chandelier and looked around to take her husband's hand. She screamed.

Kathy was looking past George's shoulder at the living room windows. Staring back at her were a pair of unblinking red eyes!

At his wife's scream, George whirled around. He also saw the little beady eyes staring directly into his. He jumped for the light switch, and the eyes disappeared in the shining reflection in the glass pane.

"Hey!" George shouted. He burst through the front door into the snow outside.

The windows of the living room faced the front of the house. It didn't take George more than a second or two to get there. But there was nothing at the windows.

"Kathy!" he shouted. "Get my flashlight!" George strained his eyes to see toward the back of the house in the direction of the river.

Kathy came out of the house with his light and his parka. Standing beneath the window where they had seen the eyes, they searched the fresh, unbroken snow. Then the yellow beam of the flashlight picked up a line of footprints, extending clear around the corner of the house.

No man or woman had made those tracks. The prints had been left by cloven hooves—like those of an enormous pig.

14

January 2

When George came out of the house in the morning, the cloven-hoofed tracks were still visible in the frozen snow. The animal's footprints led right past Harry's compound and ended at the entrance of the garage. George was speechless when he saw that the door to the garage was almost torn off its metal frame.

George himself had closed and locked the heavy overhead door. To wrench it away from its frame would not only have created a great racket, but would require a strength far beyond that of any human being.

George stood in the snow, staring at the tracks and wrecked door. His mind raced back to the morning when he had found his front door torn open and to the night he had seen the pig standing behind Missy at her window. He remembers saying out loud, "What the hell is going on around here?" as he squeezed past the twisted door into the garage.

He turned on the light and looked about. The garage was still packed with his motorcycle, the children's bicycles, an electric lawn-mower that had been left by the DeFeos, the old gas-powered machine he had brought from Deer Park; garden furniture, tools, equipment, and cans of paint and oil. The concrete floor of the garage was covered with a light dusting of snow that had drifted through the partly opened door. Obviously it had been off its frame for several hours.

"Is there anybody in here?" George shouted. Only the sound of a rising wind outside the garage answered him.

By the time George drove off to his office, he was more angry than frightened. If he had any terror of the unknown, it had been dismissed by the thought of what it was going to cost him to repair the damaged door. He didn't know if the insurance company would pay him for something like this.

George doesn't recall how he ever maneuvered the Ford van over the dangerous snow- and ice-covered roads to Syosset. His frustration at being unable to comprehend his bad luck blocked out any concern for his own safety. At the office, he quickly occupied himself with his immediate problems and for the next several hours was able to put aside any thoughts about 112 Ocean Avenue.

Before he'd left home, George had told Kathy about the garage door and the tracks in the snow. She had tried calling her mother, but there was no answer. Then Kathy remembered that Joan always shopped on Friday mornings rather than buck the Saturday crowds at the supermarket. She went upstairs to her bedroom, intending to change the linen in all the rooms and vacuum the rugs. Kathy's mind raced with the details of thoroughly cleaning her house for the first time. If she didn't occupy herself completely until George returned, she knew she'd fall to pieces.

She had just finished putting fresh cases on her pillows and was plumping them up when she was embraced from behind. She froze, then instinctively called out, "Danny?"

The grip around her waist tightened. It was stronger than the familiar woman's touch she had experienced in the kitchen. Kathy sensed that a man was holding her, increasing the pressure as she struggled. "Let me go, please!" she whimpered.

The pressure eased suddenly, then the hands released her waist. She felt them move up to her shoulders. Slowly her body was being turned around to face the unseen presence.

In her terror, Kathy became aware of the overwhelming stench of the same cheap perfume. Then another pair of hands gripped her waist. Kathy says she sensed a struggle going on over possession of her body, that somehow she had been trapped between two powerful forces. Escape was impossible and she felt she was going to die. The pressure on her body became overwhelming and Kathy passed out.

When she came to, she was lying half off the bed with her head almost touching the floor. Danny had come into the room in answer to her call. Kathy knew the presences were gone. She couldn't have been out more than a moment.

"Call Daddy at his office, Danny! Hurry!"

Danny returned in a few minutes. "The man on the telephone says Daddy just left Syosset. He thinks he's coming back here."

George did not come back to the house until early afternoon. When he reached Amityville, he drove up Merrick Road toward his street and stopped off at The Witches' Brew for a beer.

The neighborhood bar was warm and empty. The juke box and television set were silent, and the only sounds in the place were those of the bartender washing glasses.

George ordered a beer and watched while the bartender filled a glass. He was a roly-poly young man, somewhere in his late twenties, with a stomach that suggested he liked to sample the beer he sold. George took a long sip, half-emptying the tall stein before putting it down on the dark wood bar. "Tell me something," he said. "Did you know the DeFeos?"

The young man had resumed his glass-washing. He nodded. "Yeah, I knew them. Why?"

"I'm living in their house now and. . . ."

"I know," the bartender interrupted. George lifted his eyebrows in surprise.

"They ever come in here?"

The bartender put down a clean glass and wiped his hands on a towel. "Only Ronnie did. Sometimes he brought in his sister Dawn. A cute kid." He picked up George's empty glass. "You know, you look a lot like Ronnie. The beard and all. I think you're older than he is, though."

"Did he ever talk about their house?"

The bartender put a new beer in front of George. "The house?"

"Yeah, you know, like did he ever say there was anything funny going on there? Stuff like that." George took a sip.

"You think there's something bad about the joint? I mean, now after the murders?"

"No, no." George raised a hand. "I was just asking whether he ever said anything before the, er—that night."

The bartender looked around the bar as if to confirm that there was no one else around. "Ronnie never said anything like that to me, personally." He leaned closer to George. "But I'll tell you something. I was there once. They threw a big party and Ronnie's old man hired me to take care of the bar."

George had finished half of his second beer. "What did you think of the place?"

The bartender spread his fat arms wide. "Big. A real big joint. I didn't see too much of it, though; I was down in the basement. A lotta booze and beer flowed that night. It was their anniversary." He looked around the bar again. "Did you know you got a secret room down there?"

George pretended ignorance. "No! Where?"

"Uh-hunh," the bartender said. "You take a look behind those closets and you'll find something that'll really shake you."

George leaned over the bar. "What is it?"

"A room, a little room. I found it that night I was down in the basement. There's this plywood closet built up beside the stairs. I'm using it to ice beer in, see? When I bumped a keg against one end of the closet, it seems the whole wall is loose. You know, like a secret panel, something out of an old movie."

"What about the room?" George prodded.

The bartender nodded. "Yeah, well, when I bumped the plywood, it came open, and I could see this dark space behind it. The light bulb wasn't working, so I lit a match. And sure enough, there's this weird little room, all painted red."

"You're putting me on," George protested.

The bartender put his right hand over his heart. "God's honest truth, man, so help me. You'll see."

George finished his second beer. "I'll certainly have to look for that." He put a dollar on the bar. "That's for the beers." He put down another. "That's for yourself."

"Hey, thanks, man!" The bartender looked up at George. "You want to know something really flakey about that little room? I used to have nightmares about it."

"Nightmares? Like what?"

"Oh, sometimes I'd dream that people—I don't know who they were— were killing dogs and pigs in there and using their blood for some kind of ceremony."

"Dogs and *pigs?*"

"Yeah." The bartender waved his hand in disgust. "I guess the place— the red paint and all—really got to me."

When George got home, he and Kathy both had stories to tell each other. She described the frightening event in their bedroom, and he related what the bartender at The Witches' Brew had told him about the red room in the basement. The Lutzes finally realized that there was something going on that was beyond their control. "Please call Father Man-cuso," Kathy begged. "Ask him to come back."

15
January 2 to 3

Discovering that Father Mancuso was suffering from the flu—and was therefore unable to answer their call—George and Kathy discussed other ways of getting help. Both had agreed that now that they had already moved in, it would be unseemly to ask the local parish priest in Amityville to bless the house. Besides, he had been the confessor to the DeFeos, and George recalled from the newspaper accounts that he was an elderly man who pooh-poohed the thought of "voices" in the house telling Ronnie what to do. He wasn't much of a believer in occult phenomena.

At one point, George talked of vandalism. Possibly someone was trying to frighten them out of the house, using violent acts of destruction to hurry their departure. Kathy had her own opinions. When she had said *something* had touched her, had George thought it was just her imagination? He didn't. Could he explain the horrible figure burned into the brick wall of the fireplace? He couldn't. Had they really seen a pig's tracks in the snow? They had. Would he agree that there was a powerful force in the house that could hurt the family? He did. What were they going to do? When they went to bed at night, George told her he had decided to go to the Amityville police department the next day.

In the afternoon, Detective Sergeant Lou Zammataro of the Amityville police department went along with George, saw the wrecked garage door and the animal tracks still visible in the frozen snow, and then went into the house. He was introduced to Kathy and the children. She repeated her story of the ghost-like touchings and took the sergeant into the living room to show him the image burned into the fireplace wall.

Even after George and Kathy showed him the red room in the base-ment, they sensed Zammataro's skepticism. He had listened to George's version of the evil use of the hideaway, nodded when George mentioned Ronnie DeFeo as the builder of the secret room, then asked the Lutzes if they had any concrete facts to base their fears on. "I can't work on what you believe you've seen or heard. Maybe you ought to get a priest in here. It sounds more like his kind of job than a cop's."

Sergeant Lou Zammataro left the Lutz house and got into his car. He knew he hadn't helped the young couple at all. But there was really nothing he could do for them, except maybe have a cruiser stop by once in a while. There had been no use in frightening them anymore, he had told himself as he drove off. Why make things worse by mentioning that he had felt strong vibrations, "a creepy feeling," the moment he once again walked into 112 Ocean Avenue.

Immediately after Sergeant Zammataro left, George noticed that the compressor in the boathouse had stopped. There was no reason for the machine's stopping—unless it had overloaded the circuits and blown a fuse. That meant he would have to go down to the basement in the main house and examine the fuse box.

George knew the box was in the area of the storage closets and took a fresh box of fuses down with him. In the cellar he quickly discovered the blown fuse and replaced it. He heard the compressor start up again, making a loud racket as it began to churn, but he waited to see if another overload would occur. After a few minutes, he was satisfied and started to go back upstairs.

When he was halfway up the cellar steps, George became aware of the smell. It wasn't fuel oil.

He had his flashlight with him, but the lights in the basement were still on. From his position on the stairs, George was able to see almost the entire cellar. He sniffed and then sensed the foul odor was coming from the area near the northeast corner—by the plywood storage closets that shielded the secret room.

George went back down the stairs and warily approached the storage closets. As he stood before the shelving that hid the small room, the odor became stronger. Holding his nose, George forced open the paneling and shone his flashlight around the red painted walls.

The stench of human excrement was heavy in the confined space. It formed a choking fog. Nauseated, George's stomach began to heave. He had just time enough to pull the panel back into place and shut out the mist before he vomited, fouling his clothes and the floor.

George had finally managed to clean himself up after the disastrous trip to the basement. He and Kathy were sitting in the kitchen over coffee. It was after eleven P.M. and both were tired from the tension of the ever-increasing incidents. Only the kitchen seemed relatively safe; and they were reluctant to go up to bed.

"Listen," George said, "it's getting chilly in here. Let's at least go into the living room where it's warmer." He got up from his chair, but Kathy remained seated.

"What are we going to do?" she asked. "Things are getting worse. I'm really scared something can happen to the kids." Kathy looked up at her husband. "God knows what's going to happen next around here."

"Look," he answered. "Just keep the kids out of the cellar until I set up a fan down there. Then I'm going to brick up the door to that room so it never bothers us again." He took Kathy's arm and pulled her up from the chair. "I also want to talk to Eric at my office. He says his girl friend's got a lot of experience investigating haunted houses."

"Haunted houses?" Kathy interrupted. "Do you think this house is haunted? By what?" She followed him toward the living room, then stopped in the hallway. "I just had a thought, George. Do you think our TM had anything to do with all this?"

George shook his head. "Nah. Nothing at all. But what I do know is that we've got to get help somewhere. It might as well be . . ."

As they entered the living room, Kathy's scream cut off the rest of George's words. He looked to where she was pointing. The ceramic lion that George had carried up to the sewing room was on the table next to Kathy's chair, its jaws bared at George and Kathy!

16
January 4 to 5

George grabbed the lion off the living-room table and threw it into a garbage can outside the house. It took him quite a while to calm Kathy down because he couldn't possibly explain how the ceramic piece had managed to come back down from the sewing room. She insisted that something in the house had done it and that she didn't want to spend another minute in 112 Ocean Avenue.

George had confided to Kathy that he too felt uneasy about the lion's sudden reappearance. But he couldn't agree on running away without taking a chance at fighting back.

"How can you fight what you can't see?" Kathy asked. "This—this thing can do anything it wants."

"No, honey," George said. "There's no way you can convince me a lot of this isn't just our imagination. I just don't believe in spooks! No way, no how, no time!" Finally he talked Kathy into going up to bed with a promise that if he couldn't get help by the next day, they would get out of the house for a while.

They were both completely drained. Kathy fell asleep out of sheer exhaustion. George dozed off, waking every once in a while to listen groggily for any unnatural noises in the house. He says that he has no idea how long he had lain there before he heard the marching music downstairs!

His head was keeping time to the drumbeats before he realized he was listening to music. Glancing at Kathy to see if she had been awakened, he heard her breathe deeply. She was fast asleep.

George ran out of the room into the hall and heard the stomp of marching feet get louder. There must be at least fifty musicians parading around on the first floor, he thought. But the moment he hit the bottom step and turned on the hall light, the sounds ceased.

George froze on the staircase, his eyes and head swiveling frantically to catch any sign of movement. There was absolutely no one there. It was as though he had walked into an echo chamber. After the cacophony of sound, the sudden silence sent chills up his back.

Then George heard heavy breathing and thought someone was right behind him. He spun about. No one was there, and he then realized he was listening to Kathy from way upstairs.

Fear of her being alone in the bedroom galvanized George. He raced back up the steps two at a time and into their room, turning on the light. There, floating two feet above the bed, was Kathy. She was slowly drifting away from him toward the windows!

"Kathy!" George yelled, jumping up on the bed to grab his wife. She was as stiff as a board in his hands, but her drifting stopped. George felt a resistance to his pull, then a sudden release of pressure, and he and Kathy fell heavily off the bed onto the floor. The fall awakened her.

When she saw where she was, Kathy was incoherent for a moment. "Where am I?" she cried. "What's happened?"

George started to help her up. She could hardly stand. "It's nothing," he reassured her. "You were having a dream and fell out of bed. That's all."

Kathy was still too dazed to question George any further. She said, "Oh!" got back into bed, and immediately fell into a deep sleep.

George turned out the light in the room but did not return to his wife's side. He sat on a chair beside the windows, watching Kathy and looking out at the lightening sky of early morning.

Kathy was still in a deep sleep at ten the next morning. George had become worried about her condition after the past night's terrifying experience. He couldn't wait any longer. He had to call Father Mancuso again.

Danny and Chris had told their father that they heard on their radio that the Amityville schools were closed because of a heating problem. They were somewhat disappointed, because it would have been their first day at their new school after the Christmas holidays and a chance to meet some new friends.

George thought he was lucky not to have to drive the boys to school. It was clear across town, and he hadn't really wanted to leave Kathy and Missy alone in the house. He fed the children their breakfast and sent them up to play in their bedroom. Then he looked in on Kathy.

Her face was pale, drawn, with deep lines around her mouth. He didn't want to waken her and went back down to the kitchen. When he saw that it was 11:00 A.M., he decided to call the priest.

When he dialed Father Mancuso's private number, there was no answer. George called the rectory itself and was informed that Father Mancuso was visiting his mother. No, they couldn't give out her number but they would give Father Mancuso the message that George had called.

George sat in the kitchen the rest of the morning, waiting for the return call. He thought he had been a fool to mouth off about "not believing in spooks." Kathy was right—how the hell *can* you fight something that can lift you clear off the bed like a stick of wood? George Lutz, ex-Marine, admitted he was scared.

Kathy came downstairs just as the telephone rang. It was George's office, calling to ask when he was coming in. The IRS agent was due back and they did not know how George wanted to handle the situation. George squirmed. Finally he told his bookkeeper to call the accountant and postpone the appointment until the following week. As for his coming in, he said Kathy didn't feel well and they were waiting for the doctor. He ended the call by telling his office he'd get back to them later.

"Boy!" he said to Kathy, "are they ever getting fed up with me! I'll just have to go in tomorrow."

Kathy yawned and shrugged her shoulders in an effort to ease the stiffness in her body. "God," she said, "look at the time. Why'd you let me sleep so long? Have the kids eaten? Are the boys in school?"

George started counting on his fingers. "First," he answered "you haven't slept so good in weeks, so I left you alone." He held up two fingers. "Yes, they ate breakfast." Three fingers. "There was no school today. I sent them upstairs to play with Missy."

Good, he thought to himself, Kathy hadn't remembered anything about what happened last night. And I'm not going to tell her.

"I've been trying to get hold of Father Mancuso again," George continued. "They say he's at his mother's, but he'll call me as soon as they hear from him."

Father Mancuso's mother didn't disturb his needed rest until almost three in the afternoon. When he checked in with the rectory, the priest who answered the phone told him that George Lutz had called him.

Oh yes, he reminded himself, I meant to call him, but it completely slipped my mind. Father Mancuso said he'd return by evening. He then called George.

"Father, am I glad you called. We must talk to you right away. Can you please come over here now?"

"But I've already blessed your house," Father Mancuso answered. "It's not to bless the house," George interrupted. "It's more than that now." For the next several minutes George recounted what had happened at 112 Ocean Avenue since he had moved in. He sent Kathy upstairs under the pretext of getting him her cigarettes and then told the priest about her levitating. "That's why we need you, Father," George concluded. "I'm scared of what's going to happen to Kathy and the kids!"

Father Mancuso took a deep breath. "All right, George. I'll try and get there to . . . "

George didn't hear what Father Mancuso said next. Suddenly there were several loud moans on the line and then a crackling that almost shattered his eardrum. "Father! I can't hear you!" A continued moaning was the only answer George got.

George knew it was useless to wait for Father Mancuso to call back. Even if he did, they would have been prevented from talking to each other about the house. But George had one hope. He was sure he had heard him say he'd come, but he didn't know when. He'd just have to wait.

17

January 6

Your story is very interesting, Frank, but if I didn't know your background as a pro, I'd honestly think you were a little nuts to believe in it." Chancellor Ryan got up from behind his desk and went to the new coffee machine across the room. Father Mancuso shook his head at Father Ryan's offer. Ryan then poured one black cup for Father Nuncio—the other chancellor—and one for himself.

The Chancellor sat back down at his desk, sipped some of the coffee, then looked at his notes. "In your capacity as a psychotherapist, how many times have people come to you with stories like this? Hundreds, I'll bet."

Chancellor Ryan was six feet five, with a shock of white hair crowning a ruddy Irish face. The priest was well known in the diocese for his open manner in speaking to the other clerics, be they young parish priests or the bishop himself.

Chancellor Nuncio, on the other hand, was the exact opposite; short, stumpy, black-haired, young at forty-two, while Father Ryan was well in his sixties and with a seriousness to his approach that perfectly complemented the other chancellor's softer touch.

The two had listened to Father Mancuso's recounting of the episodes that George Lutz had said happened at 112 Ocean Avenue, and they were impressed with his fears that the phenomena had a demonic taint to them.

Chancellor Ryan looked up from the pad on his desk and spoke to the troubled priest. "Before we offer any suggestions on how you should handle this as a participant and as a priest, Frank, I think you should know the ground rules." Father Ryan nodded to Father Nuncio.

The other priest put down his coffee. "You seem to think that there's something demonic going on in the Lutzes' house, that the place is possessed somehow. Well, let me reassure you that first of all, *places* and *things* are never possessed. Only people." Father Nuncio stopped, reached into his jacket, and withdrew several short cigars. He offered them around, but the two priests declined. He lit up, puffing and talking at the same time. "The traditional viewpoint of the Church sees the devil in a number of ways: he tries through *temptation,* by which he is seen to prod men toward sin in the psychological battles with which I'm sure you're familiar."

"Oh, yes," Father Mancuso nodded. "As Father Ryan mentioned, I've seen and heard many who've come to me as a psychotherapist and as a parish priest."

Chancellor Ryan picked up the thread. "Then there are the so-called extraordinary activities of the devil in the world. Usually these are material things around a person that are affected; that might be what your're up against. We call it *infestation.*"

"*Obsession*," Father Nuncio put in, "is the next step, in which the person is affected either internally or externally. And finally there is *possession*, by which the person temporarily loses control of his faculties and the devil acts in and through him."

"In investigating cases of possible diabolical interference," Chancellor Ryan went on, "we must consider the following: one, fraud and deception. Two, natural scientific causes. Three, parapsychological causes. Four, diabolical influences. And five, miracles.

"In this case, fraud and trickery don't seem plausible. George and Kathleen Lutz seem to be normal, balanced individuals. The possibilities therefore are reduced to psychological, parapsychological, or diabolical influences."

"We'll exclude the miraculous," Father Nuncio broke in, "because the Divine would not involve itself in the trivial and foolish."

"True," said Father Ryan. "Therefore the explanation would seem to include hallucination and autosuggestion—you know, like the invisible touches Kathy experienced—and when George thought he heard that marching band. But let's take the parapsychological line.

"Parapsychologists like Dr. Rhine, who works at Duke University, define four main operations in the science. The first three come under the general heading of ESP—extrasensory perception. They are mental telepathy, clairvoyance, and precognition, which could explain George's visions and 'picking up' information that seems to coincide with known facts about the DeFeos. The fourth parapsychological area is psychokinesis, where objects move by themselves. That would be the case with the Lutzes' ceramic lion—if it *did* move," he added.

Father Nuncio got up to refill his cup. "All of what we've said, Frank, is part of the suggestion we have for the Lutzes. Have them contact some investigative organization like Dr. Rhine's to come in and look at the house. They'll do extensive testing and I'm sure they can come to some conclusion short of diabolical influence."

"But what about me?" asked Father Mancuso. "What do *I* do?" Chancellor Ryan cleared his throat and looked kindly at the priest. "You are not to return to that house. You can call the Lutzes and tell them what we suggested. But under no circumstances are you ever to go there again."

After breakfast, Kathy dropped the boys off at their new school, then drove over to her mother's with Missy. George was alone in the house. He had gone down to the cellar to clear the odor with two fans. But when he went down the stairs, there was no trace of any of the terrible stench that had made him vomit the day before.

He sniffed but could detect nothing, even when he went directly to the secret red room. George pulled the plywood paneling back open and flashed his light about the red walls. "Damn!" he said. "It couldn't have disappeared just like that. There's got to be an air hole down here somewhere."

George was searching for that possible airvent when Father Mancuso dialed his number. After the meeting, the priest had driven back to his own quarters in North Merrick, intending to call George with the chancellors' recommendations. He heard the telephone ring ten times before he finally hung up. Father Mancuso thought he'd try again later when the Lutzes came home.

George was home all right, but he never heard the telephone ring. The door to the basement was open, and usually the ringing telephone could be heard anywhere in the house.

George had no success in finding any opening where the stench could have escaped, but under the area where the front steps to the house had been constructed, he did discover something interesting. When the contractor had laid the foundation for the house at 112 Ocean Avenue, it seemed he had covered over a circular opening with a concrete lid. By squirreling around the dirt piled up against this protuberance, George accidentally loosened some of the old gravel around the base and heard it fall into water far below. He flashed his light and saw the beam hit against a wet, black shaft. "A well!" he said. "That doesn't show up in the blueprints. It must have been left from the house that was here before."

He returned to the first floor and looked at the kitchen clock. Strange, he thought, it's almost noon and I still haven't heard from Father Mancuso. I'd better try him myself.

George called the rectory. The priest picked up on the first ring. George was surprised when Father Mancuso told him he had just called and that there was no answer at the house. Then George asked Father Mancuso when he was coming, and they got down to Father Mancuso's report. He said he'd been to see the chancellors of his diocese and repeated their recommendations that George find an organization to conduct a scientific investigation of the house. Father Mancuso gave George the address of the Psychical Research Institute in Durham, North Carolina, and suggested he get in touch with the group immediately. George agreed, but pressed the priest to come to the house.

When George called Kathy at her mother's, he told her what the priest had said but snorted that he wasn't going to bother with anything like that. But Kathy felt they should pursue the chancellors' recommendations, telling George that he should listen to what the Church suggested.

Finally George agreed, saying he would drive to his office on his Harley chopper and type out the letter to the people at Duke. He didn't tell her he also wanted to talk to Eric, the young fellow at his office who said his girl friend was a medium.

George rode to his office and mailed the letter to the parapsychologists, using the chancellors' names as his reference. He didn't really expect an immediate response to his request for an investigator, so he only put a regular stamp on the envelope instead of an airmail one. Then he telephoned Eric's girl friend, Francine.

She was terribly interested in what he had to say. Sure that she could contact whatever—or whoever—was making his and Kathy's lives miserable, she promised to come to the Lutzes' house in a day or so.

Then the young woman said something that really made George's ears perk up. Out of the clear blue, she mentioned that George should look around his property for an old, abandoned, covered-up well. He didn't admit that he had already found such a place, but asked instead *why* she wanted him to do the searching.

Her answer shocked him. "I think," she said, "that your spirits may be coming from a well. You can cap it off, you know, but I bet if you do find a well under your house, there is a direct passage to it. And somehow, even if it's a tiny crack, that's all it takes. With that, 'it' can climb out when it wants to."

After thanking the girl and hanging up, George made a phone call to the Psychical Resarch Institute and told them of the letter he had just sent. They agreed to send a field investigator as soon as possible. In turn, George agreed to pay the field man's expenses.

18
January 6 to 7

Earlier that day, Kathy had returned from her mother's house in time to pick up Danny and Chris at their new school in Amityville. The boys were eager to tell about their teachers, schoolmates, and playground facilities. The yard had been cleared of snow and the children had been able to enjoy some activities outside. Missy, jealous at having to stay home, kept pumping her brothers about what the girls at the elementary school were like.

The whole family ate together at six-thirty. George told Kathy what he had done about Father Mancuso's suggestion and that he had also spoken to the girl who could contact spirits. Kathy was glad that he had called the parapsychology people instead of just waiting for an answer to his letter. But she wasn't too happy about a stranger coming into her house to talk to ghosts—particularly a young girl like Francine.

After they had finished dinner, Kathy told George she really wanted to return to her mother's until she felt the house was safe to live in. George reminded her that it was ten degrees above zero outside and snow was forecast by morning. Even though East Babylon wasn't too far up the road, he didn't think she could make it from her mother's house back to Amityville in time to get the boys to school in the morning.

Danny and Chris chimed in that they wanted to stay home—they had some homework to do, and besides, their grandmother wouldn't let them watch television after eight o'clock. Kathy finally gave in to their arguments, but felt uneasy about staying in the house another night. She told George she didn't think she could sleep a wink.

Harry had been in the kitchen with them while they were eating, and Kathy had given the dog all the scraps of meat left over from dinner. Before they went to bed, George thought that Harry might be better off staying inside that night. It was bitter cold out and would only get worse if the snow fell. Harry hadn't been served his usual dry food, and George thought the dog might be more alert after having some meat.

While the boys did their homework, Missy took Harry up to her room to play. But Harry didn't want to stay there. He was nervous and sniveling, Kathy noted, particularly after Missy had introduced Harry to her unseen friend, Jodie. Finally the little girl had to close her door to keep Harry from running out. He crawled under her bed and remained there. Finally Chris came down for him. Harry scampered out of Missy's room and, with his tail between his legs, ran up the stairs to the third floor, where he remained the rest of the night.

At twelve, when George and Kathy finally went up to bed, she went out like a light for the third night in a row, quickly falling into a deep sleep, her breathing heavy. George, lying on his side, his back to Kathy, was wide-awake, his ears alert for any signs of the marching band.

When he first noticed the snowflakes falling outside the windows, he saw it was one o'clock on his wrist watch. The wind was rising, whipping the flakes about. Then he heard a boat moving on the Amityville River. But the bedroom windows didn't face the water, and George didn't feel like getting up from his warm bed to look out from Missy's or the sewing-room windows. Besides, the river was frozen, so George ascribed the sound to the vagaries of the wind.

At 2 A.M. he began to yawn. His eyes were getting heavy, and his body was getting stiff from lying in one position. A short while ago he had looked over his shoulder at Kathy. She was still flat on her back, her mouth open. Now in the darkness of the room, George could see Kathy wasn't in bed. He could see that she was levitating again, almost a foot above him, drifting away from him!

Instinctively George reached out, grabbed her hair, and yanked. Kathy floated back to him and then fell back onto the bed. She awoke.

George turned on the night-stand light next to him and gasped. He was looking at a ninety-year-old woman—the hair wild, a shocking white, the face a mass of wrinkles and ugly lines, and saliva dripping from the tooth-less mouth.

George was so revolted he wanted to flee from the room. Kathy's eyes, set deep in the wrinkles, were looking at him questioningly. George shuddered. It's *Kathy*, he thought, this is my wife! What the hell am I doing?

Kathy sensed the fright in her husband's face. My God, what does he see? She leaped from the bed and ran into the bathroom, flicking on the light above the mirror. Staring at her own face, she screamed.

The ancient crone George had seen was gone, her hair was upset, but it was blonde again. Her lips were not drooling any longer, nor was she wrinkled. But deep, ugly lines ran up and down her cheeks.

George, following Kathy into the bathroom, peered over her shoulder at the image. He too saw that the ninety-year-old visage had faded, but the long, black slashes still cut deeply down Kathy's face. "What's happening to my face?" Kathy yelled.

She turned to George, and he put his fingers up to Kathy's mouth. Her lips were dry and burning hot. Then he ran his finger tips gently across the deep ridges. There were three on each cheek, extending from just below her eyes down to just under the jawline. "I don't know, baby," he whispered.

George took a towel from the rack next to the sink and tried to wipe the lines away. Kathy spun about and looked into the mirror. Her scared face stared back at her. Running her fingers down her face, she began to cry.

Kathy's helplessness stirred George deeply, and he put his hands on her shoulders. "I'm going to call Father Mancuso right now," he said.

Kathy shook her head. "No, we mustn't involve him in this." She looked at George's face reflected in the mirror. "Something tells me he could get hurt. We'd better go and check on the kids," she said calmly.

The children were all right, but George and Kathy were unable to go back to sleep that night. They stayed in their bedroom, with the lights out, watching the snow fall. Every once in a while Kathy would hold her hands to her face, checking to feel if the ridges were still there. Finally the cold dawn broke. The snow had stopped, and there was just enough light for George to make out Kathy when she touched him on the shoulder. "George," she said, "look at my face."

He turned from the position he had taken in a chair near the window and looked at his wife. In the dawn's weak light, George could see that the lines were gone. He put his fingers up to her face and touched her skin. It was soft again, with absolutely no trace of the disfiguring scars! "They're gone, baby," he smiled gently. "They are all gone."

In spite of what Kathy had said, George called Father Mancuso in the morning and caught the priest just before early Mass.

George told him that he had spoken to North Carolina, where a Jerry Solfvin had promised to have an investigator come to the house immediately. Then he brought up the incident of the night before. Father Mancuso was aghast about the second levitation and the alterations of Kathy's face. "George, " he said urgently, "I'm worried about what could happen next. Why don't you just get out of the house for a while?"

George assured the priest he had been thinking of doing just that, but first he wanted to see what Francine the medium had to say. Maybe she could help as she had claimed.

"A medium?" Father Mancuso asked. "What are you talking about, George? That's not a scientific investigation."

"But she said she can talk to spirits," George protested. "In fact, Father, do you know what she said yesterday? She told me there's a well hidden under my house. She's right! I found one under the stoop and she's never even been here!"

Father Mancuso became angry. "Listen!" he shouted over the phone. "You're involved in something dangerous! I don't know what is going on in your house, but you'd better get out!"

"You mean, just leave everything?"

"Yes, just go for a while," the priest persisted. "I'll talk to the chancellors again and see if they can send someone, maybe a priest."

Later that evening, Eric, the young engineer who worked at George's company, arrived at the Lutzes' home with his girl friend Francine. George immediately hustled the young couple out of the bitter cold and into the living room to warm themselves in front of the big fire.

They brought an infectious cheerfulness that had been missing at 112 Ocean Avenue. George and Kathy responded and soon the four were chatting away like old friends. But under George's exterior warmth, there was an urgency. He wanted Francine to look over the house.

As she was trying to turn the conversation around to her experience with spirits, Francine beat him to it. Suddenly she got up from her seat on the couch and motioned to George. "Put your hand gently over here," she said. George bent over and waved his hand where she had pointed. "Do you feel the cold air?" Francine asked.

"Slightly," George answered.

"She's been sitting here. Now she's left. Now follow the couch. Feel it over here?"

George put his hand near a pillow. "Oh, yeah, it feels warm."

Francine beckoned George and Kathy to follow her. The three entered the dining room while Eric remained in the living room. Francine stood next to the big table. "There's an unusual odor here," she said. "I can't quite place it, but it's here. Whew! Do you smell *that?*"

George sniffed. "Yeah, right here. It's a smell of perspiration."

The girl headed for the kitchen, but hesitated before going into the breakfast nook. "There's an old man and an old lady. They are lost spirits. Do you smell the perfume?"

Kathy's eyes widened. Quickly she looked at George, who shrugged. "Evidently these people must have had the house at one time, " Francine continued, "but they died. Only I don't think they died in the house." She turned to George and said, "I want to go to the basement now, okay?"

When George had first spoken to Francine on the telephone, he told her that mysterious things were happening in his house—but without ever really spelling out what the phenomena were nor what had actually taken place with Kathy and himself. He hadn't discussed the touchings in the kitchen nor the smell of perfume Kathy had experienced. In any case, Francine had said she would rather draw her own conclusions after visiting the house and "talking to the spirits who live there."

Now Francine descended the stairs to the cellar. "The house is built on a burial ground or something like that," she said. She pointed to a large area of the basement where the storage closets were built. "Is that new?" she asked George.

"I don't think so. As far as I know, it was all built at the same time."

Francine stopped in front of the closets. "There are people buried right here. Something is over them. There is an unusual odor. This should not be stuffy at all like this." She was pointing directly at the plywood paneling that hid the secret room. "Notice the chill?" Her hands were moving now, touching the wood. "Somebody was murdered, or he could even be buried under here. But this seems like a new part, like a new part has been added on, and over this grave."

Kathy wanted to run from the basement. George noticed her discomfort and reached for her hand. Francine solved their dilemma. "I don't like this spot at all. It's better that we go upstairs now." Without waiting for a response, she turned and headed for the staircase.

As they went up to the second floor, Eric joined them. Francine stood in the hallway, holding on to the banister. "I have to say that when I came up here, there was a whirling sensation. I felt a tightness on the right half of my chest."

"A pain?" Kathy asked.

Francine nodded. "Very slight, very quick. Right as you turn the corner. It disappeared quickly." She stepped to the closed door of the sewing room. "You've been having problems in here."

George and Kathy both nodded. He opened the door, half expecting to find the flies in the room. But there were none, and he and Francine walked inside. Kathy and Eric hung back in the doorway.

Suddenly Francine appeared to go into a trance. Out of her mouth came a different voice, heavier, more masculine: "I would like to make one suggestion to you. Most people find out who their spirits are and they find they like them. They don't want them to get lost or to go away. But in this case, I feel this house should be cleared or exorcised."

The voice coming from Francine began to sound familiar to George. He couldn't quite place it, but he was sure he had heard it before. "Somebody's little girl and boys . . . I see bloodstains. Somebody hurt themselves badly here. Someone tried to kill themselves or something . . . "

Francine came out of her trance. "I would like to go now, " she announced to George and Kathy. "It's not a good time to try to talk to the spirit. I have a feeling I should go. I was born with a Venetian Veil, you know." George didn't know what she meant, but she promised George to return in a day or so—"When the vibrations are better," she explained. The couple departed almost immediately.

Back in the living room, George and Kathy were silent for a long time. Finally Kathy asked, "What do you think?"

"I don't know," George answered. "I just don't know. She was hitting things right on the head." He stood up to put out the fire. "I have to think about it for a while."

Kathy went upstairs to check on the children. Again Harry was staying with the boys since it was too cold out for even a rugged dog. George made his usual check of all doors and locks, then turned out the lights on the first floor.

He started up the steps, then stopped before he reached the second-floor landing. George saw that the banister above him was wrenched from its moorings, torn almost completely from the floor foundation.

At that very instant, he recalled whose voice had been speaking to him through Francine. It was Father Mancuso!

19
January 8

On Thursday, Jimmy and his new bride, Carey, returned from their honeymoon in Bermuda. They called Kathy from Mrs. Conners', and Jimmy told his sister he would drop over later in the day. One of his first questions was whether she and George had found his $1,500. He was disappointed when Kathy told him there was no trace of the envelope.

It had taken George all morning to fit the broken posts of the second floor bannister back in their sockets. When the boys came down for breakfast, both wanted to help, but George shooed them out of the way, telling them they had to go shopping for new shoes with their mother.

No one—Danny, Chris, Missy, or Kathy—had heard the banister being wrenched from its posts during the night. What had caused this latest damage in the house remained a mystery. George and Kathy had their own ideas but did not voice them in front of the children.

Finally Kathy gathered herself together and herded her brood out to the van to go shopping. George took the opportunity to call Eric. He reached him at home and asked the young man if Francine had said anything after leaving their home. George was troubled to hear that the girl had been very upset with what she felt in the house. She had told Eric she didn't ever want to go back there; the presence was much too strong. She feared if she tried to talk to whatever was at the Lutzes' she would be in danger of a physical attack.

"Eric," George asked, "what's the Venetian Veil she mentioned just before you left?"

"From what Francine's told me," Eric answered, "that's a caul some babies are born with—a kind of skin covering, like a thin veil over the face. It can be removed, but Francine says that that person is somehow blessed with a highly developed degree of clairvoyance."

George hung up and sat in the kitchen for over an hour, trying to think of where or how he could get help before it was too late.

Then the telephone rang. It was George Kekoris, a field investigator for the Psychical Research Institute in North Carolina, who said he had been told to contact George and arrange to set up some scientific tests at the Lutz home. Kekoris also said he couldn't make it that day, since he was calling from Buffalo, but would try to get there the next morning.

After speaking to Kekoris, George felt as if he had received a last minute reprieve. Then, to pass the time until Kathy returned, he busied himself by taking down the Christmas decorations from the tree standing in the living room. Tenderly he placed the delicate ornaments on spread newspapers for Kathy to repack in cardboard boxes, taking special care of his great-grandmother's beautiful gold and silver piece.

By four o'clock, Kathy had returned from shopping. Since the Lutzes still had Jimmy's car, there was no way for the honeymooners to travel unless they were picked up. Kathy volunteered to go after her brother and his new wife.

George vetoed her suggestion—the icy roads to her mother's in East Babylon were still in a hazardous condition, and Jimmy's car had a stick shift—a gear system Kathy had never really mastered. George drove instead and was back in Amityville within the hour.

Kathy was delighted to see Jimmy and Carey again and spent the next hours eagerly chatting with them. The newlyweds also had a bundle of Polaroid snapshots to go through, with a detailed explanation behind each one. Jimmy didn't have a dime left, he said, but they had some memories that would last a lifetime. Naturally thay had brought some presents for the children, and that kept Danny, Chris, and Missy out of the adults' way for most of the evening.

Rather than spoil the pleasant visit by recalling their own weird experiences since the wedding, George and Kathy simply shared the excitement of the other two. Eventually Kathy and her new sister-in-law went upstairs to change the linen on Missy's bed. Jimmy and Carey would be staying overnight in Missy's room, while the little girl slept on an old couch in the dressing room down the hall.

Jimmy explained to George his plans for moving out of his mother's house. He wanted to rent an apartment situated exactly between his mother's house and his new in-laws, who also lived in East Babylon; this way, both families would be placated for a while.

Everyone retired fairly early. Before turning in, George and Jimmy checked the house inside and out. George showed Jimmy the damaged garage door but didn't offer any explanation beyond the theory that it was caused by a freak windstorm. Jimmy, who had been victimized of his money by an unknown source, was suspicious of something else, but he too kept silent and followed George as he checked the boathouse.

Back inside, they continued their tour of doors and windows until both were satisfied with the security of 112 Ocean Avenue. It was eleven o'clock when the couples said goodnight to one another.

George knows that it happened at 3:15 A.M. because he had been lying awake a few minutes and had just checked his wristwatch. It was then that Carey woke up screaming.

"Oh, God, not her too!" he muttered to himself. George leaped out of bed, ran to Missy's room, and snapped on the light. The young couple were huddled together in bed, Jimmy cradling his sobbing wife.

"What's the matter?" George asked. "What's happened?"

Carey pointed to the foot of Missy's bed. "S-s-something was sitting there! It touched m-m-my foot!"

George approached the spot Carey had indicated and felt the bed with his hand. It was warm, as though someone had been sitting there.

"I woke up," Carey continued, "and I could see a little boy. He looked so sick! He was trying to tell me to help him!" She began to cry hysterically.

Jimmy shook his wife gently. "Come on Carey," he said soothingly. "You were probably having a dream and—"

"No, Jimmy!" Carey protested. "It wasn't a dream! I saw him! He spoke to me!"

"What did he say, Carey?" George asked.

Carey's shoulders were still shaking, but gradually she looked up from her husband's arms. George heard a noise behind him and a touch on his shoulder. He jumped, then looked around. It was Kathy. Her eyes were misty, as though she too had been crying. "Kathy!" Carey cried.

"What did the little boy say?" Kathy prompted her.

"He asked me where Missy and Jodie were!"

At the mention of Missy's name, Kathy bolted from the bedroom and ran to the other side of the hallway. In the dressing room the little girl was fast asleep, with one foot sticking out in the air. Kathy lifted Missy's blanket and bent her leg back under the covers, then leaned down and kissed her child on the head. George came into the room. "Is Missy all right?"

Kathy nodded.

In about fifteen minutes Carey had quieted down enough to fall asleep again. Jimmy was still nervous, but soon he too drifted off.

George and Kathy had returned to their own bedroom. Immediately she went into the closet and took out the crucifix that hung inside. "George," she said, "let's bless the house ourselves."

They began on the third floor, in the children's playroom. In the eerie predawn silence of the cold room, George held the crucifix in front of him while Kathy intoned the Lord's Prayer. They did not go into the boys' room; Kathy said they could wait until the next day to bless that room and those in which Missy and Jimmy and Carey were sleeping.

They moved on to their own bedreoom and then to the sewing room on the second floor. Warning his wife to be careful of the newly repaired banister, George led the way to the first floor, still brandishing the crucifix as he supposed a priest would during a holy procession.

When they completed their blessing of the kitchen and the dining room, it was just starting to get light outside. Even without turning on the lights, they could see the living room dimly visible before them. George marched around the furniture and Kathy started to recite: "Our Father who art in Heaven; hallowed be thy—"

She was interrupted by a loud humming. Kathy stopped and looked about her. George halted in midstride and looked up at the ceiling. The hum swelled into a jumble of voices that seemed to engulf them completely.

Finally Kathy clasped her hands to her ears to drown out the cacophony, but George clearly heard the chorus thunder: *"Will you stop!"*

20

January 8 to 9

After speaking to Father Nuncio, Father Mancuso called George to tell him that both men felt he should vacate the house. He let the telephone ring for a long time and was ready to give up when George answered. The priest assumed the phone was up to its weird tricks, so he was surprised that he had gotten through without interference.

George said that they had just returned from seeing Jimmy off to East

Babylon. Then George repeated the results of their impromptu blessing ceremony the night before. Dismayed, Father Mancuso urged George to heed the chancellors' advice and get out of the house then and there. "And George, " he said, "don't ever do that again. Your evoking God's name in the manner you did can only anger whatever is in your house. Let a priest do that. He's a direct intermediary between the Lord and the Devil. . . ."

"The *Devil*?" George interrupted. "Father, what are you saying?" The priest could have bitten his tongue for the slip. The chancellors had confined any discussion of the Lutzes' case to scientific causes, and there would be a long period of investigation before the Church would acknowledge demonic influence. He hadn't meant to express his own personal fears. "I'm not sure," Father Mancuso corrected himself. "That's why I plead with you to leave your house now until some determination can be made, scientifically or . . ." The priest hesitated.

"Or what?" George asked.

"It may be more dangerous than any of us realize," Father Mancuso answered. "Look, George, many things happen that none of us can really explain away. I admit I'm very confused about what seems to be an evil force in your house. I also admit that it may be caused by more than our imaginations." The priest paused.

"George? You still there?"

"Yeah, Father. I'm listening."

"All right, then," Father Mancuso began again. "Please get out. Let things cool down for a while. If you get away, maybe we can all think this thing out with more rationality. I'll tell the chancellors what happened last night and maybe they'll send someone right . . . "

Father Mancuso was interrupted by Kathy's scream over the telephone. George blurted "Call you back!" and the priest heard him bang down the receiver. George stood there in his living room, wondering what unnatural act was now being played out at 112 Ocean Avenue.

Running up the stairs to the third floor, he reached the landing, and saw Kathy in the hallway shrieking at Danny, Chris, and Missy.

George could see why: on every wall in the hall were green gelatinous spots, oozing down from the ceiling to the floor, settling in shimmering pools of greem slime.

"Which one of you did this?" Kathy fumed. "Tell me or I'll break every bone in your bodies!"

"We didn't do it, Mama!" all three children chorused at once, dodging the slaps she was aiming at their heads.

"We didn't do it!" Danny yelled. "We saw it when we came upstairs!" George stepped between his wife and the children. "Wait a minute," he said gently, "maybe the kids *didn't* do it. Let me take a look."

He went up to one wall and stuck his finger into a green spot. He looked at the substance, smelled it, and then put a little against the tip of his tongue."It sure looks like Jello," he said, smacking his lips, "but it doesn't have any taste at all."

Kathy was calming down. "Could it be paint?" she asked.

George shook his head. "Nope." He tried to get the feel of the jelly by rolling it against his finger tips. "I don't know what it is, but it sure leaves a mess."

He looked up at the ceiling. "Doesn't seem to be coming from up there . . . " George stopped. He looked around him as if realizing for the first time where he was. In a rush, he recalled the conversation he had had with Father Mancuso a few minutes before, and the dreaded word "Devil" almost slipped from his lips.

"What'd you say, George?" asked Kathy. "I didn't hear you."

He looked at his wife and children. "Nothing. I was just trying to think . . . " He began to edge the others toward the staircase. "Listen," he said, "I'm hungry. Let's go down to the kitchen and have a bite. Then the boys and me'll clean up this gook. Okay, gang?"

George had been so absorbed in his thoughts that he had completely forgotten to call Father Mancuso back. By that evening, sitting beside the fireplace, Kathy was all for leaving for her mother's. But when she suggested they get out of the house that night, George suddenly went beserk. "Goddammit, no!" he shouted, jumping up from his chair, his face red with rage.

All the pressures that had been building within him finally exploded. "Every goddamn thing we own in the world is in this house!" he stormed. "I've got too much invested here to give it up just like that!"

The children, who were still up, cringed and ran to their mother's side. Even Kathy was frightened by a side of George that she had never seen. He had the look of a man possessed.

Absolutely livid, he stood at the foot of the staircase and screamed so that he could be heard in every room in the house. "You sons of bitches! Get out of my house!" Then he ran up the stairs to the third floor and into the playroom and threw all the windows open wide. "Get out! Get out in the name of God!"

George ran into the boys' bedroom, then down to the second floor and repeated his actions, shoving up each window in every room, bellowing, "Get out in the name of God!" again and again.

Some of the windows resisted his push, and he banged furiously on the the frames until they loosened. Cold air poured in from outside, and soon the whole house was as frigid as the outdoors.

Finally George was finished. By the time he returned to the first floor, the anger was leaving his body. Exhausted from his efforts and panting heavily, he stood in the center of the living room, tightly clenching and unclenching his fists.

While George was on his errand, Kathy and the children had been rooted to a spot near the fireplace. Now they came up to him slowly, encircled him, and he lifted his arms and embraced all four frightened people.

Over the following hour, 112 Ocean Avenue warmed up again. The heat from the radiators finally overcame the frigid air that had invaded the house, and once more the thermostat read 75 degrees.

The boys had been dozing in front of the fireplace while Kathy held little Missy in her arms, rocking the sleeping girl. At ten o'clock she checked the children's bedrooms and decided that Danny and Chris could now go to bed.

Since his tirade, George had been completely uncommunicative, silently staring at his blazing logs. Kathy left him alone, realizing her husband was trying to resolve their dilemma in his own way. After the children were tucked away upstairs, she finally went to him and gently tried to urge him out of the room.

George looked at Kathy and she saw the confusion and anger in his face. His eyes were misty; George seemed to be crying over his frustration. The poor guy deserves a break, she thought. He shook his head at her suggestion to go up to bed.

"You go," he said softly. "I'll be up in a while." His eyes returned to the dancing flames.

In her bedroom, Kathy left the lamp on George's night stand burning. She undressed, slipped into bed, and closed her eyes. Kathy could hear the wind howling outside. The sound slowly relaxed her so that in a few minutes she began to doze off.

Suddenly Kathy sat bolt upright and looked at George's side of the bed. He still wasn't there. Then she slowly turned her head and looked behind her. She saw her image reflected in the mirrors that covered the wall from ceiling to floor, and she had the urge to get the crucifix out of the closet again.

So strong was the feeling that Kathy was halfway out of bed when she stopped and again stared into the mirrors. Her image seemed to take on a life of its own, and she could hear it saying: "Don't do it! You'll destroy everyone!"

When George went up, he found Kathy asleep. He adjusted the covers about his wife, then went to her night stand and removed her Bible from its drawer. He turned out his light and silently left the room.

George returned to his chair in the living room, opened the Bible, and began at the beginning, the Book of Genesis. In this first book of God's revelations, he came upon verses that caused him to reflect upon his predicament. He read one aloud to himself: "And the Lord God said to the serpent: because thou hast done this thing, thou art cursed among all cattle, and beasts of the earth: upon thy breast shalt thou go, and earth thou shalt eat all the days of thy life."

George shivered. The serpent is the Devil, he thought. Then he felt a hot blast on his face, and he snapped his head up from the book. The flames of the fireplace were reaching out for him!

George leaped off his chair and jumped back. The fire he had left to die was roaring to life again, the blaze filling the entire hearth. He could feel its searing heat. But then he was stabbed in the back by an icy finger.

George whirled about. Nothing was there, but he could feel a draft. He could almost see it in the form of a cold mist coming down the staircase in the hallway!

Gripping the Bible tightly, George raced up the steps toward his bedroom. The cold wrapped itself about him as he ran. He stopped in the doorway. The room was warm. Again he was struck by the icy finger.

George ran to Missy's bedroom and flung open the door. The windows were wide open, the below-freezing air pouring in.

George grabbed up his daughter from her bed. He could feel her little body was icy and shivering. Rushing out of the room, he ran back to his bedroom and put Missy under the covers. Kathy woke up. "Warm her up!" George yelled. "She's freezing to death!"

Without hesitation, Kathy covered the little girl with her own body.

George ran out of the room and up to the third floor.

The windows in the boys' bedroom, were also wide open. The boys were asleep but burrowed completely under their blankets. He gathered both in his arms and staggered down the stairs to his bedroom.

Danny's and Chris's teeth were chattering from the cold. George pushed them onto the bed and got under the blankets with them, his body on top of theirs.

All five Lutzes were in one bed, the three children slowly thawing out, the two parents rubbing their hands and feet. It took almost a half-hour before the children's body temperatures seemed back to normal. Only then did George realize he was still holding onto the Bible. Knowing he had been more than warned, he flung it to the floor.

21

January 10

On Saturday morning, Kathy's mother received a frantic call from her daughter: "Ma, I need you immediately." When Mrs. Conners tried to question Kathy over the phone as to what had happened she said only that there was no way to explain; her mother had to see for herself. The older woman took a cab from East Babylon to the house in Amityville.

George let his mother-in-law in and hurried her upstairs to Kathy's bedroom. Coming back down, he cautioned Danny, Chris, and Missy to finish their breakfast. When he left the kitchen to join the two women upstairs, the children were unnaturally subdued and meekly obeyed their father. But judging from the way they were eating, they had evidently recovered from their freezing experience the night before.

When George entered the bedroom, his mother-in-law was examining Kathy, who lay on the bed naked beneath her open bathrobe. Kathy watched as her mother's finger traced the ugly red welts that extended from just above her pubic hairline to the bottom of her breasts. The streaks were flaming red, as though she had been burned by a hot poker slashed laterally across Kathy's body.

"Ow!" her mother winced, jerking a finger back from one of the welts on Kathy's stomach. "I burned myself!"

"Be careful, Mama!" Kathy cried. "It happened to George too!"

Kathy's mother looked at him, and George nodded. "I tried putting some cold cream on them," he said, "but even that didn't help. The only way you can touch her is with gloves."

"Did you call the doctor?"

"No, Ma," Kathy answered

"She didn't want her doctor," George broke in. "She only wanted you."

"Does it hurt, Kathy?"

The frightened girl began to cry. George answered for her. "They don't seem to. Only when she touches them."

Kathy's mother put a hand to her sobbing girl's hair, stroking it gently. "My poor baby," she said. "Don't you worry now, I'm here. Everything's going to be all right." She leaned forward and kissed Kathy's tear-stained face. Then she closed Kathy's bathrobe, softly folding it over her inflamed body. She stood up. "I'm going to call Dr. Aiello."

"No!" cried Kathy. She looked at her husband, her eyes wild. "George!"

George put his hand out to Mrs. Conners. "What are you going to tell him?"

Kathy's mother was confused. "What do you mean?" she asked. "You can see she's burned all over her body."

George was insistent. "But how are you going to explain it to him, Ma? We don't even know how it happened. She just woke up that way. He'll think we're nuts!"

He hesitated. If he told Kathy's mother any more about what had happened during the night, he would have to disclose the demonic events that were plaguing the house. Knowing Mrs. Conners' heavily Church-oriented background, George felt sure that she would insist upon Kathy and the children leaving until she could talk to her priest. George had met the cleric and knew him to be very much like the elderly confessor at St. Martin of Tours in Amityville—unworldly when it came to anything beyond simple parish duties. In reality, George would have welcomed a priest, but not the one from East Babylon. And he did expect to hear momentarily from George Kekoris, the psychical investigator.

"Let her rest a while, Ma," he finally said. "The marks seem to be easing up from what they were before. Maybe they'll go away soon." He was remembering the slash lines on Kathy's face.

"Yeah, Mama," Kathy said, also fearing to involve her mother any more deeply. "I'll lie here a little longer. Can you stay with me?"

Kathy's mother looked from her daughter to George. There's something going on that they're not telling me about, she thought to herself. She would have liked to tell Kathy that she had never liked this house; that each time she was here she felt uncomfortable. She just did not trust 112 Ocean Avenue. Looking back, Mrs. Joan Conners now knows why.

George left the two women upstairs and went back down to the kitchen. Danny, Chris, and Missy had finished their food and had even cleared off the table in the breakfast nook. When he came in, there were questions in their eyes. "Mama's all right," George assured them. "Grandma's going to stay with her."

He put his hand on top of Missy's head and turned her toward the doorway. "Come on, gang, " George said, "Let's go out for a while. We gotta get some things at the store, and I want to stop at the library."

After George and the children had driven off, Kathy's mother left her daughter alone for a few minutes and went dowstairs to the kitchen to call Jimmy. Her son would want to know why she had rushed off to Kathy's so hurriedly. Jimmy had wanted to drive Mrs. Conners to Kathy's but she said he should stay at home in case she needed anything from her house.

Over the phone, she told Jimmy that Kathy only had some stomach cramps; she'd call him later when she was about to leave. Jimmy didn't believe her and said he wanted to come over with Carey. He was *not* to come, his mother yelled at him, and he wasn't to bring Carey. She didn't want the report that Jimmy's family was a little crazy to get back to her son's new in-laws.

Kathy, lying in bed, could hear her mother downstairs, shouting into the telephone at her brother. She sighed and opened her robe once more to look at the burning red marks on her body. The welts were still there, but they did seem fainter. Then she tried touching one of the slashes under her right breast. Her finger rested on the ugly spot. It seemed to Kathy that the sensation wasn't as severe as before. The reaction was more like putting her finger under very warm water.

Kathy was about to close her bathrobe when she sensed someone was staring at her nakedness. The feeling of a presence came from right behind her, but Kathy couldn't bring herself to turn and look. She knew the mirrored wall was there, and she was afraid that in it she would see something terrible. Paralyzed with fear, she was unable to even raise her arms to draw the robe about her. She remained that way, her body completely exposed, her eyes tightly shut, cringing inwardly, waiting for the unknown touch.

"Kathy! What are you doing! You'll catch your death of cold!" It was her mother, back from the kitchen.

Even after the red welts had completely disappeared, Mrs. Conners didn't want to leave Kathy. When George returned with the children, she argued that the whole family should leave 112 Ocean Avenue. *He* could stay if he wanted, but she insisted her Kathy and her grandchildren go.

By then, Kathy was asleep upstairs, and after the latest episode, George didn't want to awaken her. "Let her sleep a little longer, Ma," he said. "We'll see about coming over later."

His mother-in-law had agreed reluctantly, getting him to promise to call her the minute her daughter awoke. "If you don't, George, I'll be back!" she warned him. He called her a cab, and she returned to East

Babylon at four in the afternoon.

At the Amityville library, George had been able to secure a temporary borrower's card and take out one book—on witches and demons. Now that his mother-in-law had gone home, he sat alone in the living room, deep in the subject of the Devil and his works.

It was after eight in the evening before George finished his borrowed book. During the afternoon, Kathy's mother had prepared spaghetti and meatballs that George set out at suppertime. Danny, Chris, and Missy ate while George continued reading. The last time he had looked in on Kathy, she stirred a little, and he thought she was about ready to awaken from her much-needed rest. Now he was in the kitchen and the three children were in the living room watching television.

George had made notes while going through the book, and now he looked at what he had jotted down. On the pad was a list of demons, with names he had never heard of. George tried to pronounce them aloud, and they rolled strangely off his tongue. Then he decided to call Father Mancuso.

The priest was surprised that the Lutzes were still at 112 Ocean Avenue. "I thought you were going to leave the house," he said. "I told you what the chancellors said to do."

"I know, Father, I know," answered George. "But now I think I know how to lick this thing." He picked up the book from the table. "I've been reading about how these witches and demons work . . . "

Good Lord, Father Mancuso thought, I'm dealing with a child, an innocent. Here the man's house is about to explode under him and his family, and he's talking to me about witches . . .

" . . . And it says here if you hold an incantation and repeat those demons' names three times, you can call them up," George went on. "There's a ceremony here that shows you exactly what to do. Iscaron, Madeste!" George began to chant. "Those are the names of the demons, Father . . . "

"I *know* who they are!" Father Mancuso blurted.

"Then there's Isabo! Erz, erz—this one's hard to pronounce, Erzelaide. She has something to do with voodoo. And Eslender!"

"George!" the priest cried. "For God's sake! Don't invoke those names again! Not now! Not ever!"

"Why, Father?" George protested. "It's right here in this book. What's wrong with . . . ?"

The telephone went dead in George's hand. There was an unearthly moan, a loud clicking, and then just the sound of a disconnected line.

Did Father Mancuso hang up on me? George wondered. And what's happened to this guy Kekoris?

"Was that my mother?"

George turned and saw Kathy standing in the doorway. No longer in her bathrobe, she had combed her hair and was wearing slacks and a sweater. Her face was slightly flushed.

George shook his head. "How do you feel, honey?" he asked. "Have a good sleep?"

Kathy lifted up her sweater, baring her navel. "It's gone." She stroked herself. "They're not there anymore." She sat down at the table. "Where are the kids?"

"They're watching television," George answered. He took her hands in his. "You want to call your mother now?"

Kathy nodded. She felt strangely relaxed, almost sensual. Ever since she had the sensation of being stared at in her bed, Kathy had been in a languorous mood, as if she had been completely satisfied sexually. It had even carried over into her recent nap, she mused, when she had unconnected visions of making love to someone. It wasn't George . . .

Kathy dialed her mother's number while George went into the living room with the children. He heard a loud clap of thunder. Looking out the windows, he saw the first raindrops strike the panes. Then somewhere in the distance, a flash of lightning hit the darkness and again, a few moments later, came another boom of thunder. George could make out the silhouettes of trees swaying in the rising gusts.

Kathy came into the room. "My mother says it's raining cats and dogs there," she announced. "She wants us to use our van rather than have Jimmy come for us."

The rain was coming down much harder now, beating heavily against the windows and outside walls. "From the sound of that," George said, "none of us is going anywhere at the moment."

When she had left her bedroom, Kathy opened the windows about an inch to air out the room. Even if there wasn't much room for water to get in, with the coming storm she wanted to play it safe. "Danny," she called. "Run up to my room and close the windows tight. Okay?"

George himself ran out to bring Harry inside. In spite of the sheets of icy rain that lashed at him, George could feel the cold spell was breaking up. The rains would wash away the dirty piles of accumulated snow. There was a problem living right on the river though, for such a heavy rainfall could add to the frozen waters and overflow the bulkheads.

George came back inside, with Harry gratefully shaking himself, just in time to hear Danny, still upstairs, cry out in pain. Kathy raced ahead of George up the stairs to their bedroom. Danny stood at a window, the fingers of his right hand trapped under the window. With his left he was trying to push up the heavy wooden frame.

George pushed Kathy aside and ran to the boy who was yelling and trying to pull his fingers free. George tried to slide the window back up, but it refused to budge. He hammered at the frame but instead of releasing itself, the window vibrated, only hurting Danny more. In his frustration, George became furious and started to curse, shouting obscenities at his unseen unknown enemies.

Suddenly the window came free on its own and shot up a few inches, freeing Danny. He grabbed his fingers in his other hand, cradling them and crying hysterically for his mother.

Kathy took the injured hand in her own. Danny didn't want to open his fist, and she had to shout at him. "Let me *see*! Open your fist!"

Averting his eyes, the boy extended his arm. Kathy screamed when she saw what his fingers looked like—all except the thumb were strangely flat. Even more frightened by his mother's anguished cry, Danny jerked his hand away.

George exploded. Running like a madman again from room to room, he screamed invectives, challenging whatever was doing this to his family to come out and fight. There was as much of a storm raging inside 112 Ocean Avenue as outside, as Kathy chased after her husband, asking him to call a doctor for Danny.

The rage within George soon spent itself. He suddenly became aware that his little boy was hurt and needed medical attention. He ran to the kitchen telephone and tried to call Kathy's doctor, John Aiello. But the line was dead. As he later learned, the storm had torn down a telephone pole, locking the Lutzes in their house even more effectively.

"I'll drive Danny to the hospital," George shouted. "Put his jacket on!"

The Brunswick Hospital Center is on Broadway in Amityville, no more than a mile from the Lutzes' house. Because of the hurricane-force winds raging through Long Island's South Shore, it took George almost fifteen minutes to get there.

The intern on duty was amazed at the condition of Danny's fingers, which were flattened from the cuticle to the second knuckle. But though they certainly looked crushed beyond repair, they were not broken, with no smashed bones or cartilage. He bandaged them securely, gave George some children's aspirin for Danny, and suggested they return home. There was nothing more he could do.

By then, the young boy was more frightened from the way his fingers looked than from any pain. While George drove home, he held his hand stiffly against his chest, sobbing and moaning. Again it took George close to twenty minutes to drive back to 112 Ocean Avenue. The winds whipped the front door of the house back against the building, and he had trouble trying to close it behind him.

Kathy had put Chris and Missy in her own bed and was waiting in the living room. She picked up her eldest and rocked him in her arms. Danny finally cried himself to sleep, exhausted by the grueling pain and fear.

George carried Danny up to their bedroom. Taking off only the boy's shoes, he slid him under the covers next to the other two children. Then he and Kathy sat down in chairs by the windows and watched the rain smash against the panes.

They dozed fitfully all the rest of the night. They had to stay home—it was impossible to try and get to Kathy's mother's or to any other place to sleep—but they were alert to any other dangers that might threaten their children or themselves. Toward dawn both fell asleep.

At six-thirty George was awakened by the rain spattering against his face. For an instant he thought he was outdoors—but no, he was still inside in his chair by the window. Jumping up, he saw that every window in the room was wide open, some frames torn away from their jambs. Then he heard the wind and rain coming through in other parts of the house. He rushed out of the bedroom. Every room he went into was in the same condition—window panes broken, the doors on the second and third floors smashed open—although every one had been locked and bolted! All the Lutzes had slept through what must have been a terrible racket.

22

January 11

The Lutzes had lived at 112 Ocean Avenue for twenty-five days. That Sunday was one of the worst.

In the morning, they discovered that the battering rain and wind of the night before had left the house a complete mess. Rainwater had stained walls, curtains, furniture, and rugs, from the first to the third floor. Ten of the windows had broken panes and several had their locks bent completely out of shape, making it impossible to shut them tightly.

The locks to the doors of the sewing room and playroom were twisted and forced out of their metal frames; these couldn't be closed at all. If the family had any intention of leaving for safer quarters, that idea had to be shelved in order to get the house back in shape and secured.

In the kitchen, some of the cabinets were soaked and warped. Paint was chipped on the corners of almost every cabinet. Kathy hadn't really thought about those problems yet; she had her hands full mopping up almost an inch of muddy water that had accumulated on her tile flooring. She hoped she could dry the floor before the tiles peeled loose from their cement backing.

Danny and Chris had two large rolls of paper towels and were going from room to room wiping down the walls. When they had to reach beyond their arms' length, they used a little kitchen stepladder. Missy trailed along with the boys, picking up the wet towels they discarded and throwing them into a large plastic garbage bag.

George took down every set of curtains and drapes in the house. Some could be machine-washed, and those he carried downstairs to the basement laundry. The others that would have to be dry-cleaned were put in a pile in the dining room, the driest room in the house.

The Lutzes were strangely silent while they worked that day. This newest disaster had only made them more determined to survive in 112 Ocean Avenue. Nobody said it, but George, Kathy, Danny, Chris, and Missy Lutz were now ready to battle any force, natural or unnatural.

Even Harry was putting on a show of toughness. The half-breed malamute was on his lead in his compound, stalking back and forth through the mud, his tail high, teeth bared. The growls and snarls that came from deep within his heavy chest were signs that the dog would tear to shreds the first person or thing he didn't recognize. Every once in a while, Harry would stop his pacing, stare at the boathouse, and let out a wolf-like howl that sent shivers down the spine of everyone who lived on Ocean Avenue.

When George finished with the sodden curtains, he began to work on the windows. First he cut heavy plastic sheets to cover the broken panes and sealed them to the window frames with white adhesive tape. It wasn't a pretty sight from the inside or out, but at least it kept out the steadily falling drizzle.

George had guessed right. The temperature had risen with the storm. and it was now above freezing. A lot of damage had been done to the trees and bushes along Ocean Avenue, and looking up South Ireland Place, George could see that it too had its share of broken branches lying in the street. He did note, however, that the neighbors on either side of his house had no broken windows or any other exterior damages. Only me,

George thought. Terrific!

The locks on the windows and doors were a more difficult matter. George didn't have the hardware to replace the catches on the windows, so he used pliers to twist off the smashed pieces of metal. Then he hammered heavy nails into the edges of the wooden frames and challenged his unseen foes: "Let me see you pull those out, you sons of bitches!"

The locks to the sewing room and playroom doors he removed completely. In the cellar he found some one-inch pine boards that were perfect for his needs. The doors opened outward into the hallway, so George nailed the boards diagonally across both. For whatever might have remained in the two mysterious rooms, there was no longer a way out.

George Kekoris finally telephoned, saying he'd like to come out and spend a night. There was only one problem—since Kekoris had no equipment with him, the Psychical Research Institute would have to consider the visit an informal one. He would have to draw conclusions without the rigorous controls required for scientific evaluation.

George said that didn't matter; he just wanted confirmation that all the weird events in their house weren't the product of his or Kathy's imagination. Kekoris asked George whether any sensitives had been there, but George didn't understand what he meant by that term. The field investigator said they would go into that when he came to visit.

Before George hung up, Kekoris asked whether there was a dog in the house. George said he had Harry, a trained watch dog. Kekoris said that was good because animals were very sensitive to psychic phenomena. Again George was puzzled—but at least he had the first tangible evidence that help was on the way.

Kathy's mother called her around six o'clock, wanting to know if they were coming to her house to spend the night. Kathy took it on herself to say no: the house was still in a mess after the storm and she would have a lot of washing to do the next morning. And besides, Danny and Chris would have school, and they were missing too many days as it was.

Mrs. Conners reluctantly agreed, but made Kathy promise that she would call if anything out of the ordinary occurred; her mother would then send Jimmy over immediately. After Kathy hung up, she wondered aloud to George if she had done the right thing.

"We're gonna stick it out," he said. "Before you send the kids to bed, I'm going to go through the whole house with Harry. Kekoris said dogs are very sensitive to things like this."

"Are you sure you won't make them mad again?" Kathy asked. "You know what happened when we went around with the crucifix."

"No, no, Kathy, this is different. I just want to see if Harry can smell or hear anything."

"And what if he does? What are you going to do then?"

The dog, still in his aggressive mood, had to be kept on his leash. Harry was very powerful and George had to take a snug grip just to keep from being pulled along. "Come on, boy," he said, "sniff me out something." They went down to the basement.

George removed the leash from Harry's collar and the dog leaped forward. He circled the cellar, sniffing, sometimes scratching at spots along the bottom of the walls. When the dog came up against the storage closet that hid the red room, Harry again sniffed at the base of the paneling. Then his tail dipped between his legs, and he sank to his haunches. Harry began to whimper, turning his head to George.

"What is it, Harry?" George asked. "You smell something there?" Harry's whimpers grew more frantic and he began to crawl backwards. Then he barked at George, stood up, and ran up the cellar steps. He waited at the top, quivering, until George came up and opened the door for him.

"What happened?" Kathy asked.

"Harry's afraid to go near the secret hideaway," George told her. He didn't put on the leash again, but walked Harry through the kitchen, dining room, living room, and enclosed porch. The dog's spirits picked up and he friskily sniffed around each room. But when George tried to take him upstairs, Harry hung back on the first step of the staircase.

"Come on," George urged him. "What's the matter with you?" The dog put one paw on the next step, but wouldn't move beyond that.

"I can get him upstairs!" Danny shouted. "He'll follow me!" The boy climbed past the dog and beckoned to him.

"No, Danny," George said. "You stay here. I'll handle Harry." George reached down and jerked the dog's collar. Harry moved reluctantly, then ran up the steps.

The dog walked around freely in both the master bedroom and the dressing room. Only when he approached Missy's room did Harry hang back. George put both hands on the dog's haunches and pushed him, but he wouldn't enter her room. Harry behaved the same way in front of the boarded-up sewing room. Whimpering and whining with fear, Harry tried to wedge himself behind George.

"Goddammit, Harry," he said, "there isn't anyone in there. What's bugging you?"

As soon as Harry went into the boys' room on the third floor, he jumped up on Chris's bed. George chased him off. Shooed out of the room, the dog headed directly for the stairs, passing the playroom without so much as a glance. George couldn't catch up with him.

George arrived downstairs behind the dog. "What happened?" Kathy asked.

"*Nothing* happened, that's what happened," he said.

As the day came to a close, the whole family was again in the master bedroom. The three children were in bed, and George and Kathy were sitting up in chairs next to the damaged windows. The room seemed overly warm and everyone's eyes had begun to sting. George and Kathy thought it was from fatigue. One after another, they drifted off—first Missy, then Chris, Danny, Kathy, and finally George. Within ten minutes, everyone was fast asleep.

But very shortly, George was rudely shoved awake by his wife. She and the children were standing in front of his chair, tears in their eyes. "What's the matter?" he mumbled sleepily.

"You were screaming, " Kathy said, "and we couldn't wake you up!"

"Yeah, Daddy!" cried Missy. "You made Mama cry!"

Not fully awake, feeling almost drugged, George was completely befuddled. "Did I hurt you, Kathy?"

"Oh, no, honey!" she protested. "You didn't touch me."

"What happened, then?"

"You kept yelling, 'I'm coming apart!' And we couldn't wake you up!"

23
January 12

George couldn't understand. Why did Kathy say he was yelling, "I'm coming apart"? He knew perfectly well what he had said was "I'm coming *unglued*."

Now he remembered he had been sitting in the chair when suddenly he felt a powerful grip lift up the chair with him in it and slowly turn him around. Powerless to move, George saw the hooded figure he had first seen in the living-room fireplace, its blasted half-face glaring at him. The horribly disfigured features became clearer to George. "God help me!" he screamed. Then he saw his own face emerge from beneath the white hood. It was torn in two. "I'm coming unglued!" George yelled.

Now still groggy, he began to argue with Kathy. "I know what I said," he muttered. "Don't tell me what I said!"

The others backed off. He's still asleep, Kathy thought, and he's having a bad dream. "You're right, George," she said gently. "You didn't say that at all." She pulled his head to her breast.

"Daddy," Missy broke in, "come in my room. Jodie says he wants to talk to you!"

The urgency in Missy's voice broke the spell. George snapped out of it and jumped up, almost bowling Kathy over. "Jodie? Who's Jodie?"

"That's her friend," answered Kathy. "You know—I told you she makes up imaginary people. You can't see Jodie."

"Oh, yes, Mama," Missy prostested. "I see him all the time. He's the biggest pig you ever saw." Then she trotted out of the room and was gone.

George and Kathy looked at each other. "A pig?" he said. It struck them both at the same time. "The pig's in her room!" George ran after Missy. "You stay here!" he yelled at Kathy and the boys.

Missy was just climbing on the bed when George stopped outside her bedroom door. He didn't see Jodie or anything like a pig. "Where's this Jodie?" he asked Missy.

"He'll be right back, " the little girl said, settling the covers around herself. "He had to go outside for a minute."

George let out his breath. After the weird dream of the hooded figure, he had expected the worst when he heard the word "pig." His neck felt stiff and he rotated it, trying to work out the tight feeling. "It's all right!" he yelled back at Kathy. "Jodie's not here!"

"There he is, Daddy!"

George looked down at Missy. She was pointing to one of her windows. His eyes followed her finger and he started. Staring at him through one of the panes were two red eyes! No face, just the mean, little eyes of a pig!

"That's Jodie!" cried Missy. "He wants to come in!"

Something rushed past George on his left. It was Kathy, screaming in an unearthly voice. In the same move that it took her to reach the window, she picked up one of Missy's play chairs and swung it at the eyes. Her blow shattered the window and shards of glass flew on top of her.

There was an animal cry of pain, a loud squealing—and the eyes were gone!

George rushed to what was left of the second-story window and looked out. He saw nothing below, but he still heard the squealing. It sounded as if it was headed for the boathouse. Then Kathy's crying whimper caught George's attention. He turned to his wife.

Kathy's face was terrifying. Her eyes were wild and her mouth was tightly screwed up. She was trying to choke out words. Finally she blurted: "It's been here all the time! I wanted to kill it! I wanted to kill it!" Then her whole body slumped.

George caught his wife and silently picked her up. He carried Kathy into their bedroom, Danny and Chris following. Only Chris saw his little sister get out of bed, go to the smashed window, and wave. Missy turned away only when George called her to come into his bedroom.

Kathy was determined that Danny and Chris should go to school on Monday morning. Ready to fly apart herself, she stiffened her backbone and did her duty as a mother. While George slept on, she awakened the boys, fed them breakfast, and took all three children with her in the van.

George was up when she returned with Missy. As she had coffee with him, Kathy realized he was still in a zombielike state after the previous night's affair. For the moment, Kathy was determined to be strong for both of them. She talked to her husband in everyday terms, slipping in the reminder that he had to fix the smashed window in Missy's bedroom. Later there would be time to deal with the decision of moving from 112 Ocean Avenue.

Upstairs, George had just nailed plywood over the shattered window frame to protect the room from damage by the weather when Kathy called up from the kitchen that his office in Syosset wanted him on the telephone. The company's accountant reminded George that the Internal Revenue agent was due to come by at noon.

Not wanting to leave the house, George asked the accountant to handle the tax situation himself, but the man refused. It was George's responsibility to determine how to pay the taxes. George hesitated, certain that something would happen if he left. But Kathy signaled that he should go.

After he hung up, Kathy said that the appointment shouldn't take too long. She and Missy would be all right while he was gone. She would call a glazier in Amityville to drive over and fix the broken panes in Missy's window and throughout the house. Meekly, George nodded at his wife's advice, then left for Syosset. Neither had mentioned Jodie's name.

While Kathy was giving Missy her lunch, George Kekoris called. He was sorry he hadn't been able to get there as he'd promised George, but he said he felt he'd picked up the flu in Buffalo. Kekoris's bout of illness had forced him to cancel all his appointments for the Psychical Research Institute. He was sure that he'd be fine by the following day, however, and planned to stay at the Lutzes' Wednesday night.

Kathy half-listened to his explanation. She was watching Missy eat. The little girl seemed to be having a secret conversation with someone under the kitchen table. Every once in a while Missy would extend her hand beneath the plastic tablecloth to offer her sandwich. She didn't seem to be aware that her mother was watching her movements.

From her position, Kathy could see there was nothing under the table, but she did want to ask her daughter about Jodie. Finally Kekoris was finished and she hung up.

"Missy," Kathy said, sitting down at the table. "Is Jodie the angel you told me about?"

The little girl looked at her mother, confusion on her face.

"You remember," Kathy continued. "You asked me if angels speak?"

Missy's eyes lit up. "Yes, Mama," she nodded. "Jodie's an angel. He talks to me all the time."

"I don't understand. You've seen pictures of angels. You saw the ones we had on the Christmas tree?"

Missy nodded again.

"You said he's a pig. So how can you say he's an angel?"

Missy's eyebrows grew together as she concentrated. "He says he is, Mama," she nodded her head several times. "He told me."

Kathy hitched her chair closer to Missy. "What does he say when he talks to you?"

Again the little girl seemed confused.

"You know what I mean, Missy," Kathy pressed her daughter. "Do you play games?"

"Oh, no," Missy shook her head. "He tells me about the little boy who used to live in my room." She looked around to see if anybody was listening. "He died, Mama. The little boy got sick and he died."

"I see," Kathy said. "What else did he tell you?"

The little girl thought for a moment. "Last night he said I was going to live here forever so I could play with the little boy."

Horrified, Kathy put her fingers to her mouth because she wanted to scream.

George's session with the IRS man had not gone well. The agent had disallowed deduction after deduction, and George's only hope lay in the appeal the agent said he could file. It was a temporary reprieve, at least. After the man left, George called Kathy to say that he'd pick up the boys at school on his way home.

When he arrived after three, Kathy and Missy had their coats on. "Don't undress, George," she said. "We're leaving for my mother's right now."

George and the two boys looked at her. "What happened?" he asked.

"Jodie told Missy he's an angel, that's what happened." She began to push the boys out the front door. "We're getting out of here."

George held up his hands. "*Wait* a minute, will you? What do you mean he's an angel?"

Kathy looked down at her daughter. "Tell your father what the pig said."

Missy nodded. "He said he's an angel, Daddy. He told me."

George was about to ask his daughter another question when he was interrupted by loud barking from behind the house. "Harry!" he cried. "We forgot about Harry!"

When George and the others reached him, Harry was barking furiously at the boathouse, frantically running around his compound and jerking up short every time he reached the end of his steel leash.

"What's the matter, boy?" George said, patting the dog's neck. "Someone in the boathouse?" Harry twisted out of his grasp.

"Don't go in there!" Kathy yelled. "Please! Let's get out of here now!"

George hesitated, then bent down and snapped the leash off Harry's collar. The dog leaped forward with a savage snarl and ran out of his gate. The door to the boathouse was closed and the best Harry could do was leap against it. Again he started his wild barking.

George was all set to unlock the door and fling it open. Instead, Danny and Chris ran past him and leaped on Harry, wrestling the big dog away. "Don't let him go in there!" Danny screamed. "He'll get killed!"

George grabbed Harry's collar and pulled him to a sitting position.

"It's all right!" Chris kept assuring the powerful, agitated animal. "It's all right, boy!" But Harry would not be calmed.

"Let's get him inside the house," George panted. "If he can't see the boathouse, he'll stop!"

As he and the boys were drawing Harry into the house, a van pulled into the driveway. George saw that it was a window repairman. He and Kathy looked at each other. "Oh, my God," Kathy said, "I forgot all about having called him." They hadn't reckoned on this kind of delay.

His pudgy face and broad accent gave away his Slavic descent. "I figured you folks needed the fixing right away," he said, "what with the bad weather we been having. Yah," he continued as he opened his rear doors, "better to fix now. If everything inside get wet because of outside, it cost you more money."

"Okay, that's fine," George said. "Come on in and I'll show you the windows that got busted." "The wind the other night, yah?" the man asked.

"Yeah, the wind," George answered.

It was almost six P.M. before the man was done. When the new window panes were scraped free of putty, he stepped back to admire his work. "I'm sorry," he said to George, "I could not fix window in little girl's room. You need carpenter first." He gathered up his tools. "You get him, then I come back, yah?"

"Yeah," George nodded. "We'll get him and you can come back." He reached into his pants pocket. "How much do I owe you?"

"No, no," the man protested. "No money now. You neighbor. We send bill, okay?"

"Okay!" George said, relieved. His cash *was* very low at the moment.

Somehow the glazier's kindness and friendliness left its mark on their spirits that night. After he left, Kathy—who had been sitting in the kitchen with her coat on all the time he worked—suddenly got up and took it off. Without saying a word to George, she began to prepare supper.

Kathy took out hamburger meat for herself and the children. As she worked preparing the meal, she kept Danny and Chris with her in the kitchen, insisting they do their homework in the nook. Missy sat in the living room with George, watching television while he built up a fire.

The glazier had been just the reassurance they needed. After all, nothing had happened to *him* while he was in the playroom or the sewing room. The Lutzes realized that maybe their imaginations were too fired up and they were panicking unnecessarily. All thought of abandoning their home had momentarily disappeared.

Just to be on the safe side, George and Kathy decided the children should sleep in the master bedroom again. With Harry inside, down in the cellar, Danny, Chris, and Missy were put to bed. George and Kathy made themselves as comfortable as they could: Kathy stretched out on two chairs; George insisted he was all right with one. He told Kathy he planned to stay awake all night and sleep in the morning.

At 3:15 A.M., George heard the marching band strike up downstairs. This time he did not go to investigate. He told himself it was all in his head, and when he went down, there would be nothing to see. So he sat there, watching Kathy and the children, listening as the musicians paraded up and down his living room, horns and drums blasting away loud enough to be heard half a mile away. All during the maddening performance, Kathy and the children did not awaken.

Finally, George must have dozed off in his chair, because Kathy awoke to hear him screaming. He was yelling in two different tongues—languages she had never heard before!

She ran to her husband's chair on the other side of the bed to shake him out of his dream.

George began groaning, and when Kathy touched him, he cried out in another completely different voice: "It's in Chris's room! It's in Chris's room! It's in Chris's room!"

24
January 13

George is positive he wasn't dreaming. From his position he was sure he could see clear up to the boys' bedroom on the third floor. He had been watching a shadowy figure approach Chris's bed.

He tried to rush to his sleeping son's side and grab him away from the menacing shape. But George couldn't get up from his chair! He was pinned to the seat by a firm hand on his shoulders. It was a struggle George knew he couldn't win.

The shadow hovered over Chris. George, helpless, shouted: "It's in Chris's room!" No one heard him.

"It's in Chris's room!" He repeated. Then the pressure on his shoulders lifted and George felt himself being pushed. His arms came free and he could see Chris was out of bed, wrapped inside the dark shape.

George swung his hands wildly about, again screaming: "It's in Chris's room!" He felt another violent push. "George!"

His eyes snapped open. Kathy was leaning over him, pushing at his chest. "George!" she cried. "Wake up!"

He leaped free of the chair. "It's got Chris!" he yelled. "I've got to get up there!"

Kathy grabbed his arm. "No!" She was pulling him back. "You're dreaming! Chris is *here*!"

She pointed to their bed. The three children were under the covers. Awakened by George's shouting, they were now watching their parents.

George was still agitated. "I wasn't dreaming, I tell you!" he insisted. "I could see it pick him up and . . . "

"You couldn't have," Kathy interrupted. "He's been here in bed all the time."

"No, Mama. I had to go to the bathroom before." Chris sat up. "You and Daddy were asleep."

"I never heard you. Did you use my bathroom?" Kathy asked.

"Unh-unh. The door was locked, so I went upstairs."

George went to the bathroom. The door *was* locked.

"Upstairs?" asked Kathy.

"Yeah," Chris answered. "But I got scared."

"Why?" his father asked.

"Because I could look through the floor and see you, Daddy."

The Lutzes remained awake for the rest of the night. Only Missy fell back to sleep.

Danny and Chris did not go to school in Amityville that morning. Kathy kept them home again because she wanted to pack as soon as possible. George said they'd leave as soon as he called the police to tell them the family would be away for a while. He also wanted them to have Mrs. Conners' telephone number in case of any emergency. But when he picked up the telephone to dial the police department, the line was dead.

When her husband told Kathy the phone was out of order, she became extremely nervous. Hurriedly she dressed the children and then, without taking a change of clothes, herded them out to the van.

George brought Harry from the cellar and put him in the rear of the van. Then he went around the house and checked to make sure all the doors were locked. Finishing with the boathouse, George climbed behind the wheel of the van. He turned the ignition key but the motor wouldn't turn over.

"George?" Kathy's voice quivered. "What's wrong?"

"Take it easy," he said. "We got enough gas. Let me take a look under the hood."

As he got out of the van, he looked up at the sky. The clouds had grown dark and menacing. George felt a cold wind picking up. By the time he lifted the hood, the first raindrops were hitting the windshield.

George never got a good look at what could have caused the van to stall. A huge gust of wind blew in from the Amityville River in the back of the house, and the hood was slammed down. George had just leaped aside to avoid the falling metal when a lightning bolt struck behind the garage. The clap of thunder was almost instantaneous, and the clouds broke in a solid sheet of water that drenched George immediately.

He ran for the front door and unlocked it. "Get in!" he shouted to his family in the van. Kathy and the children bolted for the open door, but by the time he managed to close it behind them, all were soaking wet. We're trapped, he thought to himself, not daring to voice the thought to Kathy. It's not going to let us go.

The rains and wind picked up in intensity, and by one o'clock in the afternoon, Amityville was hit by another storm of hurricane strength. At three, the electricity went out, but fortunately the heat remained in the house. George switched on the portable radio in the kitchen. The weather report said it was 20 degrees and that sleet was pelting all of Long Island. Since the radar showed an enormous low-pressure system covering the entire metropolitan area, the weatherman could not predict when the storm would subside.

George dealt with Missy's broken window as best he could, shoving towels into the spaces where it hung away from the frame, then nailing an old blanket over the entire window. Before he had finished, his fresh dry clothes were soaked again.

In the kitchen, George looked at the thermometer that hung beside the back door. It read 80 degrees and the house was getting uncomfortably warm. He knew that with the electricity off, the oil burner's thermostat wouldn't operate. But when George looked again at the thermometer, it was up to 85 degrees.

To cool off the house, George had to have some fresh air. He inched open the windows on the enclosed porch—the only room that faced away from the storm's main onslaught.

From the time the storm broke, it had remained dark outside, and even though it was daytime, Kathy had lit candles. At four-thirty it was as if night had already settled over 112 Ocean Avenue.

Every once in a while she would pick up the telephone to see if it was working again, but she really had little hope that it would be—the storm would prevent any repair crews from going out on call. The children weren't fazed at all by the darkness. They treated the whole affair as a holiday, noisily running up and down the staircase, playing hide-and-seek. Since the boys were much better at hiding themselves, Missy was usually "it." Harry happily joined in the romping, finally irritating George to the point where he cuffed the dog with a newspaper. Harry ran off and hid behind Kathy.

By six in the evening, the storm still hadn't slackened. It was as though all the water in the world was being dumped on top of 112 Ocean Avenue. And inside the house, the temperature was up to 90 degrees. George went to the basement to look at the oil burner. It *was* off, but it didn't matter; the heat continued to rise in all the rooms except Missy's.

Desperate, he decided to make a final appeal to God. Holding a candle,

George began going from room to room, asking the Lord to send away whoever didn't belong there. He felt mildly reassured when there was no sinister reaction to his prayers.

After the playroom door had been damaged during the first storm, George had removed the lock. Now as he approached the room to recite his appeal to God, he saw the green slime was back, leaking from the open hole in the door and oozing onto the floor of the hallway. George watched as the pool of jellylike substance slowly wound its way toward the staircase.

He pulled off the pine boards nailed across the door and threw it open, half-expecting to find the room filled with the slimy material. But its only source seemed to be the empty lock hole in the door!

George gathered some towels from the third floor bathroom and stuffed them into the opening. The towels soon became saturated, but the jelly stopped flowing. He wiped up the slime that had accumulated in the hall-way and had managed to flow down the steps. George had no intention of telling his wife about this latest discovery.

All the time her husband was going through the house, Kathy sat by the telephone. She had tried opening the kitchen door a little to let in some air, but even when it was only slightly ajar, rainwater showered into the room. She began to doze from the oppressive heat.

When George finally returned to the kitchen, she was almost fast asleep, resting her head on her arms on the breakfast table in the nook. Kathy was perspiring, the back of her neck damp to his touch. When he tried to awaken her, she lifted her head slightly, mumbled something he couldn't understand, then let her forehead fall back on her arms.

George had no need to check whether the rain and windstorm had let up. Torrents of water were still smashing against the house, and he some-how knew they wouldn't be allowed to leave 112 Ocean Avenue that night. He picked Kathy up in his arms and took her to their bedroom, noting the time on the kitchen clock. It was exactly 8 P.M.

Finally the 90 degree heat got to Danny, Chris, and Missy. Their run-ning about the house most of the day had worn them out, so shortly after George had taken Kathy upstairs, they were ready for bed. George was surprised to find it was somewhat cooler in the boys' room on the third floor. He knew that hot air rises, and on the top floor it should have been well above ninety.

Missy sleepily climbed into bed beside Kathy, but refused to be covered with a sheet or blanket. Before George went back downstairs, she and the boys were asleep.

George and Harry were now all alone in the living room. For a change, the dog didn't seem to be about to fall asleep early but watched his owner's every move. He, too, was suffering from the excessive heat. Whenever George rose from his chair to go into another room, Harry would not follow, but remained stretched out in the cool draft beneath the living room windows.

George thought of running outside to the van to see if it would start. It was still standing in the driveway and George knew its engine would probably be wet by now. But the real deterrent was his suspicion that once he left, he might not be able to get back into the house. Something warned him that he'd never get the doors open again.

Suddenly, at ten o'clock, the 90 degree heat began to break. Harry noticed it first. The dog stood, sniffed the air, then walked over to the unlit fireplace where George was sitting, and whimpered. His pathetic sounds broke his master's concentration on the van. George looked up and shivered. There was a definite drop in the house's temperature.

A half hour later, the thermometer read 60 degrees. George started for the basement to get some logs. Harry trotted along behind him to the cellar door, but would not descend the steps with George. He remained in the open doorway, constantly turning his head as if to see if someone was coming up behind him.

George used his flashlight to search out every corner of the basement, but there were no signs of anything unusual. With several logs in his arms, George climbed back upstairs and tried the telephone in the kitchen. It was still dead. He was all set to relight the kindling wood in the fireplace when he thought he heard Missy cry out.

When he reached his bedroom, the little girl was shivering; he had forgotten to cover her when the house got chilly. Kathy on her stomach, was sleeping like a drugged person, not moving or turning in bed. George also tucked blankets about his wife's cool body.

When he finally went back down to the living room, George decided not to make a fire. He wanted to be free to stay near Kathy and the children. Tonight, he thought, I'd better be ready for anything. George put on Harry's long metal leash and took the dog up to the master bedroom. He left the door open, but knotted the leash so that Harry blocked the doorway completely. Then George kicked off his shoes, and without undressing, slid into bed beside Missy and Kathy. Rather than lie down, he sat up with his back resting against the headboard.

At one o'clock, George felt he was freezing. Because of the raging storm outside, he knew there was no hope of heat in the house that night from the oil burner. He began to weep about the sorry plight he and his family were in. He now realized he should have fled when Father Mancuso originally warned him. "Oh, God, help us," he moaned.

Suddenly, Kathy lifted up her head. While he watched, she got off the bed and turned to look in the mirror on the wall. George saw in the candlelight that her eyes were open, but he knew she was still asleep.

Kathy stared at her reflection for a moment, then turned away from the mirrored wall and started for the bedroom door. But she stopped when she came to an obstacle: Harry was fast asleep, stretched across the threshold, blocking her path.

George leaped from the bed and seized his wife. Kathy looked at him with unseeing eyes. To George, she seemed to be in a trance.

"Kathy!" he cried. "Wake up!" When George shook her, there was no response or reaction. Then her eyes closed. Kathy went limp in his arms and gently he half–pulled, half–lifted her back to the bed. First he sat Kathy down, then straightened her legs so that she was lying flat. Her trance–like state seemed to affect her whole body. She was like a rag doll.

George noted that Missy, in the middle of the bed, had slept through the whole episode. But then his attention was diverted by a movement in the doorway. He saw Harry struggle to his feet, shake violently, and then begin to retch. The dog threw up all over the floor but kept gagging and trying to force out something that seemed stuck in his throat. Restricted by his leash, the poor dog was only twisting the chain more tightly about his writhing body.

The odor of vomit caused George to gag too. He fled into the bathroom, gulped a mouthful of water, took a deep breath, and came out with towels from the rack. After he mopped up the floor, George untied Harry and set the dog free. Harry looked up at George, wagged his tail several times, then stretched himself out on the floor of the hallway, closing his eyes. "There's not much wrong with you now," George whispered under his breath.

He listened, but everything was quiet throughout the house—*much* too quiet. In a few moments, George realized the storm had stopped. There was no rain, no wind. The stillness was so complete it was as though someone had turned off running water in a sink. There was a vacuum of silence at 112 Ocean Avenue.

With the storm gone, the temperature outside began to drop and in a very short time, the house became ice cold. George could feel the bedroom become even chillier than it had been. He still had all his clothes on when he slipped back beneath the covers.

There was a noise above George's head. He looked up and listened. Something was scraping along the floor of the boys' bedroom. The noise became louder, and George could tell the movement was faster now. The boys' beds were sliding back and forth!

George managed to throw off his covers, but he could not lift his body out of bed. There was no pressure as there had been before when he sat in the bedroom chair. George just didn't have the strength to move!

Now he heard the dresser drawers across his room begin to open and close. A candle was still on his night stand and he could make out the drawers rapidly sliding back and forth. One drawer would fly open, then another, then the first would bang shut. Tears of frustration and fear flooded George's eyes.

Almost immediately after that, the voices began. He could hear them downstairs, but couldn't make out what was being said. He only knew that it sounded as if people were thronging on the first floor. His head began to roll as he tried to reach over and touch Missy or Kathy.

Then the marching band struck up downstairs, its music drowning out the unintelligible voices. George thought he must be in a madhouse. He could distinctly hear musicians parade around the entire first floor—and then their first steps as they began to mount the staircase!

George was screaming now, but he heard no sounds coming from his throat. His body whipped back and forth on the bed and he could feel the terrible strain on his neck muscles as he vainly tried to lift his head from the mattress. Finally George gave up. He realized the mattress was soaking wet.

The beds were banging around above George's head, and the dresser drawers in his room were flying back and forth as the band headed up the steps. But that was not all. Despite all the noise, George now heard doors throughout the house beginning to slam back and forth!

He saw the door to the bedroom swing wildly as though someone were yanking it open and then immediately slamming it shut. George could also see Harry lying outside in the hallway, completely undisturbed by the racket. Either that dog is drugged, George thought, or I'm the one who's going mad!

A terrible, blinding flash of lightning lit up the bedroom. George heard the thunderbolt strike something close outside. Then there was a smashing blow that shook the entire house. The storm was back, with torrents of rain and wind lashing 112 Ocean Avenue from top to bottom.

George lay there panting, his heart thumping loudly in his chest. He was waiting, knowing something else was about to happen. Then George let out a horrible, silent scream. Somebody was on the bed with him!

He felt himself being stepped on! Strong, heavy feet struck his legs and body. George shut his eyes. He could feel the pain from the blows. Oh God! he thought. They're hooves. It's an animal!

George must have passed out from fright, because the next thing he remembers was the sight of Danny and Chris standing beside his bed. "Daddy, Daddy, wake up!" they were crying, "there's something in our room!"

He blinked his eyes. In a glance he saw it was light outside. The storm had stopped. The dresser drawers were all open, and his two sons were pleading with him to get up.

Missy! Kathy! George turned to look at them. They were still next to him, both still sound asleep. He turned back to the boys, who were trying to pull him out of bed. "What's the matter?" he asked. "What's in your room?"

"It's a monster!" Danny cried. "He doesn't have any face!"

"It tried to grab us," Chris broke in, "but we ran away! Come on, Daddy, get up!"

George tried. He almost got his head off the mattress when he heard Harry bark furiously. George looked past the boys through the open doorway. The dog was standing in the hallway, snarling and growling at the staircase. Even though he was unleashed, Harry did not head for the stairs, but continued to crouch in the hallway, teeth bared, barking at something or someone George couldn't see from his position on the bed.

With a tremendous burst of determination, George finally heaved his whole body off the mattress. He arose so suddenly that he crashed into Danny and Chris. Then he ran for the door and looked up at the steps.

On the top step stood a gigantic figure in white. George knew it was the hooded image Kathy had first glimpsed in the fireplace. The being was pointing at him!

George whirled and raced back into the bedroom, grabbed up Missy, and shoved her into Danny's arms. "Take her outside!" he shouted. "You go with them, Chris!"

Then he bent over Kathy and lifted her off the bed. "Hurry!" George yelled after the boys. Then he too ran from the room, Harry following him down the steps.

On the first floor, George saw the front door was open, hanging from its hinges again, torn away by some powerful force.

Danny, Chris, and Missy were outside. The little girl, just awakening, was squirming in her brother's arms. Not knowing where she was, she started to cry with fright.

George ran for the van. He put Kathy on the front seat and then helped the children into the rear. Harry jumped in behind them, and he slammed the door on Kathy's side. George ran around to the other side of the vehicle, jumped in the driver's seat, and prayed.

He jammed in the ignition key. The motor turned over immediately.

Spraying wet gravel, George backed out of the driveway. When he hit the street, he skidded, spun the wheel, and stepped on the gas at the same time. The van teetered for a moment, then all four tires grabbed and smoke shot up from the rubber treads. In another instant, the van was tearing up Ocean Avenue.

As he steered the van toward safety, George looked into the side view mirror. His house was fast disappearing from his sight. "Thank God!" he muttered to himself. "I'll never see you again, you sonofabitch!"

It was seven o'clock on the morning of January 14, 1976; the twenty-eighth day the Lutzes had lived in 112 Ocean Avenue.

25

January 15

A sharp tug on his sleeve interrupted George's thoughts. It was Missy. "Here, Daddy," she said. "I made Jodie like you said."

"What?" George asked. His daughter was holding up a paper drawing. "Oh, yeah," he said. "Jodie's picture. Let me see it."

George took the paper from Missy. It was a child's rendering of a pig, distorted, but clearly a five-year-old's idea of a running animal.

He raised his eyebrows. "What are all these things around Jodie?" he asked. "They look like little clouds."

"That's snow, Daddy," Missy answered. "That's when Jodie ran away in the snow."

Jimmy and Carey went to stay at her mother's house that night. But before they left, there was a small celebration at Mrs. Conners' house. Because of the dramatic feeling of relief that swept over the Lutzes just to be free of 112 Ocean Avenue, it was practically a party.

George and Kathy now wanted to talk about their experiences, and in her family they had a sympathetic and credulous audience. Events spilled from their lips in a flood as they tried to explain what had happened to them. Finally, George revealed his plans to rid his house of whatever evil force remained there. He told his mother–in–law and Jimmy that research groups would be invited to participate but they would have to conduct their investigations by themselves. Under no circumstances would he or Kathy ever enter 112 Ocean Avenue again.

Danny, Chris, and Missy were to sleep in Jimmy's room. The boys were exhausted from the harrowing appearance of the "monster" the night before and from the excitement of fleeing to their grandmother's. But they didn't want to talk about the white–hooded demon figure. When George pressed them to tell their version, both boys fell silent and looks of fear came over their faces.

Missy appeared to be entirely unaffected by the whole affair. She adapted easily enough to the new adventure and made herself right at home with a few dolls she had cached at her grandmother's. She wasn't even perturbed when Kathy questioned her further about Jodie's picture. The little girl would say only, "That is what the pig looked like."

George and Kathy took their baths early. Both luxuriated in the hot water and soaked for a long time. It was a dual cleansing: their bodies and their fright. By ten P.M., they were in bed in the guest room. For the first time in almost a month, the Lutzes fell asleep in each other's arms.

George awoke first. He felt as if he was having a dream, because he had the sensation of floating in air!

He was aware of his body being flown around the bedroom and then landing softly back on the bed. Then, still in his dreamlike state, George saw Kathy levitate off the bed. She rose about a foot and slowly began to drift away from him.

George reached out a hand to his wife. In his eyes, the movement was almost in slow motion, as though his arm was not attached to his body. He tried to call to her, but for some reason, he couldn't remember her name. George could only watch Kathy fly higher toward the ceiling. Then he felt himself being lifted, and again he had the sensation of floating.

He could hear someone calling to him from a great distance. George knew the voice. It sounded very familiar. He heard his name again. "George?"

Now he remembered. It was Kathy. George looked down and saw she was back on the bed, looking up at him.

He began to drift toward Kathy, then felt himself slowly settling back down on the bed beside her. "George!" she cried. "You were floating in the air!"

Kathy grabbed his arm and pulled him off the bed. "Come on!" she shouted. "We've got to get out of this room!"

As though he was sleepwalking, George followed his wife. At the head of the staircase they both stopped and recoiled in horror. Coming *up* the steps toward them was a snakelike line of greenish–black slime!

George now knew he had not been dreaming. It was all real. Whatever he thought they had left forever back at 112 Ocean Avenue was following them—wherever the Lutzes fled.

EPILOGUE

On February 18, 1976, Marvin Scott of New York's Channel 5 decided to investigate further the reports on the so–called cursed home of Amityville, Long Island. The mission called for spending the night in the haunted home at 112 Ocean Avenue. Psychics, clairvoyants, a demonologist, and parapsychologists were invited to participate.

Scott had originally contacted the recent tenants, the Lutz family, and requested permission to film activities at their deserted house. George Lutz agreed and sat down at a meeting with Scott in a small pizzeria in Amityville. George refused to reenter 112 Ocean Avenue, but said he and his wife, Kathy, would wait for the investigators the next day at the Italian restaurant.

To provoke the overpowering force said to be within the house, a crucifix and blessed candles were placed on the dining–room table.

The researchers held the first of three seances at 10:30 P.M. Present around the table were Lorraine Warren, a clairvoyant; her husband, Ed, a demonologist; psychics Mary Pascarella and Mrs. Alberta Riley; and George Kekoris of the Psychical Research Institute in Durham, North Carolina. Marvin Scott also joined the group at the table.

During the seance, Mary Pascarella became ill and had to leave the room. In a quaking voice, she said "that in back of everything there seems to be some kind of black shadow that forms a head, and it moves. And as it moves, I feel personally threatened."

Mrs. Riley, in a mediumistic trance began gasping. "It's upstairs in the bedroom. What's here makes your heart speed up. My heart's pounding." Ed Warren wanted to end the seance. Mrs. Riley continued to gasp, then quickly came out of her trance and back to normal consciousness.

Then George Kekoris, the psychic researcher, also became violently ill and had to leave the table. Observer Mike Linder of WNEW–FM stated that he had felt a sudden numbness, a kind of cold sensation.

Clairvoyant Lorraine Warren finally voiced her own opinion: "Whatever is here is, in my estimation, most definitely of a negative nature. It has nothing to do with anyone who had once walked the earth in human form. It is right from the bowels of the earth."

Lorraine and Ed Warren also found a source of discomfort in the living room. Mrs. Warren thought some negative forces were centered in statues and nonliving things: "That whatever is here, is able to move around at will. It doesn't have to stay here, but I think it's a resting place." She also thought there was something demonic in the inanimate objects. Mrs. Warren indicated the fireplace and banister on the second floor, without being forewarned of their connection with the Lutzes' problems.

As some people slept in some of the second–floor bedrooms, a photographer shot infrared pictures in the vain hope of capturing some ghostly image on film. Jerry Solfvin of the Psychical Research Institute wandered about the house with a battery lantern, searching for physical evidence.

At 3:30 A.M., the Warrens attempted another seance. There was nothing unusual reported, no sounds or strange phenomena. All the psychics felt the room had been neutralized. The atmosphere, they said, simply wasn't right at the moment. But they definitely felt that the house on Ocean Avenue was harboring a demonic spirit, one that could be removed only by an exorcist.

When Marvin Scott returned to the little pizzeria, the Lutzes were gone. By March, they had moved clear across the country to California. They left behind all their belongings, all their worldly goods, and all the money they had invested in their dream home. Just to be rid of the place, they signed their interest over to the bank that held the mortgage. Pending its resale, its windows were boarded up to discourage vandalism and to prevent the curious, the morbid, and the warned from entering.

In April, 1976, Father Frank Mancuso was transferred by the bishop of his diocese to another parish. It is nowhere near 112 Ocean Avenue, in Amityville, Long Island. The priest still bears the fear of whatever happened in that house.

Now, Missy gets upset when she is asked about Jodie; Danny and Chris can still vividly describe the "monster" who chased them that final night; and Kathy will not talk about that period in her life at all. George has sold his interest in William H. Parry, Inc. He finds it difficult to leave his family alone for too long. But he does hope that those who hear his story will understand how dangerous negative entities can be to the unwary—to the unbelieving. "They *are* real," he insists, "and they do inflict evil when the opportunity presents itself."

SIMON MEYER GUGGENHEIM (1792–1869)
m. (1) SCHÄFELI LEVINGER
m. (2) RACHEL WEIL MEYER

MEYER GUGGENHEIM (1828–1905)
(From Schäfeli Levinger)
m. BARBARA MEYER (1834–1900)
(Daughter of Rachel Weil Meyer
by her first husband)

ISAAC
b. 1854

DANIEL
b. 1856

MURRY
b. 1858

SOLOMON R.
b. 1861

JEANNETTE
b. 1863

BENJAMIN
b. 1865

SIMON
and
ROBERT
(twins)
b. 1867

WILLIAM
b. 1868

ROSE
b. 1871

CORA
b. 1873

Simon Meyer Guggenheim

Meyer Guggenheim

Barbara Meyer Guggenheim

THE GUGGENHEIMS
AN AMERICAN EPIC

A condensation of the book by

John H. Davis

CHAPTER 1

OUT OF THE GHETTO

The valley of the River Surb winds gently through green pastures and orchards of pear, apple, cherry, peach. In the spring the apple trees blossom into little white clouds; buttercups and dandelions appear in the bright green meadows; geraniums and daisies sprout in the window boxes of red-roofed farmhouses. Summer brings rich gardens of celery, endive, and cabbage to the low, rolling hillsides, and clumps of brown-and-white and Swiss brown cows to the pastures. In the fall, the vineyards turn red and gold, and the bare trees reveal the sparkling Surb tumbling through the little valley.

Here and there along the road following the river stand wooden crosses bearing pallid, bleeding Christs: the canton of Aargau is predominantly Catholic. Now and then slim, onion-domed spires of churches peep from behind quiet hillsides. Forested uplands range the far distances, never rising high enough to become mountains, never distracting attention from the bright serenity of the valley below.

One of the two villages in the valley of the Surb is Lengnau, a community of some 1,700 souls. Crossing a narrow bridge leading from the main road, one arrives almost immediately in the *Dorfplatz* of the tiny village, dominated by the synagogue. The little white-washed housefronts surrounding the *Platz*, one of which belongs to the *Gasthaus*, display the *Fachwerk* typical of German-speaking Switzerland, a design of crisscrossing wooden beams resembling Tudor-style architecture. There are geraniums sprouting from these window boxes too. A fountain plays in the tree-lined *Platz*. There is rarely much going on. Every once in a while a farm boy drives a flock of sheep, or a few cows, up to the *haupstrasse* bordering the square. Or a motorbike comes to a blustery halt in front of the *Gasthaus*. Otherwise the village is still, save for the constant tumbling of the stream, the trickling of the fountain. . . .

An idyllic setting. But this gentle Swiss land, this benign village, was once not very gentle or benevolent to people like the Guggenheims.

Simon Guggenheim, tailor, lived and worked in house No. 64, near the bridge over the Surb, from 1830 until his emigration to America in 1847. His ancestors had lived and worked in and around the same area for at least 150 years.

Like most of the houses in Lengnau, Simon Guggenheim's was a multiple dwelling and had two entranceways, one into a hall serving the first-floor apartments, the other into the hall and stair to the apartments above, one for the Christians living in the building, one for the Jews. For centuries in Lengnau the Christians had refused to enter and leave their houses across the same threshold as that used by their Jewish neighbors.

During the sixteenth and seventeenth centuries, one Swiss community after another expelled the Jews from within its confines, blaming population pressures. By 1776 only one state of the Swiss Confederation, the earldom of Baden, remained open to them. But even in Baden they were not entirely welcome. Eventually they were restricted to only two communities within the state, Lengnau and Endigen. These two villages of the Surb valley then became ghettos for the whole of Switzerland.

Lengnau and Endigen were both farming communities, but Jews there were not permitted to engage in farming. In fact, they were not permitted to possess real estate other than their own homes. Households in the two villages were limited to 108, which meant that a Jew often had to wait for years before he could own his own house. Furthermore, a Jew's house had to have a straw roof rather than a tiled one, and could be bought only after it had been offered at auction three times and no Christian had taken it. Once bought, a Jewish home could not be enlarged, nor could its exterior be altered.

When a Jew traveled beyond the borders of Lengnau, as he was often compelled to do to earn a living, he had to pay a special "Jew toll." The army of the Swiss Confederation did not accept Jews; nevertheless, a Jew had to pay a special fee for the privilege of not serving in the army.

To add insult to insult, few occupations were open to the Surbtal Jews to earn a living. They could be moneylenders, peddlers, grocers, tailors, but little else. They could not be doctors or professors. They could deal in money but they were not allowed to mine or smelt the metals coins were made from. Most of them were peddlers, who left their homes Sunday afternoons and traveled throughout Baden and the other cantons during the week, accumulating guldens and paying them out in Jew tolls and special peddling taxes, and then returning home Friday evening with what was left.

It is assumed, but it has never been proved, and probably never will be, that the Guggenheims of Lengnau, and later of Philadelphia and New York, originally came from the village of Guggenheimb, now Jugenheim, in northwestern Bavaria, a hilly, densely forested area that has long been known as excellent country for hunting quail, deer, hare, and wild boar, and is the ancestral home of the Battenberg family, progenitors of Prince Philip, Duke of Edinburgh. The supposition that America's greatest Jewish family originally came from this small south German town rests upon the undisputed fact that Jews in Germany were not given surnames during the Middle Ages and, in the Renaissance, when they were required to have them, they were forced to take the name of the town in which they lived. Firm proof, however, remains impossible since the records of the births, deaths, and marriages of Jews in Guggenheimb have long since been destroyed by zealous Christians.

Most likely it was during the savagery of the Thirty Years' War—surely one of the bitterest and bloodiest wars in all history—that the Guggenheims of Guggenheimb emigrated to then-safer Switzerland. Where they first settled in Switzerland is not known. All that is known is that by 1696 they were in the ghetto village of Lengnau in the valley of the Surb.

For it is in the year of 1696 that the name Guggenheim first appears in the official documents of Baden in the form of an entry referring to "der Jud Maran Guggenheimb von Lengnau."

Whether Maran Guggenheimb is a bona fide ancestor of the American Guggenheims is open to question. More than likely he was, for in 1702 a certain Jacob Guggenheim, authenticated ancestor of the American branch, was brought to court for illegally owning the house of Maran Guggenheimb and owning, as well, with his brother Samuel, a vineyard on Wettinger Hill, just outside the village. Later in 1702 a mob of Christians burned down Jacob Guggenheim's house.

Jacob Guggenheim, it appears, was a leader in the Jewish community of Lengnau. He was a *parnas*, or elder, of the Lengnau synagogue, and was considered a genuine *lambden*, or scholar, of Hebrew studies. When the Lengnau ghetto's charter expired in 1732, Jacob Guggenheim and one Raphael Pickert were selected by the approximately 250 Jewish families of the Surb valley to testify on their behalf before the Diet of the Swiss Confederation in Zurich. There was danger that, reacting to ever-mounting Christian pressure, the *Landvogt* might expel all the Jews from the two Surbtal communities.

Jacob Guggenheim had to resort to blatant flattery and submit to equally blatant blackmail to save himself and his fellow Jews from expulsion. Once before the Diet, he praised the *Landvogt* extravagantly and finally gave in to what the *Landvogt* wanted all along, a much higher price for "his Jews" to remain in the Lengnau ghetto.

Not long after these events, one of Jacob's sons, Joseph Guggenheim, was involved in a controversy which, for a while, was discussed all over Switzerland.

Jacob had sent Joseph to a Talmudic school in Metz, in Alsace, and while he was there he was invited to Zurich by one Johann Caspar Ulrich, a Protestant pastor who had met Jacob when he had spoken so eloquently before the Swiss Diet. Pastor Ulrich, a Christian of missionary zeal, attempted to convert Joseph Guggenheim to Christianity, and, after many vicissitudes, including two nervous breakdowns on the part of Joseph, succeeded, much to the outrage of Jacob and the entire Jewish community of Switzerland. For his heresy the Guggenheims of Lengnau subsequently struck him from the family's rolls. (Joseph, unknowingly, thus became the herald of things to come, the first of many Guggenheims, stretching to the present day, who renounced Judaism in favor of Christianity.)

Jacob was so enraged over his son's conversion that he was led into direct confrontation with Pastor Ulrich and the Christians of Switzerland. After endless debates, reported widely in the journals of the day, the *Landvogt* demanded that Jacob be compelled to purchase the privilege of remaining in Lengnau for 600 florins, a considerable sum in those times. Jacob paid the toll.

One of Jacob's sons was Isaac Guggenheim, who, by 1800, had become the richest Jew in Lengnau. Isaac, a pitiless moneylender all his life, known as "Old Icicle," was a patriarchal figure in the Lengnau ghetto. Solemn, taciturn, bearded, habitually wearing skullcap and caftan, he ruled unofficially over both the Jews of the village and the Guggenheim family. When he died in 1807 at the age of eighty-four, he left an estate valued at 25,000 florins.

Isaac Guggenheim's oldest son and principal heir was Meyer, who married a German woman, a certain Fraulein Vogel from Gailengen, in 1775. Meyer and his wife had eight children, one of whom, Samuel, is commemorated in the Partners' Room at Guggenheim Brothers in New York for having rescued a child from a fire, and another of whom, Simon, at age fifty-five was to leave Lengnau with his son, Meyer, to begin the Guggenheims' grand adventure in America.

By the time Simon began working as a tailor in house No. 64 by the Surb, the fortune that his grandfather, Old Icicle, had accumulated had dwindled to a very little, and the Guggenheim family had to rely wholly on Simon's meager earnings to survive.

Thirty years later, in 1847, Simon's economic position was little better than it had been when he first began tailoring. His wife, Schafeli Levinger, had died in 1836 and so he had had to raise his son, Meyer, and five daughters alone. Young Meyer, now twenty, worked as a peddler, traveling through Switzerland and Germany, but the daughters were a burden. They would not be permitted to marry in Lengnau unless they were provided with sufficient dowries.

Even fifty-five-year-old Simon himself was not allowed to marry in Lengnau. He had become attached to a forty-one-year-old widow, Rachel Weil Meyer, who had three sons and four daughters. But though she posessed some money, and Simon did own his own shop and furnishings, Simon was not able to convince the Christian authorities of Lengnau that they had enough money to marry.

Simon's frustrations were so great that he and Rachel were compelled to take desperate action. They decided to pool their limited resources and take themselves and their children to America. By that time word had come back to Lengnau from other emigrants that there were no ghettos in America and no proscriptive laws against Jews.

It was an enormous step for a fifty-five-year-old widower and a forty-one-year-old widow who had both spent over half their lives in a tiny Swiss village to take, but they took it. Simon sold his little house and shop by the Surb, and, pooling his resources with Rachel's, traveled with twelve of their children to Coblenz on the Rhine. From there they went by riverboat to Hamburg and from Hamburg they took a sailing ship to Philadelphia.

Once in America, the Guggenheims, like thousands of other European immigrants from oppressed classes, would take their unconscious revenge against the ruling class of their native land. Without individualizing their former oppressors in their minds, they would nevertheless show the *Landvogt* of Baden, the Diet of the Swiss Confederation, the stuffy, moralistic Christians of the valley of the Surb what kind of people they had prevented from marrying, from owning land, from freely choosing a profession, from accumulating capital, from living where they wanted to, from mining and smelting silver and gold. And what is more they would show them on a global scale. They would live in grander and more magnificent palaces than the *Landvogt*'s. They would own properties larger than the entire valley of the Surb. They would not have to plead for their lives before diets; they would serve in the Senate of their new country's confederation. They would not only mine and smelt metals used in coins, they would own and operate the largest and richest silver, copper, and gold mines in the world. And as they progressed in their adopted country they would acquire riches and honors and splendors so vast as to make the self-satisfied Christians of Lengnau look like beggars, slaves.

So tightly did the centuries of restriction, repression, and persecution of the Jews wind the spring of Guggenheim ambition that it would take many a generation before the spring would wind down, the momentum give out. And then, even in the family's twilight, there would still be bursts of energy, flashes of talent, such as few of the good Christian burghers of Baden had ever known, or imagined.

CHAPTER 2

THE HAVEN CITY

It took over two months for the ship on which the Guggenheims and the Meyers sailed from Hamburg to reach Philadelphia. Years later Meyer Guggenheim would tell his children about the unbelievably crowded conditions below decks. There was little or no privacy. At night the steerage passengers huddled against one another in rat-infested holds. For sustenance there was only hardtack, dried fruit, fish, and strictly rationed wine and water.

But, Meyer would add with a twinkle, these discomforts and privations scarcely bothered him, for it was during the voyage that he fell in love with fifteen-year-old Barbara Meyer. For Meyer and Barbara the long days passed quickly. They used all their ingenuity to find ways of being together, away from the other passengers and away from the prying eyes of their families. By the time they sailed up the Delaware River they had decided to get married, once Meyer had enough money.

First, however, it was Father Simon's and Mother Rachel's turn to marry. The ceremony was performed shortly after arrival and then the combined family—fourteen persons in all—settled down in a rented house in a nameless laborers' district outside Philadelphia.

The year was 1848. James K. Polk was President. Most of the recently expanded nation he presided over was still undeveloped and unsettled. The continent's thick forests, brawling streams, wild, lonely mountains were still unscarred and undefiled. The United States, victors in a two-year trumped-up war, had just swindled Mexico out of largely untouched California, Nevada, Colorado, Arizona, Utah, and New Mexico. In the two years prior to the Mexican War the U.S. had annexed Texas and acquired the Oregon Territory. "Manifest Destiny" it was called. The Gold Rush was just beginning. The Indians had not yet been exterminated. Women could not yet vote. Blacks were still enslaved.

Few of the great American families, whose ranks the Guggenheims would join in the twentieth century, had yet attained wealth and influence by 1848. Patrick Kennedy, great-grandfather of John F. Kennedy, had arrived on Noddle's Island, Boston Harbor, only one year before and was still as poor, if not poorer, than he had been in famished Ireland. The forebears of Henry Ford had arrived fifteen years before, also from Ireland, and were still humble dirt farmers. John D. Rockefeller, son of a New York trader, was only nine years old. Only the Astors, Du Ponts, and Vanderbilts were already on their way to great riches.

The Philadelphia to which the Guggenheims came in 1848 was one of America's most attractive and tolerant cities. It was the financial center of the seventy-two-year-old nation, though it would soon yield this last distinction to New York.

As soon as they were settled domestically, Simon and Meyer went to work as peddlers. Most housewives in Philadelphia in those days bought their household goods from door-to-door salesmen, rather than make the trip into the center of town to buy at the dry-goods store. Peddling seemed to Simon and Meyer the quickest and surest way to accumulate some money. And so the fifty-six-year-old Simon began peddling on the streets of Philadelphia, and the twenty-one-year-old Meyer began peddling in the more arduous, but more lucrative, Pennsylvania anthracite country.

Simon would come home every day, but Meyer would remain away all week, leaving every Sunday with his backpack full and not returning until the celebration of the Sabbath, which began with a family meal Friday evening. Father and son peddled a bit of everything: shoestrings, lace, stove and furniture polish, ribbon, pins, spices, needles.

Meyer's German stood him in good stead with the Pennsylvania Dutch. He soon built up a solid clientele of coal miners' wives and their local suppliers, and a few Pennsylvania farmers. He did not have to pay a

Jew toll coming and going from Philadelphia and, though he must have met with endless indignities and discomforts, he prospered.

For some reason, probably because the iron coal-burning range had only recently superseded the kitchen fireplace, Meyer's best-selling item in his backpack became stove polish. Sales of stove polish were most satisfying, but it did not take long for Meyer to realize that while he made only one or two pennies out of each can sold, the manufacturer was making thousands of dollars out of the innumerable cans *he* sold. With the mixture of intrepidity and good judgment that was to guide him to commercial success after commercial success all his life, young Meyer decided to manufacture his most popular item as well as sell it. Forthwith he traveled to a German chemist in Bethlehem, who analyzed the formula of the polish Meyer was selling and instructed him how to make it. Not long afterward Meyer discovered a way of making stove polish that would not leave a residue of black lead on a housewife's hands, and, not long after that, Simon was staying home making the polish with a secondhand sausage-stuffing machine and Meyer was out selling it. Soon Meyer was making eight cents profit on a can rather than a penny. The Guggenheim stove polish business was established.

As soon as Meyer began making good money out of manufacturing and selling stove polish, he plunged into something else. This time it was selling essence of coffee. By 1852, four years after his arrival in the United States, Meyer Guggenheim had made enough money from stove polish and coffee essence, and was well-enough established in both businesses, to be able to marry his beloved Barbara.

The marriage was celebrated at Keneseth Israel Synagogue in downtown Philadelphia and then the couple left Simon and Rachel's menage and went to live in a rented house by themselves. Meyer was twenty-four, Barbara was nineteen. Together they would found one of the greatest industrial dynasties of modern times.

CHAPTER 3

ROASTED PIGEONS
DO NOT FLY INTO ONE'S MOUTH

Once Meyer and Barbara had settled down to married life, Simon and Rachel gradually faded out of the Guggenheim picture. In time their other children married and produced children whose descendants' modest lives would stand out in sharp contrast to the splendor in which Meyer and Barbara's progeny would live. Simon died in 1869 at seventy-six, a worn-out but presumably contented man. He had accomplished his principal objective of giving his children and stepchildren a new start in a new world, and by 1869 there were eight grandsons to carry on the family name. When Rachel died is not known: the records are mute; she may even have returned to Switzerland.

During Simon's declining years Meyer gradually assumed the center of the Guggenheim stage and would hold it until his death in 1905.

Meyer Guggenheim was a caricature of the nineteenth-century Jew. He was a small, reticent, suspicious loner with long, curly brown hair, long rabbinical whiskers, and a beard. When he became prosperous, he always wore a long, black frock coat (perpetually flecked with cigar ashes) and a floppy, wide-brimmed black hat. He was single-mindedly devoted to making money. Contemporaries observed that his love of money bordered on the pathological. It has been said that no American multimillionaire started out quite so humbly as Meyer Guggenheim (at first he was really little more than a beggar) and no one, not even his near contemporary, John D. Rockefeller, pursued wealth quite so obsessively.

Physically Meyer was not particularly prepossessing or impressive: a short, slender build, slightly stooped from years of trudging through Switzerland, Germany, and Pennsylvania with a heavy pack on his back; a longish, triangular face, refined in its contours, and with lively, slightly humorous brown eyes, but with a heavy, potato nose (which was to reappear in nearly all his descendants), and very full lips; a kindliness in his overall expression, especially as he grew older, but also a coldness, at times a terrible coldness. Meyer Guggenheim was capable of love—on occasion—and pleasure—he enjoyed music, fresh shellfish, and cold white wine—but no one, *no one* would ever put one over on him.

Other characteristics. He was, according to a son, "taciturn by nature," "he wasted few words," and "kept his own counsel." Generally he shrank from wide public contact and had no appetite for large groups of people, especially great crowds. Infinitely wary, wary to the point of paranoia, he trusted the motives of no one outside his family. He was always on the alert for an ulterior purpose on the part of both friend and foe. The reverse side of every proposition had to be examined carefully for its lurking peril. Every promise carried a concealed menace.

It was a cardinal point of Meyer Guggenheim's creed—conditioned by centuries of oppression and tyranny in Germany and Switzerland—that safety and happiness in this world lay only in money. It was a harsh, dog-eat-dog world and only money could protect you from being devoured or swept away. Thus, acquiring money, more and more money, became to him a kind of consecration to the exclusion of all other concerns. A vigilant opportunist, he remained ever on the alert for every chance that might come his way. "Roasted pigeons," he never tired of repeating, "do not fly into one's mouth." You must shoot the birds first, then roast them, before you can eat them. For Meyer it was no sacrilege to do business on the Sabbath. On the contrary, he would work hard every Saturday of his life. Some of his best pigeons flew his way on the Sabbath, when his rivals were at rest with their guns across their laps. Business was the very breath of his life, his very being. It was Meyer Guggenheim and his family against the world, with no quarter asked and no mercy expected from either side. "He kept books of small, neat figures," one of his sons was to write in 1934, "and knew that every change he had made had improved his financial status, had moved him a little nearer to his goal." Tenacious and daring in earning money, he was correspondingly cautious in spending it. Deep down he always remained a Swiss penny pincher. Every penny, so hard won, should be spent reluctantly, prudently. Except to earn more money. Investment was another matter. Spend only to earn, then and only then could one spend lavishly, recklessly.

And what of Barbara? From all accounts Barbara Meyer was the perfect complement to Meyer Guggenheim. In the early days she was the eager confidante and supporter of all his hopes. Later, after the children were born, "her every energy and thought was bent toward making agreeable the lives for which she was responsible." Joyously dedicated throughout her long life to her house, her husband, and her children, she took little interest in Meyer's business affairs, less interest in public affairs, and never sought to rival her husband or challenge him in anything. He was supreme in his role as head of the family and chief provider. She was supreme as head of the household and loving wife and mother. Being "liberated" from the home and from household chores would have seemed like utter madness to her.

Barbara Guggenheim was a pleasant-looking, but not beautiful, woman. The shape of her head and the cast of her features were heavy, Germanic. More than likely there was a strong dose of German blood in her veins, as there undoubtedly was also in Meyer's. She had a variation of the same potato nose as her husband. She was inclined toward plumpness. As a girl and young woman she had lovely, long auburn hair and unusually fair skin. Her brown-and-gray eyes were warm and benevolent.

If marriage was life's supreme business to Barbara, charity was life's next more important concern. All her life she denied herself personal indulgences and gave liberally to the poor. In the words of a son, "charity was as natural to Barbara Guggenheim as industry was to her husband. If he laid the foundation for the future world-wide Guggenheim business enterprises, as certainly did she sow the seeds that would one day grow into the equally widespread Guggenheim philanthropies."

As Meyer prospered, he and Barbara moved to a small house at 433 Green Lane in the suburb of Roxborough. Here Meyer opened a grocery store and in 1854 Barbara presented him with their first son, whom they named Isaac. Three more sons followed in rapid succession, Daniel in 1856, Murry in 1858, and Solomon in 1861.

When the Civil War broke out, Meyer—still operating his grocery store and conducting his stove polish and coffee essence business—began speculating successfully in clothing items and foodstuffs—shoe pegs and mustard seeds, among other things—needed by the Army of the Potomac. Meyer himself never went to war. True to his creed, he made money from the war.

So successful, in fact, was he in making money from the war, that he was able to accumulate enough capital to become a major wholesale merchant of spices, his next business.

Meanwhile, four more children were added to his responsibilities. Jeannette, his first girl, was born in 1863, Benjamin in 1865, and twin sons, Simon and Robert, in 1867. Meyer was only thirty-nine and Barbara thirty-four, and they already had seven sons and a daughter. But they were far from finished. After the twins were born, they moved to a better house on Franklin Street in Philadelphia, and promptly had three more children, William in 1868, Rose in 1871, and Cora in 1873. Twice more they moved, always to more fashionable addresses: first to North Seventeenth Street and finally to North Sixteenth Street.

By 1873, Meyer, at forty-five, was a prosperous wholesale spice merchant, with little reason to venture into something new. Nevertheless, in that year he went into still another business, the manufacture of lye. Housewives in those days made their own soap out of lye from wood ashes and fat derived from home butchering. Why not manufacture lye and thus produce another household necessity? There might be good money to be made in such a venture. Roasted pigeons do not fly into one's mouth, however, and so Meyer, with characteristic resourcefulness and ingenuity, quickly bought up certain patent rights that were going begging, bought a small factory, and soon was putting a new product on the market cheaply and in large quantities, under the name of the American Concentrated Lye Company.

Before long, however, the Pennsylvania Salt Company, which also sought to manufacture lye, brought suit against Meyer for what they claimed was patent infringement. After a sharp battle, the courts sustained Guggenheim. Frustrated, Pennsylvania Salt offered to buy Meyer out. For a while Meyer played hard to get. Then he sold his American Concentrated Lye for $150,000 and promptly retired from the lye business forever.

Soon more pigeons fit for roasting flew his way. He realized that railroads represented the most lucrative investment of the day. Someone gave him a tip on the Hannibal and St. Joseph Railway, a small line that hauled freight in and out of booming Kansas City, and which the financier Jay Gould was interested in. The company was in trouble, earnings were dropping, dividends were being passed, the stock had slumped to twenty dollars a share. Owners of the stock had begun to dump. Meyer bought as they dumped and came up with 2,000 shares.

Meanwhile Meyer's tip proved genuine. Jay Gould was trying to put together a great new rail system, to be known as the Missouri Pacific. The Hannibal and St. Joseph was a necessary link in this system. Gould and his associates began buying Hannibal stock. Meyer let the titans in New York buy and buy while he held. After a while, Jay Gould, impatient to gain full control, sent a lieutenant to Philadelphia to coax Meyer into selling his shares. Meyer held. The stock continued to go up. Finally Meyer sold for the top dollar, realizing a whopping profit of $300,000.

Now Meyer had about $450,000 in capital. The stage was set for his next business: importing laces and embroideries from Saxony and Switzerland.

It was a time when women of every age *had* to adorn their petticoats, pantalets, summer dresses with rows upon rows of dainty embroidery and cutwork—what came to be known as "Hamburg edgings." By the 1870s one of Barbara's uncles in Switzerland had established a small factory for embroidering by machine. The Jews of Switzerland had been emancipated from the ghettos and all proscriptive laws by proclamation in 1863 and were rapidly seizing opportunities everywhere in Europe. Barbara's uncle had acquired the embroidery factory, had made a success out of it, and had sent Meyer samples, suggesting that he import the product and sell it in the United States.

Ever quick to spot a lucrative new opportunity, Meyer entered into partnership with one Morris Pulaski and soon the firm of Guggenheim and Pulaski, importers of fine laces and embroideries, was flourishing.

More than flourishing. It was a gold mine. Guggenheim and Pulaski was the first to enter the field and it held its lead. The dainty Swiss laces and embroideries poured into Philadelphia and the profits poured into Guggenheim and Pulaski's accounts. So much money did Meyer make from this business that he was able to take two giant strides into the future: move across North Sixteenth Street and buy a horse and surrey.

Meyer and Barbara had brought up their children with a good balance of discipline and indulgence. So far as religion was concerned, Barbara saw to it that the children were brought up in Judaism—she herself was profoundly religious—but Meyer, who wasn't at all religious, was more concerned that his children receive the best education available and so rather than send them to the Hebrew schools, which were not considered particularly good in those days, he sent them to the better Catholic day schools where, of course, they were indoctrinated in another religious viewpoint. The Guggenheims' synagogue, the Keneseth Israel, in which the Ashkenazic ritual was observed, was considered the most lax of all the synagogues in Philadelphia, and so it is safe to say that the Guggenheim children did not receive much of a grounding in the religion of their forefathers.

Though they were to become wizards in business, none of the Guggenheim boys, except William, liked school or showed any particular aptitude for schoolwork. What irked the older boys most was that the Philadelphia high schools condemned them to "useless" classical studies, when they would have much preferred a "practical" education in business.

After a while Meyer, always a shrewd judge of character, realized that none of his sons, save the studious William, would ever become much of a scholar, and so he put the oldest, Isaac, to work with an uncle (one of Barbara's brothers); sent Daniel to Switzerland, where the ghettos had been abolished, to perfect his German and study the embroidery business; sent Solomon too to Switzerland, and specifically to the Institute Concordia in Zurich, where he too was to polish his German and study business; and sent Murry also to Switzerland, to St. Gall, the embroidery center, there to study embroidery manufacture firsthand.

This left the younger seven children at home, Jeannette, Benjamin, the twins—Simon and Robert—William, Rose, and Cora. From this time on a sharp division between the older and younger Guggenheim sons, which had, in a way, always existed, was accentuated. Isaac, Daniel, Solomon, and Murry, who were destined to mastermind the Guggenheim empire one day, were trained in Europe, and in European manners and customs, while Benjamin and William and Simon, who would not play such a conspicuous role in the business, remained in America. Robert, Simon's twin, died from a fall off a horse at age eleven. The girls were eventually sent to the Sacred Heart Convent in nearby Torresdale, and then to finishing schools in Paris, to prepare them for marriages into wealthy Jewish families.

In time the older boys came home from Switzerland, full of first-hand knowledge of embroidery and lace manufacture, with their German and their manners polished, and Morris Pulaski retired from the embroidery-importing business of Guggenheim and Pulaski. Meyer then formed the firm of M. Guggenheim's Sons in 1877 (later incorporated in 1882) giving each son an equal share in the partnership. At first, only the four oldest—Isaac, Daniel, Murry, and Solomon—were qualified to work in the business, and divide its profits, but Meyer assured each of his younger sons that there would be a place in the business for them too and that they would divide the profits equally with their older brothers. This arrangement annoyed Isaac, the oldest, who had been working in Guggenheim and Pulaski for several years already, and felt that on the basis of seniority he was entitled to a greater share of the profits. But Meyer was convinced that any inequalities in the partnership would only breed discontent among the brothers and overruled Isaac's objections. "True," Meyer said, "when the younger ones first come in they are more bother than they are worth. During this period the older ones must carry the load. But in time all that changes. The day arrives when the older ones wish to retire. Then the younger ones must carry the load. Besides, let us not forget the wives! If the wife of one partner hears that the partner-husband of another is making more money, trouble follows."

One day, to emphasize his point, so the story goes, Meyer gathered his seven sons around a long mahogany table in his office, and, after a brief pause, gave each a stick. He then told them to break the sticks and they did as he told them. Another pause, then he produced a bundle of seven sticks held together by a band, and asked each son to break the bundle. The bundle was passed around. None of the sons was able to break it.

"You see, my boys," Meyer said, "singly the sticks are easily broken, together they cannot be broken. So it is with you. Together you are invincible. Singly, each of you may be easily broken. Stay together, my sons, and the world will be yours. Break up and you will lose everything."

It was a lesson five of the brothers were to heed to extraordinary advantage. The two who did not heed it, or who were perhaps obstructed from heeding it by the others, were to have radically different destinies.

And so by the late 1870s M. Guggenheim's Sons, importers of fine laces and embroideries, was firmly founded, with four sons in the business and three more about to join. The business thrived, as did Meyer's other concerns, for he remained also an importer of spices, a dry-goods merchant, and a stove polish manufacturer. By 1879 Meyer Guggenheim, at fifty-one, thirty-two years after leaving the Lengnau ghetto, was a near-millionaire: he had, perhaps, around $800,000. The Guggenheim family was well established in its adopted country and again Meyer had every justification to simply sit back on his laurels and let the money pour in. But, as it turned out, the Guggenheims were only just beginning their extraordinary climb to dynasty and empire. None of them, however, was even remotely aware of this, for in that prosperous year of 1879 there was still nothing on the Guggenheim horizon that even barely hinted at the immense riches to come.

CHAPTER 4

BONANZA IN COLORADO

A single, sudden decision, taken in nearly total ignorance of what its consequences might be, a decision, which, on its face value, was nothing short of wild speculation, was ultimately responsible for what the Guggenheims became and what they are today. Had this decision not been taken, the Guggenheims would, more than likely, have remained in Philadelphia as modestly prosperous lace and embroidery importers, and, like the descendants of Meyer and Barbara's sisters and brothers, would have remained in nearly total obscurity as well.

Meyer Guggenheim probably did not know that the great full tide had come in his affairs when, in fact, it did come, but, knowingly or unknowingly, he took it at the flood.

The full tide came in the form of a mining speculation. In 1881 Meyer bought a one-third interest for $5,000 in two lead and silver mines, the "A.Y." and the "Minnie," in California Gulch on the outskirts of the booming mining town of Leadville, Colorado. He bought the interest from an old Quaker acquaintance, Charles D. Graham, a grocery-store owner and speculator in Western mineral lands, who had borrowed to buy this two-thirds interest and then couldn't pay half the note when it was due. The mines had been fair to middling producers, nothing extraordinary, and had so far been very expensive to operate. Leadville itself had been thriving for over a decade. By the time Meyer took his flyer with the A. Y. and the Minnie the town boasted 120 saloons, 150 gambling houses, 1 opera house, and 35 whorehouses. It even had a *Deutsch Zeitung*, which pleased Meyer no end. Famous writers and actors occasionally recited in the opera house, Oscar Wilde among them. He delighted his readers back home by reporting that in one saloon he spotted a sign reading "Please do not shoot the pianist, he is doing his best."

Meyer Guggenheim knew absolutely nothing about mining at the time he entered into his Leadville speculation. Friends, relatives, and associates, regarding mines as worthless get-rich-quick traps for the unwary, thought he had finally made a mistake.

A few weeks after he bought his interest, little Meyer, in his long frock coat, floppy hat, and muttonchops, was in California Gulch standing among a crowd of grimy miners peering down a seventy-foot shaft and listening to a stone dropped by the mine superintendent splash in the water below. The mines were flooded. To "unwater" them would cost around $25,000. Meyer's partners did not have the money. So Meyer bought out one partner, thereby obtaining control of the mines, and, with four oil-well pumps, each driven by a twenty-five-horsepower engine, began unwatering both the A. Y. and the Minnie. During the pumping he returned to Philadelphia.

After the unwatering, Meyer received reports that miners were taking about fifty tons of ore a day out of the Minnie alone. This compared very favorably with the two hundred tons a month the two mines had been producing before they became flooded. But along with these reports there were also more requests for funds to effect repairs and further unwatering. Meyer sent the money, and waited hopefully for more favorable reports. There were more requests for money. Meyer paid. Before long he was growing very anxious about his investment. He had already sunk anywhere from $30,000 to $70,000 (reports vary) into the venture.

Then one warm August Friday in 1881 a telegram from Leadville arrived at Meyer's office. Meyer was sure it was another request for funds from his superintendent. Instead the telegram announced:

RICH STRIKE FIFTEEN OUNCES SILVER
SIXTY PERCENT LEAD

It was a bonanza.

The A. Y. and the Minnie, named after the original pioneer owners, A. Y. Corman and his wife, Minnie, who had sold their property for practically nothing, were indeed extraordinary mines. The ore in them, though highly refractory, was nevertheless found to have a higher silver content than any of their neighboring properties. In fact, they had the highest silver content of any mine in Leadville. This was due to the presence in very large quantities of pure native silver. The white metal seemed to run everywhere in the black depths of both mines. Sometimes it appeared in the form of great, twisting, silver wires. Frequently, it was spun into the shape of birds' nests. Sometimes long white wires of almost pure silver ran from nest to nest to nest, terminating in great white webs of spun metal.

Soon Meyer was earning $17,000 a month from his mines—about $100,500 a month in today's money—and he found himself a celebrity in Philadelphia.

Meyer worked the mines from his office in Philadelphia, assisted by 130 miners and supervisory personnel in Leadville, and by 1887 they had produced 9 million ounces of silver and 86,000 tons of lead. Two miners on a single twelve-hour shift could pull down enough ore from the stopes to pay all the mines' expenses for one day. The miners went on strike time and again, and time and again the strikes were broken, usually with the aid of armed state militia or hired thugs. Meyer never had much patience with striking workers. He himself had been a worker, the lowliest of workers, and he had never struck, only worked harder and harder.

By 1888 the A. Y. and the Minnie were earning Meyer about $750,000 a year. Before the mines were exhausted they would yield the Guggenheims over $15 million. And they were just the beginning of the family's mining ventures, the first tentative steps toward a worldwide empire of copper and silver and gold.

It did not take long, after the mines had become profitable, for Meyer to take his next giant step.

Quickly he realized, much to his annoyance, that the Holden Smelter at Denver, to which he sent his ore to be refined, was eating up most of his profits. The smelters were, of course, the middlemen of mining. Solution: build his own smelter; own both the raw material and the means to refine it. Accordingly Meyer sent his third-youngest son, Benjamin, to Colorado to investigate and negotiate. On Benjamin's recommendation, Meyer bought stock in the Denver smelter and together with Edward R. Holden formed a new company, which they called the Philadelphia Smelting and Refining Company. Forty-nine percent of the stock went to

Holden and an associate. The remainder, with control, passed to Meyer Guggenheim. Forthwith, Meyer began building, at a cost of $500,000, a new smelter at Pueblo, Colorado. It was the first step toward the Guggenheims' control of the smelting industry in America.

Now Meyer did an extraordinary thing, which exemplified what in William's words was "his ruling passion—the advancement of his sons." He signed over his controlling share of the Philadelphia Smelting and Refining Company to the lace and embroidery importing firm of M. Guggenheim's Sons, stipulating, again in the words of William, "that the three younger brothers be admitted as equal partners in the new venture also." Once more complaints from the older brothers, who, according to William, "had begun to lose track of the fact that their places in the sun had been bought with Meyer's foresight and kindness rather than with their personal efforts." Once more Meyer remained adamant. Once more he told them that "they were like single sticks easily broken, but that bound together they could resist whatever force could be brought to bear on them." "It is my desire," he said, "and my resolution to see you so united as to assure your invincibility."

The older sons gave in, as they would always do, to Father Meyer. Benjamin and William, both in their early twenties, were then sent into field service in the new venture. Benjamin, the first Guggenheim to go to college, left Columbia University's School of Mines to become the A. Y. and Minnie's bookkeeper. William, upon graduating from the University of Pennsylvania, went to work in the assay and laboratory department of the mines and later at the family's new smelter at Pueblo. The older boys were, at first, too busy with the lace and embroidery business to hurl themselves immediately into mining and smelting. They remained behind, in Switzerland, Philadelphia, and New York, attending to various administrative matters.

Soon, however, it became apparent that the lace and embroidery business had to be gradually phased out so that Meyer and all his seven sons could concentrate wholly on mining and smelting. By then Isaac was married and had three daughters; Daniel was married and had a son, and both were working, along with the as yet unmarried Solomon, in the family's recently established New York office. Murry was still in Switzerland looking after the remnants of the embroidery business there. Simon was in Spain, acquiring some European polish and a knowledge of Spanish that would stand him in good stead when the Guggenheims invaded South America.

Meyer ordered Murry and Simon back to America and commanded all his sons to concern themselves with the new business.

What made the new concentrated deployment of M. Guggenheim's Sons so imperative was the inescapable and terrifying fact that the Guggenheims' smelter business was beginning to lose money and soon threatened to entirely wipe out Meyer's fortune. There were labor troubles. There were management troubles. The smelter workers, for instance, struck against the twelve-hour day, ore piled up in the yards, prices went down. William Guggenheim, fresh out of college, his head full of unworkable theories, was constantly quarreling with the smelter superintendents. Before long, losses from smelter operations were soaring as high as $500,000 in six months. When the Guggenheim boys assembled in New York they were aghast at what was happening. They could not believe that one of their father's enterprises could suddenly turn so sour, could threaten even to reduce them to paupers.

So alarmed did Meyer's older sons become that they began incriminating their father for going into the smelting business in the first place. What were they doing in this business they knew nothing about when they had a perfectly sound, predictable lace and embroidery business already well established?

In response to this Meyer gathered his sons around him in M. Guggenheim's Sons' New York offices and told them to stand fast. William described the meeting:

> He was no longer young and the wealth which was being swept away was more the fruit of his labors than that of his sons. He sought to dissipate their fears and to instill in them the confidence with which he himself faced the future. Very quietly he went about reassuring the doubters. The loss had been enormous: that there was no denying; but they must not be discouraged. He impressed upon them the fact that everything he possessed was back of them in this—even the A. Y. and Minnie mines would be sacrificed, if necessary. His offer to toss the mines into the scales in their support allayed the panic which had seized them and clinched the point. They began to plan again, determined that they would not be beaten in their ambitious undertaking.

Later Meyer told them that if they were content to remain just respectable lace importers, no one would ever hear of the name of Guggenheim. *He* wanted the name of Guggenheim to ring out over the whole country, over the whole world! He wanted each son, all seven, to become millionaires. They could never become millionaires selling laces all their lives. They had to go out and take fortune by the throat. "Roasted pigeons do not fly into one's mouth."

Several months went by, then operations slowly began to take a turn for the better. The workers, coaxed by armed strikebreakers, agreed to remain on a twelve-hour day and went back to the furnaces. The surplus stocks of ore began to diminish. The price of silver stabilized.

It was at this time that Meyer's smelter partners, frightened at the terrible losses they had recently sustained, offered to dispose of their 49 percent interest in the Pueblo smelter to the Guggenheims. Meyer immediately gave his sons the money to purchase this minority interest and the smelter became wholly owned by M. Guggenheim's Sons.

The Guggenheims in 1888 and 1889 then pulled up their stakes in Philadelphia and moved to New York. By this time New York had replaced Philadelphia as the financial capital of the nation and had rapidly become the nerve center of American big business. It was essential now that the

The Guggenheims in 1888 and 1889 then pulled up their stakes in Philadelphia and moved to New York. By this time New York had replaced tainly no Jew, could hope to get even close to it, no matter how wealthy he became. Socially, nothing had changed since Meyer arrived forty years before, nor would it ever change. Old Philadelphia families like the Biddles, the Cadwaladers, and the Ingersolls formed a closed aristocracy. New York society was and always would be much more open. Not birth, but wealth and talent were what counted in Manhattan.

Consequently, in 1888 Meyer closed out the embroidery business, moved the last remnants of M. Guggenheim's Sons of Philadelphia to 30 Broad Street in downtown Manhattan, and the following year he and Barbara moved into a large brownstone with a garden in back on West Seventy-seventh Street opposite the American Museum of Natural History. Sons Isaac, Daniel, and Solomon already had brownstones of their own in Manhattan's West Fifties, just off Fifth Avenue.

The stage was now set for the first great test of the Guggenheim brothers' "invincibility." Meyer was getting old and would soon relinquish all responsibility for the mining and smelting operations to his seven sons.

CHAPTER 5

THE CONQUEST OF MEXICO

It took only three years after the completion of the first smelter in Pueblo before the Guggenheims had built up a powerful machine capable of undertaking most any mining enterprise. In the words of William, "each of the brothers was proficient in his own way and the division of labor among them followed the lines indicated by their various talents." Isaac, the oldest and most conservative, acted as treasurer, attending to bank loans and credits. Daniel, the most energetic and ambitious, became chief organizer and negotiator. Murry, with an inborn taste and aptitude for statistics, handled and sold the metals. Solomon, the "hearty good fellow of the family," became "the popular contact man." Benjamin had developed into an excellent operating superintendent. Simon, affable and easy-going at this as yet trouble-free point in his life, "devoted his attention to the purchase of ores and the maintenance of friendly relations with the miners." William, the kid of the family, had a technical metallurgical education from the University of Pennsylvania, and firsthand experience with the A. Y., the Minnie, and the Pueblo smelter.

Behind them all was Meyer, officially retired, but always there, guiding, counseling. And Barbara, inexhaustible source of encouragement, of compassion, of love.

Behind them, also, was luck, consistently one of the Guggenheims' closest allies. Precisely at the time when it appeared possible that the Guggenheims could go down in premature ruin, Congress, in the spring of 1890, passed the Sherman Silver Purchase Act and in so doing gave the Guggenheims a sudden, unexpected shot in the arm. By this act the Treasury agreed to buy 4 million ounces of silver each month. Soon the price of silver rose from 90 cents to $1.25 an ounce. And the net profits of the Pueblo smelter rose to $60,000 a month, or $500,000 a year.

Before long it became the most profitable smelter in the West, "The A. Y. and Minnie of smelters," as William put it. With single-minded determination and unstinting energy Meyer and his boys squeezed every last penny out of both mines and smelter. They beat the railroads down on freight charges, threatening to stockpile ore and often carrying out the threat. By force of arms they evicted miners who squatted on their claims. Time and again they employed armed strikebreakers to force striking miners back to work. They fought, and won, all suits brought against them by miners, workers, other mine owners, and partners.

So encouraged were the Guggenheims by the successful Pueblo operation that they soon decided to take another giant step: plunge into mining and smelting in Mexico.

For some time the Guggenheims had been importing lead and silver ores from Mexico for their Pueblo smelter. The ores were metal rich and yet, thanks to peon labor, relatively cheap. But then the McKinley Tariff

Act of 1890 was passed, and suddenly a heavy duty was slapped upon imported ores. The other American mine owners, the Guggenheims' competitors, had done their lobbying in Washington, and, among their fellow Christians, had found ample support. Bringing ore in from Mexico now would not be so cheap.

The Guggenheims' response to this sudden reversal of good fortune was characteristically quick and daring. Build smelters in Mexico with cheap Mexican labor and smelt Mexican ores there, not far from where they were hauled out of the Mexican earth. Profit margins could conceivably be enormous.

Accordingly, Dan and Murry made a rapid tour of Mexico, with Meyer's blessing, but not with Barbara's (she feared bandits), and concluded that several mines should be leased or bought in the north, near Monterrey in Nuevo Leon, and a smelter built in Monterrey, and several more mines should be leased or bought in the south in Jalisco, near Aguascalientes, and a smelter built in Aguascalientes also.

The matter was discussed exhaustively at a meeting at M. Guggenheim's Sons, in their new offices at 2 Wall Street, and approved by old Meyer and all seven sons. Now all that was needed to get started was a concession from the Mexican government. It was decided that Dan should go down and obtain the concession, which would be the first of its kind, directly from the president of Mexico.

Not long after he arrived in Mexico City, Daniel Guggenheim found himself surprisingly at home, more at home, in fact, he later confessed to his family, than he had felt in his own country. Dan's ten years in Europe had given him a social polish and assurance, an appreciation of elegance that stood him in good stead in Mexico City's aristocratic society, and benefited him much more than it had in the rough-and-tumble, vaguely anti-Semitic society of New York.

He had his first meeting with Díaz in the sumptuous National Palace on the Zócalo, in the heart of the Aztec city Cortez had conquered 369 years before. Other meetings followed and there were dinners, banquets. By the time it was all over Dan had all he wanted . . . and more. He had twisted the wily Díaz around his little finger. Not only did he get the concessions for the two smelters at Monterrey and Aguascalientes, he also received permission for the Guggenheims to "undertake the exploration and exploitation of any mine they may want to lease or buy in Mexico." And he got Díaz to agree to let the machinery for all mines and smelters come in duty free. And to exempt from state and municipal tax all capital that would be spent in Monterrey and Aguascalientes. The agreement was signed December 12, 1890.

Upon Dan's triumphant return to New York the brothers met with Meyer and reorganized themselves into a more efficient unit. Isaac, now a quiet, ultraconservative family man of thirty-six, was assigned to look after the last remnants of the embroidery business and made treasurer of the new smelting business. Daniel, thirty-four, was unanimously chosen to oversee the entire mining and smelting business from New York and to plan future expansion. Murry, thirty-two, was made Western manager in charge of sales. Simon, twenty-three, just back from study in Spain, was made mining representative in Denver, chief buyer of ores and supplies, and chief contact man with Western miners. Benjamin, twenty-five, was put in full charge of the Pueblo smelter, and William, at twenty-two, was made his assistant. It fell to Solomon, thirty, to get the Mexican venture underway. He would go forthwith to Monterrey to lease and purchase mines and build the new smelter. Then he would do the same thing at Aguascalientes.

Meyer, sixty-two, at the time, could not have been more delighted with the way things had worked out. He was in total agreement with the new reorganization and in total sympathy with the new venture. Jubilantly he told his boys that *now they must have no other ambition than to control all mining and all smelting on the North American continent.*

When young Solomon Guggenheim arrived in Monterrey in 1891 to erect the town's first big smelter (there was already a small one in existence) he found a poor dusty adobe community of 25,000 inhabitants with unpaved streets, open sewers, and no hotel. Eighty years later this sleepy community was to become Mexico's more important industrial city, boasting the country's largest steel mill and a population of over one million.

For Sol Guggenheim, Monterrey was his first great challenge, his first real opportunity to show his father and his brothers what he was made of.

At thirty, Sol was short, robust, active, with steady, determined eyes and a long, curled-up moustache. He had charm and manners, liked good wines and beautiful women, and was often taken by the Mexicans as a Latin, rather than a gringo, to his consistent advantage. Already he was known for his courage. Throughout his life, Sol was never afraid of anything or anybody. He used to beat up schoolboys in Zurich who teased him because he was a Jew. Years later, when Frank Lloyd Wright was planning Sol's museum in New York, Sol's daring and courage were the qualities Wright extolled most to intimates.

Before Solomon left New York the Guggenheims had organized the Compañia de La Gran Fundición Nacional Mexicana. Now, for this new company, Sol began purchasing and leasing plant sites, importing machinery, looking for ore. For days he rode over deserts, up mountains, sleeping in straw huts, eating tortillas and frijoles, combating dysentery, insects, rashes, bandits, wearing a loaded revolver in his belt. In time he purchased a site for the smelter, obtained the all-important water rights, and made the necessary railway agreements for freight and sidings. He also leased four mines, the "Cedral" for iron, the "Reforma" for lead, and the "Parena" and the "Encantada" for silver. Then he called for William to come down and supervise the actual construction of the smelter. Will said he would come if the brothers gave him the title of general manager for Mexico. They did. He came. Sol, his work done, his worth proved, returned to New York. For the next four years he would shuttle back and forth between the two countries building up the Mexican properties until they ran themselves.

There were labor problems, of course, all of which were eventually solved by Will. For instance, the Mexican laborers, never much motivated by the work ethic, toiled for about a dollar a day. They realized that at that high wage they would only have to work a quarter as many days as they would for someone else and so that is what they did. Finally Will had to offer them free housing and low prices at a company store to keep them on the job full time. But there was stretches when even that didn't work and thugs had to be employed to herd the peons into the blazing smelters at gunpoint.

The Mexican miners, all Indians, were not easy to deal with either. They loathed work and loved tequila as much as the smelter workers. After a while the Guggenheims had to hire a private militia to keep the peons hauling ore out of the earth. Sometimes jealous local mine owners would send their militias into battle against the Guggenheims'.

But in the end, all was completed, the ore was mined and delivered, the great blast furnaces were blown in and the first plume of black smoke drifted over the Monterrey sky to the cheers of the assembled populace. In the first year of its operation the Guggenheim smelter at Monterrey paid off its entire capital investment. Old Meyer was pleased to note that whereas the Pueblo smelter's payroll was $19,200 a week, the Monterrey payroll was only $3,840.

On the basis of these encouraging results, Solomon went to Aguascalientes, where he bought the famed Tepezala copper mines, a herald of things to come, purchased a site for another smelter, and created a second company, the Gran Fundición Central Mexicana. Again Will was brought in to supervise the construction of the new smelter. Again there were problems—this time one of the engineers was shot by a Texas outlaw who was also gunning for Will—but again all went well in the end and two smelters went up, one for copper and one for lead.

By 1895 the Guggenheim smelters at Pueblo, Monterrey, and Aguascalientes were bringing in a net profit of over $1 million a year and the Guggenheims had become the foremost industrial power in Mexico.

CHAPTER 6

STRUGGLE FOR POWER

Despite his sons' spectacular successes in Mexico, old Meyer Guggenheim was still far from satisfied. He had wanted each of his seven boys to become a multimillionaire and it was unlikely they would do so by dividing the profits of only three smelters. Furthermore, had he not told them that their ambition should be nothing less than the control of all mining and smelting in North America? They were still far from realizing that goal.

While the Guggenheims had been carving out their mining and smelting empires, other business interests had been carving out their mining and smelting empires. Toward the end of the century the inevitable clash between the Guggenheims and "the others" came. Meyer and his boys were quick to perceive that in this clash their great moment had arrived.

In 1889 the Guggenheims had formed the Guggenheim Exploration Company, or "Guggenex," an independent corporation whose purpose was to search for potentially profitable mines throughout the world, purchase them, develop them, and then invite public participation in them. Dan Guggenheim was made president. Before long people like King Edward VII of England were buying shares in Guggenex ventures.

At about the same time, Henry H. Rogers, an associate of William Rockefeller, and Adolph Lewisohn, an important copper producer, had formed the United Metals Selling Company, a trust formed to dominate the sale of metals in America. The success of this trust led to the formation of a still-larger trust, the American Smelting and Refining Company (later called ASARCO), a trust consisting of twenty-three different smelting concerns designed to give Rockefeller interests control of all mineral resources under the American soil. It was an era of combination. The powers in U.S. business, like J.P. Morgan and John D. Rockefeller, were against "wasteful" competition. Combination, "Morganization," as it was later called, was the solution. The Guggenheims were asked to join the new smelters' trust. They declined.

ASARCO was formed and the huge new company declared it was worth $65 million. H. H. Rogers was mastermind; William Rockefeller was its chief backer. Both were determined to ruin the Guggenheims because they were trying to go it alone and because they were Jewish.

Now the Guggenheims were greatly challenged. They could compete favorably against individual mines and smelters. But could they compete successfully against this giant?

Daniel Guggenheim mulled the matter over. The more he thought about it, the more he realized that ASARCO was not so much a threat, but an opportunity, the much-longed-for opportunity for the Guggenheims to win complete control of mining and smelting in America.

Dan realized that the Guggenheims were simply too big now to be squeezed out. ASARCO had to come to terms with them. And Dan would make sure the terms would be tough. The war was on.

Dan, with Meyer solidly behind him, mobilized his brothers for the battle. And immediately there were two casualties. Ben and William defected. They were frankly frightened of such grandiose schemes, which would inevitably cause the Guggenheims to enter into partnership with outsiders. They wanted the Guggenheims' concerns to remain strictly a family business limited to family-owned properties.

And so now there were five Guggenheim boys against the world. As it turned out, they made an unbeatable team. As one member of the ASARCO trust later put it, "What one Guggenheim missed, another was sure to think of. As soon as you thought you were out-smarting one, another would be putting one over on you!" Luck played a vital role. In 1900 workers struck the ASARCO trust for two months. Dan quickly seized his chance. He convinced mine owners throughout the West and in Missouri and Kansas to sell their ore to the more stable and unstruck Guggenheims. He increased production, especially in Mexico. Soon the Guggenheims were flooding the world with cheap lead and silver, driving down prices everywhere.

At the end of 1900 ASARCO profits were $3.5 million and Guggenheim profits were $3.6 million. One hundred thousand dollars more for the Guggenheims and they owned only one-quarter as many mines and smelters as the trust.

ASARCO shares fell. And Dan and a new associate, William Whitney, began buying up shares. Soon the Guggenheims owned a sizable chunk of ASARCO, enough, at least, to make themselves felt at stockholders' meetings, if necessary.

The Rockefeller interests, seriously worried now, made another attempt to buy out the Guggenheims. Dan said he would sell for $45 million, which was what the courts had capitalized the Guggenheim business as being worth on the basis of a net annual profit of $3.6 million.

But Dan stipulated that the trust would not receive the newly organized Guggenex, a firm with a vast potential, nor even all of the rich new Mexican properties. If the trust wanted these *they also had to take the brothers Guggenheim, the whole lot of them, and put them on the board.*

There followed months of courtroom battles, boardroom battles . . . When the smoke cleared the American Smelting and Refining Company and the Guggenheims were one. Daniel Guggenheim was chairman of the board and president. Solomon Guggenheim was treasurer. Isaac, Murry, and Simon were members of the board. William Whitney was on the board. Daniel was also chairman of the executive committee, which contained, as well, three other Guggenheims. And the Guggenheims and their allies owned 51 percent of the stock.

The Guggenheims were now firmly in control of mining and smelting in America and each of the brothers, including Ben and Will, who retained their shares in the old business, was, on paper at least, a multimillionaire.

CHAPTER 7

THE GOOGS OF NEW YORK

While their sons were sporadically putting together one of the great industrial empires of modern times, Meyer and Barbara Guggenheim entered their last years together in the unfamiliar surroundings of New York's upper West Side.

Barbara had not wanted to move from Philadelphia, but Meyer had insisted on it, not for himself and Barbara, but for the boys.

What most appealed to Meyer about New York was, of course, the opportunities for making money. Opportunities to make money were almost limitless in New York in the 1890s. Meyer dabbled in the stock market and lapped up shares of Tennessee Iron, American Cotton Oil, American

Tobacco, Texas and Pacific Railroad; the list was endless.

Opportunities for social advancement were also much greater than in staid old Philadelphia. Philadelphia society was one of maintenance, of status quo, whereas New York society had become one of attainment. In New York a sort of Jewish aristocracy, some would prefer to label it a plutocracy, had already been formed by the 1890s. It was headed by a group of families, all of German origin, whose extraordinary ability to make money had thrust them to the pinnacle of the New York social order, to a place equal to, though separate from, the established Gentile elite. Among these families, who later came to be known as the "Crowd," were the Seligmans, the Strauses, the Goldmans, the Sachses, the Loebs, the Kuhns, the Schiffs, the Lewisohns, the Lehmans.

The Gentile elite, people like the Astors, the Vanderbilts, the Whitneys, the then-*nouveau* Rockefellers, tended to stiff-arm this emerging Jewish aristocracy, but so did the Jewish aristocracy tend to stiff-arm them.

One member of the Crowd took the trouble to describe the chief differences between the upper classes in terms not particularly complimentary to the Gentiles, stating that the Vanderbilt-Astor people were characterized by "publicity, showiness, cruelty, and striving," whereas "ours was based only on family and a quiet enjoyment of the people we loved."

Meyer was, as we have seen, interested only in money. Nevertheless, he and Barbara were very much interested in seeing their children marry well. "Why aim low?" Meyer would always ask. If his children were ambitious in business, they should also be ambitious in marriage.

But how could their children meet the scions of the great Jewish families of New York? Answer: at the synagogue. Not long after Meyer and Barbara arrived in New York they divested themselves of the orthodoxy of their forebears—Meyer was never very attached to Judaism anyway—and became Reformed Jews, members of the fashionable Temple Emanu-El on Fifth Avenue, the richest Jewish congregation in the world. It was here, in this citadel of Reformed Judaism, that they began to mingle with people like the Seligmans, the Schiffs, the Loebs, the Lewisohns.

Meyer and Barbara, however, did not cut very fashionable figures. Meyer never wore anything but a rumpled Prince Albert frock coat whose lapels, we have already noted, were perpetually white with cigar ashes, and was constantly chomping on a usually unlighted, wet cigar. He talked very little—had no small talk whatsoever—and when he did say something he revealed a pronounced tendency to utter his favorite little Swiss-German axioms, like Roasted Pigeons Do Not Fly Into One's Mouth.

Barbara also spoke with a thick *Schweizer-deutsch* accent and never wore fashionable clothes.

But their sons and daughters were a different breed. True, they were not an especially handsome lot (with the exceptions of Ben and William) —they were all cursed, in varying degrees, with the Guggenheim-Meyer potato nose. Still they had acquired a gloss, a manner, lacking in their parents. Even though the Guggenheims were considered terribly *nouveau* by other up-and-coming Jewish families, who referred to them contemptuously as "the Googs," the boys and girls were at least a cut above the cigar-chomping Meyer and that dumpy Swiss *hausfrau* of his.

It fell to the younger ones to make the most "social" marriages. Isaac and Dan were already married to nice, unpretentious, not-very-wealthy Jewish girls from Philadelphia: Carrie Sonneborn and Florence Shloss. In 1890 Dan and Florence had their second son, the future standard-bearer of the family, Harry. Murry had married a European girl, an Alsatian, Leonie Bernheim, while working in Switzerland. Simon married well enough, to Olga Hirsch, daughter of a rich New York realtor and diamond merchant. And so had Solomon, whose bride was Irene Rothschild, daughter of a prosperous New York businessman, not a relation to the European family. But these marriages, socially speaking, were nothing compared to the marriages of Rose, Cora, and Ben. Rose Guggenheim, Meyer and Barbara's tenth child, returned from Madame Bettlesheimer's finishing school in Paris and promptly married Albert Loeb, nephew of Solomon Loeb, one of the founders of Kuhn Loeb & Company and the sponsor of the Loeb Classical Library. Cora married Louis F. Rothschild, founder-to-be of the investment banking house, L. F. Rothschild & Company, again not a relation of the European Rothschilds, but destined to approach them in wealth. And in 1895 Benjamin, aged thirty, married the socially impeccable—from the Jewish standpoint—Florette Seligman, daughter of the millionaire financier James Seligman, and in so doing joined the Guggenheims to the aristocracy of New York Jewry.

By the time Dan engineered the family's great coup in gaining control of the American Smelting and Refining Company, the Guggenheims had finally made it into the inner sanctum of New York's wealthiest and most influential Jewish families. They had been accepted, with some reservations, by people like the Loebs, the Schiffs, the Kuhns, the Seligmans. They were "Googs" no longer, they had made it into the Crowd. Later Meyer's grandchildren would marry into other, even grander, Jewish families—the R. H. Macy's Strauses and the Gimbel's Gimbels—and would spread out into prominent Gentile families as well, including the British peerage.

But even though they became accepted members of New York's, and therefore the United States' Jewish elite, there was always something that set the Guggenheims slightly apart, aside from the fact that they became far richer than anyone else. For one thing, all the other families in the Crowd were Germans; the Guggenheims, though possibly German in the remote past, were Swiss. For another, all the other families were in either finance or merchandising. The Guggenheims—alone among the great Jewish families of America—were in heavy industry. The Guggenheims somehow sensed the difference, for, in contrast to the other princely Jewish families, they alone did not limit their social life to Jewish society. The sons' generation soon found they were quite accepted in Gentile society and came to count among their close friends people like William Whitney, Charles Lindbergh, Theodore Roosevelt, Averell Harriman. Dan's son Harry became, with relative ease, the first Jew to be admitted to the overwhelmingly WASP New York Jockey Club.

For Meyer and Barbara, however, social life in their closing years meant family and only family. Almost the only times they mingled with the Crowd were at Temple Emanu-El.

Every Friday evening the entire Guggenheim clan then present in New York would meet in the brownstone at 36 West Seventy-seventh Street for a great family dinner. The boys' wives, always in intense competition with one another, would dress up in their latest finery for the occasion, and the whole family, as many as seventeen, would sit down at a long table surrounded by ferns under an enormous, blazing crystal chandelier. If there were grandchildren present, Meyer would question them like a drill sergeant, exacting clear answers and enforcing a strict discipline. He was the grand patriarch, founder not only of a business empire, but a dynasty, and expected and received deference from everyone. These reunions did not have anything to do with religious observance. Meyer never approved of Orthodox Jewish religious observances, which, he claimed, set Jews too much apart. So far as he was concerned, anything that interfered with his and his children's becoming throughly assimilated into American life was to be avoided at all cost.

Meanwhile his boys had built vast and splendid palaces for themselves on a forlorn stretch of Jersey shore and Meyer would visit them during the summer months. Barbara, who had diabetes, was usually not well enough to join him.

Each of the boys had tried to outdo the other in splendor and magnificence. Daniel had built an ornate Italian *palazzo* at Elberon, a sort of Jewish Newport. He named his new estate Firenze, after his wife and her favorite Italian city. Solomon, fresh from his triumphs in Mexico, had countered with a huge Victorian mansion called The Towers, after its Moorish onion domes and gables, also at Elberon. Simon put up a reproduction of a Southern Colonial mansion à la *Gone With the Wind.* And Murry, the quiet one, outdid them all with his marble reproduction, complete in every detail, of Le Petit Trianon at Versailles. Meyer would go from one establishment to another, pleased beyond words at these visible symbols of his sons' success. Yes, they had made up for those ghetto laws forbidding Jews to own property in Lengnau.

Years later, Peggy Guggenheim dismissed the whole Elberon enclave as a "dreary ghetto," which, in a sense, was what Newport was to become also.

By the turn of the century Barbara Guggenheim's health had begun to fail seriously, and she would have to retire early from those Friday-evening family gatherings that had become her chief joy in life.

On January 2, 1900, her youngest sons, Benjamin and William, temporarily forsaking the family business, sailed for a pleasure trip to Europe. Thanks to their pioneering work in Colorado and Mexico, both were going to live it up on the Continent. Forty-eight hours after their arrival in Paris they received a telegram saying that Barbara was deathly ill. Immediately they cancelled all their plans and took the next ship back to New York. For a while after their return, she lingered on, fighting her diabetes, in a time when there was no insulin. Then, on March 20, Barbara Guggenheim died.

Her death had a shattering effect on everyone, particularly on her younger children. Rose suffered a nervous breakdown—nervous prostration it was called in those days—and remained confined to her bedroom for months. The carefree Benjamin temporarily became a recluse. The sensitive William, in his own words, "finding that consolation only intensified his anguish, kept to his room and refused to see anyone." Referring to himself in the third person, he lamented:

> He knew that she must die, and he had come face to face with death before, but not with such terrible intimacy. He realized for the first time man's ultimate helplessness. The time of mortals is limited; the termination of everyone's uncertain journey lies only with the will of God. In his bitter sorrow Will felt all foundations swept away and his soul lost.

It had been only a year before her death that Will had designed and had built the grandiose family mausoleum in Salem Fields, Jamaica, Long Island, at a cost of over $100,000, or about $635,000 today. The huge, octagonal structure, worthy of a Roman emperor and the largest in the cemetery, large to accommodate generations and generations and generations of Guggenheims, larger even than the neighboring Seligmans' mausoleum, was constructed of white marble in Italian neoclassical style—it has been called a free version of the Tower of the Winds in Athens—and it was to it that the Guggenheims brought their beloved Barbara on March 23, 1900. Only one member of the family had preceded her to the mausoleum, her firstborn daughter, Jeannette, who had died giving birth to a daughter in 1889.

Barbara Guggenheim had exemplified all those virtues of woman it is fashionable to minimize and deride today. She had never wanted to be anything more than a good wife and a good mother, and in these high roles she had excelled beyond anything her husband or her children demanded or expected. In the words, again, of William, the only Guggenheim son who ever bothered to write anything down, "her whole life, her whole affection, revolved about her family . . . riches did not spoil her, her graciousness and sweet unselfishness remained intact."

As a memorial to their mother, the brothers Guggenheim gave $350,000 ($50,000 each) to Mount Sinai Hospital in New York for a wing to be named after her. For his memorial, Meyer contributed $60,000 more to the $50,000 he had already given to the Jewish Hospital in Philadelphia. Will, acting apart from his other brothers, gave the United Hebrew Charities $50,000 toward a permanent endowment to be known as the Barbara Guggenheim Memorial Fund and pledged another $50,000 in matching funds for every $50,000 donated to the fund. The income was to aid poor Russian Jews, who, at the time, were beginning to pour into the United States in unprecedented numbers.

These charities, inspired by the life of Barbara Guggenheim, were the first of hundreds of individual bequests, amounting to millions upon millions of dollars, which the Guggenheims were to dispense in America and throughout the world. Barbara herself had inaugurated those charities as a young woman in Philadelphia, giving to the neighborhood poor, and, in so doing, had instilled the example and spirit of charity in her seven sons. In a very real sense, the five Guggenheim foundations flourishing today, more than 130 years after Meyer and Barbara left the Lengnau ghetto, are but one vast memorial to Barbara and her living example of what a woman should be.

CHAPTER 8

DEATH OF A PATRIARCH

After Barbara was laid to rest in the great mausoleum at Salem Fields, Meyer returned to his brownstone on West Seventy-seventh Street, there to live out his last lonely years, visited occasionally by a son, a daughter, a grandchild, an old friend.

His principal consolations now were music, his trotting horses, the business successes of his sons.

In his retirement Meyer would go to Carnegie Hall to hear Wagner. What probably appealed to Meyer Guggenheim about Wagner was the composer's power and grandiosity, qualities which he, Meyer, was not devoid of.

Trotting horses were his other diversion. He kept a stable of them on West Seventy-seventh Street and almost every day he could be seen flying through Central Park in his barouche, cigar in mouth, muttonchops and Prince Albert coat trailing in the wind.

And, of course, there were always the diversions of the stock market. Meyer kept an office in his son-in-law Albert Loeb's Wall Street firm and there he would do a little trading and fondling of his stock certificates, which were kept in the firm's vault.

Satisfactions Meyer had in abundance during his closing years, chief of which was, of course, the growing wealth of his sons, but there were also many disappointments. He was dismayed when Will turned up married to one Grace Brown Herbert, a Gentile divorcee from California.

It is not known how or where Will met his bride. All that is known is that he married her in Hoboken on November 30, 1900, and promptly installed her in a suite at the Waldorf-Astoria, while he continued to live at home with his father, where he had established temporary quarters upon his return from Mexico. For a while he was afraid to tell Meyer. He knew the old man would be furious over the fact that Will's wife was a Gentile, a divorcee, and a *nobody*. Hadn't Meyer told his sons to aim high? But after a few weeks Will told Daniel and Daniel was just as furious as his father would have been.

Daniel took charge. He conferred with his lawyers. Then he commanded Will to go to Europe and Grace to go to North Dakota, where it was easy in those days to get a quick divorce. Dan assured Grace she could have all the money she needed after the divorce was final. Grace pleaded that she didn't want money, all she wanted was her darling Will. Finally the imperious Dan had his way, as usual. He shipped acquiescent Will off to Europe where Will promptly had an affair with a French baroness in Paris, and convinced Grace to get a Chicago divorce. The divorce was granted on March 20, 1901, and immediately thereafter the Guggenheims settled $150,000 on the divorcee, a princely sum in those days.

Old Meyer was severely shaken by the whole affair. He had been fond and proud of his youngest son, the only Guggenheim to earn a college degree, and to have him betray that opinion of him was bitter indeed. As for the divorce settlement . . . was this how his hard-earned money was going to be thrown away? Was this a portent of what was going to happen to the Guggenheim fortune?

It appeared so, for no sooner had the William Guggenheim-Grace Brown Herbert affair been settled than old Meyer himself was sued for $100,000 by a certain Hanna McNamara, a forty-five-year-old lady who claimed she had been Meyer's mistress for twenty-five years. In court she asserted that Meyer had promised to marry her after Barbara's death, then did not keep his promise. Meyer was outraged and publicly offered $10,000 to anyone who could produce convincing evidence he and Hanna were ever together. Friends and relatives went around snickering and for a while it appeared the Guggenheims would lose another $100,000 to a fortune hunter. In the end the judge threw out the case on the basis of insufficient evidence. (Later Meyer's granddaughter Peggy asserted that Hanna McNamara was definitely not his mistress; his cook was, and had been, even before Barbara's death.)

In 1904, he began to fail. He had prostate trouble and other old men's ailments. He stayed at home. Doctors, friends, associates, relatives came and went. He had two operations, both in his own home: he was suspicious of hospitals. Now, while convalescing, he could reminisce about his life, about his native Lengnau, and the hard early years in Philadelphia. Yes, he had stepped on many toes, and on many heads, on his way to wealth. As had the good Christians of the Surb valley stepped on the heads of his forefathers for generations. But he had made up for all that.

On Thanksgiving Day, 1904, Meyer underwent his final prostate operation. All his life he had distrusted outsiders and he was not about to develop a sudden faith in them now. He would *not* have his operation in a hospital, a captive of all those Christians; he would have it in his own home. This was agreed. When the surgeons suggested he take an anesthetic, he protested again, telling them there were "two things you couldn't sell a Jew—anesthetics and life insurance," and lay back on the dining-room table to await the knife. Agreed again. No anesthetic. As the surgeons cut in he called for a cigar. One of his choicest was thrust in his mouth. Then, as they cut deeper, he asked for music. The nurses put a record on the great tubalike phonograph. Puffing on his cigar and listening to the music—was it his favorite, Wagner?—Meyer suffered the painful operation to the end, without losing consciousness.

His recovery was slow, however, and before long he had a bad cold. The doctors ordered him to go to Palm Beach. He spent a few days there at the Royal Poinciana Hotel, did not get any better, and was then taken to a rented cottage on Lake Worth. There he died on March 15, at seventy-eight.

The funeral at Temple Emanu-El was attended by all his children, in-laws, and grandchildren, and by the elite of New York Jewry, Jacob Schiff, the Kuhns, the Loebs, the Seligmans, the Strauses, among others. Then he was buried beside Barbara in the mausoleum at Salem Fields. There were the expected eulogies, the tributes. It was proclaimed that he had not "built upon the prostrate forms of others," but most people in Temple Emanu-El that day, who had known Meyer well, and knew what the business world was all about, knew that he could not have accomplished what he had accomplished without injuring other men. Or, at least, without profiting from the sufferings of others. Hadn't he made his first significant money from the Civil War—which he had not volunteered to fight in? Wasn't it the capital thus accumulated that enabled him to become first an importer of spices, next a manufacturer of lye, then a speculator in railroad shares, and finally an investor in lead and silver mines? And had he ever shown the slightest sympathy for a mine owner or a smelter owner he forced out of business? Or for an underpaid worker who wanted more money, or for an overworked miner who wanted to work fewer hours? Or for a destitute Mexican peon who was too old or too tired to work Meyer's furnaces in 115-degree heat? No, it is only by building on the "prostrate forms of others" that great fortunes are made.

Meyer's last will and testament revealed an estate of $2,256,280 in real estate and stocks and bonds held in New York State, plus the by-now nearly exhausted A. Y. and Minnie Mines in Colorado, which he had been leasing for $60,000 a year. Most of his holdings in New York were in American Smelting and Refining preferred and common stock, railroad bonds, and stock in Tennessee Iron and American Tobacco. The greater part of his estate he left to his daughters, Rose Loeb and Cora Rothschild, and to Nettie Gerstle, a granddaughter by his deceased daughter, Jeannette. Eighty thousand dollars went to various Jewish charities. Nothing to speak of went to his sisters' families in Philadelphia, only a

$10,000 bequest to a nephew, Leon Beyle. By then the poor relations had been largely forgotten and their tracks covered up. The A. Y. and the Minnie were left to all nine surviving children, to "share and share alike."

On the surface not an exceptionally large estate. Only $2,256,280 plus the two leased and much-depleted mines. But, in addition to what he left outright, Meyer also left seven multimillionaires, all of whom he had set up in business with substantial initial stakes. At the time of Meyer's death in 1905, his seven sons' holdings in Guggenex, M. Guggenheim's Sons, and American Smelting and Refining amounted, on paper, to no less than $75 million, or over $9 million for each son. In terms of the dollar's purchasing power in 1905 relative to that of 1976, this would be roughly equivalent today to an aggregate of $476 million and $68 million for each son. [All dollar amounts for the years 1848 to 1974 have been converted in terms of their purchasing power in 1976 dollars].

CHAPTER 9

ON THEIR OWN

Back to the office. Back to the mines and smelters. On to Utah, Nevada, New Mexico, the Yukon, Alaska, Mexico again, the Congo, Bolivia, Chile. On to more and more copper, the first gold, more and more silver and lead, the first diamonds, the first tin, more copper, more silver, more gold.

A few days after Meyer's funeral the Guggenheim boys went back to their desks and business as usual or, rather, business with a vengeance.

Dan, as chairman and president of American Smelting and Refining, had two desks to go back to, one at ASARCO headquarters, and one upstairs in the same building, 165 Broadway, in the Partners' Room of M. Guggenheim's Sons. The two offices were connected by a secret stairway that opened on both ends to camouflaged doors of wall paneling hung with paintings. (Dan did not always want his left hand, ASARCO, to know what his right hand, the Family, was up to.) Isaac, Solomon, Murry, and Simon occupied the other desks at M. Guggenheim's Sons. There were no places in the room for the two defectors, Ben and Will.

From this dark-wood, leather-chaired stronghold in downtown New York, the Guggenheim boys ruled their ever-expanding empire.

Meyer's greatest asset, besides his own drive and brains, had been his sons. They had been his chief instrument of power. Given his paranoid nature, his business partners had to be blood relatives, people in whom he could place absolute trust, or else he could not work with them. His faithful and ever-fertile Barbara had given him no fewer than seven partners. Without them he could never have realized his grandiose ambition of dominating mining and smelting in North America.

Meyer was dead. Dan was quick to fill the void. Immediately upon his father's death, he assumed full and unqualified leadership of the family and its business interests. Dan, as we have seen, had already assumed the burden of family leadership even before Meyer's death—it had been he, primarily, who had forced Will to divorce his bride of a few weeks—but now he took over as absolute monarch. As chairman of the board and undisputed leader of the family, his word in matters Guggenheim was uncontested, as good as Guggengold or the tablets of Moses.

Daniel Guggenheim, destined to become one of the greatest industrial leaders of all time—his policies were to mean economic life or death to entire nations—was very short, barely over five feet, very quick and agile, bold and adventurous, and was possessed of a truly demonic energy.

Not long after Daniel Guggenheim took control of ASARCO he went out on a limb, not the first, and certainly not the last, he would go out on—the Guggenheims were forever going out on limbs—and hired for Guggenex a celebrated mining engineer by the name of John Hays Hammond at the then-highest salary ever paid an employee of a corporation in world history: $250,000 a year, plus a 25 percent interest in all mining properties Hammond discovered and the Guggenheims later acquired.

The year was 1903. When there were no income taxes and the dollar could purchase much more than it can today, $250,000 a year would be roughly equivalent to $1.6 million a year today, perhaps more. The 25 percent interest in properties discovered could, in terms of relative purchasing power, amount to anywhere from $12 million to $32 million a year for Hammond today.

Hammond's job was to comb the planet in search of rich ore bodies. By the time the Guggenheims got to him he had compiled a glittering record. He had, among his many achievements, rediscovered and reopened the fabled King Solomon's mines in Rhodesia, which he had estimated had produced over $100 million worth of gold before the industrial era, and he had been instrumental in helping Cecil Rhodes gain control of South Africa's diamonds.

Hammond was a swashbuckling character who was just as at home camping in a remote desert wilderness, accompanied by a handful of armed native guides and a pack of purposely famished watchdogs, as he was in his ten-room gilded suite at the Waldorf-Astoria, surrounded by liveried servants uncorking bottles of champagne for his girlfriends and business associates. Usually he was roaming the untouched wastes of four continents on horse- and camelback.

It took only a little over a year for Dan's investment in Hammond to pay off. In his first year with Guggenex, Hammond made $5 million for the Guggenheims and $1,250,000 in salary and commissions for himself.

With Hammond out scouring the earth for new, undeveloped mineral deposits, the Guggenheim boys sat at their desks in lower Manhattan. By 1907, two years after Meyer's death, the Guggenheim boys had reorganized and redeployed once more, and were poised on the verge of their period of greatest expansion. Dan, a peppy fifty-one, was in full control of American Smelting and Refining, Guggenheim Brothers, Guggenex, and the family; Isaac, the arch-conservative, now fifty-three, but looking and acting much older, had been relegated to what was essentially a bookkeeper's job, treasurer of American Smelting; Murry, a shy, rather dour man of forty-nine, and Solomon, an ebullient high-liver of forty-six, were, with Dan, but not with Isaac, members of the executive committee of American Smelting and Refining, and with Dan again, composed the triumvirate that ran Guggenheim Brothers and Guggenex. Simon, forty, had just purchased himself a seat in the United States Senate—it was convenient to have a member of the family looking after things in Washington—and Ben, forty-two, and Will, thirty-nine, were still out of it, trying to represent something significant on their own, but not succeeding.

Ahead lay tons of gold nuggets in the Yukon River, a mountain of copper near Kennecott Creek in Alaska, a copper canyon in Bingham, Utah, mountains of tin in Bolivia, more silver and gold in Mexico, acres of diamonds in the Congo and Angola, the Chuquicamata lode in Chile.

CHAPTER 10

GUGGENMORGANS AND MORGANHEIMS

Prospectors winding their way along Alaska's Kennecott Creek had first beheld the lode as a gleaming patch of green on a treeless mountain. There, rising out of the naked Wrangell Range, was this one, emerald-crested peak, like a mirage, the Arctic equivalent of a palmless oasis in the desert. Rumors had it that the mountain was almost solid copper.

When Dan Guggenheim got wind of this tantalizing verdigris summit he sent Guggenex' top assayer, Pope Yeatman, up to examine the property. It took months for Yeatman to make his way through the roadless, uncharted wilderness. After he examined the mysterious slope, which had not one trace of vegetation on its greenish surface, he reported that the samples of ore he had taken assayed 70 to 75 percent pure copper, and that there were millions and millions of tons of it available. It was, in his estimation, one of the largest and purest deposits of copper in existence. He was not wrong. The great "Bonanza Lode" above Kennecott Creek proved to be the richest copper deposit in the world.

To mine this treasure in that high, frozen waste, transport the ore over two hundred miles to the sea, and then ship it to the Guggenheims' smelter at Tacoma, Washington, would, however, cost more than even the Guggenheims could afford, or borrow.

Their first step was to team up with one of the reigning titans of high finance, John Pierpont Morgan.

Daniel Guggenheim was the family's envoy to Morgan. Before long a deal was set. The great "Alaska Syndicate" was formed, composed of the Guggenheims, J. P. Morgan, and a hastily recruited third partner, Jacob Schiff. The Guggenheims contributed a little over a third of the capital and all the administrative and engineering know-how. Morgan and Schiff and a few of their friends put up the rest of the money. The terms of the final agreement granted the Guggenheims the lion's share of the profits. The syndicate's first project would be the mining of Kennecott Mountain.

The difficulties of the undertaking were of staggering dimensions. First, a two hundred-mile, $25 million railroad had to be constructed over vast river deltas, over moving glaciers, through deep, unexplored canyons, from the sea to Kennecott Mountain. Then a multimillion-dollar breakwater had to be thrown across the exposed bay at the marine terminus of the railroad, and a harbor built to accommodate large freighters. Then a steamship line had to be bought or formed to transport the copper ore to the Guggenheim smelter at Tacoma. To fuel the mining camp, the railroad, the harbor, the steamships, accessible coal mines had to be found, bought, and developed. To construct camps and warehouses, make railroad pilings and scaffolding, build mining sheds, huge forests had to be bought or leased and cut down. And all this was done in one of the bleakest wildernesses on the face of the earth.

By the end of 1911, the Alaska syndicate counted a net profit of $1,658,000 from the first mining of Bonanza Lode ore. By the end of 1912 Kennecott had paid dividends of $3 million to Morgan, Schiff, and the

Guggenheims. But that was just the beginning, a faint glimmer of things to come. World War I was not far off and the Bonanza Lode and its adjacent mines, supplying the Allies with most of their high-grade copper, would rain such tons of money down upon the Guggenheims as to cause them actual embarrassment. By 1918 the Guggenheims had extracted over ten times as much money from Kennecott alone as the Russians had received for all of Alaska fifty years before.

Spurred on by their success, Guggenmorgan began buying up more potential Alaskan wealth, more coal mines, more iron mines, forests upon forests without end. If someone, something, did not stop them, the Guggenmorgans and Morganheims would someday own *all* the wealth of Alaska.

Alaska in the early years of the twentieth century had become the last frontier of the American Dream, the last place where an American could feel truly free, the last place where a man could go with just his own wits and carve out an honest, abundant, independent, self-reliant life for himself. Thus the press, the few environmentalists active at the time, and a significant portion of the American people began to vigorously oppose the Guggenmorganization of Alaska.

No one was more vociferous on behalf of conserving Alaska for the Americans rather than the Guggenmorgans than the idealistic Gifford Pinchot, who had been chief of the Forest Service division of the Department of Agriculture under Presidents McKinley, Theodore Roosevelt, and Taft. Since 1908 he had also been head of the National Conservation Commission.

Gifford Pinchot believed with all his heart and mind that the riches that lay under and upon the American earth belonged to all the American people and should not be owned or controlled by a handful of "industrial spoilers" as he termed them. The railroad to Kennecott and the mining of Kennecott was already a *fait accompli,* so he could not do much about that. But what he could do something about, he thought, was a Guggenheim-Morgan plan to buy 950,000 acres of virgin forest and a 60-million-ton coal deposit, the latter worth approximately $25 million.

There followed a prolonged battle in the corridors of governmemt and the courts of law. The debate drew the attention of the entire national press. The monsters Guggenmorgan and Morganheim appeared in more and more cartoons. The battles dragged on. . . .

Fortunately for the Guggenheims, the family had an ace in the hole. Simon, second youngest of the seven brothers, was, by the time of the controversy, a United States senator. Simon did not accomplish very much during his six years in Washington, but he did manage to squelch the conservationist Pinchot forces. In the end, Guggenmorgan and Morganheim remained lords of Alaska, as secure in their possession of the Great Land as the *Landvogt* of Baden had been in his possession of the Jews of Lengnau only sixty-five years before.

CHAPTER 11

MINING THE GLOBE

W hile the Guggenmorgans were pushing into Alaska, the Guggenheims were simultaneously pushing into just about everywhere else. There were four brothers propelling the ever-expanding empire from New York and one moving an occasional mountain in Washington. The two on the sidelines, Ben and Will, would, in addition to cashing in their ever-increasing dividends, also contribute their own two cents of advice from time to time. The mere conquest of Alaska was not nearly enough to occupy five, and sometimes seven, Guggenheim brains. There were so many other tantalizing opportunities to be taken at the flood. There were rivers of gold in the Yukon, more copper in Utah, Nevada, and Chile. There was tin in Bolivia and Malaya. There was more gold, silver, and lead in Mexico; there were acres and acres of diamonds waiting to be plucked from the Belgian Congo and Angola.

The Guggenheim business strategy, devised by Dan and rubberstamped by the others, was essentially threefold:

One, and this would always be a cardinal principle of the Guggenheims, *you always go in for big development when the business barometer is low.* (They had gone into Alaska at the time of the worst crash since the Civil War.)

Two, and using Wagnerian symbolism this might be called the Nibelheim philosophy, *you always use the cheap labor and raw materials of undeveloped countries to depress your own country's industries, to force its wages and prices down until they are so cheap you can afford to buy them up and sew them into your own monopoly.*

Three, in the metals industry *there was no use competing unless you owned everything from mine mouth to finished product. You had to own the mine and processing plant and control the marketing of the metal.*

This triple strategy worked so well wherever and whenever it was put into practice that it did not take the Guggenheims long to realize that it could be applied to control not merely the mineral wealth of North America, but also that of the entire world. Consequently, that is precisely what the family set out to do.

The American people, through their elected representatives, solemnly professed to the world in speech after speech that America sought no man's territory, that America had no imperialistic aims. Yet all the while, through the efforts of men like the Guggenheims, America was steadily building up the greatest commercial empire on the face of the earth. America covets no land, but Sherwin-Williams paints "cover the earth"; we are shown the ads with the thick paint oozing down over South America and Africa.

Thus the American empire, the most extensive and powerful commercial and military empire in world history, was willed not by the American people or their elected representatives—but by a handful of strong-minded, talented, industrious, acquisitive people like the Guggenheims.

While the Guggenmorgans were attacking the Bonanza Lode overlooking Kennecott Creek, another combination, the Guggenryans, were conducting an operation in the Congo and Angola which was, and would continue to be, equally lucrative. The story, in brief, is this:

Leopold II, King of the Belgians, wanted to organize a company to develop the natural resources of the Congo, known in those days—the early twentieth century—as Leopold of Belgium's personal slave camp.

Leopold, terribly busy keeping his mistresses happy, summoned the great American capitalist, Thomas Fortune Ryan, to take charge of realizing his ambitions. When Leopold proposed to him that he help develop the natural resources of the Congo, the discussion eventually turned to metals, and Ryan, being more of an expert in commodities, suggested that the Guggenheims handle this sphere of activity. The King, well aware of who the Guggenheims were, was in complete agreement.

Upon his return to America, Thomas Fortune Ryan summoned Dan Guggenheim to his Fifth Avenue mansion. The result of their meeting was the formation of the Société Internationale Forestière et Minière du Congo, often referred to as "Forminière." King Leopold retained 25 percent interest in the company for himself, 25 percent was kept by the kingdom of Belgium, and the remaining 50 percent was split fifty-fifty between Ryan and the Guggenheims.

The final agreement granted the Guggenheims and Ryan exclusive rights to prospect for minerals in an area roughly forty-five times as large as Belgium, with the proviso that the mines found and developed could be worked by Ryans and Guggenheims for ninety-nine years.

Subsequently Guggenryans formed two companies: the American Congo Company, which would exploit minerals, and the Intercontinental Rubber Company, which would exploit commodities. Dan and his brothers were in charge of the first, Ryan the second.

The Guggenheim boys always liked to have lots of different metals from lots of different places cooking in their furnaces at the same time. If one mix did not boil into profits, another would. And so while the great Alaskan and Congo gambles were being risked, for richer or for poorer, the boys mounted still another gigantic operation, this time in the Klondike, to dredge the gold-bearing sands of the Yukon River's fabled Bonanza Creek. Gold worth $100 million had already been sifted and sucked out of these sands, and Hammond the Omniscient estimated there was at least another $100 million left to be taken.

Consequently, it was not long after Hammond's appraisal that the Guggenheims began moving hundreds of laborers and tons and tons of heavy equipment into yet another vast, empty wilderness. Dan and Sol personally made the long trip north to inspect the operation. In time, several colossal river dredges—the largest ever constructed up to that day—were erected from matériel that had traveled in hundreds of wooden crates for five thousand miles; a two-thousand-kilowatt-power hydroelectric plant was built, and living quarters, warehouses, laboratories, sheds, and offices were put up along sixty-two miles of Yukon River flume, ditch, and pipeline. For a while the venture paid off. By 1916 the Yukon Gold Company had disbursed $7,583,000 in dividends to the Guggenheims and other stockholders, but finally labor and development costs became so high that they cut profits to nil and the operation had to shut down. The dredges were then towed to Malaya and set to bringing up tin instead of gold. They are still dredging, in what is known today as Malaysia, under the banner of Guggenheim-controlled Pacific Tin.

The Yukon Gold Company was the first Guggenheim *partial* success. Until then, everything had been Midas-touch, inexhaustible bonanza. From now on there would also be some failures.

The family had realized that the increasing use of electric cables would make copper one of the most sought-after metals in the world. The Guggenheims never did anything halfway. Not with Dan in charge. If they could, they would corner all the copper in the world. And so, in 1907, the year of a severe stock-market crash (remember, always go in for big development when the business barometer is low), they had bought a substantial interest in the Braden mine in Chile, and then in 1910, they had made their grandest gamble of all by buying the great Chuquicamata copper mine, 9,500 feet up in the Chilean Andes, for $25 million. Again the extraordinary Guggenheim luck had held.

But again the difficulties in exploiting the property were overwhelming. Chile was a poor, undeveloped country with no roads or rails in the interior, no electricity, except in the largest coastal cities, and very little water. Chuquicamata was forty-five miles from the nearest water supply, and fifty-five miles from the nearest source of electric power. It was one of the driest and most desolate places in South America, a vast waste of sand and rocks.

The Guggenheims eventually overcame all difficulties, as they had in Colorado, Mexico, Alaska, the Congo, Angola, and Utah, and made Chuquicamata into the most productive and profitable copper mine on earth.

By the first rumblings of World War I, the Guggenheims were in control of 75 to 80 percent of the world's silver, copper, and lead and could literally dictate the price of all three of these essential metals.

CHAPTER 12

HARVEST OF WAR

Daniel Guggenheim had known war was brewing and had positioned himself well to collect maximum rewards from the upheaval for the House of Guggenheim.

When hostilities actually broke out, he found himself taking the baths at Carlsbad, his favorite German spa. Hurriedly he returned to the United States and announced breathlessly to the press: "For the first time the world's marts lie at our feet uncontested. Our European competitors are hopelessly crippled for the time being and it is up to us to reap the benefits."

If the rest of America, always slow to understand the implications of war, was not ready to reap the benefits, at least Dan was. Kennecott had already swung into full production. The vast open pits of Bingham Canyon were, amid intermittent guerrilla warfare between miners and state troopers, also in full production. The smaller mines in Nevada, New Mexico, and Chile were churning away. Now, with constant prodding, Dan was readying Chuquicamata to be the greatest producer of them all.

By now Daniel Guggenheim was listened to in all the halls of power of the Western world. His business policies could affect the destinies of entire nations, such as Chile, and it was said he could make or break a government with a telegram.

Napoleon had once declared that the three most important things in war were money, money, and money. The Guggenheims were ready with money also. The firm of M. Guggenheim's Sons was one of the first corporations in America to subscribe to J. P. Morgan's $500 million Anglo-French war loan of 1915. The Germans had no idea what an enemy they had in Guggenmorgan. And Dan's wife, Florence, went out and personally sold $4 million worth of war bonds.

By the time of the loan, the first big new orders for Guggenheim copper began coming in from Britain and France. The Guggenheims were not caught napping. On March 1, 1915, mighty Chuquicamata finally moved into full production. Braden Copper, the family's smaller operation at Rancagua, Chile, was already producing. In Alaska, the fabulous Bonanza Lode of Kennecott was producing, in record volume, the purest copper the world had ever seen. Soon the Guggenheims were shipping hundreds of millions of dollars' worth of copper to England and France.

The unprecedented wartime demand for Guggenheim copper resulted, among other things, in the need for a reorganization of M. Guggenheim's Sons. Accordingly, on March 7, 1916, the old firm and Guggenex were dissolved and a new partnership formed which called itself "Guggenheim Brothers." The partners were Daniel, Solomon, Murry, Simon, and Isaac plus an injection of fresh new blood—Dan's young son Harry, aged twenty-six, and Murry's boy, Edmond, twenty-eight, and one outsider, William C. Potter, a former vice-president of Morgan Guaranty who had collaborated with the Guggenheims in Alaska. The organization of Guggenheim-controlled American Smelting and Refining remained substantially the same.

During the years 1915 to 1918 the Guggenheim mines and smelters worked night and day at top capacity. In 1916 alone American Smelting and Refining sold $234 million worth of metal to Britain and France. By the end of the war Guggenheim coppers—not to mention Guggenheim leads and silvers—had paid more than $210 million in dividends, or $52 million a year.

At the height of the war the Guggenheims found themselves much criticized in the press and in the halls of Congress for being profiteers. This criticism was applied, by extension, to the Jewish people, since the Guggenheims had become, by then, perhaps America's most prominent Jewish family.

There was also widespread suspicion that the German-Jewish plutocracy—so devoted to German culture—secretly favored Germany in the war and was also helping the Bolsheviks undermine the tsar.

As a consequence of these criticisms and suspicions, a wave of anti-Semitism broke over America that threatened to erase many of the social gains Jews had made since the turn of the century.

The press, Congress, the people, and finally President Wilson himself demanded that they lower their prices. At this the Guggenheims were quick to argue that the law of supply and demand held even in war. In the end, it was only when a furious Wilson threatened nationalization of the metals industries that the Guggenheims agreed to peg the price of copper at 23.5 cents a pound, when the price could easily have risen to over 30 cents. The prewar level had been 12 to 14 cents a pound.

When the smoke of World War I drifted away from the battlefields, council chambers, mines, smelters, and factories, the Guggenheims, though scarred by many battles—military, economic, political—emerged vastly, inconceivably rich.

How rich? It is difficult to say. It is not easy to assign precise worth to mines, which deplete in value much more rapidly than other assets. Averaging out a composite of several historians' and economists' estimates, and judging, as carefully as possible, the evidence at hand, we can put the family's net worth at the end of the war as something in the neighborhood of from $250 million to $300 million, or from $850 million to $1 billion in today's money, which was enough to rank them, financially, second only to the Rothschilds among Jewish families.

This enormous economic advancement, of course, left the family extremely vulnerable.

Though the Guggenheims considered themselves patriots who had supplied the Allies with vital raw materials without which they might not have been able to win the war, others considered them merciless Shylocks, exacting every pound of flesh for their metals.

Foremost among these accusers was Henry Ford, an admitted anti-Semite. Not long after the war ended, Ford—whose immortal utterance was "History is bunk"—published the spurious, scurrilous "Protocols of the Elders of Zion" for the first time in America in his privately owned paper, the *Dearborn Independent*. The "Protocols" was essentially an inaccurate survey of Jewish history, which assigned the Jews the diabolical ambition of wanting to rule the world.

In more or less the same breath—at least in the same publication—Ford asserted that men like himself, who made factories, really owned them, but the exploiters of mines and other natural resources, like the Guggenheims, were profiteering from property that really belonged to all. In Ford's own words: "Why should such men as the Guggenheims be paid for ore in the ground in the state of nature?"

The Guggenheims took this slur in stride, as they had taken countless others, ever since they were hounded out of Guggenheimb, Germany, and Lengnau, Switzerland, and forced to emigrate to Philadelphia.

So far as they were concerned, they had done a lion's share in "making the world safe for democracy," and were entitled to their rewards.

CHAPTER 13

THE GREAT SCHISM

Meyer Guggenheim had always urged his seven sons "to be as one." "Together," he had told them, time and time again, enacting the fable of the sticks and the bundle of sticks, "you will be invincible. Singly, each of you may be easily broken."

It took many years for the Guggenheims to understand fully the implications of this paternal admonition. When they finally did understand, it was too late. The sticks had come apart, sone were easily broken, and they could not be bundled together again.

The first defection in the ranks—Will and Ben dropping out of active partnership in M. Guggenheim's Sons in 1901—did not hurt the family too much at the time. But it was to have serious consequences in the future.

The reader must recall that the Guggenheims ran two organizations. One was the family-owned Guggenheim Brothers, a sort of holding company, and the other was the giant New York Stock Exchange-listed American Smelting and Refining Company.

A curious relationship existed between the two business concerns. Daniel was chairman and president of American Smelting and Refining, and also chief operating partner of Guggenheim Brothers. A secret stairway, still in existence, connected Dan's office in American Smelting with the Partners' Room of Guggenheim Brothers, one floor above. The door to this stairway opened onto a length of wood paneling, hung with paintings, in the Guggenheim Partners' Room. Evidently Dan scurried back and forth between his two offices, using only this stairway, and not the principal means of access serviced by elevators.

This fact attains some significance only when we consider that in 1922 the board of directors of American Smelting and Refining accused the Guggenheims of quietly and surreptitiously milking the company, and at a stockholders' meeting had the family voted out of control. The charge was that Guggenheim Brothers had milked American Smelting and Refining by letting it carry expenses and take huge risks in the discovery and exploitation of natural resources, then to skim off the cream of those discoveries for themselves.

To be sure, several Guggenheims remained on the board, but they and their allies were no longer a majority. Not long after this unpleasantness, Daniel Guggenheim "retired" from his eminences in the company, and brother Simon became president of American Smelting and Refining, assisted by Dan's son-in-law, Roger W. Straus.

The matter was much publicized in the press, which noted that though the Guggenheims still played an important role in American Smelting, all they actually controlled any longer was Guggenheim Brothers.

Guggenheim Brothers was, however, still a very powerful outfit. The partners owned, among lesser properties, tens of thousands of shares of Kennecott Copper Corporation, Utah Copper Corporation (Bingham Canyon), Diamang (diamonds in Angola), almost all of huge, seemingly inexhaustible Chuquicamata, and a huge block of American Smelting and Refining.

In 1923 the Guggenheim partnership was composed of Daniel, Murry, Solomon, Simon, and William C. Potter, representing the old guard, and Harry and Edmond, representing the new generation. Isaac had died the year before at sixty-eight.

By 1923 the older brothers, smarting from their loss of control of American Smelting and Refining, had begun to think about taking their profits, while they were still able, and retiring or, at least, semiretiring, and turning over most of the work to the young bloods, Harry and Edmond.

It was precisely at this time that Anaconda Copper Corporation came forward with an offer to buy 2 million of Chile Copper's 3.8 million shares for $70 million cash.

Receiving $70 million clear, while still keeping 1.8 million shares, was most tantalizing, especially to the older Guggenheims. Dan, Sol, Murry, and Simon had been through the wars and wanted to retire someday on a little more than paper. Accordingly, Dan circulated a memorandum among the partners expressing favorable interest in Anaconda's proposal and calling for a meeting to consider it.

The meeting took place around the long mahogany table in the Partners' Room on the thirty-fifth floor of the Equitable Building, the same table around which Meyer had assembled his seven boys some forty years . before and talked of bundles of sticks. It turned out to be the most violent, momentous partners' meeting in Guggenheim Brothers' history.

The two sides were soon drawn. On the side of selling: the oldsters, Dan, Murry, Simon, and William C. Potter. On the side of holding on: the youngsters, Dan's son Harry, and Murry's son, Edmond. Sol, who sympathized with the young, and was usually reluctant to sell anything, tended toward holding on as the discussion began.

The meeting lasted hours and hours. Dan, heading the old guard, argued passionately for not holding out for the top dollar, for taking a healthy profit and running. Did the younger ones have any conception of what a *risk* their fathers had taken, developing a mine 9,500 feet up in the Chilean Andes, with no readily available water or power, no roads, no trained labor force? That they were now able to collect $70 million for this gigantic gamble was too good to be true, much too good to turn down.

But to the young bloods, selling the richest copper mine on earth, for *any* price, was sheer folly, was madness. Steadfastly they opposed it, backed up by Sol. If Chuquicamata was sold, why should they remain partners of Guggenheim Brothers? What would there be left?

Discussions, arguments . . . the Partners' Room of Guggenheim Brothers that day shook with the conflict between young and old. Little Dan pounding on the table, getting up, storming around the room, his son Harry, tall and blue-eyed, trying to shout his father down. Stolid Murry seconding Dan. Edmond seconding Harry. Small, dark Simon repeating over and over again; "There's no choice but to sell, there's no choice but to sell." The good-natured Sol trying to pacify both sides.

In the end the old had their way. Dan, Murry, Simon, and William C. Potter drew Sol over to their side and voted down the young five to two. A two-thirds majority was all that was needed according to the articles of partnership.

Thus was the vast and rich-beyond-all-imagining Chuquicamata sold by the Guggenheims to Anaconda Copper on March 1, 1923. (Anaconda then ran it most profitably until it was nationalized by Salvador Allende in 1970. Under the subsequent military dictatorship the company did not get back the mine but did receive some compensation.)

And thus did Harry and Edmond, a few days later, carry out their threat and resign from Guggenheim Brothers. Their fathers and uncles had had their way, but in so doing they had lost the business allegiance of their sons. Losing that allegiance spelled the death of Guggenheim Brothers, but no one in the family realized it at the time.

At the time of the Great Sale, Dan was sixty-seven, Murry was sixty-five, Sol sixty-two, Simon fifty-six. Each was worth around $50 million. Harry, thirty-three, and Edmond, thirty-five, were living off funds given to them by their fathers.

Not long after the controversial sale Dan suddenly bounced back from "retirement" and from the ignominy into which he had been relegated by his son and his nephew, and he declared that Chuquicamata profits would not be salted away but would be ventured into still another field, nitrates. You could not keep Dan down for long.

"Chilean nitrates," he exulted, "will make us rich beyond the dreams of avarice!"

Dan was wrong. When the family strayed from metals and went into chemicals they suddenly lost their Midas touch: the nitrates did not turn into gold.

The Guggenheim family was now divided. The bundle held only four sticks, Dan, Murry, Sol, and Simon. Isaac and Ben were dead. Will was totally alienated, and had been for some time. Sol was not nearly as enchanted by big business as he had been before: he would soon branch out into art. And Harry and Edmond, temporarily fed up with their elders, were going their own separate ways.

From now on the Guggenheims, acting more as individuals than as a family, would devote themselves more to spending than to making.

They had a great deal of money to spend and, with the exception of a few inevitable playboys, they would spend it even more grandly and courageously, and certainly more nobly, than they had made it.

CHAPTER 14

A FORTUNE TO SPEND

The plump, middle-aged lady walks into the corset shop and asks for "one of those Guggenheim foundations." The slender young woman, newborn infant in her arms, walks into the foundation office and is greeted with: "Frankly, Miss Ellis, the Guggenheim Foundation had been led to expect a book of poems."

The cartoons, which appeared in the mid-1930s, were in agreeable contrast, so far as the Guggenheims were concerned, to those that had appeared before and during World War I depicting the family as vultures tearing at the carcass of Mexico and polar bear monsters about to gobble up all of Alaska. They reflected the great change that had occurred in the Guggenheim style and ethos since the family had acquired its place in the capitalistic sun. Now the Guggenheims were no longer heartless exploiters of man and nature, but respected benefactors of humanity, or, as in the case of Ben and Will, harmless spendthrifts whom one could criticize but not dislike.

No sooner had the Guggenheims reaped their immense harvest from World War I, and ascended into the heaven of the American superrich, than they began to move from the Jersey Shore to the North Shore of Long Island, from Elberon, the Jewish Newport, to more fashionable Sands Point, near Port Washington, preserve of people like the Goulds, Whitneys, Pratts, Astors, Woolworths . . . and the setting for Fitzgerald's *The Great Gatsby*.

William, who was to adopt the Fitzgeraldian pseudonym Gatenby Williams, was the first to move, followed by Isaac, Daniel, Solomon, and, much later, Simon.

As the war was drawing to a close Will bought a fifty-acre estate on the Sound—a large white Colonial house with farm—and promptly began throwing huge Gatsby-like lawn parties there under striped tents. Isaac then bested him by building, in 1918-19, a vast, ornate, $2 million, forty-room Italian Renaissance palace on a hill overlooking Hempstead Harbor, adjoining the Woolworth property. He surrounded his palace with marble fountains and statues, carefully manicured Italian gardens, a nine-hole golf course, and a hundred more acres of pine and oak woods. He called it Villa Carola. Later, Solomon, who liked to summer in Britain, renting a different castle each year, would buy the place from Isaac's estate for $610,000 cash and rename it Trillora Court. In the meantime, Daniel outdid everyone, including his WASP neighbors, by purchasing the kingly, unfinished Castlegould from the financier Howard Gould. A colossal stone edifice in a mixture of Jacobean and Gothic styles, the main house—there were several houses on the property—contained seventy rooms, was surrounded by a moat, approached by a drawbridge, and was situated on 350 acres of farm and woodlands bordering the Harriman estate and, like Villa Carola, overlooking Hempstead Harbor.

Ensconced in these monuments to their power and authority, amid the bastions of some of the more formidable names in the American WASP aristocracy, with rivers of money steadily pouring into their accounts from all over the globe, the Guggenheims could finally lean back and enjoy the exalted status they had won among American capitalists.

They had made a lot of money, but they had made much of it at the expense of the planet, often to the ruination of vast areas. Piles of debris and broken rocks, and heaps of slag, are all that remain of former Guggenheim operations in Colorado. In Bingham Canyon, Utah, where the Guggenheims created the world's first open-pit copper mine, there is now a vast devastation, the earth so gouged and lacerated as to seem the scene of some cosmic disaster. Kennecott: an entire mountain destroyed in Alaska. Chuquicamata: an entire mountain destroyed in Chile. Rivers everywhere contaminated with the detritus of Guggenheim mines and smelters. Yes, the Guggenheims had made a lot of money, but what respect had they had in their relentless pursuit of wealth for the rights of mountains and rivers and the rights of men and women to enjoy them?

They had made a great deal of money, but what had they done for beauty, justice, truth; what had they done to add to the joys, or to alleviate the sufferings, of their fellow man?

Not very much. In fact, a good case could have been made—and was, by many journalists and biographers—that much of the Guggenheims' colossal fortune had been made at the cost of grievous human suffering. Furthermore, had their exploitive undertakings enhanced the earth and its life, or had they had the opposite effect and changed "the soft airs and green mosses of verdant valleys" into smoke, slag, and filth?

To be sure, and fair, they had already been charitable to a certain extent. Mother Barbara, it will be recalled, had sought to instill a spirit of charity in her children from the very beginning, and they had responded first by erecting memorials to Barbara's and Meyer's lives, and then by donating large sums in their memory to Mount Sinai Hospital in New York, the Schweizerische Israelitisches Alterasyl in their ancestral Lengnau, and others. But these were relatively insignificant compared to what their resources could accomplish if put to good use, and they knew it.

Clearly it was time now to do something else with their money rather than just make it earn more money. Having gouged the earth of its resources for over forty years, wasn't it time now to begin plowing some of the wealth back?

Yes it was, and once again it was the four consuls of the Guggenheim empire—Dan, Sol, Murry, and Simon—who showed the way, Isaac and William proving to be as fainthearted in spending, unless, as in William's case, spending on women, as they had been in earning. Ben, having gone down with the *Titanic,* never got a chance to show what constructive use he would have made of *his* money.

It has been said that what makes the Guggenheim fortune different from all other American fortunes is the speed with which it was put together and the daring with which it was spent. Thus, just as they had been pioneers in business, always plunging into the unknown, constantly discovering and developing new natural resources with the most up-to-date technology, so Dan, Sol, Murry, and Simon, each in his own way, would become pioneers also in philanthropy (in a time when income and estate taxes were far from confiscatory), each finding, to his surprise, a second career for himself, one fully as exhilarating as the first, the four of them setting forth on such uncharted seas as aviation, rocketry, support of individual scientific and artistic creation, and nonobjective art, seas on which no other American millionaires had yet sailed.

Such, in fact, became the Guggenheim brothers' zeal and gusto in paying the money back, each trying to outdo the other as they had done in building their summer homes, that by 1975, fifty years after they had begun unburdening themselves of their wealth, the foundations that Dan and Harry had created were each worth four or five times as much as any of their descendants.

In the end, it was in giving, rather than in making, that the Guggenheims were to redeem their image and reputation and earn an honored place in the history of their country.

So famous and influential, in fact, became the Guggenheims' laboratories, university institutes, museums, hospitals, and foundations that by 1975 their early business career had become almost totally obliterated from the public memory, and even those thousands of people who benefited from Guggenheim munificence had little or no idea where the money originally came from.

CHAPTER 15

ISAAC: ON DAUGHTERING OUT

Of the seven Guggenheim brothers, the one who most emphatically did not lead the way in giving was Isaac.

Isaac Guggenheim, as Meyer's firstborn son, and first hope for the continuance of his business and his family, was expected to head the family, head the family business, and perpetuate the family name. He accom-

plished none of these. His life was, in a sense, a triple failure, if only because hopes for him had been so high, a long, quietly unfolding drama of
insecurities never conquered, of expectations never fulfilled. As a consequence, though he became very wealthy, riding on his more adventurous
brothers' coattails, Isaac never felt secure enough in himself to accomplish anything very significant with his money. Not even remotely approaching his four middle brothers in giving, he spent a major part of his
fortune bolstering his own insufficient ego by building, furnishing, and
maintaining his palatial $2 million Sands Point estate, and subsidizing a
worthless grandson, whom he vainly hoped would carry on the family
business, and, above all, the family name.

If, as the psychologists like to point out, every family has its victors, survivors, and victims, Isaac most certainly must be classified as something
between a survivor and a victim, though, admittedly, not so much a victim as his youngest brothers, Ben and Will.

First Isaac was victimized by his father, then by his brother Dan, then
by his wife, then by nature, then by the WASPs of Sands Point, and,
finally, after his death, by his grandson.

Victimized by his father. Born and brought up when Meyer was still far
from being a rich man, Isaac had to bear the burden of his father's high
expectations, and therefore suffer periodically from Meyer's frequent disappointments over the way he was not measuring up. As a child Isaac got
to know the whip, the belt, and the hairbrush more frequently than his
younger brothers. The slightest transgression, the slightest hint that he
might not be living up to his role as future standard-bearer of the family,
the slightest indication that he might think that roasted pigeons *would* fly
into his mouth, and he would be across Meyer's knee with his pants down
getting what was coming to him.

Nevertheless, despite the frequent punishments he had to endure for
his transgressions and, above all, for his shortcomings, Isaac was still led
to believe for much of his youth that he would someday take his rightful
place as head of the family. Until Meyer realized what sort of stuff Dan
was made of. . . .

Then, for Isaac it was downhill all the way. As soon as Dan came of
age, he quickly displaced his older brother as family leader and held that
position, undisputed, until his death.

But Dan was only one usurper Isaac had to contend with. After Dan
came five others. Murry, Sol, and Simon also proved to be stiff competition. And then, when Isaac had grown into manhood, his mother, whom
he adored, had to give all her attention to the last two upstarts, Benjamin

and William. Not to mention the three girls.

It was all too much for poor Isaac. His insecurities inevitably got the best of him. Bernard Baruch, reminiscing about the brothers Guggenheim, with whom he had transacted much lucrative business, described Isaac as "taller than the others, and perhaps the best looking, but their inferior as a businessman . . . He was a good man, Isaac, but overly conservative, and I doubt if he would have gone very far on his own."

As it happened, the strong one in the Isaac Guggenheim branch of the family turned out to be Isaac's wife. Carrie Sonneborn, daughter of a prosperous Philadelphia merchant, was a dynamic little red-headed woman with loads of excess energy and a sharp tongue. She was geared to a faster tempo than Isaac, was also more thick-skinned, and, soon after their marriage, she began bossing him around. As the years went by she put on a lot of weight, and with the authority of this extra bulk, she bossed him even more. So much did she come to boss him that Isaac was compelled to take frequent "business trips" to maintain his equilibrium and self-esteem. But, unhappy as he was, he never left her. Nor, unlike some of his brothers, did he console himself by dallying with other women. Puritanical to the core, and perhaps a bit masochistic, he took his victimization in marriage on the chin, just as he had taken his victimization in the parental nest.

If only Carrie, or God, or nature had given him a son, there would have been some compensation. Isaac desperately wanted to produce a male heir, a strong, capable son to carry on the Guggenheim name and someday take control of the Guggenheim empire. His father had expected this; he, too, had expected it, but once again, he was destined to be victimized, this time by nature. Try as he would, he and Carrie were unable to produce other than three daughters. Healthy, vigorous daughters, but still only daughters. Their names were Beulah, Edyth, and Helene. Isaac loved them, but he could never get over the disappointment that at least one of them was not a boy.

Fortunately, his three daughters married well and he was able to project his dynastic ambitions onto his sons-in-law, and finally onto one of his grandchildren. Beulah married a New York businessman by the name of William I. Spiegelberg, and glory be to Jehovah, had a *son*, William L. Spiegelberg, Jr. Edyth married the wealthy banker turned naval officer, Louis M. Josephthal, founder of Josephthal & Company, investment bankers, who eventually became Admiral Josephthal, and Helene, after marrying and divorcing Edmund Haas, married Lord Melvill Ward of Great Britain.

When William I. Spiegelberg, Jr. grew into young manhood, Isaac, with pathetic insistence, convinced him—and his parents—to change his name to Isaac Guggenheim II. It took some convincing. At first, Spiegelberg senior opposed the idea and was seconded by his son. But Isaac held the trump card: money, inheritance. If Spiegelberg junior would change his name to Isaac Guggenheim II he would receive a major legacy from Isaac's estate, about $5 million. Otherwise, little or nothing. This was enough to tip the scales, and, after the necessary documents were drawn up and the young man was shown the will, William I. Spiegelberg, Jr. accepted his bribe and duly changed his name to Isaac Guggenheim II.

With that all-important piece of dynastic business settled, Isaac turned his remaining energies to what would be his most enduring achievement, the construction, immediately after the war, of his princely $2 million, 205-acre Villa Carola, at Sands Point, a villa that would cost at least $6.7 million to build today, probably more.

Yes, now he would build a monument that would fittingly proclaim the power and glory of the House of Guggenheim to the world. After securing his majestic hilltop site, he summoned the foremost architects and interior decorators of the day and drew up plans. It was decided to reproduce, with a few variants, a great Italian country villa in high Renaissance style. The outer walls would be of terracotta, the roof of red tile, and there would be an observation tower and a porte cochere. Inside, on the main floor, long vaulted galleries, supported by marble columns with finely carved capitals, would enclose a paved court with fountain.

The house would contain forty rooms in all and would be surrounded by geometrical Italian gardens with sculpted hedges, marble statues of the Renaissance and early baroque periods, fountains, and thick groves of pine and oak. The property would be entirely surrounded by stone walls and high iron fences, and would contain also two gatehouses, a beach house, and a private yacht landing, stables for as many as twenty horses, two garages, two greenhouses, two barns, and other outbuildings to be used as servants' and groundkeepers' quarters.

While work on the place was underway, Isaac made discreet inquiries about applying for membership in the exclusive, overwhelmingly WASP Sands Point Bath and Golf Club, where he hoped to play golf, a sport he enjoyed very much. To his profound shock and dismay, he was informed he would be turned down because he was a Jew.

Victimized now by his WASP neighbors—the Woolworths and the Astors owned property adjoining his and were members of the club—Isaac's grandiose plans for Villa Carola suddenly lost their promise.

Isaac's spunk, however, was not yet all used up. After catching his breath, he reacted to the unspeakable slight by canceling much of his landscaping plans and creating his *own* private nine-hole golf course on the property. Not only that, he also hired the best golf-course designer in the country to lay out the course, ordering him to duplicate what he considered were the finest holes in the United States.

In his lordly villa Isaac Guggenheim passed the last years of his life. He and Carrie gave small, quietly sumptuous dinner parties in the gold-paneled, red-damask Louis XVI dining room. Often, in the evening, they would invite a few friends in and listen on the great living room organ to some of the finest organists of the day play Bach, Handel, and Frescobaldi. The daughters and their families would come out on weekends and during the hot summer months, and then the great marble galleries would ring to a sudden new life. Isaac liked to garden and would often personally attend to the more than one hundred potted plants surrounding his villa. During the winter he went about in heavy Scottish tweeds closely overseeing the cultivation of fresh fruits and vegetables in the greenhouses; he delighted in serving his *own* Brussels sprouts, lima beans, strawberries, and greengage plums at his 410 Park Avenue apartment when there was snow on the ground. During the summer he and Carrie and the girls would take daylong trips on the Sound in the family yacht. And, whenever he got a chance, Isaac would play golf on his magnificent course, often with brothers Solomon, Murry, and Dan. During the last two years of his life, no fewer than 18 servants and 104 grounds keepers toiled for him and his not-too-large family at Villa Carola.

But Isaac was not destined to enjoy his estate for long. He died on a visit to England in the fall of 1922, at sixty-eight, only three years after his monument was completed, leaving $18 million in securities plus Villa Carola to his heirs.

Isaac Guggenheim II was expected to go into Guggenheim Brothers and, as one of the major stockholders in Caracoles Tin, was also expected to take a leading managerial role in that company. But as it turned out, he took no interest in Guggenheim Brothers, Caracoles Tin, or even in bearing the name of Guggenheim. Five years after Isaac senior died, he sold his shares of Caracoles Tin for about $4 million, changed his name back to William I. Spiegelberg, Jr. and was banished from the heart, mind, and rolls of the Guggenheim family forever.

It took years after this double cross, after this last victimization, for the line of Isaac Guggenheim to redeem itself. Finally, generations later, a great granddaughter of Isaac's by the name of Iris Love came along who, with her grandmother Edyth's encouragement and financial aid, blossomed into one of America's most daring and accomplished archaeologists, the discoverer of the Temple of Aphrodite on Knidos, among many other ancient remains, and the identifier of the hitherto unidentified head of Aphrodite in the British Museum.

Not long after the settlement of Isaac's estate, many of Villa Carola's paintings and furnishings, which had cost around $250,000, were sold at auction for $75,000 and brother Solomon bought the villa and its grounds and golf course from the estate, again at auction, at the bargain price of $610,000 cash. Solomon and his family then lived in it, during the period in which Solomon began collecting modern art and planning his museum, until his death in 1949.

Villa Carola, bought by Thomas Watson, Jr., president of IBM, now serves as both IBM's Management Training Center and as a country club for the company's New York State employees.

CHAPTER 16

DANIEL AND FLORENCE: A FIRST STEP INTO SPACE

When Saturn V slowly lifted off its launching pad and streaked into the heavens, on its way to disgorging the space capsule that landed the first human being on the moon, few people were aware that some two hundred patents to Saturn's rocket system once belonged, in part, to a foundation created by Daniel Guggenheim in 1924.

Many of these patents had been infringed by the United States government during the acceleration of its guided missile and space programs throughout the 1940s. In 1951 Mrs. Esther C. Goddard, widow of rocket pioneer Robert H. Goddard, and the Daniel and Florence Guggenheim Foundation, which had financed Goddard, filed a joint claim for government infringement of Goddard's work. Ten years later, the litigation ended with an award of $1 million to Mrs. Goddard and the Guggenheim Foundation, the largest settlement in the history of U.S. patents.

The long suit clearly established the crucial importance of Goddard's work to the space effort, and vindicated, once and for all, Daniel Guggenheim's faith in the future of rocketry. Thirty-two years before the settlement of the patent-infringement suit, Dan had risked his reputation and his money by financing the unknown, and frequently ridiculed, rocket pioneer at a time when no one else in America, least of all in the government, was farsighted and bold enough to back him.

It was typical of Dan to spend his money chiefly on advanced technological research. Not for him, as it would be for two of his brothers, the subsidization of such elusive pursuits as nonobjective painting and avant-garde verse. No, Dan had spent a lifetime discarding obsolete technological processes and searching for, and applying, new ones. The new reduction processes he had employed at Bingham Canyon and Chuquicamata had revolutionized the copper industry. But never, in his most feverish bursts of enthusiasm, did he imagine that the money he had put into rockets in 1929 would someday result, for better or worse, in landing a man on the moon.

One of Wall Street's favorite quips during the heyday of the Guggenheims was to describe the brothers as resembling the numeral one million, a one followed by six zeros.

The characterization was, of course, unfair for the hydraheaded intelligence that was the brothers Guggenheim, unfair, decidedly, to the shrewd, genial Solomon, and, to a lesser degree, unfair also to the steady, financially acute Murry, and to the latently inspired Simon, but it did do justice to the last three zeros—Isaac, Ben, and Will—at least so far as the later development of the business was concerned, and most certainly it did justice to the one, the indomitable, the inexhaustible "Mr. Dan."

"Mr. Dan," as he was known in lower Manhattan, and in the worlds of mining and smelting, was one of those fortunate men who are able to live up to all their era expects of them. During the heroic years of Dan's career—1890–1923—the ideal American male had to be a businessman—professional men, artists, academics were not very highly regarded—who was hardworking, individualistic, resourceful, "progressive" (in business, not politics), expansionist, "moral" (sexually), and acquisitive. He was not expected to be much of a team player. He was supposed to hurl himself into the fray, no-holds-barred, and get what he could get, not exclusively for himself, of course, but for himself and his family. Dan fitted the ideal in every way. He was an indefatigable worker; often he worked sixteen hours a day. He was very independent, very autocratic, always insisting on having his own way, and almost always getting it. He was dynamic and "forward-looking": ruthlessly he would discard obsolete methods and employees. He was conservative politically, but adventurous in business.

In his vast Castlegould, which he renamed Hempstead House, Daniel Guggenheim lived like the emperor he was, surrounded by a Rembrandt, two Rubenses, a Van Dyck, herds of cattle, flocks of sheep, stables of horses, a golf course, peacocks and pheasants, servants, farmers, and grounds keepers by the score.

The great stone house with its central tower, its turreted walls and battlements was situated on a promontory of Sands Point overlooking Long Island Sound, not very far from Villa Carola.

Howard Gould had built the castle in 1901, importing twenty-eight Italian stonecutters, masons, and sculptors to carve its windows, portals, cornices, battlements, columns, capitals, towers, gargoyles. For Dan, who bought not only the castle, its outbuildings and their 350 acres, but almost all the contents of the house as well, Castlegould represented an extraordinary bargain. Dan loved the place. It was the appropriate monument, already packaged, to his grandiose ambitions and worldwide achievements. The great entrance hall, with its high-vaulted Gothic ceiling in gray stone and immense silver pipe organ, was worthy of any monarch in Europe. As was the enormous palm court with fountain on the ground floor, which Dan filled with over 150 rare plants and orchids. As were the precious sixteenth-century Flemish tapestries, the paintings—Rembrandt's "Portrait of an Old Woman," Van Dyck's "Portrait of a Nobleman," two huge canvases by Rubens. As were the guesthouses, the amusement houses, the huge stone barns, stables, and storehouses. Yes, worthy of any monarch in Europe, worthy, a dozen times over, of the *Landvogt* of Baden.

Dan built a nine-hole golf course with clubhouse (he did not even bother to try to join the local country club). He built tennis courts. He built a bowling alley. He built a beach house in rustic clapboard in which he installed a swimming pool. He built another stone barn, which he decorated with stuffed moose heads and in which his son set a brilliantly painted Sicilian cart depicting the triumphs of another monarch, Charles V, King of Spain, Italy, and the Netherlands, and Emperor of the New World. He spruced up the casino, the piggery, the hennery, the pheasant and peacock houses, and built an amusement house which he called Tally-Ho. And on his 350 acres he raised thoroughbred horses, ran a dairy, slaughtered his own cattle, hung his own beef, cured his own hams, sausage, and bacon, raised his own fruits and vegetables, canned his own preserves, killed and ate his own hens and pheasants. Seventeen servants and two hundred farmers and grounds keepers helped him in these efforts. And there were also in residence a golf pro, a tennis pro, and a riding master.

As grand patriarch of the House of Guggenheim, Dan loved nothing so much as to gather his entire immediate family aroung him at Hempstead House and enjoy watching them run around the grounds, bowl, ride, swim, play tennis and golf. By the mid-1920s that family consisted of his wife, Florence, three married children—M. Robert, Harry Frank, and Gladys—and eight grandchildren—four boys and four girls. M. Robert, by that time, had given every indication that he would turn out to be the spectacular playboy he became; Harry had proved both his mettle and his versatility by playing a vital role in readying Chuquicamata for production, earning two degrees from Cambridge, and winning his wings as a naval aviator; and the reliable, capable Gladys had shown her good judgment by marrying Roger Williams Straus, son of Oscar Straus of the R.H. Macy Strauses, U.S. ambassador to Turkey under three presidents, and member of Theodore Roosevelt's Cabinet, and the first Jew in American history to occupy a cabinet post. Reminiscing about his youth at Hempstead House, Gladys Straus' younger son, Roger W. Straus, Jr., the publisher, recalls the castle, the golf course, the stables, the tennis courts, the bowling alley, the indoor pool, the beach, and sighs: "Yeah, it's been downhill ever since."

Recognizing that Harry, not Robert, would be the one who would carry on the leadership of the House of Guggenheim after his death, Daniel, in 1923, gave Harry and his wife 90 of his 350 acres, plus $250,000 to build and furnish their own house. The result was the magnificent reproduction Norman château Falaise, perched on a cliff overlooking the Sound, and destined to play a central role in the Guggenheim drama to come.

With that bit of dynastic business taken care of, Dan turned his attentions, for the first time in his life, toward giving away some of his fortune.

For years he and his wife, Florence, had been contributing sums of money, some large, some small, to certain charities that were close to their hearts, particularly Florence's heart. In 1924 they decided to institutionalize this giving by establishing the Daniel and Florence Guggenheim Foundation for "the promotion, through charitable and benevolent activities, of the well-being of man throughout the world."

The first grants of the new foundation went mostly to organizations in which Florence was interested. These included the free Goldman Band concerts in New York's Central Park, the American Women's Association (Florence was a member of the board and a fighter for women's rights all her life), such Jewish associations as the Jewish Theological Seminary, the Hebrew Orphan Asylum, and the United Jewish Campaign (Florence took much more interest in Jewish affairs than Dan did), the New York

Botanical Gardens, the Symphony Society of New York, the Catholic Writers' Guild.

In time the Daniel and Florence Guggenheim Foundation took over total support of the popular Goldman Band concerts, which became Florence's favorite benefaction. A gracious lady with an authoritative, aristocratic bearing, taller than Dan, she attended every opening night until her death in 1945. Today the concerts are held principally in the Guggenheim bandshell in Damrosch Park, Lincoln Center.

By 1975 the foundation had made over four hundred grants to ninety-eight organizations in the United States and abroad, including hospitals and medical institutes in Chile, the Congo, and Israel.

But Dan's bold stroke in giving turned out not so much to be the Daniel and Florence Guggenheim Foundation—with its rather conventional agenda of bequests—but his creation, in 1926, of the Daniel Guggenheim Fund for the Promotion of Aeronautics.

It was his son Harry who first led Dan into the unexplored territory of aeronautics. For Dan it soon became every bit as exciting as prospecting for copper in Alaska.

Harry had become intoxicated by the possibilities of aviation as a naval pilot in World War I. When he returned to the United States after the war he was appalled to find American aviation far behind that of Europe, languishing for lack of enthusiasm and money. The government seemed to be totally ignorant of its potential, and a surprisingly conservative American public balked completely at the idea of a commercial airline.

Burning with an evangelistic passion to do something important to promote aviation, young Harry Guggenheim conceived the idea of creating a school of aeronautics at New York University, which would be the first of its kind.

On June 15, 1925, Daniel's gift of $500,000 to New York University was announced and American's first school of aeronautics was born. Encouraged by the favorable reception to his gift—the press lauded it from coast to coast—Dan then took an even bolder step and proposed to the U.S. government the establishment of a $2.5 million fund for the promotion of aeronautics.

Calvin Coolidge was President at the time and when Harry approached him with the idea, seeking official government sanction and moral support, Coolidge was at first not particularly impressed. But in the end the President gave his blessing, if somewhat half-heartedly, and on January 16, 1926, the Daniel Guggenheim Fund for the Promotion of Aeronautics was established with an initial grant of $500,000. Later, $2 million more was added, and, still later, another $475,000. The purpose of the fund was "to provide for aviation at a critical period of its infancy immediate, practical, and substantial assistance in its commercial, industrial, and scientific aspects."

Harry wasted no time in getting down to work. He opened an office on Madison Avenue, hired Ivy Lee, the public relations wizard who had done such a superb job enhancing the Rockefeller image, and by the end of 1926 the fund was financing and publicizing its first projects.

One of Harry's first projects was to popularize flying by sponsoring tours of famous aviators. After Comdr. Richard E. Byrd made his spectacular, round-trip flight over the North Pole on the *Josephine Ford,* piloted by Floyd Bennett, Harry sent Bennett out in his plane on a tour of forty U.S. cities. Later, after Lindbergh, whom Harry had encouraged, made his historic transoceanic flight, Harry financed Lindbergh's subsequent tour of forty-eight states and twenty-three state capitals in his *Spirit of St. Louis.* Harry also put Falaise at Lindbergh's disposal so that he could write *We,* the log of his flight, in peace, away from the lionizers who continually pounced on him.

The Fund financed the perfecting and manufacture of the first gyroscopic compass for aircraft; a $100,000 prize for the manufacture of the safest aircraft; a model weather-reporting service; the first American commercial airline—Western Air Express—operating between Los Angeles and San Francisco; and schools of aeronautical engineering at MIT, Georgia Tech, California Institute of Technology, the University of Washington, Stanford, Harvard, Syracuse, and the University of Michigan. It also financed the Hungarian aerospace engineer Theodor von Kármán, inventor of the wind tunnel, smooth flight, designer of the DC-3, and first recipient of the National Medal of Science.

On February 1, 1930, in the seventy-fourth and last year of Daniel Guggenheim's life, the fund was liquidated, having accomplished its goals. American aviation was at last on a firm footing; the public attitude had changed from apathetic indifference to enthusiastic support; and Harry could rejoice that he and his father had been largely responsible for these achievements.

The Guggenheims' efforts on behalf of aviation were far from over, however. While the Daniel Guggenheim Fund for the Promotion of Aeronautics was being phased out, the Daniel and Florence Guggenheim Foundation took the boldest step of all and made a grant to an obscure physics professor in Massachusetts who was experimenting with rockets he hoped would one day land a man on the moon.

The professor, Robert H. Goddard of Clark University, was a frail, solitary, withdrawn, prematurely bald genius who, since youth, had dreamed of ushering man into an era of journeys beyond the earth.

Goddard proved, for the first time, with an ingenious experiment employing a vacuum-sealed tunnel, that rockets could propel themselves in a vacuum, and hence, in outer space. Then, in July, 1929, he hauled a strange-looking contraption called "Nell" to his Aunt Effie's cabbage patch in Auburn, Massachusetts, and, amid roaring flames, sent the world's first liquid-fueled rocket into the air. The event was quickly followed by the arrival of police cars, fire trucks, ambulances. Aunt Effie's neighbors had complained of the tremendous explosion. One of them, an old lady, said that "waves" from Goddard's rocket "had pierced the apex of her heart." A Boston newspaper headlined: MOON ROCKET MISSES TARGET BY 238,799 MILES. After the smoke cleared, Goddard announced to the press: "If we had a million dollars, we *could* send a rocket to the moon, but where would we get a million dollars?"

When Lindbergh got wind of Goddard's experiment and comment he knew just where to go for the money. Daniel Guggenheim received Lindbergh in his library at Hempstead House. There, before a fire in the great high-ceilinged, wood-paneled room with its Gothic, leaded windows and shelves upon shelves of books, Lindbergh told the aging capitalist about Goddard's experiments and his future plans and needs.

After the presentation Dan asked Lindbergh, in his usual blunt manner—the same manner he had used for years in interrogating prospectors, explorers, engineers, about ore properties—"You believe these rockets have a real future?"

"Probably," Lindbergh replied. "Of course one is never certain."

"But you think so . . . and this professor of yours, he really seems capable?"

"As far as I can tell he knows more about rockets than any man in this country."

"How much does he need?"

"For a four-year project, he would need twenty-five thousand dollars a year."

"Do you think it's worth my investing a hundred thousand?"

"Well, of course, it's taking a chance. . . . But if we're ever going beyond airplanes and propellers we probably have to go to rockets. . . . Yes, I think it's worth it."

Dan trusted Lindbergh implicitly and made up his mind on the spot. He would give $50,000 "seed money," as he called it, for the first two years and $50,000 for the next two if Lindbergh and Harry and their advisory committee, reviewing Goddard's work, still agreed. Lindbergh immediately telephoned the news to Goddard. It was the first significant financial support the professor had received.

Shortly thereafter the Daniel Guggenheim Fund for the Measurement and Investigation of High Altitudes was formed, with funds advanced from the Daniel and Florence Guggenheim Foundation, and Goddard moved to Roswell, New Mexico, where more favorable conditions for firing rockets existed than in his Aunt Effie's cabbage patch.

At Roswell, Goddard rented a pueblo-style ranch house with what he called a "nice little field"—about 16,000 acres—attached. Here, on this, America's first rocket proving ground, he conducted his experiments, with support from the Daniel and Florence Guggenheim Foundation, for the next eleven years. Out of these experiments came both the bazooka and the multistage rocket.

Not long after Dan made his momentous decision to finance Goddard, the stock market crashed and J.P. Morgan, Jr. asked the Guggenheims to contribute to a $250 million pool to help shore up the market. Guggenheim Brothers, led now by Murry, for Dan and Sol had both retired, was the only nonbanking institution invited to participate in the pool, which was quite an honor, and it made its contribution, confident the market would soon turn around. When it failed to do so, a collective shudder passed through the family, for, as usual, they were way out on a limb.

The Crash was bad enough—as it turned out the Guggenheims suffered heavy paper losses in their major holdings, Braden, Kennecott, and Anaconda—but what hurt them most in 1929 was the discovery that same year, by a German scientist, of a way to make synthetic nitrate cheaply.

It will be recalled that after the Guggenheims sold their controlling interest in Chile Copper to Anaconda in 1923, against Harry's and Edmond's objections, they then went into the nitrate business.

Dan concluded a $373 million deal with the Chilean government to control all the private nitrate output of the country. Nitrate, a prime source for fertilizers, was also an essential ingredient for munitions, and given the congenital belligerency of men and nations, Dan thought it would have a limitless future. Before long, Guggenheim Brothers owned 98 percent of the nitrate in Chile and controlled 85 percent of the world's production.

For a while it looked as if the Guggenheims had cornered still another vital natural resource, but after the discovery of the synthetic process, their monopoly was broken and the world was soon flooded with cheap nitrate. Consequently, the Guggenheims lost much of their market . . . and their investment. And Harry, noting incredulously that Dan had finally lost his Midas touch, had a chance to tell him "I told you so."

By the middle of 1930 Daniel Guggenheim, who had been suffering intermittently from heart disease and ulcers for the past few years, had become aware that he was not going to live forever and that, though he was still a very wealthy man, he was definitely not going to become, as he once phrased it, "rich beyond the dreams of avarice."

About the only piece of good news Dan received at the time of the Crash was the appointment of his son Harry, by President Hoover, to be United States ambassador to Cuba. Dan had made a healthy contribution to his friend Hoover's campaign and he was gratified to see the investment paid off. It also made up, in a way, for the rift with Harry over Chile Copper and the subsequent nitrate fiasco. To celebrate the appointment Dan gave a sumptuous, gold-plate dinner for fifty at Hempstead House, after which the young ambassador was sent on his way to Havana.

As the clouds of economic depression and the failure of the nitrate gamble began more and more to darken the great halls of Hempstead House, Daniel Guggenheim suffered a further decline in his health. By the middle of September, 1930, he was feeling feeble and depressed. The end came suddenly, at eleven o'clock in the morning of September 28. Dan was talking with his doctor, Florence, and Harry when a heart attack came and he just lay back in his chair, smiled, and died.

A few days before he died he was discussing Goddard with his daughter, Gladys Straus, and said: "I'm not going to live to see it, but you'll live to see the mail shot over to Europe."

Two months after Dan died, a black Ford truck, called "the Hearse," hauled a liquid-oxygen-propelled rocket called "Nell" onto the launching pad of America's first rocket-testing center at Roswell, New Mexico. Nell was the most advanced rocket the world had ever seen and it had been assembled thanks entirely to Guggenheim money. Now it went up, thanks to Guggenheim money, to the then-unheard-of altitude of 2,000 feet, achieving a maximum speed of five hundred miles per hour, the greatest speed of a man-made contrivance up to that time. After the test, Robert H. Goddard wrote an exuberant report to Ambassador Harry F. Guggenheim in Cuba, informing him of the success of the launch.

Among the pallbearers at the packed funeral in Temple Emanu-El were Dwight W. Morrow, Bernard Baruch, John Hays Hammond, Elihu Root, Jr., and Charles Lindbergh. President Hoover, struggling with the deepening Depression, had given up going to millionaires' funerals and cabled his condolences and regrets.

Mr. Dan's net worth during the last decade of his life had oscillated between $20 million and $50 million, depending on market conditions, but when he died, eleven months after the Crash, his estate was almost insolvent. He had given away around $10 million during his lifetime . . . to members of his family and to his foundations. Now stocks were way down and the Chilean nitrate venture, in which Dan had invested several millions of his own capital, was all but dead. It took almost ten years for the estate "to come back," and when it did, it came back to something in the neighborhood of $25 million, which would be around $89 million in terms of relative purchasing power today.

Of Daniel and Florence's three children, M. Robert became one of America's most charming wastrels; Gladys, the public-spirited wife of the president of American Smelting and Refining and the president herself of the Daniel and Florence Guggenheim Foundation; and Harry, the versatile Guggenheim standard-bearer from 1930 to 1971, furtherer of his father's businesses and philanthropies, and foster father, even more than Dan, of U.S. aviation and the country's grand adventure into space.

By mid-century, Harry, using funds from his father's foundation, had established the Daniel and Florence Guggenheim Aeronautical Laboratories and Jet Propulsion Centers at Princeton and Caltech, the latter known as GALCIT, and had endowed Robert H. Goddard professorships at both institutions. By then virtually all of America's senior aerospace engineers were graduates of Guggenheim-sponsored schools.

CHAPTER 17

MURRY AND LEONIE:
CHILEAN NITRATES AND
THE CHILDREN OF NEW YORK

Murry Guggenheim, third of the sons of Meyer and Barbara, usually played it safe. In business he had the unenviable function of being the no-man of an incredibly dynamic organization, the brake on the impetuous engine Dan. Rarely, if ever, would he initiate an idea or project of his own. Sentimentally he was equally unadventurous. Unlike his four younger brothers, all of whom enjoyed a richly diversified love life, he knew and loved only one woman during his entire lifetime, and that was his Alsatian–born wife, Leonie. So attached was he to the tall, statuesque Leonie Bernheim, whom he had courted as a young man along the shores of Lake Lugano, that, in the words of a nephew, "he never gave another woman so much as a passing glance." Socially he was also very conservative. He did not make friends easily and did not nurse the slightest wish to be part of society, Jewish or Gentile (one is tempted to say that he probably would not have cut a very dashing figure in either society, had he chosen to join). Ninety-eight percent of the time he preferred only the society of his wife. As might be expected, when it came to spending money, whether his own—which amounted to a considerable fortune—or his firm's, he was something of a tightwad. Though his benefactions were munificent, he did not part with his money easily, and gave only after his brothers set the example . . . and estate taxes went up.

Murry's forte was dealing with numbers. He had a mathematical mind, liked statistics, was the sort of man who did a lot of paper work in his head. He was one of the country's foremost experts on copper sales, having a special sense for that fine, ephemeral moment when copper should be either bought or sold. In addition to being chairman of the finance committee of American Smelting and Refining and a partner of Guggenheim Brothers, he was both a director of, and agent for, Kennecott Copper, of which he was, of course, a major stockholder.

Given his rather cramped personality, it was unlikely that Murry would spend his money daringly, and he didn't. What he eventually spent it on was eminently praiseworthy, but, unlike Dan's blind leap into space, also eminently safe and acceptable: he established a free dental clinic for the poor children of New York.

First, however, and in this he did resemble his older brothers, first, before philanthropy, he took care to establish his children as impregnably as possible.

In keeping with his less-than-exuberant nature, Murry did not bother to create a Villa Carola or buy a Castlegould for the greater glory of the House of Guggenheim. True, he had once erected a copy of the Petit Trianon on the Jersey shore, chiefly out of competition with brothers Isaac, Dan, and Sol, but after he sold it at a decent profit, he ceased entertaining vast building projects. About the only significant luxury he permitted himself was his $100,000 yacht, *Leonie*, which he kept at St. Petersburg, Florida. No, it was not in Murry's character to spend hard-earned money recklessly on ostentation. It was in Murry's character, instead, to *conserve* money. And conserving money meant, among other things, not letting the government get what he had.

Thus in 1917, while the Great War was pouring unprecedented profits into the Guggenheims' accounts, Murry established two $6 million trust funds for his beloved son, Edmond, and his beloved daughter, Lucille.

The two trusts, Murry took care to stipulate, were revocable. They were not absolute gifts, for at any time the settlor could regain title to their principal sums.

This made Edmond and Lucille a little nervous. Each was earning anywhere from $300,000 to $350,000 a year from his/her trust and neither took kindly to the idea that at a moment's notice their father could legally take their income away from them. Therefore, in 1925, they both brought pressure to bear on Murry to make the trusts absolute by revoking his power to cancel them.

Meanwhile, in 1924, Congress included in its revenue act of that year a provision calling for a tax on all gifts valued at $50,000 or more.

Murry, cognizant of this, called his lawyers and asked if revoking his power to cancel his children's trusts would subject his children to the recently enacted gift tax. The lawyers said it would not. So Murry made the trusts absolute.

Not long after he made them absolute, the federal government demanded and, after a long legal battle that went all the way to the Supreme Court, collected a gift tax from Murry Guggenheim of $3,449,000, the largest gift tax ever paid by a single individual up to that time.

A year later, in 1926, Congress took the gift tax off the books and kept it off until 1932. Thus Murry had been compelled to pay a gift tax that he could have avoided by waiting until 1926 to make the trusts absolute.

After paying up, Murry, though still a very rich man, thought of himself as destitute. According to his lawyer, Leo Gottlieb, "he did not buy a single suit for over a year."

Between taxes and legal fees, Murry had to part with some $5 million all told. In the end, the two gifts had cost him a total of $18 million. For Murry the tightwad this was a bit too much, and so, in addition to not buying a new suit for a year, he took his legal business away from the firm of Gottlieb and Cleary forever.

Edmond and Lucille, of course, felt little pain over their father's defeat by the Internal Revenue Service. They now owned their trusts outright and very nice trusts they were. So sagely did Murry invest them that even in the depths of the Depression Edmond's trust earned him $332,000 per annum and Lucille's $327,000. These incomes made Edmond and Lucille the wealthiest members of the third generation during the 1930s.

Murry had pinned high hopes on Edmond—a tall, muscular man who would have been quite handsome had it not been for the inevitable potato nose—expecting him to take a leading role in managing the Guggenheim empire, and was sorely disappointed when he dropped out of Guggenheim Brothers in 1923, in protest over the sale of Chile Copper, which he had helped develop. Since Edmond was earning over $300,000 a year from his trust, he saw little point in continuing to work for what he thought was a much-depleted Guggenheim Brothers and giving most of his income from the partnership to the government.

Besides, Edmond liked sports too much to be happy spending eight hours a day sitting at a desk in gloomy Guggenheim Brothers. He had been a star second baseman on the Yale baseball team. And he was a good amateur boxer and an excellent golfer. Accordingly, upon his resignation from the firm in 1923, at the age of thirty-five, he "retired" on his bountiful income to devote the rest of his life to golf.

Edmond married three times. His first wife, Marron Price, was a high-spirited girl who bore him his only child, a daughter, Natalie, and became a passionate devotee of the airplane. In 1934 she set out to do "the loop" around South America with the handsome, dashing pilot Russell Thaw. That was enough for Edmond and he divorced her, much to Murry's annoyance, for Guggenheims did not divorce. His second marriage, to Jeanne Russell, also ended in divorce in 1952. Three years later he tried again, this time with Marion Kaufmann, with whom he remained until his death. The third Mrs. Edmond Guggenheim now lives quietly in Scottsdale, Arizona, and Westbury, Long Island.

Daughter Natalie was even less fortunate in marriage than her father. First, she eloped with one Tom Gorman, son of a Manhasset, Long Island, railroad baggage master. The marriage enraged both Murry and Edmond, and they forced Natalie to have it annulled immediately. She then went on to marry an acceptable young man of Park Avenue parentage by the name of Robert Michael Studin, whom she eventually divorced. Later she married Frederick Talbert of San Francisco, who died. She is now Mrs. B.B. Short of Honolulu and the possessor of her father's 1917 trust, plus many more millions.

Murry's only daughter, Lucille, fared no better in marriage. First she married with great pomp and divorced with much publicity Fred A. Gimbel of the department-store Gimbels. Then she married and divorced Jack E. Bonar, father of her only child, Jean. Later she became Mrs. Peter P. Summerer. She died a wealthy lady of seventy-eight.

It took a while for Murry to recover sufficiently from the gift-tax debacle to feel he could spend some more money. Finally, after his brothers' philanthropic examples, especially Dan's, had goaded him, and the new estate tax laws had goaded him even more, he decided to establish his own foundation in 1919, with an initial gift of $2 million, or $11 million less than what he had given his two children.

The general aims of the Murry and Leonie Guggenheim Foundation, purposely kept flexible, were "the promotion, through charitable and benevolent activities, of the well-being of man throughout the world," and its specific aim was "charitable and benevolent assistance to the children of greater New York through the practical application of dentistry and oral hygiene."

This later aim took the form of the establishment of the Murry and Leonie Guggenheim Dental Clinic at 422–28 East Seventy-second Street between York and First avenues in New York.

Murry Guggenheim died in 1939 at eighty-one. During his last, much-embittered years, the Murry and Leonie Guggenheim Dental Clinic had become the ruling passion of his life. Murry used to like to go to the clinic and see the Board of Education buses unload the children—mostly blacks, Hispanics, Italians, and Lower East Side Russian Jews—after school. He would stand there in the entrance hall, his derby hat on, a fragrant flower in his buttonhole, and watch the children on their way to the dental chairs.

Because of the terrible losses the Guggenheims had sustained in Chile, Murry's estate at the time of his death was much depleted. But thanks again to Hitler's war, it came back eventually to something in the neighborhood of $30 million. Of this, $5 million went to the dental clinic; Edmond got a bequest of $400,000; sister Cora Rothschild collected $100,000; and the "rest and residue" was divided into two trusts for Leonie. The first trust specified that upon Leonie's death the principal would go to Edmond, and upon his death, to his daughter, Natalie. The other specified that upon Leonie's death the principal would go to Lucille's daughter, Jean Bonar. Thus Lucille herself was left out of the will. She had by then annoyed Murry so much with her marriages and divorces that he had decided her 1917 trust was all she was ever going to get.

After Murry's death Edmond took over the presidency of the Murry and Leonie Guggenheim Foundation and its dental clinic, helped by his mother, Leonie, and daughter, Natalie, both of whom sat on the board. He then ran the clinic very ably for the next thirty years, finding the work almost as exhilarating as golf, and much more satisfying than mining and smelting nonferrous metals. By 1962, 39,388 children a year were coming to the clinic for free treatment, sometimes a thousand a day. By 1969 the foundation's assets stood at $40 million . . . and Edmond, now eighty, had begun to tire of the responsibility of administering them.

In the last years of his life, with the advent of welfare and Medicare, which, in a sense, preempted the work of the clinic, Edmond Guggenheim presided over the disposition of the principal of his father's trust. First, he closed the clinic on Seventy–second Street and donated the building and much of its equipment to New York Hospital. Then he gave $22 million toward a new building and endowment fund for Mount Sinai Hospital, and $12 million for a new pavilion at the Mayo Clinic. The sum given to Mount Sinai was the largest ever given to that hospital by one man.

The rest of Murry's wealth ultimately ended up in the purses of three women: his daughter, Lucille, her daughter, Jean Bonar, and Edmond's daughter, Natalie, each of whom came to control sizable fortunes.

And so the ultimate beneficiaries of Murry's share in the great pioneering struggles in Colorado, Mexico, Utah, the Yukon, Alaska, and Chile, were, besides the clinics and hospitals, three multimarried women who had taken no part whatsoever in these struggles and knew very little about them. The same could be said of Isaac's share, since his wealth also passed largely to women. None of these third– or fourth–generation heiresses, it should be pointed out, established a foundation of her own.

CHAPTER 18

SOLOMON'S SECOND SPRING

B ehold Solomon R. Guggenheim in all his glory.

Here he is, the most stylish of the brothers, immaculately turned out in a Savile Row gray pinstriped suit, vest, high white starched collar, gray silk tie, and pearl stickpin, sitting in the living room of his huge eight-room suite at the Plaza, the principal suite, opening onto the balconies and flags above the main entrance, the rooms filled with precious Old Masters, the entire staff of the hotel at his push-button beck and call. Here he is spending a week or two in January at his lovely 1828 Greek Revival "winter place" on the East Battery in Charleston, South Carolina. Here he is playing golf on the private course of his 205-acre estate at Sands Point, Trillora Court, formerly brother Isaac's Villa Carola, driving the ball past mossy baroque statues and fountains, formal Italian gardens, stands of pine, oak, and birch. Here he is in the early fall shooting grouse in Scotland at his lodge and preserve on the Glenkinde Moor. Here he is a month or so later, hunting again, this time geese, ducks, and sage chickens, at his vast 8,000-acre cattle ranch and game preserve near the Snake River at Island Park, Idaho. Here he is shooting deer and ducks at his 1,200-acre plantation, Big Survey, in the moss-hung woods of Yemasee, South Carolina. Here he is on his 305-foot ocean-going yacht, the *Trillora*, a former World War I destroyer, the fastest yacht in the world, capable of whisking him to his office in lower Manhattan from Sands Point in only forty minutes. Here he is with his handsome wife, Irene, his three daughters, one of whom is married to a British earl, being entertained at his son-in-law's four-hundred-year-old ancestral estate in Ulster. Here he is at his desk in the vast wood-paneled Partners' Room at Guggenheim Brothers, surrounded by gilt-framed portraits of his brothers, his father, his grandfather, himself, discussing with brothers Murry and Simon a $50 million nitrate deal in Chile, the latest financial reports from their diamond mines in the Congo and Angola, their tin mines in Bolivia and Malaya, their rubber plantations in the Congo, their huge holdings in Kennecott and Anaconda Copper.

Here he is, one of the great princes of the American empire, blessed with everything his countrymen ever dreamed of possessing; here he is, at sixty-five, only one generation removed from a European ghetto, holding the world in his hands . . . and he is bored.

Something is missing. He has everything. And nothing. He is semiretired from business—the pioneering, the buccaneering are over—now all he has to do is hold on to what he has, and that is not a terribly exciting occupation. His wife, Irene, is a fine woman, a good wife and mother, but also a dull woman: it has been a long time since she has stimulated him, either physically or intellectually; the marriage is comfortable but stale. In the last analysis, what does he have to look forward to but increasing enfeeblement, failing powers, old age? Oh yes, there are his daughters and grandsons . . . their lives are important to him, but he has the rest of his own life to live. His fortune. Ah, how much of his fortune would he give for youth? What good are riches to an old man if they suffocate him, if they do not bring him more health, more stimulation, more *life*?

Enter a thirty-six-year-old, blue-eyed, red-headed German baroness and painter. Enter like a hurricane, sweeping away, in one great cleansing wind, all fatigue, all despair, all world-weariness. Enter, take possession, and, in return, give the aging king energy, hope, enthusiasm; give

485

the old buccaneer a second spring.

Solomon Guggenheim first met the baroness Hilla Rebay von Ehren-wiesen in New York in 1927. She had come from Paris, where she had been exhibiting her works, with a letter of introduction from Irene's sister, Gertrude de Paats. Solomon was immediately impressed by her and asked her to do his portrait. She declined because she did not like realistic portraiture anymore; she had put that mode behind her and was now painting only nonobjective works. Whereupon Sol, who enjoyed needling, joking, piqued her by saying, "No, it's probably because you don't know how to do a portrait anymore." Whereupon she rose to the bait, they discussed the fee, he gave her much more than she asked—$9,000— and she executed the portrait, making him look much younger than his sixty-five years. The painting was later destroyed by Solomon's heirs.

While she painted him (weekends at Trillora Court) they discussed art. Solomon, who possessed the most refined sense of style of all the Guggenheim brothers, loved great painting, but he did not know much about it. Irene knew more and her taste ran to Old Masters. So Sol had bought Old Masters, some works of the late medieval and early Italian Renaissance periods , some fifteenth-century Flemish panels, some paintings of the Barbizon School, a Joos van Cleve, some Audubon prints and Oriental illuminations . . . and some Watteaus, as many Watteaus as he could get his hands on.

The baroness did not hesitate a second to tell him that what he had been collecting was all wrong for a man of his vision and means. Why, a man of his immense wealth and pioneering spirit should be helping *contemporary* artists, the artists of the future.

Her emphasis on pioneering struck its mark As the weeks went by, and her portrait of the Grand Old Man neared completion, she unfolded her self-styled "revolutionary" ideas about nonobjective art with the passion of an evangelist, and, in the end, won Solomon over. Yes, by Jehovah, if he had pioneered in mining and metallurgy all his life, why should he not be a pioneer, also, in art?

It was not long before Hilla introduced him to the abstractions of the Polish-born Rudolf Bauer, the Russian-born Wassily Kandinsky, and the Hungarian-born Laszlo Moholy-Nagy, all of whom were living outside the countries of their birth. Solomon was vastly impressed by an abstract watercolor by Bauer and later he dated his conversion to nonobjective art from first beholding that work. (Time was to prove that he had been far more expert in judging ore bodies.) One thing led to another and, in 1929, Solomon found himself in Germany, with Irene and the baroness, visiting "the father of abstract art," Wassily Kandinsky, who was teaching at the Bauhaus in Dessau. At the meeting, which was to have momentous consequences for all present, as it was for all modern art, Solomon took Kandinsky by the hand and, delivering a little formal speech, said: "Mr. Kandinsky, you and I have something in common. You have made a revolution in art, I and my brothers, by sponsoring the development of new methods of mining, have made a revolution in that industry." He then purchased Kandinsky's "Composition 8" and two other paintings, thus beginning a collection of Kandinsky, now housed in the Solomon R. Guggenheim Museum, which became the largest in the world.

The baroness now virtually took charge of Solomon's life, and his money, and, rushing him here and there, brought him into face-to-face contact with all the up-and-coming nonobjective painters of the day, introducing him into exhilarating new worlds he had never even approached before, and encouraging him always to buy, buy, buy. In the process, she collected healthy commissions from the painters, the first trickle of money of what was to become a very substantial fortune earned off Mr. Sol. Years later, Sol's youngest daughter, Barbara, who had no use for the baroness, would say: "Well, she came over here to find a rich American, *and she found one!*"

It would be unfair, however, to characterize Hilla Rebay as a mercenary. True, she needed money, like everyone else, and spotted in Solomon a bottomless pit of it, but it is even more true that she was an utterly, even fanatically, devoted soldier of art. Art was her life, her religion. Before Sol met Hilla, he did not know what to do with his money, or with the rest of his life. Thirty-two years after he met her his money had collected the most extensive private collection of modern art in existence and had erected the most daring art museum in the world.

Hilla Rebay possessed a certain genius, there was no doubt about it. She had an inexhaustible zest for life and art, a sort of volcanic enthusiasm, and very few inhibitions. She was extremely talkative, and spoke her mind, with no concessions to diplomacy, in a thick German accent, making dozens of charming mistakes. When she was talking about something that interested her very much she would often get extremely excited and her words would come out in waves, torrents. When she did not know the correct English word she would supply German and French words without bothering to make any explanations. In conversation she was capable of abrupt metamorphoses of mood. She might be expatiating with wild enthusiasm on some painter, her eyes shining, a look of ecstasy on her face, then she might suddenly remember some past injury or insult and would shift to a mood of violent rage. Now her words would slash about the room, her eyes would bulge, her face redden, and the past offender would be buried under an ocean of abuse. Like many German women, she was either at one's feet or at one's throat.

Intellectually, she was dogmatic, authoritarian, and somewhat bigoted. She held certain fixed prejudices and beliefs and would not waver from them, or suffer opposition to them. Though her closest friends and associates were Jews, she frequently uttered anti-Semitic statements. She liked to dominate conversation and she liked to give orders. Few people could resist her, least of all Solomon Guggenheim. When she wanted something from Sol she got it. In the end she got hundreds of paintings, millions of dollars, and a museum.

It had not taken Hilla long, after first getting to know Sol, to observe how free-spending he was with his fortune. Solomon Guggenheim had no false humility or shame about being very rich. The baroness soon saw that Solomon was no tightwad. Now it was up to her to give his spending some meaning and direction.

Fortunately for her goal, Solomon Guggenheim, at sixty-six, fell madly in love with her. She was so different from the people he normally came in contact with, so different from the staid Irene. All his life, with the exception of the Mexican adventure, he had had to deal with relatively sober, rational businessmen, people who kept their emotions under strict control. Now he had this wild, instinctive, half animal-half angel on his hands, a person who reacted, passionately, to everything, and it refreshed him no end.

Soon he was writing her letters, addressing her "Dearest Hillachen," and signing them "with much love, Sol." Soon they were taking excursions together on his yacht. Soon she was visiting him, alone, at Big Survey, deep in the privacy of the Yemasee, South Carolina, pinewoods.

Whether they had sex together remains an open, and perhaps irrelevant question. Hilla, responding angrily to the inevitable gossip, insisted that they didn't. But, knowing Solomon's lifelong penchant for the well-turned leg, the ample bosom, the . . . one is inclined to assume they did. That Sol enjoyed many affairs during his married life was no secret. He did not tell his wife for some time that he had bought his yacht because he liked to entertain his girl friends on it. Whatever the case—sex or no sex—a very tender love developed in Solomon's breast for Hilla. His letters to her, hundreds of which are on file in the Hilla Rebay Foundation's archives, attest that he became genuinely devoted to her, that he held her in high esteem and warm affection. To back up that esteem and affection with something concrete he rented an apartment in New York for her, gave her a monthly stipend, both lent and gave her scores of valuable paintings, and eventually built her a magnificent estate in Connecticut and left her a million dollars in his will.

Certainly Hilla's philosophy of nonobjective art could not have appealed much to a mind as orderly and logical as Solomon Guggenheim's, so it must have been her other qualities that won him over.

Armed with her innate dogmatism, her energy, and Sol's money, the baroness Hilla stormed into the art world of the 1930s with Sol in tow and bought up every promising nonobjectivist in sight. By 1939 she had coaxed Solomon into buying fifty Kandinskys, fifteen Gleizeses, six Légers, five Moholy-Nagys, three Chagalls, four Delaunays , two Feiningers, and every work, scores and scores of them, that ever came off the easel of Rudolf Bauer.

At first the paintings were hung in Sol's Plaza suite (the Old Masters were confined to Irene's room, while the new masters were hung everywhere else), but soon the walls outside Irene's domain got overcrowded and it became necessary to rent space for them in some offices at Carnegie Hall. As the collection grew and grew, Sol pondered its future, and in 1937 institutionalized it by creating the Solomon R. Guggenheim Foundation "for the promotion and encouragement of art and education in art." Finally, in 1939, spacious quarters were rented at 24 East Fifty-fourth Street, the entire collection was gathered there, and, on June 1, it opened as "The Solomon R. Guggenheim Collection of Non-Objective Painting" with Baroness Hilla Rebay von Ehrenwiesen in charge.

It was at about this time that Sol's entire collection of Old Masters was sold at auction for $341,000.

Irene, as might be expected, was most displeased. As she had been displeased all along by Sol's mad infatuation with the baroness and his equally mad venture into nonobjective art. Oh, how she was annoyed that day at the Plaza when Hilla barefacedly seized her antique silver teapot and poured tea for her—Irene's—guests at the head of her table, while she, Irene, had to stand dumbly by. Once Solomon tried to explain it all to her. He had been a pioneer in Mexico, prospecting for mines. He had been a pioneer in Alaska, in Chile, always prospecting for promising ore bodies. Now he was a pioneer and prospector in art. He was prospecting for new artists, promising mines of art. Sometimes a mine becomes exhausted and you have to look for something else. Irene took the whole thing personally. So she and her Old Masters were exhausted. And Hilla and her nonobjectivists were still to be explored. Well, I'll tell you, Solomon, whom she habitually referred to in her correspondence as her "worser half," you'll never find mines as rich as Watteau and me. As she silently took Hilla and Moholy-Nagy on the chin. Poor Irene. Here Sol was, enjoying his second and third springs, and she was having to witness it all as a spectator, and witness it alone, without her Old Masters to comfort her. But he was always kind and generous to her and this was a consolation in the winter of her life, without the slightest chance for a change of season. Years later, Gladys Straus defended her uncle by saying: "Sol was getting old and tired and without purpose in life. Aunt Irene was so stodgy. Hilla gave Uncle Sol a new existence, and it was so *good* for him. All of us saw how much he perked up after Hilla came on the scene."

Good for him in more ways than one. For not only did Hilla give Solomon back his youth, but she also gave him something almost as important, something that had eluded him so far, and that was fame.

Solomon Guggenheim had been a capable businessman, but not a

great one, and, as we know, he had been consistently overshadowed by brother Dan all his business life. Now, with the Solomon R. Guggenheim art foundation and museum of nonobjective painting firmly established, and the baroness holding exhibitions of the Solomon R. Guggenheim collection in Sol's native city, Philadelphia (1937); his winter city, Charleston, South Carolina (1938); and his daughter Barbara's adopted city, Baltimore (1939), the name Solomon Guggenheim was suddenly in lights. The press celebrated him for his pioneering in modern art, for giving the American public its first exposure to contemporary European nonobjective painting. It was in art, finally, that Sol won the fame that had passed him by in business.

But it was not long before Solomon's newfound fame began to backfire, thanks chiefly to the misplaced enthusiasms and mystic double-talking of the originator of his fame, Hilla, and to the increasing presence in his collection of Hilla's favorite painter, and favorite lover, Rudolf Bauer.

Meyer Guggenheim and his seven sons. From left to right:
Benjamin (1865–1912)
Murry (1858–1939)
Isaac (1854–1922)
Meyer (1828–1905)
Daniel (1856–1930)
Solomon R. (1861–1949)
Simon (1867–1941)
William (1868–1941)

Daniel, above, head of the Guggenheim family from 1905 to 1930, and Florence Schloss Guggenheim, his wife. Their estate, Hempstead House, top, in Sands Point, Long Island, with the magnificent stables of the estate, below.

Simon Guggenheim

Benjamin Guggenheim

Murry Guggenheim

William Guggenheim

William Guggenheim with two of the former show girls to whom he left his estate. Wherever Will stayed word soon got around that a very rich American was in residence. Below, Solomon R. Guggenheim and the Baroness Hilla Rebay von Ehrenwiesen.

*Harry F. Guggenheim, portrait be-
low, was publisher and editor-in-
chief of Newsday and president of
the Guggenheim Museum and three
Guggenheim foundations. Harry
with Robert H. Goddard, rocket pioneer, and Charles A. Lindbergh, in
New Mexico, 1935.*

GUGGENHEIM BROTHERS

GUGGENHEIM BROTHERS

Peggy Guggenheim, opposite page, on her marble chair, in the garden at the Palazzo Venier dei Leoni, Venice. Her father, Benjamin, perished with the Titanic. Above, Peggy with one of her grandsons, Nicolas Helion, Pegeen's son, and an unidentified friend. Left, Peggy in 1924. Below. Iris Love on Knidos, Turkey, 1976. Iris was the discoverer of the Temple of Aphrodite.

When he created his art foundation Solomon stated that he had done it "to the end that this country may become one of the great art centers of the world and may be accelerated in the process of developing its own great art works as the older nations have done."

This noble, if somewhat chauvinistic, intention was, unfortunately, not fully realized. The arbiters of the New York art world had difficulty taking the baroness, her catalogues, and her favorite painter, seriously. When she would state blithely in a catalogue that "the three principal nonobjective objects—the circle, concentrated continuity in itself, the square, a more spiritual form in relation to space, and the triangle, perhaps less spiritual—were all perfected absolute forms of purity and beauty" the critics would get their backs up.

Years later, Wassily Kandinsky's wife stated that Hilla's twofold concept of the Guggenheim Museum was first, as a realization of Bauer's dream of a new Bayreuth and second, as a showplace for Bauer's work.

Bauer and Kandinsky knew each other in the Der Sturm days. At first they were good friends, but, gradually, owing to Bauer's outrageous behavior in Kandinsky's regard, Kandinsky came to detest him.

In the first place, Bauer blatantly plagiarized Kandinsky and tried to pass his Kandinskyesque style off as wholly his own. Second, when, through Hilla, Bauer heard that the fabulously wealthy Solomon R. Guggenheim was interested in buying Kandinskys, Bauer went to Kandinsky and bought some of his paintings cheaply, pleading that he was "just a poor artist" who admired Kandinsky's work and wanted to study it. Then he turned around and sold the paintings to Solomon at an enormous profit. Third, after Bauer had thoroughly insinuated himself into the heart and mind of Hilla, and the mind and collection of Solomon Guggenheim, he tried to see to it that Solomon stopped buying Kandinskys and bought only Bauers.

After a while, Sol, on Hilla's suggestion, was buying all of Bauer's production. By 1939 Solomon had no fewer than fifty-eight Bauers in his collection, and in 1942 Max Ernst, who by then was living with Sol's niece Peggy, was prompted to dub the museum of nonobjective art "the Bauer House."

With the proceeds from these sales and resales of cheaply bought Kandinskys, Bauer built himself a magnificent villa in Berlin's West End and put over the entrance the inscription "Home of the Spiritual in Art," another plagiarism, for Kandinsky had written a book in 1912 entitled *Concerning the Spiritual in Art*. The exuberant, spendthrift Bauer then filled the House That Sol Built with extravagant furniture.

Came Hitler and the war and Bauer promptly got in trouble with the Nazis. He began speculating illegally in marks and dollars. Irritated by the Nazis' attitude toward the Jews, he hung an American flag out his window as a military parade passed by in review. Soon he was in a concentration camp doing forced labor, awaiting the gas chamber.

Whereupon Hilla the Loyal went into action. By now—1941—Hilla's brother, Baron Franz Hugo Rebay von Ehrenwiesen, was an officer in the Nazi Ministry of the Interior. Hilla got in touch with him and told him that she and Solomon Guggenheim wanted to get Bauer out of the camp and to America "at any price."

Franz Hugo responded that the price might be his head, but he would try. He did not sympathize much with Hitler anyway, especially the Führer's attitude toward the Jews. Letters, hand-carried messages, packets containing American dollars passed across the Atlantic. Franz Hugo did put his head on the block (later he himself was thrown in a concentration camp), Solomon put part of his bankroll on the block, some Jew-killer high in the SS pocketed his very substantial payoff—if you could sell a Jew for good money why bother to gas him?—and miraculously, Rudolf Bauer landed in Hilla's arms some months later.

(With Sol's inexhaustible resources, Hilla also claimed to have sponsored the flight of Marc Chagall from Nazi-occupied Paris and the escape from the Nazis also of Klee and Léger.)

There were, of course, some difficulties to overcome before Bauer was able to settle down. He had brought quite a few pornographic paintings with him which U.S. Customs would not let through; he had been detained at Ellis Island; and there had been a fight over the questionable paintings, which Bauer lost before he was released.

Once Bauer got past customs, however, Hilla persuaded Solomon to buy him a "nice house" on the New Jersey shore "to make up for the one he lost to the Nazis." Since Bauer had suffered so much at the concentration camp, she also convinced Sol to buy him "the two Duesenbergs he deserved." And she persuaded him also to give the genius a monthly income in return for his production, which would be enough for him to retain a live-in housekeeper.

So here was Rudolf Bauer, now installed in a big house near Elberon, not far from where Sol had built his Victorian mansion, The Towers, with a handsome income and a beautiful live-in housekeeper catering to his every need.

Hilla was beside herself with joy. Every weekend, when her duties at the museum were over, she would rush out to New Jersey to see her beloved Rudolf, anxious to inspect his production, and perhaps bring some of it back triumphantly to Sol, anxious also to fold herself into his arms.

She would leave no stone unturned to comfort her genius lover. Once, at the end of a long, laudatory letter to Sol, extolling him as a prince of art—"you have all your life been so constructive, so visionary, so wise and considerate of others, so hopeful"—she asked him to send $5,000 to Bauer right away "to make him feel good."

Things went along swimmingly for a while, then, for some mysterious reason, Bauer's "production" began to dry up and, worst of all, he no longer seemed terribly enthusiastic about Hilla's visits.

The reason for this surprising turn of events—after so many risks had been taken and money spent to save the artist from the gas chamber—was that Bauer had fallen in love with his lissome live-in housekeeper. Not only had he fallen in love with her, but he then committed the unthinkable and married her.

When Hilla was asked to accept the unacceptable she went to war. She wrote Solomon a letter referring to her former lover as "this foul fool who runs to everyone because he can't judge, even to his worst enemies, like your niece Peggy Guggenheim, who pokes fun at him without him even knowing it," and asking him to cut off Bauer's monthly stipend, which he did. She also persuaded him never again to purchase another Bauer. And she wrote Rudolf a letter calling his housekeeper-wife a tramp, a whore.

Mrs. Bauer then counterattacked with a suit against Hilla for libel and defamation of character. Hilla asked Sol for legal aid. Wary of bad publicity and gossip, he passed his own lawyers by and selected an obscure New Jersey attorney to handle the matter. After an expenditure of $11,000 Hilla won her case.

Of course the whole episode exhilarated the eighty-one-year-old Solomon no end. Yes, the days of adventure and struggle were not over.

Not over by far. Immediately after his wife's defeat, Bauer himself went into action against Hilla, to gain revenge. He denounced Hilla, an alien, to the FBI for spying for the Nazis, and before long she was in prison.

The sequence of events was as follows:

Hilla had, in the meantime, been established by the magnanimous Solomon in a lovely fourteen-acre estate at Greens Farms (near Westport), Connecticut, which he had paid for and which she had named Franton Court. The main house had eighteen rooms and twenty-eight Bauers.

After Bauer informed on Hilla, FBI agents sneaked into her Greens Farms property, climbed into her linden trees, and, armed with binoculars and telescopes, kept her under twenty-four-hour surveillance.

Hilla was a bird watcher; she kept notes on the birds she observed at Franton Court, and she told Solomon in a letter that she believed "some cranes" had nested in her linden trees. (She was a trifle nearsighted.)

It was the time of the great submarine scare. Not long before, a German submarine had been sighted, and positively identified, in *Long Island Sound*! Hilla had some curious habits. At night she used to go from room to room in Franton Court turning lights on, looking around the room, spilling a tear or emitting a growl over Bauer, then turning the lights off. The FBI agents perched in her trees took this on-and-off light switching as signals to Nazi submarines. One night, after Hilla had switched a dozen lights on and off, they moved in with guns drawn and bloodhounds slavering, and took the dirty Nazi submarine signaler.

In the process of taking her, they discovered in a loft over her garage 1,400 pounds of sugar, 500 pounds of coffee, and three huge cases of tea, the principal supplements to her vegetarian diet, the foods she absolutely could not do without, and the next day the papers labeled the curator of the Solomon R. Guggenheim Museum of Nonobjective Art a hoarder.

Hilla was then taken to Boston and was incarcerated, without trial, in a federal prison as an enemy alien.

Enemy alien! Why, she protested, going into sputtering, stuttering fits, she had applied for American citizenship, was director of an American museum of modern art, and was a sworn enemy of Hitler and his henchmen. *Mein Gott!* she exclaimed, exploding with indignation, members of her family in Germany had risked their lives to get Jewish artists out of Hitler's clutches.

Solomon Guggenheim loved Hilla Rebay and, loyal to her to the last, he went to bat for her. He wrote a strong letter to Attorney General Francis Biddle.

Not receiving much satisfaction from the Attorney General, he went all the way to the top, to President Franklin D. Roosevelt, and pleaded his case. Solomon Guggenheim was a conservative Republican, but he made it known to Roosevelt that he and his family and his millions really looked rather kindly on him and his Administration. Not long after the visit Hilla was released.

Hilla came out of the whole thing temporarily disillusioned, but still very much intact, still full of idealism and ambition, and ever more full of devotion and gratitude to Sol. Yes, Sol had never let her down, and she knew now he would never, never let her down. After a pause at Franton Court to catch her breath, she was ready with her next project, the most grandiose of all.

As for Bauer, the gods eventually had their revenge. His wife left him and, shortly thereafter, he went insane and had to be committed.

After one Bauer-dominated show, *The New York Times*' Aline Saarinen had had enough and suggested in an article that "The Museum of Non-objective Painting turn over its collection and its funds, including those set aside for the erection of its permanent home, to one of New York's established museums specializing in modern art."

Solomon was hurt and offended by these remarks. Now his patronage of nonobjective painting was earning him more bad publicity than good, more ridicule than praise. The subsequent newspaper reports of his director's arrest and incarceration for being a Nazi collaborator and the discovery of her hoard of sugar, coffee, and tea did not make matters any better, especially for a member of one of New York's leading Jewish families.

In very tactful, diplomatic letters Solomon suggested that Hilla resign. He would continue to support her and protect her, and use her as his "artistic advisor," but she must leave her post at the museum.

Hilla, however, had absolutely no intention of resigning. Far from it, she wanted Sol to build a larger, permanent museum for his collection, wanted him to commission the world's greatest architect to build it and, once it was built, wanted him to put her in complete charge.

This, in the end, was what he did. With their differences temporarily reconciled, they then set their minds to planning what was to become the most controversial art museum in the world.

The Grand Idea. Whose was it? Members of the Guggenheim family today will resolutely tell you that it was Irene's idea to get Frank Lloyd Wright to build his extraordinary memorial to Solomon.

However, given Irene's antipathy toward nonobjective art and her jealousy of the baroness, it seems unlikely. Besides, there is a wealth of indirect evidence suggesting the museum was wholly the baroness's idea.

By the time—early 1940s—Solomon Guggenheim first got in touch with Frank Lloyd Wright about building a permanent museum for his collection, Wright enjoyed a reputation as "the greatest architect in the world." He himself, never one to underestimate his abilities, would go a bit further and intimate he was the greatest architect of all time.

At their first meeting Solomon Guggenheim and Frank Lloyd Wright hit it off beautifully. Each developed a profound respect for the other that was to stand them in good stead during the endless troubles ahead.

Solomon was getting a breath of fresh mountain air at Peckett's Hotel in Franconia Notch, New Hampshire, when Wright brought him the first plans. According to Wright, "When the Grand Old Man saw the first sketches I made he went over them several times without saying a word or looking up. When he did look up there were tears in his eyes. 'Mr. Wright,' he said, 'I knew you would do it, this is it.'"

Solomon formally accepted the plans by letter in 1944. The building was not to be erected until sixteen years later.

In 1944, Sol selected and bought an empty lot at Fifth Avenue and Eighty-ninth Street (subsequently adding two adjoining lots), which was to become the permanent site of the museum.

The site selected, Frank Lloyd Wright then produced the scale model of the museum. It was unveiled at a luncheon at the Plaza and a photograph was taken of Wright, Hilla, and Solomon beaming upon the revolutionary construction. It was a scene out of the Italian Renaissance: Julius II examining Michelangelo's model of Saint Peter's, with Vittoria Colonna looking on.

Not long after selecting the site and approving the scale model, Solomon got cold feet about the project. "We've got to wait until building costs go down," he wrote Hilla, "before we can start construction."

A little while later he wrote Wright the same thing and enclosed a check for a thousand dollars as a retainer, and "evidence of good will."

Two years passed and Solomon still had cold feet. On July 5, 1949, he wrote Wright: "My great fear is that unless we in this country are more careful, the politicians will bring the United States to the same pass as Germany and France. While I have provided liberally for both the museum building and its endowment, it could be that, when the time comes for materialization of our plans, the money in this country will have much less value than today."

Solomon had so far given $3 million to his foundation and museum and he had earmarked another $5 million for them in his will. As Solomon's health began to fail—he had cancer of the prostate—Hilla did not want to take any chances and asked him point-blank how much he had left the museum and her in his will. He told her, and while she was satisfied with her legacy, she was not at all content with what he had left the foundation and museum. At her insistence, he left $8 million.

Three months after changing his will, on November 3, 1949, Solomon died at Trillora Court at the age of eighty-eight.

Solomon Guggenheim's passing was much mourned by his family, his associates, and his friends. He had been the most amiable and well-liked of the seven sons of Meyer and Barbara, as well as the most versatile. His daughters and grandsons speak of him today in affectionate terms.

There were many tributes, but the greatest tribute of all came several years later, from Frank Lloyd Wright. "Solomon Guggenheim," said Wright, "was the only American millionaire I ever met who died facing the future. All the others cuddled up to the past."

The will was an elaborate document, sixty pages in length, which must have made a lot of people very happy indeed.

The ranch and Island Park Land and Cattle Company in Idaho, and the Elgebar Company (El for Eleanor, Ge for Gertrude, Bar for Barbara) and Big Survey plantation in South Carolina went to daughters Eleanor and Barbara (Gertrude had died). Trillora Court and the house on the East Battery in Charleston were to be put at Irene's disposal for the rest of her life, then willed to Eleanor and Barbara. Each child of Rose Loeb received $50,000 and $50,000 went to each child of Cora Rothschild.

Two trusts, amounting to approximately $10 million each, went to the families of Sol's two surviving daughters in a very complicated arrangement that awarded the actual monies to Eleanor's and Barbara's children with the stipulations that a certain percentage of income would go to Irene and, upon her death, to Eleanor and Barbara, before the grandchildren came into full possession of their money. By this arrangement only one estate tax was paid over a span of three generations.

All Sol's paintings not yet in the Museum of Non-objective Art went to his foundation, with the exception of a few Old Masters that he had kept in Irene's rooms at the Plaza, and which went to Irene.

Eight million dollars—two for the construction of the new museum, and six for permanent endowment—went to the Solomon R. Guggenheim Foundation. And 6,000 shares of Kennecott Copper, 1,500 U.S. Rubber preferred, 5,000 U.S. Rubber common, 1,400 Standard Oil of New Jersey, 5,000 Anaconda Copper, and 400 Barber Oil, with a market value at time of death of approximately a million dollars, went to Baroness Hilla Rebay von Ehrenwiesen.

CHAPTER 19

KING SOLOMON'S MUSEUM

Harry Guggenheim, Sol's nephew, succeeded to the presidency of the Solomon R. Guggenheim Foundation and immediately collided with the museum director, the baroness Rebay. Thus it was left to two natural enemies to realize Solomon's plans for a permanent museum.

Harry and Hilla were light-years apart temperamentally and intellectually. Harry was a capable executive, and a man of considerable energy, but he knew precious little about art, least of all nonobjective art, and did not have much sympathy for the artistic temperament. Being dogmatic and somewhat dictatorial himself, it was only natural he would clash with his exceedingly dogmatic and dictatorial museum director.

The Hilla-Harry battle was waged over a period of fifteen years. Fortunately for posterity, it is all preserved in the Hilla von Rebay Foundation archives in New York.

At the height of the battle Hilla let loose her most violently anti-Semitic invective against Harry, calling him every insulting name a Jew has ever been called, and not sparing the other trustees either.

The upshot of it all was that Hilla first lost her job as museum director, then her position on the board, and finally all her emeritus titles.

In retaliation Hilla kept some four hundred paintings, sculptures, and other works of art Solomon had lent her, including some of his finest Kandinskys, at Franton Court, which was in direct violation of a written agreement Sol had made with her before his death. According to the agreement, in return for the approximately one million dollars' worth of securities he left her in his will she was to give back all the paintings he had lent her during their twenty-three years of association.

Harry appointed James Johnson Sweeney, a curator at the Museum of Modern Art, to succeed Hilla as director, and under him the Guggenheim Museum took on a new authority and professionalism. In addition to relegating the Rebays and the Bauers to the cellar, Sweeney added some 250 new paintings, including some superb Picassos and Cezannes.

Meanwhile the Great Project for the Frank Lloyd Wright-designed museum was getting nowhere. First of all, Sol's estate was not settled until 1952, and thus it was not until then that the money for the museum was transferred from the estate to the foundation. Secondly, the application for a building permit, made immediately after the transfer of funds, was quickly turned down by New York's Department of Building and Housing on grounds that Wright's plans transgressed the metropolitan building code in no fewer than thirty-two ways.

On hearing this latter bit of news Frank Lloyd Wright went into a rage. To Harry he exploded: "Architecture, may it please the court, is the welding of imagination and common sense into a restraint upon specialists, codes, and fools." And he urged him to do something about the New York City government's specialists, codes, and fools. Harry told him to go back to work.

Wright did go back to work. At the Frank Lloyd Wright architectural schools at Taliesin in Wisconsin, and Taliesin West in Arizona, the master's assistants worked overtime to revise the plans.

Permit hearings then dragged on for four years. It almost seemed as if the bureaucrats really *wanted* to obstruct the work of the genius.

Wright, at the time, was not too complimentary about New York. "It is fit only for cockroaches," he declared, "indeed is inhabited only by cockroaches, and is well on its way to becoming so crowded that soon the cockroaches will have to walk on the tops of the taxicabs." His formula for improving New York? "Bomb it."

Finally, on March 13, 1956, the New York City bureaucrats came through with the permit. But then, just as all problems seemed to have been solved, Wright and Sweeney began to squabble.

Wright wanted to create an architectural masterpiece that would publicize, down through the ages, the names of Frank Lloyd Wright, architect, and Solomon R. Guggenheim, donor. All museum-man Sweeney was interested in was a satisfactory space in which to display paintings, and also store paintings, and administer museum affairs.

Sweeney did not like Wright's curved walls and cantilevered ramp. He did not believe these architectural innovations, however daring they might be, would show paintings off to their best advantage. Wright retaliated by stating that only this way could you display a large collection of paintings "without any intervening interruptions," such as doors, elevators, pillars, staircases, hallways, and so on, and that it was certainly more restful for the body and the feet to view them this way, "with gravity doing part of the work." In the end Wright won his point with the trustees, and Sweeney was presented with a virtual *fait accompli*: the ramp and sloping walls would remain in the design.

As the building neared completion, Wright began to tell Sweeney exactly how he should hang the paintings. This infuriated Sweeney and he got the trustees to agree to hold a competition. Sweeney hung two bays, Wright hung two bays. The trustees chose Sweeney's method. Not long after that Frank Lloyd Wright took seriously ill at Taliesin West, and on April 9, 1959, died in a hospital in Phoenix.

The gala opening, which had been preceded by a preview and a reception, was held on October 21, 1959. Among the notables present were Bernard M. Baruch, Mrs. Wassily Kandinsky, and Harry F. Guggenheim. Absent were the three people ultimately responsible for the building, the donor, the architect, and the inspirer.

Mrs. Wright was present, however, and she told reporters that had her husband lived he would have preferred to stay away rather than have to look at the alterations effected against his will by director Sweeney.

As for Hilla . . . she viewed the proceedings from Franton Court with utter contempt. Later, when the foundation asked her to give back at least some of the paintings Solomon had lent her, she retorted, "Why should I take down the precious paintings from the walls of my house and give them to a pigsty?"

The Solomon R. Guggenheim Memorial Museum—so named by Harry, who rejected the name Museum of Non-Objective Art—soon became, and has since remained, one of the most controversial buildings ever constructed in the United States. It has been likened variously to a snail, a turnip, a cement mixer, a child's sand castle, a nuclear power plant, an inverted cup and saucer, a bird house for vultures on Mars.

Sol's niece Peggy Guggenheim did not like it very much. "The museum resembles a huge garage," she wrote. "It is built on a site that is inadequate for its size and looks very cramped, suffering from its nearness to adjacent buildings. It should have been placed on a hill in [Central] Park . . . the rising ramp, Wright's famous invention, coils like an evil serpent. The walls bend backwards and a cement platform keeps one at a respectful distance from the pictures. Nothing could be more difficult than viewing them from this angle."

Emily Genauer, art critic for the *New York Herald Tribune*, called the museum "the most beautiful building in America." London's *Art News and Review* said: "It was fascinating in broad daylight, while at night a surrealist element is introduced by the rivers of light that flow between the curved darkness of the spiralling ramps." Philip C. Johnson, one of the two architects of the Seagram Building, and director of the department of architecture and design at the Museum of Modern Art, called the interior "one of the greatest rooms created in the twentieth century." Moscow's *Izvestia* was all sneers: "The art of the fat ones . . . soiled with lines and blotches that do not express anything."

Whatever its merits and demerits—and there are certainly plenty of both—it is an incontestable fact that the Solomon R. Guggenheim Collection and Museum have had an enormous impact, for better and for worse, on the artistic taste of mid-twentieth-century Americans, perhaps more than any other single institution of their kind. On the for-better side they exposed American artists and the American public to the seminal abstract works of such twentieth-century masters as Kandinsky (170 paintings in the collection), Klee (140), Léger, Mondrian, Moholy-Nagy, for the first time on a significantly large scale, and in so doing helped create a welcome revolution in taste from the eclecticism that preceded them.

Throughout the 1960s Hilla had waged a constant battle with the trustees of Sol's foundation and museum to retain at Franton Court some two hundred paintings Sol had lent her. The battle was eventually settled after Hilla's death in September, 1967, with the sale, by Hilla's executors, of a large part of her collection, including the best Kandinskys, to the Solomon R. Guggenheim Foundation, for a million dollars, a bargain for the museum.

By the end of her seventy years Hilla Rebay had become a very wealthy woman. The million dollars in gilt-edged securities Sol had left her in 1949 had ridden the bull market of the 1960s so well that by 1969 it was worth over $5 million.

On an income of $250,000 a year, Hilla lived out her last days as a sort of High Priestess of Art, visited by artists and art scholars from all over the world, enjoying her renown, her visitors' sympathy over the cruel way the Solomon R. Guggenheim Foundation had treated her, her vast collection of abstract paintings, the fourteen-acre nature preserve and bird sanctuary Solomon had given her.

CHAPTER 20

BENJAMIN: ON DROPPING OUT

The portrait of Benjamin Guggenheim in the Partners' Room of Guggenheim Brothers is the smallest in the room. It displays a handsome, if somewhat soft, young face in a high Edwardian collar and rests in a simple oval frame, without a trace of gilt, above a door leading to the hall of the minerals. The meager square footage of the portrait places the subject far below Isaac, Daniel, Murry, Solomon, and Simon in importance, but not entirely in last place. William is not even represented on the walls.

Though clearly in sixth place among the brothers, Ben held a number of firsts in the family that entitle him to his own special claim to attention. He was the first of the seven brothers to go to college, the first to go into mining, the first to drop out of the family business, the first to lead a life more oriented toward pleasure than work, the first to collect paintings, the first to produce a child with outstanding abilities, the first to become an expatriate.

Packed off to Columbia in 1882, Ben did not take to college. He found most of his courses—emphasis on metallurgy—unexciting, soon became restless, and dropped out after his second year. Meyer, sorely disappointed, then offered him a job in the New York offices of M. Guggenheim's Sons, but Ben found laces and embroideries dull, the offices gloomy, and the Wall Street area "depressing."

There was only one thing to do with him and that was send him off to the mines in Leadville, Colorado. Since the other brothers were still principally involved with laces and embroideries, Ben thus became the first Guggenheim to work directly in mining.

As it turned out, Ben found the Cloud City very much to his liking. He was assigned as a bookkeeper to the A. Y. mine, a fairly big job—ten acres of land, three shafts, and one hundred men. He would sit in a shack near shaft number three, with a revolver strapped to his belt, keep track of the mine's income and expenses, make out and handle the payroll. At night he would go down to Tiger Alley in "The Row" and dance with prostitutes at fifty cents a dance, or play three-card monte with miners and mule skinners at Crazy Jim's, or drink corn whiskey at the Comique Saloon at twenty cents a glass.

In due course, Ben advanced to the position of manager of the family smelter at Pueblo (which he had also helped build), an important responsibility, and a key step in the formation of the Guggenheim empire. In this capacity he acquitted himself rather well, proving to be a shrewd judge of character (he hired an excellent superintendent), and a respected leader of men. He also proved to be a fine connoisseur of Rocky Mountain females, becoming, with brother Will, a favorite with the most sumptuous belles at Peppersauce Bottoms.

He did not, however, prove to be as good a judge of ore bodies. In 1900 he was offered a piece of Bingham Canyon. On asking how high the copper content ran, he quickly lost interest when told it was only 2 percent. It remained for Dan to buy the mine—then the largest in the world—for thirty times the money some years later.

Eventually Ben was brought back from Colorado and put in charge of the new Guggenheim metals refinery at Perth Amboy, New Jersey, which also put him within easy striking range of New York. Handsome and rich, with a seemingly limitless future before him, young Ben Guggenheim had no trouble cutting a swath through the wealthiest and most beautiful Jewish girls in Manhattan.

After a season or two of playing the field, he settled on the financially promising, but by no means beautiful, Florette Seligman, daughter of

James Seligman, brother of the great Joseph, of J. W. Seligman & Company, then America's richest Jewish bankers.

The Seligmans were ambivalent about the marriage, which was celebrated in 1895. They considered "the Googs" upstarts without polish and tradition—why Joseph Seligman had dined with Abraham Lincoln!—but were pleased with the idea of the money the great mining and smelting family represented. When the engagement was announced, the American Seligmans wired the European Seligmans: "FLORETTE ENGAGED GUGGENHEIM SMELTER." The telegram arrived garbled: "FLORETTE ENGAGED GUGGENHEIM SMELT HER."

Six years after the marriage, in 1901, at the culmination of Dan's great campaign to wrest control of American Smelting and Refining from William Rockefeller, Ben, distrustful of Dan's grandiose plans for expansion, upset about going into partnership with outsiders, piqued by what he felt was Dan's conscious effort to deny the younger brothers significant responsibility in future ventures, and desirous of tasting the pleasures of Europe, resigned as an active partner in M. Guggenheim's Sons, and, at the age of thirty-six, retired on an income from his mining investments of approximately $250,000 a year.

It was a fateful decision, for in dropping out so early in the game Ben and his heirs were to miss out completely on the grand era of Guggenheim business expansion—miss out on Kennecott, Bingham Canyon, the Congo, Angola, Bolivia, and Chile Copper—and Florette, and daughters Benita, Peggy, and Hazel were to suffer the financial consequences.

After a trip to Europe to celebrate his new freedom from his brothers, Ben established himself and his family in a lavish, five-story townhouse on the corner of Seventy-second Street and Fifth Avenue in New York. For neighbors there were people like the James Stillmans, the William Rockefellers, and President Grant's widow.

In this house Ben and Florette raised three daughters: Benita (named after Ben), Marguerite (known as Peggy), and Barbara Hazel (known as Hazel), to add to the Guggenheims' ever-burgeoning store of females. In this house, also, Florette held interminably long and insufferably dull (according to Peggy) tea and bridge parties for the ladies of New York's German-Jewish *haute bourgeoisie,* and Ben installed a slim, red-headed trained nurse, in a room of her own, to massage his chronically neuralgic head, and administer to those other needs which Florette was either unwilling, not expert enough, or not asked to fulfill.

In regard to Ben's penchant for the trained nurse, and others like her who followed, Harold Loeb, a nephew, once observed: "Of all the Guggenheims, Ben was the most extravagant in his amorous divagations, even introducing them into his own house . . . women were drawn to him, partly because of his warm smile, but principally, I suspect, because he really liked women, they sensed he did, and women like to be liked."

Since Ben's marriage to Florette was essentially a marriage of two family fortunes and never pretended to be otherwise, we can easily excuse Ben's "divagations." Besides, Florette, it appears, possessed several unappealing traits. One of these was—odd for a rich girl—an excessive attachment to money. She loved to receive money, but she was very stingy about spending it. She habitually underpaid her eleven servants and undertipped waiters and hotel porters. In France the porters got wise and marked her bags with X's, so at the next hotel the luggage would mysteriously not arrive in her room. She judged her daughters' suitors wholly in terms of their financial resources. A young caller might be acceptable in every way—family, profession, salary—but if he had no money, no *capital*—salary, no matter how high, meant little to her—if he had no capital to speak of, he was labeled "N.G.," No Good, and asked not to call again. The good life for a woman, was, to Florette, living off substantial *unearned* income, and living meant mostly long bridge parties in her Louis XVI parlor, with equally long intermissions for gossip and tea.

Florette, however, was almost normal in comparison to some of the other Seligmans, a family some members of which had slipped quickly into decadence in only three generations, thanks probably to Florette's mother. This strange lady—a torment to James Seligman all his life—had the habit of going around to shopkeepers in her neighborhood and asking, day in and day out: "When do you think my husband last slept with me? Answer me, when do you think it last was?" Her sister was an aspiring soprano, and would sing scales standing at bus stops and walking along Fifth Avenue. This sister's husband, after fighting with her for over thirty years, finally tried to kill her and one of their sons by striking them over their heads with a golf club. When they refused to die he ran to the Central Park reservoir and drowned himself by plunging into the water with heavy weights tied to his feet. Then there was Florette's perennially unemployed brother, who ate almost nothing but charcoal and, as a result, had coal-black teeth and a black tongue. For drink he guzzled whiskey before his charcoal breakfast and sucked ice during the day, carrying his ice in a zinc-lined pocket. An incurable gambler, he threatened time and again to commit suicide unless Florette's father made up his losses. He finally shot himself after losing a sum James Seligman had given him that was supposed to last him the rest of his life. Ben's daughters and grandchildren were destined to suffer periodically from this legacy.

Ben's reaction to Florette and her relatives was to philander and travel. Often he did both at the same time. Ben had taken a liking to Paris, where he had also taken an apartment and established a business, and it was there that he had his most notorious affairs. One of them was with a certain Marquise de Cerruti, whom Peggy has described as "neither pretty nor young . . . but she had the same agreeable quality (maybe sensuous) of the trained nurse." Florette was not so kind. She habitually referred to her as "the monkey" and noted frequently that she possessed "black teeth."

Ben, in his early forties, had blossomed into a very good-looking man, full of pep and fun. Daughter Hazel today describes him as "smallboned, blond-skinned, gray-haired, with light-colored eyes . . . all the other brothers were dark and did not look nearly as Aryan as my father."

In his expensive English-tailored suits, high collars, foulard ties with stickpin, boutonnieres, spats, patent-leather shoes, he was a curious sort of hybrid, an American-Jewish Edwardian swell.

It is a credit to Ben's honesty, though not to his good sense, that he did not hide his amours from his family. Florette and the three girls were perfectly aware who the Marquise de Cerruti was, as they had been fully aware of who the trained nurse was, and the role both played in Ben's life.

Peggy, twelve at the time, remembers bumping into *la marquise* all over Paris, at Rumpelmayer's, while Peggy was gorging herself on ice cream, at Lanvin's with her mother, while they were trying on dresses, in the Bois, where the whole family would take a Sunday stroll.

After Marquise de Cerruti came a "young blond singer." For a while Florette seriously contemplated divorcing Ben, but the other Guggenheims, descending on her en masse as was their custom in times of crisis, talked her out of it, claiming it would be "so bad for the business," and hence for *her* bank account also. Florette was therefore compelled to accept her husband's philandering. According to Peggy, she became a terribly unhappy woman.

Benjamin Guggenheim had the typical playboy's syndrome. His older brothers did not grow up as a rich man's sons, but he did. He therefore was never aware of the intense struggles his father had had to go through to earn his fortune. All was so easy. Furthermore, being a late child, he was spoiled by everyone, especially mother Barbara, whose inexhaustible love and compassion was, at this stage, not always counterbalanced by Meyer's severity, as it had been with the other children. Early Ben became used to a life of self-gratification.

This is not to say, however, that Ben spent all his time merely playing around. He also cultivated business interests of his own. In Paris, which he came to prefer to New York, he had established the International Steam Pump Company, an organization which, among its diverse activities, made the elevators for the Eiffel Tower. Nevertheless, his playing around must have interfered seriously with his business, since it wasn't long after its founding that International Steam Pump began to falter and Ben found himself pouring more and more of his capital into what proved to be a bottomless pit.

In the spring of 1912, Benjamin, who had been away from his wife and children for eight months, presumably looking after the affairs of International Steam Pump in Paris, decided to return to New York to celebrate daughter Hazel's ninth birthday. Accordingly, he booked passage on a steamer from Le Havre to New York. Because of a wildcat stokers' strike he had to change ships at the last minute, and so took a place, or rather three places, the other two for his gentleman's gentleman, Victor Giglio, and the young blond singer, on the White Star Line's *Titanic*.

It was the *Titanic*'s maiden voyage and the White Star Line had billed it as the safest ship afloat. The list of distinguished passengers included Isidor Straus, co-owner of R. H. Macy's and uncle of Gladys Guggenheim's husband, Roger, Bruce Ismay, president of the White Star Line, and John Jacob Astor 4th.

The captain of the vessel was determined to set a world record for a transatlantic crossing. With engines at full speed ahead, he tore across the North Atlantic shipping lane heedless of the gigantic icebergs that drifted down that time of year from the thawing Arctic.

On the night of April 14, one of these silent monsters, showing an insignificant, unthreatening head, barely visible through the fog, tore open the *Titanic*'s bottom with its immense underwater bulk and, a few minutes later, the vessel had shipped so much water and had listed so heavily to starboard, that it was quite clear to the captain and everyone else it would sink.

It was during the next frantic minutes that playboy Ben Guggenheim showed the other side of his character—the traits he had often displayed during his brief mining career in Colorado and Mexico—and became, literally overnight, a hero to his family.

Events followed one another that night with a terrible urgency. Soon it was apparent that there were not enough life jackets for all and that there were not enough places in the lifeboats for more than 600 of the 2,100 passengers aboard.

Benjamin Guggenheim and his gentleman's gentleman were sleeping when the *Titanic* struck the jagged underwater bulk of the iceberg. Shortly after the almost noiseless collision, Ben's room steward, John Johnson, awakened Ben and Giglio, told them what had happened, and urged them to get dressed.

He then handed them life preservers and they strapped them on. Ben complained his hurt his back and took it off. When Johnson suggested it was time to go, Ben said he wanted to collect a few more precious belongings and would meet him on deck.

By then Ben and Giglio had decided how they were going to meet their fate. They both discarded their life jackets, combed their hair, put on some cologne, dressed in their evening clothes, went up on deck, gave their life jackets to two women and told Johnson they were going down with the ship "like gentlemen."

A short while later, Johnson spotted Ben walking briskly along the deck helping women into lifeboats. "Women and children first!" "Women and children first!" he was shouting, while other men hurled women aside in their frantic rush to gain places in the lifeboats for themselves.

Finally an officer ordered Johnson to man an oar and Ben went up to him and gave him a message for Florette: "Tell her I played the game straight to the end and that no woman was left on board because Ben Guggenheim was a coward."

A few minutes later the waves began crashing over the decks and within an hour of the collision 1,517 people were drowning in the twenty-seven-degree waters as the *Titanic* sank beneath them.

All the Guggenheims knew Ben was on the *Titanic*.

Florette, Benita, Peggy, and Hazel were going home from James Seligman's birthday party, crossing from the West Seventies to East Seventy-second Street, when they passed a newspaper boy shouting "Extra! Extra!" According to Hazel, "My beautiful sister Benita, who must have had a sort of ESP, begged my mother to stop and buy the extra, saying 'Something terrible must have happened to Poppa's boat.' . . . My mother assured her nothing could happen to the *Titanic* as it was foolproof. This occurred eight hours before the *Titanic* hit the iceberg."

After word of the sinking did reach New York, Daniel Guggenheim wired the *Carpathia*, which had picked up many survivors, and asked if Benjamin Guggenheim was aboard. No, was the answer. This news was then relayed to Ben's daughters, but not yet to Florette.

Refusing to believe Ben had gone down with the ship, a contingent of incredulous Guggenheims, Dan's son M. Robert, Rose's son Harold, and

Murry's son, Edmond, went down to meet the *Carpathia*'s survivors in the last-ditch hope that Ben would be among them. Alas, he was not, but all was not lost, for a young blond, introduced by an officer as "Mrs. Benjamin Guggenheim," did come down the gangplank announcing that Ben had given up his life to save hers.

Later this news was confirmed, in a modified form, by steward John Johnson at Daniel Guggenheim's suite in the St. Regis. Florette was present, and when Johnson gave her Ben's message, he went no further, never mentioning the young blond singer.

In Ben's defense, if he needs any, no "Mrs. Benjamin Guggenheim" ever turned up on the official passenger list of the *Titanic* and the young blond singer, if she ever really existed, was never heard from again.

Ben Guggenheim's death at forty-seven was a catastrophe for his little family. Peggy and Hazel suddenly became very religious and, for the first time, began going to services at Temple Emanu-El regularly. Both have subsequently confessed that they never fully recovered from the disaster and have been searching for a father ever since. Hazel, at seventy-three, still has nightmares about the *Titanic*. Peggy, at seventy-six, says she thinks of her father's horrible death every day of her life.

Catastrophe in more ways than one. It was found immediately after Ben's death that his business affairs were in almost total disarray. Not only had he forfeited what would have been a colossal fortune had he remained in the family business, but he had also lost most of the money he had invested in International Steam Pump. The relatively small amount left was tied up in high-growth, low-yield stocks that were so depressed they could not be sold.

The last news was kept from the money-conscious Florette and so she continued to live in the same sumptuous manner as always. Meanwhile the brothers went to work to salvage what could be salvaged. Even Will, who had invested in International Steam Pump, was pressed into service, the situation was so desperate.

Without telling Florette where the money was coming from, Daniel, Murry, Solomon, and Simon advanced her funds from their own accounts to meet her considerable current expenses. When Florette heard about this, her Seligman pride flared up. Seligmans did not take handouts from anyone. She told the Guggenheim brothers to stop giving her money and drastically cut down on her scale of living. She left the big house on Seventy-second Street and into a small apartment. She let most of her servants go. She sold many paintings, tapestries, and jewels. She began dipping into her own personal funds.

During this difficult time Peggy developed "a complex about no longer being a real Guggenheim." "I felt like a poor relation," she wrote later, "and suffered great humiliation thinking how inferior I was to the rest of the family."

Four years after Ben's drowning, the situation was saved by the death of Florette's father, James Seligman, who left Florette a small fortune, around $2 million. Florette immediately reimbursed Daniel, Murry, Solomon, and Simon for the funds they had advanced her.

It took seven years for Ben's six brothers and their lawyers to finally settle his tangled, debt-ridden estate. Solomon and William bore the brunt of the work. When the papers were finally cleared off the desks there remained only $1,850,000 for distribution to Ben's heirs. Benita, Peggy, and Hazel each received $450,000 in trust, and $500,000 went to Florette. It was estimated by Sol and Will that Ben had lost something in the neighborhood of $8 million.

Their comparatively meager inheritances (remember, Dan's children were to get $2 million apiece, and Murry's well over $8 million apiece) and their missing out on such future Guggenheim bonanzas as Chile Copper, made Peggy, Hazel, and Benita among the poorest Guggenheims of their generation. Florette, however, alleviated their financial distress somewhat by leaving each of them $500,000, in trust, so, in the end, each daughter had $950,000 at her disposal. What Peggy then did with her money was nothing less than miraculous. Showing herself to be a *real* Guggenheim after all, she parlayed around $250,000 in income from her inheritance (she could not touch the principal) into a $30 million collection of modern art.

And then, later, driving home the point—by God, she was going to show the world who a *real* Guggenheim was—she created her own foundation, the Peggy Guggenheim Foundation, and willed to it her entire collection, plus her galleries in Venice.

CHAPTER 21

SENATOR SIMON,
OR DEMOCRACY IN AMERICA

Simon Guggenheim's campaign in 1907 for the U.S. Senate was so barefacedly corrupt (if we accept the premise that elections are supposed to represent the will of the people) that there is something almost refreshing about it. He did not try to fool anybody. "I have preserved a list showing the names of every person to whom I have paid a dollar, and what it was paid for," he was quoted by the Denver *Post* as saying in a speech. "If I am not nominated I will publish the list. And I want you to understand that if you nominate another man, I will spend $300,000 to defeat him."

Given his strong position in Colorado—the Guggenheims literally ruled the wealth of the mountain states—and the influence of money in U.S. politics, winning high public office was, for Simon, not an unrealistic ambition. Especially since the greatest political issue of the day was silver and Colorado was a silver state and Simon Guggenheim's family owned the choicest silver mines in Colorado.

The silver issue boiled down to a matter of inflation versus deflation, cheap currency versus hard currency, easy credit versus tight credit. In 1873 the U.S. government, trying to contract the money supply as a deflationary measure, refused to coin any more silver, thus threatening the "Silver Princes" of the Western states and their miners and minions with possible ruin. The gold standard had temporarily won the day. But then in 1878, and again in 1890, the government was forced to expand the money supply and went back to coining silver, thus threatening the gold standard, and causing outcries from all sustainers of deflation and tight credit.

It was no surprise to anyone when Simon Guggenheim, Silver Prince, took his political stand as a silver Republican, an advocate of unlimited coinage of silver.

First he tried for lieutenant governor of Colorado, but was forced to withdraw because, at twenty-nine, he was underage. Then he tried for governor and was forced to withdraw again, this time by his older brother, because his "silverism" was making too much trouble for them in the hard-money, gold-standard climate of Wall Street. Then he began laying plans to capture a seat in the U.S. Senate.

Meanwhile events in New York suddenly brought the Guggenheims a surge of popularity in the Western states. The family refused to join the hated, Rockefeller-financed smelters' trust, which enforced, among other disagreeable things, the twelve-hour workday, and, to embarrass the trust, the Guggenheims embraced the eight-hour day, to the joy of every miner in the West.

Sensing from this approval that his moment had come, Simon, who had just married the vivacious, talented Olga Hirsch, began purchasing his Senate seat in earnest.

Not long before his marriage he had given five hundred new suits of clothing to the poor boys of Denver. On his wedding day he had gone a step further and presented free turkey dinners to one thousand poor Denver boys. Now he financed lavish parties for the employees of the Denver *Post;* he donated buildings to the University of Colorado, the Colorado School of Mines, and the State Agricultural College. And, most important of all, he began promising and distributing largesse to the members of the Colorado state legislature, the body, in the days of indirect election of senators, which he hoped would elect him.

Simon's method was simple. He would personally finance any state legislator's campaign for reelection in return for his vote, and once he, Simon, was elected, would help his electors and their families in any way he could. One bewildered state senator, a farmer by the name of Morton Alexander, was naive enough not to fully understand how this worked at first, and, upon asking Guggenheim's campaign manager, "What about the people?" was told, "To hell with the people." Then, when he protested he had almost no financial resources of his own to sustain another political campaign without broad popular backing, Alexander was told, "Don't worry, the Guggenheims will take care of everything." Later Alexander balked at supporting Guggenheim and was surprised one day to return to his farm to find his fence torn down and his lawn trampled.

More tractable legislators were to find themselves sudden owners of stock in Guggenheim-controlled companies, all of which were booming at the time. These fortunate men finally elected Simon Guggenheim senator from Colorado by a vote of sixty-eight to twenty-seven.

Many were outraged by the election.

Simon himself quietly defended his purchase of his Senate seat stating, with his usual candor: "The money I have contributed has helped to elect these men and naturally they feel under obligation to vote for me. It is done all over the United States today. I do not consider that it is wrong and neither do I think that it can in any sense be called bribery." Later he said: "I wish to state clearly that I am going to Washington to represent all the people; that I am free and untrammeled and under obligation to no interest, company, railroad, or corporation."

Not long after the election, American Smelting and Refining, now controlled entirely by the Guggenheims, went back to the twelve-hour workday in Colorado, a double cross that earned the Guggenheims the undying enmity of the Western miners.

And so Simon Guggenheim took his place in the United States Senate, along with eighteen other multimillionaires, including Nelson W. Aldrich of Rhode Island, father-in-law of John D. Rockefeller, Jr., Henry DuPont of Delaware, Henry Cabot Lodge of Massachusetts, and, two years later, Elihu Root of New York. These eighteen millionaire senators were the ones who headed the committees dealing with federal finance, taxation, and tariffs. Now, with Simon in their ranks—and his family's fortune was larger than any of theirs—they had a powerful new ally. Ninety-six times did Simon vote for the ultraconservative schedules of the Payne-Aldrich tariff. His speeches on such subjects were usually blunt and brief. "It is of importance," he once declared, in one of his shortest addresses, "to keep out the cheap Spanish lead and also the Australian lead."

Not long after they settled in Washington, Simon and Olga Guggenheim established a reputation for themselves as a host and hostess on a grand scale. No other politician in Washington, including the President, commanded such vast resources for entertaining. When the Silver Prince threw a big party it was always *the* social event of the season.

Simon at the time was a short, dark, stocky figure with a black moustache, a prominent chin, and, of course, the almost inevitable Guggenheim potato nose. The most Semitic of all the brothers in appearance, he was also one of the most sensual in his tastes and habits. He liked gourmet food, fine imported wines, Havana cigars, and beautiful women. In Spain—where the farsighted Meyer had sent him for two years to learn the language spoken south of the Rio Grande—he had grown used to a southern European manner of living. He took time over the pleasures of the table and saw nothing wrong in maintaining an *amante*. People found him quiet, elegant, and courteous, yet at the same time a bit of a rough diamond. He smoked too many cigars and had too vigilant an eye for the ladies. The "old" families of the Denver Club had never accepted him and, though he entertained so lavishly in Washington, certain WASP strongholds never tendered him invitations. His tall, long-necked, stately wife, Olga, was an accomplished linguist, a perceptive connoisseur of the arts, a superb hostess, a good amateur musician, and, fortunately for Simon, was southern European enough in outlook herself to be able to tolerate his many mistresses, some of whom rivaled even brother Solomon's in their glory. She gave two sons to Simon—John Simon and George Denver.

As many had predicted, Senator Simon Guggenheim did not contribute very much to his nation during his lone term in the Senate. He rarely made a speech, and when he did, it was usually very brief. He did not sponsor any significant legislation. Perhaps his most sustained effort was to lead an unsuccessful filibuster against the bill that established the Department of Labor. (It was not for nothing that he was known as "the most conservative man in the Senate.") But he did manage to capture plenty of federal construction projects for his state, take care of the financial needs of the Colorado state legislators, attend to the problems of his Colorado constituents, and keep employment at high levels in Colorado's mines and smelters.

And, of course, he never failed to safeguard the worldwide interests of the House of Guggenheim, to his older brothers' everlasting thanks. During his incumbency the U.S. government purchased plenty of silver, allowed copper and lead prices to soar, slapped high tariffs on all foreign metals, and, after a bit of an environmental skirmish, let Guggenmorgan and Morganheim get away with unrestricted exploitation of the natural resources of Alaska.

One of the most applauded acts of Simon's career in the Senate was his vote for the constitutional amendment providing for the direct election of U.S. senators, an amendment that was a direct outcome of his own election as senator. (He was, in fact, the last senator to be elected indirectly.) Privately he confided to friends that the amendment would make little difference in the composition of the Senate. It might even result in more millionaire senators, he opined, because it would cost even more money to conduct a political campaign among the entire population of a state than among a few dozen state legislators.

Simon, of course, was right. Seventy years after he had decided to put his money into a Senate seat rather than into a Villa Carola or a Hempstead House, seventy years later, in the year of the United States Bicentennial, the United States Senate was still the most exclusive millionaires' club in America, with some 30 percent of its membership possessing assets in excess of one million dollars. And, just as it was in Simon's day, it is these millionaire senators who continue to occupy the most important places on the committees of finance and taxation.

Simon Guggenheim did not run for reelection in 1912 and resigned his Senate seat on March 1, 1913. By then he had accomplished his purpose. His older brothers had finally accepted him. To honor their distinguished younger brother, Daniel, Murry, and Solomon created the new positions of chairman of the board of American Smelting and Refining, chairman of the board of American Smelters Securities, and chairman of the board of Guggenheim Exploration Company, and appointed Simon to all three positions. Thus Simon could now go back to the far more serious business of making money. And with an added feather in his cap. Henceforth he would be referred to exclusively as "the Senator," a title that would remain with him until his death.

Heaped with so many honors, titles, and appointments, it appeared to everyone that Simon Guggenheim, at forty-seven, had reached the culmination of his life and career. However, a far different, and infinitely more noble, climax awaited him eleven years later, one that would all but obliterate his careers as a senator and a businessman and earn him a lasting place in the history of his country.

CHAPTER 22

ALL SIMON'S SONS

One spring day in 1922 John Simon Guggenheim, seventeen-year-old son of Senator Simon Guggenheim, died suddenly of pneumonia and mastoiditis at Phillips Exeter Academy in New Hampshire. He had done well at Exeter, showing promise as a scholar, and had been admitted to Harvard for the following year.

Seventeen years later, George Denver Guggenheim, thirty-two-year-old son of Senator Simon Guggenheim, and heir to one of America's greatest fortunes, went one November morning to the Abercrombie & Fitch sporting-goods store in New York, purchased a big-game hunting rifle, took a room in the Paramount Hotel, and, several hours later, placed the gun to his head, pulled the trigger, and blew his brains out.

Olga Guggenheim had waited almost ten years to give birth to her first child. During this time, as each year brought fresh disappointment, she had consulted the most eminent gynecologists in America. When the boys finally were born—in 1905 and 1907—she and Simon had been exultant. Simon had wanted sons desperately. He had seen his brothers Isaac, Solomon, and Ben produce nine daughters among them. He did not think much of one of Dan's two sons, and did not consider Murry's son, Edmond, especially brilliant. Who was going to lead the House of Guggenheim in the years to come? When John Simon was born in 1905 Simon was so jubilant he celebrated the event by giving $80,000 to the Colorado School of Mines.

Subsequently he made it quite clear to his two boys that he expected them to measure up. The day would come, he never tired of repeating, when they would be called upon to help lead the greatest mining and smelting empire in the world.

John did measure up, in his own fashion. Though he did not give much indication of becoming an industrial leader—he was much too sensitive—he was an excellent student and had shown he was capable of hard work.

George Denver was a very different type. Erratic, rebellious, and very high-strung, he had often incurred his father's wrath by showing far too strong an inclination toward play rather than toward work. At Harvard, where he was a member of the class of 1929, he was well liked, but he was an indifferent, aimless student. A fellow classmate described him as "all dressed up and no place to go."

After George Denver graduated from Harvard, Simon took him into Guggenheim Exploration Company as a trainee, then assigned him to the nitrate fields in Chile.

It did not take long for the dapper, pleasure-loving George, used to the amenities of Cambridge and New York, to tire of the rigors of the desolate, parched, oven-hot nitrate deserts of Chile. Before long he complained of illness and was back in New York, fooling around. No, he told his father, who was now president of American Smelting and Refining, having succeeded Dan, no, he was *not* going back to the gloomy offices of Guggenheim Exploration.

Simon came down hard on him. When Simon was tough, he could be very, very tough. He reminded his son that the Guggenheim family was short on males in his generation and that since John Simon had died, he, George Denver, was all there was left to carry on Simon's line. He reminded him also that he had already given him a million-dollar trust fund, and had left him $10 million in his will, so he would have the necessary resources to fulfill his responsibilities and uphold his name as a son of the House of Guggenheim. And he reminded him for the one-hundredth time that he was expected to take his rightful place in *the family business*.

It was an old litany for George Denver. A tiresome litany. But there was not much he could do but give in. Reluctantly he went back to work for Dad. Though George accomplished very little, Simon nevertheless made him a member of the executive committee of American Smelting and Refining—*that* looked nice on the masthead—and a director of a subsidiary, the General Cable Corporation.

But George's real interests lay elsewhere. His million-dollar trust fund enabled him to lead a gay life in Manhattan and he began keeping very late hours, making the rounds of New York's night spots and speakeasies. He was frequently seen in the company of equivocal people: call girls, bootleggers, and especially homosexuals. He turned to drink and dabbled in drugs. Before long his personality—never too stable—began to disintegrate and he became manic-depressive. Physicians were consulted and he was given insulin shock treatment, which made him worse. He became acutely paranoid, suspicious of everybody. After several suicide attempts, a male nurse was assigned to keep him under constant guard. Somehow he escaped the nurse that cool November morning in 1939 when he managed to make his deadly purchase at Abercrombie & Fitch and check into the Paramount Hotel.

It was the assistant manager of the hotel who discovered the body. Guggenheim had not informed the hotel when he was checking out and, after repeated calls had failed to rouse him, the assistant manager entered the room with a passkey . . . to find the fully clothed body of George Denver on the floor with a .300 magnum big-game rifle under him, the original store wrappings not far away.

In George's pockets were his calling cards, his driver's license, and $325 cash. Although his driver's license listed his address as his parents' apartment at 630 Park Avenue, it was discovered that he really lived at 146 Central Park West, and that he shared the apartment with a man.

The deaths of their two sons were cruel shocks to Simon and Olga and could well have ruined their lives. It is a tribute to both of them that they were able to transform the double tragedy into one of the most inspired benefactions in American history.

There had been little or nothing in Simon Guggenheim's career even to hint that he would one day create something as noble as the John Simon Guggenheim Memorial Foundation.

For the dynastic-minded Simon, the destruction of his sons was a catastrophe of enormous magnitude. What was his immense wealth for if it was not for his sons? What were his labors at Guggenheim Brothers and American Smelting and Refining for if not to provide vehicles for the advancement of his sons?

But these considerations were, in a way, peripheral. Simon had yearned for his boy, he had waited almost ten years for him, and he loved him very much.

After John's death, Simon, in his acute sense of loss, began to withdraw into himself and ask questions of himself and his Creator he had never paused to ask before. He also turned his attention and his hopes to George Denver, and realized, to his additional sorrow, and to George's frustration, that the poor boy, already nervous and high-strung and of indeterminate sexual leanings, could not be counted on.

Gradually Simon evolved the idea of creating a memorial to his lost older son and began consulting with his closest friends and associates as to what form that memorial should take.

It is not known for sure, and it probably will never be known for sure, but it appears reasonably certain that the original idea for the John Simon Guggenheim Memorial Foundation came, in part at least, from Carroll Atwood Wilson, a Rhodes Scholar and general counsel for both American Smelting and Refining and Guggenheim Brothers.

What *is* known for sure is that Carroll Wilson suggested to Simon that he consult with two other Rhodes scholars to formulate definitive plans for the new foundation. After several months of gestation, the Senator agreed on a format for the foundation, and on March 16, 1925, the day of the foundation's incorporation, Simon endowed it with an initial gift of $3 million worth of securities, an amount destined to multiply forty times.

Fellows were to be selected by juries of experts in their fields. Then they were to be given money for whatever they wanted to do, even if it was doing nothing. A Fellow could paint, write, compose, or experiment, or he could simply travel, read, or contemplate. Or, as Peter Lyon once put it, he could "just go abroad and moon through European galleries and spend Guggenheim's good American dollars in European cafés." (Though it was hoped that such types as these last would not get past the screening.)

By the end of 1976, 39 Guggenheim Fellows had received the Nobel Prize and 90 had received the Pulitzer Prize. Of the 80 National Book Awards given through 1976, 44 have gone to Guggenheim Fellows. And of the 1,066 members of the National Academy of Arts and Sciences, 349 have held Guggenheim Fellowships. In the light of these figures, it is easy to understand why a Guggenheim Fellowship has come to be regarded as not merely a financial assist, but virtually a form of intellectual knighthood in the United States.

It is difficult to imagine what might have been the state of America's cultural life over the past fifty years had the John Simon Guggenheim Memorial Foundation not existed. Certainly the United States government did precious little during the period to foster individual scientific and artistic creation, other than to grant foundations tax-exempt status (except for the Fulbright program, which was modeled after the Guggenheim Foundation and which is now being allowed to expire). And the other foundations were, on the whole, more generous to institutions than to individuals.

Simon Guggenheim died of pneumonia in 1941, at seventy-three, and was rewarded by a page-long, double-column obituary in *The New York Times.* By then his foundation possessed assets of $8 million. In his will Simon had made his foundation the residuary legatee of his estate, which was valued at approximately $50 million, the largest of the seven brothers', and so the John Simon came into another $20 million after Simon's death. Ten million of this had been destined for son George Denver, who had shot himself two years before. (There would have been more for the foundation, but we know by now what Chilean nitrates did to the Guggenheims' fortune.) In succeeding years, as Simon's mistresses began to die off, the foundation was further enriched by the trust funds he had established for them. Then, when Olga died in 1970, at ninety-three, without immediate heirs, she left the bulk of her estate, some $40 million, to the foundation. These combined funds, some $70 million, were then so well invested by the treasurer, Ernest H. Lundell, Jr., that the foundation's net worth by 1972 was something in the neighborhood of $120 million. It is presently around $100 million due to the drop in the stock market. From earnings from this sum the foundation is able to distribute approximately $4.5 million worth of fellowships each year.

CHAPTER 23

WILLIAM, OR GATENBY WILLIAMS

There may not have been a portrait of William Guggenheim in the Partners' Room at Guggenheim Brothers, but Will made up for that by writing his own illustrated autobiography, under the pseudonym Gatenby Williams, publishing the book himself, under the imprint of the Lone Voice Publishing Company, and mailing inscribed copies to each of his surviving brothers. Whether Solomon, Murry, or Simon then placed a copy in the Partners' Room to make up for their previous omission is anybody's guess.

The portrait that emerges from Gatenby Williams' book is that of a cheerful, intelligent, somewhat spoiled, idealistic prig, who was a bit removed from reality and not overly pleased with his Jewish ancestry.

Early in his book Will noted that all the Guggenheim brothers except Benjamin and himself were dark and that anyone seeing his "light complexion and the cast of his features would not have surmised his Semitic ancestry." Most observers, in fact, agreed that Will was the handsomest of the Guggenheim boys and noted that his face did have a decidedly

Germanic, even Anglo-Saxon, rather than Jewish, cast. He was also fortunate to have escaped, to some degree, the Guggenheim potato nose.

Will took his un-Semitic appearance seriously and consciously strove to be as un-Jewish as possible. In his middle years he ceased going to Temple Emanu-El, ceased observing the Jewish holy days, and frequented, for the most part, Gentile society. He even gave himself a WASPian pen name. One wonders where in the devil he got Gatenby from. Had living in a Scott Fitzgerald setting been too much for his perfervid imagination?

Will's life was a three-way dropout, but one would never surmise that from his autobiography. First, he dropped out of the family business, then he dropped out of the family, then he dropped out of his own religion and race. But the only hint of this triple defection in his book is a remark that "Will was always the exception."

He was scholarly and contemplative, whereas his brothers had "no head for book learning." He got higher marks than any of his brothers at school, almost always stood at the top of his class. He was the only brother to graduate from college. By his own autobiographical admission, he was "more sensitive to the innerness of things." "Few pause for beauty in the quest for gold," he wrote. Frequently in his book he refers to his "fundamentally artistic temperament."

Will was always at odds with his brothers, was utterly overwhelmed by them. Given his sensitive temperament, to have had five aggressive older brothers always ganging up on him must have been a trial.

First Isaac had objected to Will's being brought into the firm on an equal basis with the others. Then Daniel, playing the role of meddlesome mother-in-law, had forced him to divorce his first wife. Then Isaac, Dan, Sol, Murry, and Simon had concealed the true value of Chile copper from him, so as not to share the profits with him, and he had been forced to haul them all into court.

Was there any wonder why Will "retired" from M. Guggenheim's Sons in 1901, at age thirty-three, to enjoy his income of $250,000 a year, and devote himself to the things that were closest to his heart: literature, philosophy, the theater, and women?

As it turned out, Will was destined to have his fill of episodes with women, especially with his first wife.

Grace Herbert Guggenheim had collected a $150,000 divorce settlement from the Guggenheims and had promptly married a young Frenchman, Jules Roger Wahl, who proceeded to get rid of the $150,000 as if it were nothing but a case of Chablis. Broke and disgusted, Grace managed to get the marriage annulled.

Meanwhile Will had married Aimee Lillian Steinberger, a friend of his sisters Cora and Rose. The two settled down to wedded life in a $700,000 Italianate townhouse at 833 Fifth Avenue, assisted by twenty-one servants and two chauffeurs, and three years later they had a son, William, Jr.

By this time Grace was flat on her back in one room reading lurid, tempting accounts of Benjamin Guggenheim's marital troubles (Florette was threatening a costly divorce because of the young blond singer) and she decided to strike again.

The papers reported that Grace would be disposed to settle for $250,000. If Will would not fork over, she would attempt to annul her divorce, obtained in the state of Illinois, on the grounds that since neither partner was a resident of Illinois, the divorce was obtained by fraud.

This latter threat alarmed the entire Guggenheim family because if Will's divorce was found illegal, he and his wife, Aimee, would be living in bigamy and their son—one of the precious few males of the third generation—would be illegitimate.

Dan put Guggenheim Brothers' top legal talent on the case, and, after a long battle, which caused Will's name to appear in headlines in all the major newspapers, was victorious. The divorce decree was upheld.

Though the judges upheld the divorce decree, they emphatically did not approve of the way it was obtained: "The decree of divorce . . . was obtained as the direct result of frauds and the procuring of said decree was an outrage against the laws of the state of Illinois and a fraud upon the Circuit Court in Cook County."

This was, of course, another way of saying that Guggenheim money could accomplish almost anything, even the purchase of illegal divorces.

From troubles with Grace Herbert to troubles with Aimee.

Aimee Guggenheim was a very domineering woman who had kept her innate bossiness under wraps until William junior was born. After that major dynastic event—the name of Guggenheim would live on!—Aimee began pushing Will senior around. She had the bulk, as well as the personality, to do it. Aimee was a big lady, taller and heavier than her husband, and made herself look even taller and bigger by habitually wearing great bird of paradise-feather hats and ostrich-feather boas.

Aimee did not get along with the other Guggenheim brothers—they were, after all, impossible in-laws—and let her husband know it. She would frequently observe that Will was the only brother with a college degree and the others—a bunch of ignoramuses, in her opinion—had no respect for Will's culture. She complained also that the other brothers bullied and even cheated Will, which was true. She was a prime instigator behind Will's $10 million suit against his brothers over Chile Copper. Gradually Aimee succeeded in alienating Will from the other Guggenheims. She wanted him all to herself. So *she* instead of his brothers could bully him. By the time Will junior was nineteen, Will senior could not take his wife's bossiness any longer and they separated. Will then bought himself a four-story mansion at 3 Riverside Drive where he lived the remainder of his life.

That remainder was devoted to a curious mixture of philanthropic, intellectual, artistic, and amorous pursuits.

Will named the principal rooms in his new house after the principal metals upon which his fortune was based: the *Salon d'Or*, the *Chambre de Cuivre*, the *Chambre d'Argent*, the *Bureau de Plomb*.

In the *Chambre de Cuivre*, which he used as his studio, he devoted himself to his philanthropic, intellectual, and artistic pursuits. The *Salon d'Or* was reserved for Love.

Lover at large. Prince Billy had begun his amorous career in the mining camps of the Wild West and Mexico. After many vicissitudes, including two attempts at legitimate union, he picked up where he had left off years before at Peppersauce Bottoms and the plazas of Monterrey and Aguascalientes, this time in the more luxurious setting of the *Salon d'Or* at 3 Riverside Drive in New York City.

Will loved the theater and in his later years he became one of its most generous angels. One of the fringe benefits of this form of philanthropy that he liked best was being able to entertain showgirls, in the *Salon d'Or*, rationalizing it as business.

The plays Will financed were not always commercially successful and after a while he began to suffer heavy losses. These, combined with the large presents he was compelled to give his "protégées," substantially reduced his capital. When the Depression came, and wouldn't go away, and some of his major holdings, like Kennecott, Anaconda, and American Smelting, began to pass dividends, Will found himself having to tighten his belt. He eliminated two manservants and a secretary from his staff, keeping only his gentleman's gentleman and three maids. He sold his estate at Sands Point.

In the midst of these troubles, however, an event occurred that brought Will great joy. His son, William, Jr., married into the old New York aristocracy—she was a Beekman—and in 1939 the couple produced a son whom they named William Guggenheim III.

In his autobiography Will summed himself up in his late sixties:

> William Guggenheim, aside from his silvery hair and a somewhat rounder waist-line, looks nearly the same as he did thirty years ago. . . . He is wise enough to keep fit by leading a sane and regular existence. . . . He rests upon his laurels. . . . His career is sharply divided by two amazing contrasts: one of harsh hazardous struggle in the rugged West and undeveloped Mexico; the other of a creative, cosmopolitan club-man in the very heart of ease and civilization. . . .

Not long after penning this self-appreciation, Will's perceptions did begin to cloud a bit and he ceased living a sane existence. By the time he entered his seventieth year, he had, in fact, gone completely gaga.

What was left of his fortune was being steadily drained away by a succession of showgirl protégées. If the miracle of miracles could be accomplished in the *Salon d'Or,* the girl could have all she wanted.

By the time of Will's final illness there were four miracle workers left. They were two long-stemmed showgirls and two beauty-contest winners, Miss America of 1929, and Miss Connecticut of 1930. Assiduously did they attend the bedside, in turn, of their dying angel.

Not long after Will finally succumbed, on June 27, 1941, the Associated Press flashed photos of Will with two of his protégées to all subscribing papers, with the caption:

> GUGGENHEIM WITH TWO GIRLS NAMED IN WILL. William Guggenheim, of the famous copper family, who died last month at 72, is shown here with two of the former showgirls to whom he left his estate. . . . The will was filed yesterday, but there was no assurance that the estate's estimated $1,000,000 value would stand up.

The estate's estimated million-dollar value did not stand up. At least for the protégées. Aimee Guggenheim saw to that. She challenged the will in court and received the share to which she was entitled by New York State law, and saw to it that her son got his rightful share also. After these shares and all debts and taxes had been paid, all there was left for the four girls was $1,305.04 apiece. During Aimee's suit it came out that since Will's retirement from M. Guggenheim's Sons in 1901, the seventh son of Meyer Guggenheim had run through some $8 million.

Fortunately for Will and Will III, there remained the iron-clad, not-to-be-borrowed-against, automatically-passed-down-to-descendants trust fund of a million dollars established by Simon for Will and his heirs.

Will had always been lovable, but . . . look what he did with all that hard-earned money, all that copper, gold, silver, and lead that had been torn out of Colorado, Utah, Mexico, Alaska, and Chile.

Ah yes, but look what Will alone among the brothers did for the family in posterity. Look what he did for history. The autobiography by Gatenby Williams! None of the other brothers ever bothered to keep any records or write anything down. They were always too busy making money to take the time to record what they were doing, either in business or in philanthropy. And they had almost no sense of history.

But Will did take the time. If it were not for *William Guggenheim* by Gatenby Williams, much of the early history of the Guggenheims in Philadelphia, the early pioneering in Colorado and Mexico, would have been irretrievably lost. Perceptively, William wrote:

> The House of Guggenheim—Meyer, Barbara, and their children—has been unique in American annals, having faintly an old-world, indeed one might almost say a feudal flavor about it . . . . It is improbable that the tale will ever be paralleled.

CHAPTER 24

COLONEL BOB

As long as the bonanzas and the sons kept coming, the Guggenheims could walk on clouds, soar among the stars. But when their luck turned sour, when the hoped-for bonanza became a certified bust, when the hoped-for sons became daughter after daughter after daughter, the family went into reverse. The decline began. By 1939 only the Guggenheim foundations were flourishing. The businesses were immobile or dying, and the grandsons were not doing much of anything.

> Every wealthy family supports at least one gentleman in leisure.
> I have elected to assume that position in mine.

With these words, pronounced in early manhood, M. Robert Guggenheim, elder son of Daniel and Florence and heir apparent to the Guggenheim dynasty, expressed the philosophy that would guide the conduct of his life.

Ah, the tales that are told of M. Robert. Taking time out from his short-lived job at the Tacoma smelter to break the transcontinental speed record racing a car from Seattle to New York. Running up staggering restaurant and nightclub bills against Guggenheim Brothers. Becoming a Catholic to marry his second of four wives, then divorcing her shortly thereafter. Owning five seagoing yachts in succession, each with the same name, *Firenze*. Pinching the behinds of all the old bags at Washington cocktail parties (termed by *Confidential* magazine "the American pincers movement"). Devoting his remaining energies to raising prize Schipperkes and Bedlington terriers. Invading the décolletage of aristocratic ladies at official dinners while serving as U.S. ambassador to Portugal. Entertaining his mistresses at smart Washington restaurants in full view of his fourth wife.

Why the son of Daniel should have turned out this way is best left to the psychoanalytical diggers to explain. It is not easy to be the firstborn son of a famous and important father. Much is expected of you, and often you feel overwhelmed by the importance of your father. What can *you* do, with your meager gifts, to attract attention?

Well, for one thing, you can be mischievous; you can be a hellion. This will attract plenty of attention, and might even land you a special place in your mother's heart, since mothers usually prefer wild sons to lambs.

Thus was M. Robert—always so overshadowed by his father and brother—compelled to a childhood of unremitting mischief. Sister Gladys recalls that he was always getting into trouble. At Hempstead House he would let animals out of their pens. He would flip silverware in the air at table. He would invade the servants' rooms. He would tease the cats and dogs, and his sister Gladys. He would play practical jokes on Father's houseguests.

Of course, all of this brought the hard fist of fatherly disapproval down on his head repeatedly, but mother Florence, stimulated in some curious way by Robert's naughty antics, still preferred him to her younger son, Harry. When Dan was not around she would indulge him shamelessly. If there was a last piece of dessert to be given out it would be slipped to Robert, not Harry.

This combination of condemnation and approval bred in young Robert, as might be expected, a dislike of his father and an inordinate love of his mother.

Whatever Dan made M. Robert do, M. Robert did halfheartedly, or not at all. Dan made him go to the Columbia School of Mines, and, though he graduated, he did not do at all well in his studies. It was only because he was a Guggenheim that he managed to scrape by. Dan put him to work in Guggenheim Brothers and he worked so lackadaisically it was embarrassing. Setting up a million-dollar trust fund for him, so he would not be compelled to make a fool out of himself in another job, Dan accepted his son's gleeful resignation.

All was not lost, however, during this abortive period. For M. Robert did make his contribution to the family by marrying Grace Bernheimer of New York and producing two sons, in a family that desperately needed sons, Daniel II in 1906 and M. Robert, Jr. in 1910. But no sooner was this dynastic feat accomplished than M. Robert's roving eyes and affections killed his marriage and he was forced to give his wife a substantial alimony and award her the custody of his sons.

His two boys then grew up outside the Guggenheim orbit and ethos, and so the dynasty, for all practical purposes, lost its logical fifth-generation heirs. Later, in 1925, young Daniel II died of a heart attack at eighteen during a track meet at Exeter, becoming the fourth Guggenheim male of his generation to die before producing any offspring.

Meanwhile M. Robert had gone to war as a lieutenant in the 69th Regiment. Going overseas, he became, in the words of his commanding officer, "the best goddamned general's aide in the United States Army." The accolade referred mostly to Robert's abilities as a party giver. It was at one of these parties that he got to know Lt. Dwight Eisenhower, a man who was to have a crucial influence on Robert's later life.

In a very real sense, Bob Guggenheim discovered himself in the army. It was something wholly his, something that had nothing to do with the family. And people who knew him at the time recall today that he definitely had a "command presence." After the war he remained in the reserves and eventually achieved the rank of colonel. From then on he was known as "the Colonel." In 1925 he graduated from the War College, and from 1932 to 1935 he served on the staff of the War Department.

With his million-dollar trust fund churning out dividends and interest for him, there was not much need for Bob to do anything after World War I but look for another wife. He found her in one Margaret Weyher, a Catholic from Scranton, Pennsylvania. To marry her, Bob renounced Judaism and became a Catholic. As soon as this conversion was announced, reporters descended on father Daniel at his suite in the St. Regis for comment, and the old tycoon told them: "I'm delighted. My son has always been a very bad Jew. I hope they'll make a good Catholic out of him." M. Robert and Margaret then settled down to raising horses and dogs on Robert's Firenze Farms near August Belmont's estate at Babylon, Long Island. The marriage lasted only three years.

The divorce occurred in 1928 and Bob wasted no time in finding a replacement. This time it was a spirited horsewoman, and somewhat less-spirited Lutheran, Elizabeth Eaton, who was only too delighted to become the mistress of Firenze Farms with its stable of twenty hunters and jumpers.

When boredom with Elizabeth Eaton—brought on by the excitement of his other girl friends—reached the point of exasperation, Bob divorced her and promptly took a fourth wife, who was married at the time he began courting her. She was Mrs. William Bird van Lennep, nee Rebecca de Loatch Pollard, a doll-like blond from Virginia, whose father had been one of the pioneers in the development of Virginia Beach and whose mother was a member of the Colonial Dames. Few women can resist oceangoing yachts, vast estates, multimillion-dollar fortunes, and so it was not difficult for Robert to persuade "Polly" to divorce William Bird van Lennep and marry him. The wedding ceremony took place on board the *Firenze* in Miami, and the long, oceangoing honeymoon included stops at all the Central American countries, including Cuba, a hurricane that almost sank the happy couple, and a trip to California and back.

From 1938 to 1941 Bob and Polly Guggenheim lived exclusively on the *Firenze,* traveling all over the world, finally coming to rest in the Potomac in 1942. They then settled in Washington in a thirty-six-room Norman manor in Rock Creek Park which they called Firenze House, and in which Polly lived until 1976.

In addition to Firenze House, Colonel Bob also maintained an 1,800-acre plantation near Charleston, South Carolina, called Poco Sabo, a lovely old place, trees dripping with Spanish moss, an ancient Colonial house, a 10,000-acre hunting preserve nearby on which Bob killed a thousand birds a year hunting on tack ponies that stop as soon as the dogs point. Former guests at Poco Sabo remember lavish six-course, three-wine dinners, attended by antebellum characters, which would begin at eleven, "after three hours of drinking," and last through the consumption of as many as sixty birds shot that afternoon.

It was now, in the mid-1940s, that the final, ultimately disastrous phase of M. Robert Guggenheim's career began. In the vastness of Firenze House—which included a grand ballroom, a paneled library with engravings said to be by Christopher Wren, a dining room that could seat thirty, a four-table billard and pool room, and a bowling alley—Bob and Polly Guggenheim entertained and entertained. Among their closest friends, and most frequent guests, were Dwight Eisenhower, Speaker of the House Joe Martin, Gen. Curtis Le May, and Hubert Humphrey.

By this time, Robert could count on an income from his investments of around $800,000 a year. Since $250,000 went for the yacht, he had around $550,000 left, minus taxes, with which to amuse himself, Polly, and his friends.

By the time Eisenhower was elected President, Colonel Bob Guggenheim was a certified member of that unofficial circle in Washington that runs everything, including the country, known as the Club.

Bob and Polly had worked hard to get Ike elected. Polly raised more money for him than any other woman in Washington, and Bob contributed a healthy $100,000 to his campaign.

As a reward for helping him into the White House, Eisenhower offered Robert an appointment as United States ambassador to Portugal and Robert accepted. The year was 1953.

It was, all things considered, an incredibly irresponsible appointment, as so many of Eisenhower's diplomatic appointments were. Guggenheim had a well-known reputation for offending people at parties. Polly says today she was always having to go around "pouring salve" on people's hurt feelings. Robert had never worked steadily at anything in his life. He had never run an organization or even an office. He had never held a diplomatic position. The only qualification he possessed to become U.S. ambassador to Portugal was his money. Together with Simon's Senate seat and Harry's ambassadorship to Cuba, Bob's ambassadorship was the third public office the Guggenheims had purchased.

Right away, as soon as he got to Portugal, he started off on the wrong foot. In his maiden speech in Lisbon he told a stunned audience, which included the president of Portugal, that, of course, he would have preferred the Court of St. James's, but Portugal was not such a bad second choice.

This remark, however, was soon drowned in the endless rounds of cocktail parties and dinners Ambassador and Mrs. Guggenheim gave at the embassy and at their official residence. Bob and Polly entertained with style and gusto, always serving the finest of everything. The Portuguese were only too happy to drink their champagne and eat their caviar. Soon they reconciled themselves to Bob's booming voice, his backslapping, his practical jokes, his gaffes, even his American pincers movements.

But then the inevitable happened. People in the embassy, noting his often childish behavior, had been predicting it would come sooner or later.

A splendid state dinner in the palace of the Portuguese president. The crème de la crème of the Portuguese aristocracy present. Tiaras and jewels. Sashes and decorations. Rare wines. The presidential cuisine.

At a certain point in the festivities, United States Ambassador to Portugal M. Robert Guggenheim suddenly reverts to the mischievous little boy of Hempstead House, places two teaspoons end-to-end on one another, and flips one in the air . . .

. . . It falls into the cleavage of one of the noble ladies.

Silence at table.

Then, instead of letting the noble lady fish the spoon out herself, the Ambassador leaps to his feet and reaches into the cleavage himself, fumbling between her breasts for the utensil.

What happened next has not been recorded. All that is known is that a day or so later M. Robert Guggenheim was declared persona non grata in Portugal and was asked by the president of Portugal to leave the country.

The White House subsequently accepted the Colonel's resignation on August 10, 1954. In his letter of resignation, according to *The New York Times*, Colonel Guggenheim wrote to Eisenhower that he was "resigning for personal reasons and because of the factor of health. "

And so Bob and Polly, divested of their ambassadorial stature, packed their bags and slipped back to Washington. It did not take long before word of what *really* happened began to make its way among members of the Club, Washington society, and the Guggenheim family. Yes, Bob had done it again. It was as if his whole life had been nothing but a series of rehearsals for this one tremendous faux pas.

Bob Guggenheim's reaction to the Great Disgrace was to simply go gaga, like his uncle William.

Now he would appear in top Washington restaurants with his mistresses, literally flaunting them for all to see, whereas before he had kept them under wraps. "Dad, O.K., but not in public," his son, Robert junior, would exclaim. And Robert senior would say: "Hell, I'm proud of it!"

Sometimes, while out with his wife, he would make sure in advance that his favorite girl friend would be at the table next to him, just so he could admire and wink at her from time to time.

Having no other opportunities in life to make conquests but women, and being in constant need of boosting his ego, M. Robert eventually fell into a kind of sexual frenzy. One woman after another. Each reaffirming his waning faith in his masculinity.

Toward the end, any creature who could perform the sort of miracles Uncle Will's protégées performed for him in the *Chambre d'Or* became the most important person in Bob's life. When death came in 1959, it was while M. Robert, at age seventy-four, was boarding a taxicab in George-town after visiting one of his favorites. It had been a strenuous session, much too much for his aged heart.

Can anything more be said about Colonel Bob? Is it really true that he had no ambitions beyond his own self-gratification? Taking a closer look, and something of a psychological gamble, do we not perceive that he may very well have fulfilled an ambition he never consciously stated to him-self, or to anyone else, an ambition held, also unconsciously, by many members of his religion and race? And that was to be fully and uncondi-tionally accepted into the Gentile upper class. His family had made it into the Jewish upper class long ago: there remained that heaven-on-earth of American Gentile social status to be scaled and attained.

Did M. Robert attain it? Yes, as thoroughly as any Jew has attained it , before or since. Step by step. Choosing the overwhelmingly WASP mili-tary as his preferred milieu. Renouncing Judaism in favor of Catholicism. Marrying three Gentile girls, the last a member of the Colonial Dames. Going around with people like Dwight Eisenhower and Omar Bradley. Getting into all the right clubs and getting invited to all the right parties in WASPian Washington. Allowing his son, M. Robert, Jr., to be brought up an Episcopalian. Had M. Robert had an ambition after all? It seems so. And, in keeping with the triviality of his life, what a trivial ambition it was . . . to pass for a WASP.

CHAPTER 25

PEGGY: LIBERATED IN EUROPE

She was young, she was attractive, she was intelligent, she was finan-cially independent, and she was free, at last, in Europe.

It had taken her Guggenheim uncles seven years to untangle her fa-ther's chaotic estate. Finally, in 1919, in her twenty-first year, she came into the first of her many inheritances: a $450,000 trust fund from Daddy, $22,500 a year for life, assuming the trustees remained competent, more if they were more than competent. The beginning of her fortune. After Peggy collected her birthright her mother—who would one day leave her an additional $450,000—was most upset. She could no longer control her. First liberation.

Clear out of her mother's apartment. Take a trip. Go across the United States. Niagara Falls to Chicago. Yellowstone Park. California. The Canadian Rockies. Mexico. Fall in love. Get engaged. Get disengaged.

Fix up her face. That damnable Guggenheim potato nose. That clown's nose. Everything about her face all right but the nose. On to Cincinnati, to the famous plastic surgeon who could give you a new nose.

Choosing the plaster model of the nose she prefers. A nose "tiptilted like a flower." In the middle of the operation, performed under local anesthetic, the surgeon asks her to choose again: he is unable to tip-tilt that potato into a flower. She says stop and leave things as they are. After the abortive operation the nose remains painfully swollen and she refrains from going to New York where it might be seen. Hiding in the Midwest, waiting for the swelling to go down.

An heiress, but what to do? Cousin Harold Loeb, Aunt Rose's son, has a little radical bookshop, The Sunwise Turn, near Grand Central Station. She likes Harold because he is too somewhat of a rebel; becomes a clerk in his store. Her Guggenheim aunts come by and purchase books "by the yard." They bring in dimensions of their empty bookcases and order in bulk, without knowing what they are buying, to fill up the spaces.

Those Guggenheim aunts! Carrie. Florence. Leonie. Irene. Olga. Rose. Cora. Each with who-knew-how-many millions. That New York Swiss-German and German-German Jewish *haute bourgeoisie.* The Suffocators. Peggy snubs them. Lets them buy books by the yard, but refuses to go to their luncheons, teas, and bridge parties. Second liberation.

After a while Cousin Harold's bookstore becomes a bore. She goes to Europe, where she is to remain first for twenty-one years, then, after a brief interlude in New York, for the rest of her life. At the age of twenty-three she loses her virginity—third liberation—to the man who will become her first husband. There, for a while, the liberating process ceases.

The man to whom young Peggy Guggenheim gave up her virginity was Laurence Vail, twenty-nine, a painter who had not yet found himself, and a writer who had not yet found himself, but who knew all the painters and writers who had found themselves, one of those types who knows everybody but themselves, who lived in Paris and was known there as "The King of Bohemia." His mother, in Peggy's words, was "an aristocratic New England lady," and his father was a neurasthenic painter, perennially in and out of institutions, who was half Breton-French, half American. Laurence lived off a one-hundred-dollar-a-month allowance given him by his mother, who was financially independent.

Before long, Peggy decided, in her usual headstrong way, that she was going to lose her virginity to *him.* After all, at twenty-three, it was about time she lost it to *somebody*. "I had a collection of photographs of frescoes I had seen at Pompeii. They depicted people making love in various positions, and, of course, I was very curious and wanted to try them all out myself. It soon occurred to me that I could make use of Laurence for this purpose."

She found her moment one day when he came to visit her at the Plaza-Athenée Hotel in Paris, where she was staying with her mother. Since Mother was out, she was able to "arrange herself" so that Laurence would want to make love to her. "When he pulled me towards him, I acquiesed so quickly that he was surprised by my lack of resistance." However, there was always the chance that mother Guggenheim might return at any moment, so she suggested they go to his hotel instead: "I think Laurence had a tough time because I demanded everything I had seen depicted in the Pompeian frescoes."

It wasn't long before Peggy wanted Laurence Vail for keeps, and so when he nervously and impetuously proposed to her one day on the top of the Eiffel Tower (for which father Ben had built the elevators) she said yes at once. This surprised him, and he immediately took back his proposal. But Peggy wouldn't stand for any backtracking. She wanted him, and, in the end, she got him. The wedding took place in 1922 at the *mairie* of Seizième Arrondissement and the reception at the Plaza-Athenée.

No sooner was Peggy married, however, than she felt "extremely let down." "Now that I had achieved what I thought was so desirable, I no longer valued it so much."

The couple went to Italy for their long honeymoon. In Rome Peggy looked up her favorite cousin, Harold Loeb, who had sold The Sunwise Turn and was now publishing a literary review called *Broom* in the Italian capital. Since Peggy wanted to retain her independence, she looked up all her former beaux in Rome, and Laurence, in retaliation, looked up some of his former girl friends.

In 1923 Peggy had her first child by Vail, a boy to whom they gave the impossible name Sindbad, apparently Vail's idea.

It was at about this time, immediately before and immediately after the birth of Sindbad, that Peggy and Laurence began fighting more than usual. Laurence had a violent and uncontrollable temper and he liked to create scenes. Something of an exhibitionist, he especially liked to foment a ruckus in public. Some crippling sense of inadequacy was constantly gnawing at the root of his being.

What was causing these continual displays of impotence on Laurence Vail's part? Probably money. He was, after all, living wholly off Peggy. It was only a matter of time before the marriage would break up and Peggy would experience her fourth liberation.

But before the inevitable, they managed to patch things up sufficiently to be able to take a few long trips. Peggy insisted on avoiding the northern countries as much as possible. "I really feel happy only in southern towns, or at least in Latin ones." Among the places they visited, besides Italy, were Egypt and Palestine, with Peggy, of course, paying the bills.

After Palestine it was back to Paris, and rounds and rounds of "fantastic Bohemian parties." Endless hours spent talking, drinking, arguing, fighting at the Café du Dôme, La Coupole, the Select, the Dingo, the Deux Magots, the Boeuf sur le Toit. Trips to the Tyrol and to Venice, then pregnancy again and temporary residence in the Beau Rivage Hotel at Ouchy on Lake Léman to have the child. Laurence wanted a girl and got one this time. She was named Pegeen, and she was destined to lead a tragic life.

After Pegeen was born, Peggy and Laurence and their little family moved to a small village in the country, Pramousquier, not far from St. Raphael on the Côte d'Azur, making frequent trips into Paris in one of their three cars—the Lorraine Dietrich, the Hispano, or the Citroën. Laurence liked to drive very fast and he usually drank while he drove, rarely forgetting to bring along a plentiful supply of wine. It was, all things considered, a stupid, futile life. By comparison, the hated Guggenheim uncles to whose shrewdness, daring, and financial acumen Peggy and Laurence owed their wealth, were, for all their supposedly "dull bourgeois lives" (Peggy's words), paragons of purposefulness and sanity.

Peggy consulted a fortune-teller in Paris who told her she would meet a man in the South of France who would be her next husband. The fortune-teller was right. The man was John Holms, an Englishman, married, a writer manqué, of whom Edwin Muir said: "Holms gave me a greater feeling of genius than any other man I have met, and I think he must have been one of the most remarkable men of his time, or indeed any time."

While Laurence was away on one of his jaunts to St. Tropez, Peggy invited Holms and his wife, whom she had met a few weeks before, to her house at Pramousquier. There were also other guests in the house. One night they all went swimming together naked. Somehow, in the words of Peggy's autobiography, "John and I found ourselves alone on the beach and we made love."

The divorce agreement—concluded after seven years of marriage—made Peggy the guardian of Pegeen and Laurence the guardian of Sindbad. It was further stipulated that Peggy was to have Sindbad live with her for sixty days a year. No stipulation was made for Pegeen to live with Laurence. Peggy had to pay both lawyers. Hers cost $10,000 and Laurence's $5,000, In addition she had to give Laurence a monthly allowance, since he had no means of support.

With this nasty business settled, Peggy went to live with John Holms.

In her autobiography, Peggy was philosophical about the whole thing. Although the marriage had been "stormy," to say the least, she admitted she gained three very important things from it: one, her two children; two, a lasting friendship with Laurence Vail (they became much better friends after the divorce than they had been during the marriage), and, three, "total liberation from my early Jewish bourgeois upbringing," and from the suffocating tyranny of the Guggenheim family and their world.

Yet, we shall see there was a profound contradiction at the center of Peggy Guggenheim's sense of liberation from her family. Though almost the entire first half of her adult life was nothing but a long, drawn-out rebellion against her New York *haute bourgeois* upbringing and the Guggenheims, during the second half of her life she became the proudest and most self-consciously *Guggenheim* Guggenheim of them all, as well as by far the most famous Guggenheim of her generation.

Once Peggy was liberated from the frantic Laurence Vail, she virtually enslaved herself to John Holms. It was a typical rebound situation. Confronted with the tremendous void of having Laurence no more, she could not face life alone and so collapsed into the arms of the only other man around for whom she felt some sympathy and affection, and collapsed so completely that she all but lost her identity in his. During the first two years of their relationship, she and Holms did almost nothing but make love and travel, sometimes bringing little Pegeen along, more often leaving her with her nurse. Slowly Peggy fell completely under his spell. He was very intelligent, in an impractical, abstract sort of way, and possessed an enormous fund of general knowledge. He wanted desperately to be a writer, but lacked the willpower to ever get anything down on paper. His trouble was alcoholism.

Fortunately for Peggy, though she did not realize it at the time, Holms died in 1934, at only thirty-seven, from minor injuries sustained in an auto accident.

After his death Peggy felt very guilty, as if she could have done something to prevent it. Overwhelmed with misery, she soon fell into the arms of another man, a friend of John's with whom she had already made love, unbeknown to John. His name was Douglas Garman, called "Sherman" in her autobiography.

Douglas Garman, alias Sherman, was an Englishman five years younger than Peggy, a doctor's son who was interested in Marxism, and who was very poor. After the relationship had really become a relationship he made Peggy buy a cottage near South Harting. "Soon after this step," Peggy wrote, "I decided to commit suicide, I was still so unhappy about John. I therefore put the house in Sherman's name, as I intended to die."

After a while, Sherman, who for a year had been reading Karl Marx to the exclusion of everything else, joined the Communist Party. "All the money I gave him," Peggy wrote, "which formerly went to paying for the building he had done on the house and on other things, now went to the Communist Party. . . . I had no objection to that at all. I merely got bored listening to the latest orders from Moscow, which I was supposed to obey." After a while Peggy herself enrolled in the party "just to please Sherman."

But life with "Sherman," in the end, did not work. One weekend Peggy and he had a row about communism, and, in Peggy's words, "I got so bitchy that he hit me. I slipped and fell. There was blood everywhere."

CHAPTER 26

PEGGY AND GUGGENHEIM JEUNE

She was thirty-nine years old, and all she really had to her credit was an unhappy marriage, two unhappy children, and half a dozen momentarily exhilarating, but ultimately foolish, love affairs with penniless, footloose men. Plus the trust fund, of course.

It was in her thirty-ninth year that Peggy finally decided to do something more with her money than to throw it away on impotent painters, paralyzed, alcoholic nonwriters, and British communists.

What to do after fifteen years in and out of various, ultimately worthless beds? A friend, Peggy Waldman, suggested she either go into publishing, like Cousin Harold, or open an art gallery.

Since starting a publishing house would be too expensive, she decided on the art gallery. It would be the first gallery devoted exclusively to contemporary art in London.

Even that was an expensive proposition however. But precisely at the time she was debating the art gallery idea, mother Florette died, leaving her another $450,000 in trust. That gave Peggy $900,000 altogether. The stuffy, bourgeois uncles, whom Laurence Vail wanted hurled down Tiberius' cliffs (and who were ultimately responsible for sustaining his entire life, through the allowance Peggy gave him), invested their niece's money at roughly 5.5 percent, giving her an unearned income of nearly $50,000 a year, not bad at all in prewar Europe.

So now she *did* have enough money to open her own art gallery. After a brief search, she rented a second-floor gallery on Cork Street in London and engaged an old friend, Wyn Henderson, as secretary. It was Wyn who named the gallery "Guggenheim Jeune."

Opening an art gallery was not *such* a great departure from Peggy's former life because, after all, she had always liked, and had been interested in, painting and, of course, painters.

Peggy wanted to devote her first show to Brancusi, but Brancusi was away from Paris at the time and so Duchamp suggested Cocteau instead. After Duchamp introduced her to Cocteau, it was settled: the opening show of Guggenheim Jeune would be his. Duchamp hung the show and it caused quite a stir in London and put Guggenheim Jeune on the artistic map. Before, during, and after the show Duchamp was Peggy's chief artistic mentor, teaching her "everything he knew about abstract and surrealist art." Later Peggy gave exhibitions to Wassily Kandinsky and the young surrealist, Yves Tanguy, and held shows of sculpture by Antoine Pevsner, Henry Moore, Alexander Calder, Constantin Brancusi, and Jean Arp, all of whom where relatively unknown at the time. She also held a collage show displaying works of Ernst, Picasso, Braque, and Miró.

Meanwhile, she had to fall in love again. This time it was with "a fascinating Irishman with green eyes, a thin face, nose like an eagle," who was a friend of James Joyce. In fact, he had even been in love with Joyce's daughter. He was another "mad drunk." He was another penniless one. He was another writer who could not bring himself to write. Peggy called him Oblomov, after Goncharov's hero who did not even have the willpower to get out of bed. To complete his misery, ever since his birth "he had retained a terrible memory of life in his mother's womb." Sometimes this memory "smothered him" and he was unable to speak. His name was Samuel Beckett.

Beckett, who later snapped out of his paralysis of will to write several contemporary masterpieces and win a Nobel Prize, was destined to play a vital role in Peggy's life, not so much as a lover as an adviser. It was he who convinced her to buy the work of contemporary artists, insisting she had a moral duty to interest herself in the art of her day.

Since Beckett, when Peggy asked him what he was going to do about their life, invariably replied "Nothing," and since "he never seemed to make up his mind whether or not he was going to have me," Peggy finally had to give him up.

So back to the gallery and a show for Kandinsky. It had been Marcel Duchamp again who had introduced her to the great Russian abstractionist, who would be so avidly bought by her uncle Solomon.

Peggy's next big show after the Kandinsky was given during the second year of Guggenheim Jeune and it was for the promising young surrealist Yves Tanguy. "Since," in Peggy's words, "Surrealism was beginning to become known in England at the time . . . his show was a great success, and we sold a lot of paintings. . . . As a result, Tanguy suddenly found himself rich for the first time in his life and began to throw money around like mad. In cafés he used to make little balls of one pound notes and flicker them about to adjacent tables. Sometimes he even burnt them."

Peggy picked up a few Tanguys relatively cheaply, just as she had bought several Duchamps, Cocteaus, and Kandinskys, also at bargain prices. Often when she gave an artist a show, she would receive a painting free. It was in this rather inconspicuous way that one of the great private collections of modern art began.

Peggy might have been buckling down to work, at last, but she was nonetheless never one to let an interesting love affair float by when one happened to swim toward her net.

Now it was the turn of Yves Tanguy. Tanguy was married, but an inconvenience like that never hampered Peggy Guggenheim very much. After one of the many parties held during the time Tanguy's show was on in London, he and Peggy spent the night together in Peggy's flat. "After that," Peggy wrote in her autobiography, "it was difficult to see Tanguy alone because of his wife. Wyn [Henderson] came to our rescue and invited Mrs. Tanguy to lunch and kept her occupied all one afternoon."

In the midst of this affair, Beckett returned, appearing suddenly at Peggy's country house. When he saw a photo on the mantelpiece of Peggy and Tanguy looking happy together he threw a fit. Although he could never quite summon the willpower to "have" her, to use her expression, he was nevertheless extremely jealous—like most impotents—of the other men in her life.

The complexity and absurdity of this situation was unwittingly emphasized by Peggy in her autobiography: "Every morning Tanguy came to my house to fetch me. We spent the whole day together, then he went home to his wife. I was living in Beckett's apartment. He [Beckett] had gone to Brittany with his mistress in my car. I was still terribly in love with him. Tanguy once said to me: 'You don't come to Paris to see me, you come to see Beckett.'"

What happened to Peggy's children, psychologically, during this period is not revealed in her autobiography.

The bare facts are: Sindbad continually saw his father with a different woman, and his mother with a different man; Pegeen saw the same.

Meanwhile, in the midst of all this juggling, Peggy found the time to fall for a well-known British collector of surrealists whom she called in her autobiography "Donald Wrenclose." Peggy described him as "extremely attractive, quite good-looking, had great success with women, and was always having affairs . . . " She went on.

> He had one eccentricity . . . when he slept with women he tied up their wrists with anything that was handy. Once he used my belt, but another time in his house he brought out a pair of ivory bracelets from the Sudan. They were attached with a chain and Wrenclose has a key to lock them. It was extremely uncomfortable to spend the night this way, but if you spent it with Wrenclose it was the only way. . . . Once we slept under my favorite panting of Delveau's, the "Women with the Lamps." I was so thrilled, I felt as if I were one of the women.

Alas, in the end, everything palls, especially the wildest loves. After a while, Wrenclose-of-the-tied-wrists palled. Beckett-Oblomov palled. Tanguy palled. And Peggy, now facing life, the abyss, with *nobody*, fell for a married English sculptor by the name of Llewellyn, and "slept" with him right away.

By the end of 1939, Guggenheim Jeune, a year and a half after its founding, had become a losing business and Peggy closed the gallery. What next?

Back to Paris, which was expecting a German invasion at any minute. Not much time to lose. Now was the time to add to her collection some things she could not afford before. Artists were selling their works for whatever they could get. She bought a Brancusi bird for only $1,000, a wonderful Léger also for $1,000 the day Hitler invaded Norway. Other artists were only too willing to unload. She acquired an Arp, a Giacometti, later some Max Ernsts, for almost nothing. Her war babies. Yes, no matter how much she rebelled against the family, Peggy certainly *was* a Guggenheim. Guggenheims always know what to do when a war is threatening, or on. The immortal words of Mr. Dan: "Always go in for big development when the business barometer is low."

It was during this frightening, profitable period that Peggy ran into her future husband, Max Ernst, whom she had met briefly before. Meeting him again with the Germans about to invade France and carry them both off to concentration camps was an exhilarating experience for Peggy. "Ernst had a terrific reputation for his beauty, his charm, and his success with women," she wrote in her autobiography. "He had white hair, big blue eyes, and a handsome beak-like nose, that resembled a bird's." It was not long before she was—yes, she was far from cured—"madly in love with him."

Soon, however, things became too dangerous for love or art or anything but getting out alive.

Although she was, of course, concerned about her own safety, and that of her children, Peggy seemed more concerned at the time about her collection than anything else. Frantically she went to the Louvre and asked them to take her paintings and hide them in the secret place in the countryside where they were storing their other treasures.

To her immense surprise and disgust the Louvre sniffed its nose at the Peggy Guggenheim collection. In Peggy's words: "The Louvre decided my pictures were not worth saving and refused me space."

What they considered not worth saving were a Kandinsky, several Klees and Picabias, a cubist Braque, a Gris, a Léger, a Gleizes, a Marcoussis, a Delaunay, a Severini and two other futurists, a Mondrian, and several surrealist works by Miró, Max Ernst, di Chirico, Tanguy, Dali, Magritte, and Brauner. Her sculptures—by Brancusi, Lipchitz, Giacometti, and Moore—were not even considered.

In desperation Peggy got a friend to store the collection in a barn near Vichy. By then it was already apparent that southern France would collaborate with, rather than fall to, the Germans.

Peggy herself got out of Paris only two days before the German tanks arrived, taking her two children with her. During the preceding week over two million Parisians had fled the city in cars, bicycles, buses, trains, on foot.

Soon it appeared certain that her paintings were far from safe in the barn near Vichy and she had them removed to a small provincial museum in Grenoble. But after the fall of Paris, and the humiliation of the "peace treaty," it was doubtful if they were safe even in Grenoble.

There was no time to lose. Word was reaching southern France that the Nazis would be there any minute and no Jew or his/her property would be safe from concentration camp and confiscation.

At the last minute Peggy found there was a way she could ship her paintings from Marseilles to New York as "household objects," without inspection, and got them off this way in the nick of time.

Peggy, on hearing that Ernst had reached Marseilles with most of his works intact, immediately took upon herself the responsibility of helping to finance his escape to America. She did the same for Andre Breton and his family.

In exchange for her financing his escape, Ernst let Peggy choose "a great many pictures from every period." She bought them all for only $2,000 and it was that $2,000 that enabled him and his remaining paintings to reach the United States. After that lucrative transaction—these paintings were to be worth hundreds of thousands one day—she and Max celebrated his fiftieth birthday at the *vieux port*, "drinking wine he had brought from the Ardeche, and eating oysters."

"I felt extremely attracted to Ernst," she confided in her autobiography, "and soon discovered I was madly in love with him: from then on my only thought was to save him from Europe and get him to New York. . . . When we arrived in New York on July 14th, 1941, it was fourteen years since I had set foot in America."

CHAPTER 27

PEGGY IN NEW YORK

The house was a 1940s version of father Ben's five-story, pre-*Titanic* Fifth Avenue mansion. A remodeled brownstone on the East River at Fifty-first Street, near Beekman Place. It had, in addition to the usual appurtenances, a huge living room that, according to Peggy, might have been "a baronial hall in Hungary," and a "chapel two stories high," which overlooked the river from a terrace. Pegeen had a whole floor to herself (Sindbad was with Laurence Vail in a house Peggy had rented for them in Connecticut). Max had a "beautiful studio" to himself. Peggy had so many rooms to herself she was able to hang her entire collection in them.

It was in and around this New York brownstone, and in the gallery Peggy later opened on West Fifty-seventh Street, that the American, and to a certain extent, the European art world of the early 1940s revolved. This was the vital center. It was here, in these two places, that Max Ernst was launched in America, that the New York abstract expressionists got their first big chance, that Jackson Pollock was discovered, financed, bought, beatified, and canonized.

By now Peggy was "delirious" over the handsome, infinitely talented Max Ernst. The man had captured her affections totally, and, once he knew he had her hooked by the gills, he proceeded to torture her without mercy. It was yet another of Peggy's seemingly endless succession of sadomasochistic relationships. She had the power—the house, the money, the connections; he had the genius. He was dependent on her for his very life (the escape from Europe) as well as for his livelihood. She was dependent on him only for his love. And he resented her material power over him.

Though Max was able to escape the European war, he was unable for some time to escape the war in Peggy's East River brownstone.

That war broke out as soon as the combatants took possession of the house. The weaponry. On Peggy's side: money (her unearned income, before taxes, oscillated during the early 1940s from $50,000 to $85,000 a year, depending on how much the government let her war babies—oh, that *copper!*—get away with); prestige: by now the Guggenheim name was synonymous in New York with money, power, class, and big art patronage. On Ernst's side: artistic genius of the first rank, a ferocious wit, an overheated, sometimes diabolical imagination, a secondary talent for irony, torture, revenge.

The circumstances. Peggy was a woman who desperately needed a man in her life. Why? Was it the early, sudden, *Titanic* deprivation of her father? She thinks so. As soon as one man set, now always in a warm glow, another *had* to rise up, in blazing radiance, over her horizon. She could not do without him, whoever he might be. But it was always one man at a time, seldom two at once. Max, on the other hand, was a man who liked, or perhaps needed, to have several women in love with him at the same time. His first marriage, to former schoolmate Louise Straus, which had given him his only child, Jimmy, had broken up because of this preference. Before his relationship with Peggy he had been juggling two mistresses at once, the painters Leonor Fini and Leonore Carrington. Also, as a rule, Max further complicated his love life by showing a decided preference for stupid, young, bitchy, vulgar girls over older (thirties, forties) women of intelligence, sophistication, and taste. So far as money was concerned, he simply did not have any. As soon as he sold a painting, he spent the proceeds.

Max and Peggy got married in 1941, impulsively, in a small town in Virginia against the advice of Sindbad, who told his mother Max was as vain as she was and "the whole thing wouldn't work."

Marriage vows exchanged, it was right back again to war in the brownstone. Max refused to pay household expenses because Peggy was still supporting Laurence Vail, whom he detested. Thus, Peggy, much to her annoyance, was forced totally to support two men. As if this were not enough, Max refused to make love to her. A marriage *in bianco*, as the Italians say. Why, why, why? He wouldn't say. But he was not above disappearing occasionally with a cute little thing who caught his ever-vigilant eye. Once, when Peggy asked Max to inscribe some books of reproductions of his painting, he merely wrote: "For Peggy Guggenheim from Max Ernst." This upset her because she remembered the loving words he had used in inscribing a book to Leonor Fini. "He always made me feel that he would have liked me much better if I had been young and vulgar. He admitted he liked stupid, vulgar girls."

So here was Peggy paying good Guggenheim money for a sexless marriage, and here was Max accepting the money and spending it on a bunch of little tramps.

Was there any wonder the "fights were awful and often lasted forty-eight hours, during which time we would not speak to each other"? These fights, Peggy admitted, "were about nothing of importance"—only he living totally off her and giving her no sex. As the marriage wore on, or rather wore out, things got worse and worse and worse. More scenes. More sorrows. In the end, it took an art exhibit, entirely devised by Peggy, to precipitate the final break-up, which break-up, it must be emphasized, she never wanted because she sincerely loved Max Ernst.

Peggy had opened her avant-grade Art of This Century gallery on West Fifth-seventh Street, and—good women's liberationist that she was—had decided to hold a show there for thirty-one women painters. This proved to be her undoing.

For among the thirty-one painters was a lovely young married woman who was destined to turn Max inside out. Peggy had foolishly given Max the Womanizer the job of "going around to all the women, choosing their paintings, and carrying them off in the car to the gallery." As Peggy later wrote, "he adored this, as he loved women, and some of them were very attractive. . . . There was one called Dorothea Tanning. . . . She was pretentious, boring, stupid, vulgar, and dressed in the worst possible taste, but was quite talented and imitated Max's painting, which flattered him immensely. . . . She was so much on the make and pushed so hard, it was embarrassing."

One night Peggy opened a special delivery letter from Miss Tanning (her real name) and addressed to Max. Enclosed was a piece of blue silk, which Dorothea claimed was her hair. It made Peggy "wild with jealousy." "After reading the letter I hit Max's face several times as hard as I could."

Now nasty event follows nasty event in rapid succession. For a while Peggy could not sleep at night without massive doses of drugs. Max continued to paint every day in his studio in Peggy's house, then would dress up and go out with Dorothea Tanning. Once Peggy went to an opening at Julien Levy's gallery where she saw Miss Tanning "with her hair dyed turquoise . . . Inserted in her blouse, which was specially cut for this purpose, were little photographs of Max. . . . This really was too much for me. I was so disgusted that I decided I had had enough of the whole affair . . . and decided to put an end to it."

The end came upon the unexpected arrival of a new man in Peggy's life, an independently wealthy (her first of this genre) British writer by the name of Kenneth McPherson. After a "wild evening" with Kenneth, Peggy phoned Max at Dorothea Tanning's "asking him to find himself a studio and not come to the house anymore." That was it. Suddenly the War of East Fifty-first Street was over, and there was peace.

After their respective divorces, Max married Dorothea Tanning and remained married to her until his death in 1976 at the age of eighty-six.

Under the steadying and, at the same time, enriching influence of Dorothea, Max Ernst went on to one of the most creative periods of his life, one which culminated in the vast retrospective exhibition of his works held at the Solomon R. Guggenheim Museum in 1975, under the auspices of Solomon's grandson, Peter O. Lawson-Johnston.

For Peggy, the end of the war with Max meant not so much beginning with Kenneth McPherson, who turned out to be predominantly homosexual and eventually fell in love with one of Peggy's male houseguests, but going back to the gallery. Yes, it had been a long and bitter fight. But she had never let the battle deflect her from what she now believed was her primary mission in life, to bring the best in contemporary painting and sculpture to the attention of, if not the world, at least *le Monde*, the dimensions of which she knew so well.

On with work.

The work was Art of This Century, a top floor on West Fifty-seventh Street between Fifth and Sixth avenues (only three blocks from the Bauer House), which Peggy's ambition and money, and few people of extraordinary talent, had transformed into the most original art gallery on earth.

What an opening it had been! *Tout le Monde*—that international village Peggy had lived in for over twenty years—was no longer in Nazi-occupied Paris, but was in New York, and *tout le monde* came. A few of the Great Unwashed were also invited. Some came. Some did not. Hilla Rebay, though invited (to please Uncle Sol), did not come, but other Guggenheims showed up: Uncle Sol, Aunt Irene, Aunt Olga, Cousin Harry, Cousin Harold, Cousin Gladys. Peggy wore a white dress especially made for the occasion, and wore one Tanguy earring and one made by Calder, in order to show her "impartiality between Surrealist and Abstract Art." The press came in force and gave the show what Peggy termed "overwhelming" publicity. In a matter of forty-eight hours Art of This Century had easily replaced Uncle Sol's establishment as the capital of the New York avant-garde.

After the ill-fated show for thirty female painters, plus Dorothea Tanning—the show that Peggy says convinced her to renounce feminist altruism forever—Peggy organized a "spring salon" for young American artists. It was kind of a contest to pick out the most promising young talent in America at the time. It was from this "salon," or show, or horse race, or whatever you want to call it, that three of the great luminaries of American art of this century emerged: Jackson Pollock, Robert Motherwell, and William Baziotes.

Soon after this event, Art of This Century became *the* center for all avant-garde American painters and sculptors in New York, almost a club. These eager young people, luckily but a sable-hair's breadth too old to be dragged into the European and Pacific slaughters, had been profoundly influenced by such European abstract and surrealist painters as Max Ernst, Marcel Duchamp, and André Breton, all of whom, with help from Peggy Guggenheim, had taken refuge from the European slaughter in New York. Under this influence these young Americans unwittingly started an entirely new school of painting, which Robert Coates, art critic of *The New Yorker,* called, and thus baptized for all time, "abstract impressionism." It was, most certainly, a typically American art. Immediate. Discordant. Unharmonious. Experimental. Sensational. "Stripped," as Max Ernst once put it, "of all the dreadful baggage of history."

What happened next to Art of This Century, after Pollock, Motherwell, and Baziotes, was something of an anticlimax. For the record, Peggy discovered and gave first one-man shows to Hans Hofmann, Clyfford Still, Mark Rothko, and Adolph Gottlieb. And she also held one-man shows for such old-timers as di Chirico, Arp, Giacometti, Morris Hirschfield, and not forgetting her own, Laurence Vail and daughter Pegeen, who had decided to follow more in her father's footsteps than her mother's and become not just a collector but a painter in her own right.

But what was all this compared to *the* great discovery of the spring salon? In Peggy's words: "It soon became evident that Pollock was the best painter," and by this she meant not just the best painter in the salon but the best in the United States.

Which comes first, the patron or the painter? In the case of Peggy and Pollock it is anyone's guess. It was, in the end, just one of those happy, infrequent coincidences.

Pollock was an unknown, poor, down-and-out carpenter who worked in her uncle Sol's museum on East Fifty-fourth Street, and painted on the side. After his first one-man show at Peggy's place Pollock was virtually canonized. Alfred Barr purchased one of his works—"The She Wolf"—for the Museum of Modern Art; Motherwell wrote a most enthusiastic piece on him for *Partisan Review*; Sweeney wrote a most complimentary piece on him for the official catalogue of Peggy's collection.

A last show for Pollock at Art of This Century, and Peggy was ready to return to Europe. One by one they were all drifting back: Max Ernst and Dorothea Tanning, André Breton, Marcel Duchamp, Laurence Vail, and Pegeen Vail, now Mrs. Jean Helion. "Much as I loved Art of This Century," Peggy wrote, "I loved Europe more than America, and when the war ended I could not wait to go back."

CHAPTER 28

PEGGY IN VENICE

Almost every summer afternoon at about four-thirty a splendidly appointed gondola leaves the moss-stained steps of the Palazzo Venier dei Leoni and glides out onto the Grand Canal. Usually there are only two people aboard, the gondolier—in full livery—and *la padrona,* a lively, white-haired lady in her late seventies. But sometimes, when *la padrona* feels lonely, which happens more often now than ever, there are one or two other passengers: an old friend, an old lover, a famous artist, an unknown artist, a critic, a curator, a dealer, a cousin, a grandchild, her son.

It takes about an hour for Gino, the gondolier, to prepare the gondola for her ride. An hour to bail out the gondola and wax its varnished hull; to clean the frieze of carved black lions along the gunwales, affix the two carved black lions with their little brass collars to the prow, and install the two prancing brass lions holding spears at the sides; to lay the black carpet and put in place and wax the black headrest with the boldly carved winged lion of Saint Mark flanked by two lions rampant; to polish all the brass. Gino accomplishes it all with consummate pride and skill. In the morning he is Venice's chief corpse carrier, bearing the bodies of deceased Venetians through the canals to the churches and cemeteries; a dreary, unprestigious occupation. But now, in the afternoon, in his white blue-buttoned sailor's jacket, horizontal-striped shirt, white trousers, with blue waist sash trailing in the breeze, he is the carrier of no less a personage than "La Dogaressa" herself, and this fills him with a deep sense of importance. *Ecco, guarda,* they exclaim from the bridges, as the boat glides below, *e la Guggenheim . . . sta facendo il giro in gondola.*

This afternoon La Guggenheim is taking her ride with one of her prized little Chinese Shih-Tsu terriers, and with her favorite grandson, the handsome Nicolas Helion, who is currently filming a TV documentary on his grandmother's life and times. These much-appreciated passengers are symbolic of the only things Peggy has ever really cared for in her life: her daughter, Pegeen, and her dogs, her "babies." And her art? The collection? Ah, Lord, how many paintings would she gladly dump into the canal to have her beloved Pegeen back again? Pegeen . . . her petite, charming, talented, blond artist darling, killed by her own hand at only forty-one years of age.

Peggy directs the gondola with a regal wave of her hand, never looking back at the gondolier, or uttering a word. If she wants to go into the next canal on the right she simply raises her right hand and waves in that direction. . . . Grandson Nicolas looks up at the parade of palaces, full of admiration, taking notes for his film, his grandmother smiling benignly on him, the shaggy little Shih-Tsu prancing about, the tall, muscular gondolier rowing on with a steady rhythm, keeping a sharp eye out for obstructions—mooring piles, other boats—his blue sash floating in the air behind him. . . . People are gaping from the *Fondamente* as the gondola glides by. There are few, if any, gondolas like this, with such splendid regalia, remaining in Venice.

Two hours gliding through the narrow canals of San Polo, then back up the Grand Canal to the Palazzo Venier dei Leoni. . . .

The Palazzo Venier dei Leoni. Heavy, sepulchral, white marble structure stained green-black at the base, ivy dripping from the roof. The widest space of any palace on the Grand Canal, but only one story high. Peggy bought the *palazzo* for only $80,000 in still-depressed 1949 (the Venetians were afraid Tito would try to annex Venice to Yugoslavia), having to break one of her trusts to make the purchase. She had returned to Europe in 1946: "Much as I loved Art of This Century, I loved Europe more than America, and when the war ended I couldn't wait to go back." By now she had to admit she had become a confirmed expatriate. The previous Guggenheims had desperately wanted to be such *American* Americans, but she had none of that eagerness. She had become a European American, an international American, and was quite satisfied with that identity. With Peggy the Guggenheims had come full circle. One hundred years after Meyer and Barbara had abandoned their native Switzerland, their most celebrated granddaughter had come back to settle permanently only a few hundred kilometers from their birthplace. Furthermore, this granddaughter's own eight grandchildren were being raised not as Americans, but as Europeans—Sindbad's children as British citizens; Pegeen's as French.

The Palazzo Venier dei Leoni. As soon as Peggy was first shown the place she realized it would make the ideal repository and showcase for her paintings and sculptures. The rooms were airy and spacious, and, unlike so many other Venetian palaces, the walls and ceilings were unadorned. No gilded paneling, stucco friezes, or frescoes to distract from the paintings. And the little courtyard in front of the palace, and the large garden in back, seemed specially designed for displaying modern sculptures. Furthermore, where in America, or anywhere else for that matter, could she, with her relatively limited resources, buy a large eighteenth-century palace for only $80,000? Being one of the poor Guggenheims had always been a problem for Peggy. Unlike her more affluent cousins, she always had to settle for cut-rate elegance.

A year before Peggy installed herself and all her paintings and sculptures in the Venier dei Leoni she was invited by Count Zorzi, then ambassador of Venice's Biennale Art Exhibition, to show her entire collection at the Twenty-fourth Biennale. The year was 1948, the one-hundredth anniversary of Simon and Meyer Guggenheim's emigration to the United States. The Biennale was at the time the most important international exhibition of contemporary art in the world. Each participating nation maintained its own pavilion in Venice's wooded Public Gardens, in the northeast section of town.

Peggy's show received enormous publicity and literally put her and her collection on the international map. Her remarks about the event in her

Confessions of an Art Addict were a giveaway to her otherwise unacknowledged Guggenheimism: " . . . But what I enjoyed most was seeing the name Guggenheim appearing on the maps of the Public Gardens next to the names of Great Britain, France, Holland, Austria, Switzerland, Poland, Palestine, Denmark, Belgium, Egypt, Czechoslovakia, Hungary, Rumania. I felt as though I were a new foreign country."

In the meantime, daughter Pegeen had married the French painter Jean Helion, a realist turned abstractionist who eventually turned realist again, and so it was all but inevitable that Peggy would give a show for her son-in-law.

Pegeen had first met the talented Jean Helion in New York during World War II. Helion, a former soldier in the French army, had been captured by the Germans and had been interned in a Nazi work camp, from which he managed to escape and flee to America.

They were an attractive couple, the young Helions, with a seemingly limitless future ahead of them. As soon as the war ended the couple left their Greenwich Village walk-up and returned to Europe, first to a farmhouse in the South of France, then to Paris, where they both painted furiously and produced three sons, Fabrice, Nicolas, and Davide.

Pegeen was the most precious being in Peggy's life; she loved her three little grandsons almost as much as she loved Pegeen; and, she sincerely admired Helion's painting. But, almost as a prophecy of the tragedies to come, the show was a disaster from start to finish.

Behold Peggy Guggenheim in her mid-fifties, in the mid-1950s. A lively, intelligent, sensual, trim, still-attractive multimillionaire (she now had around two and a half million in trust, plus the *palazzo,* and her collection was worth at least ten or fifteen million), with an international reputation as a patroness of modern art and a somewhat less widespread reputation as connoisseur and patroness of men. She is, as we have said, still undaunted. All her life she has reached out for art and life and love and she is not about to give any one of them up now.

But now, for Peggy, as with the Guggenheim family as a whole, luck was beginning to run out. Whereas once whatever a Guggenheim touched suddenly doubled, quadrupled, centupled, in value, whether it was a mine or a lover or a work of art, now what the family, and Peggy, touched, not only did not bloom and multiply, but often died before it was born.

Three people did Peggy love and patronize during her fifties and sixties and all three met violent ends. By a process of alchemy of unknown formula and justification, her Midas touch had begun to metamorphose into a distinctly unlucky caress. The first unlucky one: Raoul Gregovitch, handsome, vital, sexy, ten years younger than Peggy, and, in Peggy's own words, "only interested in cars."

Give him a key to the *palazzo*. Introduce him to a lot of high-class people. Buy him a snappy new car. Set him up in business. It is the early 1950s in Italy; *il miracolo economico* is just beginning to gain momentum. Italians are buying cars as never before. Fiat is now producing hundreds of vehicles a day. The ugly modern Venetian mainland suburb of Mestre badly needs a new garage. Raoul has the idea, but not the money.

La Guggenheim takes him on as a lover, buys him a fast new sports car. He gets into his car, speeds out onto the flat, green plains of the Veneto, hurtles down long tree-lined lanes, and wraps himself and the car around a tree: dead on arrival at the Mestre hospital. Go to Ceylon and India to forget: several months wandering around Ceylon and India, continually besieged by aspiring painters, then return again to Venice, having presumably forgotten, and take on another lover, this time the young Italian painter from Feltre in the Veneto, Tancredi Parmeggiani.

Peggy had begun to sponsor Tancredi in 1952 on recommendations from a friend. He was a quiet, sensitive young man in his early thirties, very talented, given to sudden fits of temper, and entirely without funds. Peggy put him on a monthly salary in exchange for two gouaches—his favorite medium at the time—per month. Eventually she also gave him use of a studio in the cellar of her *palazzo*. After a number of experimental starts, taking as full advantage as possible of his new freedom, Tancredi evolved a style of his own, becoming what the Italians call a "Spatialista," a spatial artist, painting highly original abstractions ("I *detest* objects," he used to tell everyone), somewhat in the manner of Pollock.

Tancredi was extremely temperamental and had a number of impossible eccentricities. He would drive Peggy's servants out of their minds by walking all over her *palazzo* "with his feet covered in paint of every conceivable color." Often, in one of his periodic fits, he removed all his paintings from the palace—and there were scores of them—only to bring them back in a few days. No sooner would Peggy give him money than he would spend it all on a sudden binge of eating, drinking, and buying, then, immediately after the spree, come back begging for more.

Now things in the Peggy branch of the House of Guggenheim begin to get very complicated. Daughter Pegeen, as we know, was married to the French painter Jean Helion, whom she regarded as "a genius" (it had always been her ambition to marry a great genius). Soon Sindbad was married to a French lady by the name of Jacqueline Ventadour. The two couples were both living in Paris and saw a good deal of each other. In time, Jean Helion fell in love with Jacqueline Ventadour. There followed a double divorce and Helion married his ex-brother-in-law's ex-wife.

Shattered by this experience—after all, how often in life does a woman lose her husband to her sister-in-law?—small, thin, blond Pegeen moved to Venice with one of her sons, Nicolas, leaving the other two with Helion. Happy, at this critical moment in her life, to be near Mother, she soon met and married, on the rebound, a British painter by the name of Ralph Rumney, a man of whom Peggy disapproved, and by whom Pegeen soon had a son, Sandro, her fourth, born in Venice.

Pegeen was by now an excellent painter in her own right. While in Venice she worked in both her own studio-apartment, alongside Rumney, and at her mother's, in a studio next to Tancredi's. He was so charming, interesting, and talented. It wasn't long before the unthinkable happened. Pegeen fell in love with her mother's lover and protégé.

Peggy was very proud of her painter-daughter, whom she often confessed she loved more than anything, or any being, in the world, and apparently never suspected until it was too late that Pegeen's relationship with Tancredi was anything more than just friendship between two artists, even though Pegeen had shared other men with her mother before.

For Pegeen was always, in her mother's mind, very much the artist and, in a very real sense, Pegeen was, after Tancredi, Peggy's only other protégé. She bought her daughter canvases, brushes, and paints, showed her work to influential people, exhibited her paintings in her galleries, and, in general, promoted her as best she could. Pegeen, in turn, did well. During her brief career she held one-man shows in New York, Paris, Milan, Venice, Padua, Merano, Palm Beach, Vicenza, Stockholm, and Toronto.

At about the time Pegeen was beginning to take more than a sisterly interest in Tancredi, her mother completed the construction of her art pavilion in her garden, which she called her *barchessa,* after a certain type of building in the Veneto, usually a wing to a great villa.

To these salons came, of course, daughter Pegeen and protégé Tancredi. People who attended the parties noticed how nervous and ill at ease little Pegeen often appeared. The poor girl certainly had her problems at the time. The divorce from Helion had been a harrowing experience—especially losing her husband the way she did, to a sister-in-law and supposed friend—and the rebound marriage to Rumney was not working out. Now, just to add another problem to her life, she was in love with her mother's lover and protégé. And she had two young sons with her to raise, Nicolas Helion and Sandro Rumney, with very little support, moral or financial, from their fathers. Furthermore, she had to endure separation from her other two sons—Fabrice and Davide—who lived with Jean Helion. To top it off, she did not have much money: her mother, though a generous supporter, as we know, of art and artists, kept both her children on very tight financial strings.

It was, all things considered, a tense family situation, and so Peggy was only too happy to make a trip to New York in the fall of 1959 to attend the grand opening of her uncle Sol's museum.

As it turned out, Peggy missed the continually postponed opening, but did have a chance to see the museum (with cousin Harry as guide), to visit several other Guggenheim cousins as well, and to take in the art scene in New York.

As for the New York art scene, she was utterly repelled by it.

> I was thunderstruck; the entire art movement had become an enormous business venture. Only a few persons really care for paintings. The rest buy them from snobbishness or to avoid taxation. Prices are unheard of. People only buy the most expensive, having no faith in anything else.

Concluding her melancholy thoughts on the contemporary art scene, at the end of her *Confessions of an Art Addict,* Peggy declared,

> . . . one cannot expect every decade to produce genius. The twentieth century has already produced enough. We should not expect any more. A field must lie fallow now and then. Artists try too hard to be original. That is why we have all this painting that isn't painting any more. For the moment we should content ourselves with what the twentieth century has produced. . . . Today is the age of collecting, not of creation. Let us at least preserve and present to the masses all the great treasures we have.

Among those great treasures, Peggy has distilled a list of the top ten modern masters. They are: Picasso, Miró, Kandinsky, Klee, Duchamp, Braque, Ernst, Matisse, Pollock, and Magritte.

As for Old Masters, her top ten is tilted heavily toward the great Venetians: Titian, Tintoretto, Giorgione, Carpaccio, Velásquez, Rembrandt, Giotto, Botticelli, Dürer, and Michelangelo.

It was good to get back to her beloved Venice, but unfortunately she also had to face a continuing and steadily worsening family crisis.

Son Sindbad Vail, having lost his first wife to his brother-in-law, and having had to bring up his two young sons, Clovis and Mark, alone, had recently married a lovely British girl by the name of Peggy Angela Yeomans, with whom he soon had two daughters, Karole and Julia. He was living and working in Paris, on very little money, as an insurance surveyor, something he never particularly wanted to be.

And daughter Pegeen, still having troubles with her marriage, and still very much enamored of her mother's darling Tancredi, was desperately trying to keep her head above water in her efforts to raise two sons on bits and pieces and scraps of money coming in sporadically, if at all, from Helion, Mother, and infrequent sales of her own work.

Peggy, at this point, could have well afforded to help her children financially—she now had over $3 million, having inherited additional trusts from her sister Benita, and a cousin, Nettie Knox—but she continued to keep both son and daughter begging. Not that she did this intentionally; it was just that she was so immersed in her role as Grand Patroness of modern art as to have only leftover thoughts for her children's needs. Her palace and *barchessa* were now open to the public three afternoons a week, from three to five, and the crowds were often enormous. In season she was receiving eight hundred visitors a day—mostly Americans and Japanese—and selling eighty catalogues at five thousand lire each, for a total daily take of six hundred and fifty dollars, not bad at all.

Sindbad, with two sons and two daughters to support and educate on his earnings as a free-lance insurance surveyor in Paris, gently requests, in vain, that his mother give him, or bequeath him, at least two or three paintings—a Picasso, one of the Pollocks, an Ernst—to help care for and educate his four children, now, when they need help the most, and also cushion his oncoming old age. No, the collection says. No, I am sacred. I must remain intact.

Pegeen. Pegeen . . . Pegeen needing money desperately. Her sons. The two with Helion she rarely sees. The two with her and Rumney she must support herself. On what? Mother, disapproving of her daughter's life, holds onto her money. Tancredi. Yes, Pegeen loves Tancredi. Now Peggy is jealous of that love. The two women contend for Tancredi. Rumney knows what is going on and moves Pegeen, Nicolas, and Sandro to Paris.

The sensitive, temperamental Tancredi, torn between two hopeless loves, resentful of Peggy's financial hold over him, suffering from Pegeen's move to Paris, goes to Rome, and in a sudden fit of despair, throws himself into the Tiber and drowns.

Now little Pegeen, too, begins to drown. She has lost Jean Helion. She has lost possession of two of her sons. She does not love her husband. She has lost Tancredi forever. Now *he* was a true genius. She has no money. One evening in 1967 she is finally overwhelmed, and, after a drunken spree, takes an overdose of sleeping pills in her apartment in Paris. The French police rule it a suicide. Peggy receives news of her daughter's death the following morning. Four times before had Pegeen tried to kill herself. Now, at last, she is successful.

After the funeral, held in Paris, with the yellow press hovering about, son Nicolas goes to live with his father, Jean Helion, and his brothers, Fabrice and Davide. Sandro Rumney goes to live with an "aunt," Katy Vail, Laurence Vail's daughter by his second wife, the writer Kay Boyle.

Usually the most dreaded things do not happen. But now, for Peggy, the very worst has happened. Peggy, returning to the Venier dei Leoni, is terribly distraught, but she is a Guggenheim of the old stamp and such Guggenheims do not allow themselves to be defeated; they bounce back. They are of hearty stock. They are survivors. Peggy Guggenheim, at sixty-eight, still has much to do for and with the collection. Her greatest achievements and triumphs are still awaiting her: the creation of her foundation in 1968; the showing of almost her entire collection at Uncle Solomon's museum in New York in 1969; and then the spectacular showing of the entire collection at the Orangerie in Paris in 1974.

And so, a year after Pegeen's death, the Peggy Guggenheim Foundation is born in Venice. The Palazzo Venier dei Leoni, the *barchessa,* and all the paintings and sculptures in them—over 250 works of art, worth over $30 million—are donated "in perpetuity" to the new foundation. Later, in accordance with an agreement worked out with her cousin Harry, they are willed to the Solomon R. Guggenheim Foundation in New York, with the proviso that they are to remain forever in Venice, "unless Venice sinks," in which case they may be removed to New York. Peggy's pride in her achievement is immense. In her generation the only Guggenheims who created foundations were herself and Harry, and she started with less money than any of the others.

Then, in 1969, the great triumph in New York. Almost the entire collection crated, insured, and shipped to Uncle Sol's museum. Nationwide attention from the press.

From the triumph in New York to the triumph in Paris in December, 1974, the great revenge exhibition at the Orangerie, which she called "Twentycento." Revenge because, it will be recalled, back in 1941, when the Germans were about to invade France and Peggy was compelled to flee to the United States, the Louvre had turned down her request to leave her paintings in their secret hideaway on the grounds that they "were not worth saving." Two hundred thousand visitors to "Twentycento," paying nine francs a head, the name of Guggenheim emblazoned over all the newspapers and magazines of France. Peggy, now seventy-five, present at the opening wearing Chinese-red tights, knee-high boots, and a blue shift with crimson embroidery. Yes, she had shown those snobbish museumocrats what was not worth saving!

Yes, Peggy was a true Guggenheim. The poor relation, overwhelmed in her youth by the power and wealth of the uncles and their children, those uncles who had done her out of all that Chile Copper money, the poor relation had come out on top. The uncles were all dead and their children, though wealthier than she, had not, with the exception of Harry, accomplished half of what she had accomplished.

An accolade more flattering than that Peggy could not have demanded. Now, in the year 1976, in her own seventy-seventh year, she could quite easily lean back on her white leather settee with white sheepskin cover with her beloved dogs all over her and rest on her achievements. But no, she still had lots of ambitious things to do. She had to update her autobiographical Out of This Century with fifty fresh new pages on her life in Venice; she was collaborating on her official biography; she was also collaborating with grandson Nicolas Helion on that fifty-minute television documentary on her life and times; and she was making plans to exhibit her collection in Zurich, and in other European cities.

Journalists and writers are perennially hungry for her views. On modern art, on American civilization, on herself. She obliges.

Contemporary art. It has gone to seed, to hell. Pop art "the commercialization of a very stupid idea." The most recent manifestations of the abstract expressionist movement, a negation of art and life. The contemporary Venetian Biennale: "A communist insult to painting and the human spirit."

American civilization. Almost as uninspiring as contemporary art. Peggy finds American life and culture at the country's two-hundredth anniversary "narrow," "drab," "faddish," "racist" ("very anti-Semitic"). "Simply nothing of enduring value being created."

Herself. Yes, she knows where she and her family stand in the twentieth century, and makes no bones about it. "The Guggenheims are a twentieth-century royal family." No other female patron in Western Europe, or the Americas, has had a greater impact on the visual arts of her time than she. "I have supported the greatest geniuses of our times. I have put together a complete survey of nonrealistic art of our times. All the valid tendencies are represented in my collection."

CHAPTER 29

HARRY THE MAGNIFICENT:
THE LEGACIES

Toward the end of his long, varied, and productive life Harry Guggenheim was frequently overwhelmed by the problems of what was going to happen to the Guggenheim heritage after his death. So, in the last decade of his life, from 1960 to 1970, as his once very considerable powers declined, and death gradually began to overtake him, he came to reflect more and more on his family's achievements and, at the same time, began to set his mind to ways of perpetuating and memorializing them.

It was principally at Falaise, his splendid Long Island estate, that Harry, alone since his third wife's death in 1963, began spending more and more time contemplating his own and his family's past and what he could do to enhance its influence and *memorialize* it.

Harry had been fortunate to have benefited from an independent income since his twenty-first year. By the time he was fifty-five in 1945 his unearned income from securities that were conservatively invested was around $500,000 a year, quite enough on which to pursue one's interests and passions unhampered by economic need. Still later, he had seen his wealth quintuple, so that by the late 1960s he knew he would be able to leave something in the neighborhood of $50 million to his heirs.

Yes, his family's wealth had enabled him to lead a unique career, one with infinite facets and implications, one as varied and exciting as several members of the Medici family had been able to lead in Renaissance Florence five hundred years before.

His last career, that of newspaper publisher, had given him the most satisfaction of all. That career had begun with his third, and most fortunate, marriage, to Alicia Patterson.

Harry had to admit that his marriage to Alicia Patterson in 1939 had been a rare bonanza for a family that had been steadily running out of luck for the past ten years. What a bright, talented girl she had been. And what a background. Great-grandfather Joseph Medill, founder of the *Chicago Tribune*. Grandfather Robert Patterson, editor-in-chief of the same paper. Father Joe Patterson, founder and editor-in-chief of the New York *Daily News*.

Soon after the marriage—he was forty-nine; she was thirty-two—Harry realized Alicia could never be happy merely as the mistress of Falaise. She was too high-strung, too bright to spend all her time and talents looking after servants, antiques, Guggenheims, and peacocks. And so he had decided to give her a newspaper of her own, if only to give her something with which to occupy her time and her mind. But he had been clever. He hadn't given it to her entirely. Shrewdly he had kept 51 percent of the stock, letting her have 49 percent. The year was 1940. During its first seven years the paper operated in the red. Harry had had to pour $750,000 into it. And then, miraculously, it began to turn around. The mass exodus of New Yorkers to the suburbs, especially Long Island, after World War II was the cause.

Yes, it had been a great adventure, *Newsday*. Harry had enjoyed seeing his investment grow and grow and grow, especially after seeing his family's investment in nitrates go to pieces, had enjoyed seeing Alicia happy in her work, and enjoyed having a chance to get his own two cents in now and then in an editorial, which he often placed next to one of Alicia's expressing a diametrically opposing viewpoint. And then, he might as well admit it, he enjoyed being in full control of the paper after Alicia died of cancer of the stomach in 1963, and enjoyed no end the prospect of selling the paper for one hundred times what he paid for it (that, most certainly, was in the Guggenheim tradition) and selling it to an organization that shared his conservative political and economic philosophy.

But what to do about perpetuating all these achievements? Not simply his own, but those of his grandfather, father, uncles, and cousins. And about getting the record down, and publicizing it, about letting the world know what the Guggenheims had wrought during the past one hundred and twenty years?

Central to Harry's problem was, as we know, the search for a son and heir; for a strong, intelligent, dependable young man to succeed him as head of the family and perpetuator of its traditions. His first two marriages had given him nothing but daughters, three of them, and so he had been forced to cast around among various relatives, friends, and associates in his quest for a successor. One by one he had tried out candidates—his nephew Oscar Straus II, his 1960s' counterculture grandson, Dana Draper, his too liberal *Newsday* editor-in-chief (after Alicia's death) Bill Moyers—and one by one they all failed him, in various ways. Then, as we know, at the eleventh hour, he settled upon his uncle Sol's grandson, Peter O. Lawson-Johnson, to whom he simply gave the entire world.

Finding a son and heir to carry the Guggenheim businesses and foundations into the future was only one part of the solution to Harry's problem, however, albeit a very important part. While he searched for a son there remained the problem of memorializing the achievements of the Guggenheim past.

"Look at what we have done!" Harry seemed to cry out. "Look at what we have contributed . . . and nobody seems to know anything about it, or even care to know anything about it."

What was even worse, not even his own immediate family seemed to care. By the time he had begun to think seriously about disposing of his wealth and preserving the Guggenheim heritage, Harry had succeeded in alienating his closest kin to such an extent that they wanted to have little or nothing to do with him or what he stood for. It was that egotistic, authoritarian, dogmatic nature of his. With so much energy and family pride in his character, and so much money at his disposal, he simply could not accept opposing attitudes, opinions, wants, desires. If his wife of the moment, or one of his daughters, had a thought or wish contrary to his own, she was just wrong that's all there was to it. His first marriage, to Helen Rosenberg, had been a bitter, quarrelsome affair that took a severe toll on Nancy, one of the two girls born from it, who committed suicide in her forty-first year. His second marriage, to Caroline Morton, daughter of Paul Morton, Theodore Roosevelt's Secretary of the Navy, and member of the family that founded Morton Salt, was another quarrelsome union, ending in divorce, and one which must have had an unhappy influence on its one offspring, Diane, now Mrs. William Meek. Diane turned her back on her father and exiled herself to Ireland, where she has been living for the past twenty years, and where she is currently running a monastery school. As for Alicia, former friends and associates say she and Harry argued without let-up, that the marriage was a virtual marathon of quarrel, and that it was a combination of *Newsday* and Harry that led her to an early death at fifty-six.

The Harry Frank Guggenheim Foundation, now possessing assets of $20 million, is the most daring and visionary, and also the most vague, of all the Guggenheim foundations. The premise, or assumption, from which its many programs derive is that in the area of "man's relation to man," "man has failed to keep pace with the extraordinary progress of this era in science, engineering, medicine and surgery, agriculture, industry, transportation . . . and other fields of human endeavor."

Harry's relations with his fellow human beings, whether they were wives, children, associates, had always been contentious and abrasive. He was not an easy man to get along with, and he knew it. Was it partly a gesture of atonement for the many injuries he inflicted on people during his lifetime that he became so obsessed with human relations he decided to dedicate the bulk of his fortune to studying the problem?

It was throughout the 1960s that Harry took steps to perpetuate the name and achievements and influence of the House of Guggenheim. Then, on March 12, 1970, he put the final seal on them in his last will and testament, which confirmed Nassau County in its possession of Falaise, all its contents, and its ninety acres, and named Peter O. Lawson-Johnston and the Harry Frank Guggenheim Foundation as his principal heirs.

A little less than a year later, on January 23, 1971, Harry F. Guggenheim died at Falaise, after a long fight with cancer in his eightieth year.

CHAPTER 30

AFTER HARRY:
A FAMILY IN FRAGMENTS

With Harry Guggenheim's death in 1971, the grand era of the Guggenheims in America appeared to be over. Now there remained not much else for the family to do but hold onto what they had and make sure their businesses, investments, and foundations did not go astray.

To be sure, there was still money, energy, and talent in the family for further creative achievement—as the extremely successful careers of Roger W. Straus, Jr., in publishing, and Iris Love, in archaeology, attest.

And there was at least an outside chance that Harry's principal heir, the personable and capable, and now affluent, Peter O. Lawson-Johnston, could eventually revitalize the Guggenheim name, finances, and influence. But the heroic days of empire building and daring, innovative leadership in the arts and sciences did, nevertheless, seem to be gone forever, as they may well have been gone forever for all of the United States.

Who, and what, was left of the Guggenheim dynasty, and the institutions its founders had created, after Harry's death?

To begin with, it must be remembered that the fourth and fifth generations of Guggenheims were decimated generations. No fewer than eight Guggenheims from these generations died either premature or violent deaths before their forty-first year. John Simon Guggenheim, Senator Simon's firstborn son, the one after whom the foundation that distributes the fellowships was named, died at seventeen. Daniel Guggenheim II, Colonel Bob's first son, died at eighteen. Benjamin's two grandsons, Hazel's children Terrence and Benjamin II, died at four years and fourteen months respectively. William, Jr. died at thirty-nine. George Denver Guggenheim, Senator Simon's younger son, died a suicide at thirty-two. Pegeen Guggenheim died a suicide at forty-one. And Nancy Draper, Harry's middle daughter, died a suicide at forty-one.

Who, then, was left besides the vast number of men and women descended from Guggenheim females, people bearing surnames like Short, Smith, Meek, Johnson, and Butler, that legion of great and great great grandchildren of Meyer and Barbara living off money the Guggenheim brother had made but having little or nothing to do with the Guggenheims?

First of all, there was Harry's principal heir, Solomon's grandson Peter O. Lawson-Johnston, a slim, handsome, fair-haired young man in his early forties, firmly ensconced behind the principal desk in the Partners' Room of Guggenheim Brothers and behind many other desks besides. Then there was Colonel Bob's peppy, sixty-year-old son, M. Robert Guggenheim, Jr., and *his* capable, thirty-four-year-old son, Daniel M. Guggenheim, the two living luxuriously and productively at Newport Beach, California, far from the family power center in New York. There were Gladys Guggenheim Straus's offspring, the ebullient Roger W. Straus, Jr., and the quieter, more reserved Oscar Straus II, and their sons, Roger W. III and Oscar III, all of whom sat on the boards of one Guggenheim foundation or another. There were Harry's surviving daughters and grandchildren, who, with the exception of Harry's eldest daughter, Joan, did not much identify with the heritage Harry had spent the better part of his lifetime trying to conserve and promote. And then there was Isaac's talented great granddaughter, Iris Love, regarded by some as the most inspired female archaeologist in the world. Lastly, there was William's (Gatenby Williams') grandson, William Guggenheim III, a self-styled religious mystic, living in Florida with a wife and their infant son.

As for what was left of the Guggenheim institution, there remained a number of relatively small businesses, bits and pieces of the former mining and smelting empire, such as Guggenheim Brothers, the Feldspar Corporation, the Anglo Company, and Pacific Tin Consolidated, and then five foundations, the John Simon Memorial, the Daniel and Florence, the Solomon R., the Harry Frank, and the Peggy. The foundations with combined assets of approximately $700 million, including two museums and thousands of paintings, were worth more than all the surviving Guggenheims put together. Peter O. Lawson-Johnston is currently head of all the businesses and two of the foundations.

As for the fifth and sixth generations of Guggenheims in the Bicentennial year (one of whose chief events, the Viking landing on Mars, could be traced back to the Guggenheims' support of Robert Goddard), they were not necessarily going up, or down; they, like the nation, were just about holding their own.

But where to go from 1976, other than to the planets beyond Mars?

For Roger W. Straus, Jr. and his cousin Iris Love there was not much of a problem. Both were fortunate to have had very clearly defined vocations since their teens, which, partly thanks to the money behind them, mostly thanks to their own exceptional talents, they have pursued successfully.

For the Guggenheims of the West Coast, M. Robert, Jr. and Daniel M., it was a slightly different situation. Neither was involved in a calling as specialized and glamorous as publishing or archaeology. Life and work for them in the mid-seventies consisted of making money, putting what Robert had inherited, which was considerable, and what Daniel was currently earning, which was also considerable, to work, hoping by hard work and shrewd investment to bring their share of the family fortune back to where it had been during the lifetime of their extraordinary forebear, the bold and visionary Mr. Dan.

Peter Lawson-Johnston, of course, faced the most formidable challenge of all. As Harry's principal heir, not only to his fortune but also to "the Guggenheim heritage," it was up to him to pick up the pieces of the fragmented Guggenheim empire and try to put them back together again. It was up to him to revitalize moribund Guggenheim Brothers, up to him to lead the other Guggenheim businesses, like Anglo Company and Pacific Tin, to ever brighter futures, up to him to see that the Guggenheim Museum remained solvent and continued to be a vital, innovative artistic force, up to him to do something constructive with that biggest Guggenheim question mark of all, the Harry Frank Guggenheim Foundation, up to him to choose a successor to carry on in the next century. All this in a time of steadily increasing competition from the multinationals, ever-burgeoning and ever-interfering big government, diminishing acceptance of the work ethic, diminishing natural resources.

Such monumental challenges were the price Lawson-Johnston had to pay for being Harry's heir. They were certainly quite remote from the dividend and interest collecting that has become the principal challenge of most of the other members of the family. Even more remote were these challenges from the world of the young man who might be called, without melodrama or exaggeration, "the last of the Guggenheims," William Guggenheim III, the only male left in the family bearing the name Guggenheim who possessed sons. For Will III was not only the last Guggen-heim with offspring capable of perpetuating the Guggenheim name, he was also the only member of the family headed in a radically new direc-tion. To come from a family that had made its fortune exploiting the nat-ural riches of the earth, then used that fortune to support themselves in royal style, and support the arts and sciences . . . and then turn one's back on all that came before, and embark upon the lonely path of reli-gious mysticism, that, for a Guggenheim, was indeed a new direction.

A century ago, Meyer Guggenheim had gathered his seven sons around that long mahogany table in his office and acted out the parable of the sticks and bundle of sticks.

"You see, my boys, singly the sticks are easily broken, together they cannot be broken. So it is with you. Together you are invincible. Singly each of you may be easily broken. Stay together, my sons, and the world will be yours. Break up and you will lose everything."

This philosophy was heeded by all the brothers, with magnificent re-sults, for several decades, then it was abandoned, gradually by the broth-ers themselves, then precipitously by their children, grandchildren, and great grandchildren. By 1976 many Guggenheims had been broken. The family had by no means "lost everything," but it had lost much, and it was now far from "invincible." Now there was really no such thing anymore as the Guggenheim family. There were, instead, several different fami-lies, each stemming from one of the original seven brothers, and each go-ing in a different direction from the other. There were no more big family reunions embracing every one. It was a family in fragments and though it might well continue to produce men and women of ability, it most cer-tainly would never regain the strength and sense of purpose it had en-joyed in those exuberant days when several young men, sons of a poor refugee from a European ghetto, boldly set out together to conquer the mineral wealth of the new world.

CHAPTER 31

IRIS LOVE: BONANZA ON KNIDOS

For over six hundred years the goddess of love stood in her temple on Knidos facing the sea. The temple was on high ground, above a succession of rugged cliffs, and so it could be seen over great distances by sailors, who regarded it as their special shrine. The statue it enclosed was so beautiful—it was the first nude statue of Aphrodite ever wrought—that emperors, kings, and poets came from all over the world to see it. So prized did it eventually become that King Nikomedes of Bithnya offered to pay off the entire debt of the city of Knidos, which was considerable, in exchange for the statue. The Knidians preferred to remain in debt. Years later, the Roman historian Pliny wrote: "With this statue Praxiteles made Knidos a famous city." The work had, by then, attained the reputation of being the most beautiful statue ever made. In time, the larger-than-life-size work was copied and copied and copied so that by the fourth century A.D. it had become the most copied statue in the Greco-Roman world. For at least six centuries, perhaps more, the Knidian Aphrodite excited the passions of pagan civilization. Then, with the decline of Greece and Rome, the Theodosian decree ordering the destruction of all pagan temples throughout the Roman Empire, and the rise of Islam, Knidos suffered depredations, the temple fell into ruin, and Praxiteles' incomparable statue disappeared.

Well over a thousand years later, in October, 1970, Iris Cornelia Love, tall, blond, husky–voiced great granddaughter of Isaac Guggenheim, attracted worldwide attention by announcing she had found the head of the statue in the basement of the British Museum.

For the past three years Miss Love, a professional archaeologist, had been excavating what was left of the ancient Greek city of Knidos, now Tekir, on the southwestern coast of Turkey. Hoping she would find Praxiteles' statue, fifty–two known copies of which are still in existence, and largely frustrated in that hope (although she thought she had discovered the foundation of the temple), she went to the British Museum with a cousin, Margot Love Marshall, to inspect its large collection of Knidian antiquities, which had been lifted from the ancient site by a British archaeological expedition led by Sir Charles Newton in 1858. Perhaps this hoard of over three hundred and fifty pieces would contain some important clues to what was left on Knidos.

Again she was frustrated. Nothing on display proved particularly enlightening. So, catalogue of the Sir Charles Newton collection in hand, she and her cousin descended into the museum's enormous, crowded basement to see what pieces of the collection had been stored there. "It was dark and dank, with bare electric light bulbs breaking into the gloom at long intervals," Iris later told the press, "and spooky too, with all those white faces in tiers of shelves looming." At length she came upon a head, catalogued as number 1314, "covered with a cloth and the dust of ages." Iris pulled it out, took away the cloth, looked at it, and screamed, "Margot, it's here! It's here!"

According to Miss Love, the head, which was missing its mouth, chin, nose, most of its hairdo, and a good part of the back of its skull, was carved of the same fine-grained white Persian marble favored by Praxiteles, and the quality of workmanship, the late-classical style and type of hairdo, "the delicate folds in the neck," and the slightly larger-than-life dimensions, all indicated it came from the chisel of the supreme master.

The curators of the British Museum were not all that convinced. Or pleased. They maintained that the head had been found originally at the Temple of Demeter, goddess of agriculture, about a mile from where the Temple of Aphrodite was supposed to have been. And they were very upset at the implication in Miss Love's sensational announcement that they neither knew nor appreciated the value of the thousands of artifacts stored in their basement. "To imply that we didn't know we had this piece, and that it was unstudied," said Denys Haynes, Keeper of Greek and Roman Antiquities, and custodian, among other things, of the Elgin Marbles and the Rosetta Stone, "is simply untrue. We're overcrowded with material, but we know what we have . . . I'm very cross at her," he went on, "if she wants to put her points down on paper we shall examine them, as we should arguments of any member of the public."

Undaunted, Iris hurled back more reasons why she knew the head was what she claimed it was. "The slight burnishing that gives the impression of flesh," she elaborated, "the folds in the neck, they all agree with copies I have examined in the Louvre and the Vatican Museum."

Undaunted as well, the British Museum, hauling the head out of the basement, dusting it off, and putting it on display, marshaled evidence that it was the head of Persephone, daughter of Demeter, and got the noted Austrian archaeologist Prof. E. Schwarzenberg to back them up. The dispute has never been resolved.

How did it all come about? How did this great granddaughter of Meyer and Barbara Guggenheim become perhaps the foremost female archaeologist in the United States, if not the entire world?

The story of Iris Love in relation to the Guggenheim family is almost too appropriate to be true. For three-quarters of a century the Guggenheims had mined the globe for the metals of the earth. Then, at a certain point, they stopped digging, and, for the most part, sat back and lived off the dividends of their efforts. At precisely this juncture a member of the sixth generation came forward to dig again, not for metals, but for antiquities, not for financial gain, but for knowledge. At precisely the time when the mining bonanzas ceased, the archaeological bonanzas began.

But to get at the phenomenon of Iris Love, we must go back a few decades to her great grandfather Isaac, who, it will be remembered, was the eldest and perhaps the least effective of the seven sons of Meyer and Barbara Guggenheim.

Isaac died in 1922, leaving each of his three daughters $2 million. One of these daughters, Helene, married Lord Melvill Ward, becoming the second Guggenheim daughter to marry into the British aristocracy. Another, Beulah, married William Spiegelberg (it was their offspring, William, Jr., who was bribed to change his name briefly to Isaac Guggenheim II). The third daughter, Edyth, it will be recalled, married the banker and naval officer Louis M. Josephthal, who eventually became Admiral Josephthal, commandant of the Naval District of New York. Admiral and Mrs. Josephthal had, in turn, two daughters, one of whom, Audrey, became the mother of Iris Love.

Audrey Love, a keenly intelligent woman, summa cum laude and Phi Beta Kappa at Smith, and her husband, Cornelius Ruxton Love, brought up their precocious daughter in a museumlike atmosphere in their opulent New York maisonette. As a child Iris found herself surrounded by priceless collections; there was scarcely a corner of the two-floor apartment that was not occupied by an important work of art.

Audrey Love's mother, Edyth Guggenheim Josephthal, besides inheriting that $2 million from her father, went on to inherit substantial sums also from her mother and her husband, becoming in her later years an extremely wealthy old lady. Recognizing her granddaughter's precocious sense of history and markedly superior intellectual curiosity, she singled her out among her grandchildren and left her a substantial trust in her will, which was sufficient to guarantee Iris financial independence for life.

Grandmother Edyth died in 1960. Immediately thereafter, Iris came into her trust fund. She was only twenty-five and she was free to dedicate herself, with no financial impediments, to her great passion, classical archaeology.

Being a Guggenheim was, Iris later found out time and again, not always an asset. When she began trying to raise funds for her archaeological campaigns, individuals and foundations to which she appealed for money would often say, "But you're a Guggenheim, why are you asking *me* [or *us*] for money?"

It was not always easy for Iris to explain that though her Guggenheim grandmother did leave her a handsome trust fund, it netted her no more than $25,000 to $30,000 a year before taxes, or just enough to meet her personal expenses, certainly not enough to finance major archaeological expeditions. (A three-month campaign on Knidos costs a minimum of $50,000.) In addition, she could not count on significant financing from the living members of her family. Furthermore, she would be compelled to explain, just because she was a great grandniece of foundation founders Daniel, Solomon, Murry, and Simon Guggenheim, did not mean she had access to funds from their foundations. In fact, she would probably be the *last* person the Daniel, Solomon, or John Guggenheim foundations would finance.

Iris first saw Knidos from the prow of a caique in the summer of 1966. She was traveling with Askidil Akarca, a granddaughter of the last sultan of Turkey and a fellow classical archaeologist at Istanbul University. For the past nine summers Iris had been a jack-of-all-trades at the New York Institute of Fine Arts expedition on Samothrace. Now she had begun looking around for a site to excavate herself.

Landing on the little peninsula, she was immediately awestruck by the ancient city's great walls and their more than thirty towers, all still in an excellent state of preservation. Within the walls she was charmed to find farmers were growing cotton, tobacco, and sesame among the ancient ruins, oblivious to their significance, as if they were only so many stones in a field. Interspersed among the stones grew oregano, thyme, sage, and rosemary. Flocks of geese and turkeys were wandering in and out of a crumbled Greek theater and goats grazed among the ruins of the ancient agora. Then and there she made up her mind to excavate Knidos.

Iris at the time was an assistant professor of art history and archaeology at C. W. Post College, Long Island University. When she returned from her summer in Greece for the fall term, she screwed up her Guggenheim courage, and, after a series of impassioned pleas reminiscent of her great granduncle Daniel's petitions to J. P. Morgan to raise money to develop Kennecott Mountain, she succeeded in persuading Long Island University and the steamship magnate Jakob Isbrandtsen to finance a full-fledged archaeological expedition to Knidos for the summer of 1967. The following year Iris won additional financial backing from the Old Dominion Foundation, the Ingram-Merrill Foundation, and two archaeology buffs who were friends of hers, Win Nathanson and David Fromkin.

And so, beginning in the summer of 1967 and continuing to the present time, Iris Love has been pitching her "smelly, hot U.S. Army tents" among the stones and potsherds and flowers of ancient Knidos, living and working, sometimes in 120-degree heat, with her staff, and overseeing a force of Turkish laborers that has grown from thirty to one hundred.

And Iris is most emphatically boss of her expeditions. She raises the money, starting from scratch for each expedition. She writes up all the reports for the Department of Turkish Antiquities, sees to it that the objects she recovers reach the museums the Department designates, takes roll call, is the paymaster on payday, makes sure the water arrives at camp (there is only one freshwater spring on Knidos), buys all the food—she picks up okra, peppers, tomatoes, melons, eggplant, grapes, figs at the local market in her Land Rover—and even does the cooking, her specialty being barbecued wild boar with orange sauce. She always buys the wine, which is very good at Knidos, as it has been for millennia, because, as Iris likes to point out, "the vine is native to Turkey, not Greece, contrary to what most people think."

Iris' first summer on Knidos was primarily exploratory, and so it was not until the second summer that she began to make important finds.

Her first spectacular bonanza came during the first week of August, 1968, when a group of workers under the supervision of staff member Marie Keith, an indexer at the Frick Art Reference Library in Manhattan, unearthed a small marble sarcophagus inside of which gleamed a magnificent gold funeral crown, in perfect condition, not even tarnished, along with gold ornaments, and a rare two-handled glass wine goblet.

The second bonanza came in the summer of 1969 when Iris and her crew unearthed, in rapid succession, a beautiful bronze statuette of Priapus, a perfectly preserved marble statue of a woman, an exquisitely carved Hellenistic bone portrait ring of a matron, a marble head of a boxer, and a splendid larger-than-life-size statue of a young woman, possibly a goddess. They also discovered a strange round temple which Iris—holding her breath—intimated, but did not state at the time, might be the fabled Temple of Aphrodite.

On Iris' birthday, August 1, 1968, seven geese waddled into her tent "in single file, stood there cackling for a while, then turned around and waddled out again single file." Iris interpreted this as an exceptionally good omen since the goose, along with the dolphin, was one of Aphrodite's holy animals—she was often depicted riding one—and the number seven was sacred to the ancient gods.

A good omen indeed. For Iris' principal ambition on Knidos was to find the Temple of Aphrodite and, she hoped, Praxiteles' statue, or at least a part of it. In 1970 she finally reached her goal. It was her biggest bonanza and it landed her at age thirty-seven on the front pages of the major newspapers of the world.

The discovery of the temple actually took place on July 20, 1969, but Iris was not a hundred percent sure it was Aphrodite's sanctuary that she discovered at the time, although she had a strong hunch it was.

On that torrid July morning Iris and a member of her staff, Rolf Stucky, a Swiss archaeologist and mountain climber, struck out for a steep height they had not yet explored and which had not been assigned any importance on Sir Charles Newton's 1858 map of ancient Knidos. Climbing northward through steep, rocky fields covered with holly oak, thistles, yellow gentian, and stinging nettles, they eventually came to the base of a sort of terrace, and immediately felt a soft, refreshing breeze from the sea. The view was magnificent: to the north a series of steep cliffs plunging into the blue Aegean, and then immediately behind them, the parched white stones of ancient Knidos.

Climbing up the rock terrace wall, Iris' keen eye spotted something at eye level that took her breath away and made her tremble: a spill of stones, in what appeared to be a circular configuration, the remains, perhaps, of some collapsed structure.

What sort of structure would the Greeks have built on such a high eminence as this? Only a temple. A temple to a very important deity. Immediately Iris began poking about in the holly oak bushes that covered the terrace and found in one bush the top of what appeared to be a statue base. Was this the base of Praxiteles' statue of Aphrodite?

That evening, on returning to camp, she confided her hunch that she had at last found the temple of Aphrodite and announced her intention to dig an exploratory trench on the site the following day.

Iris will never forget that hot July day. It was, among other things, the day the Apollo astronauts landed on the moon and she had mused after returning to camp on how gratified her cousin Harry must have been by that event: another Guggenheim hunch had paid off.

Iris arrived at the site charged with almost unbearable emotion. It was a scorching morning and the rocks blazed in the sun. The scent of sage and thyme was heavy in the warm air. Carefully she and her workers began digging the exploratory trench.

Before long it became apparent that the structure she had had only a dim hint of the day before was indeed circular. Iris knew from ancient literary sources that the Temple of Aphrodite at Knidos was circular and so, as the dimensions of the marble courses were gradually revealed, she knew she had found what she had been searching for for three years.

That conviction was confirmed in the summer of 1970 when she unearthed the statue base she had discovered the summer before and found it contained the partial inscription: "PRAX . . . NUDE . . . ABOVE." Examination of the base revealed its construction was contemporary with that of the temple. The inscription had probably been etched much later, possibly as a guide to pilgrims and tourists. Later on, beneath a staircase leading to a terrace below the temple, Iris found a slightly larger-than-life-size fragment of a Parian marble hand, the dimensions of which almost exactly matched those of the known copies of the Aphrodite of Praxiteles. And not far away she also found "an overlife-size Parian marble female finger" and "an exquisite fragment of Parian marble drapery, both of which may have been parts of the original statue."

Iris made the official announcement of her discovery of the temple at the annual meeting of the Archaeological Institute of America in San Francisco, and a day later a photograph of her standing in a miniskirt alongside a Greek statue (having nothing to do with Aphrodite) was on the front page of *The New York Times,* accompanied by an article headlined "TEMPLE OF APHRODITE FOUND IN TURKEY."

Other publications had great fun with the event. "LOVE FOUND LOVE," "A LOVELY COUPLE," "MISS LOVE FINDS LOVE ON TURKISH COAST" ran some of the headlines. "THE LOVE AFFAIR" was *Time* magazine's headline. Only *The New Yorker* did not attempt a pun on Iris' surname. "Archaeologist" was the title of their subdued article on the find.

After the sensational discovery—one of the two or three most important Greek archaeological discoveries since World War II–and specifically during the campaigns of 1971 and 1972, Iris went on to make still more sensational discoveries. Excavating very carefully within the precincts of the temple itself in 1971, she found scores of beautiful terra-cotta female heads dating from the archaic through the Hellenistic periods. Many were the heads of young women at the zenith of their beauty. Some depicted groups of young women. One group represented the birth of Aphrodite aided by Horae. There were representations, also, of Aphrodite's son, Eros. The find was so large and varied that Iris was able to introduce an entirely new school of coroplastic sculpture to the archaeological world, which she has named the Knidian School.

Then, the following year, in a trench dug southeast of the altar of Aphrodite, a cache of several hundred terra-cotta statuettes, some intact, some fragmentary, was unearthed. Most depicted young females clutching their breasts. One was a double figurine showing two nude reclining figures, perhaps a bride and groom. Another group included divine female musicians carrying lyres and kytherai, playing double flutes, and carrying tambourines. And in the supposed gardens of Aphrodite to the northeast of the sanctuary, wherein aphrodisiacs were once grown, other appropriate items, such as "a jug with its spout in the form of a phallus, as well as phalli of all sizes" (some as long as four feet), were found. It was not for nothing that Pseudo-Lucan had written in the second century: "I took two authorities on love and went about Knidos, finding no little amusement in the wanton products of the potters, for I remembered I was in Aphrodite's city."

With the discovery of the temple in 1969, the discovery of fragments of Praxiteles' statue and its pedestal in 1970 and 1971, all the terra-cotta heads discovered in 1971, all the figurines in 1972, and the discovery, as well, of four other Hellenistic and Roman temples, two theaters, a council house, a colonnaded marketplace, a stoa, and scores of pieces of gold jewelry and painted pottery, Iris had made a strike on Knidos comparable, in archaeology, to the Bonanza Lode of copper above Kennecott Creek.

Today the work goes on: in 1976 Iris made several sensational finds of female statues, one of which, a terra-cotta head of Aphrodite, ranks as a masterpiece. Meanwhile the honors and awards poured in. In 1973 Iris was cited for "exceptionally valuable work regarding Turkish culture" by the Turkish minister of state, upon the fiftieth anniversary of the Republic of Turkey. In 1974 she was appointed John Hamilton Fulton Lecturer at Middlebury College in Vermont. Invitations to lecture continue to reach her from all over the United States. And she has won much acclaim from members of her own family. Peggy Guggenheim considers her "the foremost Guggenheim of her generation." Which she most decidely is, and appropriately so in this era of women's liberation (in the first two generations, the achievers were all men, in the later generations the women have come into their own). All this has been most gratifying, of course, but still Iris frets occasionally over the fact that the official archaeological community has never fully accepted her. Archaeology's *enfant terrible.* No, there are certain things they simply will not forgive or condone. For one, she never got her Ph.D. Now, for all those Ph.D. holders to accept someone who did not go through what they had to go through is a bit much to ask. For another, she has had the blatant audacity time and again to challenge—publicly!—such eminent Ph.D.s, people twice her age, as the heads of the Metropolitan and British museums, about matters she really knew very little about—after all, she never wrote a doctoral

575

thesis—which, of course, has been and continues to be absolutely unforgivable.

In addition to not having been fully accepted by her so-called peers, Iris has also continued to take her knocks from other directions.

One of the biggest jolts came from Alexander Liberman, sculptor and editorial director of *Vogue*. Liberman, it seems, invited her to write the text and captions for a book he was pasting together about Greece, under the imprint of Viking, entitled *Greece, Gods, and Art*. After she accepted, he gave her much encouragement and an advance of $1,000, in two installments, assuring her she would be given full credit for her work. For months she slaved over both text and captions. Then, when the book came out, she was appalled to find only Liberman's name on the jacket, when all he had done was take the photographs.

But despite the envy and skepticism and false snobbery of many of her colleagues in the profession, and the knocks she has had to take from the likes of Messrs. Rorimer of the Metropolitan and Liberman of *Vogue,* Iris still wears that delightful air of perpetual wonder (and vulnerability) on her face that has endeared her to her friends, her staff members, and her workers for many years. And no one, regardless of where his Ph.D. is from, not even the heads of the Metropolitan or British museums, can diminish the remarkable achievements that have been hers at such a young age, achievements that rank her alongside her great granduncle Daniel, her cousins, Harry, Peggy, and Roger, as one of the ablest Guggenheims of all.